TRI-AXIUM WRITINGS 3

TRI-AXIUM WRITINGS 3

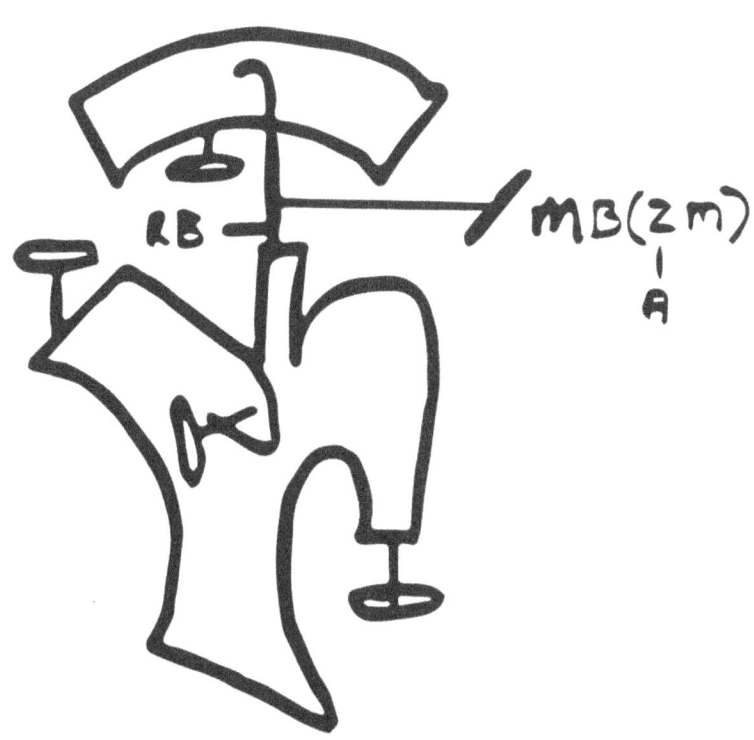

ANTHONY BRAXTON

TRI-AXIUM WRITINGS 3

1985 first edition: Synthesis Music

1985–2023 distributed by Frog Peak Music

2024 second edition: Frog Peak Music

Paperback ISBN 978-0-945996-26-2

Tri-Axium Writings 3

Contents

1	Preface & Acknowledgements (second edition)	
3	Introduction	
15	Glossary Integration	

chapter prefix

I. Alternative Functionalism — ALT(FT)
    A. Level One
25	1. Black Notated Music	BK(NM)
73	2. Creativity and Science	CS
107	B. Level Two	ALT(FT)II
145	C. Level Three: Questions & Answers	ALT(FT)III

II. Progressional Significance and Re-Definitions — PR.S(RD)
    A. Level One
163	1. Evolution	EVOL
203	2. The Teaching of Improvised Music	T(IMP)M
247	B. Level Two	PR.S(RD)II
315	C. Level Three: Questions & Answers	PR.S(RD)III

III. Popular Music from the Black Aesthetic — PMBA
    A. Level One
337	1. Popular Music from the Black Aesthetic	PMBA
379	2. The Phenomenon of Jazz-Rock	JR
	B. Level Two (no Level Two)	
413	C. Level Three: Questions & Answers	PMBA(III)

IV. Transformation — TRF
    A. Level One
429	1. The Reality of the Creative Woman	TRF(CW)
465	B. Level Two	TRF(II)
511	C. Level Three: Questions & Answers	TRF(III)

527	Glossary

PREFACE & ACKNOWLEDGEMENTS

The *Tri-Axium Writings* were approached as the beginning of a re-philosophic system that could map out fresh options and choices for the friendly experiencer on the tri-plane. This is not a system of thought that tells the individual what to think or do, but rather a set of choices that can be interpreted by a friendly experiencer based on one's individual experiences and individual value systems. This system is not a forming religion, but rather an attempt to create a model that is trans-idiomatic with flex options to suit the needs of the individual in real time. The word here is "agency."

I thank the creator of the universe that the Tri-Centric community has come into my life. What we have here is a movement of positive spirits who believe in the power of creativity and the wonder of radiant hope—and these artists are activists who are not simply waiting for public acknowledgment and/or faux celebrity status. The key word here is "action," with old-time serious groundwork and planning. The men and women of the Tri-Centric Foundation are foot soldiers for third millennial evolution and reconstruction—based on a love of composite humanity and world unification. I have no doubt that the good work of the Tri-Centric Foundation will inspire the creation of new artistic models all over the country and will continue the tradition of exposing our citizens to the challenge of composite creativity as a separate subject from marketplace focus and/or popular music—which I also love, but there's no lack of support for this community and we do not have to worry about its survival. Even so, let it be said that there is creativity all over: in America—from sea to shining sea—and in the world beyond. We have the people and the energy to evolve fresh visions to explore every focused discipline and strata.

I want to thank the Tri-Centric Foundation for the profound help this organization has given me—both in initiating the re-publication of

Tri-Axium Writings, and for the effort to literally save my creative work from the last sixty years and some. Because of their dedication I can now hope to have my music and writings documented safely into the future so that anyone interested in my effort can assess the material in the classic sense of research and discovery. In thanking my colleagues I am referring to Taylor Ho Bynum, James Fei, Kyoko Kitamura, Carl Testa, Zach Rowden, Jean Cook, Jonathan Piper, Jeanette Vuocolo, Rachael Bernsen, Tyler Rai, Chris Jonas, Chris McIntyre, and Andrew Raffo Dewar.

I would also like to thank Frog Peak Music (a composers' collective) for the support they have given me since the first publication of the Tri-Axium Writings in 1985. A special thank you to Jody Diamond and Larry Polansky for the great courage and dedication they have shown in the nearly forty years since Frog Peak Music began.

For this new edition, I am especially grateful to John McGhee for copyediting and proofreading all three books, to Carl Testa for making new schematics, and to Jody Diamond for designing both the print and digital versions. Proofreaders for Book One included Scott Campbell, Andrew Dewar, Michael Heller, Forrest Larson, and Carl Testa.

There is a difference between talk and action. All of these people can be viewed as real champions of global values and free expression—they are all artists in their own right and deserve more support as we move forward through the vibrational challenges of the recent time period.

We seem to be coming to a new era of vibrational realignment and sub-specialization. There is now a struggle to redefine reality and fantasy from a two-dimensional perspective that might not be in our best interest. More than ever, we need the input of the artist community to balance the spectrum of possibilities in a given political moment. This is a challenge that must be defended. Together, we have the creativity and the talent to succeed in every vibrational space.

Anthony Braxton
Hamden, Connecticut
2021

INTRODUCTION

Writings Three is the third book in a set of three on creative music and its related information continuum. Hopefully, this series of books will be viewed as a positive contribution to the reality of information surrounding creativity. More than ever before, there is a need for alternative viewpoints on this most important subject, and unless efforts are made to restore a more practical—and positive—basis for viewing creativity in this time period, serious repercussions will await us in the near future. The release of this book is the end result of seven years of struggling—and involved more than four complete rewrites (and more on given sections). Needless to say, I am extremely grateful to have completed this project, and I hope that the thrust of this work will be viewed as worth the effort. I believe the future will see more musicians become involved in writing about creative music, for the present reality of this subject—and especially creative music from the black aesthetic—has never been more in disarray. We have now entered what can only be called a very serious period in the progressional continuum of world creativity, and the challenge of redefinitions can no longer only be left to the so-called experts. I have written this book—and this series of books—as a response to the present state of things, with the hope that my viewpoint will inspire other efforts—this is what is needed. The writings which have helped motivate my interest in this area have all come from people who were (and are) involved in the dynamics of creativity, and I feel the special insight that creative people must have—by virtue of their involvement with creativity—can be beneficial to restoring a more correct and just viewpoint about this most important subject. I believe if more people were exposed to the writings of creative people, many of the present distortions surrounding creative music would not have materialized. To read the works of thinking musicians like Rex Stewart, Harry Partch, and Leo Smith is to gain a viewpoint from people whose lives are not separate from what they wrote about. The inspiration I have received from their work gave me the strength to complete this project, and hopefully this work will serve as a positive source to others.

I originally began this series of writings in response to the reality of information surrounding creative music in the early seventies—especially the misinformation that characterized creative music writings in monthly periodicals and newspapers. It seemed to me at the time that the level of accurate commentary had gone from bad to worse, and it also seemed as if the smearing of post-Ayler creativity was more than a series of unrelated coincidences, but instead a co-ordinated attack. My first efforts on this book took place in Paris in September 1973, as a means to challenge what I felt to be deliberate misinformation about black creativity and black creative dynamics, and the thrust of this first effort would take over a year before completion. For if my original efforts had been directed towards combating the manipulation of post-Ayler creativity, by the end of 1974 the act of writing and researching had totally changed my own perspective of the music as well as the reality of information that supported my understanding of music. For the most basic assumption that dictated my early attempts to respond to creative music commentary was the mistaken belief that western journalists had some fundamental understanding of black creativity—or even western creativity—but this assumption was seriously in error. Rather, I now believe that the reality of African and trans-African continuance is being undermined by interpretations that seek to destroy both the dynamic implications of its information nature and the particulars of its affinity dictates. As such, the whole of my first draft had nothing to do with the real reality of western commentary, because the actualness of this phenomenon is much greater than the focus on a given argument—or opinion.

It is important to understand that the reality of a given interpretation cannot be outside of the affinity nature it purports to comment on. As such, one cannot comment on the reality specifics of non-western focuses without making serious adjustments in the vibrational nature of one's use of language, as well as the particulars underlying how a given conceptual focus is viewed. In actual fact, many of the distortions that have come to permeate black music journalism are directly related to the use of western inquiry terms that have no relevance to the reality nature of black creativity, or not in the way presently understood. Nor have I meant to imply that only black creativity has suffered from the misuse of western definitions, because the whole of world creativity has been profoundly misdocumented in this same manner. The challenge of erecting a positive basis for understanding creative music must necessarily involve a complete examination of every area of creative music—regardless of form or style. We must move to seek out a more human understanding of this subject that is free of petty accusations or racist doctrine, and the time to do it is now—not later. The act of writing this book has helped me to see how deeply I disagree with the present reality of commentary about creativity—and its related information continuum. Because the dynamic misinformation that has been generated in music commentary is not separate from what has transpired in the composite quilt of our society; that is, the misinformation presently attempting to solidify our relationship with creative invention also affects our composite relationship with fundamental information (or as this period of time would have it, "alternative fundamental information")—and this is what worries me.

By 1976—and after two more drafts—the essence of the book began to form, and I have attempted in this series of works to develop another approach for writing about creative music. That being: an approach that attempts to vibrationally and systematically view the whole of earth creativity and its related information continuums as a basis to resolidify a transformational viewpoint about this subject. Yet by no means does this book accomplish the whole of this challenge, nor have I meant to imply that my understanding of the universe is such that I have the necessary insight for such a task—because this is not what I mean. Instead the realness of this challenge will involve every sector of humanity. For to really attempt understanding of the reality of creativity is to transcend the particulars of a given focus, and instead reinvestigate the dynamics of composite earth information.

As such, the thrust of these writings is as concerned about the vibrational and philosophical implications of a given information focus (interpretation) as the particulars of its related music. Because the reality of creativity is not limited to only how a given phenomenon works but also involves the meta-reality context from which that phenomenon takes its laws. This is what concerns me, and this is what my writing is directed towards examining.

I believe the thrust of the eighties and nineties will see many more individual efforts of this sort—involving attempts to redefine every area of information and information dynamics. Nothing less than this will do—because the composite realness of present-day information is profoundly distorted—and I do not view this distortion as the result of a grand accident, but instead the end product of deliberate policies and intentions. The spectrum of this misinformation seems to encompass every area of dynamic focus—our understanding of science, music, spiritualism and functionalism. No area has been untouched—and if we are to ever shape the future then we must first correct the present: that is, we must first correct the reality of information that influences how we have come to either approach living, or approach understanding information about living. Certainly I have not meant to imply my writings will clarify all of these dynamic questions—because to imply such would be nonsense. But I do feel that the challenge of attempting to change a given state begins with the first step, and I also feel that the success of a given change indirectly relates to how many people are involved. In this series of books I have tried to the best of my ability to contribute a viewpoint that could be of relevance towards re-examining the realness of creativity. The dynamic implications of this book should hopefully stimulate the commentary scan of creative music if nothing else. This is my hope anyway. I have also deliberately not included scholastic-type footnotes in this series of books because (1) the thrust of this book is only an affirmation of what I have been learning and feeling—which is to say a snapshot of what I have been thinking from a period of September 1973 to March 1980, and (2) the thrust of this book is also conceived with respect to what I believe—which is to say I offer nothing in this book as definitively "true" (because for too long we have been deluged by so-called experts with interpretations that are presented as fact—but aren't—and this misuse of interpretation has moved to damage the whole of this time period). I have also tried in this series of books to refrain from attacking any individuals—even when I felt a given attack would clarify the nature of a particular viewpoint—because there can be no room for petty accusations if the basic focus of this book is concerned about what is really true (not to mention, the present state of things is not about any one or two given individuals).

Finally, it is important to state that none of the viewpoints written in this book are viewed as complete in any real sense. Instead I have made the decision to release this material because the completion of the entire project is dependent on what I am able to totally realize in my life—and hopefully I will have another ten, twenty, or thirty years (and some) on this planet to continue my learning, and work. After rewriting these sections for seven years, I felt this material was good enough to publish and, moreover, holding it any longer actually made no sense. But it is important to emphasize that all of these concepts are only one aspect of a much greater viewpoint—and this is really what is important. I believe the reality of commentary about creativity should give insight on more than just the surface specifics of the music but also its conceptual and philosophical implications—and this is what I have attempted in this series of writings. There are so many aspects of creative music that have been ignored in the last three hundred years that something must be done to review our present reality and vibrational position with composite information and composite information dynamics. Like most musicians, I have always thought the job of attempting to secure cultural awareness about creativity was the responsibility of so-called music journalism—and to some extent the music journalist has functioned as a positive generator for real understanding. But for the most part few, if any, of these functioning journalists have worked in the area of creative music or black creativity. As such, the thrust of journalism in the past fifty years has developed much dynamic information about western art music but very little on black creativity—or improvised music. I believe the present reality of black creativity is directly related to what information has not been developed—as opposed to what has—and this is indeed a tragedy for anyone concerned about world creativity. Rather than wait for a change of attitude by jazz journalists, I have instead made the decision to become involved in writing—and now I understand that this decision should have been made fifteen years ago. We can no longer wait for black music journalism to rise to the challenge of what it implies nor can we afford to wait on the so-called liberal white documentalists to straighten out the present state of things—for that matter, we can no longer hope for the emergence of black writers who are not afraid to speak out. We can no longer wait, because time is running out. The challenge is to solidify the correct and positive definitions that are needed now—in this time period. At present, the reality of creative music commentary has very little to do with supplying transformational viewpoints—let alone transformational solutions. As such—if you want something done—you must do it yourself. I offer this book—and this series of books—as an attempt to begin re-examining the composite reality of creative music. These writings are offered as only the beginning of what I hope will be a massive body of alternative literature on creative music.

Construction

Each of the books in this series of writings is constructed so as to insure maximum idea interchange. This has been done in accordance with my belief that given viewpoints must now be examined not only on more than one level or focus—but on as many levels as possible. Moreover, the thrust of this effort is conceived as a composite attempt to examine the whole of earth creativity—and as such, the reality of a given definition must necessarily "be presented in its broadest terms," because I am not concerned with only some aspect of what seems to be true—I am interested in what seems to be really true. Since the complexity of creative music commentary involves so many different areas of inquiry, I believe the challenge of transformational journalism is to find creative ways to interpret information. It is because of this belief that I have solidified this approach to my writings. For the great thrust of creative music writings in this time period is in extremely uncreative attempts at journalism, and this is especially interesting when one considers the position jazz critics have put themselves in—that being attempting to evaluate the worth of other people's creativity. As such, the basic construction of these books contains several approaches for both reading and interconnecting concepts. I have tried to construct a systematic approach that gives the greatest focus reference possible, because the seriousness of creativity demands something more than a one-dimensional viewpoint.

The dictates of these books are constructed so that the reader must read through the material in at least six different ways, and the interconnections of concepts are set up so as to give maximum diversity. In other words, the reader will be able to view a given concept from as many different standpoints as possible. The thrust of these writings is not about any one concept but instead involves the reality of cross-information, as a means to solidify the broadest possible inquiry terms. It is my hope that an approach of this nature might prove useful for establishing a more realistic look at creative music, for much of the literature I have seen on this subject seems either too simplistic or too academic. Yet, by the same token, I have not solidified this approach as a joke, nor have I included anything in these books which was not necessary. I have tried, in this effort, to view a given concept to the farthest point of my ability with the hope that either real understanding can come from an approach of this type, or that real intellectual stimulation about world creativity can be developed. I view either objective as positive.

The construction of this book is as follows:

Within each principal section or chapter (which is designated by the use of capital letters) there are what I call levels of inquiry—or simply levels. The whole of these series of writings is constructed around the dynamics of this approach. There are three inquiry sections that can be used in a given chapter, and every idea is expressed throughout each aspect of what this division means. The explanation of each level designation is as follows:

1. Level One has to do with focusing on some particular aspect of its principal chapter, and this region of inquiry can number from one to four approaches (depending on how many "particulars" are focused on in a given section). Each of these areas of focus is separated into different colors for convenience.

The code is as follows:
>brown for approach one;
>green for approach two;
>orange for approach three;
>purple for approach four.

2. Level Two investigation is a summary of the given approaches focused on in Level One. In other words, this area of inquiry can only be utilized if there are two or more approaches examined in Level One. The thrust of a given focus in this context is geared towards the composite context of what a given viewpoint might mean in a broader context (or with respect to the whole of this book and this series of books). The color of this section is blue.

3. Level Three investigation involves the use of questions and answers in a one-dimensional context as a means to include shorter viewpoints that can be integrated throughout the whole of this book. This is necessary because the basic structure of the book is systematic to the degree that "grounded definitions" can provide a healthy pivotal factor for clarification. By including this section, the range of a given focus is all-encompassing—that is, the dynamics of this total approach run from open interpretation possibilities (i.e., understanding something in your own way—with respect to one's own affinity dynamics) to closed exact definitions. The color for this section is red.

I have tried to accent many of the important concepts in bold type as a means for the reader to have easy referral to a given viewpoint more readily.

Thus, to really utilize this book in the way I have intended, the reader is expected to read this book:

(1) completely from the beginning to the end;

(2) with respect to the arguments of only one level region at a time (i.e., read only Level One sections in each chapter, later read only Level Two chapters, etc.);

(3) read the whole book interconnected with the other books in this series through what I call the integration code—which is in every section of every focus;

(4) read only the isolated concepts that have been marked by bold type;

(5) study the isolated terminology chart—or glossary of terms (at the back of the book)—to understand the systemic interconnection (as well as application) of these concepts throughout the total integration complex of all three books, as a means to better understand both my extended viewpoint as well as the logic dynamics of its total application; and

(6) the reader is asked to translate my terminology—from the glossary and throughout the whole book—as a means to view each focus in one's own terms: in other words, I am saying, "this is my viewpoint in this context, and these are my terms, but what do you think?"—with respect to your own personal viewpoint and/or perception dynamics (in the context of my terminology—as well as your own terminology) about this same information. Only after all of the approaches have been tried can the reader have some idea as to what I am trying to communicate—yet on this comment it is important to explain my intentions. I have not meant to imply that my understanding of phenomena is such that one must necessarily reach for my so-called level, because to believe this has nothing to do with reality. Instead, I have constructed these writings in this manner because the realness of what I am really trying to communicate is not about "only one point of view"—or one level of transference. I believe the traditional use of so-called deductive logic has been greatly violated in this time period. What we now need is the use of every kind of information transference affinity position—whether or not it corresponds to what is now called logic. It is for this reason that *Tri-Axium Writings* is constructed in the manner you have before you. I have also included a code for all of the signs and symbols used in this book—and series of books.

CODE

1. A straight line under a paragraph means that the focus of that particular subject has been completed; after which the next paragraph will move to another area of relevant focus.

2. A dotted line under a paragraph means that the next paragraph is an insert that is separate from the basic flow of what is being written on. As such, the end of the insert is also marked with a dotted line—and

the reader is back on the same subject material. It is possible to simply skip the material that is presented between the dotted line sections and come back to it later.

3. All of the concepts are abbreviated as a means to trace an information line in the integration charts.

The bracketed abbreviations are:

(R) = the reality of
(C) = the concept of
(IN)DE = inquiry degree
(CT) = the criterion of
(P) = point of idea completion for a given interpretation (or schematic)
(PFC) = point for future calibration
(PO) = point of
(L) = level
(P-AT) = point of activation (a physical universe term to point out where a given idea or the effects of a given idea—can take shape or become real)
(D) = the dynamics of = when viewed in the context of
    = can be viewed
    = as it involves
    = viewed with respect to
    = particulars of a given
    = (dotted line) amplifies some aspect of the main concept it is connected to
    = is connected to on the physical universe level
(P-IN) = its position in
(D-T) = determines the _____ of its _____

    The name of this system of thought is "TRI-AXIUM," which is my term for gathering axiom tenets from the past and present—to get to the future. The reality of this inquiry is perceived and offered as a bridge for re-information designation (for possible transformational observation—tenets—and/or use). For the most part, this series of writings is based on present-time affinity postulation (or affinity observation). But the whole of the completed effort—in the next ten, twenty years—or whatever time I have to work on this project—will deal with:

1. Affinity postulation:
(a) establishing basis (through physical universe observation—and research);
(b) challenging present time definitions;
(c) establishing affinity redesignation systems (that also allow for individual interpretation).

2. Axiom correlation:
(a) researching world culture information tenets for resolidification;
(b) re-establishing transformational functionalism particulars;
(c) establishing a platform for alternative investigation.

3. Reality imposition:
(a) isolating particulars with respect for respiritual participation;
(b) resecuring the significance of ritualism and symbolic participation;
(c) re-investigating spiritual dynamics as a basis to establish transformational spiritualism.

To use the integration schematics one must first become familiar with the abbreviation of terms. The basic idea of this system is that all of the concepts in this book—and this series of books—must be viewed in more than one context. The reality of a given schematic is not isolated to only what it poses for a given focus; rather, I have designed this approach as a means to keep an extended information platform—which is to say each given schematic should be viewed as axiom tenets. To read a given schematic the reader must first view it in terms of its basic designation—which has an arrow to denote its starting point. In actual fact the term (or abbreviation) with the arrow pointing to it is the subject of the schematic. In the figure below this paragraph the subject then is "vibrational dynamics" (and since there is also an [R] in brackets, the subject is "the reality of vibrational dynamics" as this concept relates to the concept of "postulation"). Whenever there is no prefix or bracket before a given abbreviation it means to view the terms as a concept—or as the concept (in this case) of "postulation."

This is then the schematic:

(R)VT. DY.------ POST.

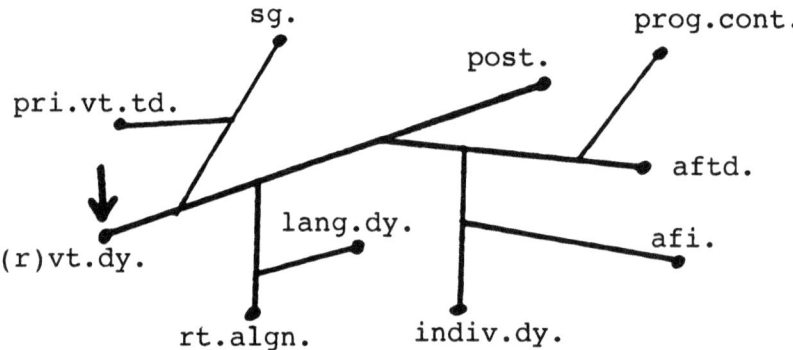

To read (or see) this schematic in words would go like this:

The reality of vibrational dynamics as this term relates to the concept of "postulation"—in three different contexts, those being: in the context of (1) SG, source initiation (involving PRI-VT-TD, primary vibrational tendencies); or in the context of (2) RT-ALGN, reality alignment (involving LANG-DY, language dynamics); or in the context of (3) AFTD, affinity tendencies (involving INDIV-DY, individual dynamics as related to AFI, affinity insight—or involving PROG-CONT, progressional continuance).

The reader is expected to probe the dynamics of this axiom as a means to better understand these terms (i.e., what is being posed in a given information complex), as well as what all of this information means when calibrated into a composite philosophy (my philosophy at first, after which the reader is expected to view this same material—and terms—[with substitutions when needed] for his or her own philosophy).

All of the various symbols that are attached to particular schematics can be found in this CODE section.

GLOSSARY INTEGRATION

See the Glossary at the back of the book for definitions of terms.

A-PR	all-purpose
ACC-DY	accelerated dynamics
ACC-FT	accelerated functionalism
ACT	activism
ACT-T	actual terms
ACT-TR	actual transformation
AF-COMP	affinity compression
AF-CON	affinity convergence
AF-NT	affinity nature
AF-POST	affinity postulation
AFI	affinity insight
AFI(1)	affinity insight—first degree
AFI(2)	affinity insight—second degree
AFL	affinity alignment
AFL-DT	affinity dictates
AFL-DY	affinity dynamics
AFN	affinity negation
AFTD	affinity tendencies
AFTF	affinity transfer
AGT	agreement
ALT-ACT	alternative activism
ALT-C-PG	alternative composite progressionalism
ALT-D	alternative definitions
ALT-F	alternative functionalism
APL-DT	application dictates
APP-RDEF	applied redefinitions
ASP-ES	aspect essence
ATT	attitude
ATTC	attachment
ATTN	attraction

BIA	bi-aitional (or bi-aitionalism)
BSCF	basic science (or basic scientific functionalism)
C-ACT	composite activism
C-AF-ALGN	composite affinity alignment
C-CONT	composite continuance
C-CULT-AT	composite culture attitude
C-FO-ACT	composite focused activism
C-HM	composite humanity
C-INFO	composite information
C-RH	composite research
CN-INFO	controlled information
COLC-FR-WC	collected forces of western culture
COS-AGN	cosmic assignment
COS-D	cosmic dictates
COS-P	cosmic particulars
CR-INFO-DY	circular information dynamics
CRT	criticism
CRTF-D	cross-transfer definitions
CRTF-PROG	cross-transfer progressionalism
CUL-TF-S	cultural transfer shift(s)
CULT-AF-BS	culture affinity basis
CULT-INFO-B	culture information basis
CULT-INFO-DY	culture information dynamics
CULT-INFO-F	culture information focus
CULT-O	culture order
CULT-SOLD	culture solidification
DE-SPTL	despiritualization (or despiritualism)
DEC	decentralization
DEF	definition
DIS-C-CT	disintegration of a culture's center
DOC	documentation
DYM-F	dynamic functionalism

DYM-SEP	dynamic separation
DYM-SPT	dynamic spiritualism
ECO-DYM	economic dynamics
EXB-H-OR	establishing high order
EXP-CONT	expansion condition (the concept of)
EXP-CONT(1)	expansion condition (composite focus)
EXP-CONT(2)	expansion condition (isolated focus)
EXP-DT	expansion dictates
EXP-DYM	expansion dynamics
EXP-INFO-B	expansion information basis
EXPM	expansionism
EXT-DYM	extended dynamics
EXT-FT	extended functionalism
EXTN	existentialism
EXTN-D	existential definition
EXTN-OB	existential observation
EXTS	extension (or nature of extension)
F	form
FUND-DYN	fundamental dynamics
FUND-P	fundamental particulars
GRAD	gradualism
HI-P	high purpose
IF-SPT	infra-spirituality
IF-ST-DY	infra-structure dynamics
IMPOV	improvisation (the concept of)
INDIV-DY	individual dynamics
INDIV-DY-RT	individual dynamic reality
INDIV-TD (or INDIV-DY-TD)	individual tendencies (the reality of or concept of)

INFO-AF-B	information affinity basis
INFO-ALGN	information alignment
INFO-COMP	information compression
INFO-CON	information convergence
INFO-DE(B)	information degrees (or information degree basis)
INFO-DOC	information documentation
INFO-DS	information dissemination
INFO-F	information focus
INFO-F-D	information focus distortion
INFO-FM (or FR)	information forum
INFO-INTG	information integration
INFO-INTR	information interpretation
INFO-OR	information order
INFO-PROJ	information projection
INFO-RT	information reality
INFO-SOLD	information solidification
INFO-TRNS	information transference
INT	intention (the reality of)
INTL	intellectualism
INTR	interpretation
INVT-DT	investigation dictates
IST-ACT	isolated activism
IST-F	isolated focus
IST-F-AT	isolated focus activism
IST-F-DT	isolated focus dictates
IST-PT	isolated particulars
IST-S-ALGN	isolated systematic alignment
JR-DYM	journalism dynamics
LANG	language
LANG-DY	language dynamics
LG-DISA	logical dissolution
LG-DY	logical dynamics

LG-EXT	logical extension
LK-IMP	linkage implications
MD-DY	media dynamics
MDT-DY	motivation dynamics
MN-DI	mono-dimensional
MPT	manipulation (the reality of)
MT-DEVF	multiple diversification
MT-DI	multi-dimensional (or ISM)
MT-IF-DB	multi-informational degree basis
MT-IMP	multi-implications
MT-INFO	multi-information
MT-INTR	multiple interpretation
MT-TFS-AT	multi-transfer shift activity
MTA-IMP	meta-implications
MTA-RT	meta-reality
MTA-RT-SIGN	meta-reality significance
MTH	methodology
OBS	observation (or reality of)
OP-SPD	option spread
P-FC	particular focus
P-PROG	particular progressionalism
PART	participation
PER-DY	perception dynamics
PER-PHY-U-FUND	perceived physical universe fundamental
PER-TR	perceived transformation
PER-TRS	perceived transition
PER-VT-U-FUND	perceived vibrational universe fundamental
PHY-U-C	physical universe context
PHY-U-FUND	physical universe fundamental
PHY-U-P	physical universe particular
POL-CON	political consciousness

POL-DYM	political dynamics
POL-OR	political order
POL-P	political policies (or execution of)
POL-SIGN	political significance
POL-ST	political state
POST	postulation
PR-INT	primary intention
PRI-AF-TO	primary affinity tendencies
PRI-INFO	principle information
PRI-VT-TD	principle vibrational tendencies
PROG-CONT	progressional continuance
PROG-EXT-FT	progressional extended functionalism
PROG-SIGN	progressional significance
PROG-TF-C	progressional transfer cycles
PROJ	projection
PROJ-CONT	projectional continuance
PROJ-DY	projectional dynamics
RC	race
RE-CONT	recontinuance
RE-DIF	redefinitions
RE-DOC	redocumentation
RE-ST	restructuralism
REL-APC	relevant application
REL-TECH	relevant technology
RES-RT	responsibility ratio
RET-AF-TD	retrograde affinity tendencies
RIT-DY	ritual dynamics
ROTP	responsibility of the position (the concept of)
RT-ALGN	reality alignment
RT-DY	reality dynamics
RT-IMP	reality implications
RT-INT-TR	reality initiative traits

RT-OP	reality options
RTD-PRD	related procedure
S-PROJ	source projection
S-ST	source shift (progressionalism) manipulation
SCI-DYM	scientific dynamics
SF-RZ	self-realization
SI	source initiation
SOC-PR	social programs
SOC-RT	social reality
SOC-RT-DEVF	social reality diversification
SOC-RT-DT	social reality dictates
SOC-RT-DY	social reality dynamics
SOC-RT-INT	social reality interpretation
SOC-RT-P	social reality particular(s)
SPT-AW	spiritual awareness
SPT-DY	spiritual dynamics
SPT-GH	spiritual growth
SPT-UNF	spiritual unification
SPTC-D	spectacle diversion
STF	source transfer
STY	style (or the concept of)
T-C-IMP	time continuum implications
T-L	time lag
T-P	time presence
T-SC	theoretical science
TECH-DY	technological (or technology) dynamics
TF-SH	transfer shift(s)
TH-AF-ALGN	thrust affinity alignment
TH-CONT	thrust continuance
TH-CONT-DY	thrust continuance dynamics
TM	terminology—or terms of a definition

TR	transformation
TR-DEF	trans-definition
TR-INFO	trans-information
TRS	transition
UNF-PI	unification (positively intended)/world unification
UPB	underlying philosophical basis
UTZ	utilization
V-SY	value system
VT-AF/ATT	vibrational affinity and/or attitude
VT-ATT	vibrational attitude
VT-DY	vibrational dynamics
VT-IMP	vibrational implications
VT-PLT	vibrational platform
VT-POST	vibrational postulation
VT-S	vibrational science
VT-TD	vibrational tendencies
VT-U-PT	vibrational universe particulars
WO-CH	world change
WO-EXP-PRI	world expansion principle
WO-MTH	world methodology
WO-UNF	world unification

ALTERNATIVE FUNCTIONALISM

(Level One) Black Notated Music

It will probably be some time before an honest evaluation of black notated music solidifies on a public level. For the particulars of this most neglected subject are not separate from the realness of present-day social reality. Thus to understand the dynamic implications underlying what has been offered through black notated music is to take into account many different factors—having to do with both the progressional misinterpretations of the western defining community, as well as how black notated music is viewed in the black community. Hopefully, as we move towards the eighties, the seriousness of this subject will take on added significance, for the reality implications of black notated music are no t separate from the general expansion principle of all creative music—that being, the projectional realness of creative music signifies and comments on the composite dynamics of people—regardless of one's perceived vibrational group. The very growth of a given group is directly related to whether its composite dynamics are allowed to expand (or simply function). The work which has been offered through the composite continuum of black creative music is important for what it signifies about black people and culture—and as such, the dynamic continuum of black notated music—and alternative scientific and methodological inquiry—is not separate from what this means as well. That this work has so often been either not acknowledged or misdocumented is a tragedy that cannot be allowed to continue. The challenge of transformation is not separate from whether or not full awareness of information dynamics is dealt with—this is true whether one is discussing the reality particulars of the black composer, creative woman, or white improvisor. It is because of the seriousness of affinity dynamics that the reality of black notated music must be re-examined. To really view this progressional continuum is to gain insight about the whole of both black creativity and world culture.

BK(NM)–2

The distortions which surround black notated music can best be understood by viewing the composite realness of western culture—especially with respect to information focus. For the collective forces of western culture have moved to create the illusion that somehow the affinity dynamics of black people cannot be viewed in the same context as those of normal people. Black people under this viewpoint are viewed as existing only in certain zones—and the creativity related to those zones supposedly has nothing to do with either methodological brilliance or "high culture." Yet I do not mean to view the reality of black notated music in one context, for obviously there is more to this subject than the collective forces of western culture. That fact is, in this time cycle very few black people are even aware of the realness of black notated music—in all of its dynamic diversifications. The present social position of black notated music cannot be blamed on any one sector of the community—but instead involves many different factors.

In the section on affinity dynamics I wrote about the relationship between a given creative spectrum to various zones of information. I wrote on this relationship as a means to better understand what a particular creative projection really is. It is fashionable in this time zone to only view a given creative projection with respect to its position in the spectacle-diversion continuum of this culture (western culture), rather than what a given form means in itself. If we are to have insight about the transformational potential of world creativity, then we are forced to re-examine our understanding of "particular" creative projections. The reality of black notated music is not separate from what this re-examination means as well—yet I do not mean to imply there is only one use of notation (or any other functional or vibrational factor) in black music, because this is not the case either. To comment on the reality dynamics of black notated music is to comment on a multitude of both forms and approaches, and this is important to understand. I am writing of a spectrum of styles which manifest the composite spectrum of a particular sensitivity. Even the use of the word "black" can be misleading if overly accented. For in the final analysis, I am only writing of creative music—and its related forces. If the present physical universe situation were different, there would be no need to focus on the so-called social implications of a given creattve thrust. But this is neither here nor there. The fact is, the present physical universe situation is directly related to the concept of race (among other things), and as such, it is important that attempts are made to clarify and expose the composite reality of black notated music.

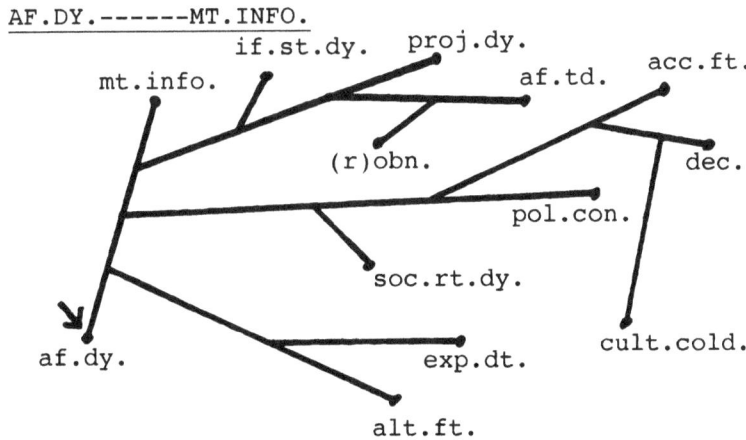

The progressional information focus that surrounds present-day western art music has moved to create the illusion that the solidification of "art" music can be viewed as completely separate from world culture. In this viewpoint, we have been led to believe that the thrust continuum of western creativity had nothing to do with any non-white initiations, and as such had no relationship to world culture. This viewpoint, however, does not correspond to actual reality. For to even lightly research the progressional realness of earth music is to find several contradictions to this viewpoint. First and foremost, the concept of notation is not the exclusive invention of western culture—let alone one person. The earliest uses of notation that have been documented go back to Egypt—which is part of the world culture community. But this is only the beginning. History tells us there have been many creative black people who have contributed to the progressional thrust of what is now called western art music.

This is also true for the functional and pedagogical basis of the music. For the foundation of western art music can be viewed as a readoption of many principles which were solidified in Egypt—having to do with the concept of harmony, the concept of form—the idea of music—and the concept of rhythm. Yet I do not mean to imply a kind of reverse racism either. Certainly the progressional continuum of western art music has seen much innovation and this is not to be disrespected—on any level. But the present vibrational stance which surrounds western art music has somehow moved towards affirming the present political realities of this time cycle—and in doing so has sought to elevate its status on untrue premises. The composite continuum of western art music must be viewed as a "great" music—but if we are to really view this thrust in meaningful terms, then western art music must be viewed as one "great" music among other "great" musics—this is my point. The cross-transfer implications of western art music are not cited here as a means to have one view of this music as "less"; rather, to really view earth creativity is to see many levels of inter-relationships (and what I call transfer-shift cycles). Nor does the pedagogical implication of western art music stop at its adoption of harmony and notation, for three-fourths of the instruments we have now come to identify as belonging to western art music can be traced to world culture as well. There are simply too many transfer cycles in the progressional solidification of western art music for one not to be aware of its world culture relationship—yet I do not mean to over-emphasize this most basic point—because there is much more to look at.

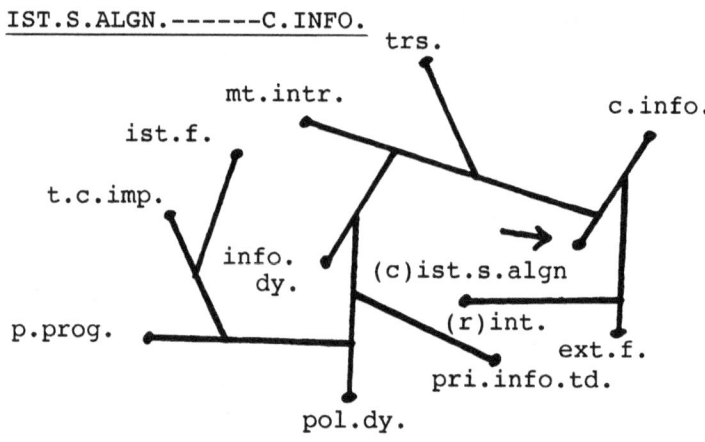

When I wrote that the emergence of the black composer was in itself not a recent development, I did not mean only with respect to events in America, or events in this time cycle. The contributions of black composers have existed in every progression of what we now call western art music. But this is not an easy task to document, for the present concepts we have of western art music have been reinforced by millions of books—and tons of misdocumentation—or simply omissions, if you like. Rather than attempt to examine the particular works of given composers—and run the risk of not mentioning either this or that composer (and I do not pretend to have all of the information that this subject needs—and as such, I look forward to many years of research on these matters)—it might be more useful to simply examine the cross-transfer implications of information exchange.

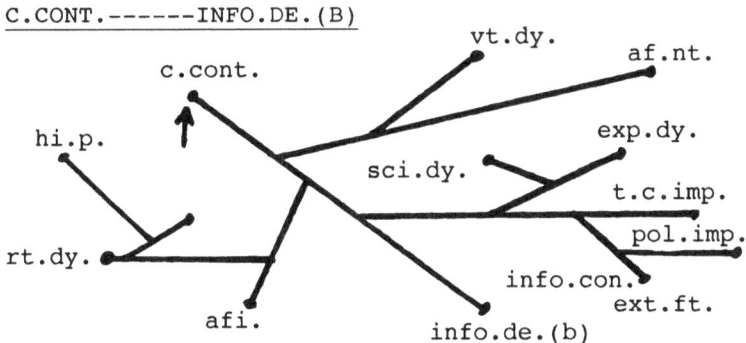

BK(NM)–6

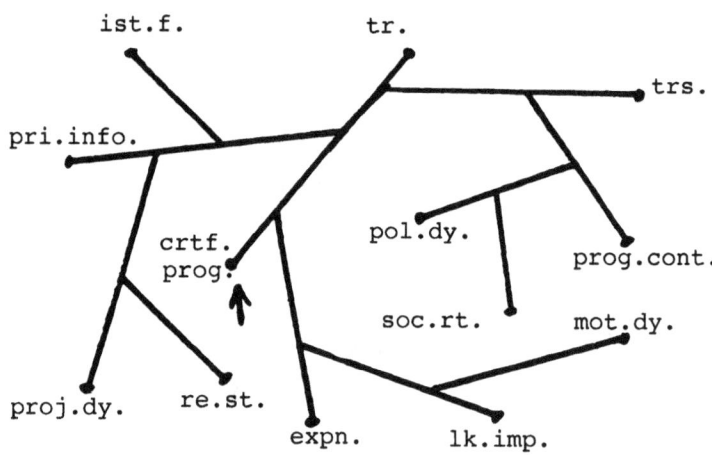

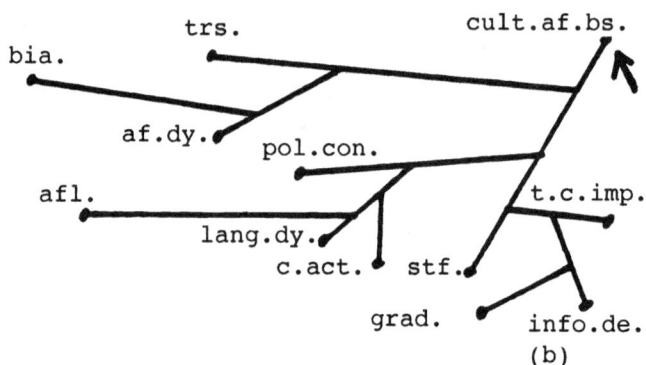

(b)

By cross-transfer implications of western art music I am referring to how the progressional solidification of the "actual" music comes about. For history can be viewed with respect to how the spread of given concepts—and practices—were brought about. This same history makes it clear that the progressional expansion of classical music can be viewed as moving northward from the region of Spain and later Italy. There can be no doubt as to the dynamic period which saw the invasion and settlement of two cycles of transitions during this same time zone. In particular, the period which saw the settlement of black people in Spain—the black Moors from

Africa—has long been documented as one of the single greatest cycles in Spanish history—for its contribution to creativity. The seeds underlying what is now called classical music can be viewed as solidifying in this cycle—which is to say, many black people were instrumental in the actual establishment of the foundation of western art music. There are tons of documentation about this most basic fact, yet few of us have ever been told of this viewpoint—for, actually, why should the fact that black people have contributed to so-called classical music be a surprise? To understand this is to view both the realness of cultural politics and racism. Every historian who has done minute research must be aware of some aspect of these contributions. Why haven't the history books included the offerings of all of the people who have contributed to the solidification of creative music? Not only are black people documented as contributing to the solidification of western art music, but the dynamics of those contributions have included many significant composers and instrumentalists in every period of western art music—but few of these people are noted in western art music textbooks. Hopefully, more research will be done in this cycle by black people, because there is a wealth of information I would like to know more about. For instance, how is it that two of the greatest composers in western art music have suddenly—through gradualism—lost all traces of their blackness because of present-day racism? Why is it that young people are not taught that both Haydn and Beethoven, by present-day western classification, are black composers (people)? The fact that this information is not known is frightening, because there would be a profound schism created in our present understanding of progressionalism—and/or affinity dynamics—if this information was brought forth. Moreover, it must be understood that practically every so-called Beethoven scholar knows something about this information—not to mention many other composers whose names we will have to dig up—which is to say, why hasn't some effort been directed towards making this information available? I believe western art music progressionalism must undergo a profound re-examination for what it poses as a multi-dynamic continuum of composite relevance. This is indeed necessary on many different levels. Because not only was Beethoven by today's definition a black man (in actual fact,

Beethoven was of German and Moorish descent—what is now called a mulatto—which is another interesting concept, since there is no strain of so-called humanity that is not a mixture of other parts of humanity—but Beethoven was not even a light-complexioned mulatto type, instead he is documented as being very dark, or dark enough to be called the "Black Spainard of Bonn"), but the violinist George Bridgetower, for whom he wrote the "Kreutzer" sonata, was considered to be one of the greatest violinists of his day and he was also black. To understand the realness of this information is to realize that many of our present-day ideas on western culture are not necessarily based on correct information.

There are many other questions about the progressional realness of western art music and its cross-sectional relationship to world culture that must be asked—for the historical factors related to the transformation cycle that solidified early Greek culture have never really been properly documented. Many people even today are not aware of the misdocumentation that surrounds the information developed in Egypt during its high culture cycle (and that information pertains to practically every area of discipline, whether we are referring to masonry, creativity, spiritualism, medicine, etc.), and many of us have not been informed even as to how the indigenous people of Africa (Egypt) looked—with respect to their physicality. The fact is, the people who inhabited Egypt during its high culture cycle are the people we now refer to as black people. Why is it that none of this historical information is made available to the greater public—and taught in our classrooms? If we are to view the progressional complications of world creativity, and if we are to understand the dynamic contributions of humanity—regardless of what sector or what so-called racial group we are focusing on—then it is essential that one has a developed understanding of actual world history. Moreover, if we are to understand the relationship of black people to process—whether that process involves notation or improvisational structures—then it is important that this understanding is not based on preconceived theories concerning whether someone has the right to a given area of information. Not only do black people have a "right" to participate in whatever area they choose, but each of us has a duty to function with respect to what is most "real" in whatever area he/she has chosen. Each of us has a duty to function with respect to what is most "real" to what we are about—or would like to be about (or what one naturally vibrates to). This is so because the historical realness of world culture seems to indicate that the dynamic spectrum of world information has come about from the composite offerings of human beings—regardless of what classification one is reduced to.

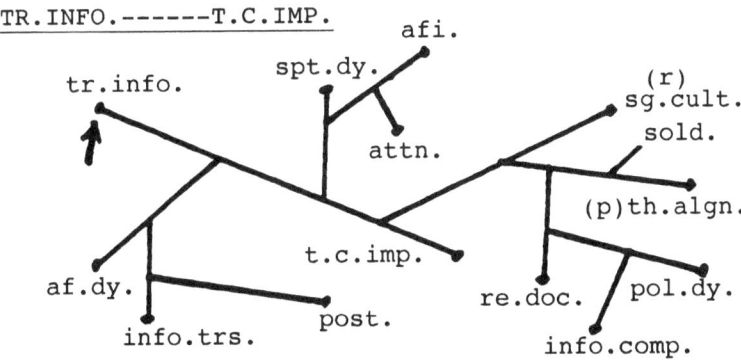

To understand the reality of the black composer in the past one hundred years is to deal with many factors. For the black composer is somehow perceived as not being related to either the black or white community. This viewpoint is understandable if the particulars of a given time zone are evaluated without respect for composite reality—yet it is not valid (if a viewpoint involves basing an opinion from something true). The black composers through the progressional continuance of time have come to be viewed as either lackeys of the western art music continuum, or simply imitators of European classical music. This is not only true for black composers alone, but extends throughout the reception of all non-caucasian composers. One can count on one hand the non-caucasian composers whose activity has gained respect in classical circles (and I mean "real" respect—not simply a nod from a friend—or two—something like "he's a real nice guy" or something). Even a composer as great as Villa-Lobos has never really been dealt with compared to what the dynamics of his work signify. Which is to say, if the collective forces of western culture can't accept Villa-Lobos, then one can imagine how black composers are viewed. Even worse, as the vibrational reality of classical music has progressed, many black composers have come to accept their position as aliens. For not very many people are able to function with respect for what they believe—and what they postulate for their goals in life (usually at an earlier age)—in the face of massive evidence about their inferiority. Only a handful of people are equipped to deal with "intensive negation"—which is to say, the physical universe reality which surrounds "how" creativity is must also be taken into account if one truly wants to understand the reality of black composers.

In the black community, the black composer has historically been perceived with respect to social-reality dictates. For to pursue the particulars of composition would necessitate greater penetration into the perceived western information complex (e.g., the university), especially as this phenomenon relates to composition study. In this context, the black composer was viewed for what he or she represented in the social structure particulars of both black and American society. As such, the black composer was perceived as one who studied extensively in the western university situation—sometimes exclusively, and embodied the characteristics of the so-called white negro. In many ways, this viewpoint is accurate, for to view the progressional realness of black notated music in this time cycle is to see a whole reality of people who were separate from the mainstream of black culture. Certainly the information focus black composers received in the university did not seek to give them—or anyone, for that matter—a worldview of creative music. Many of these people would leave the university with totally racist and distortive views about creativity—especially the creativity of non-white people. Moreover, the universities' approach to composition would necessarily stamp out alternative dynamics—which is to say, the route black composers have traveled has not been easy. To this day, the university situation can be viewed as the single most destructive factor any creative person must encounter, and this is particularly true if that person is black. The image of the black composer—and the reality of many black composers—does indeed show a marked separation from the composite realness of black culture—yet to say this as a universal fact would be a great distortion.

For the composite continuum of black notated music has seen many composers survive the "educational" experience—and more important, the composite realness of creative music has seen much creativity offered by black composers. To understand this is to understand affinity dynamics.

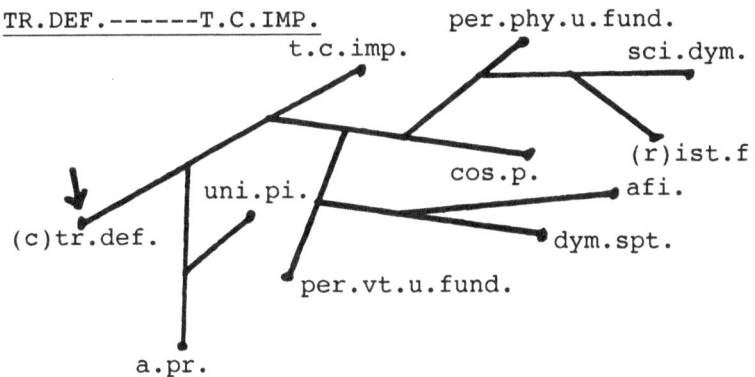

I have already stated that the historical solidification of western art music is related to world culture, and I have already stated that to view any continuum of western art music is to see a dynamic participation of many people—regardless of race—but if we are to really understand the reality of the black composer, then it is necessary that the implications of affinity dynamics are better understood. For the most basic idea that many people are dealing with in this cycle is the idea that to be involved in notation (and the reality of western art music) is to be a freak of some kind if you are not white. To agree with this viewpoint is to be totally ignorant of "progressional continuance" and transitional and transformational history. For while it is true that nine-tenths of the black composers participating in notation have suffered from how the music has traditionally been taught, it is also true that many composers have positively contributed to the thrust continuum of the music. The fact that these composers were drawn to notation and its corresponding reality in western art music, has to do with the nature of what "attraction" really means. For to view the progressional realness underlying what has happened to black people in the last three hundred (and some) years is to understand the dynamics that would surround "regrouping." When black slaves were first brought to

America there was information compression on an unprecedented level. Not only would given culture linkages be broken, but any references to Africa were suppressed. This process would continue until Reconstruction (yet it is clear that nothing has changed even as we approach the eighties)—which is to say, the move towards re-establishing affinity specifics (i.e., functional knowledge to be applied) involves several different routes. The resulting creativity that has been established by black people is something all humanity can be proud of—for the seeds underlying the foundation of this phenomenon—dynamic creativity offered from the "special situation" black people have come through—has to do with the use of affinity dynamics to tap the existing realities "of the day" (to conform with transformational alternative culture). This has been the case with the music we have come to call the blues, this has been the case with Gospel music, this has been the case with ragtime and black popular music, and this has also been the case with black notated music. Thus to understand the reality of black notated music is to understand the route it has traveled—as well as the meta-implications underlying what that route means in vibrational and actual terms. When this information is viewed with respect to progressional transition, then the reality of black notated music will be seen for the positive contributions it has made.

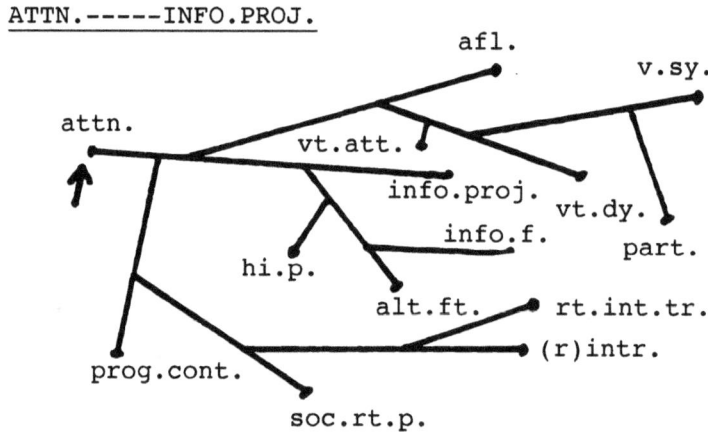

The greatest single factor that has been used to distort the significance of works by black composers is his or her relationship to the reality of western art music—as opposed to the actual music. In other words, there have been many works of great beauty offered through the progressional continuum of black notated music, but very few people have had the opportunity to experience it. To understand this is to begin viewing the particulars surrounding this reality. For while it is difficult for the average white composer to have his or her works performed—not to mention recorded—the option-spread possibilities for black composers are almost nonexistent. Most of these people have had to rely on their ability to create alternative outlets exclusively—yet this is of course not always the case. For the option possibilities of a given black composer are not separate from the social-dynamic sophistication that surrounds how that person deals with the collective forces of western culture. This is true for the progressional graduate composer as well as the student composer. In actual terms, the reality cycle of the black composer can be viewed with respect to how flexible that person can be in both risking his or her essence—postulation alignment (how one originally saw him- or herself and how one chose to pursue that image in actual life)—as well as social acuteness. This phenomenon can be seen in the very early stages in the university. For one's ability to excel in the classroom—and have one's grades be respectable—has more to do with "vibrational flexibility" than with either creativity or knowledge. It is because of this flexibility that many composers—and black college students in general—have undergone so much agony. For the progressional continuance of college education in the west moves towards the disenfranchising of one's basic affinity alignment—yet no one in his right mind would suggest that the college experience should be avoided. Because regardless of the obstacles—and there are many—if one can survive the experience, there is much of positive value that can be extracted from so-called higher education. This is also true for the reality of the black composer. For to survive the university experience and still care (or remember) about creativity is to be in a potentially positive functional position. To understand this example is to deal only with the significance of information dynamics. For the challenge of transformation is directly related to the re-securing of information lines—as a factor to reintegrate a transformational worldview. Which is to say, the significance of the university experience has to do with the spectrum of information lines to which it exposes one. The problem with getting this exposure has to do with how much stress a given individual can stand—and this is particularly true for black people. In the case of the black composer, the pedagogical implications of affinity alignment can be seen in how music functionalism is used as an identity-choking device rather than a spiritually uplifting stimulant. All of the role models that black composers are programmed to idolize are white models (or at least, this is what everyone is told), all of the works examined are by white composers, all of the learning exercises are based on the works (and even more important, the affinity attitude) of white composers, all of the composition contests (and awards) are based on how deeply one can enumerate or actualize some aspect of what one has learned as "correct" (that being, what the "masters"—who are white—have done). The reality of the black composer is filled with these incidents and many others as well.

The perceived relationship between the black composer and the western art music establishment has also brought other repercussions to the work of black composers. In other words, the use of perceived western functionalism by black composers is not separate from the composite adoption of the critical and defining community which surrounds western art music, whether or not that adoption was desired (and unfortunately in many cases it was). In this position—with physical universe factors taken into account—it was only natural that the white defining collectives would dismiss black notated music. Even to this day, any talk of black notated music is directed towards those composers whose activity fits within western words—or those whose activity can be made to conform to the aesthetical and vibrational reality of the white aesthetic. The end result of this dilemma has seen the systematic suppression of black composers. Until the black composer moves away from the collective reality of western art music (not the music but the society that surrounds the music) and until there is a conscious attempt to not accept alien definitions on one's activity, the reality of the black composer will not change. One thing is clear: the actualness of the black composer is not an accident, but rather another dynamic wing of the composite projection of black and world creativity. This is true even though there have been few efforts to expose this music to the community (either by black composers or by the people in the community). Nevertheless, the realness of this subject should help us better understand the dynamic complexities underlying actual creative functionalism—beginning with the spectrum of a "given route." The progressional continuance of black notated music can be viewed for how it has commented on the life-progression cycle of black, white, and world people—regardless of time zone. What is more, the actual creativity from this continuum has vibrationally and conceptually aided the composite reality of notated music. I am not writing of one offering of music, nor am I commenting on one form of composition. To view the dynamics of black notated music is to see a spectrum of approaches—all of which are relevant to the composite realness of black and world culture. To simply dismiss this music is not to deal with some aspect of yourself, and this is particularly true if the person reading this is black—or non-white. The work offered through the progressional continuance of black notated music is important for what it signifies about the source-transfer implications of its respective zones. This is a particular challenge that awaits all non-white people regardless of information area—having to do with the recovery of composite information and resurrection. The intensity of this challenge will one day be felt on every level of the collective reality of non-white—and, in this context especially, "black"—people (and particularly for those who are prepared—and fortunate enough to have the opportunity—to accept the academic information continuum route). The nature of this challenge will have to do with the struggle to amass information (knowledge)—no matter what affinity alignment is placed on that information—as a basis for alternative functionalism, and hopefully alternative re-examination. This challenge will be essential if indeed transformation is to be a reality (rather than a word), and the work young people are doing in this (and the next) period will determine nothing less than the future setting of the next time and reality cycle. In the case of black and non-white people, the challenge of academic rerouting is even more urgent. For unless young men and women of non-white so-called races are able to penetrate the established defining and controlling centers of western culture, there can be no hint of a positive transformation. The academic route, then, must be viewed with respect to what information it unearths as well as for what that information signifies with respect to its social implications. One's effectiveness to reshape a given culture is directly related to the option-spread dynamics to which he/she has access. This, then, is one area of challenge that the college graduate must deal with—having to do with the reinvestigation of science—astronomy, medicine, teaching, laws (both cosmic and functional), politics (and particular functionalism in government), space travel, inventions, chemistry, alternative technology, creativity (and in that category, the significance and reality dynamics of world music), improvisation—and composition. If we are to view the reality of black notated music, then our observations must be based on a total (overview) awareness of what is really taking place in this time zone.

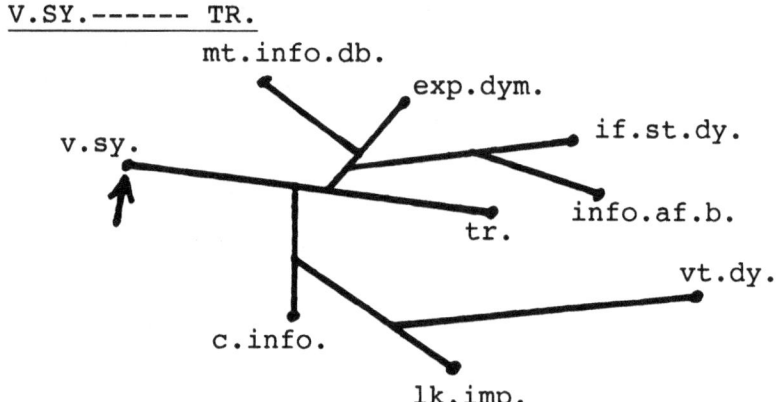

There are only a few books that devote any space to the existence of the black composer, and usually the whole reality of this subject is brushed off in one or two paragraphs (the understanding being that the music doesn't merit much focus). But if one would research alternative sources it is possible to learn about many creative composers—people whose works have rarely been heard in most cases. Nothing is more exciting than to learn about this area of music—for the neglect of this music can be utilized positively in this time zone. There is much that we can learn from the composite projectional thrust of this subject by having the opportunity to experience early (and present) examples of the music. The research related to the discovery of this information will be very important for years to come. Already, because of the research of scholars such as Eileen Southern, it is possible to view a whole spectrum of creative black composers—regardless of time zone. From this research we can begin to learn about the real progressional spread of creative notated music from the black aesthetic. It is my hope that the next cycle will see more performance of the actual music—obviously this is what is needed.

There have been many positive signs in this time zone that the reality of the black composer is about to change.

Certainly the Society of Black Composers must be viewed as extremely significant. Moreover, the last decade has seen many other attempts towards functional unification. In many respects, the reality-option functionalism that surrounds black notated music is similar to what has happened to the post-Ayler creative music continuum. For the most basic factor that has dictated the nature of alternative functionalism in both cases has been the move towards unification and redefinition. Yet I do not mean to imply that the work done in the sixties has completely laid bases for a re-examination of black notated music—because it hasn't. The struggle towards real alternative functionalism must be viewed as a progressional phenomenon. The sixties saw many organizations come together, only to fall apart in the seventies—and there are many reasons for this. For the basic political reality that permeates western culture has remained the same—which is to say, whatever surface differences exist between various musicians and composers, in the final analysis unification will be the only practical approach that can even hint of success. The seriousness of separation—whether we are referring to creative musicians, dancers, etc.—cannot be viewed as functionally sane; that is, if the alternative creativity happening in the black community is to be related to transformational world change. But to view the composite time period of the sixties and seventies is to see the beginning of what hopefully is the first signal towards real alternative functionalism. The changes taking place in creative black music in this time period aren't always apparent—as far as composite-culture awareness is concerned—but all over this country (America) one can begin to see the stirring of alternative undertakings—including notated works from black composers. It is my hope that by the middle of the eighties the total impact of this phenomenon will become apparent. For I am not commenting on the activity of one or two composers, but instead a whole reality of people who are functioning with respect to the affinity-insight (1) principle and with respect to the implications of affinity dynamics. The challenge of alternative creativity can accept nothing less—yet I am not trying to sloganize something as important as real change. The realness of the next cycle is dependent on what happens in this cycle—having to do with the nature underlying alternative activity progresses or regresses. The dynamic of alternativism is directly related to the particulars of each information region. Thus the work of black, Asian, and white composers in the next cycle must be evaluated for how it helps or hinders understanding about the next cycle. It is because of this challenge that the meta-reality implications of alternative functionalism are important. The work of black composers must be viewed from this context and is not separate from what this challenge means. At present there is a whole history of creative notated music from the black experience that has not been either integrated into the composite culture stream, or evaluated with respect to what it has offered the world community in vibrational or actual terms. This can no longer be tolerated if we are truly interested in real change.

There has been an extraordinary group of creative black composers who have been raised in this country (America). Many of these composers have had their works performed throughout the planet—although this is not the norm. Some of these composers have even had acclaim in America—

yet one can't really make too much of this (for while it is true that several black composers have had relative success, by the same token, this success has historically been used to suppress other composers—this is not only true for black composers but includes every area of cultural participation). To write of creative notated music from the black aesthetic is to write of composers like William Grant Still or Edmond Dédé, Clarence Cameron White or Ulysses Kay. All of these people, by any definition, have greatly contributed to the reality of creative music. That their work has never really been available to the greater culture is a tragedy—for without having the opportunity to experience the realness of their music—or scores—it will be impossible to learn from their contributions (i.e., focus and/or insight). But to even lightly experience the music from this sector is to become aware of a unique body of invention. These composers have not simply adopted themselves to the reality of western art music, but instead have used that medium as a basis to project the dynamics of their life and cultural experiences. To experience the music collectively produced by these composers is to experience a music that includes spirituals, Gospel, so-called jazz, world music, and, yes, even western art music. The dynamic spectrum of these contributions has yet to be dealt with, for to really view the significance of black notated music, it is important to understand the "reality position" each composer affirms in his (or her) own individual focus. All of these composers have thoroughly mastered the mechanics of their craft—having to do with the ability to write in whatever style deemed appropriate (with a mastering of the "laws" or so-called laws that constitute what a given form is supposed to be). In that light, the reality of the black composer begins to take on an interesting edge. For while the dynamic spectrum of classical music encompasses many forms and periods in itself, the black composer can also draw on another whole reality (and its related affinity dynamics). To view the composite works offered through this continuum is to see an added factor.

Among the composers whose works must be cited are:

Wendell Logan—has contributed a dynamic body of work in the time cycle of the seventies, and I view his activity as required listening for any person serious about creative music. The dynamics of his work have utilized choir music, chamber music, and solo music in both a notated and/or structured improvisational context. This is a composer who has investigated the spectrum of world creativity, and the thrust of his work will be an important factor in the direction creative music takes in the eighties. The spectrum of Logan's activity encompasses the total reality of transformational involvement—and the reality of his activity is not separate from extended world methodology (as a given function is extended from both African and/or western art music information dynamics). Logan has worked in electronic music and also functions as an instrumentalist. Any real attempt to view creative music, as we move into the eighties, must include some awareness of his work.

Talib Rasul Hakim—of the black composers who emerged in the early seventies Hakim must be considered the most successful. Many of his works have been performed throughout the United States, and it is clear that his creativity is profoundly relevant for the next cycle. Every work that I have experienced of Hakim's has been extremely beautiful and important, and the reality of this composer's involvement with creativity transcends any one context. Hakim has produced compositions for orchestra, solo music, as well as tone poems and improvisational works. I believe Hakim's activity will play an important role for composite creativity in the future. Already the works that have been produced must be considered significant. This includes his work for solo piano, piano with two percussion instruments, and two recorded orchestra works. I for one eagerly await his next record.

Alvin Singleton is among the most dynamic of the new composers in creative music today, and the thrust of his vision will undoubtedly profoundly affect the direction and reality of creative music as we enter the eighties. The spectrum of Singleton's activity includes solo music to orchestra compositions—and to date he has already completed his first opera. To experience Singleton's music is to enter a creative universe totally separate from either the serialist or repetition movements. This is a universe of creativity that has solidified its own laws and particulars. Hopefully the eighties will see more performances of this most creative composer's work—and along with more performances, I would hope that recordings will also be made available for the greater public. I view

Alvin Singleton's activity as among the most important creative outputs in this time period.

Olly Wilson is quite simply one of the most important composers writing music in this time cycle. The spectrum of his work has encompassed every area of creative music, and in each case his actual creativity has brought forth necessary invention and dynamic insight. There are only a handful of composers who are on Wilson's level in electronic music—in terms of technical mastery and, more important, dynamic invention—and there are no composers whose achievements in this field are more vital. But Wilson is not limited to only electronic music. Instead, the scope of his involvement with creativity is boundless—affecting every area. I believe that Wilson will continue to contribute significant works as we move into the eighties and nineties.

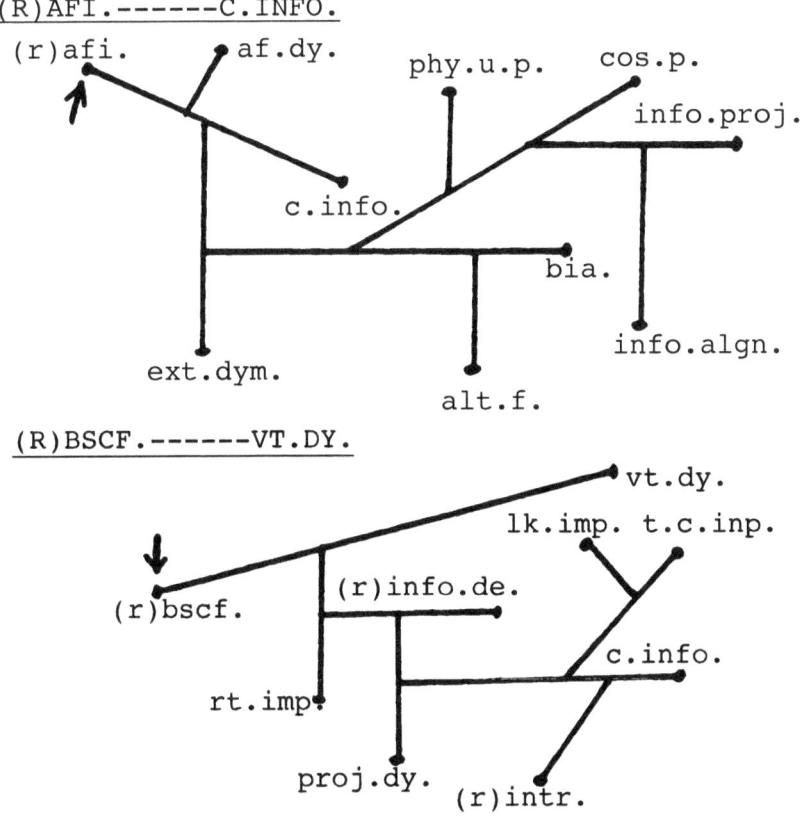

To examine the composite continuum of black notated music is to also begin developing another viewpoint with respect to the basic continuum of western art music—especially in America. For while composers like Charles Ives and/or George Gershwin are generally credited with integrating western art music to the world (or what in this cycle is called folk music of American culture), this viewpoint does not necessarily correspond to the truth. The total reality of notated music from the black perspective seems to indicate otherwise—which is to say, the work of black composers can no longer be simply dismissed as irrelevant. If we choose to wait for the collective forces of western culture to change the cultural perception of black notated music, then we will have a long time to wait. I have not introduced the use of folk and African concepts and/or melodies to imply that this example is the only area black composers have contributed to—because this is only the beginning. To really understand the dynamic implications of black notated music (with respect to its real "particulars"), one would have to deal with each composer on an individual basis (for obviously no one person has functioned in every area—which is to say, different people have contributed different aspects). The fact that there are no colleges or conservatories really teaching about this area of creative music is shameful.

Creative Improvised Continuum

In the beginning of this section, I stated that the dynamic continuum of black creative functionalism is not limited to any one area—or strata. If we are to understand what this means in actual terms, then it is important that other areas of the music are focused on—this is necessary if we are to gain a total overview about black functionalism. For this reason, it is important to view the progressional implications of creative improvised music from the black aesthetic—regardless of focus or context. Because the dynamic functionalism offered through this thrust alignment has played a major role in reshaping world creativity. At the same time, the profound influence of black music must be viewed for the source-initiation principle underlying what this reshaping has meant—as interpreted through the vibrational continuum of world culture. In other words, the reality of present-day extended functionalism must be viewed for what it implies about the oncoming planet change cycle—whether that cycle is transition or transformation—and this examination can also give us insight into the aesthetical dynamics of black creativity. For the progressional continuum of black creativity has never really been credited with the significance of its composite offerings—whatever period, and if we are to uncover the reality of this phenomenon, then the factors related to this "unacknowledgment" must also be viewed. Certainly one could cite racism as the most basic factor related to the suppression of black functionalism documentation—yet while this is of course true, it is more important to understand why suppression—and neglect—were necessary in the first place. Because while black music has never really been credited for its dynamic contribution to composite creative functionalism, the realness of its influence has still been utilized—which is to say, its dynamic functionalism has still been practiced—all over the planet. Thus any attempt to deal with the realness of black functionalism—or black creative functionalism—would involve re-evaluating just what has been realized through the progressional continuum of the music. Yet it is important that I state my own limitations as well. For I do not presume to thoroughly know all of the particulars of so vast a subject. I have only chosen to write on particular aspects of this subject. The end result of this chapter can be viewed as only an attempt to begin re-examination and nothing more. The real work that must be done has yet to materialize. If we are to ever understand the dynamic reality of creativity in this time cycle, then the particulars—the total particulars—of black creative functionalism must be dealt with. Either this is the case or the mis-documentation of this period will go unchallenged.

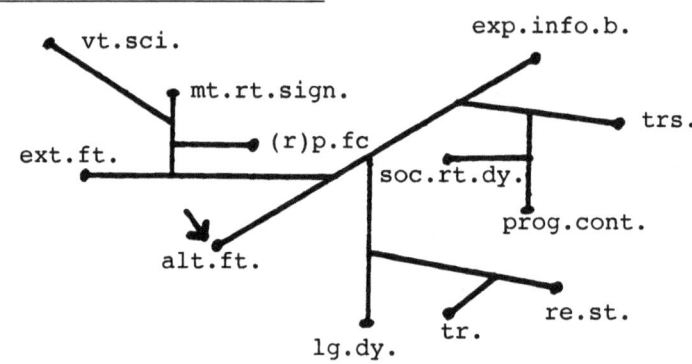

The dynamic realness of black creative functionalism must be viewed with respect to its progressional and historical brilliance. For the reality of this subject is not separate from the composite factors responsible for this time period. To focus on the dynamics of trans-African creative postulation—as this phenomenon solidified in the Americas, it is important to establish the broadest possible context for examination. For the early period of slavery established a definite progressional path with respect to the creativity of black people. By taking away the culture of black people—and also disallowing the rebuilding of anything related to Africa—the progressional resolidification of black inventions would have to do with re-adaptation—which is to say, the dynamic spectrum of black creativity would be related to what particular area a given person found him- or herself in. The two basic thrusts which would develop from this phenomenon would be (1) the group which moved to resolidify their activity from actual life experience and environment particulars, as opposed to (2) the group which penetrated into the information circle of western culture. To understand the dynamic spectrum of black creativity is to understand what has materialized from both continuums.

For the present cycle we are in (late seventies) has been directly shaped by both progressional thrusts. Any attempt to understand the realness of black creativity—and world creative invention—would also imply that the particulars of each projectional route be re-examined. Both paths can give insight into the reformational potential of black creativity as well as its relationship to the greater pattern dictating composite reformational world culture. Which is to say, the progressional implications underlying black creativity can give insight into the expansion particulars many countries are now experiencing in this time cycle (and of course this phenomenon cannot be separated from the realness of politics and transformation).

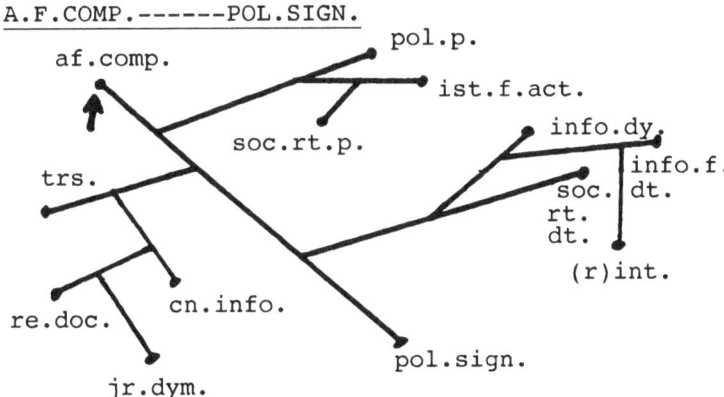

The social-reality dictates of creative black music detail the dynamic spread of both source initiation and source transfer. In this context, the progressional expansion of source-initiation postulation involves what particulars solidified in the expansion development of reformation. For the fact that black people in early America fashioned their activity from unimpeded affinity dynamics would play an important role in determining how their "forward" (coming) creative routes actualized (and proceeded). It is from this context that one can view the dynamics of what in this time zone is referred to as black folk music—also blues, early ragtime, boogie woogie, etc.

All of these projections were actualized with respect to the nature of source initiation—which is not to say there was no awareness or influence from source-transfer-related activity—obviously creativity is affected by its total environment (but the significance of a given effect is related to whether or not its terms are in the defining position). By contrast, the life route of source-transfer black creativity would involve that group of people who acquired some aspect of "formal" musical training, and practiced in so-called classical music. Many of the forms we now refer to as Gospel or harmonic improvised music would come from this thrust. Yet it would be wrong to view any of these creative routes as completely separate. For to view the reality cycle of the early periods of slavery is to see many cross-sectional developments. Practically every book I have read on this period (the early period centered, say, around New Orleans) seems to indicate there was much interplay between every sector of the black creative community. For example, there is much documentation on the "schooled" creole musician who would, when possible, "jam" with the creative musicians who functioned from source imitation. My point is that this interplay had to do with exchanging information as much as actually playing music. It would be a great error to conclude that the projectional continuance of black creative music involved a separation of its community or information dynamics. This has never been the case. However we choose to look at the progression spread of creative black music—in terms of the time zone reality of its creative notated and improvising traditions—it is important to recognize the nature underlying what has resulted from the composite music. Every tradition of creative music from the black aesthetic has functioned with respect to both its functional dynamics and its vibrational identity. We can also view—in the activity of a musician like Fletcher Henderson, for example—what amounted to the ingredients that would define the reality of this time cycle. Which is to say, the actualness of a music that would utilize the dynamics of both notation and improvisation. The seeds from this continuum would define the reality of the "jazz orchestra" as we know it today, as well as the post-Webern move towards controlled open forms.

The realness of the phenomenon is important to understand, for the essence umbrella underlining black methodology has dictated the vibrational and functional implications of present-day expansion dynamics. This is so because not only has creative black music dictated the transformational re-adaptation of methodology—with respect to how given universal and functional particulars could be utilized for a "new" music, but this re-adaptation was not separate from the affinity-insight (1) principle. Which is to say, the underlying vibrational basis of creative black music has always functioned with respect to an accented spiritual base. That base has helped to not only generate "new" forms, but the realness of what it signified would also house each extended creative projection with a transformational spiritual potential—and assignment. To understand this phenomenon is to begin to unravel the significance of alternative methodology from a black revolutionary perspective.

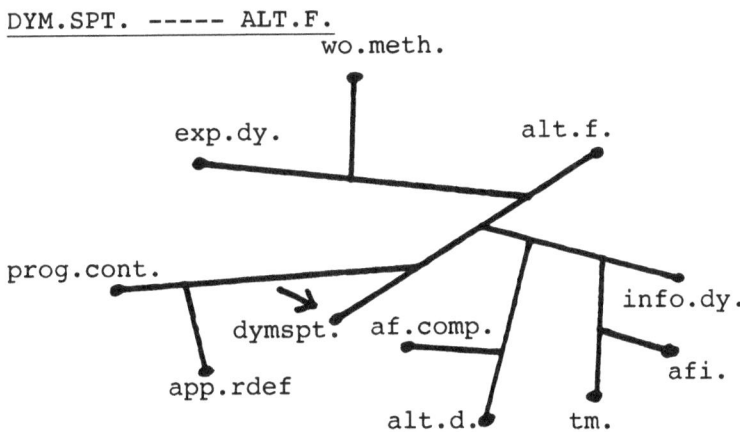

To view the dynamic continuum of creative music from the black aesthetic—regardless of projection—is to see the realness of composite continuance. For the tradition of black functionalism is not separate from the spread of its creative methodology—that is, the diversity of black methodology can be viewed as consistent with what was posed in the nature of its tradition. More so, the traditional realness of black creativity is not separate from its primary African essence foundation. The seriousness of what this means sheds light on the transformational position of black creativity (and this relationship also sheds light on why western culture has continually moved to either distort or suppress the music). For the composite thrust realness of black creativity can only view this period as one cycle in time—rather than the start of its initiation. Thus, in examining the methodology implications underlying how given processes have been utilized, it is important to not lose sight of the total continuum of black creativity. All of the realignments which have occurred in the last two thousand years (and some)—having to do with the rape of Africa to the forming of America, etc.—are only one chapter in the composite continuum of black creativity. As such, if we are to view the realness of black creativity "ised" in America, then the implications of source initiation and source transfer must be viewed in the correct context. Not only have forms been utilized and created by black people after arriving in America—having to do with resolidification and survival—but all of these adaptations signaled some aspect of the re-establishment of "composite black methodology" and how this phenomenon was and is to be brought about. To understand what this resolidification means in actual and vibrational terms is to understand why it is important to focus on the significance of black methodology and alternative functionalism. Because by focusing on these questions we are not simply viewing a given initiation—with respect to either its existence or its brilliance—but instead these matters are related to the profound implications underlying what a given participation "really" means (in its vibrational and mystical sense). It is because of "what this information means" that the realness of "tradition" must be taken into account. For by focusing on the composite progressional significance of black creativity, we are actually focusing on the path alignment underlying how given areas of "vibrational information" are transmitted and maintained. The role of tradition in this context has to do with how a particular methodology has solidified through a time continuum of thousands of years to "best" serve a particular information function. In other words, if we are to view a creative projection like (what in this time zone is called) "the blues," it is important to understand that this projection has actualized because of a particular vibrational attitude (and that attitude is related to a particular area of information—vibrational, cosmic, functional, or scientific) which has been utilized throughout a great time spectrum (and adopted because it best fulfilled the reality of its function) having to do with the affinity particulars of black culture (when that culture defines for itself what was real and how that realness is to be dealt with), and also having to do with the information that best served how to deal with particular regions. This is the blues. To view the realness of black alternative restructuralism is to bring the significance of black affinity dynamics into real focus. Only when these questions are dealt with will we—as a collective people—be able to deal with the seriousness of creative transformation—not to mention rebuilding. The reality implication of affinity alignment is not a joke. To view these questions is to begin looking at the heart of creativity.

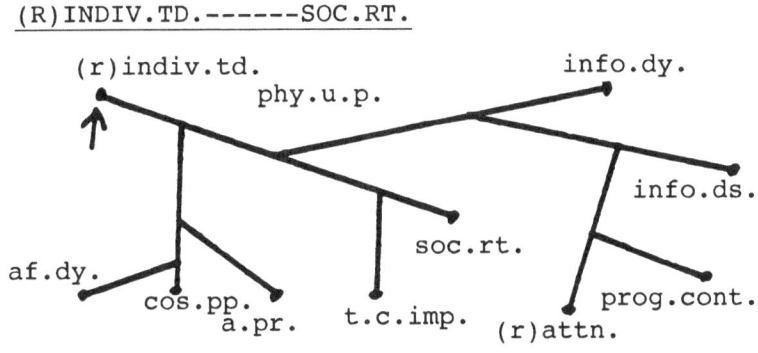

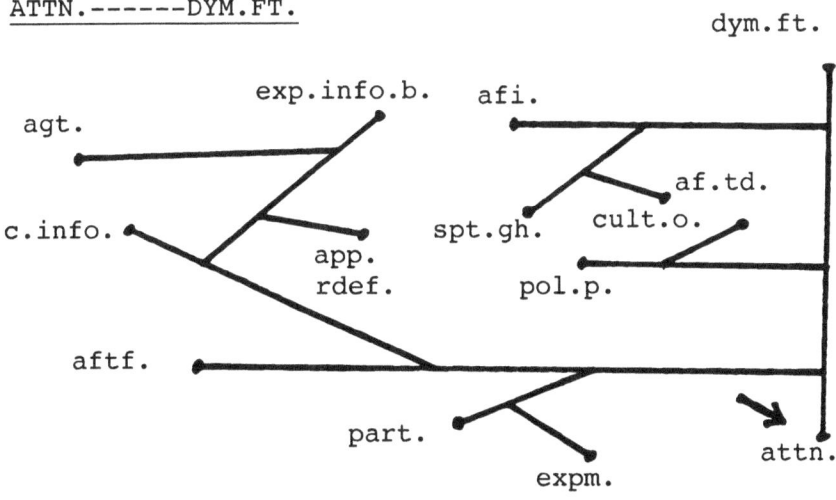

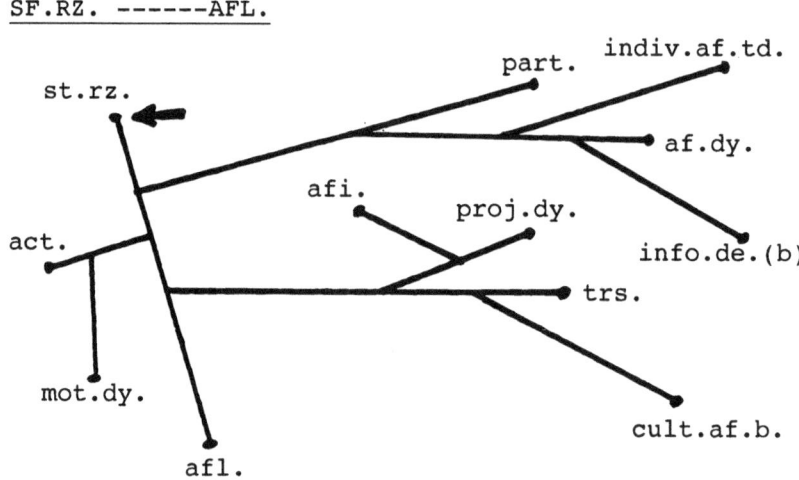

To view the early solidification of creative music from the black aesthetic is to see the forming of a dynamic continuum. The actual music from this juncture would solidify our present understanding and use of creative functionalism. This understanding would comment on every aspect of creative music, having to do with the dynamics of composition and improvisation to the use of form and creative materials. The actual "stuff" that would result from this information would be the emergence of the creative orchestra as well as the use of ensemble and group improvisation of both the affinity-insight (1) and affinity-insight (2) principles. The projectional realness of this phenomenon would also define the nature of alternative process (and alternative meta-process). All of these changes were revolutionary in their time, and remain such in this cycle. There is no so-called contemporary music on the planet that has not in some way benefited from the reality of restructuralism in transitional creative music from the black aesthetic.

The solidification of the creative orchestra is extremely important in the evolution of creative music. This medium would dynamically outline the path of extended creative music. To experience the music of composers like Henderson and Ellington is to experience the most "innovated" use of fixed material functionalism with improvised (or open) material. The realness of their activity (and others) would establish a new dynamicism for creative music. All of the subsequent extensions of this medium must be viewed for what this original dynamicism meant, for the progressional continuance of creative orchestra music—even until today—is no more than fulfilling what was implied (and practiced) in the early period of the music. As such, whether a given person decides to view present-day creative music as "more or less" advanced is irrelevant, because the composite implications of present-day so-called contemporary music were implied and utilized in its inception.

It is important to be made aware of the uniqueness of alternative functionalism as defined and practiced throughout the total continuum of creative music from the black aesthetic. For the reality of interpretation of continuum is very different from, say, western art music or Indian music. This difference not only extends to interpretation of material but permeates the total reality of the music—having to do with sensibility and meta-reality designation. I make this point not to under-rate western art music—or any music from the world community—but only to accent the nature of what has happened in creative black music. For western historians have moved to mis-document the reality implications (and functional brilliance) of this subject, with the understanding being that black music can be viewed as only an adaptation of western functionalism—with an added rhythmic difference. To state this without also commenting on the nature underlying how this adaptation was utilized is to have no understanding of black creativity (not to mention, can one really say that American black music has adopted any aspects it has not also helped to define—for I have already stated that the functional realness of western art music has learnt much from world culture). I make this point as a means to accent what has happened to black music documentation. For however one chooses to understand the many developments of the last transition cycle (especially with regards to the forming of America as the next defining culture and world power), the solidification of alternative functionalism as "ised" through black creativity must be perceived and respected as significant. The creativity that has resulted from this information has made a world impact that has exceeded any other comparable development. This is true no matter what initiation one chooses to compare it with. The thrust continuum of creative black music has clarified and redefined every "particular" in its progressional cycle—whether we are referring to the emergence of serialism, or the advent of electronic music. But this impact is rarely dealt with—especially on the level it deserves. An understanding of these contributions can shed light on the meta-reality significance of creative music from the black aesthetic—as a multi-dynamic thrust continuum.

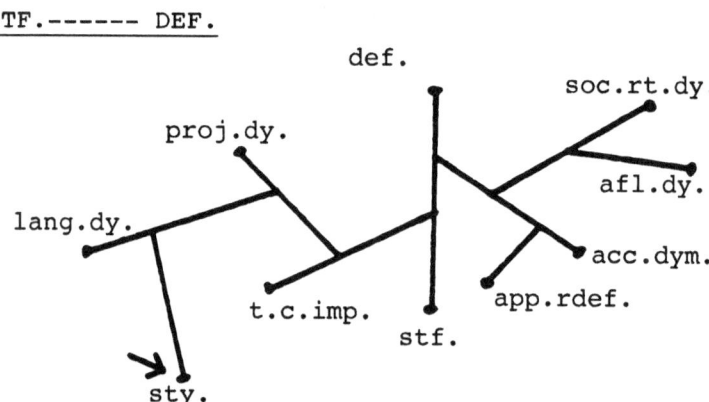

The use of notation in creative improvised music has yet to be really examined in all its different permutations. For the reality of this consideration functions on several levels that are outside of European art music. Notation as practiced in black improvised creativity is not viewed as a factor that involves only the duplication of a given piece of music—and as such an end in itself. Rather, this consideration has been utilized as both a recall factor as well as a generating factor to establish improvisational coordinates. In this context, notation is utilized as a ritual consideration, and this difference is important for what it signifies about extended functionalism. For in this position, notation can be viewed as a factor for establishing the reality platform of the music—dictating the harmonic and rhythmic sound-path of activity and also as a center factor. The result of this use of functionalism serves as a dynamic extension of contemporary process—nor am I commenting on only one alignment. For to experience the music of any creative orchestra is to see the reshifting of structural and vibrational moment-events (this can be checked by merely listening to the recordings of a given arrangement—or composition—and later hearing another version of that same arrangement but with a different order of events) as a means to have the fixed activity of a given composition re-ordered to deal (or apply) with the physical universe particulars of its performance. Today the use of re-ordering in this manner is called aleatory or indeterminism—but this practice has been utilized in creative music from the black aesthetic since its inception. Notation in this context invariably becomes a stabilizing factor that functions with the total scheme of the music rather than a dominant factor at the expense of the music. To understand this use of process is to see the composite implications of creative music—with respect to its progressional implications. For to view a consideration like what is called "the riff" is to see a functional tool directly related to African methodology—which is to say, the restructuralism implications of creative music from the black aesthetic are directly connected to world music and world meta-implications.

The dynamic implications of creative music from the black aesthetic can be viewed both with respect to its progressional continuum as well as its world culture dictates. To view the solidification of what is now called the "jazz" orchestra is to see the embodiment of one of the most significant uses of progress in this time millennium. It is by examining the works of composers like Duke Ellington where one can begin to understand dynamic extension. For his work—as well as others'—has directly aided the expansion principle of creative music. In the seventies, we see the "jazz" (creative) orchestra as sophisticated in every way—whether the focus is directed on the use of harmony or rhythm—as its European counterpart, and in many other ways even more sophisticated. Because however any particular "jazz" orchestra utilizes the dynamic of musical science (and laws), there is also the added ingredient of improvisation. That is, whatever the structural particulars of a given use of process, the "jazz" orchestra can still be viewed as a dynamic living and breathing ensemble—for the use of improvisation is a factor that sustains new life, and new actual and vibrational dynamics. This difference is important to understand—because the main emphasis of creative music from the black aesthetic has always been on the "ising" of creativity in accordance with the science of its given process and in accordance with the affinity-dynamic implications of the participants in the actual orchestra. The realness of this aesthetical alignment has always differentiated the reality of the so-called jazz orchestra from its European counterpart, because the jazz orchestra—and its use of process—has always functioned on several vibrational levels. The fact is that western art music has come to utilize its functionalism only with respect to the dynamics of re-interpretation (which in itself is most certainly beautiful and significant—any other viewpoint would be ridiculous, for I am not attempting to disrespect this or any form of music—rather, I am attempting to point out why the creative orchestra should be respected as well)—and in no way do the dynamics of interpretation compare with the freedom inherent in the functional arena of creative black music.

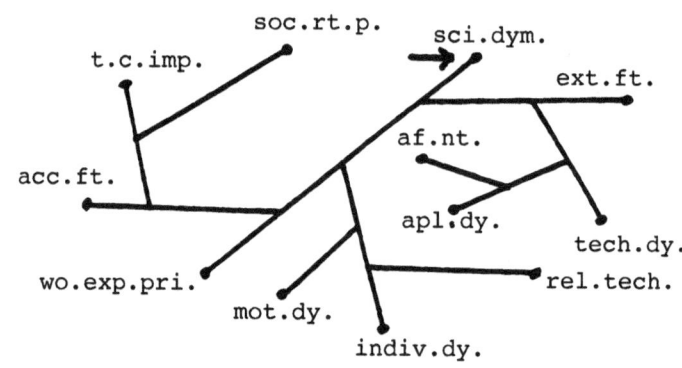

Among the many distortions that surround the progressional continuum of creative music from the black aesthetic is the notion that somehow the dynamic continuum of the music has now transported itself to the level where it now corresponds to western definitions. It is in this context that jazz is viewed as a form that has recently come to be "art" music (in the sense that the reality of its expansion dynamics has transported the music to the same aesthetical position as western art music). This viewpoint is not true. For while one can certainly view the progressional expansion of creative music functionalism as a continuum that corresponds to the dictates of universal transition (i.e., the gradual move from what is called simple use of elements—like harmony—to a later complex use of functionalism), at the same time it is important to understand that this expansion has never been separate from the needs (and reality) of the improvisor—or participants. To understand this difference is to understand that the expansion principle of creative music has not been undertaken because of the infinite possibilities of "numbers"—rather, the continuum of the music has adjusted to the "present time particulars" of its corresponding time zones. Obviously this is true because the meta-reality implication of creative music from the black aesthetic is not the same as western art music. To view the progressional continuum of creative black music is not to see an existential projection thrust—as in the post-Webern continuum—and this is also true for the form we now call bebop, because the meta-reality of all black creativity can only be viewed with respect to its actual vibrational and physical universe alignment—in other words, black creativity has never had the same relationship that western art music has with spiritual alignment. The resultant crisis that western culture is now experiencing has nothing to do with the projectional continuum and/or significance of creative black music (black people are not actually a part of western society anyway)—rather, each functional change of the music can be viewed with respect for what that change signifies about the reality and vibrational particulars being dealt with on the way to resolidification and transformation. Musicologists in this context would like to have it both ways, for on one hand jazz is put down as primitive when compared with western art music, but on the other hand when the dynamics of the music are conceded then suddenly the music is viewed as a form that in spite of itself is western (usually in these discussions there is much discussion as to "jazz" not being an African music, rather it is "much closer to western music"). These arguments are nonsense.

```
RE.DOC.------C.INFO.
       ist.f.              c.info.
               int.

                              cult.af.b.
(c)re.doc.                    pol.dy.
afl.dy.
         mt.info.      mt.info.

   indiv.td.
```

It follows that any proper evaluation of creative black music pedagogy would reveal the dynamic position of its alternative functionalism. This is, the use of process in creative music from the black aesthetic has supplied the expansion principle for freeing the total understanding of present-day dynamic functionalism. The progressional expansion of this phenomenon will one day be shown as being crucial to transformational information (dynamics and/or focus). For to understand expansion dynamics is to understand that not only has black music adopted (or re-adopted) elements from western art music in its early cycle (after being forcibly brought to the west), but the nature of that adoption is directly related to how those same elements have been expanded—and as such this phenomenon has given insight about the reality of composite alternative functionalism. We can now look at the medium of notation and deal with it as we choose, without being locked in by its historical use in any context. For notation as "ised" through the progressional realness of creative music has served as a supportive functional tool, and notation dictated through the creative music tradition has served as a basis for what can only be talked of as dynamic alternative functionalism. This consideration—notation—can now be viewed as not necessarily stagnating—but instead, something that can be used when deemed appropriate.

(R)TH.CONT. ------ T.C.IMP.------COS.AGN.

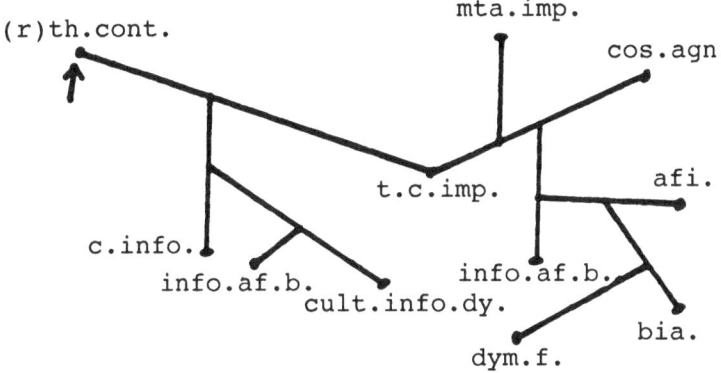

It is indeed amazing that so few critics of western culture have been able to deal with the dynamic re-alignment implications black creativity has brought to present-day creative functionalism. Instead, the most basic viewpoint we have had to deal with is the idea that black creative music could only utilize particular areas of functionalism—as compared with western art music—if it were to be successful. Very few critics have been able to deal with what has really happened in creativity during the past one hundred years. For black creativity has not only solidified the most dynamic alignment to alternative functionalism in this time millennium, but the solidification of this alignment has served as the most basic regeneration factor for all contemporary earth creativity. The end result of this phenomenon has seen a freeing of the individual, and the establishment of a creative platform for the composite forming of world creativity and also the emergence of contemporary methodology. Moreover, the progressional continuum of creative music from the black aesthetic has forecasted and actualized a whole new dynamic understanding of even the instruments themselves. It would be impossible to cite every area of what this change has signified, but even to point out the dynamic instrumental developments related to this subject can make my point. For the creative continuum of creative black music has expanded the reality of brass functionalism (i.e., increased the range and timbre of the instruments), expanded the understanding of percussion (i.e., the development of the contemporary drum kit—which was revolutionary in its inception), expanded the dynamics of the woodwind family (and in doing so showed another dynamic understanding of what this family of instruments could be about if approached creatively), etc., etc. All of these examples—and many others—have defined how creativity is perceived in this cycle—which is to say, the progressional realness of creative music from the black aesthetic has dictated the composite reality of contemporary world creativity. Nor have I meant to exclude any area of instruments, for the reality of the contrabass and violin have also been greatly altered by the music (this is true even though historians have long tried to claim that black music has never successfully utilized the violin—and this is not true; one needs only to hear the music of a Stuff Smith or Eddie South to know these statements are not accurate—there is also the work that was done in ensembles like Old Man Finney's Orchestra, which are not completely documented). There are many other areas of creative black music that must be dealt with. For the composite continuum of the music has affected many other factors—and the affinity nature surrounding those factors cannot be lumped together if one is to really understand the particulars of this subject. The solidification of ragtime is a form that is especially important for what position it occupies with respect to the continuum implications of both improvisational and notated functionalism. For ragtime in its original state was an improvised music that was formed through the actual postulations of creative musicians. Even after it became a notated form, the music continued to have a completely different sensibility than European art music. Any serious examination of a given thrust alignment would show that the functional reality underlying that projection cannot be viewed as separate from the aesthetical reality of its affinity alignment. However one chooses to view western art music, it was and is a manifestation of trans-European affinity dynamics—in terms of how they saw themselves and in terms of their relationship to affinity dynamic. In ragtime music, we see the notated principle utilized with a different aesthetic to the degree that its use represented an alternative basis for applied functionalism. In other words, ragtime music would utilize notated material and still maintain its separate vibrational identity. The seriousness of this utilization would dictate the dynamics of black notated music—regardless of time zone—and this is important to understand. For the use of this consideration (notation) does not necessarily mean that one is vibrating to the precepts and affinity reality of western art music. The emergence of notated ragtime music must be viewed as a significant actualization in the transfer cycle continuum of black creative music. For this form would be the clearest realization that, even in the early progressional development of restructuralism (starting again from the blockage of slavery), black creativity could assimilate every aspect of so-called western functionalism and still retain its own identity—and affinity make-up. This is true of ragtime and this is also true of the composite continuum of black notated music and alternative functionalism. To understand this is to deal with the progressional all-encompassing spread of black creativity.

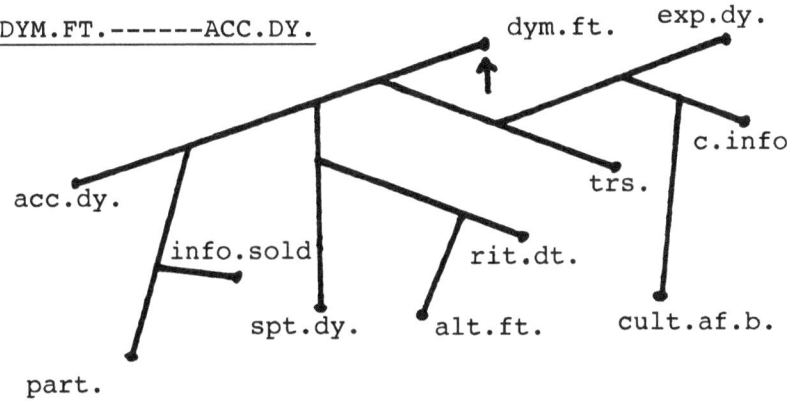

There have been many attempts by the established defining community to separate the meta-reality of ragtime music from the composite continuum of black creativity. Most of these attempts seek to disenfranchise ragtime by drawing analogies between the functional areas of the music and classical forms (e.g., Mozart). Yet however one chooses to understand the significance of these comparisons, in the final analysis the actual musics are so different that in no way can these techniques work. It is true that comparisons can be useful to help outline basic structural developments in a given period of creativity, and it is also true that there are similarities—on many levels—between the functional arenas of ragtime and western art music. But if taken too far, this type of dissection eventually can be used to distort the realness of a given form of music. For ragtime is not distinguished by its similarities to classical music but instead by its differences. Joplin's relationship with the functional arenas of western art music reveals only how alternative considerations can be a factor to transform a given creative thrust—regardless of time zone. For when I write that ragtime music was the first black music to utilize the notational functional arena after black people were brought to America, I am only commenting on the nature of source transfer as the most basic progression with regards to how any given physical universe situation can be understood. In this context, ragtime would immediately reveal itself as the first junction, with regards to alternative functional creative systems, to emerge in America: that is—the actualness of ragtime as an existing form must be looked at as an expansive and advanced consideration with regards to its functional arena—and this is what is important (and by the way—who was this German teacher Joplin was supposed to have studied under? There is no proof of this in recorded history—not to mention that even if this did happen, it could only have been for up to six months. Thus can one honestly conclude that Joplin's brilliance had to do with his studies under this mysterious German teacher?).

If the conceptual and vibrational implications of ragtime are understood, then its position in the creative continuum of American culture must also be dealt with.

For the emergence of ragtime represents America's first creative thrust to utilize the notational functional continuum of western methodology (even though the functional continuum of western functionalism is not exclusively western) with respect to what is implied in alternative functionalism. In other words, ragtime is America's first creative thrust that utilizes the scientific affinity-insight (1) principle as that principle relates to source initiation (which in this case is creativity actualized in and from America)—as opposed to European culture. The implications of this thrust would later affect composite American culture, and the solidification of a creative and vibrational methodology of this type would also generate the progressional continuum of American creativity (from the affinity insight [1] projectional route). The dynamics of ragtime and its related strains would dictate design (i.e., thematic utilization and style) with regards to every existing and forming creative thrust in its time zone. The actualization of this continuum would affect the use of original material in western Euro-American classical music (e.g., Ives) or the sophistication that was to come into march music (e.g., Sousa), all the way to the actualization of the American song form (e.g., Gershwin). It is in ragtime music that we can get an understanding of the forming identity dynamics of American culture—or at least the vibrational solidification of America is not separate from what the vibrational dynamics of ragtime would postulate (with respect to what America could have been). Moreover, by viewing the realness of ragtime music, one can have some sense of what forces were forming in the composite-essence basis of transitional America. For the progressional continuum of ragtime music would move to become a total American music—with participation and contributions from the composite "culture," whether we are referring to black or white creative people—and the seriousness of this participation has yet to be dealt with. Because the actualness of ragtime functioned as the first potential alternative transformational tool of American culture—which is to say, the first projection as related to the path of its zone (the first alternative functionalism projection with respect to the affinity insight [1] principle having to do with what it signified about the methodological transformation possibilities of affinity dynamics as focused from creative functionalism—which in this case had to do with its use of notation). To understand what this solidification means is to deal with a total overview of creativity and progressional continuance (on a composite level). For if the world implications of black American creative functionalism have to do with how its solidification will transport western culture back into the dynamics—and affinity range—of world culture, then ragtime must be viewed with respect to what its solidification signals about the nature of this progression. It is for this reason that the composite realness of black creativity must be viewed as significant—whatever projection. For the actualness of black creativity has had a profound position in western culture—regardless of strain. To view the composite realness of black creativity is to view how potential transformation attitudes have affected the tone reality of American culture, as well as what particular forces have been encountered in that continuum. To understand the dynamics of this phenomenon is to have some basis for viewing the composite route of America—as it is in this cycle, and as it promises to be in the next cycle. Creativity is not simply an isolated entertainment factor but rather a beacon that comments on the total reality tone of its environment space. The solidification of ragtime is not outside of what this viewpoint means.

Implications of Process

The emergence of creative music as a factor that has helped shape the present cycle we are now in has yet to be dealt with by the established controlling forces dictating policy about creativity in the west. I believe the dynamic implications of creative music have affected the total vibrational and intellectual arena of western art music, both in terms of how we have come to see process as well as basic routes to pursue with regards to this information—and this must be understood. Nor do I mean to imply that only creative music of the affinity-insight (1) principle has been of service in this regard—but rather the composite arena of creative music from the black aesthetic. Quite possibly the historical context can better show the realness of this subject, for too often many of us have come to accept the present reality—the appearance of things as it relates to "present time"—without regard for the total factors that allow it to actualize. It is the present disregard for composite history that best characterizes the situation we are now in—not only in creativity but in general—and it must also be remembered that not only are we the effect of what we have chosen to ignore—but even a brief look at the historical progressions which have shaped this period would reveal that western culture has long depended on our short memories: in short, the realness of 'gradualism'—as a factor that depends on the re-arranging of historical information—would not be possible if more attention were paid to the historical progressions of world progressionalism. It is for this reason that the functional dynamics of black creativity have yet to be dealt with by the composite information lines of the west, and it is this same factor that will move to lay a basis for redocumenting the historical progressions of composite progressionalism unless checked.

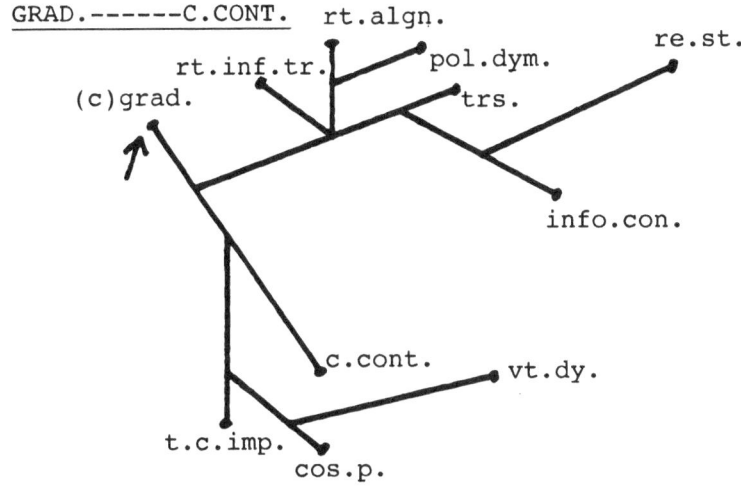

I have already written on the situation surrounding the progressions of western art music from the early emergence of that thrust—what it implied, etc.—and how it later advanced to Schoenberg. Whatever the understanding of the functional arena of western art music by western culture interpretations (as the form advanced to the post-Wagner and -Stravinsky period), we must understand that other factors were also taking place in that same time zone—factors that were important for what they would later pose for composite western creativity. For in this same time period, creative black music was not only emerging as a creative force to be reckoned with, but the functional dynamics underlying its reality dictates were a profound factor for what they implied to composite creative music functionalism. The realness of the Wagner-Stravinsky juncture in this context posed a very interesting situation for the controlling western forces of that time zone. For if process had become a choking factor in western art music at this point in its continuum, the very opposite was the case in creative music from the black aesthetic. More so, the meta-reality that defined the functional arena of composite black music addressed itself to the most basic flaws in the western functional and vibrational meta-reality: that is, creative music from the black aesthetic was a creative and notated form to the musicians who participated in it; this form was living proof that the dilemma of the creative musician in western art music—and the position of the composer—had more to do with the meta-reality of western art music than the process itself.

But to really understand what creative notated music posed with regards to the transition that occurred in the early 1900s, one would have to look at the implications of black music as a factor that has reshaped the composite community, as well as how that influence has helped to shape the present situation of western creativity. In other words, the implications underlying how process was used in creative music from the black aesthetic certainly had a profound effect upon composers from the western art music aesthetic. This has been the case with every period of creative music from the black aesthetic, but all too often the realness of what this "effect" means is forgotten—or dismissed. I am not writing that creative black music was the only factor that reshaped the functional arena of western art music—for that would not be correct—nor am I implying that creative black music was the only factor which compelled white composers to re-investigate process, because I am quite sure there are many different factors connected with how any transition is achieved. I am also aware that many individual composers had begun to see the consequences of the post-Schoenberg functional arena, and the limitations of notation as well. Certainly during the thirties, composers like John Cage were aware of the dilemma of western art music functional dictates. It was in this period that Cage was to prophesize how the advent of technology—in the form of electronics—could be of assistance to help the composer. Cage would later become the chief architect for opening up the structural arena of western art music. Yet one would have to be quite naive to think that these people (e.g., Cage, Varèse, Cowell, Harrison), however gifted and however much foresight they possessed, were not affected by the creative improvised music that was happening all around them. This is especially true of the American composers' tradition (e.g., Ives, Partch, Copeland), for no matter how separate this thrust chooses to see itself with regard to the dictates of composite American music—the fact is, creative music from the black aesthetic permeates every level of American music, and there is simply no way that these composers could not have been affected as well.

My reason for accenting the relationship between the American composers' tradition and creative music from the black aesthetic has to do with many different factors, because this relationship can give insight into the composite social and physical universe context that established extended functionalism for western creativity—and information dynamics. If one would investigate the reality particulars that dictated the transition Schoenberg and Webern personified, it would be possible to clearly see the dilemma of the Euro-American composers' strain. My point is, the only other attractive route Euro-American composers had—as a basis to claim their work was an independent creative notated music that was different from Europe's—was the actual developments taking place in American culture—especially black music. When Stravinsky embraced twelve-tone music—in his later period—there was no other route for the Euro-Americcn thrust to pursue. In other words, with the fall of Stravinsky as the strongest alternative to both twelve-tone and serial techniques, the Euro-American composers' tradition had either to embrace this same thrust (which most of them did) or move to align their activity with the composite American music thrust—not out of love but because of necessity. Add to their dilemma the fact that it was clear that the next transition cycle of western art music would involve re-aligning the functional arena of its aesthetic as a means to "humanize the position of the interpreter" (this was obviously the case when the realness of serialization became apparent), and one can better understand the Euro-American composers' reality as the time zone of the fifties became real.

After Schoenberg, and looking at the developments that occurred in America, what we see are movements (especially with the group of musicians who worked around John Cage) that immediately began to deal with the expansion of the western art music functional arena. Whether it was graphed process or rhythmic process that did not have the performer interpreting in any particular time zone—these processes have to be looked at in terms of their relation to improvised music, and these processes also have to be looked at as being the direct result of the improvising sensibility.

Cage himself doesn't really talk of his music as such, and of course he does not give any credit to black creative music, to my knowledge (if anything, Cage has shown only contempt for all things African), but if we would look at his early music—his concerto for prepared piano and orchestra, and the devices he employed—we have no choice but to put his activity in its total perspective. For when John Cage was writing this music, not only had Duke Ellington been writing but the time period of Miles Davis and Gil Evans's early orchestral works had already become known. Moreover, many of the people who would move to expand Euro-American creative music were also involved—at one time or another—in attempting to practice "jazz" on some level (the reality continuum of Earle Brown can be viewed in this context). As such, the dynamic implications of creative music from the black aesthetic are not only related to the particulars of its isolated expansion but involve a multitude of factors.

To really view the world position of creative black music—and its related methodological implications—is to view what effects this phenomenon has had on alternative functionalism (both in vibrational and actual terms). For the thrust continuum of black creativity has moved to alter the utilization of composite creative functionalism (yet I do not mean that black creativity alone has widened the total reality of methodology, because many other creative thrusts have also helped to define this point in time—but only black creativity is viewed as not related to the creative continuum of "high art") in every context—having to do with expanding how given functional considerations are viewed and utilized. It is possible to view the last one hundred years for how this influence has reshaped world creativity—and especially western art music. For the progressional continuum of black creativity has moved to create a climate for alternative and creative perception dynamics, while also re-introducing the dynamics of improvisation. I state this not as a means to distort the achievements of any given composer—or so-called new development—but only so that this subject can be put into better focus. The dynamics of both composition and improvisation in black music would forecast the restructuralism that would surround western art music—from the early 1900s to the present. Today we can view the emergence of what is now called aleatory music or "indeterminism" as an example of the influence of the composite continuum of black creativity—as well as an affirmation of the dynamics of world creativity (i.e., African, Indian, Tibetan, Japanese, etc.). The reality implications underlying black creative methodology, then, are not separate from what it has posed for transformation—which is to say, the time has come for western culture to deal with the seriousness of black creative music—whatever alignment—on all of its various levels.

(Level One) Creativity and Science

The dynamic implications of alternative functionalism are not limited to the particulars of only one aspect of creativity, nor can the realness of this subject be understood by suppressing the affinity-alignment implication of principle information. This is so because the reality of a given projection does not stop with "how" that projection works in any one context—let alone "how anything works" for that matter. Instead, the realness of this subject moves to shed insight on the real reality position of a given information strain—having to do with the functional and meta-functional particulars surrounding what a given focus means with respect to its principle center of information as well as its extended context. For this reason, the challenge of alternative functionalism cannot be limited to one area, nor can we understand the realness of this subject by viewing the nature of functionalism as it pertains only to creativity—or at least creative music. Instead, it is important to view the reality of functionalism as it pertains to the composite nature of "doing," and this is especially true for alternative functionalism. Because the real information we are looking for is not so much about the particulars of a given function (since this is really another subject and can be found in any book or so-called center of learning—that being, "how something works"), but rather the composite nature underlying what a given function really is—or at least "how a given function is." As such, the dynamic implications of alternative functionalism must be viewed with respect to what this subject really means to creative postulation—with the understanding being that creative music is only one area of creative functionalism (and even more important, this one area is not the first junction of information solidification, but instead one of two areas of necessary importance). The purpose of this section, then, is to discuss the other aspects of information solidification—as it involves creative functionalism. That area is science.

The fact is, many of us in this time period have come to view science as somehow divorced from the composite continuum of principle information—but this viewpoint is not correct. The essence of science can be viewed as not very separate from all creativity—that being, functionalism as a means to better understand the reality of things, as it pertains to either the laws sustaining "this region" or as it pertains to the greater cosmic realness of being. The reality of science is the same as all creativity—that being, "doing in the light of the greater forces" and "doing as a means to uncover what is to be uncovered"—and nothing more. If we are to positively move into the next time cycle then the reality of composite functionalism must be re-examined—regardless of region and/or discipline. This is so because everything is not necessarily separate, and the information we can learn from science can help us in every area of information dynamics, and vice versa.

In the last fifty years, so many changes have occurred in contemporary science that it would be impossible to elaborate on so "great" a subject without breaking it down. There is no area of our lives untouched in some way by new functionalism—from transportation to household products, from our clothes to food—etc., etc. To deal with the progressional realness of this subject from the last fifty years until now is to have some idea about what possibilities await us in the next time cycle. The fact is, if the countries on this planet are able to find some way to live peacefully together, there is no limit to what we can expect from science in the next cycle. This is not to be overly optimistic, for certainly the reality of science (as it is now understood) cannot be totally viewed as a positive phenomenon without its own hazards, yet the dynamic implications of this subject are mind-boggling for what it could mean for world change. If we are to really understand the reality of progressional continuance—as it relates to alternative functionalism—then it is clear that the consideration of science must be dealt with (and this is true on many different levels). For the reality of science is necessarily tied to the whole concept of creative functionalism. All of the particulars that have reshaped contemporary information lines can be viewed with respect to its relationship to basic science—yet the realness of this subject requires that serious divisions be erected, because the reality of science is composed of many different areas of research, and it would not be to our advantage to merely lump everything together. Science is not a one-dimensional relationship to either information or functionalism.

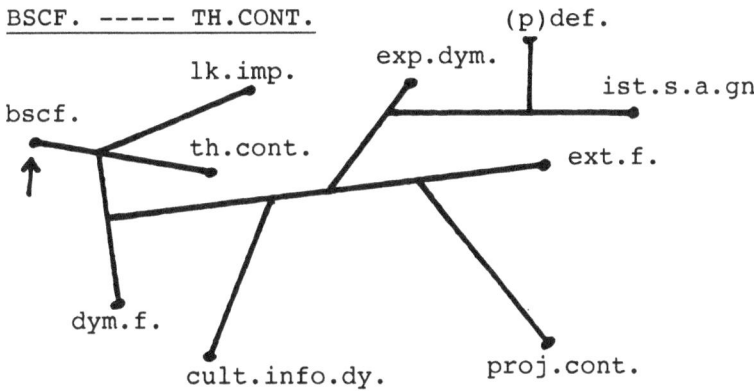

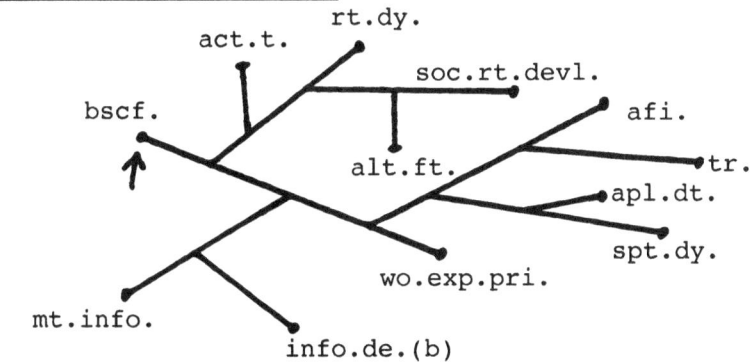

For the purposes of this essay, it will be necessary to break down the reality of science into several dynamic perspectives—for the composite realness of this subject transcends the reality of this book (and what I am looking at). The categories of science for this book can be divided into: vibrational science, theoretical science, and applied science. All of these areas make up the real reality of science as a dynamic discipline that is necessarily intertwined with the composite reality of its culture's information. As such, it is important to explain the dynamics of each category.

CS–4

"Vibrational science" is the term I give to that area of science which utilizes the reality of functionalism as that information is collated with both the affinity-insight principle and intuitive interpretation. The discipline of astrology can be viewed as an example of this kind of science, and the realness of magic, philosophy, and/or para-psychology is also related to what I call vibrational science. The thrust of this region of information has to do with understanding the necessary functionalism to penetrate the vibrational dynamics of what I will call "other forces." The realness of vibrational science moves to give individuals insight into the reality of progressionalism—pertaining to how something might happen (premonition) or how to stop that something from happening (the concept of the curse or spell)—or the dynamics of "unfinished business" (if you know what I mean). The thrust of this region of information is usually only open to particular individuals whose vibrational range is attuned "beforehand" to the "business" of this continuum—yet I do not mean to imply that this region cannot be entered, because every region is (or isn't) available to all of us!! Whatever, the thrust of this phenomenon is extremely important because the essence of a given utilization has cosmic implications. In other words, the realness of a given utilization of vibrational science moves to establish the "space" for dynamic cosmic business to be completed—which is to say, the essence of this region of functionalism can be viewed with respect for its ability to allow "divine" rule to be actualized. Yet I do not mean to limit this zone of functionalism, because obviously if a given person puts a spell on another person, then that action transcends the region of "cosmic purpose" and moves to affirm the intentions of the "spellee"; nevertheless, the realness of vibrational science is a serious area of functionalism and should not be viewed lightly.

Vibrational science and extended functionalism are two of the few areas of contemporary science not received as being "real" in western science, and this is a problem. For the composite thrust of western functionalism has moved to only be impressed by "what it thinks it has done"—as opposed to what "the real" it has done. The thrust of this attitude in the last one hundred years and some has moved to solidify outright disrespect for any area of information that can't be qualified "by the boys": the understanding being that the truth of a given function is not separate from whether or not that function corresponds to "established" scientific procedure. The end result of this attitude has been the gradual decline of vibrational information as a cultural stimulant and the over-reliance on dynamic empiricism "to see what happened." However, it would not be correct to say that vibrational science occupies no space at all in contemporary western pedagogy, for the realness of creativity cannot exist without "extended implications." The fact is, every postulation carries to some degree its own affinity dynamic implications and, as such, its "extra-affinity" outside influences as well. Nevertheless, the dynamic implications of vibrational science—and what this phenomenon implies for the formation of vibrational functionalism and vibrational postulation—have yet to assume their rightful place in western science. Hopefully the next time cycle will see a more balanced understanding of dynamic functionalism—this is what is needed.

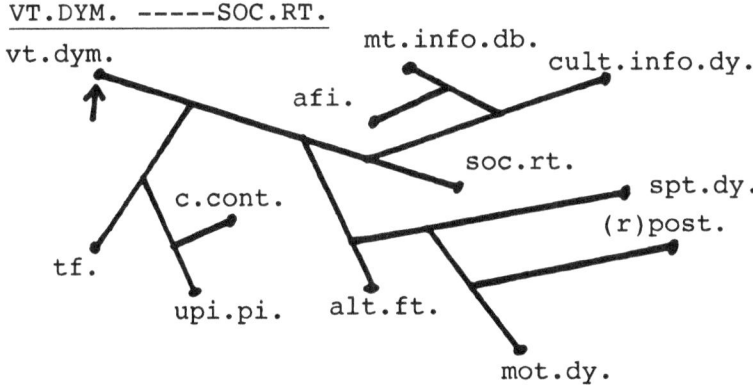

To say there is no input at all from vibrational science in western culture would be somewhat of an overstatement. For the realness of creative music is vibrational—that is, a vibrational science. This is true even though the progressional realness of time has moved the creative community somewhat away from postulation's real position in "high multi-discipline." For the last two hundred years have moved to isolate the extended implications of creativity as a necessary aspect of composite information, and in its place this period has moved to supply dynamic existential viewpoints concerning the strength of given projectional encounters—or experiences. The end result of this shift would move to solidify creativity as something separate from the composite wellspring of cultural information—but this phenomenon is not only true for creativity but pertains to every region of present-day western information dynamics. In other words, the move to isolate information—particularly in transitional western culture—would alter every reality continuum of its information focus, and in so doing, establish the reality particulars we are now dealing with in this time cycle. As such, the resulting relationship western culture developed with multi-information would move to create the "era of the specialist" and the dynamic separation of composite information. As the natural continuum of time proceeded, the creative and scientific communities would come to see their realities as being very different—even though both groups would still function from the same laws and premises (whether understood or not). This separation would extend throughout the entire region of vibrational science to both basic and applied research—and to this day, has not been resolidified.

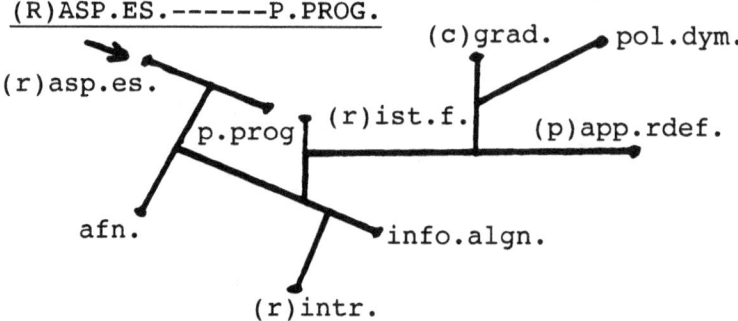

The resolidification of vibrational science and basic science is important because the reality implications of a given information line are not one-dimensional but touch on more considerations than many of us are aware of. This is not to say applied science in itself is not valid or of importance—because every area of investigation and creativity is important—rather, the essence realness of given information cannot be tapped unless there is some awareness of and empathy for its dynamic base. In other words, the "truth" of a given area of information does not end with "how that area of information works," but instead has to do with the reality of what that information means in its cosmic totality. The thrust of vibrational science must then be viewed for what it poses for extended perception and alternative investigation. It is for this reason that the real reality of creativity and science must be commented on—for the dynamic implications of the next cycle will necessitate another level of understanding.

The seed underlying vibrational science and "intuition" will come to be viewed as necessary to the progressional continuum of information discovery, and this is what concerns us. Until this solidification is actualized, western science cannot be viewed as a composite science or even a transformational science. Half is not enough.

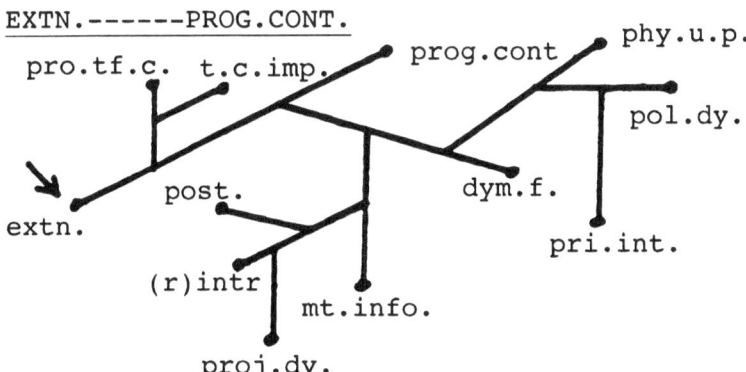

CS–8

The reality dynamics of basic science can be viewed as a continuum that utilizes investigation to better understand the "laws" of this sector (what we now call the universe). The spirit of this continuum moves with the belief that an examination of fundamental cosmic information can move to uplift the condition of humanity (with respect to the dynamics of physical universe particulars, i.e., eating, health, and working) and while doing so also provide answers about "the reality of living"—or "What is this?" To really deal with the realness of western science is to begin understanding this most dynamic area of western functionalism, for the composite thrust of this sector has determined the whole course of western progressionalism—and affinity dynamics—in the last thousand years and some. The collected realness of basic science has moved to define how we view the considerations of investigation as well as "information degrees" (axioms). As such, it is important that the specifics of basic scientific functionalism are understood—on whatever level, for the decisions which have solidified the past have greatly affected our ability to look into the future—which is to say, "the reality of decision making" underlining this time period must not be allowed to solidify a practical ideology without reclarifying the actualness of alternative functionalism—and what this information means to investigation dynamics. This is so because the infra-reality dynamics (i.e., tenets) that solidify from basic scientific investigation have a profound impact on the whole of everyone's life—whether or not one is in agreement with a given conclusion. The challenge of the next cycle demands a reinvestigation of the whole phenomenon we now call science—having to do with clarifying every aspect of both postulation and qualification—as well as the consideration of technique.

The most basic difference between basic science and vibrational science has to do with the nature underlying how functionalism is viewed. For the thrust continuum of western science has moved to draw dynamic conclusions from the actualness of empirical specifics—how a given combination of factors act in a given situation—as a means to comment on what the "reality" of that specific is; as opposed to vibrational science, which functions as a means for cosmic definitions to solidify understanding. The realness of these two approaches to investigation should not be lightly viewed, for the dynamic implications related to where a given route of information leads carry profound consequences—on every level. This is not to say "there is no truth to a given area of investigation," because one of the amazing things about this subject is that there is something of importance to be learned whichever route one pursues (and there is also something "of significance" in every route that sheds light on the realness of existence and its dynamic mysteries). Sometimes the route of a given investigation tells more about "the investigator" than it does about "what is to be revealed."

The reality specifics of western basic science can be understood by dealing with the dynamics of isolated empirical deductions as a basis to establish information tenets. Yet in itself this kind of investigation is not new, for the composite thrust of world culture—regardless of time period—has long recognized the dynamics of empirical analysis, and the composite thrust of world information can be viewed as proof of this understanding. But the use of empirical observation is only part of the uniqueness of extended western functionalism, for the composite basis for western observation is not separate from the total reality position of the culture itself. In other words, the realness of western science cannot be isolated from what events have shaped progressional continuance in western culture, because the reality of information and information continuance is directly in alignment with how a given continuance actualized (moreover, in many cases, the solidification of a given information deduction has dictated the composite nature of its time zone—or area of influence—or period of progressionalism). The most basic factor that has established the uniqueness of western science has to do with how the consideration of investigation has come to be viewed as separate from the all-cosmic implications of a "phenomenon reality"—and as such, viewed without respect for the dynamic position a given phenomenon has in regard to its meta-reality implications. The thrust of this approach (to understanding) has helped to create great advances in fundamental research, while at the same time retarding the vibrational dynamics of the very information it purports to understand. I write this not as a means to view western science negatively, because nothing is gained by imposing extra adjectives on a situation that is already bad enough—rather, it is important to establish a basis for evaluating this most complex subject. Certainly all of us have benefited from the collective thrust of western science—which is to say, there have been many wonderful postulations that have come from this sector of dynamic functionalism. It is important that my inquiry into this most vast subject is not taken out of context to the whole of what alternative functionalism poses—as composite information that hopefully will be positive and life-giving in the immediate and not immediate future, and also as necessary information for dynamic transformation. My point is only this: if we are to really understand the challenge of the next cycle, then it is important to view the particulars of this time cycle—as a means to know what to do and what not to do for further growth. The realness of basic science is not a limited consideration of no consequences to the greater society, but instead one of the most important considerations to shape a culture's reality (and destiny). As such, this consideration is too important to not examine.

To really understand the meta-reality lining of western science is to view what isolation has implied—for observation. For the deductions that have moved to reshape our lives, in many cases, were formed completely separate from the composite theatre of world information. The progressional realness of these deductions has moved to solidify a whole new area of information that draws its "degrees" (i.e., tenets) from the most radical use of observation in this time period. On the other hand, the thrust of this phenomenon has also moved to observe the forming of an alternative composite information pool—that, in its reality slant, involved the realness of information with the dynamics of spirituality. The progressional continuance of this phenomenon is related to the emergence of the "specialist" and the dynamic split of composite investigation—regardless of zone; and the realness of this phenomenon has also affected the traditional perception criterion that has determined social reality and spiritual reunification and/or relevance. To view the reality realness of basic science is to deal with the essence umbrella that determines the "footprint" of its given culture group—for the realness of this area of information cannot be limited to any one context. Basic science, which is basic research, is the consideration that determines the progressional path its cultural group will exist in—this is true whether we are focusing on the dynamics of learning, the dynamics of attitudes. and extends even onto what individual one decides to marry. In other words, basic science is not only about "how a brick works," but extends onto the reality of behavior, the reality of politics, and the dynamics of postulation. The seriousness of this consideration extends into practically every aspect of this book—even the so-called de-spiritualization of western investigation has to be understood very delicately, for the realness of this de-spiritualization has moved to function with respect to "other areas of spiritualization" (which is to say, every phenomenon is related and attracted to particular areas of—what I will call—"greater forces," and as such, it would not be true to state that western science has no "extra-vibrational attachments"; rather, it might be more accurate to say that the decisions which have characterized western scientific investigation are attached to forces "no one wants to talk about"). Nevertheless my point is: the reality implications of western basic science are indeed profound, and the challenge of the next cycle demands a reinvestigation into this most important subject.

The last area of extended functionalism, as it relates to science, is the area of applied science. This is the junction where the actualness of a given theory is given "lift"—in that after a given information line is secured, the dynamics of applied science move to actualize its focus particulars for cultural use—to be used for actual living. Applied science, then, is not concerned about the aesthetic or vibrational implications of a given information line, but instead with whether or not it can be of service. Unfortunately, it is important to understand that the reality of applied research assumes that the actualness of a given information line is true—before it begins to work. In other words, the "truth" of a given information line is considered solved before this extension of the scientific community goes to work—and while this relationship (between basic and applied science) is understandable, in the final analysis, many problems have materialized through that assumption. Because while the functional dynamics of a given information line might work, this does not mean it is true. Another way of saying this is: the dynamic implications of a given information line are true on many levels that one might not want them to be true; which is to say, there is information and there is information. On the physical universe level, this phenomenon can be understood by viewing the emergence of nuclear energy and the whole of the nuclear age. For while it is too early to comment on what this information will mean (in real broad terms—having to do with its use for a period of one to two hundred years), it is clear that something awesome has now been unleashed. The reality position of applied science must be viewed for how it has and will continue to shape the path of the western and (by de facto consent) world community. One thing is certain: unless some effort is made to re-examine contemporary science, there can be no hope of positive transformation—and there is more. The progressional continuance of the next cycle will need to solidify a transformational viewpoint concerning dynamic functionalism, in all of its aspects. There can be no positive extension without a restoration of ethics and world spirituality. This must be the goal of transformational functionalism and/or alternative functionalism. To understand this is to deal with the reality dynamics surrounding the whole of creativity and science.

The emergence of contemporary technology is also related to new creative functionalism. For the changes reshaping our lives are totally intertwined with new developments in technology. The challenge of the next cycle has to do with our total relationship to information; because science is not only about empirical theory—rather, this subject has to do with attempting to understand the fundamentals that "ised" this experience (living—or what we call living) in space. The dynamics of technology must be viewed for how it has totally altered our lives in this cycle—as a result of science (i.e., applied functionalism). Nor has contemporary creativity gone unaffected by this phenomenon, for the realness of new inventions has completely reshaped what is possible in every discipline. This is true whether we are commenting on the solidification of new projections (e.g., electronic music) or whether we are referring to the dynamic utilization of popular forms (e.g., Broadway musicals). Technology has brought us to the junction where it is now possible to write of composite world activity.

For technological dynamics are directly related to (and responsible for) the composite reality dynamics of this time period. This is true even though the rapidity of change has made us somewhat numb to the uniqueness of this time cycle. In fact, the continuum of the last thirty years has been so dynamic thanks to technological breakthroughs, that many of us have come to view it as "normal"—but it isn't. For the realness of technology is related to the affinity-insight principle—which is to say, technological dynamics are not separate from the nature underlying how transformation is forming. This factor (technology) is no less important than any other consideration in new functionalism. In other words, we could not be at this juncture of time and space unless all of the "particulars" related to how we got here were there.

The significance of new functionalism implies that every area of information particulars be re-examined—and this is especially true of the role of science and transformational culture. For the dynamics of technology are directly related to the vibrational and physical realities of a culture—having to do with the composite affinity tendencies that surround how functionalism is perceived and how information is collated. In this context, the reality of scientific research and contemporary technology cannot simply be viewed as all positive. This is not to ignore the wonderful contribution that has solidified in contemporary science—because obviously much good has been brought about through scientific research. But the realness of alternative functionalism is not only about how given information routes are to expand; instead, this subject extends into our composite relationship with perception. To view the dynamics of contemporary science is to see many existing areas utilized for creative functionalism—yet the affinity adaptations that have resulted from this same sector have opened up new problems that cannot be ignored. We are slowly coming to a point in time that will require re-evaluating scientific research and objectives. In other words, the present state of western scientific investigation doesn't necessarily correspond to what is implied in alternative functionalism, and the challenge of the next cycle will have to do with realigning creative investigation, with respect to what "postulation" can or will mean for transformational "thinking."

CS–14

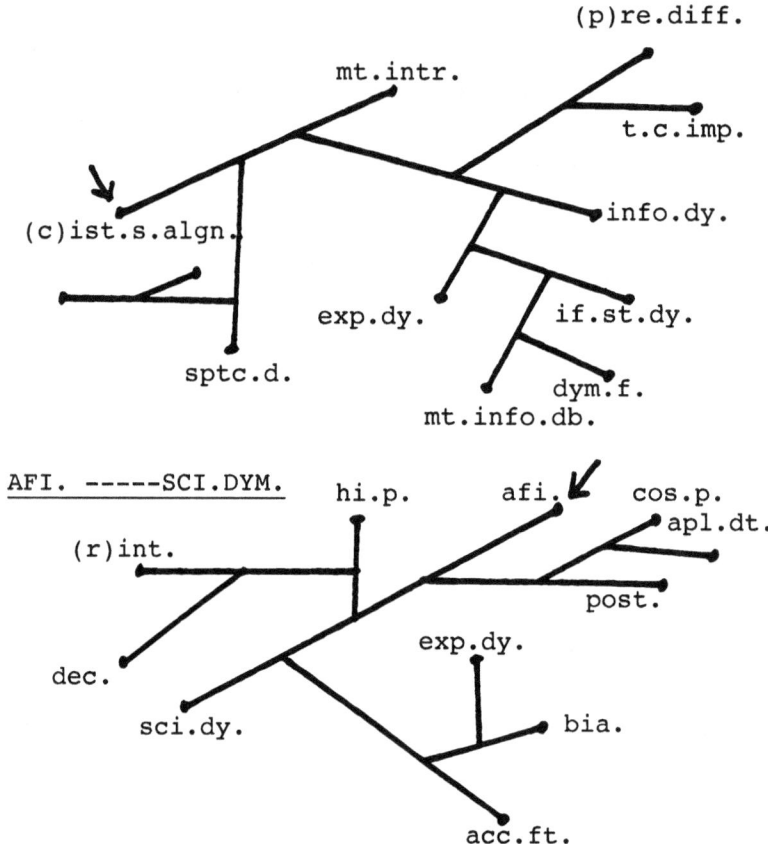

To understand the meta-reality of western science is to view how present-day information is perceived. For the affinity adaptation of western science has moved to advance the nature of aspect-essence perception dynamics.

In other words, the continuum of western scientific thought is directly based in the affinity stance of western culture—having to do with perception within an existential information focus. The end result of this focus is that information is viewed for how it seems to function—rather than with respect for its function as well as its spirituality. This is not to say the functionality of a given phenomenon has no meaning for investigation, because it does, but in the final analysis the functionality of a given phenomenon has more to do only with how something works. If the realness of science is concerned about learning universal laws (i.e., how the universe seemed to be "ised"), then it is necessary for its observation criteria to correspond to what is being observed. This is so because the universe is not about "how"—rather, this phenomenon (the universe) is not separate from its cosmic and spiritual existence. If we are to view the realness of western science with respect for its transformation potential, then we are forced to start from this point. It is not a question of attempting to knock everything western—and certainly everyone has benefited from the composite thrust of western investigation—but if science is to be a transformational tool, then it is important that its affinity focus be re-examined. This is true both for science (theory and investigation) and scientific functionalism (actual practice—and/or technological expansion).

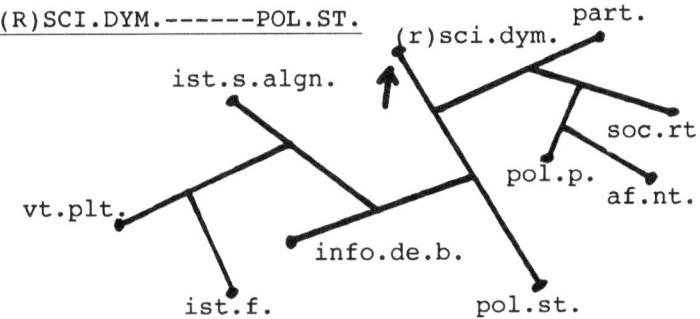

The dynamics of science are also important for the role it could play in transformational society. For the information continuum that sustains any focus substantiates how that focus will be both viewed and utilized. In actual terms, the realness of science is directly related to how reinterpretations can be brought about. For the solidification of transformation is not just an idle state of being, but involves how change is brought about (through "doing" or participation). Creative alternative science could supply the basis for realigning the meta-implications of information dynamics for world culture. In other words, alternative investigation in this time zone must be viewed with respect to both what areas of information are uncovered and what position that same information has with respect to its role in alternative perception dynamics. This use of science is important, for the solidification of "real" culture has to do with the position a given area of information occupies in the total hierarchy of its culture dynamics. Yet I have not meant to imply that research must necessarily be limited—or restricted, because the implications of dynamic investigation are important to the very essence of "being"—rather, it is a question of how given areas of information are utilized. The continuum of alternative functionalism must be related to those composite factors reshaping positive physical and vibrational universe change, for the collected information scan of various participators will ultimately move to establish a composite meta- and actual reality position. As such, the work of creative scientists in this period must be scrutinized very carefully until a unified world position emerges. Because many of the investigations taking place in this cycle are presented to us as "being true," but are only part true. There is nothing worse than postulating a reality position from information that later is found to be only half true. Certainly there are particular areas where half-correct information is not necessarily destructive (for scientific investigation deals with many different areas), and in these contexts no damage is done if a given theorem is found to be in error. But this is not always the case, and the progressional realness of creative investigation cannot be viewed as outside of cosmic responsibility.

Creative science could function as a transformational tool by providing methodological guidelines for the research of particular zones. This is really the correct posture for creative functionalism, for science in reality is no different than any other creative discipline. As such, the realness of the next cycle will call for the establishment of a general affinity stance with respect to both how information is to be collated and what guidelines can best serve investigation and also humanity—and the "cosmics" (or God). The solidification of this new functionalism must also take into account the entire world community. In other words, contemporary science must now move to open up the dynamics of composite perspective. What this means is that the realness of alternative functionalism must not degenerate into the affinity dynamics of any one group. As such, transformational science must now move to first collate world group information lines as a means to "pool" information—and this will be no easy task. For the resolidification of world knowledge is not separate from the physical universe particulars of this time period. The fact that research has not been developed (or redeveloped) in given regions of the planet must be taken into account in actual functionalism. What this means is that the responsibility of science and its related communities has to do with how it aids reconstruction. It is not just a question of a given community moving to do a good deed—for no one is interested only in so-called goodwill—rather, the composite continuum of world information is directly related to whether the unified world community is allowed to participate. For the extensions of the western scientific community are not separate from the social, political, and historical implications of source transfer. Yet this relationship is not the only reason for multi-unified investigation either.

The inclusion of the composite world community in alternative functionalism can best be understood by viewing the significance of affinity dynamics. For if the dynamics of planet Earth can be viewed with respect to how different regions perceive of given information routes, then this difference will also be manifested in investigation. In other words, the participation of composite earth—men and women from all over the planet—will move to broaden the dimensionality underlying the perception of functionalism (and this broadening of information will also affect how interpretation is viewed as well). The scientific community needs this diversification of information options, and the composite planet could only benefit from a wider affinity band for observation. For the transformational potential of alternative interpretation will underline how real change can actualize on the physical universe level. Many of us have come to view real change as something that will just come on its own, or will come through the romantic ideas we have of revolution—but real change depends on many factors. The significance of alternative functionalism has to do with the position it has for sustaining realignment. For while the first level of "transfer" might in some contexts have to do with the excitement and participation of rebellion and struggle, in the final analysis, the sustaining of

CS–18

a given shift alignment is directly related to alternative functionalism—and its position in the spiritual hierarchy of its culture (or new context). I do not mean to view isolated functionalism as more important than the essence basis that dictates its parameter—for obviously alternative functionalism is not the second degree of transfer alignment, but is after spiritual focus. But the significance of alternative functionalism should not be lightly viewed. There can be no real transformation without an accompanied new functionalism. It is important that the reality dynamics of science are viewed for the role it will have in "real" change. My point, however, is that the progressional continuum of scientific thought can no longer be divorced from its reality responsibility. Unless the scientific community opens its participation to include the information/interpretation scan of world culture, the route that transformation will take will be very difficult. Moreover, it is not just a question of opening the doors of creative research to the world community, it is a question of recognizing what has happened to the world community in the last hundred and fifty years. Unless a move is made to solidify collective research, western science will have to bear the responsibility and consequences of mis-information—in this and the coming cycles.

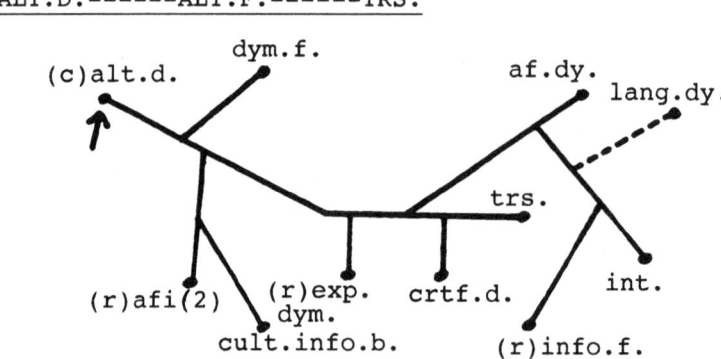

Transformational science in many ways must be viewed in the same context as creative music. For obviously in this time zone there is no world composite culture—which is to say, the significance of alternativism has to do with the nature underlying how "present-day progressionalism" is viewed. In other words, the state of "without culture" implies that progressionalism must be based on positive moves towards potential reformation. In this context, both creativity (or creative music) and science can only function with respect to what is implied in the affinity-insight principle, as a means to accelerate affinity dynamics. What this means is that investigation can no longer be locked into only conventional definitions, for the challenge of the next cycle cannot be contained in the information tenets of this period. This is not to negate the present information reality, but only to recognize the nature of our collected position on this planet. Both creative music and creative science can be of significance to positive world change if the challenge of expanded options are recognized—having to do with the significance of real invention. It is because of this significance that the affinity-insight principle is of such importance. For while it will be some time before real composite unification can be brought about—on the physical universe level, the realness of the affinity-insight principle supersedes the implementation of regionalism. In its place is substantiated a context more suitable for spiritual guidance and individual awakening. As such, the underlying factor that will dictate alternative functionalism will be the nature underlying how affinity dynamics are understood—or reshaped. The progressional continuum of creative music and science in this context must be viewed as extremely important for its ability to expand meta-reality options. For the end result of these two disciplines could underline the move (of world culture) into transformational world culture.

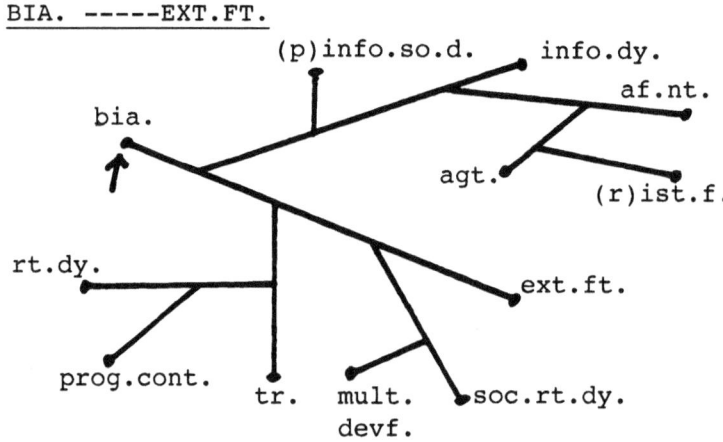

In actual terms, transformational science must be viewed for how its expansion principle vibrates to the affinity-insight principle, as opposed to set theory. The importance of this alignment cannot be overstated, for invention dynamics are related to how a given phenomenon (focus) is perceived. This is not to say that any particular scientist should simply forgo his or her established information lines, but rather each of us must realistically deal with the juncture western culture has arrived at. For western science in particular has arrived at a crucial cycle in its progressionalism—having to do with understanding how to make its extensions meaningful. As human beings begin looking to the awesomeness of the heavens—as the next juncture of extended investigation lines—and into the meaning of life (how things are really put together), many of the theories we now take for granted will no longer have any relevance. In other words, science is slowly moving towards the juncture that will necessitate a re-examination of composite information and information dynamics, as well as what basis is most relevant—significant as a stabilizing factor—to investigate from. Galactic science will involve totally re-establishing many of the fundamental ideas we have come to accept as correct. This is not to say that any one area of present-day information functionalism is not valid—because obviously it is—but rather, the functional dynamics of a given idea are not separate from the reality focus it is viewed from. In other words, what we now call laws might only be laws in one context that has nothing to do with what that same phenomenon might ultimately mean in transformational information tenets. It is really a question of how much we want to know, and it is also a question of how much one-dimensional knowing is related to real knowing, and finally it is a question of "is it ready yet?" The reality of affinity-insight investigation could be important for how these questions are dealt with, for the spectrum of observation dynamics is related to many different factors.

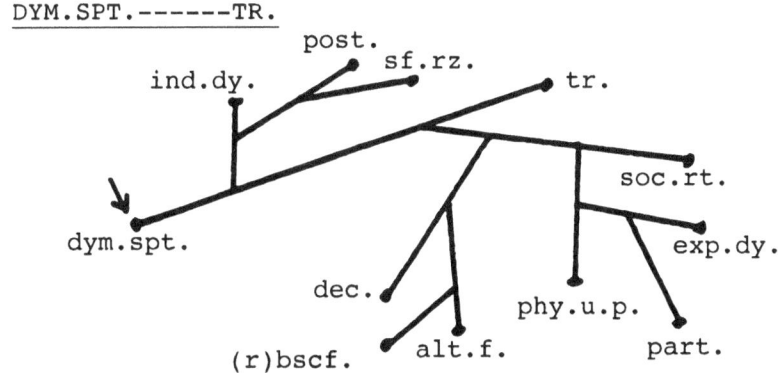

The most popular example of extra-curricular information gaps would be the research happening in this time zone concerning both the origin of the universe and the emergence of what we now call "black holes." Both of these areas of speculation will test every branch of western science, for science, as it has solidified in this cycle, is not really equipped to deal with this area of focus. The idea that something in the universe does not correspond to existing laws only shows the reality barrier of present-day information routes, not to mention that the concept of the origin of the universe is already wrong—because immediately one is transported to the one-dimensional conclusion that something must "start." All of these areas of information (and many more) will slowly move to redefine our understanding of what science really is. For the laws or so-called laws of the universe might transcend our present perception of events—by not adhering to one-dimensional empirical dictates. The challenge of transformational science will rest on its ability to provide a revolutionary new context for perception. Hopefully this new context will not isolate strict functionalism from spiritual reality—for science and spirituality are not separate if really understood. The resolidification of investigation (and "being") is directly related to the nature underlying how alternative functionalism is brought about—in both creative postulation and actual functionalism.

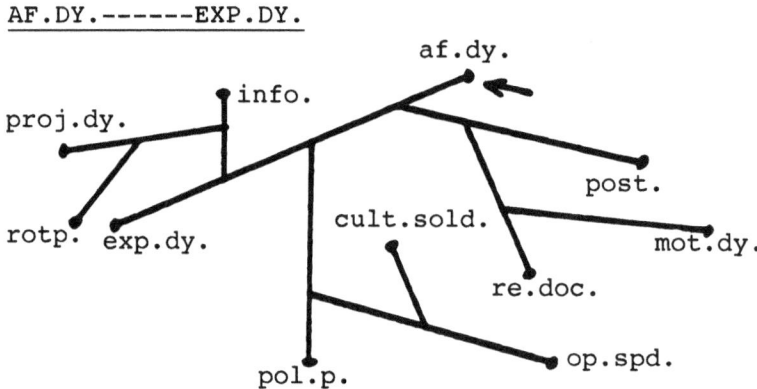

The dynamics of alternative methodology cannot be viewed in limited terms, for the composite continuum of creativity and science is related to every area of existence. If we are to view the transformational potential of technology and applied science, it is important that its use is not perceived as outside the reality of actual life. The fact is, the composite dynamics of applied science can help to reorder both our physical universe existence, as well as how we perceive of ourselves. The realness of what this means can be understood by looking at the implications of applied science to actual life. For the reality of medicine can be viewed for how transformational science could positively reshape our lives—and this area is important. There is much work to be done on the question of health and life fulfillment (or longevity), and transformational medicine will address itself to the dynamics of methodology in this area. The whole reality of how the body functions must be re-examined with respect to the affinity-insight principle. For most of us have been led to believe that the breakdown of many areas of the body implies either no regeneration or artificial replacement. Transformational medicine will help us to see how vibrational techniques can move to restore particular body functions, without the need for surgery or mechanical devices. Yet I do not mean to oversimplify a very complex subject. For transformational medicine is not only about one area of treatment but a total viewpoint concerning how to live and what to do when.

Transformational applied science and medicine must be perceived from the total content of vibrational dynamics. Investigation cannot be perceived only in masculine terms, but must also include the vibrational insight we associate with real "feminism." In other words, vibrational transference and affinity communications must be rediscovered in applied science and medicine. Sickness must not be viewed with respect to how a given function did not function, rather the application focus of transformational medicine will have to do with becoming aware of vibrational balance—both in sickness and in health. The challenge of western medicine will involve exploring vibrational sensibility and spiritual awakening.

Moreover, the reformation of transformational medicine must be viewed with respect to both its particulars—for in this period, western medicine has yet to discover women (which is to say, there will be a long path to real change in composite applied medicine)—and its total approach to refunctionalism. What we are seeking is the development of another whole attitude in applied science. For the practice of strict empirical functionalism has brought with it an inability to recognize the total context of actual life—and life sensitivity. The development of vibrational insight must not be taken lightly, for this consideration is not separate from the implications of the affinity-insight principle. This is not to say that any particular area of applied science is in itself negative, nor have I meant to discredit any of the work that has brought us to this period in time. An attack of this nature would mean nothing—and would be non-progressive. It is amazing that western research has done as well at it has—considering the seriousness of its vibrational climate. The transformational implications of new functionalism must be viewed as a cyclic progression that is related to both the forming of the next cycle and the particulars underlying its evolution.

CS–24

It is important for contemporary science to begin reviewing its responsibility to humanity. For too long, this sector has come to view itself as separated from the basic thrusts of universal and cosmic laws. As such, a given area of research is now viewed only with respect to what information route it extends, rather than what positive effect a given new development might have for actual living. This is not to negate isolated research, but we have now come to the juncture where many factors must be considered—having to do with invention and society, and responsibility. No initiation, whether it has to do with creative or functional creativity, is separate from transformation. As we now move towards the investigation of genetic coding and body transplantation, the role of present-day science threatens to become even more all-encompassing. If ever there was a point in time when the progressional expansion of information routes needed re-examination, it is now. Certainly, I am not implying that new research be simply cut off, nor do I have the right to question whether or not a given information line should be investigated. But the dynamic implication of contemporary science will affect the composite realness of the coming cycle, and the future as a whole. It is important that the community of creative scientists—whatever region or country—be in real communications with the composite "real" culture—especially in this period. Science can no longer be viewed as separate from the wholeness of creative discipline and creative extensions. A given information line will affect many different areas of our lives, and the mis-application of a given investigative route will have multi-complexual consequences for everyone. To understand this viewpoint is to understand what has happened to investigation in this cycle.

We are slowly moving into the solidification of what I will call "galactic science." In other words, the discoveries that have shaped this cycle—starting from the theory of relativity—are slowly moving to resolidify a new transformational basis for investigation. It will be this investigation that will become the basis for the next cycle of perceived extension. Already many new attempts have come forth (e.g., new ideas about time and space), and the next twenty years promise to be extremely exciting for what investigation promises to unfold. The realness of this new science will necessitate that we change many of our concepts about both the universe and existence. New information will not be seen as separate from the dynamics of spirituality, for the dynamics of new information will move to reform the affinity basis of science, as a natural extension of the composite communities alignment (i.e., transformational culture). Galactic science will thus be the new functionalism related to uncovering our greater position in the total context of "real space"—having to do with learning the next set of laws having to do with experiencing the next "reality plane." For while in this time cycle the idea of space travel and "galactic voyages" might sound unreal, this is in fact the next juncture (if we do not destroy ourselves on the way). To deal with the realness of space travel, one needs only to view how far we have already come—in only the last hundred years. At the rate information is expanding, space travel will surely be a reality within the next hundred years. The forming of "galactic concepts" must be viewed from this context, for the challenge of expansion will encompass many factors—having to do with establishing alternative basis for investigation. Moreover, the seeds for this new scientific stance are being planted in this period—which is to say, the beginning of galactic science has already started. Whether or not this information will be positively practiced depends on the reunification of information dynamics. In other words, the solidification of alternative functionalism will have to do with how composite information lines are brought together.

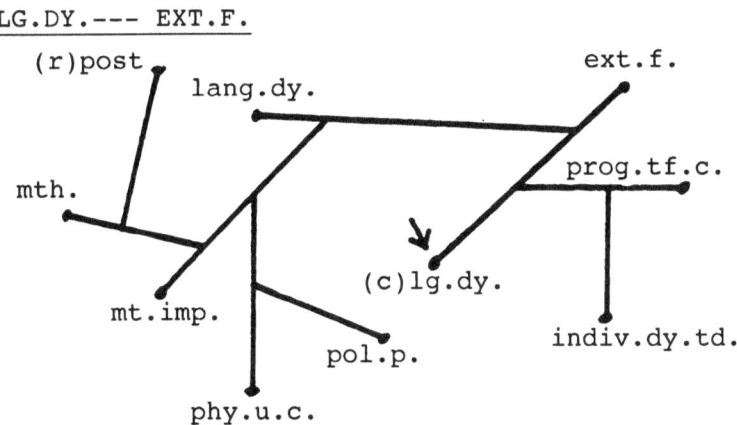

CS–26

When I wrote that the next level of new functionalism will involve the affinity-insight principle, I did not mean to limit this phenomenon to any one context. In actual terms, the affinity-insight principle will be important for what it implies about investigative attitudes.

This discipline is directly related to creative postulation (through functional science) in the same sense as for creative music functionalism. For the discovery of the next level of laws will have as much to do with vibrational and creative insight as empirical analysis. Just as the creative restructuralist musician must function with process and vibrational investigation, so will the creative scientist have to develop intuition for vibrational awareness. Because many of the decisions that will make up new functionalism will be brought about by affinity postulation of "creative intuition." The solidification of actual functionalism will be the second stage of discovery—not the first. For the opening of galactic information lines might not have anything to do with the extension lineage of empirical investigation. Alternative information gathering will imply another understanding of affinity dynamics as well as "degree coding" (or designation of significance). All of these postulation tools will accent the need for new functionalism, and greater insight. In the end, the total concept of science in the future will be very different from what we have in this cycle.

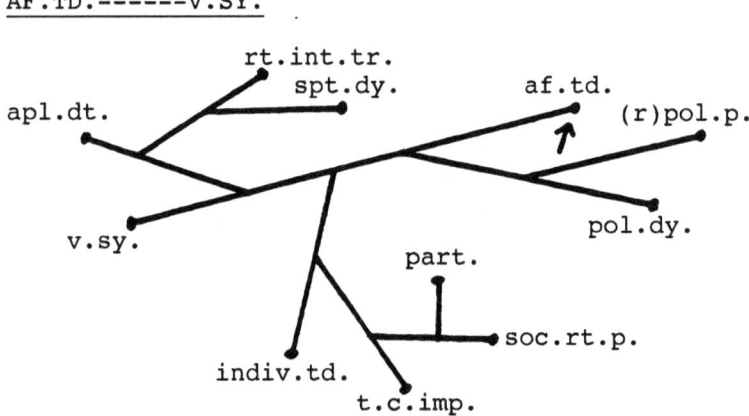

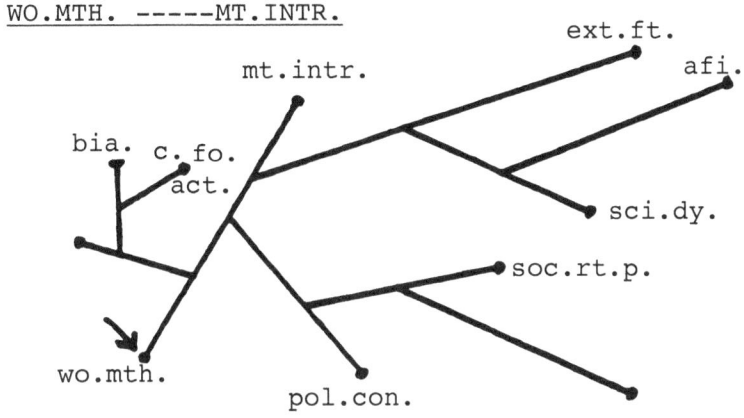

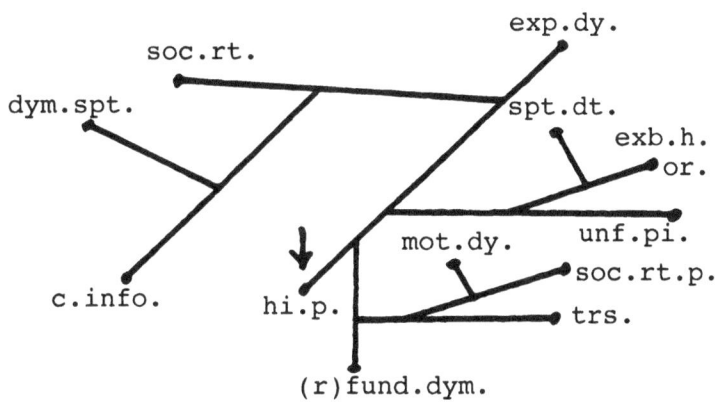

The significance of new functionalism will have to do with what affinity-insight postulation poses for empirical investigation. For the dynamics of galactic science will challenge every area of strict analytical tenets. The realness of this phenomenon will move to refocus affinity perception (and/or empirical tools)—and the vibrational sensibility that permeates how those tools are utilized. Transformational science will vibrate less to "how" than to "what." Because the implicational spread of "how" might not necessarily be of relevance to what is actually happening. In actual terms, transformational science will also affect our understanding of system and methodology. Even the concept of numbers will expand to include its feeling degree. For while many of us have come to accept that one plus one equals two, this is not necessarily correct. Transformational science will move to clarify to what degree given principles can be perceived as real. For one plus one equals two only if need be (and that need is related to what zone one is attempting to enter). Transformational science will move to reorder the effective range of empirical principles (and this reordering will even affect pre-transformational science and logic). For not only does one plus one not equal two if need be, but the whole concept of "one" must be re-examined, for western functionalism has yet to deal with the real significance of "degrees." The multi-implications of numbers have to do with many facts that are not yet practiced in contemporary science. I have no doubt that the affinity-insight principles underlying extended empiricism are directly related to the numbers one and zero (its "negative" equivalent). Transformational science and new functionalism will move to clarify this information, and in doing so, lay the basis for a totally radical awareness of numbers (and its related "axiom" tenet). All of these changes are related to galactic science, and all of these challenges are related to the dynamics of our next extension—whether that extension involves the research of extended functionalism (towards galactic space) or research into "inner space." To understand this is to deal with the reality of dynamic investigation.

The fact is, there are only two basic routes for progressional science—and the challenge of transformation is related to both directions. The first route would have to do with a re-examination of world culture as a means to uncover what information was lost, and the second route would be the expansion of contemporary functionalism as a means to uncover what we could be. Both of these information areas are important if we are truly interested in transformation, for real change cannot solidify unless it has a composite basis. Thus, if we are to understand the dynamics of contemporary science—whether that discipline pertains to the composite thrust of world creativity, or the composite information related to world functionalism (methodology)—then we are forced to consider its multi-dynamic implications. The seriousness of the next cycle necessitates that a total overview of creativity is solidified in this cycle, for the dynamics of the coming cycle cannot afford to have any discipline viewed separate from its composite transformational aesthetic base. Transformational functionalism must be viewed with this in mind.

In actual terms, the reality of alternative functionalism must be viewed with respect to the basic divisions that determine real participation—which is to say, the nature underlying a given science must be viewed in both its functional and mystical context. There are two most basic examples related to what this means: those being, the "concept of equal equal and functional equal" and the "particulars of imaginary and real numbers." The progressional continuance of extended investigation in the next cycle will undoubtedly move to clarify both of these concepts, because this information directly intertwines with the dictates of extended functionalism.

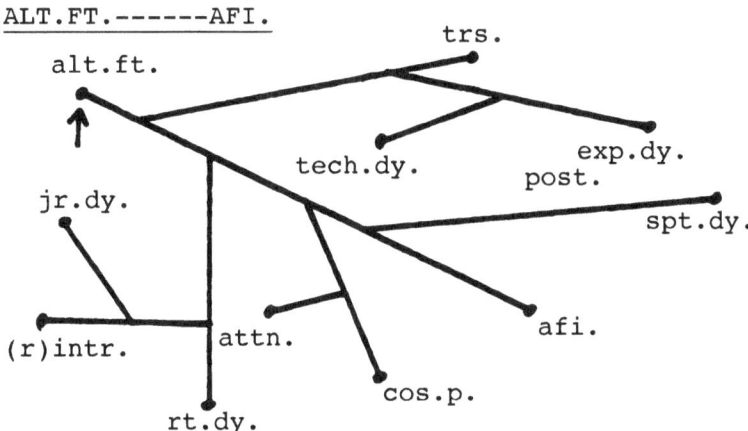

The concepts of equal-equal and functional equal have to do with my belief that there are two most basic realities connected with every functionalism, and each reality carries its own implications. It is important that we are taught what this difference is, for the dynamics of extended science will not necessarily be based on the "laws that sustain any one region of investigation." My point is this: the notion of equal-equal does not always correspond to the same point of what is now viewed as equal in functional terms, and the challenge of contemporary science will be to understand what this difference means. Furthermore I do not believe that the concept of equal can be arrived at through empirical research, regardless of approach, because the realness of this way of viewing information will necessitate spiritual growth—as opposed to mathematical proficiency. This is also true for the reality of real and imaginary numbers. For the systems that tell us one plus one equals two are the same systems that can clarify that one plus one equals one. The thrust of vibrational investigation will hopefully move to give more insight into the real reality of numbers—with special emphasis on the number one and zero. By "re-examination of world culture," I am referring to the multi-implications of progressional continuance. To lightly research world history is to become aware of the dynamic continuum of many cultures—having to do with the emergence and decline of many advanced nations, and also having to do with the information that enabled particular cultures to attain "high civilization." If new functionalism is to be grounded in what is most real about world knowledge, then it is important that attempts are made to re-examine and re-integrate composite world information. For the realness of world history seems to suggest that historical information could be extremely significant today on every level. This is not to say that documented scientific achievement in world culture is necessarily more (or less) advanced than western culture today, but rather that world history interpretations were perceived in both vibrational and empirical terms. If this is true, and all indications seen to suggest it is, then it is important to review progressional history. For the composite realness of world history seems to directly comment on the nature underlying how functionalism was perceived and practiced—having to do with the reality of discipline, the projectional dynamics of discipline, the relationship of a given discipline to its meta-reality function, and the applied functional dynamics of a given discipline, etc. At present, all of these areas of information have been lost, and in its place we have existential functionalism. The challenge of new functionalism must be viewed for its ability to restore a composite context for investigation—and in doing so, help establish the seeds for a dynamic new functionalism. There is also the realness that many of the information lines developed through world culture are still applicable today—which is to say, the study and research of world culture is relevant to alternative resolidification. It is possible to view isolated rediscoveries in this cycle; for instance, the gradual re-examination of acupuncture is slowly gaining momentum in western culture—and already its use has opened many new lines of thought (and research). For to examine the applied functionalism (as related to medicine) that has been developed in the east is to have an expanded understanding of healing. Techniques have been developed in world culture that involve "touching" rather than surgery—and when surgery has been practiced, in many cases, the patient has no need of anesthesia because of advanced "over-riding" techniques. All of this information is directly related to world culture, and western culture must at some point come to deal with this same level of applied techniques. For the heart of world information seeks to understand the proper balance between existence on the vibrational and physical universe planes. Applied functionalism in this context has to do with how that balance is maintained. For this reason, world information has made much use of "natural" remedies and "earth" materials. To examine the high culture information of the American Indian continuum is to see an extremely sophisticated use of "earth" materials and natural healing techniques—and hopefully one day western culture will be open to learn from what these viewpoints pose. Moreover, all of the techniques and viewpoints solidified through world culture have a position in the spiritual hierarchy of the composite culture—which is to say, a meta-reality basis.

Transformational functionalism is not separate from what these concepts pose—and as such, this area of information resolidification must be dealt with if we are to expand.

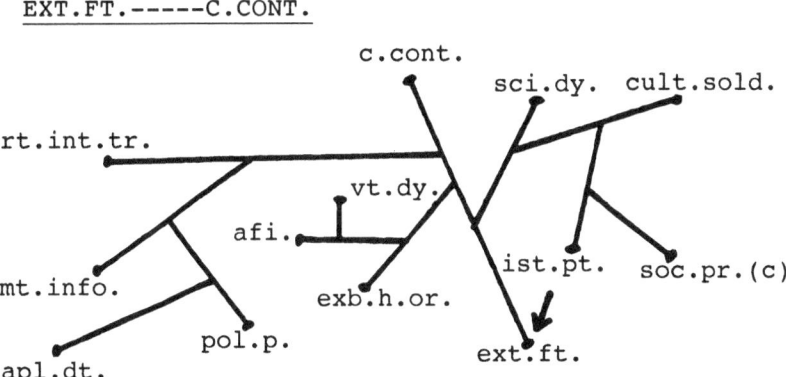

EXT.FT.-----C.CONT.

CS–32

The "expansion of contemporary functionalism," in accordance with the affinity-insight (1) principle, has to do with the implication of affinity dynamics (and what this poses for creative postulation). In actual terms, many new theories will be arrived at in much the same way creative music methodology is generated. Expansion in this context has much to do with both vibrational intuition and empirical analysis. Moreover, the realness of investigation will be resolidified with its spiritual basis—having to do with both spiritual clarification and cosmic integration. The realness of this new alignment will forecast a new functionalism on every level—for in this context, science will no longer be strictly science, but instead one aspect of composite discipline. In other words, the expansion of new functionalism implies new criteria for viewing investigation as well as cataloging information. Scientists in this context can no longer only study strict functionalism—nor can the basic university route be allowed to continue. The progressional realness of new functionalism implies a return to a composite information formation—in the sense of pre-Socratic perception dynamics. The move towards information reintegration can be brought about by installing new definition contexts—thoroughly grounded in spiritual reality. Hopefully the coming cycle will see this undertaking start, for new functionalism can no longer tolerate the extended separation we have in this period. As long as the astronomer sees him- or herself as separate from the astrologer, we cannot really consider ourselves totally released from mono-dimensionalism (yet I have not meant to comment only on one aspect of present-day functionalism, for the example of the astrologer and astronomer is only a small problem when compared with the composite scene). The challenge of new functionalism is too important to not have dynamic culture integration. Science can no longer be viewed with respect to one aspect of functionalism; instead, this subject must be seen in the "realest" possible context—involving all that is "of knowledge."

The challenge of new functionalism will not only move to broaden the reality-tone level of particular disciplines but will also call for a dynamic interplay between various aspects of transformational culture. Because not only can a given area of discipline not afford to be ignorant of its related areas, but there must be a dynamic new interchange created for composite knowledge. Scientists should be involved with creative people—and should be aware of the reality expansion of music, dance, and poetry (to name a few). Scientists and musicians in this context must learn to work together—and this is especially true for restructuralist creativity. The forming of a composite functionalism can create a dynamic new context for extension, and together, creative discipline and new spirituality will move to substantiate the vibrational reality of earth culture. This relationship is important because there is a music (or creative discipline) for every scientific focus—which is to say, the inter-relationship between science and creativity is not artificial (not to mention there is a function science—and law—for every creative projection style). The solidification of new functionalism (which in this cycle is alternative functionalism) will expand the dynamics of this new alliance regardless of discipline. The solidification of composite information is the only chance to possibly attain real "high culture"—which is to say, the challenge of reintegration is paramount to transformation (not only for music or dance, but involving every area of creative discipline).

It is clear that the progressional move towards multi-information will reshape our present perceptions about functionalism. I have no doubt that many other related developments to transformational change will also occur which have not been mentioned in this book. This subject transcends any single context, for the realness of transformational functionalism is indeed, by today's standards, revolutionary (in the most positive sense of the word). My point in mentioning this subject is only to comment on the need for re-examination—of functionalism and the role of science to composite society. I realize that the dynamics of multi-functionalism cannot be secured in a short time period—which is to say, dynamic transformation is not going to happen tomorrow. Yet at the same time, we have no choice but to postulate that which is most real—whether or not it is immediately possible. The solidification of a new transformational functionalism in the terms I have described might sound somewhat unrealistic, yet five hundred years ago the concept of the airplane was not universally embraced either. One thing is clear—we are on this planet and the composite realness of life is manifested in this experience on many different levels. It is now possible to view activity in this time cycle that already hints of new functionalism, and there is no reason to assume this phenomenon will not continue. As long as there are people who are not afraid of their imagination, there will be new areas to learn about and explore. This is also true for alternative functionalism. For the dynamic expansion of a given culture is directly related to what transpires in the cosmic zone which dictates what that culture is. In other words, the state of transformation is not only related to a word but instead has to do with how cosmic factors are manifested. For instance, how could anyone have created an Einstein—rather, his work and life came about in a much broader spiritual and cosmic context than we can now deal with. This is also the case with transformation—which is to say, the "particulars" that can solidify the next change cycle will not be about any one factor, but will instead encompass many different dynamic considerations. It is for this reason that I cannot deal with transformation as a mono-dimensional phenomenon that must fall within any particular context—because "if you can think about it, then something is already happening."

(Level Two)

To view the present reality of world creative music is to see many new developments in every area. There are so many dynamic creative areas for us to experience in this period, and there are so many musicians whose work offers us great beauty (beauty that also hints of positive transformation). The intensity of this time cycle (late seventies) seems to suggest that the next twenty years will be even more exciting for what it will pose for earth creativity—regardless of thrust continuum. Moreover, the realness of this intensity is not limited only to particular regions of the planet, but can be experienced throughout the composite planet surface—there is the creativity of the west, east, north, and south; the music in America, Europe, Asia, Japan, etc.—and all of these focuses are important if we are sincere in our love of creativity. The significance of this time zone might well have to do with whether we are able to recognize the dynamics of our position on this planet, for the seeds underlying earth creative diversity might very well be related to functional transformation. This has been my viewpoint throughout the whole of this series of books—that being, the realness of this time cycle is conducive for the forming of new alliances—alliances not based on what we perceived to be "most different" about ourselves (on the physical universe level) but instead for what similarities bind us together as a single family on this planet. To understand this viewpoint is to understand the transformational potential of earth creativity—and this is especially true in this time cycle. For the progressional realness of this period has moved to outline the dynamic inter-relationship of all earth culture, and in doing so, this phenomenon has planted the seeds for resolidification—and transformation. It is important that some attempt is made to understand what this forming resolidification might mean in actual terms. For we are slowly coming to a crucial time cycle in this planet's history (or at least in this time quadrant), and as the next twenty years come into focus, the decisions and attitudes we adopt now will have lasting effects on generations to come. As such, the reality continuum of world creativity will be of profound importance for what its continuum will signify with respect to particulars and vibrational dynamics. This is not to say that creativity on its own will determine which forces earth culture will be dealing with, for obviously creativity is not in that position—that is, there is no one factor that can claim to give total insight into the future. But certainly the realness of this subject will signify some aspect of progressional earth life—for this consideration (creativity) is not separate from the people who are creative.

If we are to understand the dynamic continuum of earth creativity in this period, and if we are to view the reality particulars of world methodology as a positive transformation tool, then this subject cannot be separated from the whole of new functionalism as it relates to transitional earth—in its composite context. This is so because while I have advanced the realness of world creativity—as a subject that has been either neglected or distorted—so that we can hopefully see the positive value offered through this continuum, at the same time no one factor will determine the vibrational realness of the next period. This is not to under-rate earth creativity but only to put its value in perspective to the composite initiations of creative disciplines. The fact is, no one creative discipline is going to determine the dynamics of world transformation—through its "natural" route. This is true whether we are focusing on the realness of so-called black, white, or Asian affinity dynamics—whatever form. For this reason, the dynamic implications of earth creativity must be viewed with respect to its world position, and its projectional implications. Nothing is more important than the world (for right now).

The new functionalism developing in this time cycle has to do with the expanded dynamic options that are available to all creative people. The actualness of this phenomenon can be viewed with respect to the changes that have transformed this period of time involving both technological breakthroughs and collective individual invention. The fact that it is now possible to be clearly informed about the particular continuum of every world culture section cannot be underestimated. Moreover, the option implications of composite information are not separate from affinity dynamics. To understand what this increased information scan means is to have a real basis for viewing progressional continuity. For while it has been fashionable of late to write of so-called fusion developments, the fact is, this phenomenon has always been a natural progressional factor in earth creativity. In other words, the cross-sectional influences of earth creativity can be viewed in every time period of earth creativity. What is different today, however, is the rate of change. For the technological realness of this period has now allowed for rapid cross-interrelated information on a level that was impossible before. The realness of this information has accelerated the dynamics of source transfer, and as such the nature of what these cross-developments will mean in future terms. Yet the dynamic implications of new functionalism must be viewed for how it has altered the option spread of creative postulation—whatever projection. (It is important that this phenomenon is understood as we move into the time zone of the eighties.) It is not simply a question of viewing the dynamics of fusion—or a particular fusion—rather, the dynamics of new functionalism will have a profound effect on every area of creative music. As such, the composite realness of world creative music must be viewed from this context as well—because if new functionalism has indeed substantiated the vibrational platform of the next cosmic continuity, then any attempt to understand the meta-reality implications of creative music from the world continuum would involve to what degree this awareness—and challenge—is dealt with. The seriousness of new functionalism must be considered in any thorough examination of transformational activity. For the net effect of a given projection will have serious consequences for the entire world community, and this is important to understand. To examine the reality of earth creative music is to view a multiple of projections that are significant for their effects on the total planet. The composite realness of earth creativity affects all of our lives—whether or not a person is consciously aware of a particular projection. As such the challenge of new functionalism cannot be evaluated from any one context, but instead must be viewed for what its realness implies on a composite level.

ALT(FT)II–4

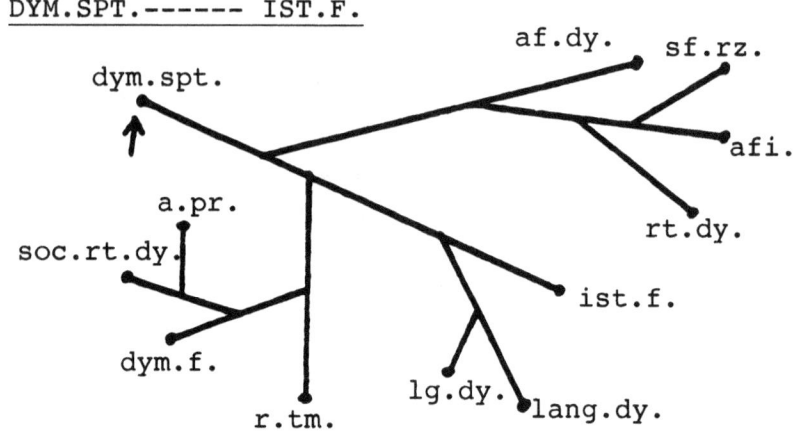

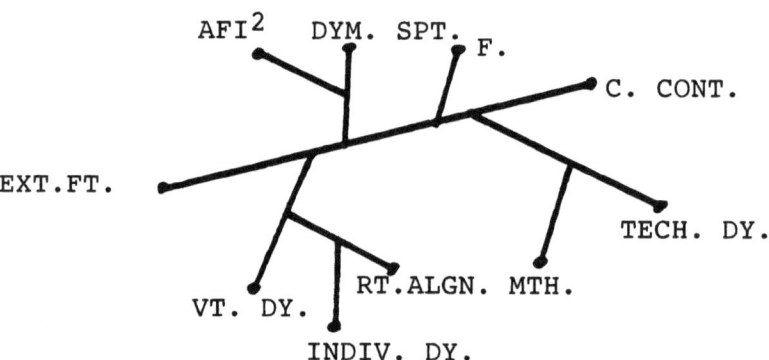

The progressional continuity of black creative music and extended functionalism is no different than any other projectional community—yet it can and must still be commented on (because its particulars are directly related to the whole of this series of books—having to do with establishing some basis to properly deal with the reality of creativity from the African experience and its relationship to transformation). For the continuity of American black creativity is especially related to how the affinity-insight principle has actualized in western culture. To understand this phenomenon is to view the relationship progressions that have surrounded every projectional strain of black music for the last hundred and some years. Each period of the music has advanced the affinity-insight principle with respect to the vibrational posture of the next cycle. It is possible to view every projection of black creativity from this context—and in particular, the emergence of bebop and the continuity that established the post-Ayler junction of music. For the dynamic implications of the African-American experience have forecasted the next composite affinity transfer adaptation—which is to say, the affinity-dynamics solidification of post-Ayler creativity would signal the acceleration of dynamic source transfer—regardless of focus. The actualness of this phenomenon is not separate from the emergence of new functionalism. For the thrust continuum of black American creativity in the time span of a hundred years has now methodologically moved to incorporate every creative continuum in its path—which is to say, the expansion principle of creative music has progressed to where its projection has become all-encompassing. The realness of this expanded vibrational (and actual) position has transformed the functional arena of the new creative musician—and this is important to understand.

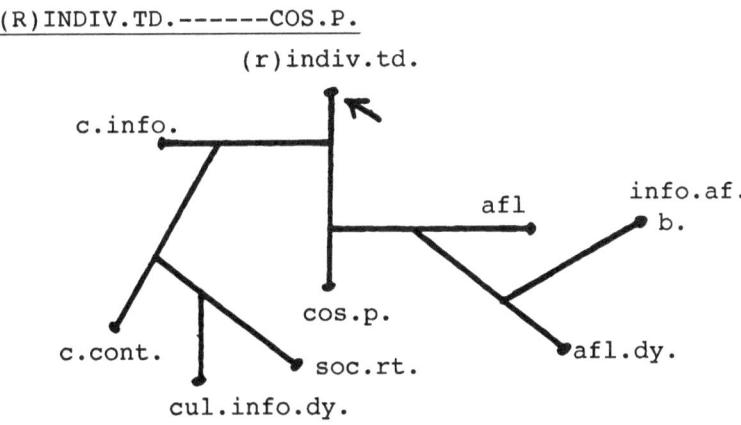

If, in the beginning, the continuity of creative music from the black aesthetic had to do with how its dynamics were reflected in its affinity-insight principle implications—as it related to black American culture (and transformational and resolidification culture)—by the post-Ayler junction of the music, one could view black creativity as a principal alternative agent for world culture (or composite transformational culture). The realness of this change would be directly related to the nature of source transfer and changing world reality. The actualness of the affinity-insight principle is not separate from what this expanded position means as well. At the heart of this subject is the realness of resolidifcation as a basis for alternative composite culture (or at least alternative transfer alignment—since it is more than possible that the next cycle will not be about everyone coming together as such—but instead, a relocation of affinity pulls). Thus to really view the post-Ayler continuum of creative black music is to deal with its position in the multi-complexual realness of composite world culture. For the nature of the affinity-insight principle in this context is not only about the reality of any single group, but rather this phenomenon comments on the whole of humanity.

The significance of multi-transfer shift activity in this context has to do with the option-range particulars underlying how creativity is perceived. Which is to say, the concept of fusion music can be viewed as the first degree of alternative functionalism. For the progressional continuity of this phenomenon seems to forecast a total breakdown of music categories as well as "viewpoints." In actual terms, the emergence of the transformational musician will have to do with an individual's ability to function throughout the composite spectrum of creative music. The reality of so-called fusion music is important for how it has utilized source transfer, and also for how it will eventually vibrationally prepare the next time continuum. Already in this cycle there has been much commotion about the dynamics of source transfer—concerning whether one has the right to change his or her activity (is it or is it not jazz!)—but, in the final analysis, these arguments are really beside the point. It is no wonder that new functionalism—as an actual phenomenon—has yet to be dealt with—or even understood—by the collective forces that dictate composite western journalism and control. For the gradual awareness of this phenomenon is always coupled with extra-curricular social-reality "particulars" (that are not always in the interest of the truth). The significance of new functionalism—in its composite state—will change the present reality underlying how creativity is viewed, and in doing so, this change will expand the option dynamics of the creative musician—and audience. The dynamic implications of creative music have already established a significant momentum—with respect to how its affinity dynamics have determined the present course western culture is now pursuing—and as such, this continuum is in an excellent position to accelerate the fundamentals of the next time cycle.

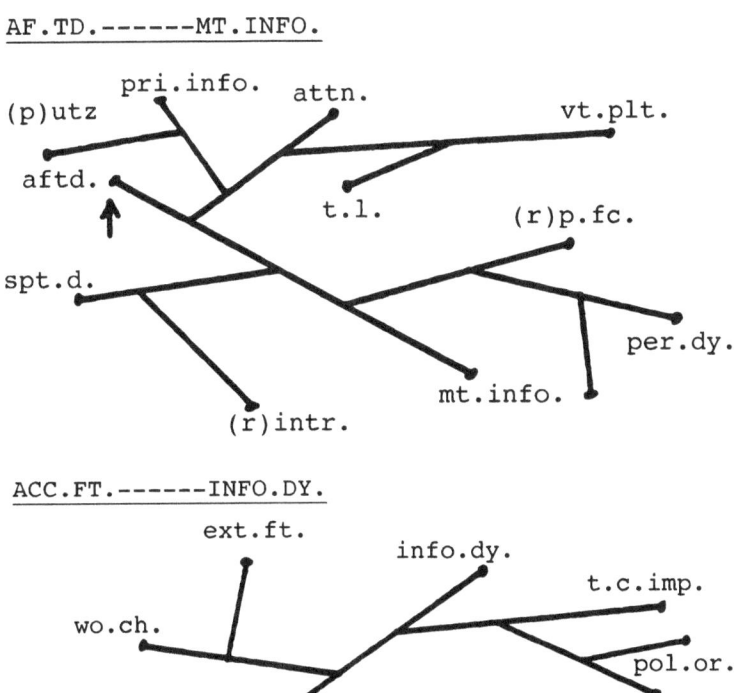

Without doubt, the emergence of the multi-instrumentalist-composer is directly related to the realness of new functionalism. To understand this development is to have insight into the progressional continuum of this time zone. For the new multi-instrumentalist-composer promises to totally reshape the composite spectrum of world creativity. This is not to say that either multi-instrumentalism or composition is something new in itself—for obviously there have always been multi-instrumentalists and composers—but rather, the dynamics surrounding present-day new functionalism have seen this consideration expand to new heights. For the emergence of new functionalism has altered the option requirements for the master creative musician. To view what this development has actualized is to view a musician who now functions instrumentally on from two to twenty instruments—a musician who composes for every type of creative situation (whether that situation involves composing for notated/improvisational situations, to strictly notated works) and eventually as a musician who has defined his or her music, extending to the creation of alternative record companies, methods of teaching, etc.). The emergence of this new musician will completely alter the composite reality of earth creativity, for the collective thrust of composite alternative functionalism on this level cannot be simply dismissed. The realness of this phenomenon will also reshape methodology, as well as the "particulars" of every sector of the music—whether that sector is the history of the music (or culture) or the economic dynamics surrounding the music—or the performance reality of alternative creativity. All of these changes are part of what I call new functionalism—which is to say, the dynamics of alternative functionalism will dictate the next creative thrust of world music—and this is what the next cycle of creative music must address.

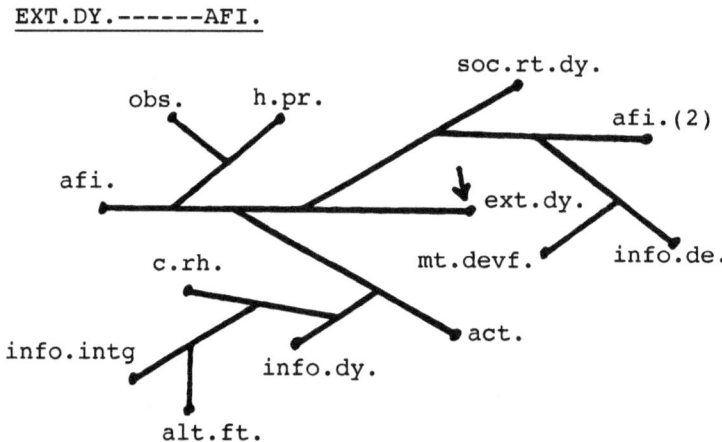

To understand the new multi-instrumentalist composer it is necessary that the composite progressional particulars of western creativity be viewed. For the reality of a given projection is not separate from the responsibility that projection promotes to its particulars. For instance, historically, the reality of the instrumentalist in western art music has progressively moved towards suppression. Solidification of "classical" music in this context would only promote the "interpretive affinity stance," so much so that individual dynamics were all but forgotten. The resulting disintegration of western art music and culture that followed is not separate from what this affinity suppression meant—for the suppression of individual affinity dynamics was not only manifested in western art music, but instead this phenomenon paralleled the composite culture tendency. In other words, this dynamic suppression was constantly applied and manifested. The solidification of the creative musician in creative music from the black aesthetic would be of monumental importance for the progressive move towards "reculture." We are still in this cycle—yet the progressive implications of creative music from the black aesthetic still have somehow not been dealt with. For to view the activity of a Fletcher Henderson is not only to view a dynamic creative composer and arranger, but his viewpoint would also allow for both collective participation and "composite affinity." Which is to say, the total continuum of creative black music must be viewed for how its methodology functions as a dynamic and composite re-unification factor—yet there is more here. My point is that before we can begin to understand the new functionalism of this time cycle, we must first understand the functionalism it is based from. This is so because by "new functionalism" I am not commenting on a factor that is separate from what was implied in the early solidification of alternative functionalism—as this phenomenon is related to the emergence of black creative music in its beginning (re-beginning) period. In other words, the term "new functionalism" is my phrase for the acceleration of the particulars that solidified "original" alternative functionalism, as defined through the collective imprint of black creativity. As such, it is impossible to examine the realness of this new functionalism if its historical implications are not understood.

ALT(FT)II–10

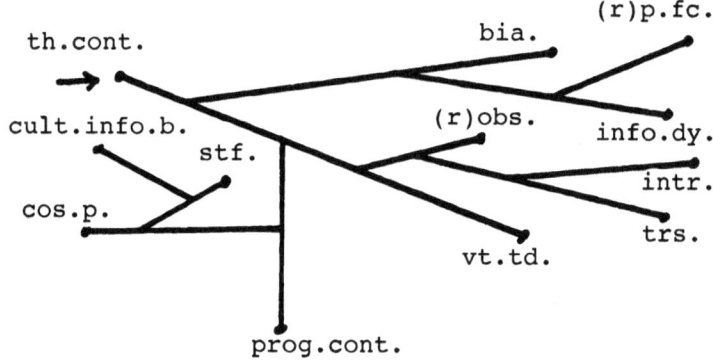

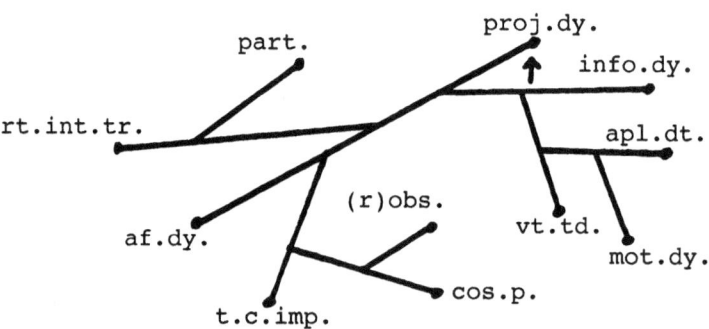

The "responsibility ratio" of creative black music is important for what it tells about progressional continuance and progressional transformation. For the nature underlying how creative musicians perceive and practice functionalism is directly related to the present position creative music has in this cycle. The very continuum of alternative creativity has to do not only with how given musicians were able to function (in the music) but also what they "did" (demonstrated) within that functioning. The importance of this distinction can be viewed in the functional "working space" of the actual music, for no matter how different a given form was perceived in the continuum of trans-African music, the actual music would celebrate the conceptual identity of the composition (and in doing so, utilize both fixed execution and improvisation—both individual and collective)—as well as the vibrational imprint of "present time" space (having to do with the actual moment at which the creativity was "ised"), as well as the collective identity of all of its participating musicians (in the actual music). The conceptual implication of alternative creativity in this context can be viewed in every developing strain of creative music from the black aesthetic. As such, the "responsibility ratio" of the creative musician would necessarily not be separate from the shape new functionalism would have to take. In terms of new functionalism, the contemporary creative musician can now be viewed with respect to the dynamics of his or her "participation dynamics." Which is to say, the post-Ayler transformational creative musician can be viewed as a direct extension of the New Orleans dynamic creative continuum. The only difference between these two examples would be in where the vibrational tone of this period has brought us—that being, how the music sounds on the surface, but not how the music "is." The dynamics of contemporary music's "responsibility function" would have to do with how new vibrational areas can dynamically give insight into the "nature" of this (and the continuing) cycle we are now living in. From this context, the implications of open-ended improvisation must be viewed with respect to what its emergence signifies for about the past fifteen years. New functionalism is related to all of these considerations, which is to say—the dynamics of the creative improviser are directly related to how one functions throughout the composite spectrum of the music. If we are to understand the continuum options of creative music, and if we are to understand the reality position of creative musicians, then the multi-dynamic implications of the affinity-insight principle must be examined with respect to what "total involvement" really means. This is so because in focusing on the transformational creative musician we are focusing on another level of involvement made possible through the essence foundation of creative music from the black aesthetic—and its tradition. Further—this continuance only accents the methodological implications of both alternative functionalism and individual affinity dynamics. This is important.

ALT(FT)II-12

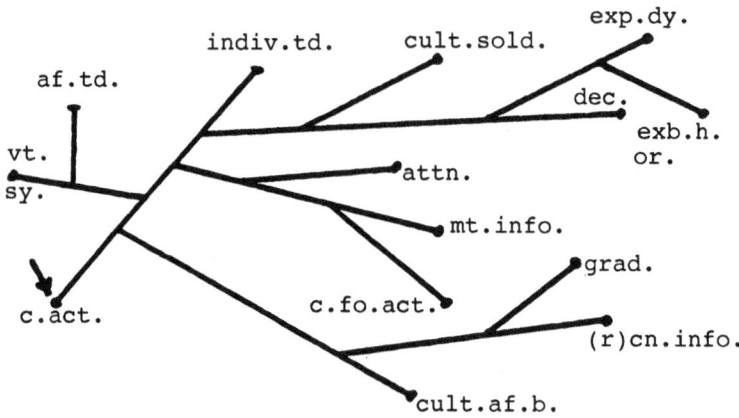

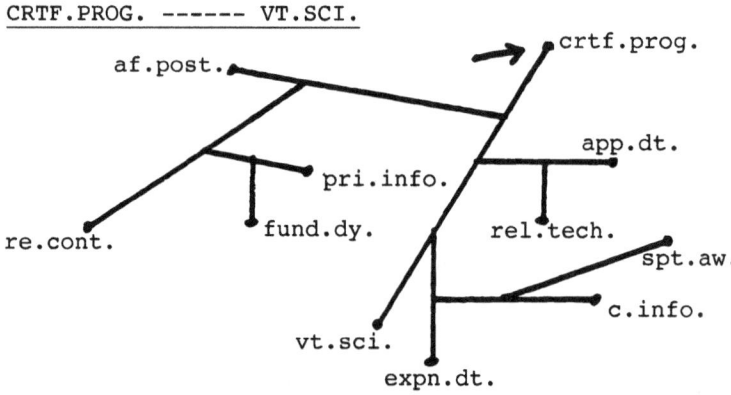

The present-day participation dynamics of the transformational creative musician should not be viewed lightly. This development is directly related to the expansion of creative dynamic options for both the individual and the music. For instance, the reality of multi-instrumentalism throughout the composite continuum of the music has greatly affected how the instrumental specialist is perceived. The realness of this phenomenon has made possible the present-day creative musician. That being, an individual who can not only function with respect to the laws of his or her given instrument (i.e., facility, ability to read or interpret), but whose dynamic contribution is not limited to one instrument. Nor am I only referring to the so-called instruments in his or her musical family (e.g., woodwind, brass). For the contemporary creative musician now functions in many areas not normally associated with what is suppose to be the natural "doubling" instruments. Ornette Coleman showed in this and many other examples what the dynamics of new multi-instrumentalism would mean in actual terms. His use of the saxophone, trumpet, violin, and bassoon is a perfect example of the expanded concept of multi-instrumentalism. Many of the post-Coleman musicians have taken this concept to other areas—in the AACM, all the musicians would become involved in percussion as well (and of course this involvement relates directly to the activity of Duke Ellington and/or Stan Kenton—for their orchestras have been expanding the concept of the multi-instrumentalist since the early thirties—and some). The realness of instrumental expansion on this level will move to have instrumentalists not view their creativity from one context. For in this cycle, many musicians have come to view their activity as not separate from their instruments (as opposed to the instrument being secondary to invention and/or purpose). I believe the challenge of the next cycle will move to promote an alternative view of functional instrumentalism.

The significance of a wide operational base will also clarify the reality position of creative music. For in this cycle, the western defining and controlling community uses the word "jazz" or "blues" as a choking factor to suppress the affinity-spectrum implications surrounding how alternative music is perceived publicly. The spread of transformational creative music will totally render these definitions useless. For the composition-dynamics implications of this phenomenon will destroy the locked definitions that these agencies have now created. Already it is apparent that the gap between the music and present-day western journalism has increased, and this trend will no doubt continue as we move to the next cycle. Creative composers are now functioning in every area of the music—writing compositions from solo to orchestra—whatever combination or instrumentation. The composite continuum of this activity will eventually move to expand the reality dynamics of creative music, for the music has never been about its "medium." The importance of this "expanded operational participation" in alternative creativity cannot be over-estimated. The emergence of the contemporary creative musician can be viewed as the single most dynamic factor that will shape alternative creativity in this cycle. For it is not a question of whether or not creative black music is a transformational projection with revolutionary potential, rather it is a question of how this phenomenon will aid composite change on the physical universe level. The solidification of the expanded creative musician must be viewed from this context. The work happening in this cycle will greatly affect the vibrational tone of progressional creativity for decades (and centuries) to come.

HI.P. -----IF.ST.DY.

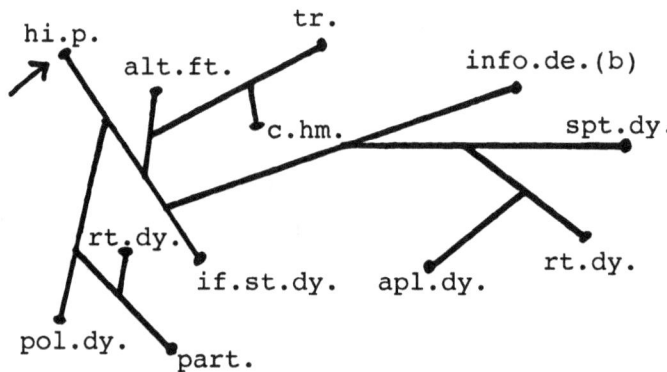

To really view the significance of alternative functionalism is to deal with the composite continuum of world creativity. This is so because the seeds underlying alternative functionalism have their roots in world culture. In actual terms, the composite continuum of western creativity must be viewed for what its breakage from world culture meant—in vibrational terms—and for the route its "particular" projections have had to travel as a result of that break. In other words, alternative functionalism is the activity that moves to resolidify composite earth culture, or information dynamics. As such, it is important to understand what western culture has lost in the last four hundred years as a means to gain the necessary perspective to view present-day events. This is not to berate western culture—or any area of world culture—but only to comment on what the disunification of world culture will mean if not corrected in the future. (Yet it is important to not give the impression that I hold western culture responsible for everything wrong on this planet—because I don't; moreover, the disintegration of world culture cannot be blamed on any particular group at this point in time, because there is no documentation that comments on whether this state of being ever even existed at all, not to mention whether any particular group can be made responsible for the resulting separations we now have in this time zone.) For the dynamic particulars of every given cultural thrust must be viewed for both what it tells about its reality path, and what it signifies about its separateness (in world culture terms). There are only two possibilities: (1) the actualness of real unification can exist and as such is a desirable state to pursue—having to do with the solidification of world culture (and with it a dynamic new political and sound order), or (2) the actualness of transformation is not about this kind of unification, rather this phenomenon has to do with the natural order of recycling that can be viewed in progressional history; which is to say, the realness of alternative functionalism can be viewed for how it will aid the nature of the next composite transfer shift. Both of these viewpoints are valid—but in either case, the realness of alternative functionalism does have a position function. Because from a historical context, alternative functionalism can be viewed with respect to its ability to aid the forming of "new" world culture (transformation) or with respect to its ability to aid the nature of the next "real" change cycle (which is also transformation). As such, if we are to view the emergence of present-day alternative creativity—whatever form—then it is necessary that the progressional continuum of this phenomenon is kept in mind. For the solidification of alternative creativity has seen momentum—and actual functionalism—for more cycles than anyone can accurately comment on (which is to say, this consideration has not sprung up from nowhere, having only to do with this time period, but instead is related to the composite continuity of physical universe life—or at least that part of life we can comment on with any degree of certainty).

ALT(FT)II–16

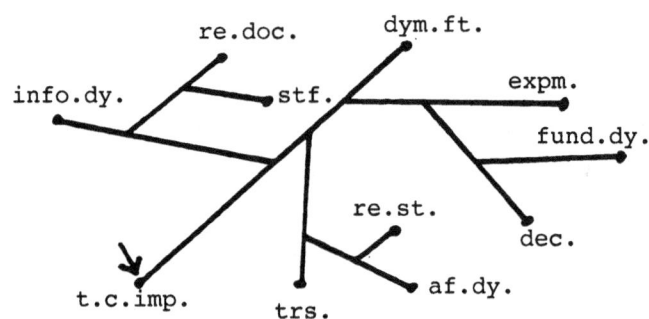

However the concept of transformation is perceived—whether this phenomenon is viewed with respect to the idea of complete unification, or with respect to the fundamentals underlying progressional world "information" ("knowledge," and as such, the multi-continuum that revolves—shifts—around that information)—this context (transformation) must function as the basis from which we can postulate real recovery. Which is to say, the realness of transformation cycles—no matter what type of transformation—does have relevance as a platform for viewing present-day events. This is so because connected to the idea of transformation is the composite continuum of world information that has provided the basis from which our present-day information lines have extended. As such, to view the last two thousand years with respect to world information is to have some basis for examining the particulars of this cycle. For this reason, the phenomenon of alternative functionalism is not separate from the information that has come forth in world culture terms. That information being: (1) the discipline of creativity and its real laws, (2) the meta-reality implications of those laws, (3) the discipline of science and planet functionalism, (4) the spiritual realness of everything, (5) what "being" really is (and can be), and (6) how to move from zone one to zone two. To view the composite continuum of world culture—and its creativity—is to see how these information areas are understood and taught. Only western culture has completely lost its meta-significance, and as such, the realness of present-day alternative functionalism must be viewed for what this loss signifies.

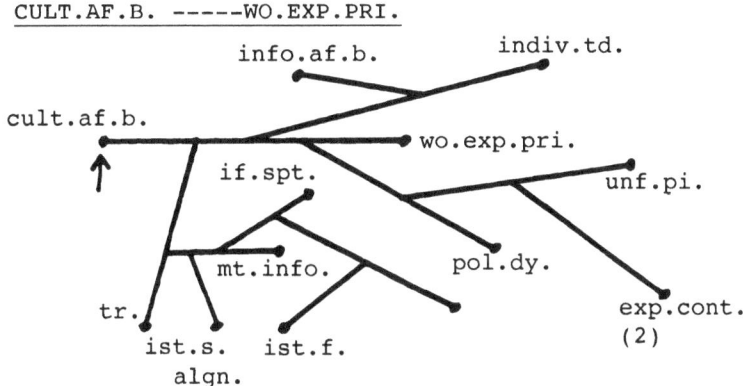

Alternative functionalism can be defined as the activity which seeks to move the vibrational tone level of western culture back into the realm of real culture—and also back into the world community. The progressional continuity of alternative functionalism can be viewed with respect to what degrees of "alignment" are focused on. In this context, the solidification of creative black music must be viewed as significant because of what its meta-reality implications pose to "re-alignment"—yet, as I have tried to state throughout the whole of this book, no one factor personifies alternative functionalism (because black people are not the only people on this planet either). The success of any real transformation will depend on how successful all six of these aforementioned information areas are re-instituted—which is to say, the realness of transformation is a progressional factor (not apt to happen within a short time zone, but instead deals with whole time periods). To view the emergence of transformational creative musicians is to see the emergence of an individual who functions on the most dynamic level with respect to his or her "craft" (if I can write it that way). The emergence of this "condition" can be viewed as significant for what it will imply for the individuals' creative range (and dynamics) and for how the results of that activity (the music, in this case) will affect the culture (or physical universe space). The fact that creative music from the black aesthetic has continually suffered mis-documentation must be viewed as a factor related to the path it has pursued for transformation. Which is to say, the reality of any projectional continuum is not separate from the time-space dynamics it has to function in. In other words, the nature of the struggle that creative black music is now dealing with touches not only the people who are open to it, but all of the people in the environment. It is for this reason that no region of American culture has escaped the influence of creative black music (and culture)—whether or not individuals were actually aware of a given influence. On the other hand, the creative reality of black people has not escaped the vibrational influence of western culture either. Thus, the "inter-relationship of multi-complexual vibrational transference" does exist in actual terms—everything is influenced by everything. And as such, the emergence of alternative functionalism has relevance as a composite transformational tool for the total planet. The seriousness of the next cycle demands that this phenomenon is understood on some level—I am not writing of "theories" that have nothing to do with our lives.

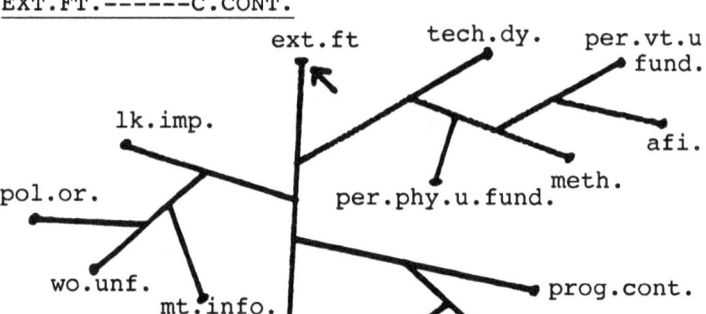

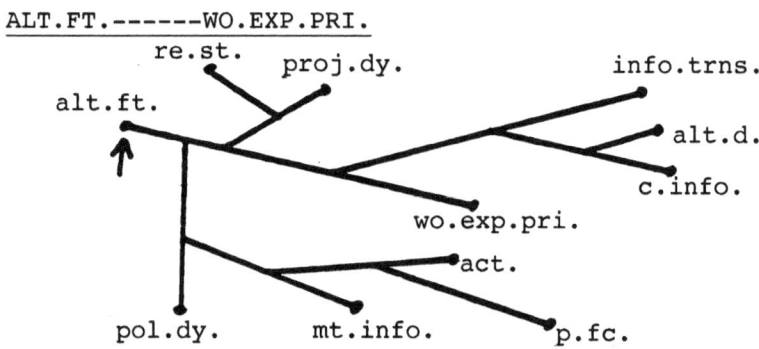

The composite solidification of world information—and what this phenomenon means when viewed with respect to the realness of alternative functionalism—is a subject that must be dealt with if we are to understand the realness of creativity. It is important that some attempts are made in this cycle to advance the re-examination of composite information lines—and this is especially true with respect to the significance of basic information or discipline focuses. For the study of creativity and its related laws is a subject that must be brought into the forefront of our conservatories and centers of higher learning. It is important that the next generation of creative people is better aware of the reality of this subject—because, strange as it seems, the information pattern of the last fifty years has moved to produce better and better technicians and fewer and fewer artists. Only by moving to refocus on basic underlying principle information will young people be able to attain the correct balance between functionalism and spiritual purpose. The realness of alternative functionalism is not separate from what this refocusing will mean in actual terms. For the reality actualness of what we call creativity is not about a mystery—there is a reason for creativity, or at least the realness of this phenomenon occupies a particular space—serves a particular purpose—and makes particular things happen. The study of alternative functionalism can move to supply the creative person with the dynamic inter-relationship between composite methodology and meta-reality dictates. In the final analysis, alternative functionalism can move to create the proper vibrational state for coming to terms with the reality position of methodological laws—having to do with not only how a given function works, but why. The challenge of supplying information of this kind will take on added importance as we enter the next cycle.

ALT(FT)II-20

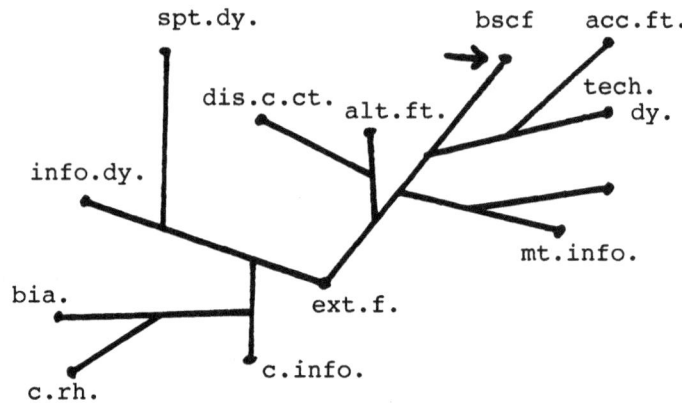

The discipline of creativity and its real laws can be viewed in every culture in every recorded time zone. The realness of what this means can help us to understand the cross-sectional diversity of world information and the multi-complexual state of things. For the reality of functionalism in creativity, if properly taught, moves to also give insight about the composite state of things. That is, the laws underlying a given functionalism are not only relevant for an isolated focus but are dynamically integrated into the whole of what we call knowledge—or better still, relevant information. The challenge of the next cycle will involve whether or not the dynamic functionalism of the last thirty years is discussed and properly integrated into the thrusts of composite functionalism—this is true for contemporary science and this is also true for contemporary creativity. However, the solidification of alternative information can materialize only by challenging the present information lines of western culture—or western media control. For the past cycle (i.e., the last fifty years and some) has seen a staggering amount of both mis-definitions as well as outright lies directed at alternative initiations—and this is particularly true when applied to world culture postulation and non- (so-called) western initiations. As such, the first junction that must be secured in the next cycle is the solidification of alternative information outputs—whether those outputs are manifested in the form of alternative books, radio, newspapers, etc., whatever. There is now a need to combat the mis-information surrounding world information—and we can no longer wait for western scholars and definers to discover universality and bail us out of this dilemma—because these people are part of the problem. The time to act is now (and it was "now" two thousand years ago).

ACT.------INFO.TRNS.

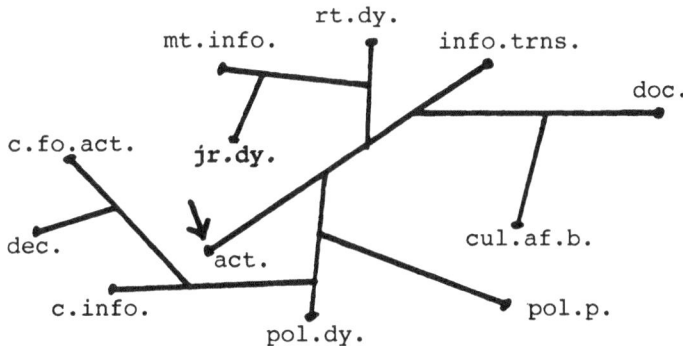

AFL.------POL.CON.

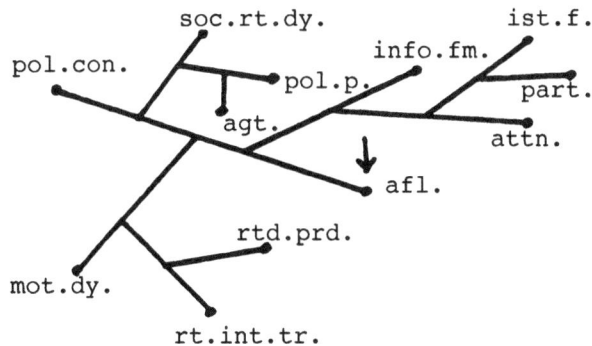

ALT(FT)II-22

RE.ST.------ TR.

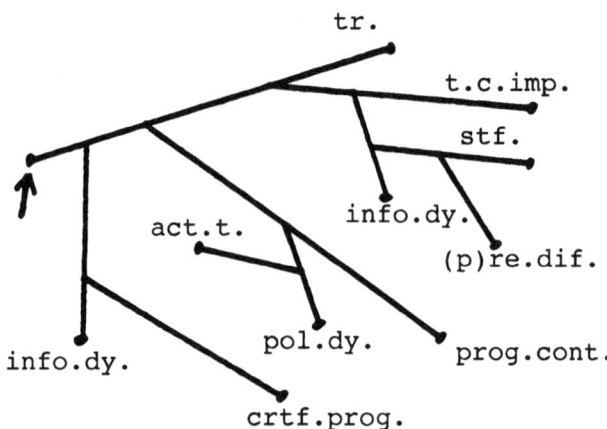

By coming to terms with alternative functionalism, the real gains of the post-Parker to post-Ayler continuum can better be understood—on every level. For it is clear that there can be no basis to deal with the post-AACM junction of extended functionalism if one is not aware of the projectional (and thrust) dynamics of the composite strain of black creativity. It is important that the next focus of post-Parker progressionalism is not undertaken with the same vibrational and empirical misconceptions—as to its reality base—as what transpired in its first encounter with western defining terms, or we will run into the same errors about this music that exist today. For the essence realness of bebop was not about how it extended, but rather its position in the composite nature of world progressionalism—having to do with the route black people would travel in physical and vibrational universe terms, as well as what form world transformation would take (or through what form the "cosmos" would direct world change). Hopefully the next level of commentary on bebop will address itself to the real dynamic implications underlying what this projection poses to extended functionalism. In this context, some attention must be directed to the reality of functionalism posed through this continuum (bebop)—for this projection was not simply an existential celebration, but instead the next cycle of applied extended functionalism: having to do with what came about from cross-information exchange through ensemble extended functionalism; having to do with the "vibrational cross-exchange" that developed between the rhythm section and the soloists (involving the utilization of what was then a new rhythmic language); and having to do with the dynamic implications of its projectional (path) reality context. To deal with these questions is to begin viewing the realness of progressional continuity in black creativity during the last forty years—in fact, during the last two hundred years.

The second degree of alternative functionalism involves viewing the realness of continuance with respect to what this phenomenon poses to the meta-reality implications of a given function—and given cross-function. In other words, if we are to ever understand the seriousness of alternative functionalism, then it is important that some effort is directed to re-examine our total understanding of "function." My point is this: there is no function separate from its vibrational and mystical implications; moreover, there is no function that does not make a given vibrational and mystical "thing" happen. In other words, every action produces a particular vibrational and mystical response, and the purpose of a given discipline is to understand the best route to a given cosmic zone of information or truth (another way of saying this is that the purpose of a given "high" discipline is to secure the zone of its given region as a means to have it available for either participation or insight). As such, the reality of extended functionalism has to do with the progressional awakening of particular routes of information as those areas are so-called discovered (but really, revealed) as a means to have that information correspond with the dynamics of "living" as it flows in accordance with the dictates of its related time period. The "truth" of a given area of information is of course "not about the information" but instead cosmic (or about God). But the reality of alternative functionalism can be viewed with respect to what it poses to the concept of "designation"—or the move to establish both proper (correct) alignments for information degrees and particulars. It is important that this is understood.

To view the nature of progressional continuum in this cycle is to have some idea as to the multi-complexual implications surrounding transformational re-interpretations. For the last hundred years have clearly shown that the source-transfer-information-shift phenomenon is not limited to any one consideration but instead involves the composite planet. In other words, the cross-sectional informational exchange now taking place in this time zone did not start in this time zone (i.e., the last thirty years), but is related to the whole of this cycle. The implications of this phenomenon should now be clear to all of us, for the acceleration of cross-information seems to clearly indicate that we (as a collective people) have come to the next level of information assimilation—and this is particularly true of western culture. Certainly one of the major problems that western culture must now move to understand is that the reality of cross-sectional information does indeed shed light on the nature of progressional continuance in the last two thousand years—and as such, challenges many of the popular notions western culture has come to accept as being true. To view the realness of cross-sectional information can help western culture make the adjustments necessary for both survival and expansion. The fact is, many of us in the west have wrongly come to view ourselves as more "developed" than what we now call the "primitive countries" (this is true even though practically all of the information that solidified western dynamic functionalism—and aesthetics—has its roots in world culture). But the last hundred years especially has moved to show the errors associated with the so-called cultural superiority mentality of the west—and I have no doubt that we are only seeing the beginning of this phenomenon. Nevertheless, the reality of progressional continuance in this time zone has moved to transport western culture to a very interesting position—for the realness of this time cycle seems to carry great dangers for the whole of western culture unless there are profound changes in the way westerners think and live. The dynamic implications of cross-sectional information seems to imply that the reality of extended functionalism in the west has now reached the point where its meta-reality dynamics must be integrated into the greater pool of world information if it is to continue. This is not only true for creativity but encompasses the whole of "real information." The fact is, dynamic functionalism without a spiritual basis means nothing; the fact is, contemporary technology without a feeling for humanity is not impressive; the fact is, dynamic productivity while half the world is starving is not just. My point is that every progression has its own dynamic implications as well as responsibility. This is true for creativity and this is true for exploration. The challenge of understanding alternative functionalism involves moving to view a given initiation with respect to what it poses—or can pose—for the composite reality of world positive change.

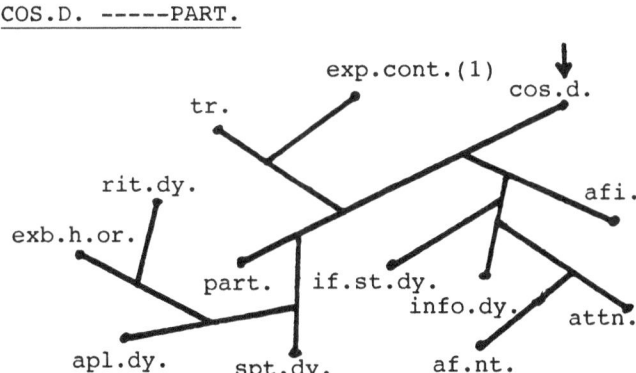

The meta-reality implications of composite functionalism is a subject that will become more and more important as we move to the next cycle. At present, the information continuum of the last one hundred years has been so overwhelming that no real basis has materialized on which to begin properly examining the multi-complexual realness of where we (the culture) are—let alone where we seem to be going. To review the meta-reality realness of cross-information is to begin examining the dynamic implications of both projectional routes as well as vibrational particulars. In other words, it is my belief that there is no such thing as "new"—that being something (i.e., a law) that did not exist before—rather, it is a question of moving to examine a given information line with respect to the composite realness of all earth information. This is especially so in creativity because the realness of a given form of activity, in world music terms, is designed to "do something," as opposed to only be entertaining. It is important that in the next cycle western culture moves to begin understanding "what it has been doing to people" in its creativity—for the effect of a given innovation is real, having nothing to do with whether or not it is understood. In other words, the use of given materials has multi-complexual implications. If there is to be a real "high culture" in western society, then the collected realness of its functionalism as well as its vibrational dynamics must be understood. Many of the problems western culture faces in this time cycle can be traced to the vacuum between dynamic functionalism and mis-intentions (I write it this way because no person in his or her right mind would consciously move to hurt someone—if he really understood what he was doing). As such, the composite realness of earth information can provide a real context for both understanding the realness of a given discipline and also understanding the spirituality related to what that discipline "activates." To examine a given phenomenon in this light is to begin viewing what really happens when a given phenomenon is practiced—as opposed to only the "experience of it" happening.

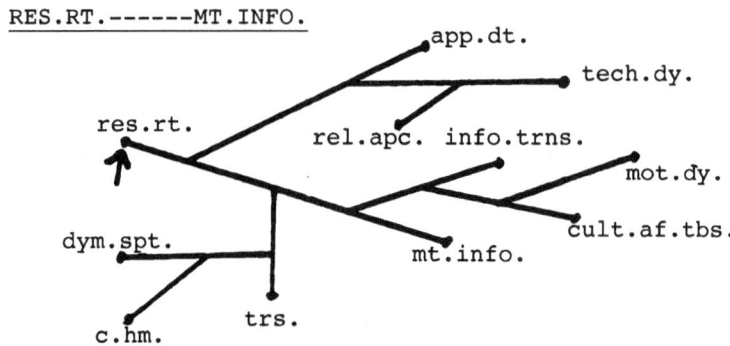

The significance of meta-reality consciousness in extended functionalism can help to bring about "deliberate moves" for future extension. In other words, a better understanding of dynamic functionalism can produce a situation where a given discipline can be utilized to bring about "a particular state." As such, the real spirituality of a given phenomenon will not be viewed as separate from what it is possible to attain in "high discipline" terms. And, of course, this idea is not new but instead borrowed from "creativity—as understood in world culture."

To really view the composite dynamics of world progressionalism is to re-examine the significance of information continuance—and what this means when applied to source-transfer innovations. It is important that cross-sectional dynamics of information continuance are not negatively viewed as alien to the basic realness of expansion—because they aren't. Throughout the whole of this series of books I have tried to challenge the notion of isolated progressionalism in every context, because this notion does not correspond to documented history. Not only has everyone (and every group) contributed to the well-being of this planet—and the tragedies that have come as a result of that so-called well-being—but the future continuance of "things" is not separate from what this cross-information has seeded. In other words, the future well-being of "this state of being" cannot be vested in any one affinity persuasion, but rather will depend on whether or not we, as a collective people, can draw on our collective experiences (and information) as a means to "find the right slot for the problem of the moment" (with the understanding being that there are more than enough problems for every slot, and some). As such, it is important to properly come to terms with cross-sectional information (source transfer), because the route of a given information line is not separate from what it reveals about "basic tendencies" (which serve as the basic motivating factor for "doing anything"). There is no information line that cannot be viewed with respect to its source-transfer implications—and this does mean something. Without doubt, the narrow interpretations we are dealing with in this time period can be traced to the vibrational state related to both nationalism and racism. But, as a collected people, we can no longer afford to limit the scope of our understanding. This is not to ignore the offerings of any particular group, nor have I tried to disrespect the uniqueness of a given participation. Rather, the dynamic realness of a given information line must be viewed with respect to what that line signifies about its real projectional continuum—as made real for the whole of its thrust continuum, as made real for the zone that dictated what that projection is really moving towards (and from)—all of these matters transcend narrow definitions about race and/or nationalism. To really view a given information line is to view that line with respect to its universal realness, and this should concern everyone.

 The collected realness of earth information, and its relationship to meta-functionalism, is important because of what it signifies about composite dynamics. My point is this: only by understanding all the dynamic utilization of a given information strain can we begin to properly understand its transformational function and value. The whole concept of alternative functionalism is not separate from what this means as well, for the meta-reality implications of a given function or methodology are not one-dimensional. Moving to solidify the composite information tenets of a given focus will help the collected realness of earth humanity be in a much better position for evaluation—and this is also true with regards to how the nature of a given function is viewed, as well as how the meta-implications of that function is revealed. The challenge of alternative functionalism is not limited to either the amassing of information or technological dynamics, but extends instead to the attitude surrounding how functionalism is to be utilized—in other words, alternative functionalism is not about revenge or retribution. The dynamic implications of this most important subject is related to positive change—and, moreover, positive intentions for making change. As we enter into the eighties, the importance of this viewpoint will become even more serious. Nevertheless, the meta-reality implications of alternative functionalism have to do with the composite solidification of earth information as a means to examine both the functional and meta-functional dynamics of that information, with the understanding being that the "truth" of a given information strain (in this period) can only be viewed by experiencing (and hopefully vibrationally understanding) the cross-realness of that information as it is manifested in world terms. The thrust of alternative functionalism cannot be limited to particular regions of the planet, or particular nations, but instead must involve a composite solidification of world information. There is no information strain that is not important, which is to say, the collective information umbrella of every nation can be of great service to all humanity—if we reach out for it.

    The meta-reality dynamics of composite information will help to bring about a situation where a given area of information can be utilized with respect to the whole of its inherited implications. Which is to say, the concept of doing can again be transported into the "ritual"—and actual living can be viewed with respect to its creative particulars. For the reality of information is not separate from its real position in the actual continuum of living. The restoration of transformational information can move to transport earth life back into either the real position life seems to have, or the real position life could have (whichever one is good for you). The understanding here being: the life we are now collectively experiencing on this planet and in this time zone is not the only option we have—and is not "what seems" to be the highest state of existence (when you think about it). The solidification of transformational functionalism can be viewed as an important step towards uplifting the basic tone level of existence.

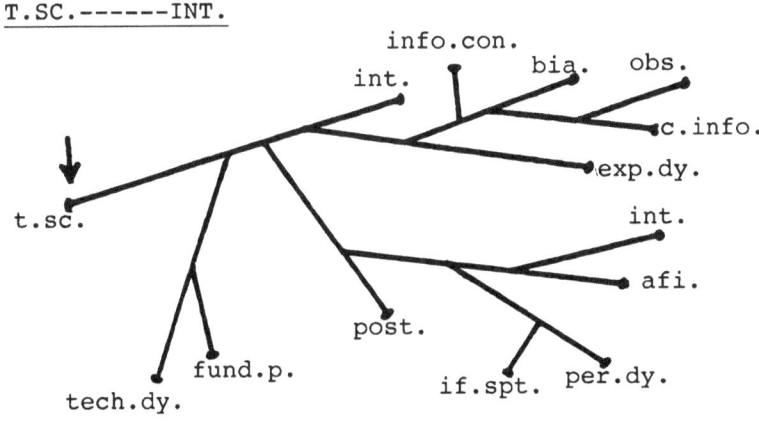

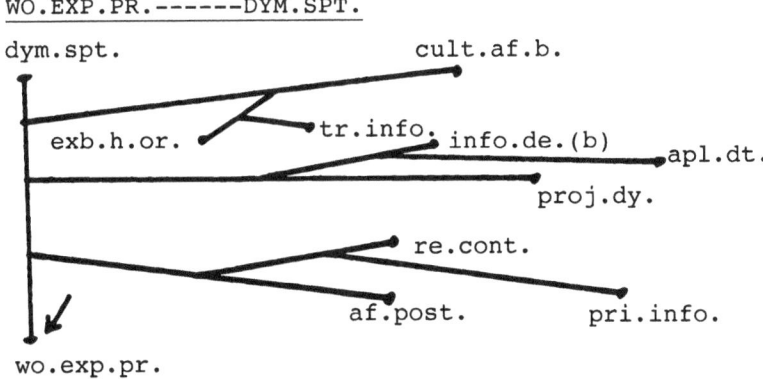

ALT(FT)II–30

TR.------INFO.DY.

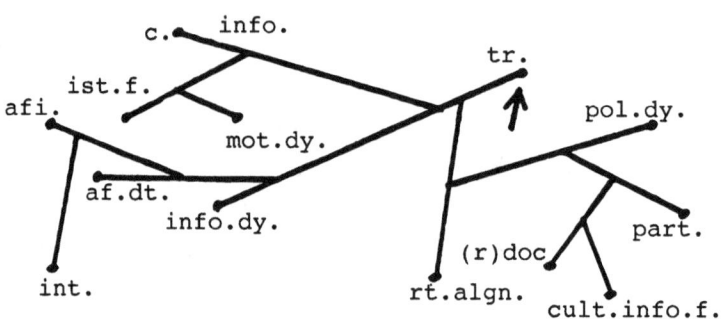

SOC.RT.DY.------TR.

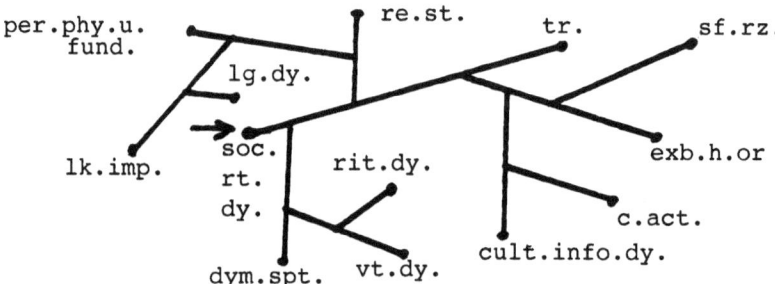

By providing a new meta-reality basis for motivation and/or functionalism, the realness of alternative functionalism can expand our total understanding of phenomenon—regardless of level. For instance, if we isolate just the consideration of medicine with respect to world information, we can begin seeing the solidification of a whole different viewpoint about healing. Because the thrust of western culture has moved to solidify a dynamic technology and functionalism that is quite different from eastern medicine (e.g., acupuncture)—not to mention the reality of this subject in places like Africa (e.g., magic and natural healing). The solidification of world healing information alone could revolutionize the science of medicine, and while doing so also provide another understanding about transformational continuance. This is what I am interested in—the solidification of composite information and the emergence of a new order as a result of that solidification. In the end, the realness of this phenomenon will move to promote a revolutionary context for continuance—involving the cross-sectional realness of all humanity. Because, in the end, real unification can come about only if there is respect for all aspects of what is unifying. Which is to say, before a given phenomenon can solidify, there must first be a vibrational state whose affinity and attraction pull is real to all aspects of that phenomenon. For human beings, especially with the state of earth life in the past five thousand years, there can be no possibility of positive change unless we are first made to see the composite state of things—as means to view what is most similar (as opposed to what is most different). By viewing the composite information of earth culture, human beings can begin to see the dynamics of this experience (living) as well as the relationship of resolidification to even deeper insight. For the net effect of exposure to composite information will move to produce universal respect for the so-called family of men and women, and this phenomenon will also move to activate the basic laws of attraction—that being, the nature of what factors will constitute transformational laws and investigation. Thus, the purpose of alternative functionalism, in its real sense, has to do with its ability to accelerate the inevitable "point of re-evaluation" for establishing a new order. This is true regardless of information region and regardless of vibrational level.

In the beginning of this section I wrote about the misconceptions we seem to have about what is now called fusion music. It is important that some attempt be made to clarify the theatre of composite earth information lines. For the emergence of this time period has moved to produce many misconceptions about the whole of progressional continuance and/or alternative functionalism. Somehow the last one hundred and fifty years have moved to complete the necessary documentation for proclaiming the superiority of western culture at the expense of the composite world group (I write "somehow" because the sophistication surrounding this maneuver cannot simply be traced to either literature—mis-literature—or mis-documentation, for the whole of the "western spell" has profoundly affected the entire planet), causing entire regions of the planet to somehow accept their supposedly "inferiority"—which is of course nonsense. Certainly the

ALT(FT)II–32

spread and eventual dominance of western culture is not separate from the manipulation and/or installation of present-day world economics and military might, but I am not satisfied that even these considerations can be made responsible for the present state of things. For the present-day concept we have of so-called fusion music vibrationally seems to hint at something out of the natural order of things. But the real truth is that cross-sectional information has long been a part of composite earth continuance—not encompassing only music, but encompassing every area of information and functionalism. This is not to take away from the west, or any region for that matter (certainly every region on this planet has moved to produce "great" things, and I am not advocating that accomplishment not be acknowledged), but only to state a fact. The real reality of our situation on earth seems to be that we are existing in a continuum that transcends the rise and fall of nations and time periods, having to do with the particular dynamics of this sector in space—and also having to do with the reality of this sector in space. The actualness of this phenomenon involves all of us, not simply one or two nations (let alone one or two so-called great nations). The particulars of present-day progressionalism, however, have reached the point (and I have no doubt this point has been reached four thousand, two hundred and fifty-seven other times "around" as well) where humanity will have to make important decisions about the future—having to do with what region we, as a composite people living on earth, want to move towards. It breaks down into this: either we move to unite and work together for the "good of our planet," or we can continue to function for the particulars of our own separate situations (and by doing so, ensure that nothing will change—not to mention, ensure the destruction of everything we think we know and/or have). In other words, the nature of the next real change seems to imply revolutionary dynamic transformation—involving not only the realness of western culture, but the total planet. The seriousness of this change will affect everything about this state of existence—which is to say, no one can afford to not be concerned about the coming cycle of earth continuance.

The progressional continuance of the coming eighties and nineties will be extremely important for what it will imply about alternative functionalism. For the next twenty years will undoubtedly be the cycle where the composite solidification of transformational information lines are developed—and applied. In other words, the composite thrust of the coming time period will probably be the time period where the empirical "stuff" of a given information line will be joined by its vibrational and spiritual "housing." The realness of this solidification will dictate the reality position of alternative functionalism and dynamic information continuance. As such, the progressional continuum of expanded functionalism in this time zone (late seventies) must be viewed as necessary, relevant, and important, for the seeds underlying new investigation will greatly affect the totalness of how we proceed into the next cycle. This is not to ignore the composite offering of world information in its early cycle—nor have I meant to under-value the significance of progressional continuance—obviously information from every period of earth history is important and should be learned (not to mention that the solidification of this time period is not separate from the information that made it possible)—because every progressional continuum has helped to bring us (western culture) to this point in time; rather, the coming of the next time cycle will involve the necessary "sorting" of those factors which are most "operative" for progressional continuance. It is because of this "sorting" that there is now the real need to qualify the reality operatives of this time period—especially with regard to particulars. Because, unless some effort is made to properly document and examine present-day information and progressionalism, the mis-conceptions will continue to be passed from cycle to cycle (and possibly from transformation to transformation). Thus my attempts to comment on the reality position and progressional continuance of western art music, world music, and creative music from the black aesthetic has to do with my belief that there is now the need for final clarification of these information continuums—and this is especially true for interpretation from outside the western information block. There is a need to interpret contemporary progressionalism and reality dynamics because our present documentations for the most part are either untrue or "almost too true" (that being "true with great holes left uncompleted").

If we are to be effective in shaping the next cycle of earth continuance—having in this case to do with forming the vibrational nature of the next transformation—then it will be necessary to challenge many of the things we now take for granted. It is not a question of simply attacking the so-called establishment, for in itself this kind of activity means nothing—not to mention that the flaws underlying the composite state of world information transcends the manipulation done in any one time cycle—rather, the re-investigation of alternative functionalism and progressional continuance is important because this subject is related to every aspect of our existence on this planet: having to do with how our attitudes have formed and towards what area focuses we postulate as desirable. It is not possible to simply block off this most important subject to any one time cycle, because we run the risk of not observing the composite reality of this phenomenon—and also how the present state of things has been constructed. For this reason, I have attempted to examine the particulars underlying our present notions of creativity as a means to hopefully supply alternative viewpoints that include in their natural interpretation a composite respect for all humanity. It is important that some effort is made to reconstruct a more human viewpoint about earth realness and progressional continuance. This is not to say my viewpoint per se is the final answer, or necessarily correct (or all correct)—because it isn't (not to mention, there is much more to write about on all of these subjects)—but hopefully the net effect of my effort will encourage other efforts (just as my reasons for even attempting this book can be traced to people like Rex Stewart and Leo Smith). Nevertheless, the realness of gradualism cannot be under-estimated, for the significance of unchallenged information can move to shape a whole society—and if not challenged (when that culture moves into its inevitable transformation), can also become a cornerstone underlying further reconstruction. It is for this reason that alternative interpretations are so important—and this is especially true for the coming changes reshaping American and western culture. Either we move to change the existing reality and information continuum of American culture, or run the risk of having our children live in alien definitions concerning both who they are and where and who they could be. The challenge of alternative functionalism is this and nothing less.

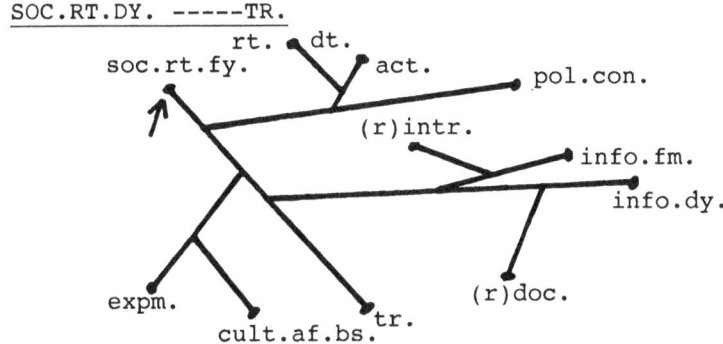

The dynamic implications of alternative functionalism can be viewed in several different contexts. For the realness of this subject transcends any one viewpoint and instead moves to supply insight about the whole of contemporary progressionalism. It is important that some attempt is made to view the composite changes reshaping earth creativity with this consideration in mind. Because initiations do not simply come from nowhere, nor does a postulation necessarily end with the natural cessation of its body continuance; rather, the route of a given continuance can take on many different forms—and in so doing, not necessarily adhere to our strict definitions concerning projectional continuity. As such, a given thrust alignment might carry the seeds of a particular message that later is continued through a completely different alignment. This is not to be confused with source-transfer progressionalism—where the functional dynamics of a given projection are co-opted by other alignments as it corresponds to the dictates of its time zone; rather, the realness of information transference has to do with how the germ essence of a given continuum progresses irrespective of its thrust on projectional "housing." In some cases, the actualness of this phenomenon transcends the dynamics of a given time period—that is, the germ information of a particular continuum is actualized and ends, and after, say, two hundred years reappears in a totally different thrust alignment reality. My point is that this phenomenon is "about something"—having to do with the dynamic continuum of "cosmic matters." It is important that some attempt is made to view the realness of alternative functionalism as this phenomenon relates to creative continuity—for the challenge of the next cycle depends on our ability to solidify a composite affinity stance for world continuance. This can be possible only if we can view the particulars of projectional expansion and dynamic change—which, in this context, have to do with the reality particulars of western art methodological continuity, world functionalism and expansion, and the role of black creativity in America as a dynamic stimulating agent for activation. My point is this: The phenomenon of alternative functionalism is directly relevant to the challenge of world change and progressional continuance.

To understand this phenomenon is to have some basis for really viewing "normal development" and/or what we call change.

My point is also this: the composite theoretical elements concerning projectional continuity in this time period also shed light on the vibrational nature of what the next cycle is. In other words, the seeds underlying the next transformation have already made themselves known—and the real question is "what do we want to do?" It is now possible to view world creativity continuity—regardless of time period—and experience the realness of what this phenomenon means. Because the dynamic continuum and meta-reality significance of world creativity is not lost. Every projectional strain moves to only further accent the realness of what can only be called the principle "germ" seed underlying composite progressionalism. In every case, that "seeding" has to do with the restoration of spiritual discipline and high ethics. That is, every thrust of projectional information (regardless of creative region or time zone) moves to outline some aspect of how that balance can be brought about. This is true for world creativity in every cycle—time and focus. The particulars of western continuance must be viewed with respect to the special problems we have been dealing with in the last two thousand years, yet even this continuum is not without its dynamic purpose. The challenge for alternative functionalism is to help sort out the real "germ" center underlying western continuance, as a means to help its people (and all people) live. For the acceleration of western so-called dynamics has moved to observe what is most basic in all of us—including its own information continuum. And as such, the matter of "sorting things out" is a serious matter indeed. The dynamic reality continuum of black creativity in the west has and will continue to be of importance in this regard, for the realness of black creativity seems to supply an important stimulating factor for the whole of western culture. The realness of this phenomenon will be important for helping to solidify a composite world position for western creativity by moving to "clarify" the germ essence underlying what this continuance (western creativity) really means. For this reason, it is important to re-investigate the whole of world progressionalism—especially the particulars of creative extension and dynamic change—because the route of a given information line can directly shed light on the reality of its solidification (and postulation)—and this is what concerns us. In other words, our present situation on earth is "not about an accident."

(Level Three)

1. Can the development of composition in black creativity be viewed as separate from western art music?

Yes. The progressional continuance of black creativity—involving the totalness of its dynamics—must be viewed separately from western art music, if it is to be understood. This is not to say there are no similarities of specifics, because of course there are. Rather, the reality of functionalism in black creativity is an affirmation of its vibrational reality position (having to do with what a given function raises about information dynamics as made real through black culture—to world culture), while the progressional continuum of western art music is an affirmation of the composite reality base of the western vibrational sensibility (as its principal interpretation sensitivity—to world culture), and they are not the same. By placing such emphasis on the meta-reality implications of functionalism I have not meant to imply that any given function is necessarily better than another function. Instead, the basis of my opinion is that the vibrational position of a given function is really fifty percent of its composite reality—which is to say, there is no way to isolate a function from its "all purpose." In actual terms, the reality continuum of black composition has long expanded from its own pedagogical basis. For the reality continuum of black creativity has proceeded with respect to both a strict notational formula and extended functionalism. The thrust of this continuum has helped clarify the dynamics of extended specifics as well. The realness of this phenomenon must be viewed in its separateness.

2. Does the use of composition take away from what is really implied in improvisation?

No. We are still passing through the final period of what has been termed the "free jazz" movement (among other things), and undoubtedly the present-day mistrust of notation is related to what this continuum has posed. But composition—as is improvisation—is only a discipline that can be either utilized if desired or ignored. The dynamic implications of composition as offered through the composite continuum of black and world creativity seems to me to attest to the brilliance of both new techniques and creative use of materials. The reality of this discipline is really nothing more than the realness of an overview—with respect to what and how given participation should take place. Which is to say, there are as many different kinds of composition as there are types of improvisation. If a given individual makes the decision to not utilize these various approaches, that is his or her right, but that decision should not be confused with the inherent dynamics of either composition or improvisation. No, I do not believe that the use of composition takes away from what is implied in improvisation, nor do I feel that the use of improvisation takes away from what is being implied in composition. Take what away?

3. Is improvisation also composition?

To really examine the creative particulars of a master improvisor is to view activity that exhibits many different levels of dynamic organization. To me, this is what composition is all about. But the implication of this question is somewhat complex—because anything that starts and ends can be viewed as adhering to some aspect of composition. I do believe that improvisation is composition but to simply state this without several levels of qualification would be an over-generalization. There are two aspects to this question: (1) compositional improvisation as based on each person's subjective relationship with perception (that being, "whatever you do I will hear it compositionally—whether or not you actually were thinking or dealing with composition," and (2) compositional improvisation as a discipline (which is to say, something that is approached compositionally whether or not it is heard that way). From this viewpoint, it is impossible to make an absolute judgment as to the exact reality of a given participation. However, it does seem to me that transformational pedagogy will imply that when a given discipline is utilized, it will also be perceived as utilized. In other words, "everyone will know what is happening" because the creativity will not be simply an existential affirmation of self, but a dynamic participation of cultural and spiritual affirmation.

4. What has been the most dynamic use of notation—in terms of the creative spectrum of possibilities inherent or discovered—in any given medium?

I must confess that in draft 509, I wrote that creative music from the black aesthetic has shown the most dynamic use of notation—as compared with any form. However, by draft 2,087 it became clear to me that this idea was nonsense. There is no such thing as what is most dynamic—at least not in this context anyway. The use of dynamic notation—or functionalism—can be viewed in every context and focus. There has been a dynamic use of notation in India, Africa, Asia, western art music (yes—western art music), the Middle East, and Australia. Certainly the composite continuum of black creativity does show a unique use of notation—in a variety of situations—but these dynamics can also be viewed (in different forms) in every other continuum as well. Rather than looking for the best (which is a concept that really means nothing), it might be more productive if we were able to simply experience— and learn to appreciate—the spectrum of earth creativity.

5. Can a black composer participate in a total notated music without being under the reality of western information dynamics? In short, can there be a notated music continuum of black music separate from western art music?

I imagine everything is possible—which is to say, theoretically a black composer could only study the works of black composers and view that information from his or her own vibrational persuasion (not to mention that it is even easier to study the composite spectrum of notated music from an individual's information and affinity position—this to me is more likely). But whether or not this is probable is another question. There are two aspects of this question that come to mind: (1) to really view the continuum of notated music—with the intent of becoming a composer as this term is now viewed—is to already have a connection with western art music (whether or not one wants to accept that connection); moreover, to only study the great works of black composers is to still have a connection to western art music, because all of these composers have—in their own studies (regardless of level)—also studied western art music, and (2) the second aspect of this response is why any individual should attempt to deny him or herself the wonder and beauty that has been offered through western art music (or any form for that matter)—especially if that person is interested in a totally notated music. To negate western art music while being interested in notation is like making the decision to invent the telephone . . . in 1980.

6. What is the function of composition in improvised music from the black aesthetic?

The function of composition in black creativity has had to do with structuralism as a means to provide the specifics for improvisational investigation—with respect to the consideration of form as well as the rhythmic nature of its base—and finally with respect to the harmonic dictates of its region as well. The functional reality of composition in black music has also involved the use of given idea configurations or alignments—that being, the dynamic use of both thematic and non-thematic materials, as well as the vibrational and actual use of particular stimulation tools (e.g., the idea of the riff, or the ritualistic structural continuum). Composition in this context has to do with the use of given coordinates as a basis for determining the skeleton of an improvisation—as well as the region of involvement (or character of involvement). The realness of this use of process is directly related to the pedagogy of world culture—with the difference being that black creativity, as "ised" in America, is a music that is vibrationally moving to both recover and reintegrate itself back into the fold of world culture; while world creativity utilizes functionalism in the same manner as noted before, but with the added ingredient of "actual culture"—which is to say, the participation of a given area of creativity is in accordance with, and about, the composite spirituality of the culture, and must be viewed as ritual.

7. *The interpretation dynamics of so-called jazz compositions have always required the interpreter to have an understanding outside of the literal translation of the notation. Has this approach also carried over to the more contemporary forms of the music?*

Yes. In fact, if anything, the challenge of interpreting the music has increased because of the expansion of contemporary approaches. The creative musician in this time zone can now participate in such a spectrum of styles, from the early forms until now, and I view this as positive. Nor should the diversity of the music be viewed as necessarily detrimental to the affinity dynamic nature of its reality. Because the spectrum of approaches now available for the creative musician only increases the dynamic possibilities of the individual (not to mention that no particular structure or path is mandatory for any musician anyway). The significance of diversity, in this context, has to do with the dynamics of what challenges (or aspects of self) the contemporary musician can now choose from. The breakdown of composite methodology that has occurred in this time cycle (the last one hundred years) has also moved to accelerate the emergence of affinity dynamics (and its related continuum of individual new approaches). Until transformational culture can set in, I view the multi-diversification of functionalism to be "the best possible non-culture situation to be in."

8. *To what degree does the composer need to deal with the individual characteristics of the improvisors who will interpret his or her music?*
There is no single point of order for the composer to function from—especially in this time period. It seems to me that the challenge of the composer in this time zone is wide enough to allow for many different interpretations and/or approaches. The basic question that must be asked is to what degree can the composer not deal with the specifics of his/her universe—and probably even in this question the answer is the same—that being, "to whatever degree that person wants to." For myself, I believe there are several different aspects of this question that can be answered—or approached. The fact is, by examining and coming to know the musicians in an ensemble, it is possible to better understand what

vibrational possibilities can be actualized in the music (which is to say, some people are better suited to particular things than other people)—yet this criterion of working with an ensemble is only one approach that might not necessarily be any better or worse than another (for instance, what happens if a given person quits the ensemble—what does that mean for a tailored part?). I believe the composer in this time period is in the same dynamic position as the musicians—there is no one criterion or focus that dominates the reality position—or possibilities—of any creative objective—or focus.

9. Duke Ellington molded his music around the individual characteristics of the musicians he worked with in his orchestra. Do you see this relationship as indicative of transformational participation?

Yes. I view Duke Ellington's reality relationship with his music and musicians as being directly related to the dictates of transformation participation and motivation. The dynamics of this relationship promote the least amount of separation between the music and its greater family (i.e., the orchestra). The realness of this approach is related to extended functionalism in the sense that the dictates of transformation will undoubtedly utilize an approach of this nature—and go even further in its implementation. I see the restoration of a real community cultural unit—all of which has to do with the composite restoration of dynamic culture, and cultural participation and responsibility. I view this development as the highest function of civilization—that being, living—as an individual as well as collective—that utilizes "doing" as a composite function for the total reality, and in "being that way" also becomes spiritual. Ellington's approach to his music seems to really understand—and respect—the realness of the orchestra. For to view the actualness of the orchestra is to view a collective family—and this should not be taken lightly.

10. What influence has style and form had on the meta-reality of creative music?

The dynamics of extended functionalism have provided the impetus for the gradual awakening of world consciousness—this is true for creative music and composite western information in general. For as the progressional development of isolated projections (styles) extends, the nature of that extension invariably sheds light on world creativity—because everything has already been done (and the research that invariably leads to expansion also leads to world music discovery). Moreover, the reality of a given functionalism is not limited only to "how it works" but extends to the vibrational path and implications of its thrust alignment—and these matters become cosmic (and as such, inter-connected to the destiny of what that functionalism really means). Nevertheless, this too must be viewed as one avenue of dynamic influence. For the most part, both the consideration of style and form gives insight as to the "route" of a given continuance—having to do with where a given continuance comes from (involving the reality of its components and vibrational assignment) and also having to do with where that consideration is going. This is so because one half of the reality of a given projection is its style and form, and the "stuff" of a given functionalism (which is the other half) is an affirmation of its meta-reality dictates. In other words, the meta-reality dictates of a given functionalism come before the influence of its particulars (style and form)—and this is what really does the influencing.

11. Has the reality position of the black composer improved?

Not really. There are no black composers whose works are regularly performed—and this is true regardless of context (i.e., traditional or avant-garde). Nor have I seen anything that could be interpreted as a change in the basic attitude of the western art music community. The black composer continues to exist as a background figure—in the shadows of the basic focus of the culture. I do not personally think the black composer will ever be accepted as part of the composite reality of western art music—and I do not see this rejection in negative terms completely. For the black composer—like it or not—is irreversibly connected to transformation and alternative functionalism. In other words, the black composer who is not afraid must necessarily create a separate political base—either this will be achieved or nothing can be accomplished. Because one cannot grow if there are no opportunities to hear what has been written. Outlets for the black composer must be created—and in the near future; not only this, but an audience must be found as well. The eighties and nineties will be an important cycle for the black composer.

12. Do you believe that a scientist's responsibility involves only the nature of his/her research, or do you see a greater criterion?

It seems to me that the reality of real science is not separate from the dictates of its composite culture—which is to say, a given area of investigation cannot be viewed as an isolated phenomenon from the greater culture. But this is only true if the vibrational or meta-state of that culture ts real—or thorough. In other words, the present state of western culture cannot justify any move to interfere with contemporary science because there is no such thing as composite ethics or spiritual morality in this time period. As such, contemporary investigation is justified in pursuing what seem to be the most "interesting" areas of research—even though, in the final analysis, all of us will have to deal with the consequences of that pursuit, both positively and negatively. The concept of transformation, however, implies another role for scientific investigation, for the composite thrust of any area of participation (in this context) must vibrate to a greater responsibility ratio than either the individual or particular community. I believe the highest responsibility of a given discipline has to do with what its involvement poses for its greater spiritual dictates—and dynamics. In other words, the reality of investigation is very serious and must always be undertaken with the greatest spiritual care—and concern. With the present state of things being as it is, the reality of western investigation will undoubtedly continue to extensively investigate the composite nature of things—and I view this with great alarm.

13. Exactly what do you mean when you write that there is a music for every information strain?

The thrust of my viewpoint in this context has to do with the dynamic inter-relationship of all composite discipline. In other words, the realness of a given fundamental is equally manifested in every area of information dynamics—and this is my point. The particulars of a given information strain can be broken down (but not separated as such) into its physical universe reality—or law functionalism, as well as its vibrational universe implications—and my point is that the coordinates underlying how given information "is" are the same coordinates (with the same meta-reality implications) that are related to the solidification of its "music type." There is a music for every information strain because there is a functionalism for every information strain—because the concept of information has to do with multi-commentary, as to the state of a given phenomenon. The question we must ask ourselves is: what areas of information (and doing) seem to be moving towards the greatest path for world unification (if this is really the state we care about)? For if every focus does have a creative affirmation, the real question is "are there paths that are more conducive to world unification than others, and if so—what does this really mean?" As such, "do we have a choice?"—or, is it "not about choice"?

14. If every information focus is an affirmation of cosmic destiny, does this imply there can be no composite basis for understanding—or establishing a base viewpoint?

I believe every viewpoint does reflect some aspect of cosmic destiny, but I also believe that the thrust (or route) of a given inquiry means something as well. If this is true, then the dictates of each given route implies some degree of limitation as a means to clarify the particulars of its path—in other words, all routes are routes, but the particulars of a given journey do focus on "what appears to be different." The realness of what this means is undoubtedly related to the concept of affinity dynamics. For the realness of this phenomenon has to do with the vibrational zones people are born into—as a means to understanding the reality of their "encounters" with either given areas of information or particulars. It is somewhere in this area that we can begin to understand the basis from which "it seems to be decided," or that "certain things should or should not be done," or "it is best to do it this way." In other words, the reality position of a given encounter seems to also be related to what degree that phenomenon has in its cosmic designation. This is true regardless of whether a given society has attained "culture"—even regarding the isolated actions of individuals and/or small groups. Even an existential context must invariably function with respect to the basic laws surrounding what "doing" is. This is true even though the weight of a given participation in existential terms can never be understood—as a discipline. Because existentialism is a state that rejects the meta-implications of any action outside of its first degree attainment (i.e., "the fact that something happens" to the existentialist is only what is focused on—in other words, "the happening" is enough).

15. Western science seems to believe that the truth of a given phenomenon is not separate from whether or not its functionalism works—in other words, if something works, then it is true. What is your opinion?

I believe that the success of a given functionalism—as perceived before its meta-basis (which probably can never be known because we are always growing, and as such "it" is always growing)—can never be true, but can be viewed as hopefully information that is leading us where we want to go. My theory of information seems to imply that a given state can be true on as many levels as one desires—which is to say, there is no real state of true information, or true functionalism. The realness of what this means will be important as we move towards the next cycle of space exploration—especially. For the laws we have come to view as indicative of this experience (on earth) might only have minor—if any—roles in the next application realm, as we move into the "systems dynamics" of galactic information. It seems to me that the truth of a given information strain transcends the reality of its functionalism and moves towards its cosmic role. As such, the only way to really understand information on this level is to move towards what we in this time period call "the mystical."

16. What does the concept of the "law" really signify or mean?

There are two degrees of the concept of the law that I believe: (1) the concept of law as it involves the particulars of a given functionalism that expresses some aspect of how the universe seems to be with respect to the appearance of what we call "motion" or change; (2) the concept of law that expresses some aspect of the will of dynamic cosmic intentions or state of being. The realness of a given law is more than simply how something works, but instead involves the basic tenets of what this experience (living) is about. In other words, the concept of laws seems to have something to do with manifesting how and "how" this experience works. The reality of this phenomenon seems to be about how the celebration of this sector (the universe) is manifested—having to do with the dynamic inter-connection of information routes and composite "all motion." The concept of the law can as such be viewed as the basis from which all functionalism actualizes, and this is also true of the concept of religion and spirituality (i.e., in terms of doctrine). For the realness of a given law comments on when something works as well as how—but not why, because "why" in this context moves to express the real intention of cosmic dictates (i.e., purpose).

17. How related is the actualness of a given discovery to some aspect of the person who is doing the discovery?

I believe there is a direct relationship between the areas of information transference a person vibrates to and what interpretations are solidified as a result of that vibration. Moreover, the concept of affinity dynamics is directly related to what this phenomenon means as well. For the nature of a given person's relationship with principle information, as well as what part of him- or herself has been developed, determines what insight (or affinity) that person will be able to extract from a given observation. This is true in every interpretation, regardless of focus. It is for this reason that the reality of information transference in western culture must open up to include the composite spectrum of information dynamics. For the realness of a given phenomenon is not about only one or two interpretations, but involves as many interpretations as there are affinity positions. The challenge of the next cycle will involve trying to better understand affinity dynamics—as applied to the spectrum of human being, and as applied to what this phenomenon reveals about information. The realness of this question is also related to individual dynamics and affinity formation. Everyone is born with different life-force regions that can be magnified (and stimulated, as a means to pursue) and suppressed (as a means to not pursue). The realness of dynamic information can better help us understand how to be—or how to make ourselves. The optimum situation would probably be to have some insight into the meaning of a given "attraction"—in terms of its spiritual significance and its actual particulars, and after receiving this understanding, act accordingly.

18. Is there a coding denominator for extended vibrational investigation in the same sense as in practical applied science?

I believe there are several extended vibrational coding denominators for vibrational investigation that have been brought over from world culture, but for the most part these informational positions aren't viewed as such—nor are they really made available except to "certain people." Certainly the thrust of contemporary religion is based on the dictates of vibrational laws, and this is true of every culture (and mystical discipline), and while most of us have come to view religion only with respect to what our religion tells us about ethics or spiritual value, in fact the tenet formation underlying what religion really is—a coding denominator for extended vibrational investigation, or doing. The last two hundred years have seen so many changes come into our lives that the need for composite spiritual re-evaluation (of all earth religions) will be necessary if we are to have a better basis for viewing the next cycle. For the present state of vibrational investigation in the west seems to not adhere to any precepts concerning "what should or shouldn't be examined." The realness of this position is extremely serious, because if there are regions of participation and observation that should not be explored, then what is the consequence for "not knowing this"? It seems to me that everything can be explored, providing one is prepared to deal with the "reality of exploration." I believe the challenge of contemporary science should not be explored without spiritual guidance and awareness. I also believe that the basic tenets supporting world culture and world mysticism are as important today as they were thousands of years before—and that contemporary scientists should be made more aware of the spiritual nature of their work.

19. Is there always a science that is able to get to the desired zone in every context? In other words, does every situation vibrate to the same reality implications—or vibrational implications (in terms of spectrum of options—leading to principle zones—as opposed to particulars)?

I believe there is always a functionalism that is related to achieving the desired objective in every situation. In other words, in every situation we can be saved or we can win (whichever feels better). But I also believe that the reality of a given functionalism can have different dictates—or reality particulars. Because nothing is divorced from the all-cosmic realness of what is. The hope and challenge of living seems to be directed not only towards understanding what aspect of functionalism is most meaningful to completing whatever objective, but, rather, the realness of living also involves whether or not certain lessons can be understood as a means to deal with "something greater." Thus, the reality of functionalism has to do with the route each person takes in his/her own life—having to do with what lessons we have to learn (or want to learn) as a means to become closer with "it." The dictates of a given functionalism in this context pales with the greater realness of "learning about living and how to live." In this final analysis, the significance of a given functionalism has to do with each individual's own separate encounter with that functionalism. In other words, there is no best route as such—rather, we all try to do the best we can with what we are able to understand. I feel this same concept is also expressed in science dynamics as well.

20. Why do you feel a composite input from all countries could benefit western science? Are you implying that all countries are on the same scientific level?

I believe that the realness of earth information could benefit from the composite participation and cross-participation of world culture because (1) I feel that the realness of composite participation would be more conducive to real understanding than interpretations that involve only particular areas of information transference, and (2) I also feel that the realness of this composite participation would provide a more healthy forum for building and re-examining dynamic information. As far as whether or not I am implying that all countries have the same scientific level of ability—I would say there is no country that cannot add something of value to transformational information. This is not to say every little culture must necessarily have physics labs as advanced as those of America or France—because of course this is not the case. But it seems to me that the challenge of dynamic information is not only about the particulars of physics—as we now view this subject—but includes many other areas that are just as important. To move to solidify a world information input could hopefully reshape our total understanding of information—and form areas we have not even begun to think about. I believe the thrust of transformational information will involve both inner perception (about ourselves as people and about the state of our consciousness and spirituality) and outer perception. I believe this because the truth of a given phenomenon is not only about how that phenomenon works, but how it "is"—or "feels" as well. The move to solidify a world information position might be the most important step that humanity can now take.

21. Do you feel that galactic functionalism will invalidate the present reality of western functionalism?

I believe that the progressional expansion of earth information will be clarified by what we learn about galactic functionalism in the next cycle. I write "clarified" because to say that the present reality of western functionalism will be invalidated seems too strong. This is not to say western information has no problems, because obviously there are many areas of information that are not understood on the level they should be, and obviously we are also dealing with many assumptions that do not pose what is in the best interest of earth continuance. But to blanketly put down western functionalism is to move into the other "extreme"—that being, "everything done in the west is bad"—and this cannot be true either. It is my hope that the next investigation cycle in earth science will move to have a deeper respect for spiritual interpretation and multi-logic. We are only at the beginning of real understanding, and the realness of the next five thousand years promises to be very exciting. I do not believe our present earth information tenets will ever be completely invalidated for what aspects they "express" (because the reality of a given functionalism need not transcend its vibrational and physical universe context). Which is to say, "if it works on earth then it can always be used in some form or another"—or, "there is nothing wrong with a body."

22. Why haven't black composers made some attempt to establish independent performing and recording possibilities?

I believe very little alternative functionalism has taken place from the black composers' sector because few of these people are able to view their own activity as significant unless it is recognized and endorsed by the white community—and this is a shame. Obviously this must be the case, for why haven't black composers produced their own records by now—creative improvising musicians have made this move long ago. It seems to me that most black composers in this time period simply feel inferior to their white counterparts, and as such are content to remain as background figures. For the most part, the only records one can find on the music of black composers are in special series devoted to "the black composer"—which are something like "handout" giveaways—as opposed to a composer having a record out of his or her music. It would be nice to simply blame white people for the ineffectiveness of this dilemma, but in actual fact, many black composers teach at the same universities as their white comrades—and make good money doing so. Why haven't any of these people produced their own records and concerts? How can a person hope that someone else will produce his (or her) creativity if he won't help himself? The dilemma of the black composer is indeed complex.

PROGRESSIONAL SIGNIFICANCE AND RE-DEFINITIONS

(Level One) EVOLUTION

IN ORDER TO UNDERSTAND THE MULTI-IMPLICATIONS of earth creativity, we must first understand the progressional path of information routes and the "affinity nature" of contemporary information lines. In other words, one's most basic "reality alignment" is the direct result of what he or she has learned through their own individual vibrational tendencies as well as collective cultural conditioning (attempts to shape through "education" and/or exposure). As such, "the transformational potential of earth creativity" implies a re-examination of our total understanding of progressionalism (that being, the expansion reality principle related to how we have come to view phenomena). It is not simply a question of examining the particulars of any one informative scan (or set of ideas); rather, the challenge of transformational creativity necessitates that the very foundation of what we have learned about this subject be re-examined. To understand this challenge is to understand the reality of definitions and/or redocumentation—as well as the realness of affinity-alignment interpretations and/or mis-interpretations (not to mention prejudice, racism, sexism, and honestly right or wrong interpretations). This is not to write that only a given historical viewpoint is necessarily non-productive—or "consciously wrong"—nor have I meant to imply that any one interpretation is necessarily more relevant then another. Rather, the challenge of the next cycle will call for another level of awareness about creative functionalism if it is to be successful. To view the reality dynamics underlying how creativity is seen in western culture is to become aware of the many extra-curricular factors that have affected our understanding of this subject. So profound is the dynamic manipulation of creativity in this time cycle that very few of us can really see him- or herself as not being affected—in one way or another. Yet the manipulation of contemporary information lines in the west is much more sophisticated than any one example. I am writing of a collective movement whose work has affected how we have come to view every aspect of earth life—whether we are focusing on the dynamics of history, mathematics, creativity, or science. Thus if we are to view the realness of creativity, we cannot divorce ourselves from what this manipulation has raised—for the last one hundred years, even, can be viewed for both given creative initiations (of transformational value) and their accomplished documentational forces (and redocumentational forces). The reality of "progressional significance," then, must be reviewed if we are to really understand what factors have helped to solidify this time period. It is important that we are able to view "world expansion principles" without alien definitions that distort the "reality position" of possible transformational information. Without this knowledge, we will be reduced to having to relearn both who we are and what we were—and I do not mean this in narrow terms. For the collective contributions of humanity are not relegated to only certain sectors, or certain people, of the planet, but instead involve everyone. The dynamic mis-interpretation lines western culture has solidified in this time zone are so overwhelming that we are now forced to completely refocus on what creativity "is" (let alone "the significance of particular creative routes"?—or creative methodologies?). Yet the work of resolidification cannot be actualized tomorrow. This challenge will probably take many years—even if everyone were "interested" and/or functioning—which does not seem to be the case.

By "progressional significance" in this section, I am referring to the collected dynamics that have been offered to us from world creativity—having not only to do with how given forms are viewed, but encompassing the methodological and vibrational significance from which all music derives its significance. Moreover, the realness of this "significance" has to do with the cross-spectrum diversity of composite information lines—for creative music is practiced in every sector of this planet (no matter whether or not it is referred to in these terms). The fact that so few of us are aware of the composite nature underlying "progressional significance" cannot be lightly dismissed, for the future continuum of creativity—and creative application—is not separate from what composite progressional significance implies. If we are to correct this condition, then we must first understand what has happened to "source-initiation interpretation," and why. **At the heart of this essay is my belief that the collective forces of western culture have moved to create a particular "reality structure" around creativity that is not conducive to composite world information.** Moreover, the solidification of that reality structure has created an attitude that is directly beneficial to the accented position of western culture—at the expense of world culture. It is for this reason that the concept of progressional significance must be re-examined. Because no matter how beautiful or important we choose to make western art music and/or western definitions, there is now a need to integrate an alternative composite basis for understanding all creativity. Mis-interpretation from the western sector has created a situation that promises to have profound consequences for the continuance of world culture. So successful have alternative redefinitions been utilized in this time period that one of the major challenges we face in the next cycle is the restoration of a practical viewpoint concerning "life creativity" and "transformational action." Yet I do not mean to over-simplify this most complex problem, for the present "reality alignment" of creativity involves many factors. The spectrum range of this subject transcends any one stratum and naturally affects every region. But the use of misdocumentation and/or redefinitions does pose a serious problem for the future of world culture. So real is the importance of this phenomenon that something must be done—and done quickly by all concerned. Each generation in America (in particular) grows up with less real information (and this is true in practically every subject area). If change is to be brought about, there is no time like the present.

EVOL–4

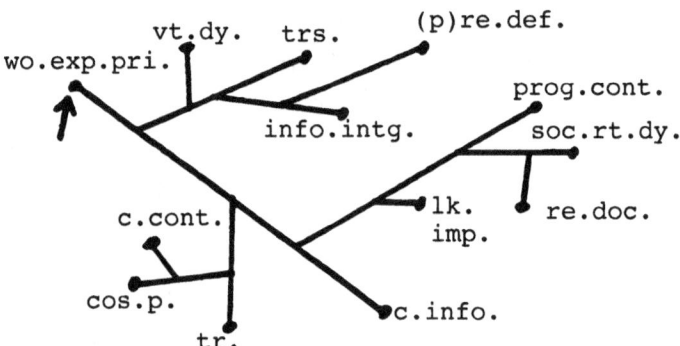

To view the accented position of western definitions in this time cycle is to be confronted with the accented position of western culture in social/political terms. Thus the geo-political manipulation that has secured the economic reality of western culture is directly related to the position western definitions and redefinitions have in this cycle. Nor am I only referring to interpretations that have progressively shaped this period. By even viewing the late seventies, we can cite four million instances of redocumentation—just in creative music. We are forced to deal with the "reality of interpretation"—as it applies to cultural viewpoints, and as it applies to source-transfer transition periods. Because when a musician like Bill Haley is credited with the solidification of "rock and roll," we must understand what the western cultural information lines are really saying. At the bottom of these mis-interpretations is the realness of "bi-culturalism"—that being, the fact that the reality tone level of western culture functions with respect to its "caucasian cultural focus" inside of its "multi-geo-culture." This does seem to be what is happening. For many of the definitions we are dealing with in this cycle make no sense if this were not the case. It is not simply a question of attacking Bill Haley or any given individual, rather it is a question of understanding the actuality of bi-culturalism. The reality of western culture, and its resultant information lines—although existing alongside the composite American culture—is in fact very different from the reality of non-white America. Yet the basic cultural "information feed" is the same. Which is to say, the collective forces of western culture control the reality of America's composite information lines—affecting every community, whether that community is white or not. This is not to say that black or Asian communities have no alternative information lines—obviously there are many such alternative lines (if this were not true, they could not have survived), but the principal information sources—whether we are referring to radio, television, public schools, magazines, newspapers, etc.—are exclusively white. Thus the dynamics of redefinition must be viewed in this context. Because I am talking about interpretations and redefinitions that are perceived to be reality, on one level, but if believed, will move to "lessen" the "affinity and reality" dynamics of any group outside of its "range interpretation." It is for this reason that the "interpretation focus" of a given initiation must be reviewed and challenged when not correct (which is practically ninety-nine percent of the time).

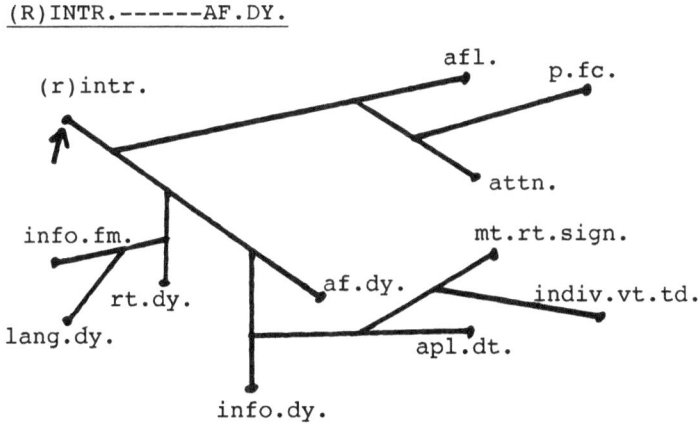

EVOL–6

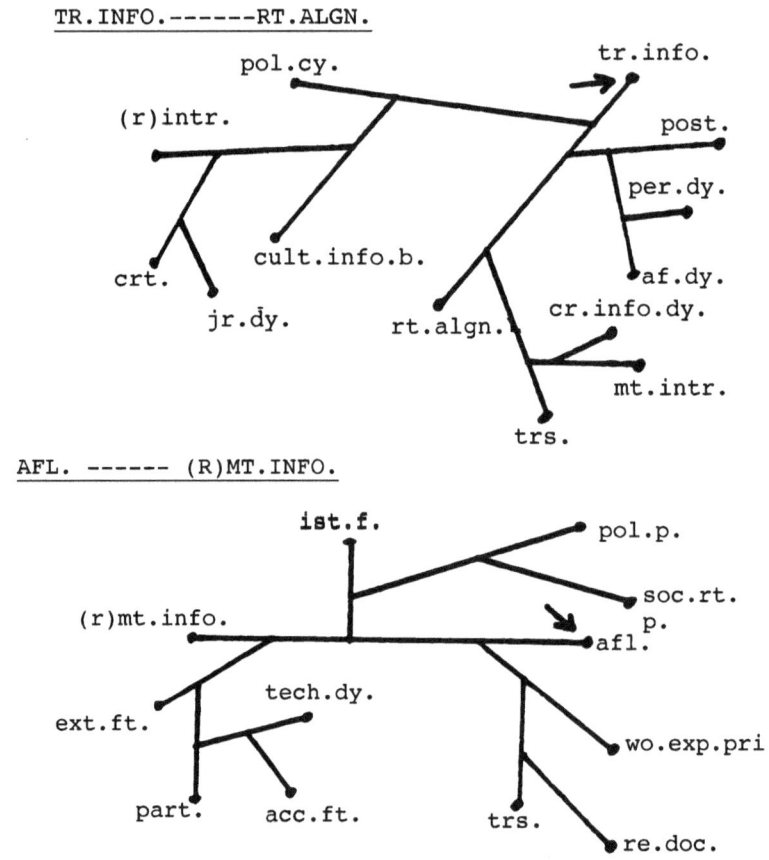

In actual terms, the reality of "progressional significance" and "redefinitions" can be approached by viewing the nature of "preferential activity." By "preferential activity" I am talking of the "isms" that spring into play after the solidification of a contemporary projection line comes into being (which could be the emergence of a "new" music form, or scientific development, etc.). The dynamics of preferentialism in this case must be viewed as significant as the "real projection." **Because in the final analysis, western culture has created a situation where "what a person says" is as significant as "what a person does."** In other words, the development of a given music or musician is no more significant in western terms than the development of the person who interprets what that music or musician does—and this is true even if the musician does not agree with what is written about him. Thus, if we are to view the reality of creative music, then we are forced to deal with the actuality of this phenomenon. For the contemporary thrust of creative journalism has become an entity in its own right. There are no information lines not affected by "contemporary interpretation"—which is to say, there are no areas where non-white people can have access to alternative information sources untampered by "western re-interpretation." Because of this, it is important that moves are made to again refocus on the composite factors surrounding the creative process. This phenomenon will not simply go away on its own.

The solidification of music journalism, and especially criticism, would move to transport the reality of western creativity to a totally separate "affinity nature" from world creativity. Yet this would not necessarily become apparent in its early stages. In the beginning, journalism did serve a positive functional role in that it functioned as an "awareness" tool for the culture. "Awareness" in the sense that as the acceleration of western art music began to take shape—bringing into focus the participation of many new (or unknown) composers—music journalism in this period did attempt to inform the greater public about the nature of this expanded participation. This is not to say that I am endorsing the reality of music journalism in its early period—or any other period for that matter—because I am not; rather, I have mentioned the early period of western journalism only to comment on the nature underlying how this alliance was perceived in its early stages. Moreover, in looking at the emergence of music journalism in its infancy, we can also see that its peripheral solidification was indeed designed to function positively for the music. In this context, a given music would be written on with the expressed purpose of helping the public to understand the "reality" of its projection. If this were the only functional objective of western journalism, I would have no trouble endorsing its existence. But many things have happened since the early alliance between creativity and the press—and if we are to really understand the collective forces of western culture today, then we are forced to probe the underlying implications surrounding what "this relationship means." It must be understood that the reality of "music journalism" today has not only transcended its original "alliance" with creativity—but that the progressional dynamics of its continuum have forced us to re-examine the reality particulars underlining its inception. As such, the reality of music journalism today can be viewed as fulfilling its "progressional dynamics." This is so because the solidification of western journalism—and especially criticism—really tells us something very serious about the "essence identity" of western culture. To deal with the reality of western journalism is to deal with the "vibrational order" and "reality position" of western culture.

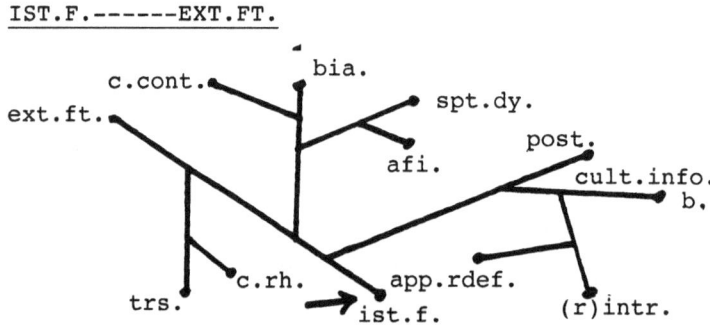

If we are to understand the reality of western journalism today, then it is important that this phenomenon is viewed in a composite context. **It is important to also understand that no other culture has solidified any "isms" comparable to what we now call western journalism.** This is not to say world creativity has never had a "level of criteria"—or "excellence"—because obviously every cultural group has. Rather, the nature underlying how creative excellence was "commented on" in world culture has to do with another vibrational and reality sensibility. Why is it that only western culture has developed this type of existential analysis—or objective criteria analysis—that we now find ourselves with today—what is the basis from which the collective western cultural sensibility derives its "right" to practice this type of analysis focus— what does the use of this type of "analysis" really mean in the context of progressional expansion—and also what does the use of this vibrational attitude signify when utilized on world creativity (or creativity that is

not western)—and what does the reality of criticism tell us about the nature of western information focus? To deal with the reality of western criticism is to deal with these questions and many more. It is not simply a case for intellectual discovery, nor have I introduced an unreasonable criterion as a tool outside of what is appropriate to ask from western criticism. The fact is, the reality of western criticism is directly related to the questions I have raised—and moreover, its inception was actualized because of what these very questions posed—to the progressional continuance of western culture, and to the perpetration of the false notion we now have that western culture is really a "culture." Thus, the reality of western journalism demands that these questions are dealt with.

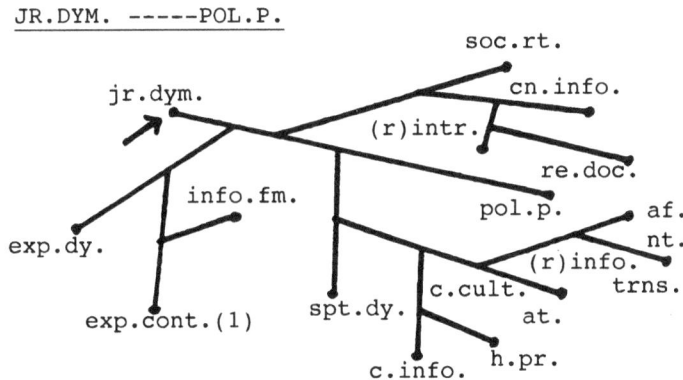

The first question I asked was "why is it that only western culture has developed the type of existential analysis—or objective analysis—that we now find ourselves dealing with today?" To understand this question, it is not necessary to view the composite planet. For the solidification of existentialism comments on the most basic factor that has necessitated contemporary "journalism." Because, rather than utilize objective analysis, world creativity has always derived its significance from its position in the composite hierarchy of its meta-reality structure. In other words, the progressional continuance of world culture has always viewed given information and projection routes with respect to its composite basis. The discipline we now refer to as music was viewed with respect for what role its "high culture" focus would have on the total "degree structure" of its implementation. Thus, there was no music without its methodological particulars and spiritual application. Another way of saying this is that the solidification of music was not outside of the composite spiritual and vibrational "alignment" of the total culture. In that context, music was not isolated and evaluated as existing in a separate context from the actual life of the people, but instead this phenomenon was viewed with respect for its total community function. Nor have I meant to imply that given individuals did not have the responsibility to teach the "particulars" of a given form or creative thrust, because obviously they did. An African master drummer most certainly had the responsibility to instruct and teach the "particulars" concerning how to execute a given rhythm as form, but there was never any question as to the existential worth of a given individual's creativity— "based off of a moment." The realness of "composite spirituality" must be viewed as representing the most basic "affinity alignment" difference that separates the nature underlying "what a comment means" in world culture as opposed to western culture. Moreover, it is important to understand what this difference says about affinity dynamics. For the realness of existential analysis tells us about the real underlying dynamics happening in this time cycle.

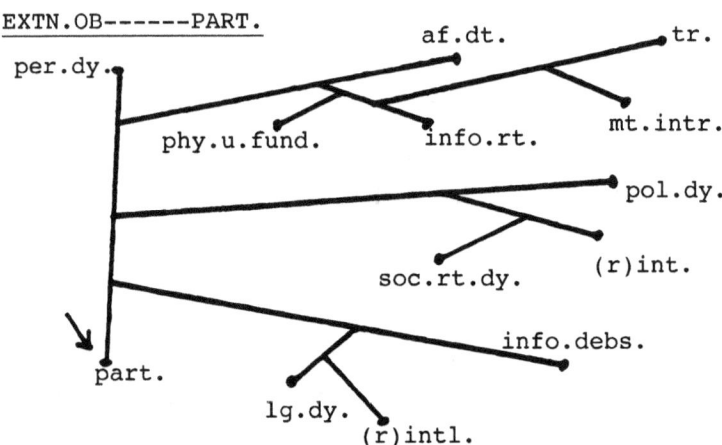

Western culture has substituted "information dynamics" for the role spirituality plays in world culture. Moreover, the emergence of contemporary journalism—and in particular criticism—only underscores the vacuum position dictating the basis from which this type of phenomenon derives its function. For journalism has long outgrown its primary role—that of serving as a positive educational factor (if indeed this were ever the case)—and has instead become more important than that from which it draws its relevance. The fact is: the reality of contemporary western journalism has made the vibrational position of western culture very clear—that being, "nothing has any meaning." For without a spiritual function, there is no real basis to determine the "reality function" of any discipline (let alone creativity). Western journalism has moved to camouflage this most basic crisis. For with the sophistication of technological developments, the press has created an "alternative reality structure" that sustained the "time and image continuum" of given cycles. In this context, creativity is something to be talked about and written on—with the variables being that someone agrees or disagrees (which also continues the basic momentum of this phenomenon as well—for if someone disagrees then he or she will have something to write about). And while all of this is going on, the momentum moves to create the illusion that somehow journalism is involved in "meaningful insight" or "necessary analysis"—but this is not the case. For to understand that without "real meaning" (that being, spiritual meaning) the whole purpose of creativity is distorted—or defeated. Moreover, without a composite spiritual context from which to maintain its affinity alignment, creativity is about "something else"—and this "something else" is important if we are to understand what is happening in this period.

I have stated in the chapter on affinity dynamics that every projection affinity moves according to the nature of its vibrational laws and cosmic destiny. If we are to understand what this means, then it is important that the "reality function" of western culture is taken into account as well. For it is important that the reader understand I have not moved to single out western culture because of any inherent disrespect for all things western—clearly this is not the case. Rather, every projectional route tells us something about the multi-dimensional reality of planet Earth (nor have

EVOL–12

I found it necessary to speak of one culture as being any better or worse than any other culture, because, in the end, none of these comparisons really serve any purpose but to fragment and/or confuse the basic purpose of this book). Obviously various culture groups have different "tendencies," and this must be respected. In other words, I have not focused on world culture at the expense of western culture. Yet the nature of the affinity-dynamic projection of western culture must be viewed in its separateness because in it we are viewing more than just a vibrational variable, but also a continuum not outside the social/political multi-context of present-day events. If we are to draw a basis for understanding what is happening in this time cycle, then it is imperative that the uniqueness of this phenomenon (the position of western culture and western affinity dynamics) is made clear. My point is that the "affinity reality" of western culture seems to be as it is because that is "as it is." If understood then it should not matter that the "high culture implications" of this unique vibrational viewpoint are important—and indeed if western journalism were only applied to western culture, one would be forced to maybe choose other arguments (against western analysis). Yet nothing can obscure the realness that the present affinity alignment which has produced the uniqueness of western journalism is possible only because of the de-spiritualized position underlying how phenomenon in this context is viewed. Why this de-spiritualization has occurred is another question—if indeed the realness of this phenomenon is universally recognized.

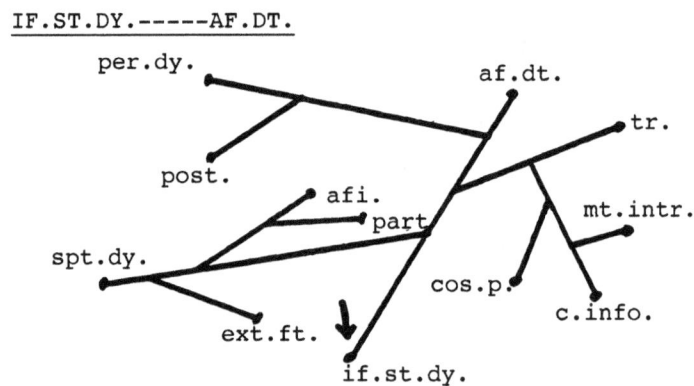

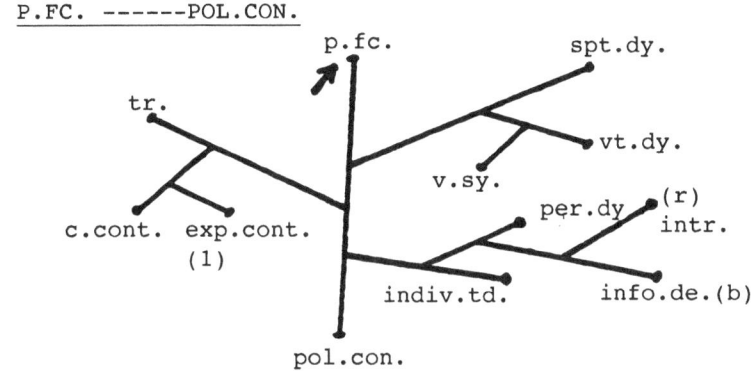

There are several ways to view the reality of spiritualism or de-spiritualism in western culture: (1) the particulars of western progressionalism have made "culture" impossible to solidify simply because not enough time has elapsed; (2) what I perceive as "culture" is not a universally accepted definition of this concept; and (3) the nature of this time cycle has multi-complexual implications—one being the realness that several different projectional and progressional factors have come into play (involving the reality of both source transfer and geo-political manipulation), which have defined what "operatives" are in the air during this cycle. Possibly on several levels all of these definitions are relevant, for it is important to understand that the progressional lineage of particular world cultures can all be viewed as having learned from and influenced one another (if indeed all of us did not start from the same place). With this in mind, we can view the progressional continuance of western culture with respect for what dynamic initiations it has brought forth. Obviously, western culture has contributed much to the continuance of world information—this is true whether we are commenting on the re-adaptation of world information, as well as the solidification of its own "information-reality continuum." To not acknowledge this is to be either deluded by "present life-intensity pressure" or simply ignorant. Yet at the same time, western culture has clearly chosen a separate "identity-information alignment" in its natural progression. For the most basic factor that western culture utilizes has to do with its ability to function from the most extended vibrational position documented in this time zone—or if that is not the case, then western culture has initiated a "revolving multi-spectacle affinity base" (having to do with its ability to use whatever is at hand with a couple of words here and there as a means to continue). If we are to understand western journalism, then it is here that we must first look.

By "extended vibrational position" I am referring to the ability of western culture to pretend both "culture" and spirituality. Nothing is more fascinating than the nature underlying how both these considerations (culture and spiritualism) are practiced and perceived in present-day western culture. Even the concept of culture and/or civilization has been reshaped—with the added feature of culture without meaning, or spiritualism without God. Yet I have not stated these positions as a means to have something to joke about. The "extended vibration position" of western culture reveals a most unique "affinity reality," for the postulations of all contemporary creative disciplines are constructed from this expanded reference. From this affinity position have come many new information lines, and it is to the credit of western ingenuity that the technology of tomorrow promises to be "of relevance." Yet all of these new information lines have come from the realness of "extended speculation" as opposed to spiritual realization. This difference is extremely important. For the nature underlying extended functionalism in western culture has no regard for the concept of "cosmic significance"—let alone "cosmic consequences." Nor am I commenting only on how investigation is perceived (e.g., the nuclear industry or the developments occurring in biology), but, rather, this extended vibrational position seems to be at the very pulse—identity base—of western culture. The end result of this phenomenon has promoted the most exciting "nothingness" of this period—or at least the progressional complexity of this time period has moved to create the most diverse "non-information" of this cycle. My point, however, is that this phenomenon does seem to be of relevance for the people who have instituted this affinity position (which is to say, it would not be fair to simply imply that this affinity and reality platform has no meaning for everyone). As such, the dynamics of this phenomenon must be respected while at the same time it is viewed in its separateness. **Because one thing is certain: no matter** how flexible one tries to be about the uniqueness of the expanded vibrational base of western culture, this alignment is not universally viewed as "real" within the composite information continuum of world culture. We can, as such, view this difference with respect to the uniqueness of the western vibrational and reality pull (and in doing so, recognize both its strengths and weaknesses), and we can also view this difference for what it tells us about the present cycle we are now in (that being, no matter how perverse one chooses to view western culture, the fact is, their techniques have put them—white people—in the best planet position in this time zone, where everyone, whether or not one wants to, has to deal with "western" reality). This phenomenon, then, lies at the heart of what is happening with the affinity-dynamic nature of its particulars. For while contemporary western culture dominates the world theatre, at the same time this position has not moved to clarify and substantiate real spirituality (which is to say, "what good is technical brilliance and political domination if there is no reason for living?").

The solidification of the "revolving multi-spectacle affinity base" vibrational position in western culture must be viewed within the total "reality fabric" of western culture. To understand this phenomenon is to understand the "reality function" of the composite non-white population as a "transfer shift" cultural-feeding stimulant. For the most basic "actual life situation" in America can be viewed with respect to the "projected image" realness of western manipulation, as well as spectacle-diversion reality decisions. It is also possible to view the composite effects of this phenomenon as related to the inability of western culture to secure "culture." For the "information spectrum" that is the outgrowth of this "reality position" is not only not conducive to the forming of essence, but also cannot be scrutinized with respect to a principle-information affinity probe (since no real information tenets have developed in western culture). This is not to say that no affinity alignment has developed in western culture—obviously it has. But if we are to understand the present cycle we are now in, then it is important to view the "reality dynamics" underlying how information is perceived. **For the most basic factor that substantiates the "reality" of a given information line is not the phenomenology of that** line, but rather the "godliness" of what that line really signifies. Thus, without a spiritual base, one only has "ideas" rather than knowledge. The spectacle development of "revolving multi-spectacle activity" is the natural outgrowth of a godless but transitional multi-ethnic civilization that is controlled yet not absorbed into the reality lining of the culture. The dynamics of this phenomenon have directly shaped the momentum and vibrational intensity of western culture—and of course to write that this development has simply not influenced the basic fabric of western culture would be false. My point, however, is that the nature of that effect has not been open to composite interpretation—that is, only white people (of a certain class) are in the position to designate "significance." As such, the multi-diversity found in western culture can be viewed as relevant only for its spectacle implications—rather than for what it poses vibrationally or conceptually for the possibility of transformational "interpretation." In this position, multiple diversification must be linked to how "spectacle diversion" is utilized—that being, the appearance of "style," or the dynamics of "interesting"—while at the bottom of this phenomenon only one basic continuity can be viewed. This is so because the progressional thrust of western culture is not about multi-diversification, but was instead designed for the exclusive well-being of its white citizens. The "culture within a culture" phenomenon is of interest only until the nature of the next reality particulars solidifies. My reason in mentioning this phenomenon is only to lay bases for attempting to examine the greater reality underlying what these ideas pose for "cross-transfer shift" definitions.

If the concept of a revolving multi-spectacle affinity base can be viewed as an integral and/or natural factor that characterizes what is happening in this time period, then quite possibly the realness of this concept can also give us some insight into the question of progressional spirituality in western culture. My point is this: the reality of this time period might have nothing to do with the "possibility" of "culture solidification"—which is to say, the revolving reality structure of western culture can be viewed as a progressional factor that is significant only when seen in its developing "over context." The realness of this phenomenon comments on the longevity of "cultural solidification"—which is to say, the concept of a revolving multi-spectacle affinity base tells us something about the nature of what forces are forming in the next (or coming) cycle. **As such, in actual terms, there are several ways to perceive of the present composite planet situation, those being: the nature of this experience (revolving reality structure) as it comments on the reality nature of a given time period, and the dynamic implications underlying what this experience signals about progressional continuance and/or coming events.** What this means is that if we are to understand this period in time, then the reality implications of progressional continuance must be understood. For the nature of what I have come to call the "revolving multi-spectacle affinity base" not only describes the reality tendencies of this time cycle, but in doing so also tells us something about the particulars and reality state of western culture, because the progressional implications of this phenomenon tell us about what is really happening on a global level. My point is that it is possible to view the progressional development (and expansion) of western culture, and, in doing so, better understand the particular dynamics concerning how that progression has shaped present-day "information dynamics," and it is also possible to view the nature of both transition and transformation as a means to view a larger signal concerning "space and time." The "revolving multi-spectacle affinity base" of present-day western culture is in itself nothing new, for it is possible to view the composite realness of world culture—and cultures—and see this same phenomenon—but directly related to this "chain of events" is the more important factor of progressional continuance. For the reality of a given phenomenon can be viewed with respect to whether it develops in accordance with its implied vibrational dynamics (and when that is done, what we have is a logical extension)—or whether that phenomenon, in its natural state (developing and taking on new properties—or becoming all-encompassing), moves outside its basic vibrational state. The difference between a logical extension and a "trans-affinity shift" is the difference between "developing" and real "transition"—with the understanding being that a "transition" of the ninth power is not only just a transition but a possible signal of composite transformation. That is what I am interested in.

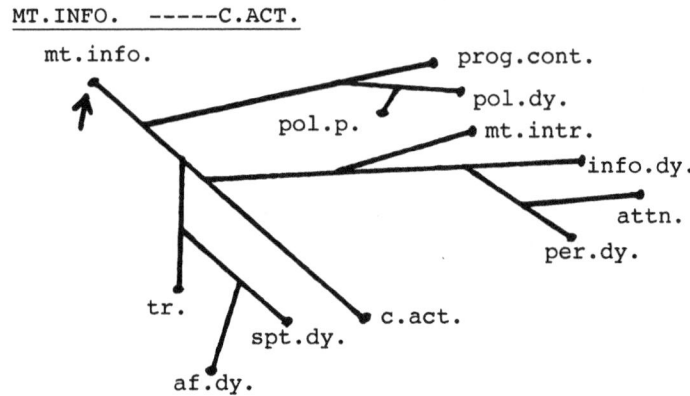

If the progressional continuance of western culture is only "logically extending," then the concept of "revolving multi-spectacle affinity" can be viewed as a factor that comments on the nature underlying how this extension is expanding. In this context, the "multi-composite reality tone" of the culture must be seen as the basis that has dictated the "particulars" surrounding how progressionalism has ensued. As such, the "essence solidification" of actual culture—or cultural lining base—can be understood as "in transition" on the first degree. That being, the changes taking place in this time zone are not necessarily signaling the basic affinity order of the culture. If that is true then the nature of western information particulars must be viewed with respect to "source transfer"—and in many ways this does seem to be the case. For to examine the composite reality alignment of western culture is to see the cross-transfer use of affinity dynamics as a means to perpetuate the western affinity pull exclusively. In this context, the composite spectrum of American (and/or western) culture—that being, all people regardless of race or nationality—functions as a dynamic diversion factor that is redefined to suit the reality position of controlling white America (or western culture). Thus it is no wonder that only certain information lines are recognized as representing the established American (or western) cultural position, for to those powers that be, these are the only people worth representing. The importance of this position should not be minimized, for the reality of information dynamics in this context is not separated from the present social and political condition of this planet.

Which is to say, it is not a question of whether or not the controlling sectors of western culture have the ability to understand "outside information lines"; rather, the present reality of events has been designed with the eventual objective of totally eliminating anything but western culture. In actual terms, this viewpoint can help us understand what is happening on one level with the present programming we are now dealing with. For unless the reality of information dynamics are dealt with, non-white people will slowly lose the ability to effectively function—in any meaningful sense. Because the sophistication of a given effective function is not separate from whether or not its information-affinity nature is respected. As such, the "logical extension" of western culture—if indeed this is the case—must be viewed as the "logical dissolution" of world culture. Moreover, since the basis of this section is "information significance," the logical extension of western perception dynamics must also be viewed as "necessarily affected" if this objective is to be achieved.

The reality of "logical extension" must also be viewed for what it poses to the concept of "cultural order." This is so because the dynamics of information control and manipulation are not separate from whether the actual "life experience" is able to take place. If there was no manipulation of information, then the basic continuum of the culture (western culture) would find itself in a somewhat difficult position. For there is no way that one affinity-dynamics persuasion can control a multi-composite group realistically. Because the natural tendency of people is to learn from one another. Thus, the use of "information manipulation" can be viewed as a natural controlling factor as well as a vehicle for programmed source-transfer possibilities. Without this regulation, western culture as we know it could not exist. Thus, it stands to reason that the logical extension implications of western culture must be perceived with respect for what it poses to the concept of "information manipulation"—yet I do not mean this on one level. Obviously the reality of source transfer implies that given information lines be re-adjusted to the affinity dynamics of the individuals or groups to which it is addressed. Which is to say, there is a natural "information schism" between various groups (as far as the meta- and vibrational affinity alignment to their information), and I have not meant to imply that the phenomenon of source transfer is necessarily negative—because it isn't. But if we are to understand the composite reality scheme of American society, then it is important that its utilization of source transfer is better understood. For the most basic state of source transfer does not imply suppression towards any affinity position—which is to say, the dynamics of composite source-transfer interpretation are not happening in western culture at present. Moreover, there is a difference between natural source transfer and controlled governmental decisions. **In other words, the progressional continuance of western culture is designed to perpetuate the affinity dynamics of what it perceives to be real to white America (or at least a particular "zone" of white Americans). What we are experiencing in this time cycle is no mere case of extended affinity dynamics—but rather, a continuance consciously designed for particular aims.**

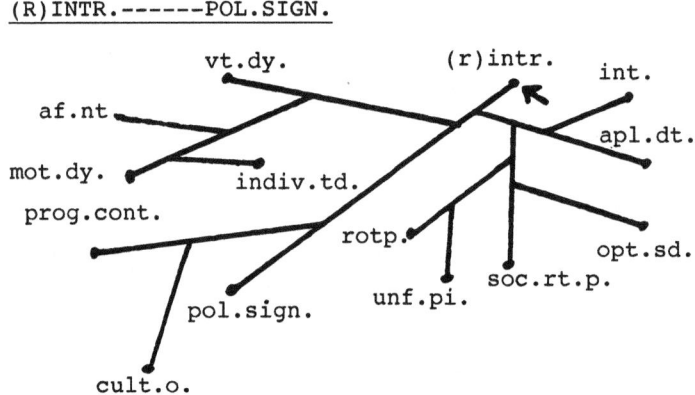

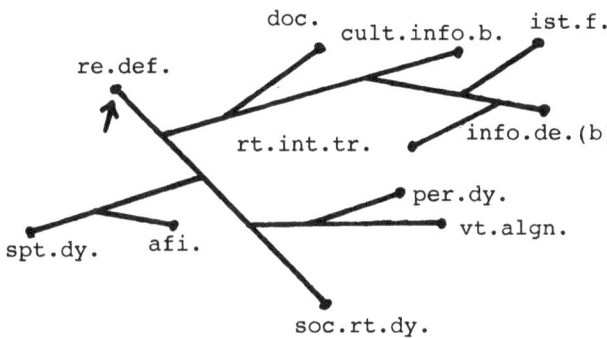

If we choose to examine the progressional continuance of western culture with respect to the concept of "affinity-convergence lines," then the reality base underlining our understanding of western culture takes on a different significance. In this context, the developing multi-vibrational affinity arena of western culture can be viewed in composite terms. It is because of the implications of "affinity convergence" that the progressional continuance of western society can be viewed as not formed. In other words, the reality of affinity dynamics transcends the reality particulars of any one time zone, and instead comments on the composite nature of world progressionalism. As such, the many changes that are reshaping earth culture are indicative of much more than isolated particulars, but instead ultimately derive their significance from transition—or, even more important, transformation. Information focus (or knowledge) in this context must be viewed within this much broader context of "trans-culture" (or forming composite culture). Which is to say, actual focused transformational definitions have not yet formed. This is so because the realness of transition is not about solidified definitions anyway. The whole of this time period can be viewed for how the concept of affinity convergence seems to be forming—understanding, too, that the nature of a particular forming is not separate from what transpires socially and politically on the physical universe level. To view the realness of progressional continuity in this context is to develop a basis for viewing the composite factors at work in this cycle.

Clearly, the manipulation that surrounds the reality of "affinity convergence" is not separate from the progressional-significance implications of general world expansion (or, simply, change). This can be understood by dealing with the realness of what affinity convergence implies. Because in its most natural state, the expansion and interplay of affinity convergence implies world transformation—threatening the established basic order. As such, the affinity-dynamic re-interpretations that surround present-day information can be viewed as a choking device to keep "real change" from occurring, Yet I do not mean this in general terms—because certainly every conscious "interpretation" encompasses more than one criterion. But if we are to view the composite reality of western culture, we cannot afford to take information re-interpretation lightly. For while it is true that an over-broad application of any concept threatens to over-simplify the composite scope of what is being dealt with (in a given interpretation)—and in doing so make wrong assertions—at the same time, no one can afford to not acknowledge the nature of dynamic manipulation now taking place in this period. The very concept of what I have come to call "the collective forces of western culture" is not simply a "new arrangement of words" but, rather, something that does exist. Moreover, it would be absurd if we did not consider how these "forces" have secured the reality tone of present-day Earth. If the basic continuance of affinity convergence does indeed have multi-vibrational consequences, then clearly those forces would challenge the composite nature and state of present-day political dynamics (economics, history, politics) and, as such, the collective forces of western culture would both oppose and actively work against it. My point is also that the reality information we are now dealing with today has to do with many different factors—the least of which is whether or not a given information interpretation is true. If we are to deal with what this viewpoint means, then we must first understand the multi-complexual implications of information manipulation and affinity dynamics. The seriousness of this phenomenon affects us from the moment we enter the planet. It is not just a question of the information manipulation that surrounds the music business, it is more a question of understanding how this phenomenon ultimately affects the totalness of our existence. The range of information manipulation and/or distortion that is taking place in western culture can be viewed starting with grammar school textbooks, on through high school (i.e., the teaching of history, mathematics, creativity, etc.), and continuing on through one's total life. Nor can we assume that partial change will threaten the basic order of western culture, because, in fact, the web of information dynamics we are now dealing with has nothing to do with one focus manifestation. My point is that the progressional continuance of affinity convergence forecasts a world transformation at its optimum position—and at its minimum, positive transition. Both of these states are not viewed as desirable for the existing power structure. Which is to say, the reality of present-day information dynamics will not be dealt with unless those of us outside the basic structure move to change it. In the final analysis, we really have no other choice. Either we change the information reality surrounding our lives or progressively become the effect of mis-documentation and/or imposed affinity dynamics. There are no other alternatives.

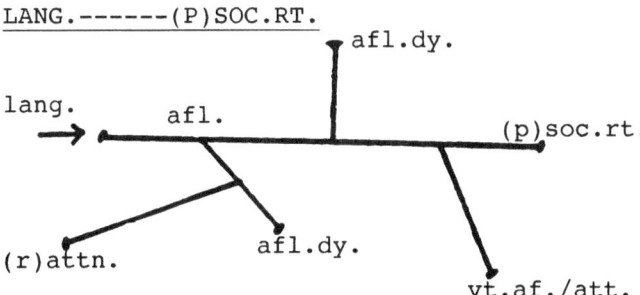

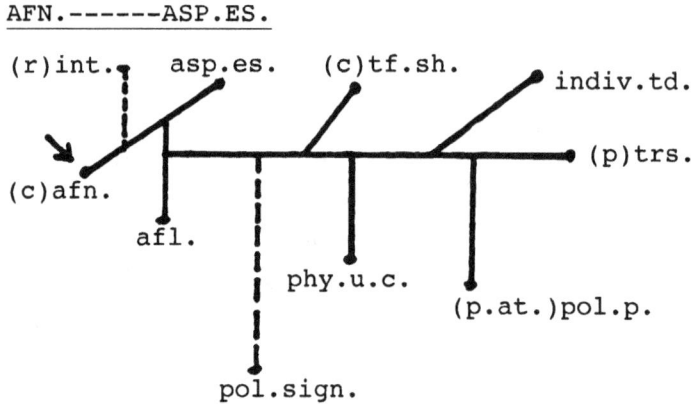

If we are to understand the basis from which western culture derives its vibrational nature alignment with phenomena, then the implications of abstract existentialism and/or phenomenology cannot be overlooked. For the "natural" continuance of western culture has moved to solidify the most "interesting" information-focus position in this time zone. **The fact is, with the desolation of the spiritual base of western culture, the concept of investigation has moved to become the "concept of assigned observation."** By "concept of assigned observation," I am commenting on how a phenomenon is perceived as well as how given information degrees are attached to the observance. For the "concept of assigned observation" is western culture's reality of information degrees (knowledge tenets). In this context, it is possible to view the "functionalism" of a given phenomenon—with respect to what that functionalism will dynamically imply—without having to deal with the spiritual degree that dictated what and how that functionalism came to be. It is this affinity posture that has come to characterize the reality of western definitions, and it is also this affinity posture that has served as a basis for the uniqueness of contemporary western expansionism. Yet to write that this affinity position has no reality value at all would be to invalidate the existence of "life activity" on this planet—especially in this time zone. For no matter how different this affinity position can be viewed, the fact is, its solidification represents something "real" for the forces that established it. We must also acknowledge that the cosmic realness of existence seems to imply that everything is as it is because it has something to do with the nature of what is really happening—in other words, there is no one way—or one correct alignment. For the solidification of a given sensibility has multi-complexual implications—it is a question of what route a given attraction is motivated to pursue, and it is also a question of all routes leading to God. For this reason, we can view how the western vibrational affinity alignment seems to function and, in doing so, attempt to draw some understanding about this phenomenon. Yet there has never been any question of whether or not any given thrust has the right to participate in its own affinity dynamics—rather, the complexity of this subject comes from its extended application on world culture. Certainly the reality lining of western culture does not exclude the possibility and realness of "spirituality" on some level besides a word. Yet the composite application of western thrust continuance has established a peculiar (at best) relationship with world culture. One needs only to look at what is happening to present-day information dynamics. **One of the most basic problems non-western people are dealing with in this period of time is the weight of attempting to "expand" under wrong definitions.** This "weight" can be reduced to the progressional continuance of western redefinitions conceived from the "special" affinity dynamics that have characterized this time zone. And this is no mono-dynamic phenomenon.

It is important to understand that the reality of affinity dynamics does not necessarily substantiate the present world position we are in on the basis of "what we have now come to call race." If this is understood, then the focus origin of western affinity dynamics cannot simply be traced to white people—as a broad generalization. The fact is, since the concept of affinity dynamics transcends the theory of race, then it is important that we view this question with respect to the "focus nature" of principle-vibrational projection lines. My point is this: if the concept of affinity dynamics is not about the origin of a given race—but rather the solidification of given forces—then what does this mean if we are to understand the meta-implications of what I have come to call the "composite western affinity alignment" (since this name itself is not "what it is about"—or since this name has been utilized only because it has been "convenient")—this is really the question.

I believe that the present composite affinity nature of western culture has to do with the vibrational dynamics signaling what period we are really in—or at least what period we have been in. For the solidification of this alignment has most certainly underlined the nature of continuance in the last two thousand years. Until we as a collective people are able to deal with the establishment of a transformational culture, this alignment will probably continue to vibrationally underline the nature of contemporary "progressional continuity." This is so because the reality of the western affinity-dynamic principle has shown itself to be able to "function"—even without center (even without meaning)—and in doing so dynamically affect the world group—even if it is negative. In actual terms, this alignment has come to rely on observing the "function particulars" of the physical universe—as a means to develop dynamic functionalism—while totally ignoring the "infra-spirituality" that permeates what a given function "really means." In itself, this type of affinity alignment must be viewed as revolutionary—but not necessarily "of life." Yet I have not meant to imply that nothing positive can come from this juncture, because obviously "you just can't say that." Quite possibly the reality of contemporary western "affinity dynamics" can best be viewed in the context of progressional continuance. For the whole of this time zone—the last two thousand years—can be viewed as a transition of sorts. Earth has yet to really solidify a composite transformational vibrational attitude—and information continuum—since the dissolution of the great Egyptian, Greek, and Chinese cultures of old. Moreover, the progressional line related to how that "period" actualized has been subjected to so many re-interpretations that I see no composite refunctional position soon emerging of trans-cultural importance. As such, we can view the vibrational particulars of the western affinity position with respect to what its implementation has meant in world terms—understanding too that in this we have no choice, for the social-political position of western culture in this cycle gives us no other possibility but to examine the underlying factors from which this dominance is based. It will be important for the world community to understand the vibrational nature of western culture—not that I am proposing something never thought of before, because obviously this question has been dealt with by many people, and this will undoubtedly continue—as we move to the next cycle, for the application and practice of contemporary information lines directly comments on the nature and reality implications of affinity dynamics. My point has also been that the reality of a given alignment colors the dynamics of both its progressional continuance as well as the composite planet's natural expansion (and/or continuance).

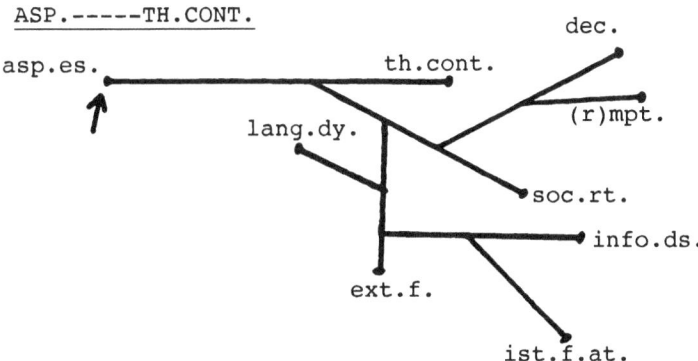

The nature of western progressionalism in this cycle can best be understood by the concept of existential evolution—which is to say, the basis from which western culture has now come to view information rests with "abstract observation." The reality of what this phenomenon poses directly collides with world affinity dynamics. For without a spiritual basis, there is no unified context to transfer composite information. It is for this reason that the "vibrational-gap spread" between the west and world group has accelerated. Moreover, the profound implications of this separatism lies at the center of my belief that western definitions now serve as a functional tool for suppressing world culture. For without a spiritual basis, information can be interpreted to suit the reality particulars of the moment—colored only by the person defining (or redefining). It is at this junction where the significance of affinity dynamics can clearly be understood, for at the base of every information line is its multi-vibrationally directed assignment—

that being: **every information line manifests some aspect of principle-vibrational—and spiritual—"realness" (and in doing so becomes "real" in the sense of how it affects a given "zone" of reality)**. This is true for the reality of information in western culture, and this is also true for the reality of information in world culture (or "not" western culture). My point is that these differences do mean something, and my point is also that the reality of information dynamics must be respected if we are to positively function for the re-establishment of the next cycle (whether transition or transformation). But this has not been the case—which is to say, the accented position of western culture in the last thousand years has necessitated a functional position with respect to the dynamics of "information focus." As such, the progressional continuance of western information—re-interpretation—must be viewed for what it has come to pose for the "developments" that have transpired on the physical universe level. In other words, information manipulation is political—and even more "about politics." **In actual terms, the redefinition that has characterized this time zone must be viewed for what it signifies in vibrational terms (the reality of source transfer)—what it philosophically poses (the reality of affinity dynamics)—what it seeks to avoid (the reality of affinity convergence)—and the nature of what its "solidification" has come to pose (the consequences being the focus on phenomenological aspects as a means to proclaim "meaning" leading to post-existentialism).** All of these variables are directly related to the solidification of western redefinitions—yet I do not mean to over-simplify this most complex problem. For the reality of multi-interpretations when applied to western culture is not necessarily the same for world culture. In other words, a distinction must be made between the reality of western affinity dynamics when applied to multi-information, and the reality of world culture to this same criterion. To not make this distinction is to risk unfairly criticizing the reality position of western culture—and this would only distort my most basic point (because I am not interested in "simply pointing fingers").

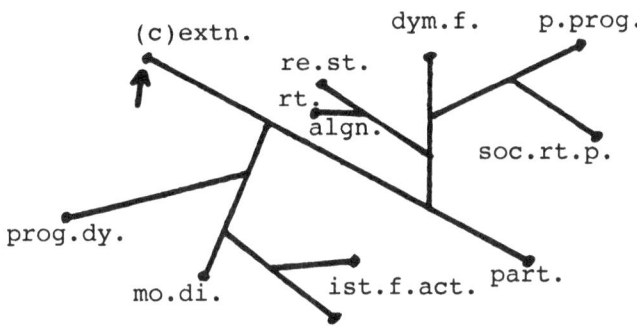

The dynamics of multi-information in western culture have to do with the nature of the present situation we now find ourselves in during this cycle, that position being "everybody can say whatever they want to say about anything" (basically this is what we are dealing with). The reality of this phenomenon comments on the dynamics surrounding how we have come to view information. **In this period, the affinity and methodological structure of western information has created a situation where "the realness of a given phenomenon has to do with what words are put on it"—as opposed to the phenomenon "being what it is"—and "you knowing what that is."** In this position, given "experts and scholars" are free to interpret phenomena either in any way that seems fit, or in any way that "makes sense." The progressional continuance of this situation further moves to create a situation where, with the natural expansion of the physical universe (that being, given individuals will "deal" with the same information and deduce completely different meaning from that information), variable interpretation tends to establish a multi-informational basis, rather than information that means "this" (or "this is this"). The end result of this "multi-informational degree basis" is that there is no central point to establish "composite grounding." This phenomenon can then be viewed as very positive for "doing something"—and also for "actual functioning"—and the dynamics of western culture are the best example of what can happen when this position occurs: "electronics, airplanes, the automobile, television, elevators"—yet this same phenomenon dictates another total relationship with "center" and/or "cultural affinity reality." Which is to say, actual living is not made any easier.

The solidification of a "multi-informational degree basis" in itself is not necessarily negative—that is, when utilized by those whose vibrational alignment sees this phenomenon as real (and it is important to understand that the essence underlying what "this"—life—is does seem to have necessitated that this zone is "operative"). In other words, the affinity dynamics of western culture can be viewed with respect to what they signify about western culture (and life in western culture), as well as what they signify about progressional continuance. In the context of western life (in its separate and exclusive state), multi-information has functioned as the basis from which the composite expansion principle of the culture is taken. As such, it can be viewed as the germ principle responsible for the "nature" and course western culture has moved to take. Thus if western culture were the only culture on the planet, there would be no quarrel with the dynamics of "multi-information" (of this type). The most basic problem of this phenomenon can be observed when the whole of the planet is taken into consideration—which is to say, "the world does exist" and as such the reality of multi-information (as it has solidified in western culture—that being, as an affirmation of western affinity dynamics) cannot be totally embraced as positive for the composite planet. It is for this reason that I have tried to probe the composite implications of this phenomenon, because obviously I am not only commenting on the whole of western culture when citing the "complications" of multi-information. But, what then does this mean?

I believe the reality of multi-information must be viewed in its most "real" composite context, for the affinity basis from which this concept derives its significance is not bound to any particular physical universe sector. In other words, it would be wrong to perceive of the concept of multi-information as solely a manifestation of western culture or necessarily indicative of isolated racial or nationalistic groups. I write this even though I have constantly associated multi-information with the reality of western culture (as a means to easily convey an identifiable factor for immediate use). Yet the heart of this concept has nothing to do with any of these "particulars." **If we are to really understand the basis from which given projections derive significance, then we are forced to investigate the essence basis that defines and dictates the "real reality" of all "affinity assignments," and this is cosmic in nature.** For to seriously deal with the reality of affinity dynamics is to have some awareness that every "projection" and/or "projection nature" (affinity dynamics) is only what I will call the second degree of a principle "force" (or "forces") alignment. Which is to say, to comment on the reality of a given projection assignment is to comment on the spiritual workings of cosmic-related concerns. As such, my observations must be viewed in the proper context—for while I have found it necessary to present my own viewpoint (which is based on one-half feeling and the other half observation and research) in this book, I have no illusions as to my non-qualification to write about these matters in "definite" terms. To really communicate about the "realness" of these matters is to have much more spiritual awareness than I now possess in this cycle. For the essence reality of affinity dynamics comments on the "real" workings of the universe. My viewpoint in these matters is based on what I sense, rather than "know"—and it is important that the reader is constantly made aware of this difference. Nevertheless, the real reality of multi-information cannot be dealt with unless some attempt is made to clarify the nature of its "context"—or, in my case, "what I feel to be a relevant context."

The underlying reality of multi-information can best be viewed by observing the nature of the physical and vibrational universe continuum. In this context, the "consequences" of a given projection are not separate from what "reality particular" each person—and culture—finds him- or herself in. In other words, the underlying factors that substantiate the reality of a given progression also comment on the "nature" or "vibrational factors" that ultimately color every person's life particulars (or functioning). Rather than run the risk of wrongly commenting about the tone level of every projectional thrust, and in attempting to do so, violate both myself and the reader, it is possible to look at the two most basic life positions related to "functioning" and/or "net purpose spectrum" as a means to clarify in actual terms the significance of multi-information. **My belief**

is this: the spectrum of a given affinity projection can be viewed with respect to those tendencies that function as a tool for world unification and what I will call positive transformation, and those tendencies that function as a tool for dynamic separation and what I will call "negative" transformation. Yet by citing the two extremes of projectional dynamics, I have not meant to unjustly distort the composite reality of information lines. Nor have I meant to simply not recognize the dynamic interplay of given projectional affinities—obviously there is much more to be said about the reality of "information dynamics." But in making such an easily recognizable division, there is the hope that I might be able to elaborate on the essence of what this concept poses. For if we are to understand "the reality of interpretation" in this time period, then it is important that the underlying vibrational implications of this concept are explored on some level. It is for this reason that I have moved to isolate only what I now call the "extremity position" of "composite affinity projections." To approach this concept in any other manner would greatly increase the possibility of mistake—for I am not on solid ground on these matters (in fact, if it were possible to discuss the reality of "multi-information" without viewing the underlying factors that make this concept significant, I would have taken that route). Yet on the other hand, if by focusing on the nature of this subject I am able to make some aspect of this concept clear, then hopefully something positive can be gained from this effort. With this stated, how are we to better understand the "extremity position" of multi-information?

The underlying significance of both affinity dynamics and/or multi-information can best be viewed by understanding what position these concepts have in the basic breakdown of what I will call "cosmic order." In other words, the realness of these concepts are significant with respect to both the nature of its origin (projectional significance) and the reality of its principle alignment (source initiation). As such, if we are to really understand the reality particulars of a given projection, then we must have some insight as to that projection's "meta-reality base." This is so because my understanding of "projection significance" has to do with "what a given route of information" really means—that is, "really means." Thus the underlying significance of both affinity dynamics and/ or multi-information has to do with my belief that creativity—regardless of projection—is not only about the "doing" and/or involvement of the individual or individuals, but, rather, the essence foundation of creativity comments on—and, indeed, is a part of—the nature of what forces we are "really" dealing with (in this zone, or life zone). This viewpoint is not only true for music or creativity but extends to every level of existence on this planet. Thus the "dynamic reality" of a given information line has to do with what factors that "line" really affirms, or another way to say this is "the reality of a given information line has to do with what 'force' that 'line' functions to realize." As such, the significance of given information must be viewed in its composite context. For with these definitions we are not only commenting on creativity, but instead we are discussing the reality of composite information. The basic viewpoint that the whole of this book has tried to advance is the notion that the reality of information lines—affinity dynamics—has to do with the significance of both methodology (with respect to what functionalism really means when viewed in a composite context) and the vibrational implications underlying what a given methodological particular really means. To understand this is to also understand why the "reality of interpretation" must be dealt with as well.

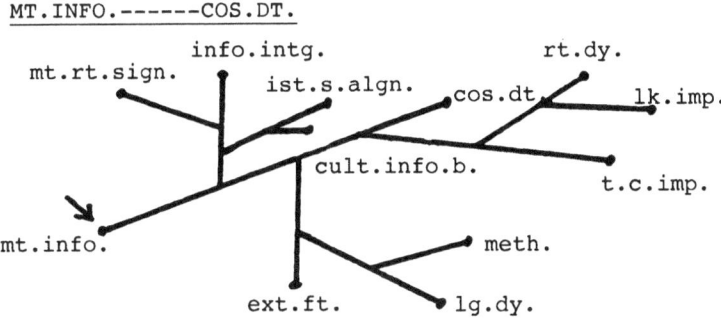

INFO.DY.------COS.AGN.

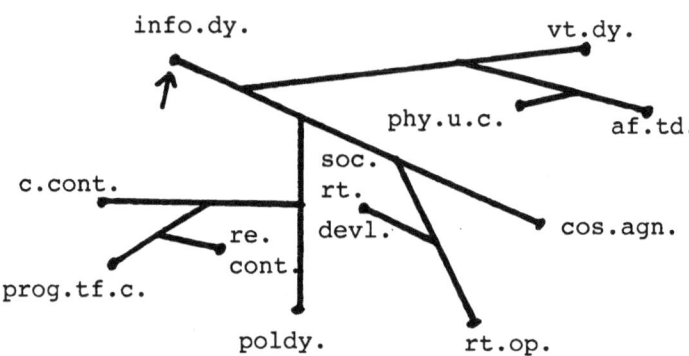

The underlying dynamic position of multi-information can best be viewed in the two examples I posed earlier—those being "world unification purpose" and "dynamic individualism." If we are to understand the "reality of information possibilities," then it is important to elaborate on what these two basic positions really mean. By "world unification purpose" I am commenting on the nature of what "principle alignment" means. Information in this context has to do with the solidification of "what is" in composite terms as a means to provide a universal basis for understanding and participating in this planet experience. It is in this juncture where one is able to view the potential functionalism of assistance for positive world transformation—or "change with respect to what is most 'of humanity' about all of us!" This is not to conjure up images of Walt Disney, nor by "world unification" am I attempting to postulate the "heaven on earth" concept! Instead, I believe that the next cycle of progressionalism can carry its own new problems, rather than the problems we have been dealing with in this cycle. Nor have I meant in this concept to imply that "everybody will be together and live happily ever after," for I do not believe our experience on this planet has anything to do with this viewpoint either. The "concept of world unification"—and the projections that move to affirm this phenomenon—only has to do with moving to collectively understand how to proceed in accordance with what "vibrational and spiritual factors seem to imply." Those concepts have to do with the "real"

laws surrounding what this experience on earth seems to imply. Which is to say, by "real laws" I am referring to the composite progressional solidification of information that has been handed down to us from world culture (that being, every culture we know about)—information which—no matter what corner of the globe it comes from—moves to have us come to terms with being on this planet, and also tell us how to live. **All of the high culture information in existence seems to comment on the same basic reality focus. That being: "how to live with each other"—how to treat each other—the concept of there being greater forces determining what is really happening (God) and the interrelationship of this information as a means to "function."** I have come to refer to all information of this type as "within the world unification purpose," or related to "this" most basic principle. This is not to say my concept of world unification is correct or all-consuming—because it isn't—but rather, I have advanced these examples only as a means to transmit something about the reality of the world unification principle as related to what I am able to understand (or postulate). My point being: all of these "particulars" can be viewed with respect to given vibrationaltory factors—and at the heart of these examples is the desire for (if you will forgive my use of word) "peace" and/or spiritual living.

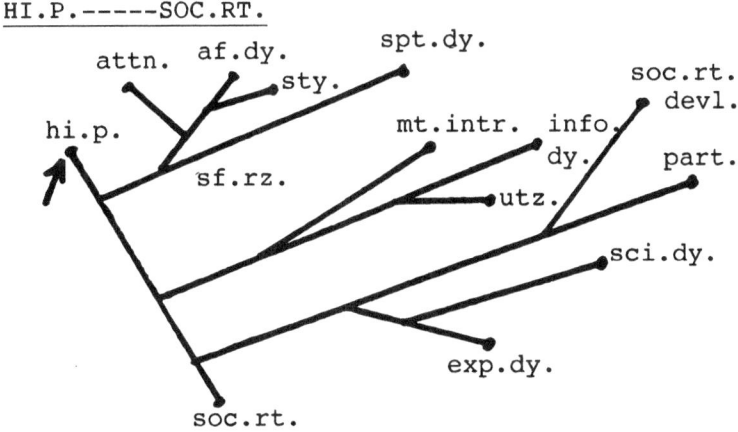

EVOL-36

DYM.FT.------HI.P.

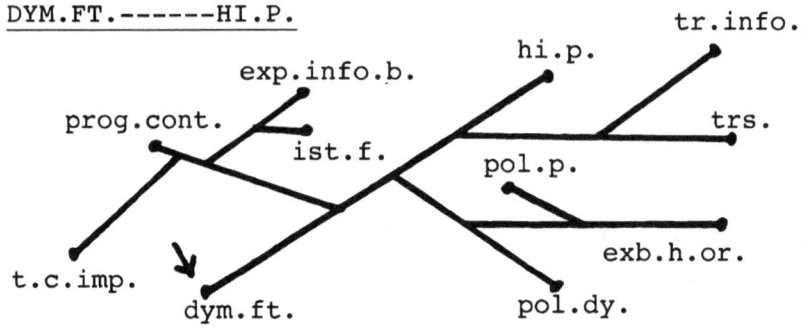

EXT.DY. -----TR.

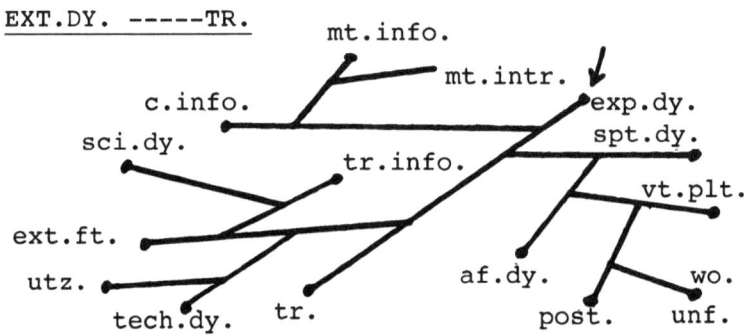

SPT.DY.------SOC.RT.

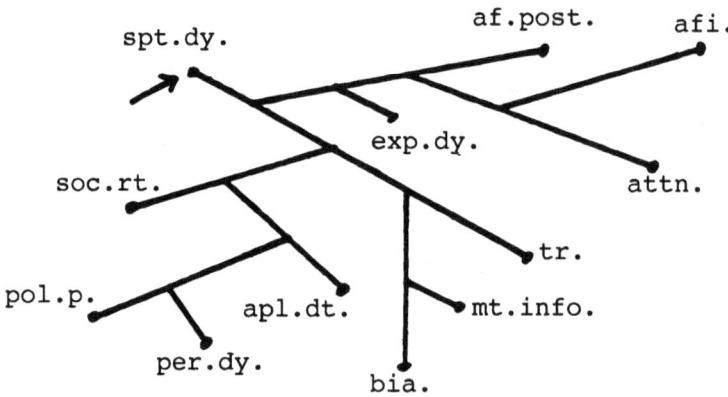

The concept of "individual dynamics" can be viewed with respect to the nature of "doing." That being, the realness of life on the physical universe level and the route individuals travel to learn about "it." The implications of this phenomenon have helped to advance the dynamics of earth life with respect to the realization of isolated "tendencies." The natural thrust of this phenomenon also moves to accelerate the separate nature surrounding how given realities "progress," and as such, this concept is important for the dynamics it has helped promote over the face of the planet. Because of this phenomenon, we can now view the various tendencies of planet earth with respect to "the appearance of things"—for example: the collected offerings of world creativity—the dynamic views surrounding religion, and its concrete solidification in functionalism. The reality implications of "individual dynamics" have helped to solidify the nature underlying how things have come together—and apart—on earth. Which is to say, this source focus has a significant role in earth participation. Yet I have not meant to imply that only two principle alignments (i.e., world unification and individual dynamics) are of importance in the total scheme of things, nor have I necessarily given the best descriptions of these two "source" positions (in every context). To really deal with this subject would necessitate creating a separate forum (since the basic focus here is primarily on creativity), but I have commented on these factors as a means to solidify some understanding about "source initiation" (and its relationship to the concept of there being two principle-projectional extremities from every "source-information line").

Thus, if we are to understand the reality of interpretation, then the underlying factors that substantiate what a given projection ultimately means must be recognized. My point is this: the essence basis of a given interpretation has to do with what aspect of its information line is understood, and for what purpose. Which is to say, the reality of interpretation is not separate from the realness of affinity dynamics—or in this case, affinity interpretation. **If the extremity position of multi-information is understood, then there can only be limited interpretation options—those being (1) interpretation with respect for positive functionalism for earth continuance, or (2) interpretation with respect**

to the reality position of given particulars. Thus, the composite nature of definitions must be re-examined if we are to understand what has happened in this last cycle (last thousand years and some). For the present time zone has yet to deal with solidifying multi-information as a means to begin the next level of composite or actual knowledge. What we have instead in this cycle are interpretations as an affirmation of a selected affinity reality, or interpretation as a means to negate the composite implications of source initiation, and, finally, interpretation as a factor to accelerate the "force or vibrational" implication of information selection. As such, the composite realness of world culture cannot afford to accept the present "reality of interpretation" of western culture—and in like terms, the realness of western culture could not afford to simply accept non-western definitions that are not correctly integrated. For the risk of wrong interpretations carries profound consequences—on many different levels.

In other words, the reality of a given interpretation is not separate from the affinity consequences of attachment—regardless of information line. The fact is, **the affinity alignments related to what a given interpretation is to mean are also related to "what principle forces will come into play" as a result of that attraction.** Thus the nature of what information is drawn on, as well as the reality of interpretation, must be viewed with respect to its multi-consequences (either vibrational or actual)—and this is exactly why I have found the dynamics of definition to be significant for what it poses for transformation.

As such, the reality of interpretation is not only about how a given individual relates to a particular phenomenon—for in this concept, we are commenting on the use of cultural education and/or music journalism (or criticism), among other things—and this phenomenon also extends to affect the composite infra-reality of its operative space. This is not to say we should not have opinions, but, rather, the "reality of interpretation" is concerned with how given information lines are interpreted for the composite culture as well as what its interpretations signal for the greater vibrational dynamics of the composite culture.

When I stated that the progressional continuance of western culture can be viewed with respect to the nature of its affinity-dynamics position,

I was also commenting on what this "nature" posed to the composite society. In actual terms, the information we have now come to deal with in our education and critical defining centers can be viewed for how it has promoted "certain" tendencies in the culture—and while many given sectors of our society have benefited from western information of this character, the whole of the greater society clearly has not.

(Level One) The Teaching of Improvised Music

THE REALITY OF MUSIC EDUCATION IN THIS TIME PERIOD cannot be understood by examining the particulars of only one region of information; rather, the dynamic implications of this subject touch on the vibrational identity and tone level of its composite culture. In other words, the realness of music education—as made real in cultural pedagogical dynamics—is not separate from the total vibrational transference of all information—having to do with the "affinity state" related to how that culture has come to view both perception as well as intention. As such, the realness of education must be viewed as the cornerstone of any living culture, because this consideration is directly related to "how that culture came to be" and "how that culture could come to be." The reality of education is necessarily connected to every aspect of its culture—on every level, regardless of time zone.

To view the present state of western education is to see one of the most dynamic areas of western culture. For the last two hundred years have seen the emergence of the transitional university profoundly altering the progressional route of western culture. Where, in the past, advanced education was available only to a limited sector of the greater public, today many people are able to receive the full thrust of any area of information—and the realness of this change cannot be over-emphasized. For the increased availability of extended education promises to be a major factor in the next cycle of transformation. The dynamic acceleration of western functionalism must also be viewed as necessarily related to the present reality of western education. Every day, new information lines are being rediscovered, and the young student of today has a staggering amount of information options—as compared to even fifty years ago. There are the developments now reshaping western functionalism, there is the information continuum reshaping theoretical information, and of course there is information about dynamic creative possibilities. So much information is now available that no one can possibly learn all of it even if a lifetime were devoted only to the pursuit of available information (not to mention new information). The realness of western education is exciting on many different levels, for, if I am correct, we are slowly moving to one of the most dynamic periods for new information and discovery in this time cycle. The challenge of this information will profoundly alter everything—which is to say, the progressional continuance of education is a subject that concerns all of us. As such, it is important that attempts are made to view the dynamic realness of this subject—especially with respect to what it poses to the basic focus of this book—that being: the reality of creativity and its relationship to transformation. This is what concerns me.

Certainly the reality of music education is not separate from the general continuum of composite progressionalism—that is, the reality of this sector of culture-information transference must be viewed in the same context as all new functionalism. For music education, like everything else, has come a long way—and the future promises even greater changes. No longer are the "effective" schools situated in only a limited sector of the country, for the last twenty years have seen the solidification of many dynamic institutions—that is, for the study of western art music—and the end result of this phenomenon has moved to establish orchestras like the Chicago Symphony as second to none. The dynamics of contemporary education in this cycle have also moved to create a whole new order of creative musicians for the western art music continuum—involving not only musicians but conductors as well—and the net effect of this phenomenon has moved to solidify the Euro-American classical community on a level few thought could have been possible—and there are many factors related to how this change has come about. For the dynamic implications of World Wars One and Two would create a situation that attracted many creative people to America from all over the world. To even attempt naming individuals who migrated to America in that cycle would only underscore the realness of this phenomenon—for dynamic conductors like Toscanini came in this cycle, Stravinsky, Schoenberg, etc., etc. The net effect of this development would dynamically change the reality continuum of Euro-American western art music. By the middle of the fifties, many of the greatest musicians and composers from Europe had collectively moved to reshape the dynamics of American creative music performance and education.

But the dynamics of present-day music education are not limited to the changes affecting only western art music continuance. For the collected implications of this phenomenon are also related to the composite reality position of all creative musics—which is to say, if we are to really understand the present reality of music education, then we must view this consideration with respect to what it poses for not just western art music but world music and, even more important, for alternative functionalism. In other words, the dynamic position of western education must be viewed with respect to its position—and responsibility—to all information—because "everyone on the planet is equally on the planet"— or at least the realness of composite information is not about whether or not one chooses to deal with it. The reality of the education process is designed to only be "dealing with it"—that is, if it is properly serving its function. Nor by raising this point have I meant to totally discredit the positive things that have and are happening in western education—for the thrust of even the last ten years has seen many changes and innovations in contemporary western education, and this must be both applauded and respected. Rather, the thrust of this section will focus on what changes and innovations have not been necessarily realigned—and why. My belief is simple: The composite state of applied definitions in the last four hundred years must be re-examined for its relationship to the progressional decline of world culture and "extended" perception—furthermore, the realness of western education cannot be excused for its role in vibrational suppression—and mis-documentation—because this juncture (western education) is directly aligned with the collective forces of western culture (and interpretation sanction). In other words, the reality of information dynamics in western education is directly related to the "present state of things" and this relationship must be challenged if we truly desire either transformation (and positive world change) or simply "real information."

T(IMP)M–4

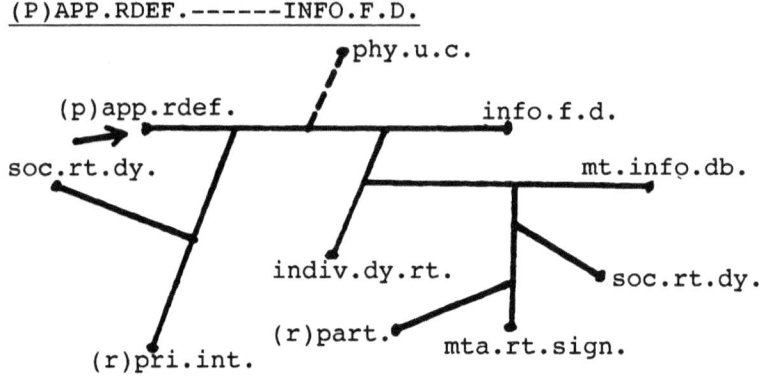

The Teaching of Improvised Music

Before the beginning of the sixties, there had been very little instruction on improvised music within the educational system (i.e., universities, conservatories) of America. For that matter, improvised music had more or less been swept under the carpet and viewed as a form not worthy of serious study. The basic curriculum of most universities was instead devoted and geared to western art music as an exclusive form. The spectrum of these courses spanned the period surrounding the Gregorian chants, the reality of composers like Johann Sebastian Bach, and the classical period of western art music. For the most part, the average curriculum in many of these schools concluded with a glimpse of Stravinsky's music (every now and then, a given school might continue to the activity of Schoenberg—but this was rare). It goes without saying that the functional reality of western art music was also taught, and in this sense American universities did provide a positive outlet for people interested in western classical music. What basis the educational system could use to not deal with three-fourths of the music on this planet is beyond me, but this was the actual situation as we moved into the sixties.

Without doubt, the neglect of creative music has to do with many factors. For while most educators have long recognized the significance of creative music as a factor reshaping American creativity, very few of these people have been able to accept the music as being on the level of western art music. It would not be far-fetched to say that the disregard for creative improvised music has much to do with racism—no matter how flexible we choose to be in looking at it. For the exclusion of creative music from the academic community is not in itself an isolated act, but rather another signal by the controlling forces which dictate how culture is to be understood, that world music is not worthy of serious examination. All of the creative forms that have emerged from Africa, South America, Japan, etc., have been neglected by our educational institutions in this same way. To understand this situation is to be aware of the nature of how cultural racism works, but at the same time it is necessary to understand exactly what culture America is vibrating towards. For if creative improvised music is American music, then one would think that by definition it would merit some degree of respect by the academic community—but this has not been the case. The fact is: the controlling forces which have designed how culture is to be taught in America have merely embraced European culture at the expense of what is happening in their own country.

The attempts to align America with the European composite culture thrust was inevitable—especially in the early periods of this country's history (it is clear that America still sees herself as the bulwark of the western culture continuance, and to some degree this viewpoint is both understandable and true)—but America has also attempted to adopt this thrust (European creativity) at the expense of what she could potentially be. This longing to be part of European culture is of the utmost importance if one really hopes to understand the vibrational reality of American culture. Not only is the educational system today the end effect of that longing, but the entire history of music school development in America was created exactly for that very purpose. In short, the real history of music schools in America would reveal the actual position of the controlling groups which have dictated the nature of our present social mis-alignment—with regards to culture. From the very beginning of America, the concept of music education has been directly linked to source transfer—and in this position, the education centers functioned as the most basic linkage factor to retain European culture. It is no wonder that there have been only a few composers from America whose activity did not simply mirror European music, for not only have European techniques and concepts been taught exclusively in America's educational systems, but the meta-reality and sensibility of this thrust were also transmitted to the students as well.

There are other problems that must be faced concerning the reality of education in America if we are to really understand the realness of this phenomenon as it relates to creative music. For the music curricula in ninety percent of the schools in this country all seem to share the same basic flaws in both their structure—with regards to the programming of subject arenas—and viewpoint. It is the student who loses in the final analysis—for at present, the academic experience does not adequately prepare people for what is really happening on the planet—and in this context, I am not simply referring to the music schools but instead the total university as the final state of preparation for real life. In short, not only do we find, in looking at the average graduate student, an inability to deal with what is really happening with creativity on the planet, but in many cases we also find a vibrational blockage in many of these same people—that is, the university experience in many cases supplies a viewpoint that is very difficult to shake off. The resulting dilemma of this situation is that many of the people who have completed their studies in music eventually wind up teaching music—and in doing this, the present educational spiral is continually re-created. After a given period of time, this situation begins to take on an elitist vibrational tone; and as a result, the university begins to look more and more like a Bastille where people are fighting to keep new ideas out—which is the opposite of what the educational experience should be. I have already discussed some of the impairing factors inherent in the structural development of the European composite aesthetic as it was manifested in western art music (since the emergence of notation), and by now one would probably think that some of these questions are being looked at in the universities—to better understand western art music if nothing else. But in fact very few, if any, universities are even aware of these questions—let alone how to deal with the problems which have solidified from this phenomenon. The functional arena of western art music is still taught today in the same way it was conceived in its earliest state.

The time-lag factor that surrounds the academic situation is not only manifested in the universities' inability to deal with world music, but extends into how the totalness of western art music is treated. In other words, it would be wrong to assume that the neglect of world creativity is the only factor that has resulted from this mis-alignment. When I stated in the beginning of this section that very few universities have attempted to teach the full gamut of western art music, I was in fact referring to another manifestation of this same problem. There are only a handful of schools that provide classes on the latest developments occurring in western art music. In short, the progressions of western art music from Schoenberg to John Cage to La Monte Young are hardly ever really commented on—this is also the case for the progressional continuum from Schoenberg to Webern to Stockhausen. Many colleges and universities, if asked about this omission, would justifiably point out the economic consequences of trying to include a complete curriculum with the money problems the planet is now experiencing. But this does not balance if examined even lightly. For the developments I have mentioned have occurred at least fifteen years ago by now—in short, there has been enough time to establish some courses devoted to contemporary music—more so: if a music school can afford to have classes on the Gregorian chants, that school could also afford to create an outlet for students to learn about Webern. I do not believe the economic situation is the basic motivating factor responsible for the neglect of contemporary music.

In short, the collective forces that move to define what the academic reality will signify—in the lives of the people who attend these institutions—is directly aligned with the consideration of "time lag." That is, the university situation can be looked at as another tool society utilizes that functions to sustain "time lag." All of the available courses seek to achieve this condition; more so, the vibrational slant of the information taught in these courses helps to sustain this same alignment as well. After studying for four years or more at a given institution, the average student graduates with an inability to deal with what is actually happening with the creative music of his/her own time zone. The basic thrust of the knowledge learned in the educational system serves as a locking factor on western art music exclusively, and this is unfortunate. The seriousness of this problem can be better understood if one examines what the university concept really implies—as well as what function the university represents with regards to the life progression of its constituents. The university represents the last juncture for society to aid in the shaping of one's consciousness. After this period, each of us are left to our own devices and life direction. Thus, if understood, the position of the university must be taken seriously not simply because this is the last educational zone—but because of how this position could be utilized in a positive manner. In short, the university, if properly utilized, could help to prepare a person for dealing with "actual" life, rather than "theoretical life." The implications of what this means with regards to creativity are all too clear. It is now time for the educational institutions to prepare young people for the realness of present-time awareness with regards to music and thus serve as a meaningful tool rather than an esoteric and useless function. I do not mean to imply that the study of western art music is not important—or necessary—for this is not my viewpoint. The historical progressions of any creative thrust are extremely important—nor am I against one learning about the functional arena of classical music, because this is besides the point. I disagree with the notion that only western art music is deserving of this kind of study, or that the meta-reality of world music is not as important as western art music and therefore can only be touched upon lightly in the eduction curriculum—if touched at all.

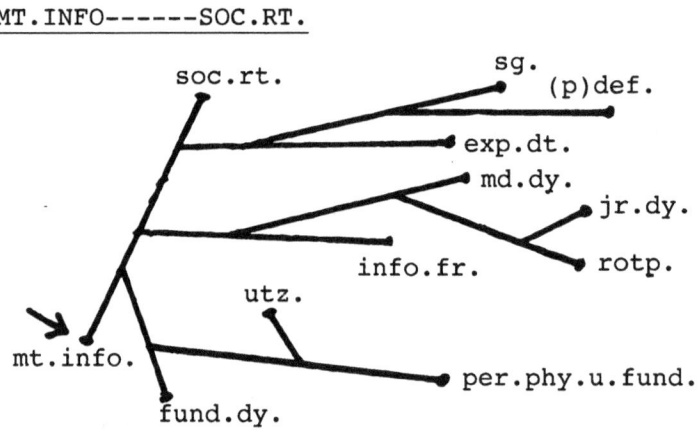

In the mid-sixties, there was an apparent change in the universities' viewpoint with regards to education, and as this time zone progressed one could begin seeing attempts by the controlling forces to alter curriculums. There were many reasons for the changes that took place in this period; for the time zone of the sixties accented the need for relevant education, and the vibrational realness of this period demanded that something be done—rather than simply discussed. In other words, the changes in university functionalism that took place in this period were directly connected to the social-political arena of the sixties. Yet the final determining factor that made universities consider reshaping their curriculums was undoubtedly the realness that college applications were decreasing at a serious rate in that same time zone. It then was not a question of adapting to the needs of the people as much as adjusting to what was necessary in order to survive. Nevertheless, by the end of the sixties many changes had been made in the educational institutions throughout America. It was in this period that many universities began to teach about creative improvised music and the significance of world music as well; and while, for the most part, these attempts towards re-alignment have been applauded by the general public, there are other factors related to this phenomenon that must be looked at if we are to really understand what the teaching of improvised music will mean with regard to source initiation. For while it is most certainly to one's advantage to be exposed to the full gamut of information dynamics, we cannot ignore the realness of the universities' position: as a defining tool that functions in accordance with the controlling forces of western culture, as a source-transfer vehicle that has never dealt with the significance of any creative music that is non-western or not white, and, finally, as a factor that couldn't teach about creative music because in actual fact the university situation has moved so far away from creativity that it is not intellectually or vibrationally equipped to deal with the subject. In other words, all of these factors must be considered if we are to really understand the adaptation of creative music into the established institutions—moreover, all of these factors must be considered if we are to really understand the seriousness of creative music as a primary tool for positive transformation.

My point is that it would be extremely difficult for a person to learn about the significance of creative music through the educational institutions of western culture because of what the relationship between these institutions and the society implies on the most basic level. That is: the western educational system is an affirmation of not only the western affinity-vibrational thrust, but the western political thrust as well. It would be ridiculous to assume that these institutions would undermine the political and vibrational structure that has given them their position. Nor should we assume that these people are necessarily qualified to teach about creative music either, because even this is debatable. I am saying that the relationship between the educational institutions and the defining and controlling forces of western culture is based upon affinity and vibrational agreement—rather than disagreement. Because of what this means, it would be foolish to believe that the university would endorse any move that might be construed as detrimental to the aesthetics and vibrational lining of American (and western) culture. To understand this viewpoint is to really understand the function and position of the educational and intellectual community as a related tool of political controlling forces. For in this context, the most basic function of the educational community is: to expand on western concepts as a means to continue culture; to examine other vibrational flows as a means to utilize source transfer (or gradualism); and, in general, to serve as a Bastille in the intellectual arena for the continuation of western ideas and culture. In short, the realness of creative music can be useful to the defining and controlling factors of western culture only if it can be molded in accordance with the composite western vibrational position—or how Americans (in this case, caucasians) see themselves.

From a geo-political context, the university must be understood as the zone that dictates how source transfer is to be applied to a given non-western information focus. In other words, the university functions as the most sophisticated juncture to re-align how given thrusts are understood. This is then the zone where a given initiation is adopted—understood—or rejected and put down. More so, if a given initiation is understood (on some level), the university can then supply what that initiation will mean in western terms (adaptation). The utilization of a given outside initiation must also necessitate redocumentation and/or gradualism as a means to secure the historical implications underlying what its adoption implies. In short, however a given vibrational thrust is perceived, the university context is the juncture which functions to apply transfer progressionalism. What this phenomenon means when applied to creative music is this: there is no way that the meta-reality of creative music can be understood by the collective forces that dictate culture in the west. For the secrets that surround the vibrational thrust of black music have nothing to do with how information is understood in western terms.

The most basic factor we can understand about the emergence of creative music in America is that the composite forces of this thrust are changing American culture. If this is true, then the position of the university structure is clear: creative music from the black aesthetic has reached the next time cycle for source transfer: that is, the thrust progression of creative music from the black aesthetic is subjected to source transfer every fifteen to twenty years—and the functional arena of the aesthetic is reduced to words—and thus made less effective (at least on the surface).

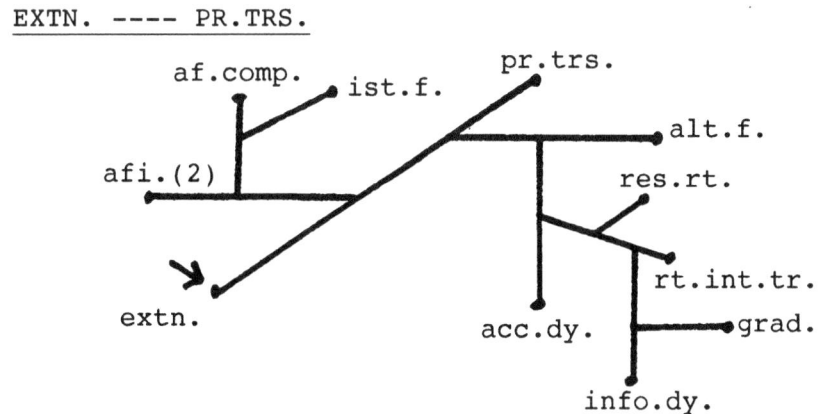

T(IMP)M–12

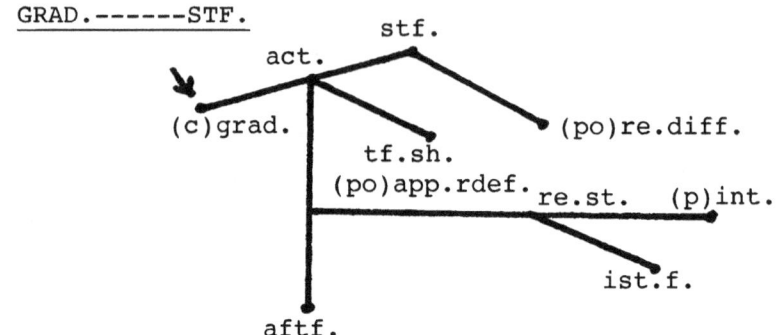

There are several reasons why I am not able to embrace the teaching of creative music by established western institutions. The most basic of these reasons would reflect my belief that there is a natural conflict between how functionalism is perceived in western terms as opposed to world music. In short, the vibrational dynamics underlying western thinking is detrimental to understanding the meta-reality and implications of creative music. Obviously this is so, for not only can we review the historical progressions related to how the source transfer of earlier creative music forms was brought about, but one needs only to look at the present situation creative music is in today to see the realness of this argument. The factors that have kept me from embracing the source-transfer shift of creative music today stem from my disagreement with how process is taught as well as the sensibility surrounding how phenomenon is perceived and interpreted by the established western educational centers. In short, there is a difference between the essence factor that dictates how functionalism is perceived in world creativity and that of western art music. This difference is not reflected in present-day teaching methods, however—and as such, the reality of world creativity (information dynamics) and its encounter with western observation must be looked at very seriously.

As we move into the time zone of the 1980s, the realness of creative functionalism will necessitate many changes with regards to how information perception and transference are practiced. That is, if I am correct and we are moving towards a new world music, then this phenomenon will necessitate many changes in how music is taught. For when I stated that the meta-reality of western affinity dynamics is not designed to comment on the dynamic implications of world music (i.e., improvisation), I am commenting on the position of western educational institutions as we move into the next transition. If this is understood then quite possibly the function of the university has to radically change, for not only is this outlet slowly becoming detrimental to understanding the positive potential of creative music, but the university—as a useful institution of learning—is slowly moving to retard the solidification of relevant interpretations. This is so because the most basic measure we can use to evaluate something must be how effective does that something function to assist/aid positive change. If this is true then the position of the university can no longer go unchallenged, for the past two hundred years have shown very clearly that the western methodological and vibrational thrust progression functions as a negative factor when applied to world music. The seriousness of the present situation in creativity makes it necessary to examine every related aspect that gives insight into the reality dynamics of this subject. We are forced, because of the suppression and distortions surrounding this subject, to ask every possible question concerning the positive and negative potential of a given medium in its relationship to creativity. The effectiveness of a given context will be directly related to how successful that context is in dealing with transformational interpretations. The realness of creative music tomorrow is directly connected to whether or not we are successful in combating the negative forces threatening composite world music in this time period.

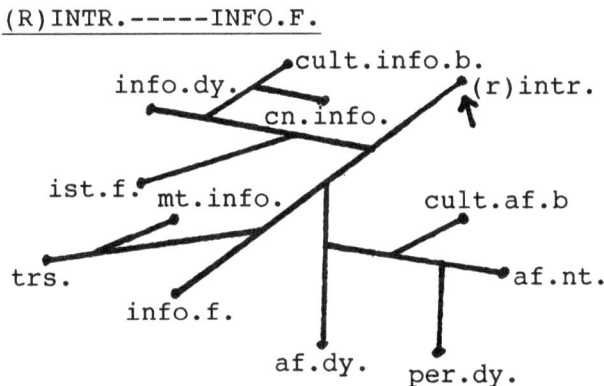

For us to merely assume that the integration of creative music into the university spectrum is a positive step would be not to deal with the historical progressions which surround creative music from the black aesthetic. Yet to simply dismiss this phenomenon is to give no credit to the university experience at all—and this cannot be correct either, because obviously the university experience must have a positive side as well. Certainly in this period the university functions as a juncture that provides insight about many different areas of western art music—especially with regards to process; and it is also a fact that if one hopes to become cognizant of a given creative thrust, this cognizance does imply some understanding of its functional dictates. But my reason for not championing the teaching of creative music in the established western universities has to do with other questions—questions that touch on the nature of what the creative experience is supposed to be about in the truest sense of affirmation, and questions that would explain the nature underlying how source transfer has been utilized in every period of creative improvised music, and why. Because I am saying that in taking a look at the philosophical and vibrational position of the western aesthetic—and looking at the progression of not only the music but the underlying factors that determine how the music was to be understood—it makes sense that the university is ill-prepared to deal with this subject. For the aesthetic that "ised" creative music from the black aesthetic runs counter to the underlying vibrational and philosophical dictates of composite western information dynamics. Which is to say, when the realness of what this difference implies is understood, then the reality of this composite phenomenon will also become clear.

I have already stated that there were earlier attempts to deal with creative music from the black aesthetic by the educational and defining institutions of America. It would be to our advantage if this period is better understood, because there are definite lessons that can be learned about this phenomenon. The fact is: the teaching of creative music through the source-transfer shift of western education has always resulted in a lower appreciation of a given form—both in itself and how it came to be viewed by the public as well. More so, the transfer-shift-cycle phenomenon is directly related to why given functional thrusts (styles) are eventually abandoned, for interpretations from this sector are always used to make the music appear "less" than it is. The end result of applied interpretations is that black musicians usually feel compelled to abandon the form, and to some degree this is understandable. For the realness of a given form is directly related to whether or not that form can function under its own meta-reality sensibility as opposed to outside definitions—it was never a question of any period of creative music not addressing itself to the "actual reality" of a given time zone. The abandonment of different forms of creative music from the black aesthetic is directly related to the nature of how source transfer is utilized in the west. To understand the seriousness of this subject, we are compelled to investigate source-transfer progressionalism. Rudi Blesh and Harriet Janis in their book *They All Played Ragtime* dealt with the incorporation of ragtime into the composite reality of American culture, and their research into this area has helped to clarify what really took place in its related particulars. Their book detailed the social-reality conditions that "ragtime" developed from, and also how composers like Joplin and Chauvin changed the direction of American music. The book also details very clearly the factors that surrounded the emergence of ragtime music as the first popular American music—and this information is directly related to the composite reality dictates of all non-western creativity. For the events that surrounded ragtime music after it became popular are directly related to the particulars underlying how source transfer is practiced in American culture today. The events I am referring to have to do with how the collective forces of western civilization create source transfer through education (i.e., literature redocumentation—gradualism) and political power (i.e., government regulation—force). The emergence of the white ragtime schools can also be looked at as one of the important factors that helped shape the transfer shift of composite ragtime music. For this emergence secured the final platform for applied alternative information dynamics—and documentation (where the total understanding of the functional and vibrational base of the music was made to correspond to the western sensibility). After a period of ten years, we arrive at a music that, removed from its sensibilities, could be talked of as America's first attempt at using a creative form from the

T(IMP)M–16

black aesthetic as a diversion factor. This, of course, is not to say that on an individual level the creative white musician did not contribute to the composite thrust of ragtime music—because many different people have helped establish the realness of this form (as a multi-vibrational thrust that reflected composite dynamics). Instead, the most basic point I have tried to raise about this phenomenon has to do with what takes place when the source-transfer solidification point of a given information line occurs. For the establishment of what we now call the ragtime schools can be viewed as the most basic point of source-transfer solidification—and, as such, this junction is the point we must re-examine if we are to readily understand the spread of ragtime in composite American culture. This is so because the solidification of ragtime as an "understood" form would establish itself as a relevant factor to the affinity-dynamic structure of western progressional continuance (i.e., the emergence of the white stylist and the resulting socio-economic cycle that has come to follow each source-initiated strain of black American creativity). My point is this: the emergence of the ragtime schools and the period we now refer to as the "ragtime period" can be viewed as directly related to the emergence of the first institutionalized efforts to teach black music by established western institutions (and in doing so, this phenomenon also represented the first consolidated efforts to apply source-transfer definitions to a projectional thrust of black creativity) as a basis to create definitions for the "forward thrust" of composite ("perceived") American culture.

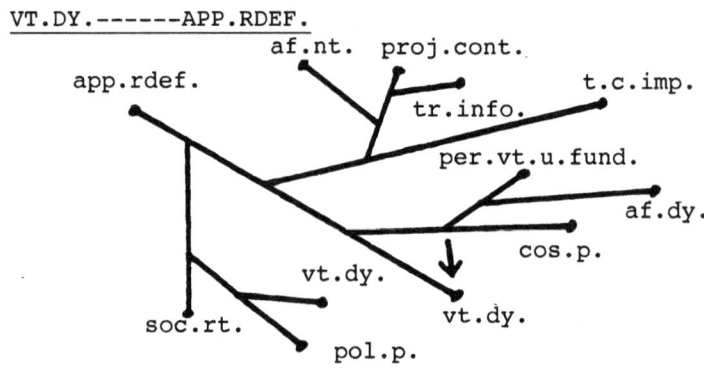

In many cases, the cross-transfer implications of progressionalism (as sanctioned through the source-transfer re-alignment juncture of western education) can be viewed as directly adverse to the source-initiation (primary) intention of the music. This can be understood by examining the dynamics of progressionalism in real terms. For the emergence of the Tin Pan Alley songs as well as the "coon" songs would move to mock the very essence of the music that made it possible (not to mention how these songs viewed black people). The mutation of ragtime and the subsequent developments that changed its progressionalism clearly showed that western culture had no real understanding of the form—and the reality distance surrounding what this phenomenon poses can also be viewed as a constant feature that is related to every projectional extension of black creativity, in its first (and second) encounter with western education. The progressional use of applied definitions would move to even alter the basic documentation and path concerning how ragtime would come to be viewed—and in doing so, this phenomenon moved to distort the essence identity of the music. By the end of the so-called ragtime era, the reality position of the form had been subjected to such a composite assault by the collective forces of western culture and extended "participation," that the real identity and route of the music no longer served the same purpose for its position in progressional continuance (as made real through the particular path that black creative musicians were dealing with at the time). The beauty and seriousness of this form would be pushed aside until much later—for the composite dynamics of the so-called ragtime period would make a mockery out of ragtime—and the realness of this phenomenon can be viewed as a precedent for "things to come."

T(IMP)M–18

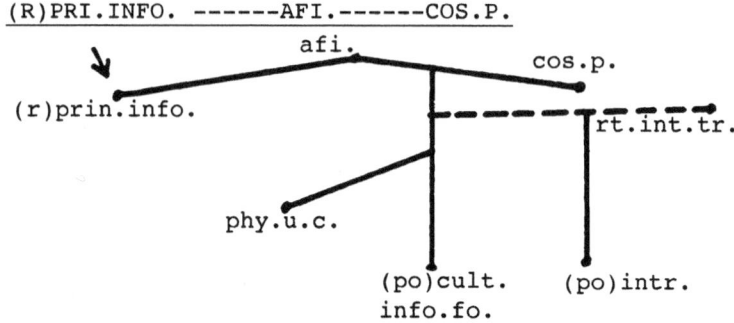

To really understand the reality of ragtime music, it is important to not lose sight of the nature of its path assignment. For the solidification of ragtime is not separate from the composite nature of information continuance. It is important to remember that ragtime was first an improvised music and only much later a notated music. The realness of composers like Joplin and Chauvin must be viewed in the same context that we have come to view all restructuralists—for the thrust of their activity would establish the progressional science of ragtime in "identifying terms"— that is, the essence of their activity would move to establish the realness of alternative functionalism (as this consideration related to black people in that time zone, and as that consideration relates to "the nature and reality position" of perception dynamics). The realness of their activity would comment on the direction of trans-African restructuralism—for basic and future extension—that being: the dynamic options of trans-African restructuralism with respect to (1) information continuance involving improvisational extension, (2) information continuance that utilizes the codification (notation) of its particulars as a basis to participate in alternative functionalism and extended technology, and (3) information continuance that involves the total isolation of methodology (strict notation) as a basis to participate in the source-transfer "natural traffic" of world information (as made real to the affinity-dynamic region that is conducive and/or attracted to—and/or actualized from—that "way of doing" things). It is possible to view every extension of black creative music within this context, for the reality position of a given phenomenon is not separate from the route its information particulars have traveled. We can thus look at the integration of black creative music into America by coming to terms with what a given initiation poses to the composite continuum of western progressionalism and/or vibrational dynamics. The realness of this information will also detail the progressional implications underlying both source-transfer initiations and multi-informational dynamics. For to deal with the emergence of Joplin and Chauvin is to deal with the same progressional phenomenon that would dictate continuance for restructuralists like Henderson or Ellington. Because the dynamic implications of each continuum of creative music would see the solidification of multi-extended functionalism—as this phenomenon relates to the reality position of alternative functionalism (that being the emergence of new information—which of course is not new—as a stimulation factor that accelerates both source transfer and source-motivated intentions, as made real through "doing"). The thrust of all of these composers would move to become part of the composite lining of American-western culture (through adaptation, or source transfer) and later would see their work used to retard the source essence of its "original intentions." For the manipulation of information dynamics, without regard for its affinity housings, has been the most constant factor that all black creativity has had to withstand. Because not only does the source-transfer interpretation of information dynamics in this time zone move to disregard the realness of its attraction (or source generator), but the intensity of this phenomenon is always accomplished by the same degree of socio-economic pressure—the end result being that Paul Whiteman has to be the "King of Jazz" ("or is it swing?"). By the time a given time period has come to an end, the significance of a composer like Duke Ellington is muddied by mis-documentation and gradualism.

Rather than dwelling on the historical dynamics of progressional continuance—as a means to comment about the reality of mis-information surrounding creative music from the black aesthetic—it would be better to view this subject in the backdrop of the sixties. For the dynamics of mis-information (as solidified in our so-called centers of learning) really clarifies the reality context of source initiation (from black creativity) as a consideration that has progressionally never been either understood or accepted in its own right. To view the progressional realness of the music we now call rock, and its relationship to source-transfer definitions, is to confront this same phenomenon in the sixties. For not only is rock now separate from rhythm and blues—in terms of its meta-reality postulations—but in many cases the dynamic potential of this form now functions as a diversion tool for suppressing black creativity. I write this not as a means to simply knock rock music—because this means nothing. The progressional continuum of contemporary rock is really a business consideration that functions solely with respect to the collective forces of western culture. The realness of rock can now be viewed as a separate strain of creativity with its own meta-reality and "reason to be" that moves in accordance with the affinity tendencies of the exclusive western sector, and this same projection also functions as the recipient of its "designations." In other words, when white people refer to the jazz age they are not commenting about the work of musicians like Count Basie but instead Paul Whiteman. By the same token, when the collective forces of western culture decide to document the fifties and sixties as the age of rock we can be sure they will not be writing about Chuck Berry. Every period of black creativity is subjected to this same pattern, and it is important that the realness of this phenomenon is understood. For the realness of this pattern focuses on the dynamic implications of information transference and affinity attachment. All of these considerations are related to the question of education.

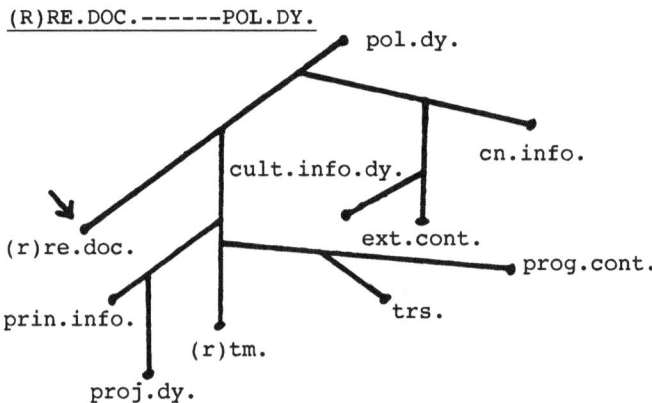

STF. -----PROJ.DY

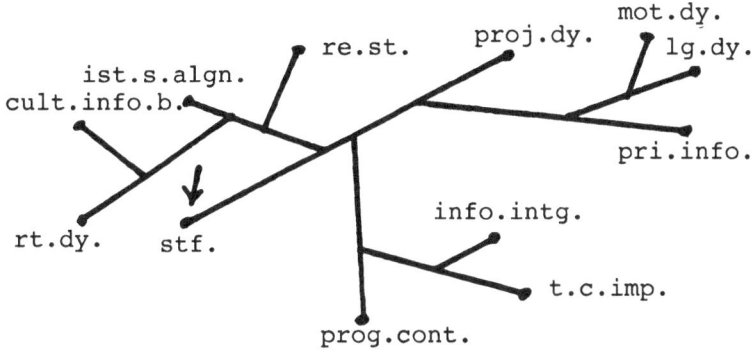

INFO.DOC.-----AFL.DYM. ------T.C.IMP.

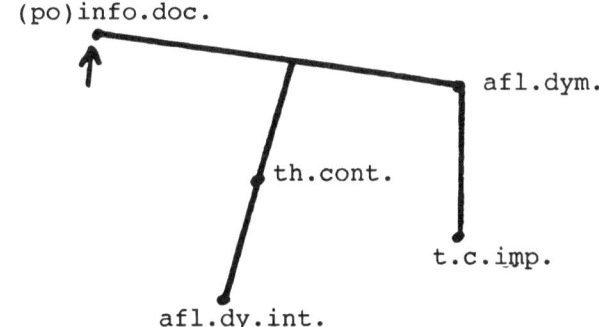

My reason for commenting on the historical progressions of improvised music from the black aesthetic is to give some understanding as to how once a form has been adopted by the controlling forces of western culture, the meta-reality potential of that form usually retards. If my theory is correct, the whole purpose of focusing on world creativity (non-western creativity) in this way is detrimental to what that actual creativity implies on a cosmic level. For although a student might be able to investigate the techniques of a given functionalism, there must be a profound distinction as to what this isolation means with regards to learning about world music as opposed to western art music; yet none of the institutions in the west make this distinction. Moreover, I have not meant to imply that the western university itself is not a useful function; rather, we have to look at what this juncture really implies for the next source-transfer cycle of creative music. For if the time zone of the sixties represented the transfer cycle where improvisation and creative music were integrated into the western educational curriculum, it would be to our advantage to better understand what this integration will mean with regards to the next time cycle of the eighties on to the next century. It is not a question of anyone being against a person participating in the educational system for whatever reasons—not to mention, the current political and social forces dictating culture have left only a few outlets where one can freely research and hopefully grow regardless of direction—it is more a question of understanding how process is perceived in the west. Furthermore, the realness that source transfer is utilized to make creative or world music "less"—while at the same time co-opting the surface aspects of its particulars—is what disturbs me about this phenomenon. We are forced to look at the educative process if the future of composite progressionalism is to be positive. For not only are the techniques of a given reality perception taught, but the composite-vibrational implications that surround that perception are also transferred.

Quite possibly, the essence of what I am saying can better be examined by looking at the curriculum of a given educational institution, especially the music institution. For when I write of the multi-dimensional complications that surround the reality particulars of a given style, I am not simply making up an interesting word—I am referring to something real. The fact is, I have never seen a university in the west attempting to unify the functional and vibrational aspects of a given form as a means to accurately teach about that form—or about the "actual reality" of that form. Instead, the basic policy in most schools is to isolate the functional mechanics of a given form as a means to examine its separate workings. The problems of this approach can become clear if we examine a given particular in actual terms. For instance, the average institution today has several required courses in what is called "ear training." These courses are designed to regulate what a given person should hear when that person hears a sound—especially a so-called musical sound. The basis underlying how the course is constructed has to do with the de-classification of sound into identifiable categories as a basis for both identification as well as musical order. This is so because ear training is related to the defining order that underlines composite western functionalism.

In other words, the resultant twelve-note arrangement that we have come to accept as normal was in fact designed in accordance to the western vibrational and methodological needs. But it is important to understand that however one chooses to deal with the concept of twelve notes representing a composite spectrum zone of western music, in no way does this concept take into account the many other available sounds that most culture groups take for granted. By this I am saying that the concept of twelve notes can be looked at as being limited or not limited when compared to other cultures—but for sure it is different. My point is also that if the concept of twelve notes representing a spectrum slice of the universe is valid for western culture, then, while that is fine (whatever that means), this concept does not necessarily reflect the reality of non-western affinity source pulls. In other words, the utilization of ear training might not have anything to do with what non-western people are hearing, and because of this, this discipline as presently taught could possibly be a negative factor—depending on whether a person liked what he or she was hearing before taking the course. So we arrive at an apparent conflict at the very beginning of attempting to understand even the most basic level of western academicism with regards to music. But we are only scratching the surface of what I am trying to raise. For if the western functional arena has designed a situation which can be fulfilled by a tempered scale of twelve pitches, we must understand that this implies either a lack of affinity with the remaining two hundred or more sounds that exist or that those who have defined these terms must not have a need for those particular sounds (there are probably many other ways to look at this as well, but my point is that because the complete sound spectrum is not used, this non-use does mean something). More so, it is understandable that the collective forces of western culture would seek to make everything correspond to their reality dictates—this is only common sense. But the vibrational particulars which allow for western civilization

T(IMP)M-24

to function as it does are different from that of the world group. In other words, the fact that world music utilized a greater sound spectrum is because that spectrum is necessary if the people of that reality are to be able to express themselves in a "real" way. If this is so—and it is—then it is possible to look at the time juncture that "ised" ragtime music, and better understand how source transfer functioned as a negative factor to the actual "meta-reality" of the music. For in this most noble context, we can ask, "How were the collective forces of western culture to know that their tampering with ragtime music would result in distorting the form?"—because many of the vibrational and cosmic consequences of ragtime were totally outside of their ability to comprehend (in other words, if the functional properties that outline how given creative thrusts are to be actualized are a necessary factor that relates to the vibrational and cosmic realness of that form, then this necessity must mean something—that is, the functional properties of a given functional creative thrust are as they are because they mean something).

MTH.------TR.

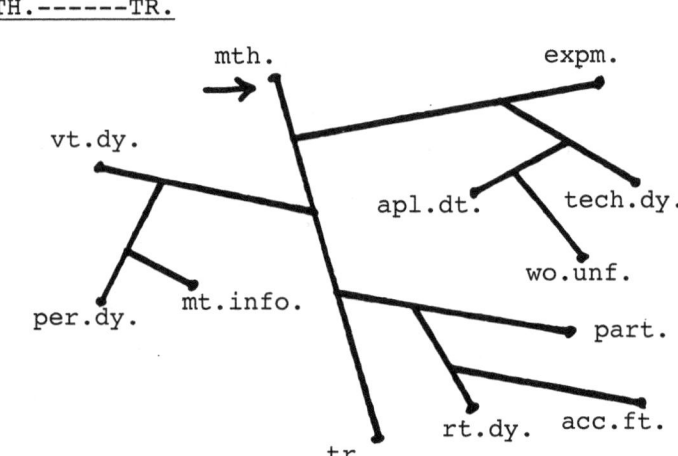

(R)SCI.DY.------AFI.

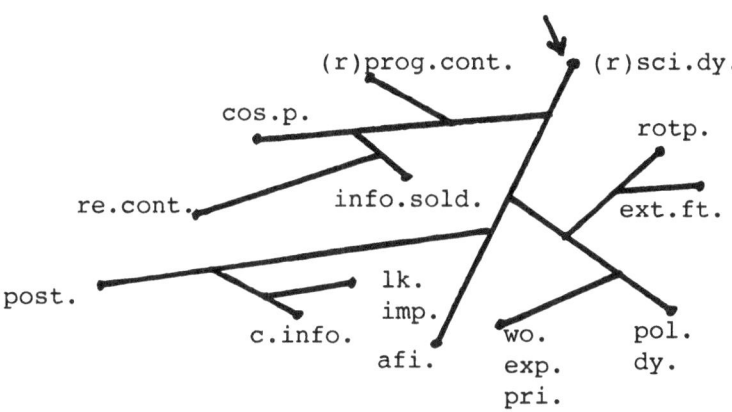

But this is not the only factor that comes into play when one considers the reality that surrounds the discipline and concept of ear training. For if there is an apparent discrepancy between the sound arena affinity grasp of western art music and world music with regards to sound material, then the basis of what this discrepancy really implies must be touched upon. In other words, I am not just referring to how a given culture relates to a particular sound or choice of sounds. My point is that the basis from which any culture derives its affinity relationship to a phenomenon has to do with the cosmic vibrational context underlying what that given phenomenon really represents. In other words, it is not a question of whether any given sound spectrum is more advanced than another, but rather, does that sound spectrum fit the vibrational and emotional needs of the culture group which utilizes it. More so, the factors which determine what all of this will mean on a physical universe and vibrational level are cosmic by nature. In other words, the science of a given form is directly related to the cosmic and spiritual considerations that determine how given cultures are to flow. On a physical universe level, this simply means that a given person might not necessarily hear the same sound in the way another person might hear it. Because what we call sound is about "something else" (another way of saying this would be: the consideration we call sound is only one small manifestation of what is "actually" happening

T(IMP)M-26

when something is heard—or experienced—especially in the creative context). In short, the realness of "vibrational alignment" is a factor that is not taken into account when most people take ear training, but this phenomenon is still present.

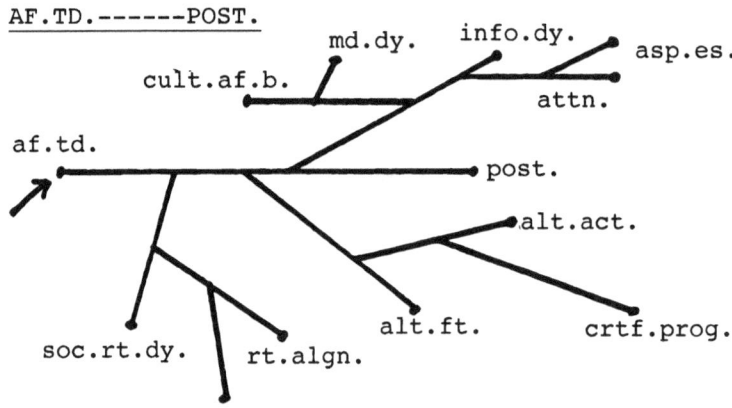

It is possible that many will find my emphasis on ear training to be somewhat out of context, and this is understandable. Yet I have no choice but to continue this path if I am to make my point clear. For at the base of my argument is the realness that all of us at some point have come to simply not challenge the existing reality of education, and instead simply accept the present reality as something that must be meaningful because it exists. I have not meant to imply that any particular course in the music institutions is not meaningful, but I do believe if we are to understand the potential of what is implied in creative music—and if we are to understand the seriousness of this subject—then we are forced to look at the situation creative music is now in and understand how it developed. I believe that the teaching of creative music is directly related to the factors that have helped obscure the realness of non-western creativity. This is so because western educational centers are designed to transfer concepts in accordance with the western sensibility, which is fine in itself—but without adjustments, this sensibility can be detrimental to understanding non-western methodological and vibrational focuses. If this is true, then it is possible to look at the university as the most dangerous distortion juncture for people interested in alternative creativity—as "ised" from the world music consideration and/or perspective. We can no longer afford not to focus on what this really means. Because if the time zone of the sixties is indicative of the shift now taking place in western culture, then it would be to one's advantage to better understand what this phenomenon will mean in both practical and vibrational terms.

My point is this: When the average person goes to a class on ear training, the understanding behind this move has to do with the concept of developing one's ear. One is then taught to recognize and relate to certain intervallic relationships between sounds as they are perceived in the western position. Not only is this function divorced from the "all-cosmic" consideration of sound, but the vibrational consequences of this function (i.e., isolated inquiry) are also taught. This explains why the higher a person goes in the educational system, the harder it is for that individual to relate to "source initiation" of non-western creative thrusts. Obviously there is something to this for, why is it that the higher a creative musician from the black aesthetic goes into the western educational hierarchy, the harder it becomes for that musician to perceive of creative black music in a different sense than western art music. This is not only true for the progressions surrounding ear training—for I have only used this course as an example—but instead, the peculiar orientation surrounding how creativity is taught is consistent with the entire educational process of the western sensibility; including harmony and rhythm. In short, the university functions as the most sophisticated factor for initiating "source-transfer." To understand this is to understand the role and actual significance of the science underlying a given vibrational thrust. For to accept and believe in creativity as taught in the west is to, in fact, accept and embrace the western vibrational and philosophic arena that allowed these perceptions to develop. The science of a given creative thrust affirms the cosmic factors underlying what that thrust addresses itself to—or from.

T(IMP)M-28

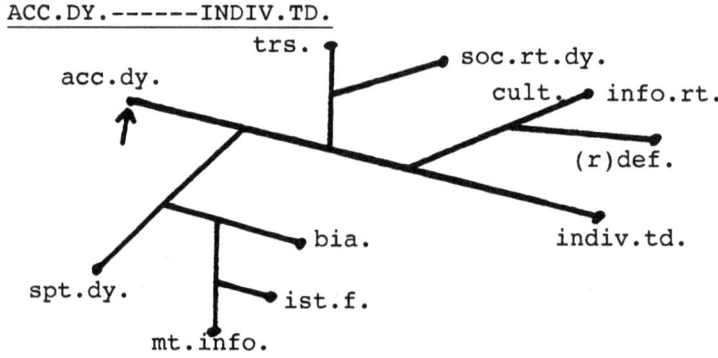

It would be to our advantage if the cosmic implications of a given teaching process agree with the source pull of where we are trying to go—or where we have come from. When we deal with creativity through sound (music)—it is the area of sound vibrations that we are really dealing with. The nature underlying how a given affinity alignment is understood has to do with what significance we attach to our own values, rather than institutionalized values. We must understand that in the music of Africa, for example—as opposed to America—the consideration governing how sound is perceived is of a completely different nature. When I stated that a person must decide on whether or not he/she likes what they are hearing—I mean precisely that. Because the actual fact I am dealing with in this context is: how can a person not hear correctly? And if a person can hear incorrectly, what is it that he's hearing? More so—what is there for us to hear? I realize that many of my concepts concerning this subject might sound different but, in actual fact, isn't the present situation we are in concerning creativity somewhat unbalanced? Unless some effort is made to re-evaluate what the teaching of creative music should really mean, nothing will change, and black people in America will continue to be subjected to the whims of the western defining and controlling alignment. We have no choice but to challenge these forces—and we must do it in this time zone, not in the next ten to twenty years.

ATTN.------AFI.

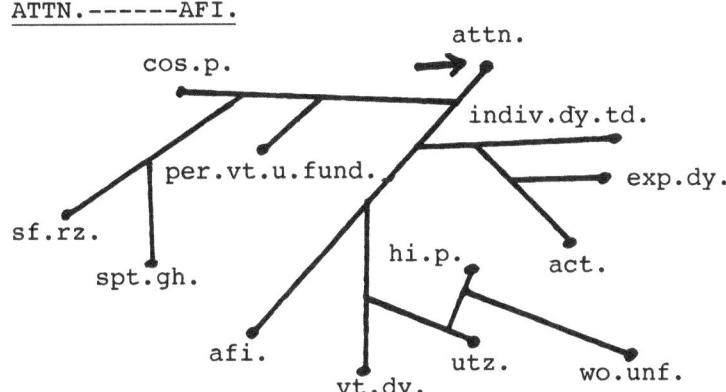

RC.------TR.DEF.

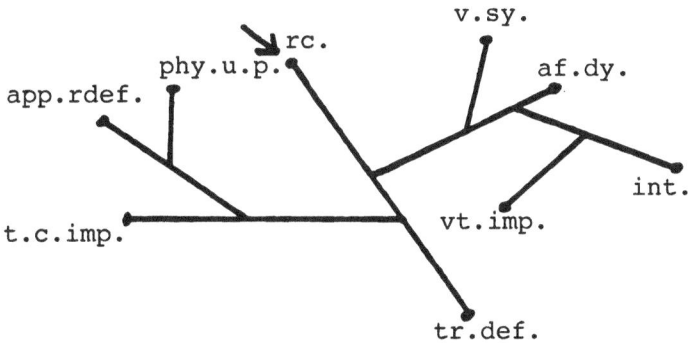

PROG.CONT.------SPT.DY.

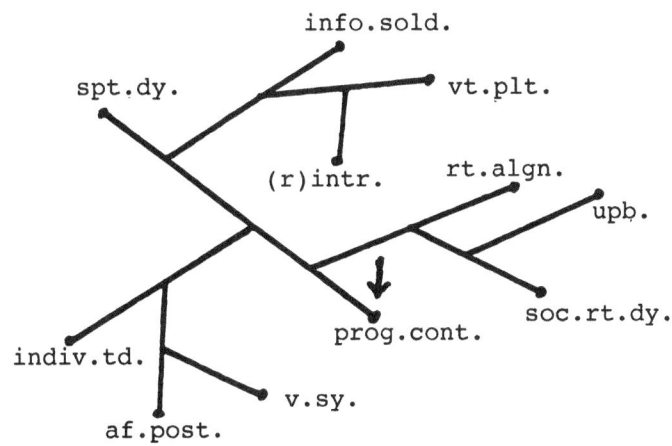

T(IMP)M–30

The factors I have chosen to comment on represent only a small example of how the western educational community has chosen to deal with teaching creative music. Yet I have not expressed my opinion about this subject with the intent of negating any area of western art music, nor have I purposely meant to negatively comment on how western caucasians have chosen to teach their own aesthetic. Certainty I understand that however one chooses to deal with western art music—or any creative thrust for that matter—it is clear that the reality of a form is directly in accordance with the physical and vibrational realness of its cultural dictates. In the final analysis, it is irrelevant whether one agrees or not with how western art music is taught—because this is simply the situation we are now faced with (and for the people who agree with these teaching methods—it is real). My reasons for focusing on the reality of the teaching situation has to do with the realness of what this methodological approach means when applied to creative music from the black aesthetic. I am interested in the total reality of this phenomenon—that being, how creative music is taught in America and the relationship of these teachings to the meta-reality of the music.

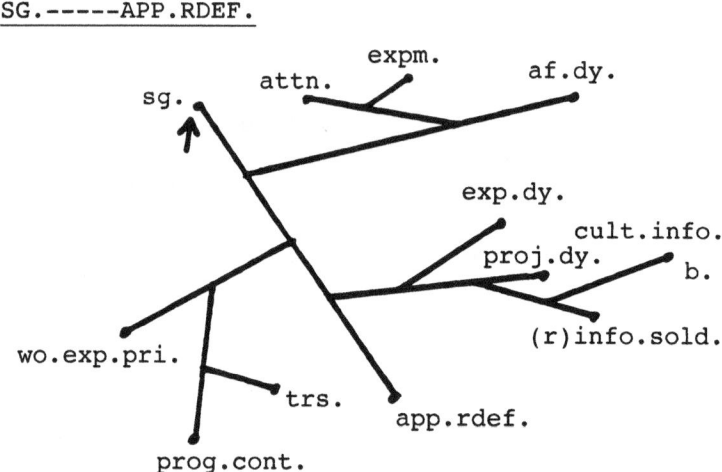

The progressional development of western art music shows us how western culture has chosen to deal with the significance underlying structural developments. Each period in the progression of western art music has to do with how the consideration of process was understood in relationship to a given functional aspect of the music—whether that understanding applied to the harmonic or rhythm aspect of form. I have written about the underlying philosophical basis that determines how the music itself is seen by the defining forces of western culture, and I have also written about the problems this approach (viewpoint) poses in understanding the meta-reality of its creativity by the greater public—or people in the culture. When I wrote that the universities today are no more than source-transfer centers that negatively function for the disruption of world creativity—I am saying that the university represents the zone where through source transfer the same factors that solidified western art music as a separate reality from world music (and later led to the dissemination of the aesthetic as a composite spiritual and meaningful music that had the potential to help the culture) are now being applied to creative music from the black aesthetic. In other words, the vibrational and functional forces that moved to de-stabilize the center factor of western art music are now focusing on creative music from the black aesthetic. Unless these forces are understood and checked, the situation in creative music will mirror that of western art music. More so, the meta-implications of creative music will also be affected by this same phenomenon (source transfer) because, in this context, the essence factor of the music will be without actual purpose but, instead, intellectually stimulating. The implications of source-transfer progressionalism also implies that black people will be affected on another level as well. For if the reality of black people in this period is constantly controlled on a political and social level already, the total co-opting of black creativity through source transfer would be the final step towards controlling the vibrational-affinity-creative thrust of black American culture (i.e., the actual situation of black people in America). The co-opting of black creativity would imply that the vibrational realness of black music through source transfer will be redirected and used in accordance with the thrust alignment of western culture. Thus, rather

T(IMP)M–32

than the vibrational realness of creative music reflecting the reality of black people, the use of this phenomenon will serve as a factor for aligning the functional arena of black creativity (regardless of period) under the American umbrella (and in this position, the black vibrational thrust will be inoperative). The net effect of this phenomenon will be a retardation of the sensibilities which allowed creative black music in America to be "ised," as well as the implications of what that retardation implies.

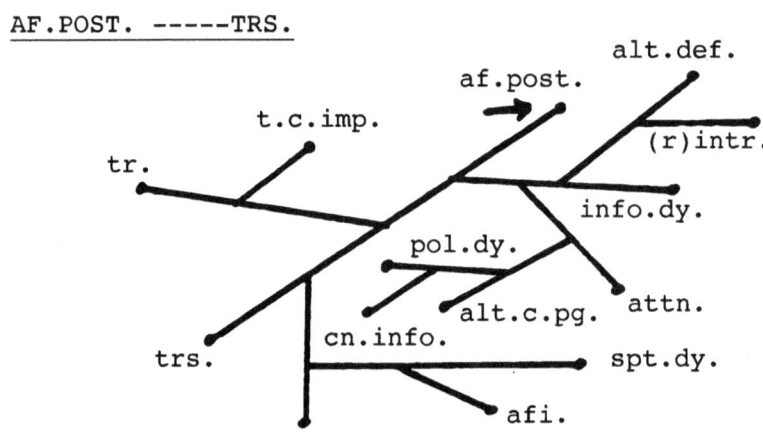

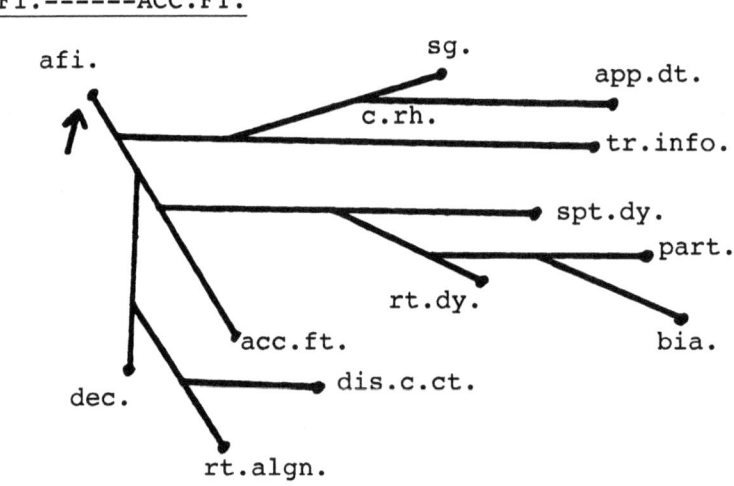

T(IMP)M–33

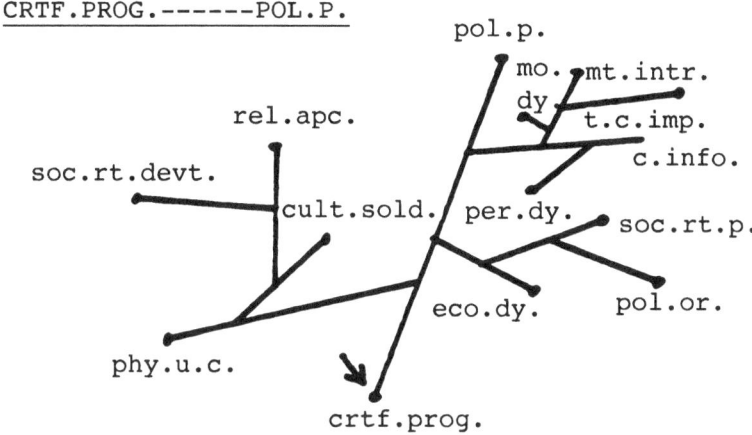

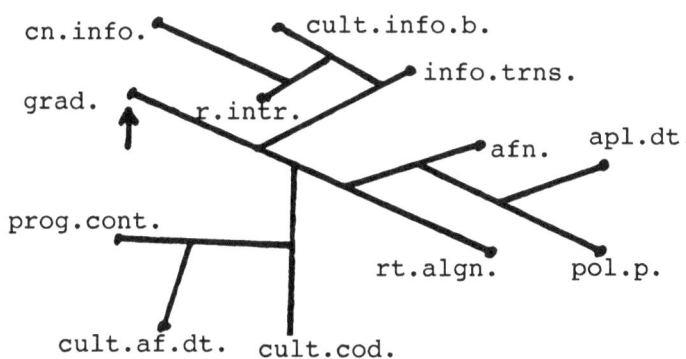

When I wrote that I am not impressed by the interest in creative music by the university composite defining structure, I am only commenting on what this interest really means. My point is that in the past ten years, we have been moved to the era where the functional arena of creative music has become fixed and "ised" by the defining forces of western culture, and we are now led to believe that these processes are understood to the degree that it can be taught in the classroom. This simply is not true. Instead, what seems to actually be happening in this time zone is that improvised music has now been fixed "in a formulated phrase" to the degree that western words can be applied to its functionalism. Given structural particulars from the different time zones of creative music are now supposedly understood by the western establishment, so that its science can be spoken of in the same way one talks of process in the western sensibility. What this implies is that improvised music from the black aesthetic has now moved to the position where it can no longer be separated from the mainstream of American or western music (or at least this is what the controlling forces would have us believe). Yet to imply there are no connections between creative black music and American culture would also be ridiculous. Because at some point creative black music must be looked at as a factor that has contributed to the meta-reality of American culture by nature of its position in America, and also by the fact that the music was "ised" in America. But the essence implications of creative black music have not at any point had the same relationship to these factors as western art music. What we see in the seventies is a gradual shift in the perception dynamics of creative music (and also a gradual shift in the interpretations underlying what creative black music implies for source-shift progressionalism).

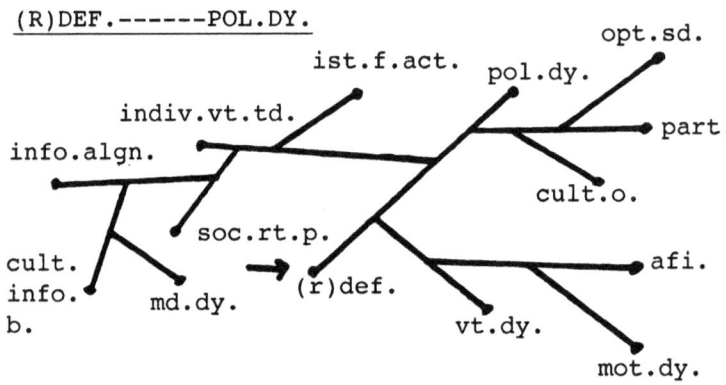

What this phenomenon means on a planet level is clear, for the source-transfer-continuum phenomenon moves as a factor to co-opt how given aspects of the music are to be understood in its "actual" sense. It is in this juncture where the functional arena of a given creative form is both adopted and reversed. This can be best explained by looking at the realness of the post-Webern post-existential period in western culture. For the most basic factor that determined the realness of a given creative thrust in this context had to do with how intellectually interesting that thrust would be if pursued. It was during this cycle when, because of the collapse in the composite spiritual arena of western civilization, the potential of "absolute" systems was thought to be attractive as a substitute basis for creative participation. The basic understanding that emerged in the post-Webern thrust was that the outward appearance of a given mathematical (or empirical) thrust—if extended—was sufficient enough to be talked of as "new." But this newness was always looked at as a separate factor from the composite spiritual realness that necessitated the actual research. In the 1900s, as the center of western art music began to crumble, we suddenly find a whole new wave of theorists. It was in this cycle where theorists like Schillinger brought forth new systems for substantiating the vibrational and cosmic reality of the western methodological thrust alignment. In short, however one chooses to understand this time zone in western art music, there can be no doubt that the reality of western art music allows for this sensibility to happen—that is: the composite realness of western culture has established a particular alignment to empiricism that is directly in accord with how it flows (as a culture—group—or as a people). And while it is possible to look at the developments in western art music as a basis for understanding how European and/or Euro-Americans related to functionalism (or the realness of what a form implies—to them)—it is also important to understand that those perceptions might not necessarily have anything to do with black creativity (and what black creativity means for black people). More so, it is also possible that this methodological and affinity alignment serves as a factor to distort the "actualness" of creative music from the black aesthetic. This has been my point for the whole of this section of the book.

It is important that the reader not misconstrue my thoughts about this phenomenon, for by attempting to clarify the dynamic implications of source initiation—as it pertains to black creativity and progressional continuance—I have not meant to disrespect the reality position of source transfer. Certainly the reality of interpretations for source-transfer initiation can be viewed as necessary to the whole of composite functionalism—and reunification. And certainly I have not meant to imply that interpretations from the collective forces of western interpretations have no validity—or are without positive implications—because every area of information continuance has both positive and negative implications. But if we are to really view the dynamic implications of black creativity, and if we are to really understand what has happened to source-initiation interpretation, then there can be no denying the nature of what factors have provided the revolving base that now threatens to distort world creativity. My point is that not only is the progressional realness of black creativity undergoing a serious challenge as to what its reality nature really means, but the dynamics of this attack move to challenge the composite meta-reality significance of world information and alternative functionalism. This is what interests me, and this is why the consideration of education cannot be taken lightly. For the reality attachment of a given definition must necessarily come through this juncture, and the truth is that very few interpretations are able to survive the collective dynamics of western scrutiny—especially if the "truth" of a given information line has nothing to do with western idea formations. The seriousness of this phenomenon is manifested throughout the composite range of information transference—having to do not only with creativity but extending to every area of necessary communication. As such, we have no choice but to come to terms with the position and reality of "western education" as a means to begin the process of reclarifying "that which must be understood" if we, as a collective people, are to survive. The challenge of coming to terms with the realness of western education is this and nothing less.

T(IMP)M–37

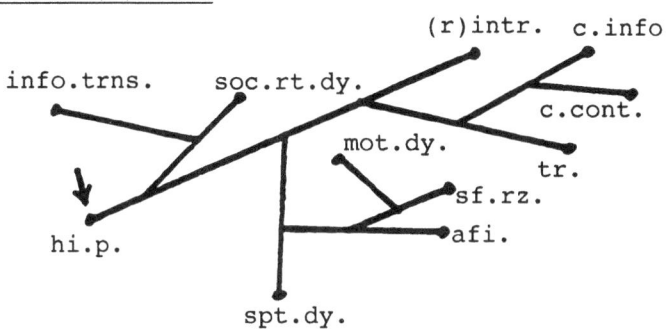

Certainly the realness of dynamic mis-definitions through western education does indeed move to affect the reality position of source-transfer information continuance, and as such it is important that the particulars of this effect are discussed. For the realness of source-transfer definitions must be viewed in the total context of information continuance—and also for what it means in the total context of social reality. On its own, the re-aligned information from the western sector does not pose a problem in the "normal context of things," for the composite history of this planet has always seen multi-level information exchange. But the dynamic position of western culture in this time zone does not lend itself to the "natural" transference of information, but instead moves to control the reality of composite interpretations. As such, in the final analysis, we are left with only those areas of interpretation that western culture does not see as threatening to the whole of its "order" (or survival). Herein, then, lies the heart of my argument, because the most basic thrust of alternative functionalism transcends the particulars of a "given state of being," but instead moves in accordance to the dictates of cosmic considerations (and real laws). What this means is that there is no way that a given multi-information alignment could not threaten some aspect of western life, because the realness of life in this period seems to clearly show the over-balanced dominance of western culture—as a negative factor for positive continuance. As such, the regulation of western information lines must be viewed as a factor that doesn't necessarily correspond to the concept of the "happy planet." In other words, the sophisticated regulation of information in this time period must be viewed as only serving the interest of western extension and dominance—but this is only the beginning. For the implications of a given information line are not limited to whether or not it is suppressed, but instead "what it poses with respect to what is." In other words, the end result of present-day information confusion has to do with the dynamic retardation of alternative functionalism—as it relates to understanding the essence of a given information route and as it relates to "doing"—that being, working to bring about change. All of these considerations must be looked at if we are to understand the reality of information and the position of what we now call education.

The net effect of cross-transfer definitions, as the only source of learning, has to do with the nature of vibrational continuance in this time period. This is so because the real reality of western education in this period has to do with re-aligning how a given function "is" to have it correspond with the "affinity attitude and alignment" of composite western culture. The end result of this phenomenon is the stagnation and eventual dissolution of alternative affinity tendencies by the world group—or by non-white people. The realness of this phenomenon is very serious for what it implies about the future. For the actualness of this phenomenon moves to narrow the spectrum underlying how a given line of information is viewed—and as such, vibrated to (or functioned from). This is exactly what is happening in progressional continuance—as this concept applies to black creative music (and its related information) in its encounter with the collective forces of western culture—and the reality position of the university is directly connected to how this phenomenon works.

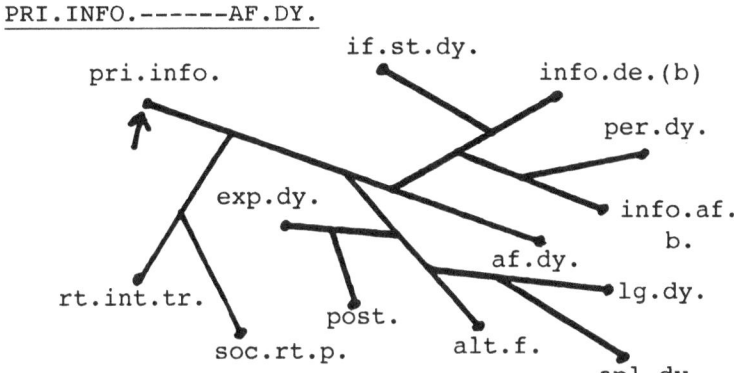

To really understand the seriousness of cross-transfer manipulation is to begin to view the realness of "applied definitions"—that being, what a given definition used to mean in its source-initiation context, and what the same definition means after its adoption into the throngs of western dynamics. For every aspect of black methodology has had to necessarily be re-aligned to become real to western functionalism—and the realness of these changes should not be viewed lightly. Where the consideration of "swing" had to do with the individual ability to tap his or her affinity-insight-principle dynamics (in accordance to the language dynamics of the form utilized) in the beginning, this same consideration would later be used to make everyone play "correctly" (e.g., play Charlie Parker or John Coltrane licks in the same places the masters themselves utilized them). Where the reality dynamics of the blues in the beginning had to do with mystical and vibrational information that could be transmitted through the use of certain areas of functionalism—having not to do with a sequence of notes as such, but instead evolving the real ability to "make a certain thing happen"—later this same consideration would be taught in classrooms—where the new understanding would involve playing the "right seventh" (with those hip "blues notes, man!")—and this is supposed to now be the blues! When, in the beginning, the reality of a given form had to do with how much that form could contain until it revealed the next level of investigation (with the understanding being that every projection derived significance through its ability to advance the necessary information related to alternative functionalism—e.g., the re-establishment of world culture, the end of non-white suppression, the solidification of real spiritualism, and the removal of affinity shackles on women)—now those same forms are perceived as isolated pockets of "fun time"; having to do with "have a good day!" The changes that have been forced upon the composite identity of creative music from the black aesthetic should not be lightly viewed. For the realness of source-transfer interpretations has altered the total reality of this phenomenon, and in doing so, has also moved to profoundly affect black culture.

Nor have the affinity-dynamic re-interpretations of the western sector been limited only to the reality realness of creative music from the black aesthetic. Rather, the nature of western functionalism has moved to penetrate the composite "state" of alternative pedagogy. In other words, every aspect of alternative functionalism has undergone scrutiny at the hands of western analysis—and the conclusions from the scrutiny have been utilized to push black creativity even farther from its path nature. For instance, the reality of harmony in black creativity has now come to be viewed in the same spirit as western art music—and as such, these mis-conceptions have moved to totally alter the base of the music. In the final analysis, the collective forces of western definitions have transported the reality of black creativity to the reality position of composite western culture—where the affinity-dynamic interpretations of the western community rule supreme. The net effect of this move has made more changes in the "vibrational lining" of black creativity than many people would care to believe. This is not to say that nothing positive is related to western culture, nor by commenting on the reality of "present events" have I meant to under-value the path of western continuance; rather, if we are to really view alternative functionalism and the role of education, then it is important that this area of information is discussed. For the manipulation surrounding alternative information poses several different real problems—concerning the cosmic destiny of a given initiation, as well as the social-reality implications of source-transfer interpretations.

It is important to understand that the information reality each successive generation of young people receives is directly related to how that generation will function. The fact that alternative definition outlets are on the decline while source-transfer definitions are assuming greater and greater significance is something that cannot be simply dismissed. In other words, very few young people have any other source of reference to properly balance the information slant now received in school, and in the case of non-white students, this problem assumes even greater proportions. Unless something is done to correct the reality of information in this time period, there is the real possibility of applied definitions becoming the only information position for the composite culture—and this would be a tragedy. Already it is possible to see serious changes taking place in the composite reality of creative progressionalism—as it relates especially to young people. Every day, the sophistication of western definitions assumes greater strength—moving to shape both the creativity of this cycle and its related continuum of alternative ideas. As such, the idea of "jazz" was greatly changed, the idea of "life's work" (intention) has undergone profound changes, and the meta-implications of extended functionalism have moved to either distortion—or worse, irrelevance. The realness of these changes is important, and does mean something.

The dynamic implications of western interpretation—and its effect on composite information continuance—can be understood by examining the recent inclusion of so-called jazz in the established university curriculum. For the emergence of institutions like the Berklee College of Music and North Texas State University are indicative of the next cycle of information transference. If we are to really understand the reality position of creative music, then it is important that some attempt is made to deal with schools of this type—for if I am correct, we are only at the beginning of this phenomenon. The realness of the last fifteen years has seen the first wave of musicians from these institutions—which is to say, the dynamic implications of a school like Berklee transcend the confines of its campus. Instead, the reality of information transference in these institutions today will be the definitions shaping the continuance of the composite culture tomorrow.

There are many things to be said about schools like Berklee and North Texas State, for the thrust of these institutions will underline the seeds of alternative pedagogy for the next cycle. This is especially true if the real objective for dynamic information exposure is to become a reality for western education—for the future of alternative education cannot be directed only towards western art music or creative improvising music, but must instead involve learning about composite world music. As such, the fact that these institutions exist at all must be viewed as a giant step forward for music education—and I have no doubt that their influence will be beneficial to the composite dynamics of information transference. It is now possible for the developing student to take real courses in extended harmony—for improvisation and/or strict composition—on a level not possible twenty years ago. The dynamics of many of these new institutions extends into every area of creative functionalism—and in doing so, moves to complete the new creative musician on a variety of levels—even the art of music copying is now taught at some of these new schools, as well as the reality of music business. To simply not recognize the incredible gains that are slowly changing music education in this time zone would be criminal—which is to say, no matter how one feels about the composite state of western information transference, there can be no doubt that some very valuable changes have emerged. This is not to say that every aspect of "new education" is positive—because it isn't; but compared to the reality position of information dynamics even twenty years ago, education has come a long way. Certainly there is still a long way to go—for the reality perspective of all western centers of learning only moves to transfer the affinity-dynamic interpretations relevant to western dynamics exclusively, and this is a serious problem. Because the whole of this section has underlined the significance of multi-information and composite affinity dynamics. The fact is, "nothing is" in only one or two given states or "persuasions." If we are to really properly transit information in the next cycle (that is, transmit transformational information), then it is important that the affinity implications of transference are observed. This is not to say that any particular interpretations are necessarily right or wrong, but rather the dynamics of a given transference are directly related to what option students will have with respect to either how an idea is to be understood ("what part" of that person will have to be utilized to "make real" a given area of information) or how that idea is to practiced. The reality of alternative education must be viewed with all of these considerations in mind, for the business of "education" is one of the most important responsibilities of any culture (or group that wants to be a culture).

In the final analysis, it is always easier to criticize a given subject than to actually participate in shaping a phenomenon—as "you see it." Certainly my assessment of education in this time period has tried to accent the many areas of disagreement I have long had with western information transference—yet it is important to restate my admiration for the men and women who have taken the challenge of this most serious profession—that being, teaching. Obviously there will always be disagreements about the nature of a given interpretation, but it is important to learn as much as possible (regardless of focus or alignment). Anyone who really believes that the challenge of teaching is an easy job should spend one day in the life of a teacher. For myself, even with the many levels of disagreements I have concerning present-day information transference, I remain deeply grateful for the reality of education. There can be no doubt that the dynamic implication of "real" education can change the world; the only problem is that, without composite affinity transference, that change might not necessarily be for the better. As such, the challenge of positive education is too important to not be concerned, for the realness of this subject has no boundaries.

(Level Two)

IF WE ARE TO EVER VIEW CREATIVITY with respect to its world implications, then we must first understand what has happened in this time cycle—and this is particularly true if we desire some understanding of the definitions and redefinitions that have solidified this time period. For the social reality that surrounds creativity is not separate from the multi-definitions that dictate how a phenomenon is to be understood—either regionally or on a planet level. As such, the realness of music journalism, and in particular jazz criticism, must be viewed for its role in helping to establish the present reality position of creative music. This is not to say only one sector of the society is responsible for the composite reality of creative music, nor have I meant to imply that music journalism in itself in necessarily negative—rather, the nature underlying how information is viewed directly affects its perception dictates (and its ability to be effective). To view the realness of music journalism is to deal with one of the most basic defining sources of western culture—whose activity directly moves to shape the total reality perception of a given creative projection. As such, the actualness of creative music must be examined with respect to the many interpretations which have been handed down from the western critical and defining community—regardless of form and regardless of time period. All of our viewpoints about creative music—whether we are discussing Louis Armstrong or Albert Ayler—have been subjected to both music journalism and criticism, and all of these interpretations have affected our relationship with this subject. Which is to say, the progressional use of applied definitions should not be viewed in isolated terms—having little or no effect on the composite culture—instead, this phenomenon must be recognized as profoundly instrumental in determining both the life (effectiveness) of a given projection and what "vibrational attitude" will be brought to it by the public. Because of this, the reality of applied definitions must be understood as important—too important, in fact, to not be dealt with. For not only have controlled interpretations determined our relationships with all of the forms we have had exposure to, but this phenomenon will also play an important role in the future. Unless some effort is made to deal with the reality of applied definitions—and what has resulted from its use—the future promises to see this phenomenon increase to new levels. This essay will attempt to understand what underlying factors have been incorporated by music journalism as a means to be effective—and why, and also how, those factors are utilized in actual criticism and/or journalism. I write this with the understanding that something is not right in present-day music journalism, and, moreover, "something is not right and designed to be so."

Without doubt, the most basic factor that dictates the reality of western interpretations is the nature underlying how world methodology has come to be viewed. It is here where one can best begin understanding what has and is happening in music journalism. **For the collected writing that surrounds the music—regardless of period—has never really taken the "vibrational reality" (and implications) of the music into account on its own terms (or own definitions). Rather, the history of music journalism can be viewed as the history of both applied redefinitions and source-transfer interpretations.** It is important that this viewpoint is understood. This is not to say the reality of redefinitions and source-transfer interpretations have no relevance whatever the context—because everything has relevance when used properly. Instead, the nature dictating how these considerations (redefinitions and source transfer) have been practiced is what concerns this essay.

To view the reality of applied definitions in creative music is to become aware of the real dilemma underlying journalism in this period. For the critical analysis that surrounds the music was not designed for the reality of world art dynamics. Nine-tenths of the definitions we are dealing with in this cycle were designed to comment on the reality of western art functionalism—as it was actualized for western society exclusively. In other words, the solidification of western journalism really had to do with interpreting the accelerated dynamics of both western methodology and extension with respect to the particulars of western affinity dynamics. As such, the nature of an applied information focus in this context involved commentary about the scientific and execution dynamics of a given particular. In doing so, western journalism was actualized to provide a valuable function. But we are now light-years away from the factors that necessitated this type of discipline—or at least the reality of this discipline in its formative stages—and the dynamics of creative music have greatly changed, even if music journalism hasn't. This is not to say there is no scientific basis from which to view a given form, nor have I meant to imply that given extensions cannot be commented on from either an executional or methodological basis. But the most basic factor that has determined the realness of world creativity is not its methodological diversity but rather its "vibrational reality." As such, any attempt to comment accurately on a given creative projection in world creativity would imply some real understanding of the affinity nature of that projection. Moreover, I am not only commenting on the superficial history of a given projection, but instead the reality of affinity dynamics as it applies to the specifics of a form. As such, the "truth" of a given methodology in world culture has not only to do with the empirical handling of its science but also must include (and respect) its vibrational attitude as well. By introducing this viewpoint as a necessary criterion for commentary, I have not meant to place an unfair prerequisite on music scholars either, because obviously a person can only write about what is "real" within one's own vibrational parameter. But it is just this "natural limitation" that we must look at. For the basis of my viewpoint is that the reality of world creative music can never be understood unless its affinity nature is included in any critique—and I do not mean this in light terms.

PR.S(RD)II–4

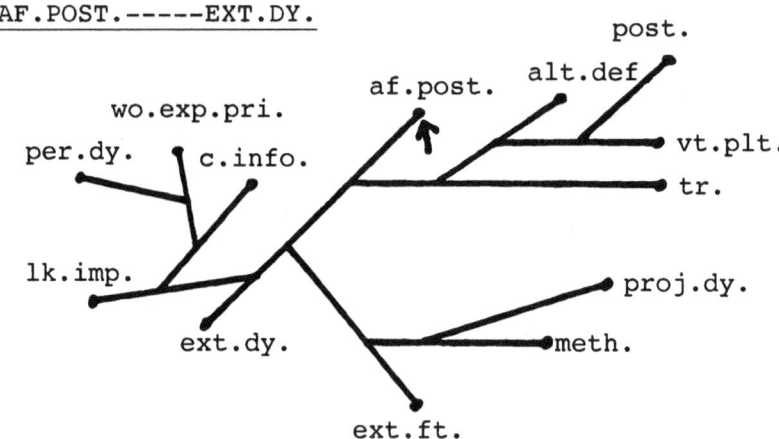

Certainly every article I have ever read about so-called jazz does include a surface acknowledgment of its reality. And, of course, everyone has written on how the music has come down the Mississippi, or jam sessions (with the commentary describing the fact that some individuals "really blew well that night"). But this is not what I meant when I stated that a given commentary must respect the affinity basis of the music. Because ninety-nine percent of the articles written on black creativity, in the final analysis, all move to evaluate the standard of excellence of that performance outside of its "real" informational and methodological reality. That being, the real reality underlying how a given participation is made "real." Instead, we are only given commentary that respects the reality and affinity alignment of what has been declared as "significant" for a selected affinity community. To understand the reality of transformational journalism is to focus on how this phenomenon has come about—and what it means.

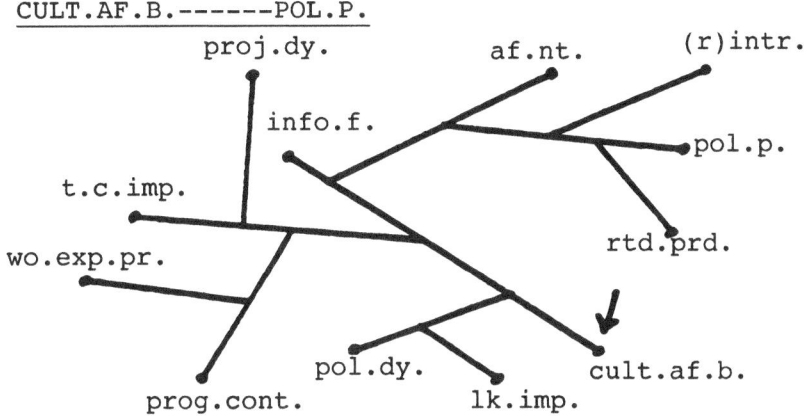

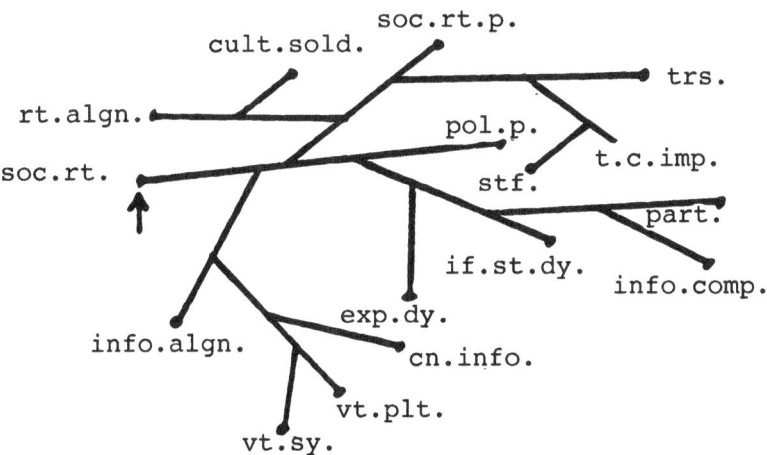

The distortions that have crept into western analysis can be viewed by understanding the essence premise that dictates its information degrees. For the journalism that comments on the methodological or executional dynamics of a given projection (form) must be seen in its composite context. Certainly the fact that there is no unified spiritual basis in this time zone cannot be lightly dismissed, for the most basic fact that has obscured the hope of relevant journalism is the realness that no single substitute can take the place of a spiritual basis. The fact is, the reality of applied journalism can only deal with the progressional route of a given creative projection rather than the ultimate worth of a given participation. Moreover, the realness of social reality implies that the affinity implications of progressionalism—even in this context—have to be respected. In other words, without a unified spiritual basis, a given participation in creativity must be viewed with respect to what it signifies about the reality of its route. This is especially important if we are to understand creative music from the black aesthetic. For the reality of black creativity—whatever strain—comments on the route black people (and transformational culture) are traveling to restore both culture and "information particulars." We are forced to view the realness of music journalism with this in mind. Because while every creative projection expands within the reality of its own affinity dynamics, the fact is that only white people of a particular vibrational persuasion are in the position to define the composite information scheme of western culture. **The progressional participation of western journalism in creative black music must be viewed for how it has (1) sought to alter the basic dynamic path of the music; (2) moved to establish the nature of source transfer; and (3) participated in and defined the application of gradualism.** To view the realness of western journalism is to look at all of these questions and more, for in looking at this area of information control, we are confronting one of the single most sophisticated wings of western culture.

There are two basic information (focus) distortion positions that characterize how western journalism has dealt with black creativity: (1) the thrust of interpretation practiced on the music has not recognized the importance of affinity dynamics—and in not doing so, made the mistake of thinking "everyone's relationship with phenomenon is the same," and (2) that the expanded functional area of creative music did not necessitate a transformational application of "commentary." Three-fourths of the mis-interpretations that surround the music can be reduced to these two basic distortions (yet I am not including deliberate racist or nationalist interpretations, since there is nothing to deal with in these categories). If we are to ever move towards necessary journalism, then the vibrational dictates underlying present-day mis-applications must be understood. The reality potential of transformational journalism depends on whether or not an expanded information basis is able to materialize.

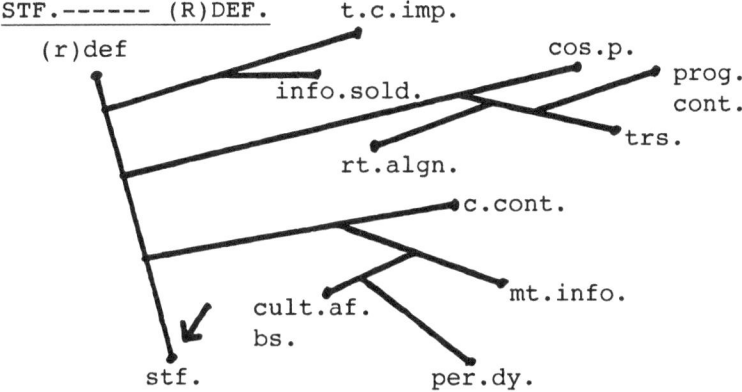

By "information degrees" I am referring to the axiom tenets that have been placed on the spectrum of methodological techniques that have been developed and practiced in the music. For instance, nothing is more obscuring than the present distortions surrounding black creativity and the concept of rhythm. Even in the early periods of the music, one can find writers who attempted to isolate a given musician's language as a means to break down one principle factor—as a measuring tool for the composite reality of the projection. In this context, a given critic would write of a particular musician as a "great swinger" or a "really hot player." But all of the classifications that would later solidify from the early period of the music concerning simple to complex rhythm really had nothing to do with what was actually happening. This is so because no matter whether the notes of a given player could be reduced for analysis (and then labeled "swinging" or "not swinging"), the essence factor that determined the meta-reality of the music was not about focusing on a moment to determine whether it is valid or not. The consideration of rhythm has been grossly misunderstood by the collective forces of western culture, because the essence of the music has never been "how" one played, but "what" one played. Which is to say, the real reality of black creativity is not separate from the implications of the affinity-insight principle. Any attempt to accurately comment on the reality of the music implies some understanding of the aesthetic basis of that reality. Western journalism has never really dealt with this most basic fact.

PR.S(RD)II–8

Nor is the consideration we call harmony really understood by the western defining community. For at every stage of the music, the science has never been viewed as a choking device but, rather, the basis from which invention could take place. This is not to say the science of a C-major scale in black creativity is different from western art music—because it isn't. Rather, the reality of a given harmonic progression has never been practiced in the way critics have evaluated. The fact is, the science of a given form in black creativity has always followed the vibrational necessity of the invention and not the other way around. All of the extended harmonies practiced today were played in the early forms of the music—with the difference being that the notes were extended because of the vibrational reality of the individual, as opposed to the individual functioning as an extension of the notes. This is not to say there was no exact science to the music, nor am I implying that the musicians did not have to deal with the discipline of the form—rather, the nature underlying how a given participation was practiced had nothing to do with how these forms have been written about. The progressional continuance of western journalism has moved to distort the basic reality continuum of the music as a means to apply a source-transfer-definition pattern on the music. The end result of these maneuvers is that few people outside of the actual reality of a given thrust are really aware of the music (that is—what is really happening in the music)—but this is only the beginning.

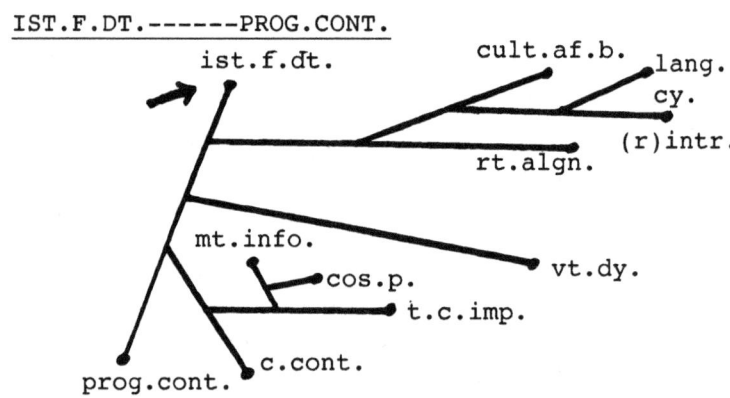

If the theoretical and vibrational basis of creative music from the black aesthetic is not understood (or has not been accurately transmitted) by the collective forces of western journalism, it is nothing compared to what has happened to the extended functional dynamics of the music. Because the most apparent distinction between the reality dynamics of world creativity and western art music is the progressional inclusion of improvisation by the world group—and the information dynamics related to that use. The collective forces of western interpretation have never been able to deal with improvisation because the whole reality of this discipline exceeds the concept of "empirical information degrees" ("this means this, and this means that"). What we have instead are attempts to make a law out of a vibrational continuum that differs from moment to moment, from person to person, and at the heart of this conflict one can begin to view the factors that have helped to solidify this phenomenon. If we are to really view the progressional mis-application of western journalism, then it is important that this phenomenon is understood.

Before we can begin to understand what has happened in contemporary western journalism's relationship with black creativity, we must first view the dynamic reality position of world culture (of which black creativity is part). This is so because the reality basis of world culture lies outside of the aesthetic functionalism of western society—which is to say, any attempt to comment on the nature of contemporary western observation implies that, first, one must establish some basis for understanding what this difference means. This is not to say there is no relationship between world creative postulation and western creativity on every level—obviously this is not the case. I have stated throughout the whole of this series of books that the inter-relationship between earth creativity—whatever region—is more profound than most of us would like to admit. But there is a difference in the nature underlying how information has come to be viewed and utilized in given cultures—as opposed to western culture—and there are also differences between vibrational cultural tendencies. My point is that these differences must be manifested in the aesthetic lining of their related pedagogy—having to do with the particulars underlying

PR.S(RD)II–10

perception dynamics (how given forms are interpreted)—and this is exactly what is not being respected in western applied interpretations. As such, the progressional interpretations of the western defining and critical community have functioned as a distorting factor for the real reality position of world culture. I am writing of a relationship that has moved to mis-document every aspect of the music—from its move to interpret earlier forms of the music until the present. Until real efforts are made to correct these mis-interpretations, the reality option of alternative creativity will continually find itself more and more separate from actual transformational involvement. Yet one would have to be quite naive to believe that real change can be brought about overnight—for in viewing the collective forces of western interpretation, we are looking at a progressive movement that has functioned intensely for many years—and cycles. One can only hope that the seeds for alternative investigation are being planted in this time period—but what of the aesthetic reality of black methodology?

The dynamic reality of black creative postulation can be viewed by understanding the relationship between what a given methodology poses for functionalism and what a given moment (time-space situation) poses for participation. It is here that one can begin to view the extended functionalism that permeates all world creativity (as separated from western society). The dynamic use of methodology coupled with the extended use of improvisation has forecasted another reality position for the creative artist. The reality situation promoted by this methodology can be viewed in several contexts—those being (1) the dynamics of methodology as a factor to promote or affirm composite culture, or (2) the dynamics of methodology as a means to vibrationally establish what route a given transformation will take. As such, the reality position of black creativity can be viewed with respect to what participation will mean for given individuals as well as for the composite culture. In either case, the truth of a given form is not about how that form is put together—rather, the science of a given form is utilized with respect to how a given utilization will advance the progressional nature of "what is being dealt with" (or, in this case, the social-reality factors that black people are now functioning under). To understand the reality position of black creativity is to view the significance of "extended functionalism"—which is to say, any attempt to accurately comment on the music must imply some real understanding of the "reality of extended functionalism."

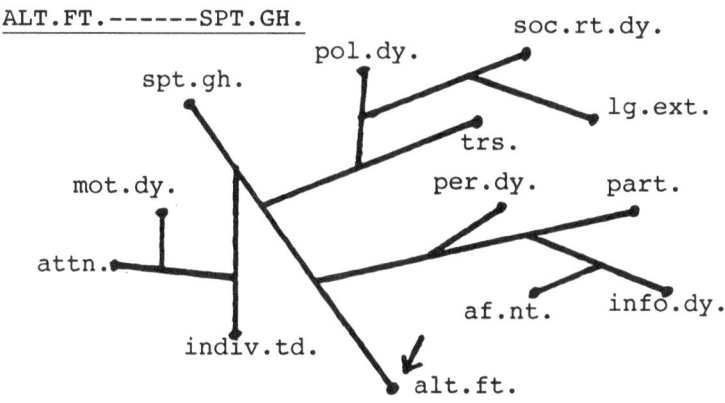

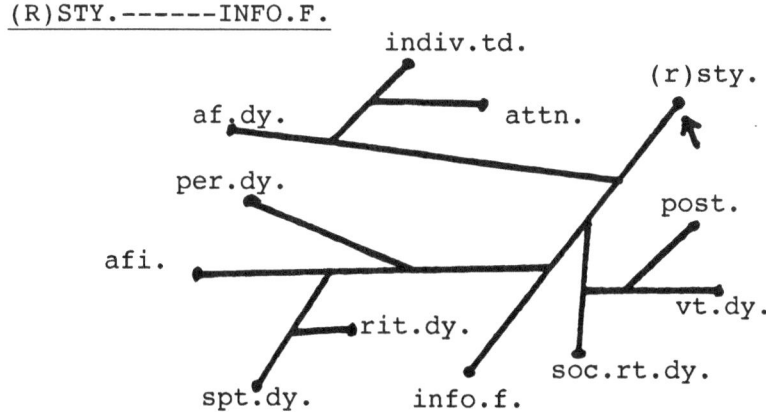

PR.S(RD)II-12

EXT.DY.------SOC.RT.DY.

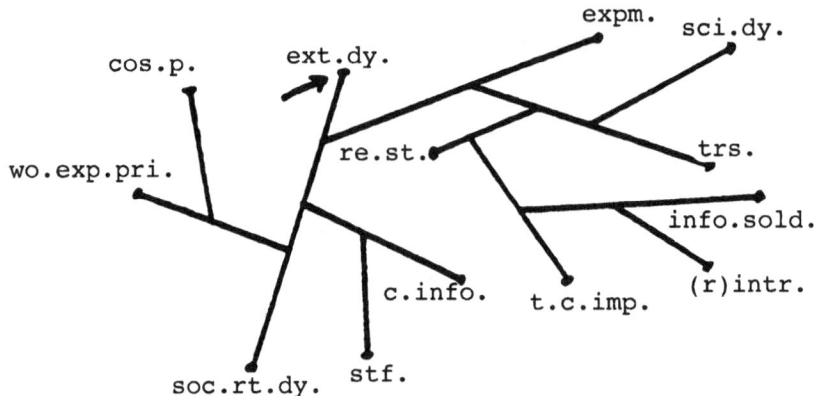

SCI.DY.------UNF.PI.

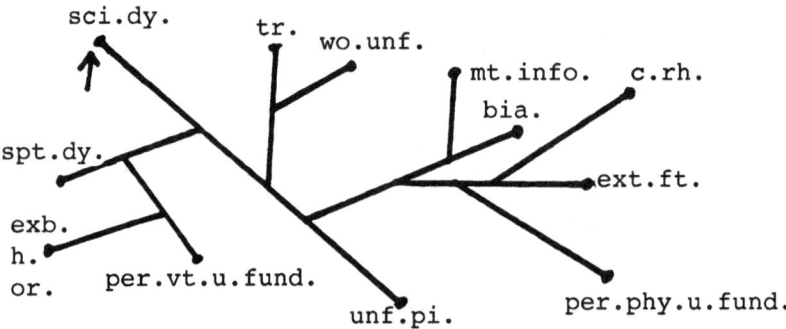

From early creative music (e.g., Louis Armstrong and Duke Ellington) until the present, western journalism has basically focused on the form and tools of the music as a means to interpret whether or not a given participation corresponds to an imposed definition of "real" (or correct). A given observation would find journalists measuring how a particular person functioned with respect to the affinity interpretation that western culture has developed in its own methodology (which in many cases runs counter to the reality participation of black creativity). Criticism in this context focused on whether or not a given player was performing correctly within the harmonic or structural science of the music—but no criterion could be developed as to the actual "nature" of the music (because "the music" is not the outgrowth of the science, but the other way around). The interpretation that developed in the critical defining community would move to completely overlook the meta-implications of "extended functionalism" and stress, instead, the affinity dynamics of execution: the understanding being that if a given individual executed the science of the music correctly, then his activity could be written on as fulfilling the reality of the music—and if not, then viewed in negative terms. In taking this position, the western defining community had wrongly assumed that the reality position of methodology in western creative postulation is the same as creative music from the black aesthetic. But the reality dynamics of improvisation have never really corresponded to this interpretation. For the progressional realness of creative music has never really moved to solidify one viewpoint—let alone one language. It is because of this extended functionalism that the transitional nature of the music has undergone so many changes in so short a time cycle. There has been no real attempt by the collective forces of western interpretation to deal with the implication of what extended functionalism really means—nor has there been any real understanding of the affinity-insight principle (and what this principle means in the music). This is so because the reality of extended functionalism transcends the criteria on which western observation is based. **The fact is, improvisation in the working arena of black creativity is related to many other factors that are outside of the actual "doing" in the music. I am writing of a functional arena that utilizes both a fixed and open operational scheme—whose ultimate significance has nothing to do with the execution of its coordinates, but is instead concerned with how a given participation is able to vibrationally affirm what is being dealt with!**

This is not to ignore the technical demands for each period of improvised music, but rather to enlarge on the composite overview concerning the "actual" reality of the music. The emphasis in creative music from the black aesthetic—whatever discipline—has never been on the "how" in the same manner as western art music—because the affinity-dynamic reality that determines information focus for particular cultures is not universally shared. Certainly every projection from the lineage of black creativity has had its functional reality, and I have not meant to disrespect what this means. But the dynamics of extended functionalism are not separate from the overall vibrational reality of the aesthetic. My point is that the commentary surrounding the music has moved to distort the reality of methodology as defined through the progressional resolidification of alternative black functionalism (which is not separate from the composite world alternative functionalism). This can be understood by reviewing the progressional development of world creativity. In Ross Russell's book *Jazz Style in Kansas City and the Southwest*, there are several examples of how the actual reality—participation—of the music was brought about. Ross wrote of many musicians who contributed to the music, and how this participation contributed to the composite fabric underlying what the actual aesthetic foundation of the music implied. All of the musicians mentioned in Ross's book can be viewed for both collective and individual dynamics—those being, no two musicians functioned with the same language, and every individual had a personal solution (or adaptation) of the principle science foundation of the music. This has always been the essence reality of creative music in world culture definitions. That being, methodology as a consideration that underlies the composite spiritual basis of the culture and, while doing so, also accents (and includes) the dynamic potential of the individual. To understand what this viewpoint means in actual terms, one needs only to view the principle relationship between how given individuals functioned and the reality of the tools utilized for the actual music. For example, in western art music, the concept of the instrument has to do with a preconceived notion as to what the reality-tone-basis implication of material is. In this context, a given musician is expected to eventually arrive at producing a "particular" sound out of his or her instrument. This attitude also extends to the reality of creative interpretation in western art music as well—the idea being that there is only one way to correctly interpret a particular composition if it is to be "real." But in the reality of creative music from the black aesthetic, the opposite of this viewpoint is seen as equally important. An instrument in this context is viewed as nothing more than a vehicle to establish the musician's spiritual and vibrational reality. Creative musicians are expected to extend the very nature of their activity—including even the sound of the instrument—until that activity affirms the whole of their "life position." Even the sound of the instrument is not viewed as existing in a fixed state—and this is only the beginning. For the progressional thrust of creative music from the black aesthetic frowns on the idea of actually trying to be "someone else"—because strict imitation runs counter to the aesthetic basis of the music (not to mention the planet).

The methodological reality of creative black music can be viewed with respect to its position in the all-composite scheme of planet discipline. For if we view this planet with respect to how the order of phenomena seems to function, we can then begin to see how given laws are interpreted. The principle laws that substantiate the functional reality of creative music must be viewed from this same context: that being—the reality of a composite methodology (what must be understood and practiced if a given projection is to be effective) and the reality of participation (the route a given individual must travel to "know" him- or herself). Any attempt to comment on the reality of creative music must respect these divisions, and also respect the underlying vibrational implications that these qualifications raise—to the reality principle of the music. Yet jazz criticism has never done this—regardless of period.

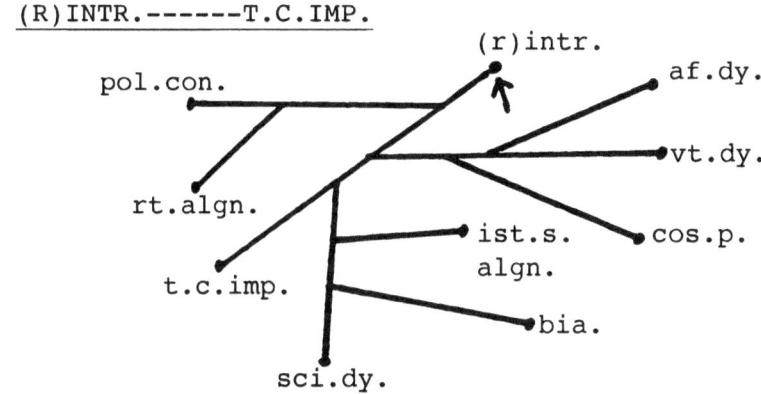

PR.S(RD)II–16

The social-reality implications of interpretation must also be viewed as directly related to the nature underlying how information is perceived. This is especially true if the reality of affinity dynamics is considered. For the progressional continuance of western interpretations has functioned almost exclusively as a defining tool for the affinity reality of its own nature. Many of the definitions that have come from this sector can be viewed as totally violating the essence reality of the music—and this is still true in this time period. Affinity dynamics mis-interpretations have helped distort every aspect of the music—from the concept of swing to the reality of improvisation. Even worse, the basic information used to either teach or comment on the music has come from this community for so long that many people have now come to accept their viewpoint as valid. **The collective forces of western culture (and interpretation) have redocumented every aspect of the music—to the point that no stone has been left unturned. This community has decided which musicians are to be viewed as important (regardless of time zone)—which musicians are the "best" of their group—which movement was important—which attitude is indigenous for the creative musician to have if he or she is to be a jazz musician—who influenced who (and how); and along with these imposed definitions, the collective forces of western culture, in applying the source-transfer-affinity adaptation of information, have also moved to establish what is the best solo played in a given moment—what is the right way to utilize the science of the music—who is the best technician (not to mention, what does the concept of technique for creative music mean as well)—what is the correct rhythm for given forms, etc.** All of these definitions have solidified in the progressive continuance of western journalism and/or jazz criticism.

It is important to state that I have no objections to any interpretation if the interpretation serves as a positive tool for the group it is relevant for. But the reality of western interpretation transcends any one strata—I am commenting on information re-interpretation that, when applied, becomes the sole criteria for the composite community. Certainly, the affinity reality of music education in America reflects the affinity-dynamic source-transfer interpretations of black music; so do the few magazines that exist as well. My point is that when the composite information-focus lines of a given culture move to affirm only one affinity persuasion and, in this case, that persuasion directly substantiates only the reality feed of a certain class of white Americans—then something is wrong. This is exactly what we are now dealing with in this time zone. Needless to say, the accuracy of a given viewpoint is somewhat diminished if the interpreter happens to also be subject to the effects of a racist culture—which is to say, the reality of a given source-transfer interpretation is not in a vacuum from the total life activity of its composite culture. For this reason, many of the most basic concepts we have now come to associate with the reality of world creativity must be re-examined. I have lately found several articles by young college graduates evaluating whether or not this or that musician was "playing the blues correctly," which is to say, where will it ever end—the musician they were evaluating was . . . Ben Webster.

It is impossible to view the reality of applied redefinitions without commenting on what effect this phenomenon has had on the basic information lining of the music. To understand this is to understand that gradually **the overwhelming machinery of the western defining thrust has come to view itself as completely separate from the composite reality of the music it purports to interpret. In many cases, there is now a total disrespect for the aesthetic from which the creativity expanded (in its source-initiation cycle).** This attitude can be viewed especially when focusing on the expansion (or restructuralist) cycle of the music. For example, much of the writing about the changes reshaping the music in the sixties and seventies contained more than just unhappiness over the direction of the music, but extended to outright hostility. When this was not the case, one could find a kind of paternalistic racism (the understanding being, "we know you don't know what you're doing—boy"—or "boy, you better get back into your rightful place") in many of the articles on the music. Both of these attitudes, in fact, are quite common to nine-tenths of all jazz journalism—and criticism in particular—and this is still true even as this book is being written. For the nature underlying how redefinitions have been designated in creativity has moved to give the western defining community an impression that they are more knowledgeable on the music than the people who actually created the music. This feeling is enforced by the nature of the documentation made available by the collective forces of western interpretation. That documentation being thousands and thousands of articles that can be utilized to substantiate a given source-transfer information line—and/or record collections that reach into the thousands. The progressional continuance of this phenomenon has moved to give the impression that, somehow, applied definitions from the transfer-shift juncture of a given projection can now accurately dictate the composite redefinitions of the whole music—and this has been happening (whether or not those definitions are relevant). The resulting schism that has developed between the musicians' (and music) and writers' communities must be viewed as a natural factor related to what has transpired in composite world interpretation. For it must be understood that every creative musician exists as a potential target for evaluation—and with present-day social reality as it is, very few individuals can afford to not be concerned about how a given interpretation (of one's music) is solidified. To view the reality of contemporary music criticism is to look at all of these questions and more. For the progressional continuance of applied redefinitions has shaped the composite reality of this subject in more ways than many of us seem to be aware of. This is not an isolated factor that is separated from the composite reality lining of the music. In viewing the sophistication of western functionalism, we are seeing something of profound importance (which is to say, something too important to not challenge).

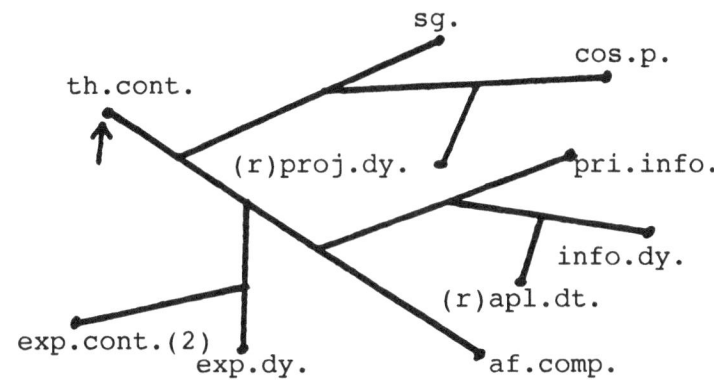

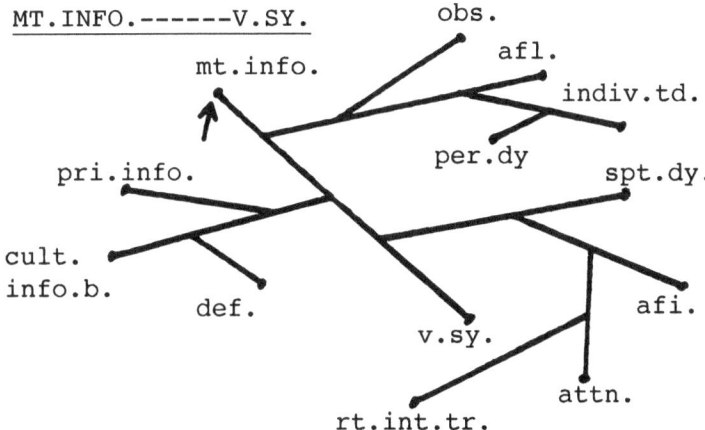

The progressional move to apply transfer redefinitions on creative black music can be viewed in the early solidification of the music. In that period, western journalism would focus on the specifics of a given performer as a means to dissect the reality of the composite music. But the nature of how this focus was applied would establish from the beginning a profound insensitivity to the actual music. Because the reality functionalism and components of creative black music, even in its early period, utilized an extended functionalism that transcended the dynamics of western definitions. This is not to say that isolated commentary—describing the particulars of a given creative postulation—in itself is meaningless; rather, the application of western definitions in the early formation of the music showed a profound disregard as to the reality of its position (as observers). Because at the heart of the music is the dynamic realness of multi-functionalism and reality dynamics, as related to the composite form and individuals practicing within that form. Western journalism—and criticism—would move to distort the nature of that relationship as a means to make the music correspond to the vibrational position of western criteria. The early period of applied definitions would see the western defining community examining individual improvisations as a means to formulate a composite basis for evaluation. But never was the real reality position of the aesthetics taken into account—in terms of the source-initiation interpretations by the musicians themselves. The investigation of a particular solo by a musician like Louis Armstrong would serve as a model to determine the artistic reality (and worth) for other musicians, as well as the primary language of the form under review (which is to say, the concept of isolating "actual time improvisation" would solidify as an investigative tool by the collective forces surrounding the solidification of American black creativity—and it is important to understand what this solidification means). For it must be understood that the dynamics of extended functionalism—as practiced and defined by the actual participating musicians—had nothing to do with applied western definitions. The solidification of transitional black creativity has always gained its reality assignment from its position in the progressional continuum of trans-African composite information and vibrational dynamics. As such, the reality dynamics of creative black music comment on the meta-reality of all black creativity—even with respect to the social-reality factors that surrounded every projectional strain. At no point did the reality of black creativity have anything to do with making a universal fixed law out of a discipline that had to do with natural postulation. For the reality umbrella of creative black music has long understood that the particulars of a given form have to do with the composite nature of the route that form travels, and the underlying forces related to what that form is. To base a universal assumption on an isolated improvisation is to totally violate the reality of what improvisation is. This is so because the reality of improvisation has nothing to do with the "good chorus." Rather, the meta-reality of improvisation has do with each person creatively postulating—through their activity—who and what they are (at that moment) and who and what they will be (understanding, too, that no two improvisors—people—are the same). This difference is the very basis of the music. Thus, if the measure of critical analysis is to be based on the initiations of any one individual and/or style, then we arrive at the apparent conflict at the very beginning—and this is exactly what has happened. **Essentially, jazz criticism can be reduced to attempts to make reality out of a process that has to do with "becoming."** Using the empirical aspect of the "how"—that being, what components are governing the nature of a given functionalism—as a controlling factor to applied alien definitions, western interpretation has methodologically moved to applied transfer definitions and redefinitions on black creativity regardless of period and/or form.

The acceleration of applied redefinitions has moved to distort the meta-reality continuum of creative black music on more levels than is generally recognized. This is not to neglect the significance of transfer definitions in every context—certainly the reality position of any projection must adjust to the particulars of its route—but only to comment on what has happened to the source-initiation interpretation of the music—as made real for black culture. The collective interpretations of western culture have moved to paralyze the meta-implications of black creativity as a positive transformation tool. This can be understood by viewing the option-spread potential of black participation in black creativity. For not only have the collective forces of western culture secured the position for dictating which musicians are to be viewed as good or bad, but more important, this same group has redocumented what position any individual participation is to have in the historical context of the music. The end result of this control is directly connected to the present situation black creativity is dealing with today—which is to say, the present reality position of black creativity cannot simply be brushed off as accidental. The present reality of creative music must instead be viewed as the logical result of the position western journalism took in the early period of the music. For the critical establishment has never been able to properly differentiate the meta-reality of black creativity from the vibrational-reality position of who they are as white people (or people who see themselves as white people), and this inability has greatly affected the nature of how interpretation is practiced. **There has long been an inability on the part of western culture to deal with the realness of "form" in non-western creativity and the actualness of what that form celebrates—with respect to its vibrational or cosmic assignment. Present-day distortions exist because western culture has never really been prepared to deal with the dynamic implications of these questions in their own reality focus—which is to say, there has been no composite basis established in western culture for viewing the realness of extended functionalism and art creativity in any real sense after the dissolution of the spiritual reality of western culture.** As such, western criticism and applied redefinitions can be viewed as unqualified and intellectually speculative—"without basis." The inability to properly come to terms with the meta-reality implications of creative music has brought about several other problems as well. For the defining group that surrounds the music has had to rely on the dynamics of comparison as a factor to establish criticism—which is to say, separation in this period is the most basic tool that has been substituted for insight. Through the flexibility of words, separation is now practiced on the most expansive plane one could possibly conceive of—and we have all suffered because of the interpretations that have come down through this practice.

Thus, to view the reality position of black creativity in this period is to view interpretations that are not only dis-advantageous to the source-initiation lining of the music, but definitions that have totally undermined the progressional significance of the music as well. The practice of intellectual separation has been used as a basis for establishing the position of such great musicians as Art Tatum and Fats Waller—and separation as a tool for establishing gradualism is the principle factor utilized to accent the activity of musicians like Bix Beiderbecke (that being—isolating a particular musical phrase executed in an improvisation as a means to claim innovation—or separate development), and this practice is still with us today. Musicians/composers like Duke Ellington have long been evaluated in terms of their structured dynamics—as applied against other equally creative musicians in that same period—but no insight has been offered as to the reality implications of the total movement of the music. In the end, the dynamic reality of the music is sacrificed for the manipulation potential of one-dimensional separation.

The "dis-reality" of western interpretation has helped solidify the nature of the relationship creativity—and especially non-western creativity—has to the continuance of culture in this time zone. In other words, the progressional applications of source-transfer definitions have established the effective perimeter function of isolated creativity. The present-day concepts we have of entertainment are directly related to the nature underlying how interpretation has been practiced, and this is only the beginning. Western interpretation has also moved to clarify the progressional expansion of black creativity with the same alien definitions it applied to western art music (i.e., the concept of "the reality of extension" implies an inherited advancement that is particularly western). But the truth is that the progressional continuum of black creativity has nothing to do with the idea of advancement as understood through western interpretation. Every period of black creativity can be viewed as "necessarily real" to the composite reality of the music. This is not to say that no given projection has expanded; rather, the reality principle that dictates expansion in black creativity has nothing to do with separation as practiced in western culture. All of the forms in black creativity can be viewed as affirming particular vibrational zones of information routes, where the only factor that has dictated the expansion principle is the realness of life itself (that being, "change" seems to be one constant of the universe—or at least the "re-adaptation of a given phenomenon" seems to be in accordance to the nature of the universe)—"but the universe itself hasn't changed (not changed)." In other words, the western defining idea of "one period of music being more advanced than another" has nothing to do with the reality of world creativity. There is no difference between the music of John Coltrane, the Art Ensemble of Chicago, and Louis Armstrong. All of these musicians affirm the same reality—and the structural differences are indicative only of the reality and vibrational particulars that are connected to the composite nature of universal expansionism. The emphasis in black creative music is on the affinity-dynamic relationship of "doing" to "is"—the "how," while continually shifting, becomes instead a tool for progressionalism. Yet there is still another argument that must be dealt with which concerns the reality of interpretation. For if the use of western criticism is to really be understood, we must view what this consideration means with respect to the composite culture. Because the practice of composite interpretation implies that there is an understood reality context of the total culture (or anti-culture)—and this is most certainly not the case with what has happened in western journalism (and criticism).

Criticism can be relevant only in an environment where the people of the culture share the same reality—and affinity spectrum. That criticism would function as interpretation of activity in accordance to the information-reality dictates of its agreed spiritual hierarchy. Moreover, the reality of criticism, even in this context, would establish the nature of what composite functionalism would mean without applying existential investigation as to the reality of a "given participation." Which is to say, the optimum position of interpretation has very little to do with what is happening at present in western society. The very idea of interpretation would have to be reshaped in transformational culture, for the consideration of "criticism" really has no place in discovering real creativity. In fact, the idea of existential criticism has nothing to do with world creativity—let alone black creativity. Because western criticism—that being, determining the worth of a given creative activity—is an evaluation based on existential exercises as it relates to intellectual juggling. The world community has never really related to the reality of observation in this manner. Every culture, with the exception of the west's, has long viewed a given creative participation as being valid in itself. Yet I do not mean to imply that no standard of excellence (or methodological discipline) evolved in world culture, because every creative projection has a procedure. But the significance of a given projection in world culture derives its position from the underlying spiritual and vibrational hierarchy that substantiated its reality. The route a given individual would travel to learn a given discipline was simply that—a route. There was no need to make an existential evaluation on the implications of a given participation—instead, the music was "focused on," rather than the individual's relationship with his or her "life particulars." The distinction between this application of interpretation and western commentary should not be taken lightly. Because the dynamic distortions that have permeated black creativity from its inception in the Americas (from its continuance period, after the dissolution of black high culture) involved establishing an information focus that was alien to the actual reality of the music. It is this alien focus that has helped to distort both the reality dynamics of the music, as well as the progressional effectiveness of the music. As long as black (world) creativity is subjected to western interpretation on this level, there can be no real hope for positive change. Western interpretation functions as an obstacle to the possibility of composite-informational dynamics—and there is more.

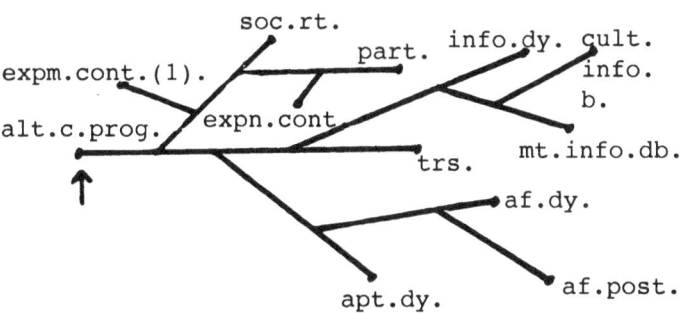

The composite application of affinity-dynamic interpretations from the western defining community moves to perpetuate the notion that music criticism is a valid practice—but this is a false assumption. In an existential society where the basis for perceiving phenomena has to do with intellectual assumption, criticism can be viewed as a regulatory device—having to do with the manipulation of information dynamics. The use of this practice can be understood as both political and/or progressive, for the net effect of applied redefinitions is not separate from how the expansion principle of any culture group is brought about. Moreover, the reality of applied redefinitions can be viewed as the first necessary junction for successfully establishing gradualism. The nature underlying how these redefinitions are practiced tells much about the sophistication of western functionalism, because the basis from which western interpretations have moved to distort world creativity has nothing to do with universal premises. Western journalism in this context functions as a regulating device to re-interpret the reality position of "principle-affinity tendencies." By performing this task, western journalism has helped to establish a profound flaw in the meta-reality position of world culture. The challenge of the next cycle will have to do with whether or not world culture can overcome false interpretations about their reality and move to eliminate western redocumentation. This will be no easy task.

By "principle-affinity tendencies," I am referring to the physical universe factors that are related to how different beings can be perceived in terms of their relationship with principle information. For purposes of this section of the book, the concept of "principle-affinity tendencies" would involve the nature underlying how given individuals function with respect to multi-information. Yet by introducing this concept I have not meant to imply that only one sector of the planet has affinity tendencies, because this is not the case. The fact is, the reality of "principle-affinity tendencies" has to do with the cosmic nature of information dynamics as it relates to the whole of humanity. As such, even the dynamics of western interpretation cannot be viewed as outside this context. The realness of this concept can put the nature of western interpretation into better perspective. That being, the use of "principle-affinity tendencies" in western culture is a reflection of the composite philosophical and vibrational nature of present-day western continuance. The distortion that has solidified in this area is directly related to how the application of redefinitions has been practiced, and sustained. In other words, the progressional continuance of western interpretation can be viewed for how it has purposely moved to apply mis-definitions about the whole nature of affinity dynamics—especially as the reality of this concept applies to non-white people. **At the heart of western interpretation we can view a consistent attempt to distort the "reality of principle-affinity tendencies" as it applies to the composite spectrum of information dynamics—and these attempts** can be viewed throughout the whole continuum of applied redefinition. As such, it remains for dynamic research to rectify what has happened in the last two thousand and some years. For the sophistication that surrounds information manipulation is in itself nothing new. But if we are to understand the dynamics of this phenomenon, it will be important to elaborate further, because by commenting on what I call "principle-affinity tendencies," I am touching on one of the most consistently utilized re-information tools in this time period—and it is important to understand what this concept really is.

The three most basic divisions of "principle-affinity tendencies" can be viewed as such: (1) **the vibrational thrust alignment that functions towards preserving the nature underlying how a given reality is maintained**—having to do with the utilization of established postulation techniques as a means to solidify the principle state of its culture group. This thrust alignment is usually viewed with respect to its ability to preserve the reality of its given principle state, and in this time period has come to be associated with the concept we now refer to as conservative; (2) **the vibrational thrust alignment that moves forward with respect to what it learns about the historical realty of the past.** This is the alignment that derives its reality function from its relationship with the composite tradition of its continuum. As such, the dynamic reality and vibrational pull from the past becomes the basis for dealing with both the present and the future—for clarification purposes, this alignment will henceforth be referred to as the "traditional affinity tendency"; and finally (3), the third tendency that completes this trilogy would be the nature of the expansion principle—that being, **the vibrational tendency that in its normal function moves towards restructuring as a means to adopt the particulars of its dynamic route.** Thus if we are to understand how contemporary western journalism has been practiced, and if we are to understand the function of transformational journalism, then it is important that the three divisions of principle-affinity tendencies are understood. For the reality of western interpretation has greatly affected our understanding of vibrational tendencies—and as such, three-fourths of the information we have been dealing with in this time zone can be viewed for the peculiar nature of its use of affinity tendencies. Quite possibly the challenge of transformational journalism will rest on whether or not an expanded information scan can be adopted—one that could move to clarify the composite reality of information dynamics, as opposed to what we now have in this period. For the problem of interpreting world information through the natural limitations of one affinity-dynamic posture has created a special barrier for western manipulation. If any credibility is to be re-established, then the collective forces of western interpretation must first develop into a composite interpretative agency in accordance to the practical functionalism of world participation.

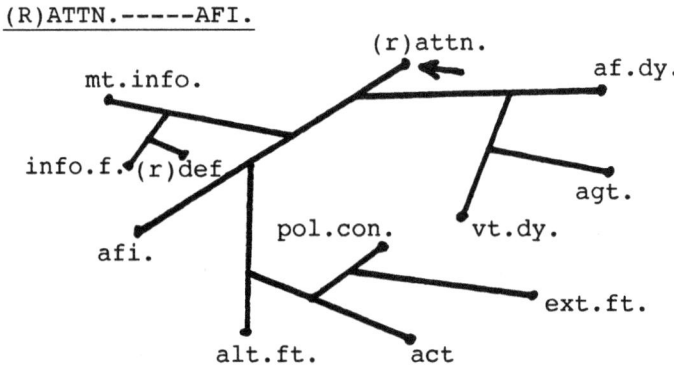

If the reality potential of world interpretation is to be solidified as a functional tool for positive utilization, then the concept of "principle-affinity tendencies" must be examined as a means to understand the nature of present-day progressionalism. This is so because the reality of interpretation is not separate from the meta-significance that dictates how a given sensibility functions—which is to say, the most basic factor that dictates how a given sensitivity "participates" has to do with cosmic matters. As such, the reality of interpretation must, along with everything else, respect what this phenomenon means. Rather than intellectually assuming what the implications of a given participation mean, western journalism could function as a meaningful factor by adhering to what "affinity tendencies" implies in real terms. In other words, the "truth" of a given participation has nothing to do with the implication of "good" or "bad"—as applied to individuals or individual participation—rather, the actualness of a given action carries its own multi-dimensional implications. Transformational journalism should function with respect to what this phenomenon means—which is to say, the purpose of transformational journalism should be to provide the most real context for observing how a given participation is practiced. By functioning in this context, journalism rises above petty criticism and instead contributes to the information scan of the culture. This is what is needed. Moreover, observation within the context of "affinity tendencies" can also be viewed as a positive regulating device—for the reality continuum of multi-information carries its own dynamics—but before one can deal with what this means in actual terms, it is necessary to elaborate on the nature of "principle-affinity tendencies" (what this viewpoint means with regards to its natural reality-function nature).

The nature of the balance function of principle-affinity tendencies reflects the life nature underlying how individuals function on the physical universe level. By this I am saying that no one tendency is more important than any other tendency, but instead, the reality of principle-affinity tendencies has to do with how given postulations are brought about— and what these postulations imply for the composite culture. This can be understood by simply viewing how progressionalism is practiced. For the balance function of principle-affinity tendencies comments on the particular nature of events that intersect the cross-sectional alignment of its information dynamics. This phenomenon then can be understood by viewing the particulars of that relationship. Which is to say, the challenge— and real purpose—of transformational journalism has to do with whether or not preparation has been initiated for establishing the balance of multi-informational tendencies. Because if unchecked, the composite nature of information dynamics moves to undermine the solidification of culture— and this is important.

In actual terms, the reality of "affinity-tendency balance" has to do with how observation and functional interpretations are utilized as a basis to sustain the "center" (or culture). As such, it is necessary to view the nature of a given "tendency" and/or the balance focus of a given combination of tendencies. For instance, if not understood, the affinity tendency of the third degree (expansion) could function as a natural detriment for culture. For the reality position of this tendency is to constantly move towards experimentation and re-introducing materials. I refer to this affinity tendency as the'"restructuralism degree" of multi-information. The primary motivating factor that underlies this sensibility has to do with the nature underlying how expanded functionalism affects progressional continuance. The understanding being: the greater the functional arena, the more people will be able to learn about what is; and also that potentially inherent in every system are the seeds for new exploration. At the heart of the restructuralism degree of multi-information (and affinity tendencies) is the natural ability to employ new approaches—and as such, the reality of restructuralism is not separate from how given change cycles are brought about. I have avoided the concept of innovation in this context because the semantical implications of this subject move to create the illusion that something has been created out of nothing, or that something was created which didn't already exist before (in another state)—and this is contrary to what I believe. The concept of the restructuralist degree of multi-information (or affinity tendencies) has to do with the progressional re-adaptation of the basic laws we are functioning with/from on this planet. As such, the nature of a given practice of restructuralism is not outside of the composite reality of information dynamics.

That people are naturally born into "restructured degrees of affinity tendencies" seems to be undebatable, and moreover, the position of restructuralism in this time zone is also directly related to how the expansion principle of cultural lineage has come to be maintained. In other words, restructuralism in this context provides a very real function with regards to a given cultural thrust, and cultural extension. This is true for physical universe reality—with respect to the appearance of things, and its progression—and this is also true for what restructuralism implies about the reality of ideas (and especially, for this section, creativity). It would be extremely difficult to recognize and understand the spectacle-diversion dynamics of western culture without having some awareness of what role restructuralism plays. The nature underlying how creativity is viewed in this cycle, and the applied separation that has determined the isolated progressional development of information dynamics, has moved to accent the reality position of restructuralism. Because, in this context, restructuralism is perceived with respect to its position in the forward stimulation of a given information scan—having to do with the initiations of new ideas for the composite vibrational lining of the culture as well as transformation technology. As such, if we are to understand what restructuralism really means, then it is necessary to examine the composite factors that dictate the reality of "principle-affinity tendencies" and its relationship to multi-information. In actual terms, it is important for us to have some understanding about the reality principle (and implications) that determines the nature of a given affinity-tendency interpretation. This is so because the concept of "principle-affinity tendencies" derives its significance from the nature surrounding how information is perceived. As such, I am not commenting on a phenomenon that has nothing to do with information focus and/or interpretation. The reality of affinity dynamics is directly related to the multi-use of redefinitions.

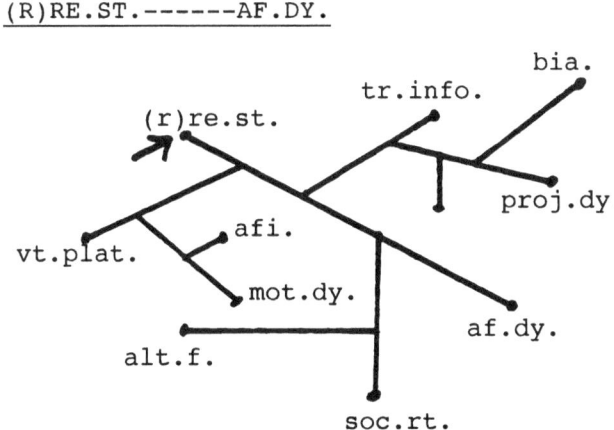

If the significance of restructuralism has to do with the ability of a given information line to initiate new concepts and areas of research, then it would be well if we understood what this phenomenon means in practical terms. My point is that **if the principle focus of a given culture group is balanced by only one sector of its composite informational**

continuum, then the total reality interpretation of that continuum will suffer. In other words, to separate restructuralism from its position in the "principle-affinity tendency" relationship to multi-information is to promote an unbalanced situation that is not compatible with actual life. Thus, if the consideration of restructuralism were to be over-accented, it would not be possible to solidify the composite reality of its principle-culture group (or culture). Because while the reality of restructuralism, by its very nature, is concerned with expansion, movement, and change, none of these considerations have anything to do with the solidification of culture if perceived in an isolated sense. In other words, motion in itself cannot become the basis for establishing a cultural vibrational identity unless that motion is viewed in relation to the composite forces that determine the total informational and vibrational reality of its culture. As such, the function of transformational journalism, with respect to restructuralism, is to help integrate new initiations into the composite realm of cultural information focus (that being, to the public and to the progressional thrust of the basic culture-informational continuum). This, then, is the real function of journalism regarding the interpretation of restructuralism, as opposed to what has been happening in this time cycle.

If journalism functioned with respect to the balance of "principle-affinity tendencies," the public would be in a better position to deal with creativity—and multi-information. Because the emergence of a new information line (or form) does not in itself necessarily have anything to do with "new" as separated from "all information." Yet the realness of a given information line does shed light (and insight) on the composite reality of its given effective space (or culture). For this reason, it is important to make the total culture aware of the dynamics of its informational base—which is to say, the emergence of restructured creativity is not isolated from the composite reality of culture information. Moreover, the realness of principle affinity tendencies implies that the reality of western interpretation be restructural as well. Because if the reality of information dynamics is not separate from the principle-affinity tendencies that determine the information route that a given individual will take, then it is important to understand what this non-separation means—which is to say, it is important that this perspective unification is included in the multi-interpretations handed down from the defining and controlling sector that dictates culture. As such, the reality of principle-affinity tendencies must be viewed because of what it tells about the nature of a given participation—and in doing so, this viewpoint will also give insight into the proper context for understanding (experiencing) creativity. This concept comments only on what seems to be the most natural affinity relationship on the planet—that being, the fact that people vibrate to different areas of given informational continuums as a means to correspond with who and what they are (in both a vibrational and cosmic sense). I have formulated this concept as a means to comment on the nature underlying how multi-information progresses in a given culture and also as a means to provide a more realistic context for understanding transformational interpretation. In its most positive sense, journalism should function as a balancing factor with regards to its ability to comment on the reality of principle-affinity tendencies. This information could provide a positive context to better understand world information and positive evolution. "Principle-affinity tendencies" and multi-information interpretations could establish a community with relevant tools for viewing the dynamics of its "reality position."

The second degree of principle-affinity tendencies is the nature of information that functions with respect to cultural solidification. This affinity position can actually be viewed as indicative of a principle-composite-cultural focus inasmuch as its "persuasion" usually permeates the "attention" of the total culture. As such, the solidification-affinity tendency consolidates the reality of a given information line as that line comes into the composite focus of its culture group—and this solidification establishes the second transitional cycle of adjustment, that being: a given information (or procedure) route has actualized (i.e., transition) and is adopted for cultural use (or awareness). This affinity tendency is also the zone where given routes of multi-information are consolidated into the basic information practice of the culture—and in music terms, this is the junction where given projections become acknowledged styles. The affinity-tendency principle of solidification functions to elaborate on (and make real) the dynamics implied in the resolidification of a given information contingency, and it is in this juncture where the "gap" between initiation and the public lessens. Which is to say, the solidification-affinity tendency can be viewed as the integration principle that moves to establish how the culture deals with information (past, present, and future), and this should not be taken lightly. For the progressional continuance and expansion of information is not separate from whether or not it is perceived as real and practiced by the people of its culture group. As such, without the solidification-affinity tendency, restructuralism would have no real meaning because the extension of a given information line means nothing in itself; rather, the meta-reality of a given function has to do with how that function participates in "actual life" and whether or not it can be practiced.

The reality of solidification-affinity tendencies can be viewed with respect to its relationship to culture identity. This is the tendency that serves as the most basic vehicle to determine the "reality" of a given time period. In fact, the reality of solidification-affinity tendencies cannot be separated from the composite reality position of a given culture's information interpretation, because by its very nature this phenomenon is dependent upon the initiation of material for development. By this I am saying that the reality of solidification-affinity tendencies derives its significance through the nature of its utilization of extension (restructuralism) and history (tradition). As such, the function of journalism is this context is to give a projectional basis to interpretation, with the understanding being, "to really understand a given function (or information particular) is to have an extended practical application of its dynamics." Which is to say, the reality pull of solidification-affinity tendencies moves to convert a given theory (or isolated application) into concrete applicational focus. The challenge of interpretation in this context is to reveal the dynamic spectrum of a given information line with the hope of having people in the culture become cognizant of the full gamut of their available expressions (and information).

(R)STY.------PROJ.DY.

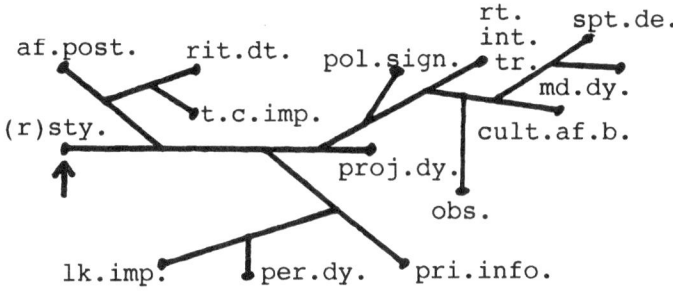

(R)STY.------PROG.CONT.

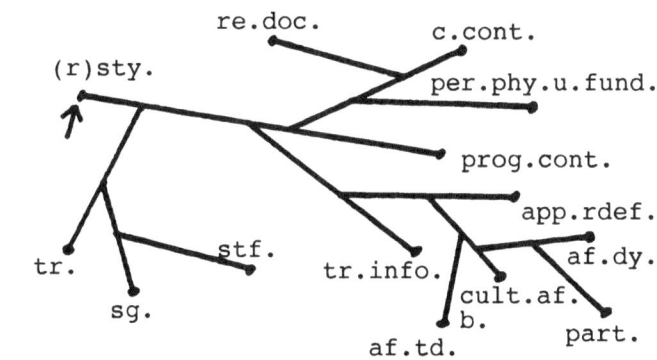

The third division of "principle-affinity tendencies" has to do with the progressional expansion of retrograde information interpretation. The nature of this tendency has to do with progressional development with respect to the vibrational lining of its principle-information continuum. The retrograde affinity tendency functions as a factor to keep the people of its culture aware of the dynamic route of its path, and this awareness also serves as a positive tool for establishing the vibrational nature of adopting "new" information. As such, the reality of the retrograde affinity tendency can be viewed with respect to its relationship with traditionalism. For the most basic application of this tendency moves to develop one's understanding and appreciation of the tradition of the culture. It is important to understand that no informational (or functional) extension could solidify without the work that took place before it. Moreover, since I have already expressed my belief that innovation, as we refer to it, does not exist—the realness of the reality base of a given projection can better give one insight into the extension solidification of that projection. Which is to say, to understand the future extension of a given projection is to have some understanding of the history of that projection. Thus the reality of retrograde affinity tendencies moves to supply a broader definition of a given information line—rather than deal with only the particulars of a given focus. Many of us have come to have a distorted view of traditionalism, and this attitude is also reflected in the information dynamics of this time cycle. As far as creativity is concerned, I have met many people who have no respect or interest in the tradition solidification of a creative projection. As such, the music we now refer to as Dixieland music, or early classical music, Gregorian chants, boogie-woogie, are seen by some as amusing rather than directly relevant. Nevertheless, to study the progressional realness of world creativity seriously is to begin seeing the multi-implications of traditionalism, for the traditional solidification of earth creativity reveals that the dynamics and elements we now associate with so-called modern creativity are common to all humanity and were practiced thousands of years before the Christian era.

The reality implications of retrograde affinity tendencies can help one understand the significance of progressionalism. For the brilliance of creativity can be viewed as equally manifested throughout the whole of earth existence. As such, the nature of affinity tendencies in this context serves to remind us of this truth as well as what this brilliance means in actual and conceptual terms. By examining the composite realness of earth creativity, we can better understand the significance of extension (restructuralism) as well as principle focus (or solidification). In this context, we will come to understand that there is no such thing as new music, and that "new" in itself is not the issue (purpose). Thus, the responsibility of retro-focus journalism is to interpret a given projection line with respect to the reality dynamics of its total continuum—and as such, integrate a composite viewpoint not separate from vibrational and social reality. This, then, is the reality of what I call principle-affinity tendencies—having to do with the nature of a given information route, as well as the dynamic factors that dictate how given individuals function. Because the basis of this viewpoint is only that given information routes are directly related to the nature—or affinity disposition—of particular individuals; moreover, every individual functions with respect to a given affinity alignment of information, and this must be respected. Finally, the nature of a given alignment tendency must also take into account the affinity dynamic implications of information and information focus. The reality of meaningful interpretation has to do with the whole of these questions, and the effectiveness of transformational journalism is not separate from the challenge to develop and practice meaningful observation and information dynamics. The fact that no real effort has been made to deal with the affinity-dynamic implications of multi-information cannot be lightly dismissed, but the seriousness of this problem should not be over-simplified either. In other words, the progressional factors which have solidified both this time cycle, and the nature (or vibrational dynamics) of this time cycle, cannot be reduced to any one aspect of existence. The problem of mis-interpretation concerns the whole of humanity—which is to say, the most basic factor everyone is dealing with is the struggle to be involved in "real" communication—with meaningful definitions—with the hope that we can be understood. The nature of how this state of being can be brought about is what concerns me, for the reality of applied definitions transcends any one information focus. This is a problem of monumental importance—and should concern anyone interested in alternative functionalism.

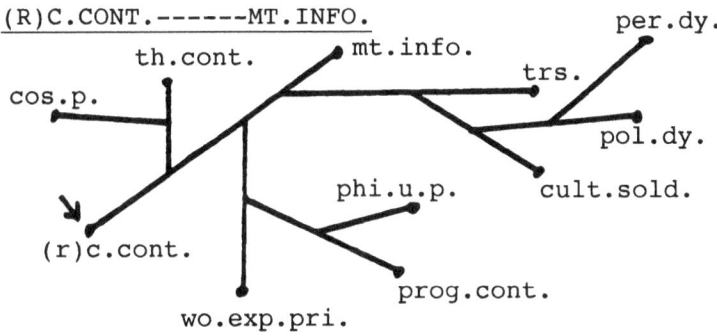

Since this book is being written in the time zone of the seventies, it would be to my advantage to comment on how journalism is being utilized as a negative factor with regards to the creativity of the last decade as well as the present. Since these frailties are operative even now—understand also that jazz criticism from Louis Armstrong to the present has not changed much either—it might be possible to get some idea about what is really happening in this area with regards to the music. In other words, jazz criticism functions in basically the same historical capacity as two hundred years ago. It would be to our advantage if some attempt is made to understand what this consideration (criticism) really means—especially with regards to the future of creative music as a meaningful and positive factor for transformation. Because there are other considerations related to jazz criticism which, if not challenged, soon threaten to completely distort the effectiveness of creative music as a lifeblood factor—having to do with the sophistication of present-day journalism that surrounds the changing social and vibratory factors (and physical and vibrational universe space) affecting black people in America. That being—the use of source-transfer manipulation as a factor to discourage black participation in creative music—and the collective forces that threaten to separate the next generation of black people from knowing about their own creativity. In other words, we have no choice but to re-evaluate the forces that surround creative music.

Jazz Criticism

If the west coast movement of the fifties represented a departure to some degree from the primal-vibrational thrust of the meta-reality of black creative music, it can also be said that the same is true of the journalism about the music in that same period. It is clear that the journalism of the fifties functioned as a negative factor with regards to providing a basic understanding of creative music—and in some cases, this sector has even functioned as an obstacle to the actual reality happening in that period. Yet it is not enough to merely reduce the antics of the critical and defining community to only racism—because if tampering with a given vibrational and creative aesthetic is understood, it is detrimental for everyone—that is, we all suffer if the legitimate manifestation of who we are is incorrectly defined. I mentioned the west coast movement because I believe the time zone of the sixties could be called "west coast revisited." I say "west coast revisited" because the present situation of creativity (with regards to the collective forces that surround how events are understood in this time zone) resembles the situation that solidified in the early fifties—especially with regards to source transfer. If there is any real difference in the situation of creativity today, as opposed to the reality of the fifties, that difference would only outline the sophistication of the controlling and defining communities' ability to regulate creative music. I believe the time zone we are in today is much more potentially destructive to creativity because of what this position implies. The controlling and defining forces of western information regulation function as a negative factor to the "actual meta-reality" of creative music.

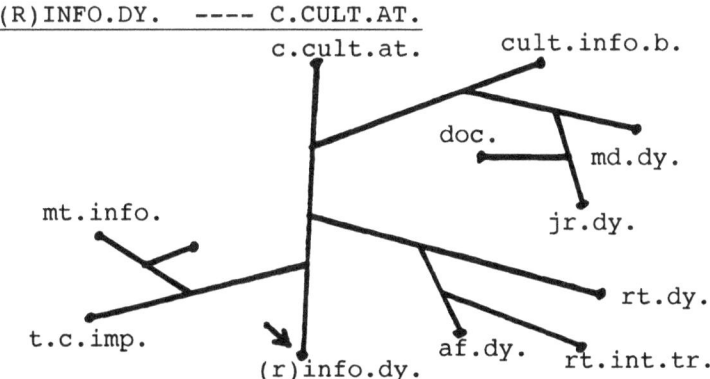

PR.S(RD)II-40

(R)DOC.------TRS.

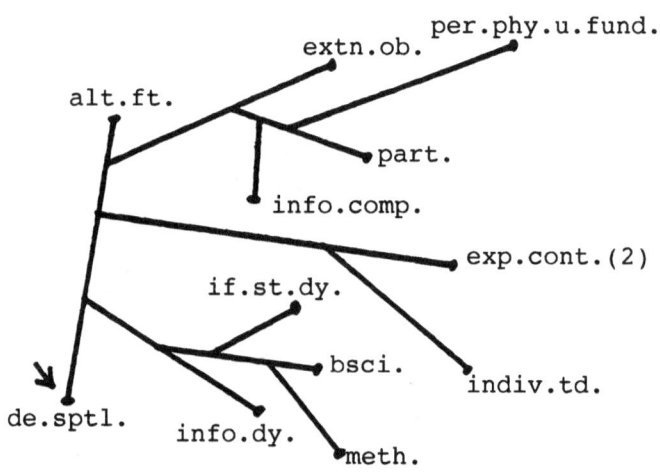

DE.SPTL.------ALT.FT.

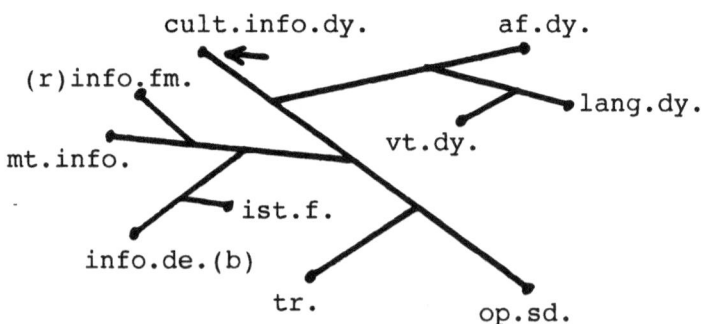

CULT.INFO.DY------ OP.SD.

PR.S(RD)II–41

The fact is—very few people seem to be aware of the significance of the transition cycle that took place in creative music during the sixties, and while there are many reasons for this, in the final analysis, the basic interpretations of the critical community have gone unchallenged. For however one chooses to deal with the ideas of this book (whether one agrees with my viewpoint or not), there can be no disagreeing with the fact that creative music in the sixties made a very real impact on the total scene in that period—affecting every form of music, as well as dictating what events were to comprise the basis for creativity in the seventies. That there was a reaction to the music is a fact, and I do not mean to imply that the majority of people who experienced the music embraced it as a positive factor either—because this is not true. But even a surface understanding of western civilization would reveal that no other reaction could have been possible. In short, the collective forces that shape American culture have created a situation contrary to what creativity really is. People have been programmed to view creative music as something foreign in the reality of the culture; new initiations are thus received in a negative light rather than as something that might be of assistance to positive transformation. In short, people have been programmed in accordance to the dictates of value systems that are not in their best interest. It was in the period of the sixties that jazz journalism secured the next level of source transfer, and it is in understanding how this phenomenon was applied—in regards to both functionalism and gradualism—that we can better understand the controlling forces which surround the music. The question then becomes: **where are these forces attempting to direct the music; and moreover, can jazz criticism be looked at as a functional tool connected to controlling factors that extend beyond merely regulating how a given thrust of the music is perceived?** It is important that the question is asked, for the next cycle of creative music seems to imply a total re-evaluation of the actual position of the jazz critic. When I say the time zone of the sixties could well be labeled "west coast revisited," I am not trying to make light of a very serious development but, rather, to examine certain basic progressions that can shed light on the nature of how source transfer has been utilized to secure the present position of western culture. More so, when I state that the sophistication of the controlling forces surrounding creative music is a factor that cannot be avoided any longer, it is necessary to understand what role criticism has played in creating the present predicament that we are now confronted with.

The journalism that affirms the contractual (retrograde) creative thrust has assumed another level of prominence in the time zone of the late sixties and early seventies. So significant is the over-balance underlying how this thrust has come to be viewed that it is necessary to examine what this phenomenon has implied to the total arena of creative music. For it must be understood that by citing the emphasis on the contractual (retrograde) creative thrust, I am actually drawing attention to which area jazz journalism has decided to exploit as a means to achieve its own end, rather than what has been used to honestly interpret creative music to the public. My point in this context being: if any aspect of the tri-vibrational balance factor is suppressed or denied, we run into the same basic distortions that have long characterized how creative black music is mis-understood; in other words, if restructuralism becomes the sole basis for creating the music, there could be no composite reality to substantiate culture, because the basics underlying how a given reality is understood would constantly be in motion. If the conservative (solidification) vibrational thrust is accented by the controlling forces that dictate culture in any given period, not only do we not advance, but we are, as Amos Moore once wrote, "Doomed and Shrouded in What Was Jazz, 1931." What we are witnessing in the time zone of the seventies is the suppression and distortion of contemporary creative music, and this is being achieved by manipulating our perception of the contractual (retrograde) vibrational arena. In short, jazz criticism has elected to accent the realness of the contractual vibrational thrust as a basis to distort the total arena of creative black music. And as the dynamics surrounding the post-Coleman continuum developed, we can now see why this route was chosen. For when I stated that the collective forces surrounding creative music have utilized the contractual vibrational thrust as a factor to distort the music, I did not mean to imply that jazz journalism is mono-dimensional. My point is this: **the misuse of the tri-vibrational arena, as it relates to the creative process, is directly** connected to how source transfer was achieved as we advanced into the seventies. My point is also this: all of the factors that served to suppress creative music in this time zone—as well as the subsequent abandonment of creative music from the affinity-insight (1) principle by many of the musicians in the late sixties, as well as the emergence of jazz-rock as a form that would substitute as a marketable creative music, as well as the rise of the next cycle of white stylist musicians who would assume power for the present time zone (the seventies), as well as the disintegration of the composite-creative-music thrust (even, in the final analysis, the word "jazz" no longer had the same meaning, so effective was the last maneuver), as well as the resulting break of the music with the black community—all this was possible only because of the sophistication of the controlling forces that surround creative black music—more so, it was only possible because of the effectiveness of composite jazz journalism.

```
APP.RDEF.------ IST.S.ALGN.
```

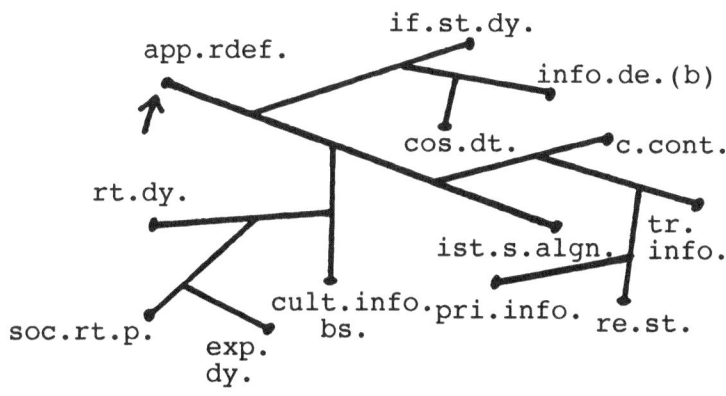

The present social and vibrational position of creative music is not separate from what it signals about the vibrational forces that control American culture. It cannot be overlooked that America would love to accept the potential of what this creative thrust implies—in fact, America is quite capable of accepting any creativity, for that matter, as long as the reality of a given thrust doesn't threaten the established meta-reality of its controlled information lines and/or ("perceived") cultural state. In other words, America can embrace any form of creativity—and has, in fact—but the principal fact remains that the utilization of any given creative thrust is only equal to how easily that thrust adapts itself to source transfer—as a factor to function in accordance with gradualism. It then is not a question of whether or not America is interested in creative black music—of whatever principle; rather, it is at what juncture a given thrust can be adopted safely without disturbing the basic vibrational lining of the culture. In other words, **America will not accept creative improvised music until the black aesthetic—that being, the meta-reality of the black aesthetic—can be reduced (1) with regard to the implications of the cosmic significance of black music; (2) with regard to the insight—"tendencies"—of this thrust on form (and what this means with regard to "actual" culture); or (3) until it can be redocumented, where the black contribution is made "less."** There are still other factors related to this phenomenon—having to do with the historical attractiveness of trans-African music as a source-transfer wellspring for western expansionalism (when the condition of source transfer has been achieved). My point is this: America can use creative black music as a stimulating agent for composite western culture. In this position, black music functions as a generating factor for teaching young people how to utilize extended affinity dynamics, and the music also serves as an expansion consideration for the functional arena of western music. When this situation is established, black musicians then fall into a supporting role (at best).

This phenomenon can be better understood if one would look at developments on the social and physical universe level, especially with regard to the educational institutions in America. On the grassroot national level, we can look at the emergence of the stage band movement as a signal about the forming nature of source-transfer progressionalism. It is here, on this most basic level, that we can view how this phenomenon will develop for the next time zone, for the emergence of the stage band movement (and I have lately been informed that many of these groups have now begun to accept the name "jazz band") represents how the last cycle of creative music (before the transition of the late fifties—bebop) will be utilized and rechanneled in accordance to the dictates of the white aesthetic exclusively. For many people, the emergence of jazz education was viewed as a positive progression that signaled the end of cultural oppression and social change. But there are many factors surrounding why creative music has suddenly become so popular on the academic level, and to understand this phenomenon is to better have a basis to view both the controlling forces that dictate progressions on the physical universe level, and the effectiveness of the critical defining community (that surrounds every aspect of creative music). The motivational thrust that has dictated the establishment of creative music in the educational institutions is directly related to how the contractual (retrograde) vibrational thrust has been utilized. In other words, not only does the stage band movement signal that the realness of the next level of source transfer with regards to the music has been met, but this juncture also represents the realness of gradualism as a factor that has successfully distorted the historical progression (and reality) of the music. What we have now are attempts to make a composite reality out of a form that was "ised" through the black aesthetic, and while I do not disagree with this objective (since this is inevitable if we are to move towards transformation), I am also aware that the forces underlying how this change moves really function with the objective of redocumenting creative improvising music with the white aesthetic in the dominant position. My opinion is this: **there can be no composite reality for improvised music as long as the position of non-white people remains as it is. America is now trying to actualize improvised music without "ising" the metaphysical basis responsible for the music.** I do not mean to imply, however, that the transitions occurring in this time zone are only related to the progressions surrounding west coast jazz in the fifties, for in actual fact, source transfer on this level can be traced back to Scott Joplin's day. I mentioned the progressions surrounding source transfer in the fifties because this period personified the vibrational forces in the air after the Second World War—and this same time zone was also the period that "ised" the emergence of bebop. In other words, the developments in the juncture of the late forties to early fifties are relevant to the situation we now find ourselves in (the transition of bebop as an American music). My commentary in this context is directed at the use of source-transfer progressionalism as a basis to understand the manipulation that permeates "sanctioned" black music documentation (and definitions). In short, the misdocumentation of black music is part of the national "state of being" of present-day jazz journalism (one need only read reviews of Chet Baker in the fifties, as a substitute for Miles Davis—or Doc Severinsen as a substitute for Miles Davis in the sixties—to Chuck Mangione as a substitute for Miles Davis in the seventies, to understand what I am saying). For the most basic factor that allowed for the phenomenon of west coast jazz to expand to the extent it did was the hope that this music could be documented as the source-transfer junction of creative music; that is, the emergence of west coast jazz was conceived as the juncture where the black aesthetic could be discarded as a primary factor in the meta-reality of the music—in other words, the collective forces of western culture were seeking to establish a junction where creative improvised music from the black aesthetic could be integrated into the mainstream of American culture. The only problem with this objective was that the solidification of west coast jazz perceived of it as a music that could be considered "above" the basic thrust of the black music that made it possible. West coast jazz was, then, a creative music from the white aesthetic which had very little in common with black music. This is what the west coast musicians sought—and to a great extent, this is what they found (although I do not believe everything worked out in quite the way it was planned). **When I stated that the present period represents a critical juncture for creative music, I make this assertion with the awareness that not only are the same forces functioning with regards to the music scene at present, but the mistakes of the west coast transfer cycle have been learned by the controlling factors. In other words, the necessary preparations for source transfer have had more attention from the defining forces that dictate spectacle diversion, and the manipulation happening in this time zone—with regards to the suppression of creative black music—is much more sophisticated than many of us are aware of.**

If I am correct, we will soon be moving into a period of confusion as to the very nature of what creative music is—not to mention the potential of creativity as a positive functional factor for transformation.

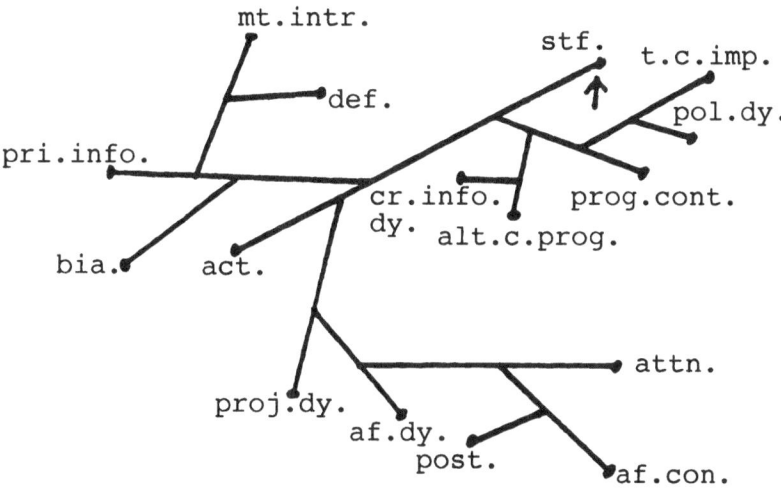

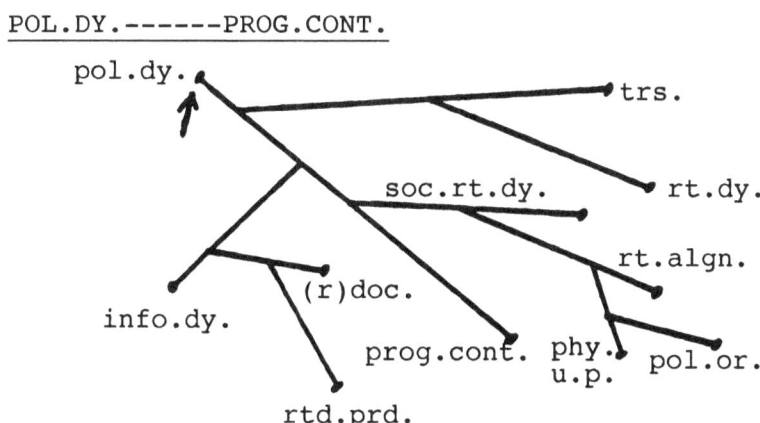

It is important that some effort is made to understand the present reality of western interpretation on non-western creativity—and especially black creativity. For the realness of western mis-definitions has so profoundly altered our understanding of creative participation that something must be done to restore alternative definitions about this most important subject. It is important that attempts are made to look at the western critics—and western commentary in general, for the present distortions surrounding black creativity are not the result of a grand accident but are instead related to what has solidified from the use of both wrong definitions and dubious intentions. We must view the contemporary so-called jazz critic for what role this medium has contributed to the present state of things, and we must attempt to view this phenomenon from every possible context. Because the nature of present-day commentary on black music gives insight into the real way western culture sees non-white people—that is, western criticism in this context transcends the particulars of a given focus and instead moves to give insight about how white people really see black people, black creativity, and black culture. If we are to understand the present nature of western commentary, then it is from this juncture that we must first begin examination.

The realness of western culture's perception of black initiations can be understood (sensed) in its first encounter by examining the early exposure particulars that solidified in early Greece and/or Rome about Africa. For Herodotus, who is documented as being one of Europe's first historians (and is also mistakenly viewed as the father of all history—the idea being that recorded history began only when white people started documentation), established the first, most basic attitude that has since been amplified from generation to generation. His basic viewpoint vibrationally could be interpreted as "a dynamic feeling of awe about Africa with emotional interpretations that sought to accent what he felt to be most unique about her culture and people." Yet I have not meant to sound negative about Herodotus, because in fact the thrust of his interpretations about Africa were meant to be (and sound) positive. In his early writings, Herodotus commented about the beauty of the land, the difference of the people, etc., etc., and all of his comments were real as far as what he "thought" he saw—but the particulars of his description—in an expanded context—take on another meaning, and still another meaning after a hundred, two hundred, or three hundred years. It is important that some attempt is made to understand just what

Herodotus, and his later followers, activated through their glorious writings about the so-called dark continent.

The progressional thrust of recorded information in that time period would solidify a vast body of data on African culture and life dynamics—on every level. Herodotus and his followers would write about the "wonder" of the continent and how it differs from Greece—in both general and particular terms. Yet the words he used to describe African music would somehow come to be viewed as "what is really happening" with black creativity—as opposed to merely one individual's viewpoint and/or experience. Herodotus, when commenting on the music, wrote of it being a richly rhythmatic music that was also "physical" when compared to his culture; he also described given ceremonial functions and particulars. Many of the viewpoints he expressed in that period have become the staple of present-day western music journalism. But more important than his particular focuses, the realness of Herodotus's writings (and those who followed him) would also establish the basis of an attitude that has moved to severely undermine the composite dictates (and dynamics) of black creativity in every sense. For the thrust of their writings would establish the concept of "black exotica"—as a means to explain their attraction to Africa, and the realness of this phenomenon would move to paralyze the information implications of black invention for decades and decades. It is past time to challenge the nature of this phenomenon and what it implies, because the dynamic implications of "exotic in this context" have nothing to do with black creativity, but instead give insight into the values and "things" of those who have felt it necessary to create those images. This is my point.

The thrust of black creativity documentation since Herodotus's early journeys into Africa has long viewed African music as a physical music with little conceptual dynamics. Even in the early solidification of Greece, Africa and Africans have been viewed in terms of what Europeans called their sexuality. Moreover, as this viewpoint began to solidify, the mystique of Africa became more important than what was really happening. I write this because Europeans, and now Americans, have long needed to view black people as exotic and "accentedly sexual." Even today, black popular music is the form white people use to "get down"—because somehow the music is about "the dreams of dynamic sexuality" or "the journey into the forbidden garden" type of ideas. Even worse, the progressional use of this viewpoint has also affected black people's understanding of who they are. The normal life for most Americans and westerners "of that sensibility" is to live, work, play, make money, and then ... when it's the right "time," sneak on down to what Henry Threadgill calls "the foot wash." The concept of black exotica is real, and it is important that some attempt is made to understand what this means.

The dynamic "mystification" of black culture would also be accelerated in the slave trade period of earth history. This would be the time zone that would see the "Dr. Livingstone, I presume" mentality throughout Africa. All of the so-called customs of black people would be subjected to the microscope and analyzed with respect to the "black exotica" mentality. Moreover, while all of this was happening, the glorification of black people's so-called sexuality coincided with the dynamic raping of composite black culture—on every level. **My point is that Europeans have historically been interested in keeping black people in the "exotica zone" as a means to not deal with the significance of Africa. It is important to understand that the mantle of "black exotica" is not separate from the notion that black people are not thinking human beings and, as such, the raping of Africa was not a negative act towards a civilized people.** The resulting functionalism that destroyed Africa need not be dealt with in this section, because obviously the realness of this subject cannot be dealt with in the context of what I am trying to look at. I mentioned this phenomenon—the raping of Africa—only as means to lay a basis for understanding what happens when the reality of black information dynamics, on its own terms, is not dealt with, but is instead violated by viewpoints that historically have come from what can only be called "different intentions."

When I write that black information or creativity has not been dealt with on its own terms, it is important to understand what this means. For the reality dynamics of black creativity in Africa were not formed as a means to "have a rhythmatic music" that white people could dance to—in fact, the methodological specifics of black creativity had nothing to do with how Herodotus viewed any aspect of black invention. Instead, the realness of black creativity was a response to the affinity dictates of black culture information and black creative dynamics. In other words, Africa was not trying to be more or less rhythmatic than Europe, because the reality of its dynamics had its own pedagogical implications. **What Herodotus called rhythmatic music and dance was only the natural music and dance of people he focused on in Africa. But the thrust of western commentary has never respected the realness of this distinction.** Rather, the composite reality of western interpretation has imposed its own criteria on black creativity and black information dynamics—and black people are still trying to recover from what this imposition has meant.

The dynamic implications of the "black exotica" mentality has had a profound impact on composite black creativity progressionalism. To understand this phenomenon is to have some insight into the reality dictates of present-day western culture. For the "black exotica" concept is not separate from the "particulars" it has attracted from the western community. In other words, **the solidification of this concept has underlined what "area of motivation" would underline those individuals attracted to black creativity.** It is for this reason that black creativity has long been the "best place in town" for those who somehow believe they are either "against the system" or heading for "against the system." **Every period of black creativity has been used to outline some aspect of western spectacle-diversion particulars—which is to say, western culture has long utilized black creativity as a lever to invoke some aspect of its own desires—either with respect to spiritualism, sexuality, rebellion, or to get individually or collectively rich. But in every case, there has been no attempt by the western establishment to view black creativity and/or its related information on its own terms.** It is important that some attempt is now made to understand what this means—because the seriousness of this phenomenon is not one-dimensional.

I believe the concept of "black exotica" has underlined the present-day position of black creativity, and I also believe this concept has moved to determine the dictates of western information dynamics. For the seriousness of the manipulation surrounding black creativity is much too profound to be only an accident, but instead signals something about how this culture (western culture) works. The thrust of this manipulation is related to what I call the "concept of the across-the-tracks syndrome"—that being, the use of black creativity as a means to "have a good time," while also suppressing the dynamic implications of the music to accomplish that "good time." In this context, black creativity is viewed as related to prostitution or the life of sensuality, and western culture is viewed as its opposite—that is, of high information and ethics. But what is interesting about this phenomenon is that black creativity has been used to fuel the composite thrust of the very people who seem to hate it the most. How many times have we heard about the fact that Al Capone listened to ragtime or boogie-woogie piano music—yet on the other hand, how many boogie-woogie piano players have you heard about who committed the same level of **atrocities** that Al Capone committed?—probably none. In other words, western information sources would have us view black creativity as low art—even though the music has never been offered in those terms—while ignoring how the collective dynamics of western culture have exploited the music. But let me go on.

My point is that the composite reality of black creativity has long been utilized as a phenomenon "at the edge of the culture," to be used to "do those things you aren't supposed to do." Black creativity—and for that matter, black culture and people—have forever become the scapegoat of this culture—regardless of context—and this can no longer be accepted by black people. Because in the final analysis, I am saying that black creativity can no longer afford to be used to further the exotic imaginations of those who have historically exploited the music for their own selfish purposes. Because Herodotus did not see a "country in sin" when he visited Africa, nor did he see "exotic dancers" or "sexually rhythmatic music"—instead, what he saw was a territory of high aspirations as well as a spiritual culture of people whose lives and actions were in accordance to what they believed. He also saw a culture whose meta-reality lining was composite—with respect to both its information and its ceremony. But somehow none of this information is generally recognized—outside of certain academic circles, or specialists—for when I wrote that Herodotus didn't see a city of sin, or exotic dynamics, I am not saying black people were not aware of sex, nor am I saying that the rhythmic dynamics of their music did not exist—because obviously they did. Instead, my point is that none of these focuses were perceived in the same context that western culture views information. The dilemma of present-day black creativity is the same as two thousand years ago—that being, the actual reality of the music—and its dictates—are not recognized, but, instead, all of our information (which of course is surface information) on this subject comes from the "concept of the across-the-tracks syndrome" and its related definitions. If we are to ever view the realness of black creativity (onto world creativity), then the distortions of this juncture must be recognized.

Certainly the most basic factor that differentiates the reality of black creativity from the imposed definitions of the "across the tracks" brigade is the nature of cross-transfer definitions. For when a given writer talks about the dynamic rhythm of Charlie Parker's music, in actual fact he is really viewing the consideration (rhythm) as separate from the dictates of the subject he is focusing on. Because the reality of a given individual in black creativity is seen as not separate from the concept of individual dynamics—in other words, Charlie Parker has only his natural rhythm, and this is not good or bad, but instead as it should be. **But the western critic evaluates a given "participation" with respect to how a given fundamental is made separate in western terms (and this has nothing to do with black creativity).** It is at this point that we can begin to understand the reality position of western observation, and it is also at this point that we can begin to see what has happened in black music journalism. For the actualness of western words and values systems (and feelings . . .) is being imposed on a continuum that has never corresponded to any of its dictates—and the losers have been black people.

PR.S(RD)II-54

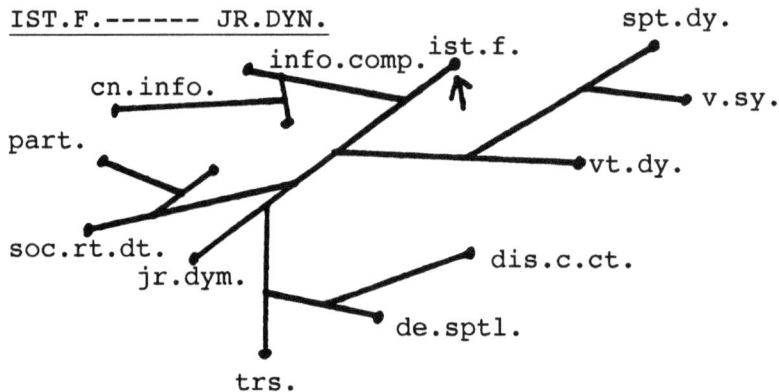

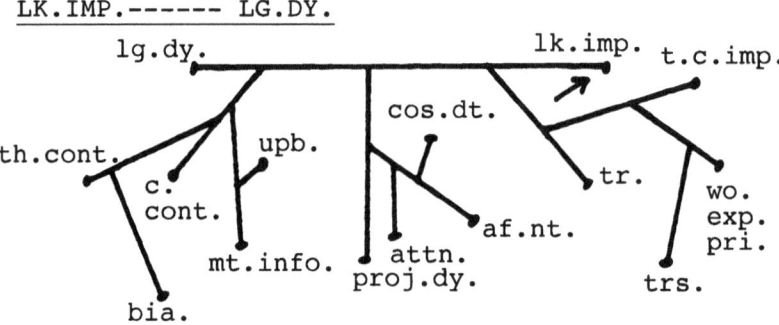

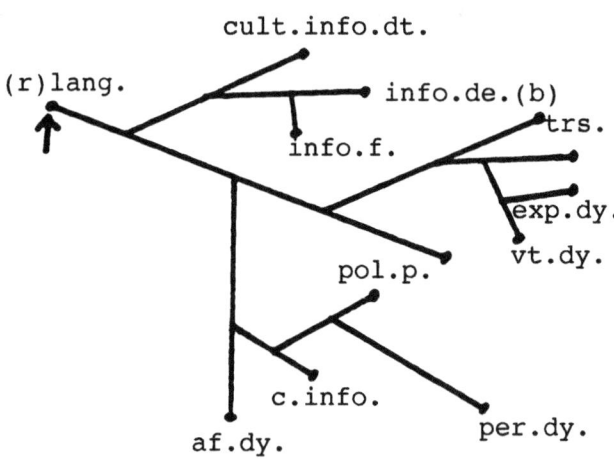

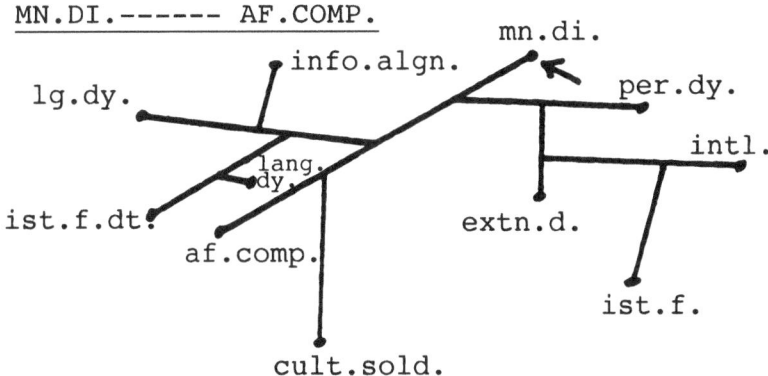

Before I can completely solidify a basis for commenting on present-day black creativity journalism, it is important to backtrack to another aspect of this most diverse subject, for the thrust of this section is intended to be about the western critic, and so far I have only vaguely focused on this subject. I have instead tried to lay basis for establishing some means to understand what affinity make-up surrounds this sector of information so that it might be possible to really understand what western journalism has done. Nevertheless, it is now time to focus on the western critic—but only in general terms at first. There are still several areas of this subject that must be looked at before any real understanding can be amassed—because we are not simply interested in surface observation. The questions we must first ask are: **(1) who is the jazz critic, (2) what are the motivating factors that underline this phenomenon (perceived intention), and (3) ultimately what is the effect of composite jazz journalism?** These are the questions that can help solidify a composite basis to examine this phenomenon, and these are also questions that can clarify the present reality of composite black culture.

It is important to understand that the progressional emergence of the western critic is a phenomenon that is completely distinct from the reality of black creativity. The average critic is a young man or woman who has (1) gone to college for journalism, (2) studied music in some capacity but did not feel equipped to be a professional musician, or (3) graduated in some area of sociology and drifted into jazz criticism as a means to begin a career. Moreover, the reality dynamics of this phenomenon—the critic—does not necessarily imply that one has completed his or her academic credentials. For many of these people have simply come to this medium because of their love or concern for alternative creativity, as a means to "set the record straight"—about the music they profess to care about. And of course, regardless of pedagogy, the basic critic must feel that his or her viewpoint is necessarily relevant to what is happening in the music. Yet the realness of this subject is more complex than it might seem on the surface. Because very few jazz critics have arrived at this juncture as a life's work, but instead as a "step on the ladder." In other words, for the student of sociology, the solidification of a jazz critic's job is seen as one step towards becoming a social critic on—maybe the greater society; or the frustrated musician critic might see jazz journalism as one step towards having his or her own record company. Not to mention, to get a job at any particular newspaper is to be paid a salary (and even for those occasions where no money is available, one can get the necessary experience in jazz criticism for better things to come). For instance, if a given music graduate or journalism graduate can write well enough in the jazz section of a given daily newspaper, maybe that individual will be "elevated" into the classical music section. There is of course more to this most complex phenomenon, but my only point is that there is a "reality of objective procedure" that surrounds the jazz critic's relationship with the commentary of black creativity—and the realness of this phenomenon is not necessarily negative, if we are trying to understand the particulars of a given individual—after all, many of these people have a real concern for the music (and besides, a guy's got to make a buck, huh!). I have mentioned some of the dynamics of the jazz critic's reality of objective procedure as a means to understand what this phenomenon has posed to the music—because it is my belief that the composite spirit of present-day jazz journalism is not separate from what the concept of "black exotica" implies, nor from what the concept of the "across the tracks" phenomenon implies. It is for this reason that this subject—jazz journalism—must be examined.

To view the reality of the jazz critic is to begin understanding the dynamic implications of the "across the tracks" phenomenon. It is important that some effort is made to understand the reality of definition that has resulted from this phenomenon. Because the dictates of present-day journalism are symptomatic of progressional vibrational fantasies that have very little to do with the realness of both black people and black creativity. We must understand that very few of the writers who have "come across the tracks" have done so only as a response to the music—because many other factors are related to decisions on this level. This is not to say that any particular sector of humanity—or white people in general—cannot be inspired by and attracted to the music without ulterior motives, because obviously to take this position is racist. Nor by focusing so closely on the white critic have I necessarily meant to imply that any given critic consciously believes his or her work to be non-positive—or non-positively intended (or offered). For it is clear that people do not simply think the same way about given focuses—and as such, my investigation in this section is not offered as a universal indictment of any particular individual. But I believe the reality dictates of the so-called present-day jazz critic must be viewed in the composite context of what is happening in our greater society, and I also believe that the present reality of jazz criticism is simply too fixed to have been arrived at by accident. As such, the realness of this phenomenon—jazz criticism—must be examined as rigorously as any other area concerning creative music—and in particular, black creative music. For the realness of this sector has profoundly affected how the composite sector of the culture views the music—and my point is that cultural perception is important.

The reason I have gone to such great lengths to prepare some basis for viewing the jazz critic is because this sector is important if we are to really view the present reality of black music commentary. There are two most basic concepts permeating the whole of this subject that must be discussed if we are to really view the present state of things, and both of these concepts are derived from the progressional continuance of the concept of "black exotica." The two concepts I am referring to are: (1) "the reality of the sweating brow" and (2) "the concept of the good night."

PR.S(RD)II–58

Both of these vibrational—and actual—positions can help us to see what has happened in black music commentary, and both of these concepts can also help us better understand the reality of manipulation surrounding present-day black creativity.

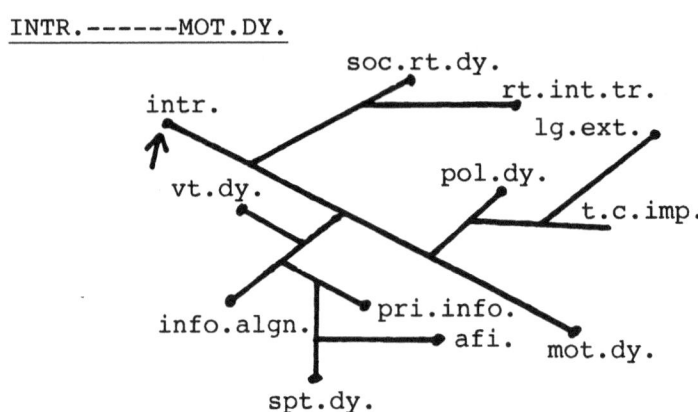

"The reality of the sweating brow" is my phrase to comment on the perceived state of whether or not a given performance—or participation—in black creativity is viewed as "real." To understand this concept is to view how differently white people have always seen black people, for the thrust of this concept moves to give insight into which images and affinity particulars determine how a given non-western (white) focus is ultimately viewed. "The reality of the sweating brow" has to do with how white writers have come to interpret whether a given black musician is accurately "doing the best" he or she can, or whether that musician is merely "coasting"—or not "really trying to be creative." What is interesting with this concept, however, is that "the reality of the sweating brow" is not so much dependent on the actual music but instead on "how" the actual "doing" of the music looks. **In other words, the progressional continuum of western journalism has moved to create a viewpoint about people and creativity that validates the actualness of a given participation on something other than the actual participation—and this is interesting, to say the least.** A black so-called jazz musician's activity (or music) in jazz journalism is viewed not so much with respect to his or her given music offering, but instead with respect to whether that person's emotional surface output is viewed as sufficient. But on this point, it is necessary to make several clarifications—because I am not making a universal blanket assertion that has nothing to do with the dynamics of particular differences. Certainly the reality of every so-called performer is expected to have some emotional involvement with his or her activity. As such, even the western art community is not impervious to the emotional creative involvement in their artists—this is true wherever we are commenting on the spectrum of western art, from Leonard Bernstein to Itzhak Perlman. But in every case, the reality of this awareness is not viewed before the actualness of the music—because white people recognize that there is no one way to be emotional—that is, white people recognize that other white people have different emotional dynamics. Some people are naturally demonstrative in their way of being, and other people are emotional in more subtle ways. This is simply a fact of life, and this is also simply how people are—which is to say, any attempt to have a reality of commentary would necessarily have to accept differences in people, because the purpose of any honest inquiry is to comment about "what seems to be true."

The reality of jazz commentary since the Dixieland period has taken another viewpoint about the realness of individual dynamics—and its related emotional particulars—and this viewpoint is most strange. For somehow those early white writers were able to solidify, even in this early period of the music, a viewpoint about black affinity dynamics that has never corresponded to who black people really were and are—viewpoints that we are still living with today. For the thrust of early jazz commentary has moved to create the idea that there is only one type of black person, and also that there is only one level of "involvement" by black people. This warped viewpoint has been able to solidify even though there have always been twenty million and some black people who did not fit this image. To really understand how these concepts have materialized, it is necessary to examine the information position of jazz commentary. The fact is, **the concept of cool jazz or coolness has long been the worst term one could put on the black creative musician, because the realness of what this concept raises is now viewed as "not in accordance to what black people are supposed to be about."** There are, of course, exceptions to this rule (for instance, Miles Davis was viewed as cool, but this was written off as "only a style" rather than a fact). For the most part, the progressional viewpoint of black creativity has been documented by the white press with respect to the idea of the musician who at every turn "blew his guts out" whenever he touched his axe (horn). This "image objective" has long since been the denominator that determined the reality of jazz criterion—from early Dixieland until today.

"The reality of the sweating brow" is a phenomenon that can be viewed every month in every so-called jazz publication. How many times can one recall some so-called review that questioned whether or not the musicians performing were "really doing it"—that is, did the dynamics of his or her performance really adhere to the involvement dictates that have solidified about black creativity? Jazz musicians are simply supposed to sweat—if they are serious—and this was especially the case after bebop solidified. Ensembles like the Modern Jazz Quartet have long been viewed from a distance—not because of the validity and beauty of their music, but because the dynamics of their involvement challenged the most sacred observation position that has emerged in black music commentary—that being, the reality of the sweating brow. It is for this reason that west coast jazz has long been viewed in mocking terms, because "obviously those white musicians could never 'get down' like those good old black musicians." The thrust of the sweating-brow phenomenon is deeply ingrained not only in the reality of black creativity, but also in every sphere of black participation—from athletes to dancing. Because somehow black people, in these viewpoints, are always viewed as "more primal," if I can write it that way (and, of course, this phenomenon is not separate from the "grand trade-off" as well).

In the late fifties, the dynamic implications of the "sweating brow" image manipulation would also crush the so-called third stream movement of fusion continuance. For somehow nothing is worse to white critics than the possibility of black music having anything to do with western art music—and this is extremely interesting. **Why is it that white writers have embraced so lovingly the source-transfer juncture of black music and Indian music, or black music and Arabian music, or** rock (which is a continuum of black creativity) and reggae—rock and country-and-western, etc., etc.—anything until it comes to western art music. I believe this vibrational rejection of western art music tells us something about what is really happening in present-day jazz commentary—because the realness of this phenomenon is consistent with the composite manipulation that surrounds black creativity. **The fact is, nine-tenths of the writers who have come to document so-called jazz continuance have come to the music as a reaction to the dictates of western art music—from the "across the tracks" phenomenon.** Many of the white critics who solidified the present dictates of jazz commentary (and composite documentation) have approached this subject as a basis to both get away from Europe, and to "not make the same mistake that Europe made." Moreover, the thrust of this phenomenon is not separate from the reality tone of actual American culture. **In other words, the resulting documentation that has characterized our present viewpoints about so-called jazz was written by Europeans who were trying to get away from Europe—but not to "those people"—or black people. The dynamics of present-day black music commentary are extremely interesting for how racist white writers have attached themselves to black creativity as a means to get away from other white people—while at the same time taking Europe's information tendencies (and nature) to keep blacks in their place while helping whites to live.** It's as simple and complex as that. If the medium of black music commentary is ever to be made positively relevant, then some effort must be made to restore both proper definitions and high intentions.

PR.S(RD)II–62

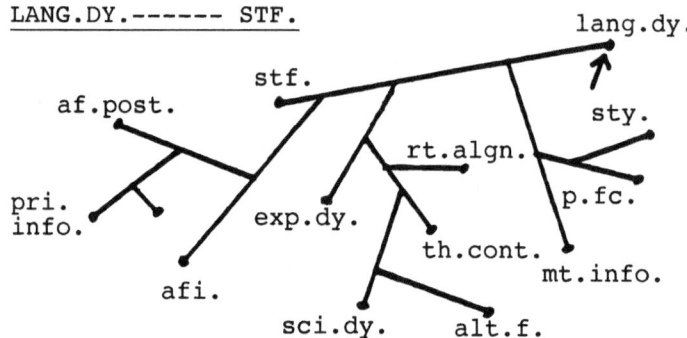

It is possible for a black musician to play a given musical idea and have two profoundly different basic interpretations. That is, (1) play the idea (note for note) but with little surface inflection, and (2) play it with as many gyrations as possible. Invariably the second treatment will be viewed as more successful in present-day black music commentary, because the present reality of information interpretation in black creativity—by white writers—is based on notions about black people that relate to the concept of "black exotica" rather than the actual music being played. Black musicians in today's music scene are viewed in the same context as black athletes. All are expected to "put out" in a way that corresponds to this so-called notion of "primal" that white people have of us. Nor is this phenomenon related to only one aspect of the music. Because black musicians are expected to live and perform in this manner all the time—regardless of context. I have read put-downs of a given individual's ballad treatment—on a given record—because that person did not "get down." In other words, every focus commentary is viewed with this phenomenon in mind—to the extent that it is isolated from the whole of what "has been done" in a given performance of record. My point is that the total reality of this phenomenon has been created by western music commentary, not by black people.

There are two related information positions that have solidified as a result of the concept of the sweating brow—and both positions can help us better understand what has and is happening in western music commentary. The first is "the concept of the good night," and the second is "the concept of non-sequence credibility." To really understand what these viewpoints are affirming is to begin seeing the profound distortions that permeate black creativity. For these viewpoints are really impositions that relate more to how white people view black people and black culture as opposed to the real dictates of blackness on its own terms, or from its own definitions—and this must be changed. "The concept of the good night" is an attitude that has long underlined how black creativity is viewed. For the realness of this phenomenon has compositely affected how any person's "participation" is viewed—in terms of its realness or its effectiveness. To really view this concept is to see something much deeper than only commentary—for the thrust of this concept moves to give insight into the intentions of the western defining and controlling community. Because the western community has successfully designed an attitude that seeks to continually downgrade individual achievement, and this cannot be lightly viewed. Only in black creativity can the dictates of a given inquiry be separate from the dictates of its vibrational dynamics. "The concept of the good night" is the observation phenomenon that seeks to evaluate a given musician's offering in a manner that contradicts the dynamics of "what that musician has offered"—and in doing so, moves to give insight into the nature of cross-transfer definitions. How is it that black musicians who utilize improvisation (that being, a discipline that utilizes "present time"—having to do with celebrating "present time" and vibrational affirmation) can be evaluated in terms of "isolating some aspect of their creative offering" by a criterion that has nothing to do with the music—and by a criterion that was responsible for why the very people writing about them have left their own so-called tradition? But this is only the beginning. How is it that great black musicians (e.g., Coleman Hawkins) are subjected to an observation criterion that dismisses the composite reality of their music offerings and instead focuses on only "what Mr. Hawkins might have played at the moment" as a means to elevate the reality of his offering. In other words, "the concept of the good night" is really a way to keep from acknowledging the wholeness of a given individual's offering, as well as a means to keep black musicians (or anyone functioning in that medium) in the position of being "boys" whose viewpoints and contributions can continually be subjected to either harassment or unnecessary challenges—even by seventeen-to-thirty-year-old white jazz critics.

It is very common to read in a review, "this is a good record, but not really the best from Mr. Parker" or "Mr. Young never played the same way after the Army," etc. etc. For myself, I have often wondered when these great musicians will ever have their activity accepted without four million qualifications. Moreover, **I have also wondered when the master musicians in black creativity will ever reach the point where their qualifications can no longer be challenged—and, as such, what they play will be viewed as "what they wanted to play."** This is especially true because the reality of improvisation in black creativity has always been directed towards the individual learning his or her tools as a means to express their lives—and indeed, give insight about both their lives and our lives. This has always been the case in black creativity, and all of the musicians have attained that level—that being, the solidification of one's functional and vibrational dynamics as a means to "affirm the realness of living." To view a given improvisor from this context is to experience the route of that person's life—through the so-called good times as well as the so-called bad times. But somehow all of this has been lost in jazz commentary. How many times do we hear "this solo was good" and "this solo was bad"? Not only that, the progressional continuance of western implication now tells us that some solos are "even great"—while others are practically nothing. This viewpoint is totally at odds with the real aesthetic of black creativity, because the reality of "participation" in black creativity has nothing to do with the "isolated phrase." Nevertheless, white producers and writers like John Hammond will write that a great musician like Billie Holiday only had a good period from her early youth until the late forties—and this is preposterous at best. Billie Holiday's activity was a total offering of her life and we are fortunate to have whatever records are available from this great musician. I mention Hammond's viewpoint only as a means to begin examining the reality of western definitions and interpretations—especially when applied to black people or black culture. Because the realness of this phenomenon has and is profoundly affecting black creativity, and it is important that some effort is made to understand what redefinitions really mean for the future of black continuance.

The reality of functionalism—and methodology—in black creativity is decidedly different from western culture, and it is time that this difference is recognized. **Musicians like Charlie Parker cannot simply be dissected into the so-called good period or bad period, because these terms have no meaning in black creativity. The fact is, to attain mastership in black creativity is to attain both a viewpoint and executional ability, as well as living credentials.** To write about a so-called bad night is to totally misunderstand black music—because "whose bad night" are we really discussing—not to mention, "bad nights are some of my best nights anyway." The realness of warped observation criterion has made a mockery out of relevant observation in black creativity, and has also helped to distort the aesthetic foundation of black creativity—and information dynamics. For the thrust of this phenomenon has put given so-called critics in the position of deciding what nights or moments of a given black master's performance are valid—and this is sickening. Every month since I have been reading about black creativity (ca. 1957), I have read articles by white critics commenting on the so-called success or failure of some given musician's musical offering. Comments like "skip this record and buy . . ." or "this is not vintage so and so because . . . ," "this session was not as inspiring as . . ." In other words, "the concept of the good night" is an observation criterion imposed by western journalism that seeks to imply that "some parts of your life, or what you were thinking about when you created a given so-called idea, are not as good as other parts," and as such, because you played the wrong part you must be penalized ("take off two stars"). This "way of viewing information" runs contrary to the dictates of black creativity, and is also harmful for coming to terms with the real music. I mention this phenomenon because it is intricately related to the information implications of western journalism.

"The concept of non-sequenced credibility" is directly related to "the concept of the good night" in terms of its observational significance, but the realness of this concept carries even greater distortions about the meta- and social significance of creative participation. For master musicians of black creativity are not viewed from the concept of what they have offered the music—in terms of the whole of their output—but, instead, every participation is viewed from the context of "accountability"—and this is both dangerous and sickening. For example, when John Coltrane began to change the functionalism of his music, one would have thought that the critical and defining wing of western journalism would have been the first sector to be open to whatever direction, or directions, that Coltrane was moving in. Because, by the middle of the fifties, Coltrane had established himself as a master musician—whose work had been embraced and respected by the composite community of creative musicians. One would have presumed that the critics' community would have been among the first sectors to focus on Coltrane's expanded functionalism—but in fact, it was just the opposite. For the thrust of negative journalism that surrounded Coltrane's activity challenged him as if he were a student without any pre-established qualifications. The reality of commentary that was transmitted to the general culture about Coltrane's activity was totally inconsistent with the state one would have thought Coltrane had long secured. This is not to say the defining community that controls so-called jazz should have been expected to like Coltrane's music—because the reality of restructuralism in western culture is not designed for extended creativity to be received immediately—but this is to say that the dynamics of criticism that ensued regarding Coltrane's music transcended the normal dynamics of rejection. For when Arnold Schoenberg extended his functionalism, no one questioned his credentials, nor did anyone try to impose their own definitions as to what his extension meant—because Schoenberg told them what his music was about, and they (the critics) believed him. As such, when the western critical and defining community said they hated Schoenberg's music—they meant just that: that is, they didn't like the music but they most certainly respected Schoenberg's ability and right to do whatever he wanted to do because Schoenberg was a master composer, and everybody knew it. But this is not the case in so-called jazz—there is no level of real acknowledgment. Instead, a given musician is viewed each time as if he had never played before in the public sector.

In the last decade, I have seen more articles violating more black musicians than at any other time of my life. I can recall articles by so-called hip jazz critics (white or black) who wrote about artists like Sonny Rollins like they were dogs or something (because that writer didn't like the direction Sonny Rollins had taken in his music). I have read articles putting down musicians like McCoy Tyner because some writer felt that "it was time for Mr. Tyner to change his music." Black artists of the highest caliber—people who have undoubtedly contributed to the composite reality of black creativity—are daily written of as if they are "on the auction block" or something. A given so-called critic will now freely give advice to a master black musician on what he or she should do in the future with his or her music. I have even read articles on a given musician's ego and how he or she has gotten "out of his/her place." To me, the present reality of black music commentary is simply incredible. For while master black musicians are being insulted daily, the composite continuance of western culture is exploiting their music—on twelve thousand different levels. Yet it is necessary to elaborate on this subject as a means to establish basis for dealing with "the concept of non-sequenced credibility."

The fact is, the offerings of a given musician must be viewed in the total context of his or her activity. This is not to say one is not free to so-called like or not like a given piece of music—because everyone has his or her own taste. But the reality of a given participation must be viewed in its total context—because the realness of an individual's music is not about one aspect of a given offering. As such, when a composer like Stockhausen offers a new composition, that composition is viewed within the continuum of his work (and inside that viewing, a given critic will like or not like his work), but in the so-called reality of jazz or black creativity, this is not the case at all. Musicians in black creativity are still viewed from the so-called cutting mentality where whoever plays the longest and strongest will "win." Like the black athlete, the success of a given participation in black creativity means that one must give every ounce of one's mettle—even to the point of having a given creative postulation not mirror "one's actual intention." Either this is done or the final critic's evaluation will view that musician's participation as "less." The effect of this phenomenon has helped to distract the composite dynamics of black creativity, because the nature of a given "offering" is geared to the dictates of false observation criteria that are separate from the music. Moreover, the composite thrust of this misperception has re-accelerated the already over-accented position of the masculine affinity slant of present-day black creativity. The end result of this phenomenon is the use of dynamic—but empty—pyrotechnics, over-long solos, over-loud dynamics, and simply over-distorted emphasis on "what is now called power"—even though in actual fact, this phenomenon retards the real power of the music. Black musicians are encouraged to prove themselves every time they take a solo, every time they make a record—and the reality of this mentality has profoundly altered the music. This is not to vibrationally knock that region of one's self where one is trying to struggle with learning and growing—for I view this struggle as related to what is most beautiful about living. Rather, it is the synthetic present-day concept of "prove it" that I am reacting to. Because in effect, this concept is one-dimensional.

There of course is much more to be said about the reality of western journalism and its relationship to black creativity. For to really understand this subject is to begin viewing the whole of what has happened in the last two thousand years—and some. The seriousness of restoring correct definitions about non-western (and western) information focuses remains one of the most important challenges for the next cycle. The thrust of this section has only touched the surface of this most complex subject—and there is much more to be written. We have now come to the juncture where every area of information dynamics must be necessarily re-examined for its transformational and real value. Either we begin this most difficult task in this time zone, or the future promises to be even more complex. For the reality of a definition is just as important as what it seeks to define. The hope of humanity is not separate from whether or not accurate information dynamics are allowed to affect the composite platform of cultural decisions and directions. Because what we think about—and how we think, as well—determines our participation in actual life—and living.

(Level Three)

1. What role can music journalism have in assisting positive transformation?
    It depends on what area of journalism we are commenting on. For the reality of so-called jazz journalism has so many special problems that its restoration will necessarily involve different particular efforts—and this is also true for so-called classical music. Probably the most basic area that must be changed is the present use of ego interpretation that permeates all western information commentary about creativity. What is needed is a change in motivation as well as focus objectives. For the realness of a given creative offering has nothing to do with whether one likes it or not—nor should this level of commentary have anything to do with the dynamics of transformation interpretation. Rather, the most basic objective of journalism should be to teach about the reality of a given thrust alignment—with respect to its history and with respect to its beauty. Music journalism must somehow come to see itself as a dynamic cultural responsibility, rather than only a vehicle for given individuals to "get over." The reality position of a given culture, in the west, is directly related to the dynamics of its information scan—which is to say, the composite interpretation of information concerns all of us. In the area of so-called jazz, there is now the need for intelligent articles—for a change—about the real reality of the music, as opposed to the spectaclization of individuals—as "they come and go." Music journalism has an important responsibility, and sooner or later, efforts must be made to make it accountable as a positive cultural tool—rather than a negative source of separation and ego gratification.

2. How did jazz criticism stunt the development of creative music during the sixties?
    The reality of composite information transference in America during the sixties created a state of being that was dynamically opposed to any

information that had the possibility to transcend established conceptual positions. This is true for creativity and this is true for many other areas of information dynamics (e.g., politics). The thrust of jazz journalism and criticism moved to paint extended creative musicians as somehow anti-music and racist. The collective mis-interpretations of the music critics helped to stunt a movement that had more than its share of troubles even before it started. If it were not for Europe, no one could guess as to what fate the post-Coleman continuum of creative music would have suffered. Jazz criticism is inextricably related to this phenomenon, because the progressional continuance of jazz criticism has helped to shape the composite nature of America's relationship with creativity. This is true regardless of what form is under consideration. This is not to say nothing positive has ever happened in this medium, nor am I commenting on anyone's particular viewpoint. Instead, the fact that jazz criticism is directly instrumental in furthering the divisiveness surrounding how we view information, as opposed to trying to help people learn about creativity in a healthy sense, is why I view this phenomenon as negative.

3. *What are the principles that could underline a more relevant approach to music journalism?*

Usually when I hear music, I find either an affinity with it or I find no affinity with it—and even this initial response is subject to change. Nevertheless, I also have found that when I have an affinity with a given composition, I will usually perceive of that piece in like terms—that is, I will probably perceive of that piece in positive terms, rather than negative terms. There is, of course, much more to this, for all of us have different ways of experiencing phenomena, and I have not mentioned my way as a means to universally fix only one vibrational criterion response. I have mentioned my relationship with informational perception and transference only to state that I have never met a person with total objectiveness to the point that when that person is commenting on something he or she likes, "something more than objectivity is taking place." In other words, to even like a piece of music is to recognize the realness of one's emotional criteria as a factor underlying responses—and this is the problem—and not the problem. Music journalists could be more positively meaningful if they channeled their energies into those areas of creativity—and particulars—they liked, as a means to help become more aware of what they themselves have discovered. I find this position much more positively conducive for transformation than the present—that being, journalists putting themselves into the position of determining what is good or bad, and in doing so, playing god while tampering with the informational and creative dynamics of the greater culture. Certainly I understand that this viewpoint runs counter to the present state of things—for music journalists today are judged by what particulars he or she likes, as well as what particulars are denounced (because everyone will know that that individual "stands for something"). But if my viewpoint has anything to do with what is true, then no one has the right to negatively put down someone's creativity. The use of this area of music journalism shows a profound misunderstanding of one's position on the planet, as well as the vibrational implications of the music they seek to evaluate.

4. Do you feel that some standard is needed in the music journalism—especially so-called jazz journalism—to elevate this medium's relationship to creative music and meaningful interpretation?

Yes. It seems to me that the only way to uplift music journalism is to establish some criteria to serve as guidelines for those special individuals who feel their viewpoint is important enough to influence others. At present, the only qualification for the jazz critic is to own ten records or more—that's about it. The situation in music journalism today is that any fool can have his or her articles printed in some newspaper or magazine—and this has dynamically affected the composite understanding of creative music—especially black creativity. Nor by criteria am I necessarily implying that the cold use of technical or mechanical devices found in classical music commentary is necessarily the highest state of observation either—because it isn't. But at least classical music commentary necessitates that the writer must know something about that which he or she professes to be an "expert" on. The jazz writer can and does write just anything—because there has been (1) no real research and documentation developed as a basis for "having the right to comment on the music," and (2) there has never been any effort to compositely view the music with respect to what it poses to alternative functionalism and/or affinity dynamics. This is a serious problem—for both the music and the musicians, as well as the culture.

5. *Would more black critics make the reality of music journalism better?*

Well—yes and no. Certainly there is a need for composite information interpretations, and it is clear that the whole of music interpretation would greatly benefit if people of every persuasion are able to participate in shaping the reality interpretation surrounding how given focuses are perceived. But the most basic factor that has moved to distort the reality dynamics of western information is the affinity-alignment dynamics that western culture utilizes as a means to perceive. As such, the problem of this phenomenon is the real factor that must be changed—or re-examined—not the so-called skin color of the person using the technique. In other words, there is not too much difference between the black writer who affirms the western information affinity position, and the white writer coming from this same alignment. For the reality of interpretation from the composite western affinity position does not lend itself to transformational interpretation, and this is the problem. This is not to say that I do not advocate the need for more non-white writers or women writers—because I do. Now, more than ever, we cannot afford the luxury of allowing only white men—of that particular persuasion—to compositely define our lives any longer. The challenge of transformation involves everyone.

6. *Why have no black magazines on creative music actualized?*

To my knowledge, the magazine *The Grackle* is the only attempt by black writers to develop a new forum for alternative ideas (I say "new" because the only other black periodical I know of—that being, *The Black Perspective in Music*—had been developed in the sixties). The failure of the black intellectual community to develop alternative publications on the music is just that—a failure. And who would we like to blame this time? We can say that the white establishment has made independent publishing impossible—we can say it is impossible to raise money in these most difficult financial times—we can say that white institutions are consciously working to keep black intellectual periodicals on either creativity or alternative viewpoints from solidifying—we can take any of these positions, or we can say the truth. It is clear to me that the transformational black writer has yet to arrive as a real actuality. I applaud the work of those few individuals who are functioning and hopefully the example of writers like Ron Welburn, Roger Riggins, and Eileen Southern will stimulate accelerated activism throughout the composite black writers' community. I keep hoping that somehow the realness of this subject has eluded me, and that there are several areas of necessary participation in the reality continuum of the black writer. I am constantly reminded of how much I need alternative viewpoints from the black writer whenever I pick up a magazine on music. Surely I am not alone in my disgust with present-day music journalism.

7. What did the rush of critics to rock in the sixties signify about the reality position of black creativity?

The composite move from black creativity to rock in the sixties simply corresponds to what everyone should already know by now. That being, the information dynamics and focus on black creativity by the composite media is only as real as the time it takes for the white community to come up with a replacement. This is true for the reality of the western information focus and this is also true for the reality of western information interpretation. Suddenly, by the middle of the sixties, the offering of acid rock came to be viewed as more vital than the composite reality of black creativity, and three-fourths of the so-called jazz critics were among the first to anoint rock as the real music of the sixties, while off-handedly laying bases for the next "jazz is dead" cycle. In other words, the rush of jazz critics in the sixties only re-affirmed the position that white people have in America with respect to information interpretation and dissemination. For the activity of children in this period would be interpreted as more dynamic than the work of musicians who had long been documented as establishing a viewpoint responsible for the reality dynamics of both popular and extended creativity. I write this not to take away from rock but only to comment on the inconsistencies that always come up when one attempts to understand the reality position of black people in America. The dynamics of the sixties information manipulation affected (1) the decline and unacknowledgment of the great continuum of blues musicians and what they have contributed to American popular music; (2) the obvious economic neglect of these same musicians until much later in the rock cycle, when a few crumbs from the economic avalanche could be thrown to certain musicians; (3) the total adoption of the functionalism of black creativity while mis-documenting every aspect of its takeover for white musicians and white culture; (4) the most dynamic information manipulation in this century concerning the use of every available outlet—for white musicians only; (5) the move to cut back or fire any musician on a record label who would not "play ball," etc. The rush of so-called critics in the sixties to rock music is directly related to how events transpired in composite America's relationship with creativity. The thrust of this period, which resecured the realness of white-dominated music—and affinity position—can be traced to the work of the white critic.

8. Do you see anything positive about the use of the jazz poll?

I imagine that the realness of a jazz poll could have a positive effect on any of the musicians who win—but even that is debatable. It is also clear that to place high on a given poll is to potentially be moving to a more visible position in the culture—as a commodity—and, with the business of music as it is in this time period, this can be viewed in positive terms. Moreover, the results of a given jazz poll are not separate from the composite reality that determines what individuals are to be candidates for particular areas of opportunity and/or exposure. For instance, I am sure that a given record company would be more open to record a musician who has won a poll than one who hasn't—yet to state this is a universal fact would be a gross over-generalization. Not to mention, there is also a difference between the reality dynamics of each poll—for the vibrational and reality implications of the critics jazz poll is very different—as far as its commercial implications—from the readers' poll. I would imagine that the dynamic implications of western media would be more available to the musician who has won the readers' poll—because this poll is really nothing more than a popularity vote. As such, these are some of the possible positive features of the jazz poll concept. But it is clear to me that, however one chooses to view this phenomenon, in the final analysis, the jazz poll must be viewed as a negative imposition that has been put on the music—at the expense of both the music and the greater culture.

9. Do you see the concept of the jazz poll as racist?

The use of the jazz poll raises many questions about the whole of the times we are living in—regardless of focus—and among the valid questions examined is, what does the application of this concept really tell us about the lining and vibrational intentions of western culture? Because if the poll mentality was equally applied to every form of music, I am sure there would be no need to even equate music polling with racism—but this is not the case. The fact is, I have never seen a poll that gauged whether Bach or Beethoven is the best composer—nor have I seen a poll that stated who should be in the composers' hall of fame—yet maybe these charges are unfair, since the poll concept was not in operation during their life cycle. But what about the composers who are alive and functioning in this time period? Why hasn't there been a poll to determine whether Stockhausen or Cage is the number one composer of this time period? Because the western intellectual community would not tolerate this kind of treatment of western art music—that's why. This is so because the poll mentality functions as a factor to take away from the significance of creativity. Clearly I have not meant to imply that the dynamics of every period have not seen the rise of particular individuals—some of whom became more "successful" than others—and surely the reality of "the favorite musicians—or object" has always been with us—regardless of culture or time zone. But in the final analysis, why hasn't the poll concept been unilaterally utilized for every music? Why is it that only black creativity—and its derivatives—is subjected to this phenomenon? Nor can we separate this usage from the composite theatre of "western living"—because no one in his or her right mind would disagree with the dynamic realness of racism as part of the American dream. If that is true—and it is—then how can we not view the use of the music poll—or jazz poll—as not having racist implications. Somehow the use of this concept moves to deny the dignity of the music, somehow the use of this concept moves to destroy the real solidarity that made the music possible, and somehow this way of perceiving black creativity lessens the vibrational significance of the music.

10. You have stated that the established methodology utilized in the normal western educational institution runs contrary to the nature of black creativity. Would you elaborate?

The gist of what I have written on this subject is only that the informational reality that sustains black creativity does not necessarily correspond to the western reality of information interpretation or affinity transference. The seriousness of this phenomenon has helped to further distort the reality surrounding how the music is taught—and as such, before any positive changes can be made, it is first necessary to understand just what has happened. Because I believe that the teaching of a given world creative projection must reflect that culture's particular vibrational alignment in information transference—which is to say, the reality that determines what the particulars are in a given aesthetic is the same reality that must underline how those particulars are to be taught. If this is understood, then it makes sense that the teaching of western art music is in accordance to the meta-reality of western information dynamics. I feel the teaching of black creativity—and world creativity—must be approached in this same manner. For no matter how similar one chooses to view these continuums (western art music and black creativity), the particulars underlying how each culture views its creativity and related pedagogy are very different. Which is to say, the real reality of harmony, rhythm, and participation in black creativity is very different from western art music—even though on many occasions both continuums will utilize the same specifics (e.g., a G7 is a G7—or a triad is a triad).

11. What do you consider to be a practical approach to teaching creative music?

First, I consider any approach that transcends the present strict "I teach, you listen" situation to be more advantageous to transformational teaching. This is not to say that I have no respect whatsoever for traditional teaching methods—because I do—but the dynamics of western education in this period are not always practical. Second, it seems to me that more emphasis should be put on open improvisation—that being, making sure that every student, no matter what level, spends one or two hours a day (or whatever) improvising. I believe that even these two suggestions could benefit the reality of present-day music education. Third, I feel it is important for young musicians to have contact with professional musicians—as a means to better understand the reality of "music living"—and as such, I would accelerate the "musicians in residence" programs throughout the country. It is important for individuals to be taught that there is no mystery surrounding what creativity is—everything can be learned and every individual's contribution is valuable. Finally, I would continue the teaching of so-called conventional harmony and instrumental development—because the information of this sector can provide the necessary basis that must be attained before real participation can take place.

12. What in your opinion is the single most important factor that must be changed in young people's musical education?

I believe the beginning of a person's musical awareness is a very important period in one's life. For the vibrational particulars that underlie what experiences and interpretations that person will have in his or her first encounter with creative postulation (and experiencing) will form the basis of that person's involvement with creativity—and extended information (maybe even for the rest of that person's life). It seems to me that the most important factor at this stage of life is positive exposure to composite creativity—as much as possible. In other words, young people should be taught to love all musics—and all things positive. I also feel that the seriousness of this question cannot end only at the point of exposure, but must also include practical involvement. In other words, young people in their music lessons should have both fun and discipline. Music and instrumental learning should not be a dreaded act, but rather a source of inspiration/creativity and learning. It is important that music teachers are developed to help students learn rather than hinder them. How many people have given up music because of the antics of an overbearing or insensitive teacher?—probably hundreds of thousands. Finally, all music lessons should include the widest possible spectrums of music. Beginning etudes, easy transcribable Bach, easy transcribable Joplin, scales, make up a song, etc., etc. In other words, a music lesson is more than simply putting a person in a straitjacket (or a snowball fight). I believe creative teaching can help to inspire creative people—and from this junction, the music will take care of itself.

13. What effect does a musician's personality have on the character of his or her music?

I have always believed that "you are your music"—which is to say, one's character is directly and dynamically manifested in every area of one's involvement. This is true whether we are referring to the imprint of one's creativity or personality traits. Once this viewpoint is stated, however, there is not much more to be said without possibly violating someone or something. Because there is really no way to put a meaning on what a particular aspect of a person's personality means—how are we to know? It seems to me that all of us, in the final analysis, gravitate towards "that which is most real to us"—having to do not with words but with natural attractions. It seems to me that "natural attraction" is even before the intention—which is to say, I believe there is also the added ingredient of a cosmic destiny consideration. Yet in these matters I am not qualified to delve any deeper. The basic vibrational character of a person's music is most certainly an outgrowth of that person's personality, as well as many other factors (e.g., the position of that person in his or her own life track, or the position of that person in terms of his/her karmic implications, etc.)—not to mention that people are so different from one another that it could be misleading to attempt to apply universal criteria to what means what. By this I am saying that a given person might be pleasant (whatever that is), but does it necessarily follow that his creativity will be any more beautiful than someone whose personality is not as pleasant? Not to mention, the history of great musicians and composers is not necessarily the history of pleasant people, or even nice people—but what does this mean? Yet I do believe a person's personality must have an effect on his or her music, but to take this question any further would not be beneficial to the question.

14. How much does the transmission of the spirit in improvisation depend on non-verbal communication?

I would say that three-fourths of the music cannot be communicated verbally. For the realness of what is actually happening in music is vibrational, and vibrationally—spiritually—oriented. For the most part, only the surface of the music can be talked about—that is, the reality of its functionalism. When it comes to the infra-reality of the music, one can only approximate zones of transference. It is for this reason that one should try to have the right musicians together, because the transfer of approximate zones of feeling and affinity is not something that can be made to happen with words. The transmission of "intention transfer" in improvised music is even more complex, because the reality of this phenomenon involves each individual's understanding of him- or herself as well as the wholeness and separateness of the music—in all of its operating theatre permutations—as well as a common understanding of the ensemble's "affinity oneness"—as a means to make a family music; while at the same time, having the ability to "surprise" the family (ensemble). Thus, the reality of this level of communication is "between the words"— because I have found for myself that "nothing is worse than someone who does what they said they would do" (in the music). Don't do it—do "it"!

15. To what do you attribute the mounting interest by young people in so-called jazz? Especially those young people who have transferred from rock to jazz?

I am not really sure of the extent of this transfer—if there is transfer— and it seems to me that this is a somewhat dangerous question. There is evidence that something is changing in composite America's attitude to creativity—but I hesitate to view this phenomenon as a concrete signal that we have successfully entered into a new period. If this change is indicative of something real, then quite possibly young people have come to that point of their lives where they are somewhat more open to different areas of creativity—maybe people are looking for another level of creativity that rock didn't offer them—but on this I have no way of knowing. This so-called new interest in jazz could also be viewed as another notch in the progressional continuum of spectacle diversion. Whatever the reason, I believe the composite culture can benefit from a greater involvement in all forms of creativity. Because it seems to me that every form of music has something to offer. I reject the viewpoint that implies that any person interested in rock must automatically leave that form if he or she is to become more aware about creativity. But I do believe if a person is interested in the diversity and spectrum of extended information, then that person must become exposed to the greater dynamics of world creativity—regardless of strain. Hopefully the mounting interest in so-called jazz is related to the forming of a composite alternative attitude about world creativity. This is needed.

16. How do you view intellectualism in relationship to jazz criticism?

Western intellectualism (ideas that are formed with respect to the reality of a perception—as that perception is viewed in so-called logical terms) has always functioned as a negative aspect to really understanding creative music—especially creative world music. Because the affinity-dynamic structure that supports western definitions does not always comment effectively on the real reality position of alternative functionalism—or world creative pedagogy. Moreover, the thrust of western intellectualism has moved to isolate and separate the reality of black music in a manner that is not real for its (black creativity) aesthetic—and in doing so, both violates and lessens the effectiveness of the music. Western intellectualism as utilized in jazz criticism is an attempt to alter the sensibility of the music and also make the music correspond to western dictates. For in the reality of western ideas, everything is true—and everything can be written on and agreed and/or disagreed with. But what is really happening with this phenomenon is that everything can be cast into the mold of western information dynamics as a means to make its continuance behave accordingly. Western intellectualism, then, is only one tool available for the western critic to help bring about this change. In the final analysis, it seems to me that this phenomenon cannot be viewed as positive.

17. What can, in the final analysis, be the only basis for criticism?

I do not believe an existential society can establish any basis for criticism—because there is no foundation to determine what a given function's value is in a vacuum. But this is not to say that observation cannot be applied in a universal context, because there is a form of activity similar to criticism that is valuable. It seems to me that in a real spiritual society, the basis for its observation and calibration is directly connected to the reality of its spiritual pedagogy. In that context, it is possible to be evaluated with respect to whatever the reality of the involvement is, but the basis of that evaluation is offered in completely different terms than present-day criticism. I am really referring to spiritual guidance, as opposed to some writer who makes the decision to put someone up or down. There is no need for the kind of commentary we have become so accustomed to—purposely hurting people, purposely putting down someone's creativity or putting it up as well (on wrong premises). The role of spiritual guidance involves consciously trying to help someone rather than destruction. For the solidification of a trans-composite music also implies a transformational pedagogical basis. The use of spiritual counselors in this context could be very positive.

18. Is there room for empirical criticism?

There is room for everything if the real effectiveness of a given consideration is not separated from how it is applied. Because if a solidified transformational basis is established for alternative functionalism, then the reality underlying what this state will mean will have its own science—or way of doing things. Thus, the use of empirical observation (not criticism) will be a necessary part of learning—and participation. The only problem with empirical observation is when there is no spiritual basis to humanize its focus. Because there is no such thing as something that "is" on the physical universe level without its motivation and spiritual radiance. (This is not to say if a person is to play a C-major scale and doesn't—or can't—that we should not be able to comment about it—because in fact this is the only area where empirical observation can be applied.) But if we are focusing on the next level of participation—that being, the music—then the basis underlining the success of a given postulation is aesthetic—not technical (as such). I believe there should be no criticism at all. In its place should be understanding and guidance (and all of this takes place before the performance, not during the performance). Individuals should be corrected in private and not made fools of in front of the composite community. Guidance should be an act of love, not ego.

19. In your opinion, what is the prime concern of the critic?

I believe that, on the first level, the prime concern of the critic is to succeed in his or her chosen job; in other words, I do not believe the first level of criticizing is to understand, or even to be concerned with whether or not criticism itself is a positive function—because obviously the critic thinks criticizing is valid. The prime concern of the critics, it seems to me, is to become established as professionals, and in doing so, move to advance both their economic and political state as "people who really know what is happening with creativity"—or "people who have the right to evaluate other people's creativity." The reality of the critic is no different than your or my reality—because in them we are still commenting about people. It is for this reason that the reality of criticism is so dangerous, because no person can feel every version or every form of creativity is positive—and no person can possibly know everything about this most dynamic subject (creativity). The dynamic problems that have come to permeate western observation are directly related to the fact that people have put themselves in positions that they could not possibly be qualified to handle. The "god position" of the western critic is not conducive to real understanding.

20. How do you view the present reality of jazz periodicals?

The present reality of jazz periodicals is much too complex to simply over-generalize, because the dynamics of every periodical is necessarily different. Yet the overall reality tone of jazz publications in this period seems very one-dimensional in comparison to what I feel is needed. For instance, there are very few real research articles in jazz publications—and I would even say that there are very few intelligent articles as well (but this is a value judgment that might not be either necessary or fair). Most of the information from this continuum relates to surface observation and social gossip—some of which is interesting, but most isn't. Some of the magazines do attempt to inform their readers about when a given musician is playing—or what musicians are playing in a given town—as well as what new records have been released, and this information is useful. But the basic tone of present-day "jazz" magazines is geared to not really dealing with what the music is, or what the realness of a given individual's music is. Instead, a given article on a particular musician will read like a feature in Pan American Airways' magazine (the ones available for reading inside the planes)—and the end result of reading this information gives little insight into the real reality state of either the musician or the music itself. I do not believe this kind of journalism is up to the level of the music, or the people experiencing the music—or the people who buy the magazines.

21. Do you see any positive attributes to the college jazz or stage band movement?

Yes. The mere fact that students today have a wider spectrum of creative contexts is in itself positive. This is true for the university as well as high and grammar school curriculums. It seems to me that if we are serious about the challenge of transformational education, then the realness of its application cannot begin only at the university level. We must attempt to inspire our youth, from kindergarten on up. The solidification of the school jazz band gives the creative student musician the opportunity to have a real context for learning about improvisation. The thrust of this opportunity can better prepare musicians for the challenge of the music—and this is positive. I see the emergence of the school jazz band as a move towards a healthy pedagogy, and I believe all students should be encouraged to participate in this phenomenon—whether or not their primary focus is towards improvisation or forms dealing with improvisation. Hopefully the reality of this development will see more attempts to gain insight into the nature or aesthetic dynamics of improvisation by the educational community. Because the composite thrust of this movement, from the sixties until now, has yet to really view itself with respect to the whole of improvisational music dynamics. For the most part, the college state band movement has functioned as a phenomenon that has very little to do with black creativity—and nothing to do with extended contemporary western art music. This is a problem, and hopefully the realness of the eighties will see a more composite attitude.

22. How important is it that more black writers write on the music?

The present reality of so-called jazz journalism can be viewed as directly related to what happens when only one area (or sector) of the greater community is put in the total position of defining. It is important that the composite people in a given environment have access to multi-information interpretation—because, especially in this time period, nothing is either one way or another. My insistence that more black writers are needed is based on what this viewpoint implies—but it is important that this viewpoint is not taken out of context. Because there is a need for more hispanic writers—and this is not a joke. The seriousness of multi-information interpretation and transference is directly related to positive or constructive continuance—for the individual as well as composite culture. Finally, the need for more black writers—or writers who are not only white men (of a particular vibrational alignment)—is directly related to what insight or affinity interpretation can be realized about the secrets of the music. If there is one thing that is needed in this period, it would be more insight into the "real information" underlying creativity, in terms of its mystical and dynamic function. We will not arrive at this point until the present reality of western interpretation is opened up to include the composite culture.

23. Do you feel there are some critics whose insights (and hence writings) into the music are more relevant than others?

I believe that critics are like the rest of us—that is, in the final analysis, we are all trying to live and learn. And also, like the rest of us, there are some critics whose viewpoint I would say is closer to "having something to do with something" than others. I cannot say a given individual's viewpoint is closer to "what is true" because to do so would imply that I am in a position to judge "real truth"—and I will not put myself in that position either. As such, probably the best overall viewpoint—that could be consistent with the whole of this book—would be that any individual, be he or she critic or mechanic, has a viewpoint, and the optimum position for a culture—in these times—would be for that individual to have a right to his or her viewpoint. My own personal belief, however, is that there are definitely writers or journalists whose viewpoints seem better thought out, better informed, more sensitively written, and intellectually broader than other writers. But in the final analysis, there is no single writer or critic—writing on a regular basis (in the jazz magazines or periodicals, etc.)—whose viewpoint I could endorse as being above the pack. On the whole, I see music journalism as being in a "sad state."

24. *If black critics have not shown themselves to be different in their approach to writing on creative music, why have you stressed the need for black critics?*

I have not stressed the need for black critics, rather I have stressed the need for black journalists. The need for black writers must be viewed in the total context of present-day social realty. For the composite documentation of black creativity has been cemented and locked by white people since black people first arrived on America's shores, and the reality of those interpretations has never been conducive to black people—or even correct. I have stressed the need for black writers and scholars to begin challenging the composite dynamics of this mis-information, because no one else will do it if they don't. Certainly it is true that many of the articles by black writers that have appeared in some of the so-called jazz magazines have revealed the same problems as the white press—and this is to be expected—especially since western culture controls the total reality of present-day education—but in the final analysis, the black scholar and journalist community will rise to the challenge of transformational definitions—because we have no choice.

25. *Why do you believe there has been a failure by black scholars to properly accept the responsibility of their position?*

    It seems to me that the reality of mis-documentation that surrounds all black creativity is directly related to the limited or non-functioning stance of the black scholar. Nor am I only commenting on one particular period of the music. Within the last ten years, even: (1) why was the book *Bird Lives!* written by a white man and not a black scholar; (2) what about the book on Fletcher Henderson; (3) why hasn't the New York critics' bloc been challenged on their successful seventies mis-documentations; (4) why hasn't the black scholar produced a body of works that interpret the reality dynamics of black music functionalism; (5) what about aesthetic interpretations and alternative criteria; (6) where are the black specialists on such figures as Lester Young, Billie Holiday, Miles Davis; (7) why haven't the black scholars developed some ideas—and implementation—towards bringing composite black creativity to the black community; (8) what forums have been developed by the black scholar to effectively deal with the real need for alternative definitions; (9) why have so few books been offered by black scholars on the composite route of significance of black creativity from Africa until today; (10) what strategic positions has the black scholar solidified as a means to change the present state of things; (11) why is it that musicians like myself (who have no writing history or training) are forced to raise questions that should have been solved two hundred years ago; and finally, (12) why have no black scholars attempted to recalibrate the methodological and vibrational dictates of composite black creativity as a means to clarify reconstruction (and where are the "Friends of Charlie Parker" societies, or the "Group to Preserve the Music of William Grant Still"—or the "Fletcher Henderson Society")? This is not to say that no individuals have contributed to the whole of positive or necessary information, because obviously given individuals have. But the actualness of the black scholars involves thousands of people. Surely the reality intensity of this time period demands that all people in responsible positions (or in emotionally near-health states) put forth some effort to change things—but where is the black scholar? ... (Huh!)

26. How do you view the present-day concept of liberal and conservative—and do you see these terms as relevant for African Americans?

One of the greatest challenges that African Americans face is separating ourselves from the value systems and affinity-dynamic tendencies of western culture—and this is true on practically every level. As for the question under consideration, I would say that, for all practical purposes, there is no difference between so-called liberal and conservative intentions. There are two most basic notions that clarify what is really happening with this phenomenon. For the concept of contemporary liberalism can be reduced to: "everything is everything (especially if it's your everything)," and the concept of conservatism can be reduced to: "this is my land . . . (and, for that matter, so is this!)." I do not believe either of these positions is transformational.

POPULAR MUSIC FROM THE BLACK AESTHETIC

(Level One) Popular Music from the Black Aesthetic

While it is generally accepted that creative music from the black aesthetic has designed the total scheme of popular music in this period, the extent of this dominance is rarely dealt with. Moreover, while the black aesthetic has defined the functional arena of popular music as a factor to help solidify "actual" culture, the extent of this defining is used to negate the significance of black creativity. To understand this paradox is to be aware of the many arguments concerning what is "high" or "serious" art, as opposed to low art. For the most basic factor used by the collective forces of western culture to balance the impact of black music is words—and the emergence of high art or low art as concepts that function in accordance to what is respectable—and these are only tools to keep the composite culture from dealing with what is actually happening in creativity in this period. Nevertheless, however one chooses to deal with the particulars surrounding this subject, it is clear that trans-African music has penetrated every level of western culture—whether we are talking of popular music for dance, music for television—movies—background music, etc., and the extent of this influence has yet to peak. So real is the dominance of black music in American culture that it is possible to talk of American music as a black music—yet the progressional continuance of the music goes even beyond this context. For the technological advances that have brought us radio, television, and the recording industry have also helped spread the availability of creative music from the black aesthetic. With the exception of China, it is possible to look at the changes black music is making on a global level—from Australia to Sweden—from Japan to Canada. Popular music from the black aesthetic is the greatest single factor for the whole of this planet.

When I write of creative black music as it has been "ised" through what we have come to call popular music, I am actually referring to the second transformational thrust projection of the black aesthetic—with regards to the implications of bi-aitionalism. By this I am saying that while there is no difference in any creativity "ised" from the composite thrust of the black aesthetic—in terms of its essence factor—there is a difference in how these thrusts are allowed to actualize with regards to physical universe particulars (having to do with how the planet is viewed in this period). To better explain: while there is no difference in the essence factor of any music "ised" from the black aesthetic, there is the realness that certain thrusts are designed to deal with certain realities—or certain thrusts correspond to particular cosmic or vibrational needs at a particular time. Thus the dynamics of a given aesthetic are directly related to whether or not it can function in a multi-spectral plane—with regards to what is actually happening on the planet level. Yet there is more here—for if we are to truly gain insight into creative black music, it is necessary to examine the cosmic and vibrational implications of black popular music with regards to its aesthetic center. The objective then becomes to comment on the significance underlying how given transformational projections function with regard to the multi-complexual realness of the black aesthetic.

What western culture has off-handedly labeled popular music in this time zone is a thrust projection of profound importance—whose implications have yet to be understood, and whose consequences are affecting the total strata of earth culture. The ramifications of black popular music must be looked at in dynamic terms—for even as this book is being written, this music is helping to reshape the vibrational and cosmic actualness of our lives. So real is the presence of black popular music in this period that no one can perceive of themselves as not affected by the music—this form has completely permeated western and world culture. If I can talk of creative black music as a bi-aitional creative thrust, having to do with composite affinity insight, and if I have commented on what bi-aitionalism means with regards to the underlying philosophical (and vibrational) implications surrounding how form is utilized, then it is necessary to examine the meta-implications connected to popular music as it relates to this phenomenon. For if what we call popular music is actually a thrust projection "ised" from the affinity insight (2) principle, then it is necessary to elaborate on what the vibrational and conceptual actualness of this phenomenon might mean—with regards to what is happening now, and what we would like to be happening now (or later). When I stated that popular music from the black aesthetic is the contemporary manifestation of the affinity insight (2) principle, I am really saying that black popular music is the thrust projection that normally would have this position if there were "culture"—or if the consideration of "culture," as an actualness, existed. I do not mean to imply that black popular music, in itself, has no culture either—for that would be ridiculous and away from my point. When I write of "culture," I am referring to the solidification of what this word means in a real-life sense, as opposed to a secular sense. More so, when I stated that black popular music functions as a substitute for the affinity insight (2) principle in this time zone, I am commenting on the realness of the transition cycle we are now living in at present. To understand the significance of black popular music is to be confronted with the realness of what the affinity insight (2) principle is all about. This is true on both a functional and cosmic level, yet it might be impossible to accept this viewpoint without an examination of the reality implications of the affinity insight (2) principle—in a varied context.

If a given creative thrust gains its significance from how it participates in solidifying reality for a culture group—how life is viewed and how activity (doing) corresponds with the ritual functions outlining particulars—as well as its spiritual alignment (in cosmic and spiritual terms), then that thrust can be viewed as functioning in accordance to the multi-dimensional realness of creativity. If the affinity insight (1) principle is the phrase I have coined to describe what this phenomenon means with regards to "essence or force" alignment (dictating how a given culture sees itself), then the affinity insight (2) principle would have to do with how this vision is manifested on the physical universe level—in actual life and "doing" terms. The thrust projection we call popular music is a manifestation of creative flows affirming how we—as a people—have chosen to move with who we are—or for this analogy, "what we see." Nor do I mean to limit the composite effectiveness of the affinity insight (2) projectional thrust by defining it only with regards to one function, for in fact the significance of any given thrust merits a separate book of its own. I have raised this viewpoint only to state that the essence factor which determined the existence of creativity—or, in this case, popular music—means something, and any serious attempt to deal with the significance of popular music would reveal some aspect of that meaning. More so, any attempt to deal with the realness of popular music would necessitate some effort to examine how given thrusts have come to be viewed with regards to the essence factor (or source projection) it affirms. It is for this reason that I have gone through such lengths to formulate definitions like affinity insight (1) and affinity insight (2). Quite possibly the best way to write about my conception of the affinity insight (2) principle would be to look at how this thrust manifests itself in 'actual' culture. For the affinity insight (2) principle is directly connected to how a given thrust projection is actualized on a physical universe level. In its optimum position, the affinity insight (2) principle would be directly connected to the social implications involving how given forms are utilized (for example, the actualness of dance is connected to the ritual implications of a given creative thrust, and I do not mean "dance" in only one context—there is dance as a spiritual function, there is dance as a social function, and there is dance as a mystical and healing function). Another example of how a given creative thrust might relate to the affinity insight (2) principle can be found in work songs, community function (or unification) music, or creativity as a vibrationaltory functional thrust (i.e., ceremony). Nor have I meant to imply that the significance of any one aspect of bi-aitionalism is more than any other aspect, because this is not what I believe either—nor would this route of thinking bear out in real analysis. My point is that the seriousness of bi-aitionalism is what we are dealing with in any attempt to investigate present-day popular music, and the realness of this subject is directly related to the actualness of popular music from the black aesthetic.

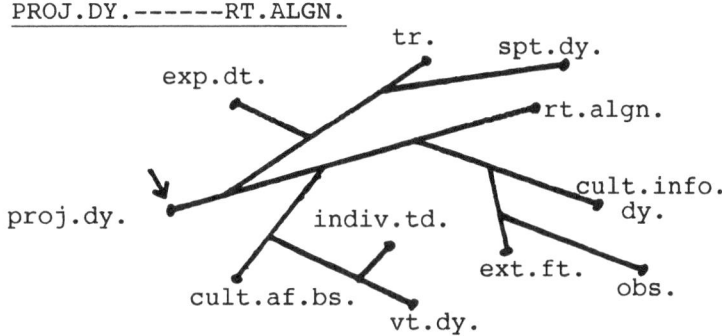

The reality implications of popular music in this time zone can best be understood by examining the source-transfer junction of the early fifties. This is so because the time zone of the fifties solidified how creative music from the black aesthetic would flow with regards to the next transition cycle in American as well as black culture, and also what this flow would mean in social terms following the Second World War. This period would thus detail the transfer-shift dynamics of black creativity as a resolidifying link between the social and political factors affecting black people in America (i.e., the solidification of the migration cycle to the north en masse, and the changing reality brought about from the participation in the war) and in dynamic terms (the need to look towards the future, and the real belief that things would get better). The emergence of black popular music in this time period would thus bridge the progressional continuity of black music—and, as such, black culture—while at the same time help lay a basis for establishing the next transition. The nature of this continuity would provide a vibrational platform from the creativity of the early forties to extended forms that could express the forces reshaping a changing American cultural continuum. To understand the vibrational dynamics of this change is to view the significance of the fifties—with regards to black American culture. The transfer junction I am referring to is the composite thrust of black creative music in the late thirties and forties. Any attempt to understand the subsequent changes that occurred in the music during the fifties must take into account what change means in the context of progressional continuity. For while the focus of this section is concerned about the actualness of change—and the transition cycle of the fifties—it would be a gross error to assume that the thrust projection of black creativity had somehow momentarily experienced a loss of motion in the thirties and forties. In fact, the opposite is true. The progressional continuance of black creative music in the forties can clearly be looked at as dynamic in every sense of the word. This was the time zone that experienced the last period of the big band development, and as this book is being written, America has yet to have another period quite like the forties. Musicians like Duke Ellington and Count Basie characterized only one progressional thrust of the music, and many people would be quite surprised at the composite spectrum and intensity of the music in that period. Nor was participation relegated to only one area of black creativity, for many of the dances that came from this period were as dynamic as anything happening today. Dances like the Hucklebuck and Charleston were only a few of the many styles practiced in that time zone. My point in mentioning all of this is only to lay the proper backdrop for looking at the post–World War developments surrounding black culture and black creative music. All of the subsequent changes that reshaped black music in the fifties can be understood by examining the social and vibrational factors surrounding the composite reality of the music—in aesthetic terms, as well as what this phenomenon means in physical universe terms.

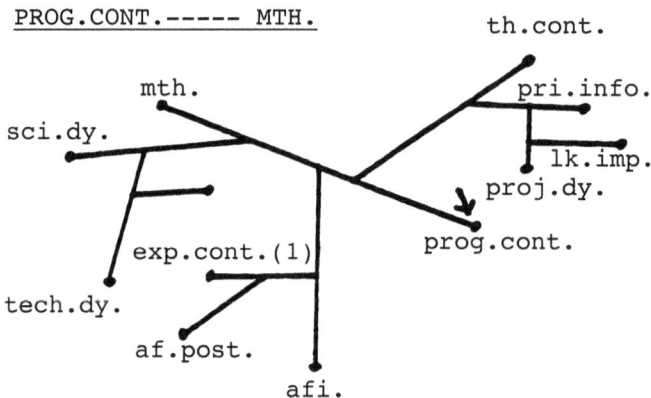

Without doubt, the thrust projection that provided the central link to the progressional continuance of creative black music—in the cross-transfer shift of the fifties—was the solidification of "rhythm and blues." Any attempt to deal with the actualness of popular music in this time zone would necessitate some effort to deal with this subject. The solidification of rhythm and blues could be looked at as a development related to the social fabric surrounding black culture in the transfer junction of the forties, and the thrust projection solidification of that which we now call "the blues" (the most basic difference between these projections has to do with how one continuum was reshaped rhythmically to function in accordance with the changing vibrational reality of black culture—this difference can be understood especially if the consideration of dance is dealt with). For the most basic factor that distinguishes rhythm and blues from blues is the realness that the "former" was redesigned to meet the changing social and vibrational ritual functions of the black community in the post-war period. Yet it must also be stated that however one chooses to deal with the realness of rhythm and blues, the essence factor which determined both of these thrusts are in fact the same. In other words, what we really mean when we used the word "blues" is also an integral factor in rhythm and blues. The progressional continuance of a given creative projection can best be viewed with regards to its change of shape—but this change must not be separated from the essence factor that solidified it. Rhythm and blues was thus a form that corresponded to the vibrational actualness of the forties, and in doing so, provided the most central link for what was to occur in the fifties.

The time zone of the fifties would thus be a period where the transfer-junction continuance of popular music would solidify as an actualness. Any attempt to deal with the present situation we are in—with regards to creative music—would imply that some effort is made to deal with the vibrational reality of the fifties. More so, if we can say that the phenomenon of transfer-shift continuance is an integral progression surrounding how a given culture is maintained—or destroyed—then we must view the time zone of the fifties as a period that provided how this shift was to occur. For the time zone of the fifties was the juncture that experienced the second thrust of technological advances to reshape American culture, and this was also a period where the controlling forces dictating American culture would secure their next thrust alignment. The significance of this phenomenon is directly connected to the changes that took place in American culture, and these developments greatly determined what was to transpire in the creativity as well. In fact, the seriousness of changing social-reality dynamics would affect the events surrounding creative music, on a level that was unprecedented. Before the decade of the fifties had passed, the magnitude of this phenomenon could be sensed, for at this point it was clear that something different was in the air.

The solidification of "rock and roll" as a term could be seen forming in the early fifties in the transfer-shift junction of creative black music—and the actualization of this form as a movement was a reality by the middle fifties. Rock and roll was thus the projection that dictated the transfer shift of black music to the composite American arena (and in doing so, supplied the basis for how the social progressions of American culture would proceed), as well as the embodiment of the next transitional continuance of American culture (towards transformation). It was thus in the fifties that the solidification of this phenomenon became "real," and it is at this juncture where we can begin to examine the factors that directly affected the period we are now living in (the late seventies). Without doubt, the progressional development of the communications and recording media played an important role in helping to establish the momentum that rock music secured by the middle fifties. In fact, the over-balance surrounding how rock and roll is now utilized in western society can be looked at as being directly related to the total social implications that the form first signaled. This is so because the emergence of rock and roll must be looked at in accordance to what its appearance meant to white America, as opposed to black America. In other words, the spread and dissemination of rock music was not a response to the composite factors shaping how the black community functioned—for rock and roll was only another projectional thrust from rhythm and blues, and as such was received as only another factor in the black community that could be experienced—but rather, the significance of this form is directly coupled to what it posed to white

America. The emergence of rock and roll would signal the nature of the next transfer cycle in western culture, and on a physical universe level, this phenomenon would manifest itself in the cross-transfer shift of black popular music. Thus, the attraction this form would have in the white community would serve as the strongest factor to solidify moves towards real alternative options (with regard to life thrust).

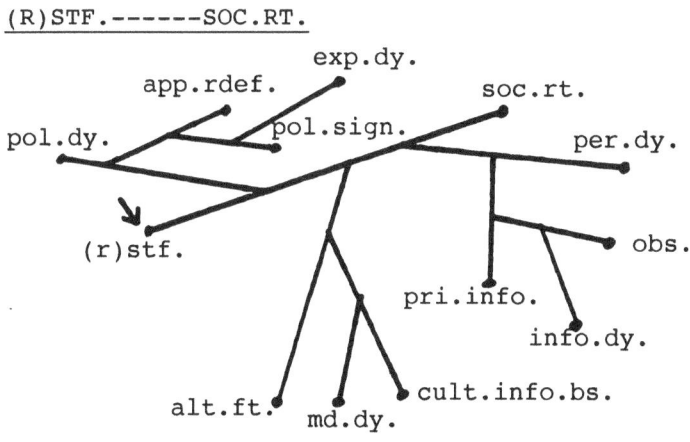

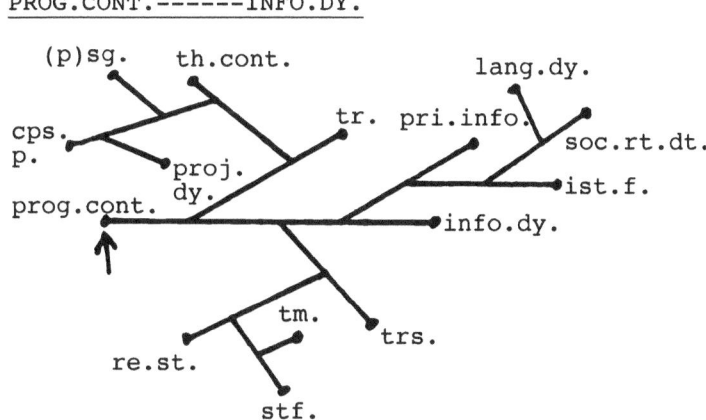

The move to embrace black popular music by the white community in the fifties cannot be looked at as an isolated development, but rather a cyclic ritual directly in accordance to the progressional dynamics of American culture. Every junction in American history has witnessed this same pattern, and yet many white people would have us believe that the phenomenon of source-transfer progressionalism (which seems to be a natural progressional development in every cultural thrust) has not overly relied on any one so-called ethnic tendency. There can be no doubt that the utilization of black creativity has been the most distinguishing factor to personify American creativity—and if this does not imply an over-reliance on black creativity by the composite forces of American culture, then I'll go on to something else. Whatever, the progressional involvement of rock and roll in American culture would directly shed light on the meta-reality of creative black music—as a transformational tool—and the attraction this form would have on the whole of composite American culture would personify the vibrational arena of the fifties (and sixties—and seventies—and . . .). In this context, rock could only be compared to—ragtime—Dixieland—swing (!)—black folk music (?)—blues (??)—in other words, there are other contexts (!). Yet I do not mean this in light terms. For if we can say that the vibrational arena surrounding the emancipation period in American history can be looked at as directly related to the situation that produced ragtime music, then we can also view the progressional developments of popular music in the fifties as the principle-thrust projection that dictated the transfer-shift juncture of the present time period (the late seventies).

By the middle of the fifties, it was possible to look at the effects of the re-formation juncture in African popular music. This was the period which saw the forming of ensembles from both black and white communities across America, and the thrust of these various groups would establish the arrival of rock and roll. Yet it must be said that even at this juncture there were basic distinctions between how the black community would relate to the emergence of this phenomenon compared to that of the white community. For if, in the beginning, the arrival of rock and roll was perceived as a new composite thrust—a coming together of the races—by the late fifties, there was a clear distinction in the music (and the factors related to that separation are also constant variables—related to every development of American culture as well—those being, the significance of the political position white people are in during this period, and the actualness of money and power as factors that do not necessarily work for unification—on any level). Nevertheless, the early emergence of rock and roll would forecast the next utilization—and adaptation—of "spectacle," as well as provide the next alignment of "style" (as a necessary ingredient that is related to the "forward" image of the music). In this juncture, we could see the arrival of ensembles like the Platters, Frankie Lymon and the Teenagers, the Del-Vikings, Fats Domino, Sam Cooke, or, from the white community, groups like Bill Haley and His Comets, and later Fabian and Frankie Avalon. By the middle of the fifties, the projectional realness of rock had solidified, and the meta-implications surrounding this phenomenon (in extended terms) would thus function in progressional sequences—that is, all of the developments that sprang from the solidification of rock as a transfer-shift junction in American culture were "ised" in the very early period of the music's arrival. By the late fifties, the vibrational implications surrounding the adaptation of rock had also crystalized—that being, rock music as a social reaction to the essence projection of western culture (or at least, rock music as a vehicle to participate in what would seem to be a rejection, but what was in fact only the peculiar progressional alignment of western continuity as manifested in style). To understand what this so-called rejection means in dynamic terms is to deal with the multi-complexual complications surrounding America's relationship with black creativity. More so, to understand the actualness of the spectacle-diversion cycle that permeates America's involvement with black creativity is to see the basic difference that separates the white community's reality from that of the black community (and from the aesthetic lining of creative black music). Yet I have not meant to imply that this involvement is mono-dimensional, because it isn't. My point is that the adaptation of black music—by the white community—provided insight into the nature of America's next thrust alignment in the fifties, and the significance of this alignment also helped solidify the post–World War Two time junction of American continuance (yet I do not mean to underestimate the effect of the Korean War). The fact is, by the middle of the fifties, rock and roll had already moved into the position of shaping the next vibrational alignment of American culture.

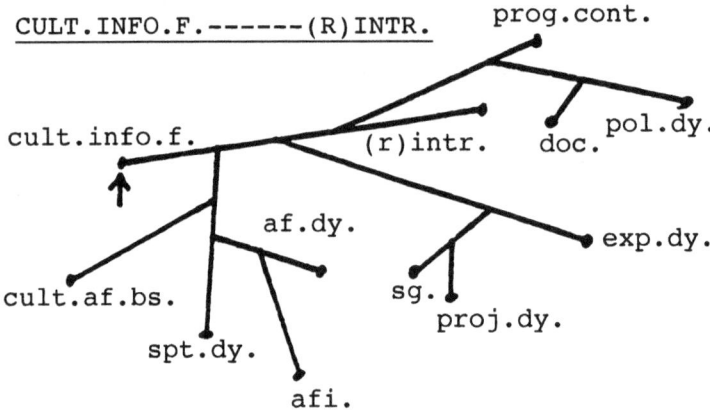

When I stated that there was a difference between how the white community embraced rock as compared to the black community, it should not be mis-interpreted that I am viewing the white community in a negative context. My reasons for citing this difference is only to examine what affinity alignment really means, with regard to the social progressions of the fifties—as well as the subsequent factors related to what this difference means for the present period we now find ourselves in. Moreover, my basic reasons for commenting on the affinity alignment of the white community is to examine what that alignment really is—in both cosmic and physical universe terms. Because I believe the affinity alignment of the white community during the fifties dictated the progressional alignment pattern of the post-war vibrational cycle—leading to the present. **The most basic difference between the affinity alignment of the white community and that of the black community—with regard to how popular music (rock) was and is perceived—is the realness that rock music is perceived as a vehicle for commenting on the social-political developments (in accordance to the spectacle-diversion cycle) in the white community, while in the black community, popular music (or rhythm and blues) is perceived of as a factor related to the natural**

progressional continuity of creative black music—and this difference is extremely important for what it reveals about the composite actualness of rock music as an American music. To understand the adaptation of rock and roll by the white community in the fifties is to become aware of what form the next progressional cycle of western culture would take—at least in vibrational terms—and this is directly related to how rock and roll would be utilized—in functional terms—as well. For when I stated that the composite affinity alignment of white culture has to do with how given social and political progressions are perceived, I am also saying that the composite utilization of rock could be viewed as a functional as well as aesthetic consideration. In other words, the basic understanding that surrounded the mass move to rock in the white community—especially in the early period—was that this move could be interpreted as an embracing of alternative resources—or rebellion. So profound would this affinity-alignment interpretation be that it would materialize as a counter-cultural thrust in the middle sixties. In the early stages of its development, rock was perceived as related to only surface forms of alternativism, such as motorcycles, slick hair, and the transfer shift occurring in language (but these manifestations were only early signals related to the basic thrust alignment of this phenomenon—in physical universe terms). By 1955, the actualness of rock was upon the composite culture, but the momentum underlying what this form would signal had yet to reveal itself—rock and roll had only just begun.

PRI.VT.TD.------MOT.DY.

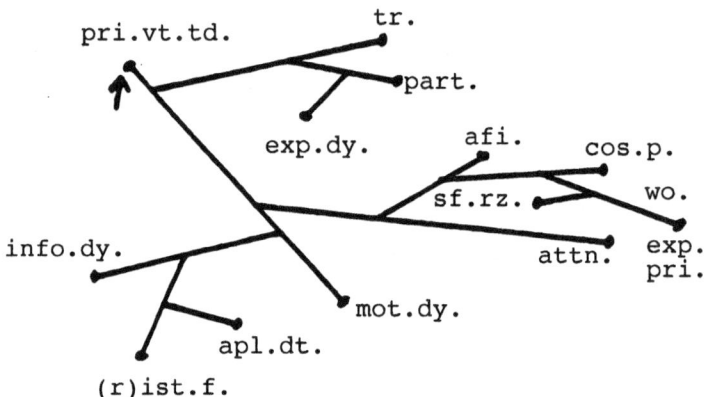

The actualness of the middle fifties transfer shift in the white community could be summed up by the impact Elvis Presley was to make on the scene—moreover, the solidification of his activity would establish the cross-transfer junction of rock and roll as a composite (American) thrust. That is, the emergence of Presley could be viewed as a signal that the second thrust projection of rock music had been secured, and that the white community would now have a dynamic alternative thrust projection from that of the black community. In other words, the actualness of Presley's activity would make it possible for young white musicians to draw from his work and thus rely only on white models—in the developing stages of learning about the meta-reality of rock and roll—rather than black models. The seriousness of this alternative was profound, for it must be understood that even up until the middle fifties, young musicians interested in rock had nowhere to go but the black community if they really wanted to learn the music. I do not mean to slight the early activity of white musicians before 1955, but it is undebatable that no single force captured the imagination of the masses before Presley. Prior to this period, the progressional sequence surrounding learning how to deal with the reality and functional dynamics of rock involved, for most, listening to black music on the radio and gradually being forced to come into the black community—like it or not. The actualness of Elvis Presley would change this progression somewhat, and the realness of his activity would allow for the next application of gradualism—that being, white form rather than black. Presley's position in the fifties could be compared to that of Frank Sinatra in the forties, in the sense that his beingness would provide the necessary symbol for the momentum surrounding white participation in rock. His music would thus be used to define what the period of the fifties would mean with regards to the white aesthetic, and his activity would also dictate the progressional development—and acceleration—of rock as a separate factor from black music—and there were many reasons for this. For obviously Presley's activity was not received in the black community in the same manner as in the white community. For most black people, his work was viewed as something either humorous or something of social significance, rather than musical. More so, it was clear that Presley's activity had been directly inspired from black creativity—which is to say, there was no real reason why black people should have viewed his activity as uniquely different, but rather another example of the source-transfer junction in American culture. For while Presley's activity solidified a whole new approach to both singing and performing popular music in the white community—laying a basis for singers like the Righteous Brothers to come to the fore—in the black community, his work represented neither innovation nor dynamics, but only a poor spin-off of black popular music (i.e., rhythm and blues)—and this response was to be expected. But if white America had been experiencing rock and roll in the closet before the dynamics of Presley's activity, this was to change completely. Presley's work would mark the beginning of a new era in American popular music.

TF.SH.------CULT.INFO.F.

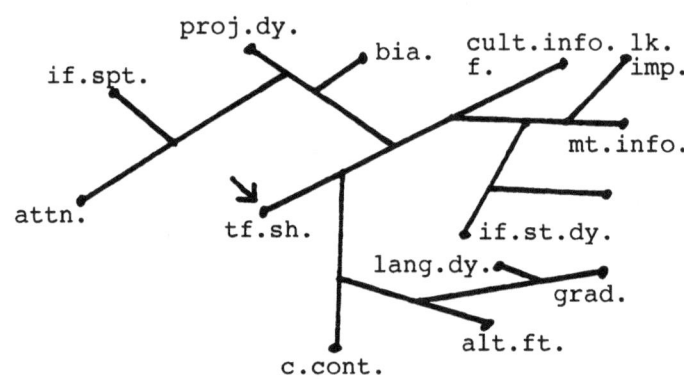

By the late fifties, the momentum surrounding the adaptation of rock as an American composite music had produced two basic effects—those being, the separation of rhythm and blues—or black popular music—as a thrust projection attached to the rock movement (even though, in actuality, this form was never really connected in the way most people thought), and the emergence of the cross-sectional thrust movement as a signal reflecting the progressional implications underlying where rock had brought us in the late fifties. Both of these factors would be of enormous importance as the time zone of the fifties concluded. For to understand the arena that determined how these factors were to be defined at this junction in time is to better have a basis to deal with the transition cycle of the sixties. When I stated that rhythm and blues had never really been a part of rock and roll, I am only saying that the affinity projection of this thrust was separate from the arena that dictated rock and roll. Rhythm and blues functioned according to the vibrational arena surrounding trans-African expansionalism and, as such, could not be perceived as being in the same vibrational arena as rock and roll. Performers like James Brown, Smokey Robinson and the Miracles, and Otis Redding functioned from a creative thrust that was very much attached to the reality base of black culture (as a separate phenomenon from composite America). This was the time zone where even the performing outlets of black and white popular musicians were separate. Thus a performer like

James Brown functioned within the "black circuit," and a given engagement would find his group playing in places like the Regal Theater in Chicago, or the Apollo Theater in New York. Moreover, I have not meant to imply that no white people listened to rhythm and blues—because this type of statement would not be in accordance to actual life—but I have meant to state that the progressional alignment of rhythm and blues could be talked of as being separate from the composite thrust of rock and roll. However, it would be wrong to assume that no activity from a cross-sectional juncture developed in the fifties. For as the progressional thrust of rock and roll assumed new dimensions, many black artists could be seen participating in the composite thrust of rock. By the late fifties, an artist like Chubby Checker could command the support of both black and white audiences, and a musician like Fats Domino would also enjoy the benefits of a composite audience. So pronounced was cross-sectional participation in rock by the late fifties that this period could be talked of as an indication of what unification (and alternative functionalism) would mean to the progressional continuance of rock in the sixties and seventies, and there were still other factors connected to this phenomenon. For the controlling forces surrounding the spread of rock had long created a progressional feature that safeguarded the economic and exposure implications surrounding popular music—which is to say, unlimited access to the basic power alignment surrounding rock was open only to those whose activity corresponded—or whose activity could be reshaped to correspond—to the desired affinity alignment that served their (the controlling forces') interest. Thus, a group like the Supremes would gain the media attention it deserved after subsequent alterations were made in their activity (i.e., moving to a zone that corresponded to the composite vibrational spectrum, rather than vibrating solely from a black perspective)—and while on the surface, this move was admirable in itself (for certainly any activity that vibrates to multi-composite overtones is something I am interested in), the fact that these alterations were forced (i.e., do it or else)—as well as designed aesthetically and vibrationally—cannot be dismissed or taken lightly.

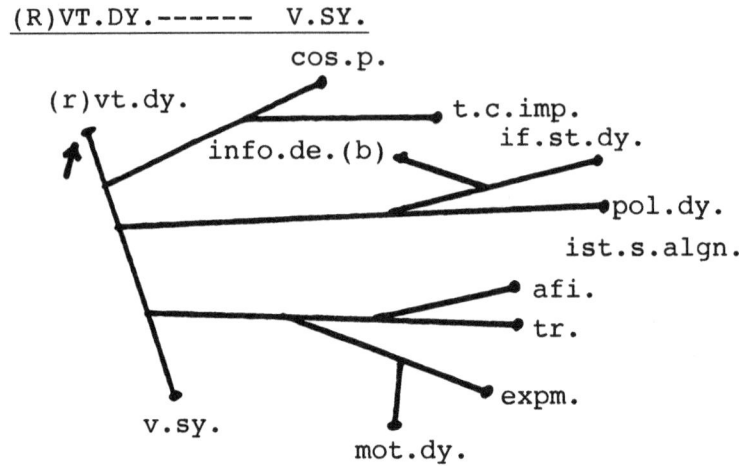

If Elvis Presley is considered to be the pivotal focus that defined the nature of white participation in rock during the late fifties, then the realness of this phenomenon would establish the source-transfer nature of present-day "perceived" rock (and "roll"?). In other words, with the entry of groups like the Righteous Brothers or Jerry Lee Lewis, it is possible to view the aesthetic implications underlying what this phenomenon posed; more so, the nature of this progression would also comment on the transfer-shift cycle surrounding rock. For if Presley's entry into the market signaled how the next progressional juncture of popular music was to solidify (as an American thrust)—and if his entry also commented on the progressional continuance that would surround the co-opting of style from black music—then the ensembles after him would solidify what this co-opting would mean in actual terms. It was thus with these ensembles where the second transformational alignment of rock music was secured, and gradually a separate music would solidify which adhered directly from the functional mechanics and actual style (dictates) of black popular music. By this I am only saying that from the early to middle fifties, there was always a clear difference between black and white popular music; and because of this difference, it was always very easy to tell whether a given performer was black or white. In other words, basic vibrational and vocal inflections served as a natural barrier between these two projections of popular music, and this factor also served as a distinctive shield that accented the separateness of black and white music. Yet as the sixties approached, this distinction would become more and more difficult to detect, for the progressional development of rock as an American thrust would reach into every area of black music, co-opting both its form and inflection dynamics. The actualness of this phenomenon would establish the transfer-shift realness that rock had now become a secured American music (that being, a music that expressed the affinity and vibrational intentions of white Americans).

The significance of the completion of the transfer-shift phenomenon in the fifties should not be taken lightly, for the developments shaping the progressional continuance of rock and roll would now be able to function from a "pure" white perspective, rather than a black or composite perspective. **For it is understood that the most basic factor determining whether or not a given consideration can be utilized by the controlling forces of western culture depends on how that consideration is viewed in "cultural terms"—in other words, the fact that rock was solidifying as a white thrust would mean the full benefits of western culture could now be utilized to advance the music—that is, the solidification of rock as a white music would mean that western words could be thus applied to the form through "gradualism"—as a means to redocument how the power structure wanted rock viewed.** The particulars that helped solidify this change were, of course, not new, for the progressional manipulation that surrounds the securing of a transfer-shift progressionalism in creativity is an integral feature in western culture. The definitions of the late fifties had actually secured the last necessary juncture for this sequence to happen. To understand the sophisticated manipulation that surrounds the securing of creative transfer shifts is to view the dynamics of the controlling forces in western culture. For the historical developments related to every period of creative music from the black aesthetic have had to deal with this same phenomenon regardless of time zone. It was in the period of the thirties that the progressional controlling forces surrounding the thrust projections of so-called jazz applied the full weight of gradualism, as a tool to redefine the composite thrust of the swing period—and as a move to define the music in accordance to the white aesthetic. The results of this effort are related to how we now perceive the thirties—with respect to creative music (and everything else). For when I stated that the progressional forces surrounding creative music in the thirties tampered with the composite actualness of the music happening in that time zone, I am also stating that this phenomenon is directly connected to the rise of many of the practicing white ensembles in that same period—not to mention that the sophistication of the collective forces surrounding that music extends even to framing how given periods of the music are compositely perceived. In other words, the labeling of Benny Goodman as the "King of Swing" in the thirties can be looked at as a progressional consideration related to the completion of the source-transfer shift of the thirties—and by the same token, the labeling of Elvis Presley as the "King of Rock and Roll" can be viewed as a factor related to the progressional continuance of this same alignment phenomenon. What is important is that we understand that all of these devices must be looked at as related to the dynamics of the controlling forces surrounding the music, and each progressional sequence provides the nature underlying how a given transfer cycle will be achieved—as related to particulars. Thus, by the end of the fifties, the situation in popular music could be looked at in a number of ways, for at this time junction, both the black and white projectional creative thrusts had solidified, as well as a composite crossover type of music, and all of this activity had been designed from the functional and vibrational arena of black music (and "matters").

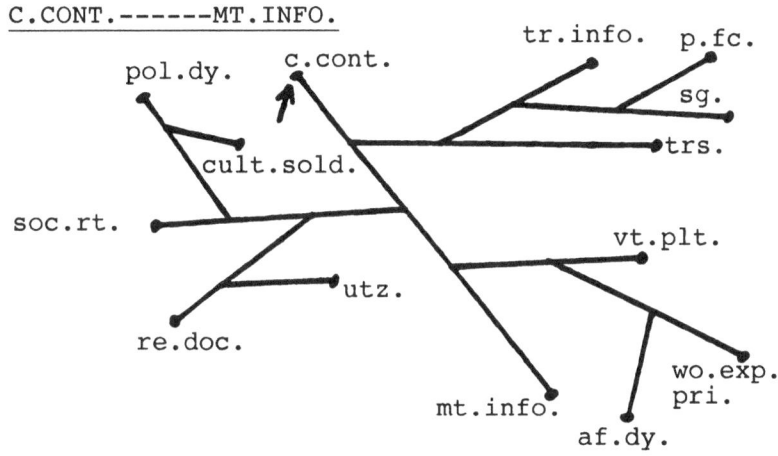

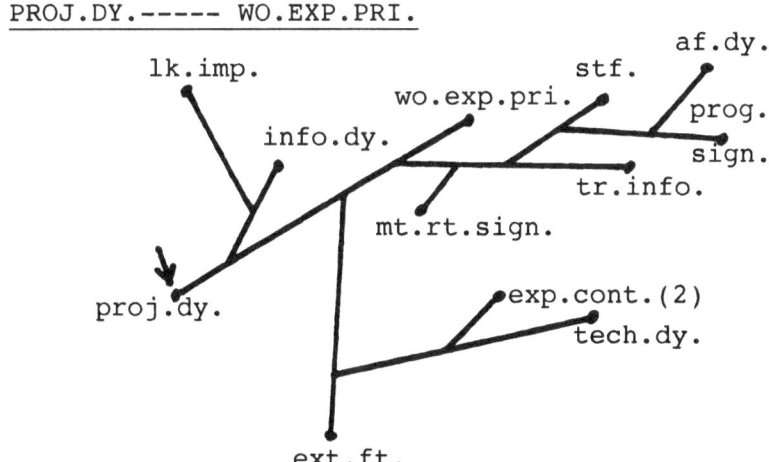

There were many other factors related to the spread and dissemination of rock music in the middle to late fifties, and all of these considerations would help define the transfer-shift implications of American popular music. For as the response of rock increased, more and more media involvement would take up the cause. By the middle fifties, rock music would find itself broadcasted daily on network television on programs like *American Bandstand*, and it is impossible to speculate on the influence this one program was to have on the white community in the transfer-shift period of the music. For the media's support of rock and roll would have a direct effect on the nature of the forming composite forces surrounding the music. The availability of rock on network television would also help solidify what form its dynamic essence factor would take as an alternative creative thrust—and what that dynamic would mean with regards to style, the spread of new dance forms, the initiation of new language (or slang), and the changing meta-reality of popular music. More important, the use of media would also outline the total cultural re-alignment phenomenon taking place in the white community—how the white aesthetic was to be redefined in accordance to the vibrational actualness of the late fifties, and how this new re-alignment would manifest itself in white creativity (as it applied to popular music)—and what this alignment would also mean in the sixties and seventies. For the end of the fifties brought two things: one, the attractiveness of rebellion as ideology (with regard to style), and two, the realization in big business that a phenomenon was occurring that was significant enough to merit adjusting by whatever degree necessary to be a part of it.

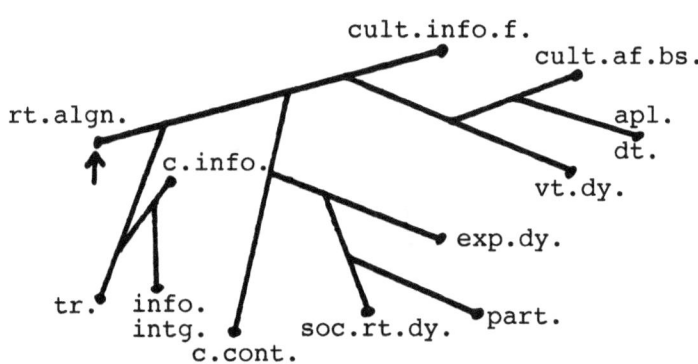

The thrust projection of rock as a national spectacle would have multiple effects on the basic social progressions surrounding American culture—especially with regard to what this phenomenon would mean in the black community. As the social implications of popular music shifted into the second degree of acceptance during the late fifties, there were several factors related to this phenomenon that could not be ignored. Certainly the most glaring aspect of this phenomenon was the separation of black popular music from white popular music, as well as what would result from this separation in the black community. For instance, by the end of the fifties, black popular music had begun to be viewed in the context of what was called "soul," as opposed to rock and roll, which meant white popular music. As the distance widened between black and white popular music (which is to say, as white rock moved on to become the most successful popular music of this period), the composite black community's reaction would become the basis for the progressional-vibrational developments that permeated the vibrational context of black attitudes throughout the sixties. By this I am saying that as the spread of white rock advanced into the next level, the understanding that developed in the black community was something akin to "we have soul, even though you have the power structure." The seriousness of this viewpoint would be an important factor that the black community would later be forced to deal with in the seventies—for no matter the inequalities that surrounded the spread of white rock, there is nothing more important than vibrating to the universal-cosmic realness of what is true about life on this planet. The subsequent developments which affected the thrust of black creativity—and the black community—would detail the progressional continuity of black creativity as a factor in the underground of American culture—even though this was not what black people in particular desired. More so, all of the factors affecting life in the black community in this period would reveal the forming progressional-alignment developments surrounding what was to be the next sequence of events for black people in the sixties. For this period formed as a response to the intense pressures that were mounting in the black community—having to do with the physical universe injustices that black people and culture were dealing with. The net effect of these various pressures would explode on the scene in the early sixties, with a venom that was to surprise the white community. But the seriousness of this phenomenon cannot be summed up in one sentence or paragraph—for to deal with the reality actualness of the black community in the late fifties would touch on many different factors.

When I wrote that the vibrational lining of the black community moved inward, I am actually commenting on the path black culture was to take as a means to deal with the reality situation of black people in the late fifties. What this isolation meant in actual terms could best be summed up by looking at the real reality of life in the black community. For the most basic factor that must be acknowledged—if one really desires some real understanding of black culture in this time period—is that the collective forces of western culture have produced a reality context which gives few options—in actual life terms—for non-white people. Thus, the average person from the black community has more than enough to deal with in just struggling with basic survival, and the collective-functioning forces in the black community would later have no choice but to also focus on basic survival considerations. Many of the concepts that would surround the understanding of "soul"—as an exclusive phenomenon that only black people had—were "ised" from the suppression of African-American culture—as well as the lack of participation in the composite spectrum of the culture. Nevertheless, the composite vibrational acceptance of "soul" would later become an important factor related to the progressional path popular black music was to take, and the institutionalizing of "soul" as a spectacle-diversion image would later provide the basis for the middle sixties to seventies transfer junction (and spectacle), as well as the later reduction of black creativity to "style" in the seventies. But during the late fifties, the concept of soul would be the rallying basis that helped to solidify the progressional alignment of black creative music. Companies like Motown Records would thus capitalize on what this new forming would mean—in both progressive and dynamic terms, and while their ability to secure a niche in the business world is to be applauded, the concept of "soul" that solidified from their activity would provide a limited framework—with regard to how black music would later come to be perceived (as opposed to what was actually happening in the dynamic spectrum of the music)—for the composite transfer-thrust developments in the seventies. This was, then, the situation as rock and roll moved into the sixties.

    If we can say that the fifties was the period that substantiated how rock and roll was to be defined, as well as the time zone that

revealed how the transfer cycle of this form would be achieved, then we could view the sixties as the time zone that transformed how that achievement would manifest itself in dynamic terms (and what it would mean in itself). For the progressions of the sixties would provide deep insight into the composite actualness of American culture. This was to be one of the most important periods in the progressional development of American culture. For while the solidification of rock and roll was to take place in this period, everything else would come to the fore as well. The seriousness of the sixties as a progressional indicator will be discussed for some time, for whether or not one agrees with my interpretation, it is clear that something of the utmost significance occurred at this junction. Moreover, any attempt to deal with the progressional implications of American popular music would imply a detailed examination of this time zone as well. For the nature of the transfer junction that emerged in this period would shed light on the progressional realness of the white aesthetic with regards to the affinity insight (2) principle and progression. Yet there is still more here, for the sixties would also be the period to witness the breakthrough of new technological developments—breakthroughs that would play an important role in helping to shape the creativity as well. Not only would new technology affect the total gamut underlying how rock music would be performed (e.g., new innovations in sound systems), but the development of the synthesizer would prove to be one of the most important new elements to appear on the scene. It is important to understand that the sophistication of technology is directly related to how the dissemination of rock was to be achieved—whether in live performances or studio recordings—and the later impact of the Beatles would attest to what these new developments meant as well. For if Elvis Presley could be talked of as rock's first real superstar, then the Beatles could be looked at as the logical inheritors of this same position in the sixties, with an impact that no one in their wildest dreams could have forecasted.

The time zone of the sixties has to be viewed as the most exciting decade of the post–World War Two period, and as the intensity of this period unfolded, it was clear that the social developments inside America would play an important role in forming the creativity as well. By this I am only saying that subsequent progressions of the sixties would in many ways promote the move towards rock music—as the most attractive creative outlet; more so, this would also be the time zone that shaped the progressional continuation of rock as a spectacle and business proposition as well. For the period that would "ise" the music of the Beatles is the same period that saw the most dynamic social changes occur in American history than in any period since Reconstruction. This was the time zone that brought us the Vietnam War, the hippies and yippies, the assassinations, and the move towards forming political consciousness, among other things; and the intensity of this period would also make a lasting impression on the progressional continuance of creativity. The realness that rock music would function as a dividing barrier between conservative and progressive forces was also a factor that would accent the thrust alignment of this form—for in practically every period of the sixties, rock music would be thought of as a form aligned with anti-establishment forces—no matter the ideology. It is thus because of the way rock music was utilized in this period that we can view the music as related to the spectacle-diversion cycle of the sixties. For the progressional development of social-political forces in this period is directly related to the vibrational thrust of rock music. Moreover, the basic tone level of American culture would also correspond to the actualness of this same phenomenon. But there is much more to the sixties than any one context, and it is important to examine the dynamic implications of this subject—as a basis to draw accurate conclusions with regard to what really happened in this period with popular music—as well as how this period has shaped the events in the seventies to the present (middle to late seventies).

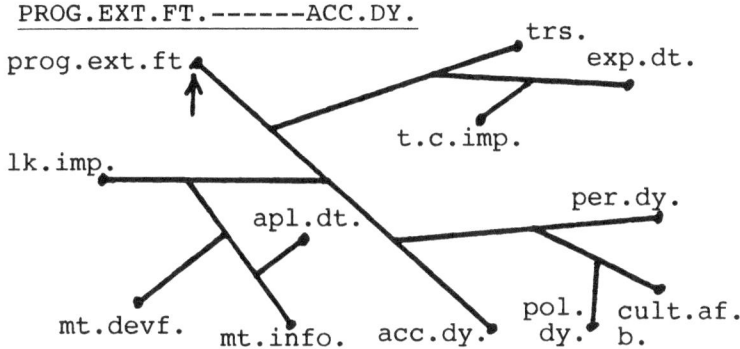

The first observation that can be made about the sixties is that this period represented the actualization of what happens when a given transfer shift is completed. For if we can view the late fifties as the time zone that saw the solidification of white rock as a thrust that existed, then we can view the sixties as the period that revealed what that existence would mean in physical universe terms. To understand this viewpoint is to deal with the gradual separation of black and white popular music in the late fifties, and later to understand how this same progression stabilized in the sixties. Thus, by the early sixties, even, black popular music was a thrust relegated to an underground position—to be used only on those occasions when a given composite thrust had spent its creative course. I am not writing that no black people were allowed to become successful, for this would not be true—certainly groups like the Supremes were moving towards some kind of peak (in audience acceptance) in that period, but this was not the norm. My point is that the basic composite alignment of black popular music functioned in the underground of American culture, even though there were some positive developments (like the founding of Motown and Stax Records, and what this would mean for exposing the thrust projections "ised" from Detroit or Memphis)—and because of this, went unnoticed by the composite culture until the late sixties and seventies. Thus, in the underground position, black music would function as a reservoir for the progressional continuance of popular music.

It would be wrong to merely reduce the initiations of white rock to the commercialization of black music, for while the realness of the transfer shift in rock is a fact, the actual life situation of this planet would not sustain such a one-dimensional generalization. For it must be understood that any composite attempt to deal with white rock includes many different factors—not to mention the actualness of its spectrum. For by the early sixties the gamut of white rock would see participation from such diverse elements that only a fool would not concede something creative was happening. The sixties would thus be the time zone that would reveal the "realness" of the developing west coast thrust (i.e., Janis Joplin, Jefferson Airplane, and the formation of what was to be called "acid rock")—as well as the invasion of the Euro-rockers (i.e., the Beatles, Rolling Stones, etc.). the composite formation of these diverse thrusts—plus the addition of various folk forms—would only underline the solidification of white rock and roll as a separate factor from the black community. And while the basis underlying this phenomenon had to do with the functional and vibrational arena of black music, it was clear that the white community in the early sixties was capable of making original and creative statements through that context as well—moreover, it was also clear that white rock could make "real" statements (that is, music creativity that moved towards "affirming" in accordance to the reality-vibrational projection of the trans-European aesthetic—and forming composite world aesthetic). Obviously this is true, for by the time the Beatles and Stones created the *Sgt. Pepper's* and "Sympathy for the Devil" records, there could be no denying the realness of white rock as a separate and serious continuum. In a sense, the sixties can be viewed as the time that saw the solidification of the composite white vibrational projection in popular music, and this period could also be talked of as the zone that actualized what this phenomenon would mean with regard to its "meta-reality" implications. For if at the end of the fifties the concept of soul had to do with the initiations of black musicians as applied to rhythm and blues—or black music—we find at the end of the sixties that the concept of "soul" and "soul music" would now only represent a "style"—moreover, a style in which the composite sector could participate. For by the middle of the sixties, the sophistication of white rock had advanced to the point where it would be extremely difficult to recognize the difference between black and white music (although this was not true in every case), and there were many reasons for this—one being the nature underlying how given transfer shifts are achieved, and another, the time factor necessary to achieve it.

Certainly black popular music did not cease to exist in the sixties, nor have I meant to imply that the progressional thrust of rhythm and blues had become entirely synthesized by the collective progressions of the sixties either—because this is not true. The fact is, the composite thrust of black popular music was simply not exploited on the same level as its white counterpart. Thus, the vibrational particulars of black popular music were focused exclusively on the black community; which is to say, the vibrational-progressional alignment of black music could be viewed as an independent projection from the composite culture. For if the most basic development that occurred in the middle to late fifties was the solidification of white rock as a social and conceptual indicator—in accordance to the white aesthetic—then the sixties would reveal what path this projection chose to manifest itself in. My point is that the actualness of white rock in this period functioned alongside the same vibrational informational dictates (of each given time juncture) as western culture in terms of the particulars of its information reality. That is, acid rock could be viewed as a thrust related to the composite reality of both western information dynamics and social reality (e.g., reaction to the war), just as punk rock in the seventies would serve as a social indicator with regard to the composite factors shaping western culture at this time (the early eighties)—and while all of these various categories were introduced and abandoned in the sixties, the progressional development of black popular music could be seen as something quite separate from this phenomenon. There were exceptions to be sure—even Marvin Gaye would record an album of social and political awareness (i.e., *What's Going On*)—but this was not the norm. In fact, the progressional alignment—and projection—of black popular music would continue functioning as a separate factor from everything—including the emergence of black power in the early to middle sixties. The realness of this phenomenon would eventually affect the social position of black people—as a composite community. For the reality actualness of black popular music—more than any other form—

understood that the progressional continuance of white and composite popular music could not shed light on the real problems black people were dealing with—nor would those thrusts have the affinity make-up necessary to understand the special problems of black people—because, in actuality, this phenomenon was "not about non-white people."

There was also a relationship between the solidification of rock music and the emergence of the black power and feminist movements of the sixties. Yet I do not mean to state that the thrust projection of rock music functioned as a positive clarification or affinity factor in this context either, because that would not be correct. Rather, rock music came to actualize the growing dissatisfaction within the country as a spectacle phenomenon. All of the other developments that were to shape the sixties could be traced back to the re-aligning vibrational identity of alternative America—which is to say, the composite thrust of rock music was directly related to many of the subsequent progressions that were to shape the sixties. That this form would play such an important role in the sixties is extremely interesting, for the meta-reality dynamics of composite rock did not necessarily have anything to do with the functional identity of many of the alternative political thrusts that were to form in this same period. Certainly there was a difference between how the composite forces shaping rock saw themselves, and how the community that embraced black power or the forces that defined feminism saw themselves, and yet the composite realness of rock would still affect the overall vibrational identity of "perceived" alternativism. Not to mention, the spectacle-diversion implications of rock music would run counter to the desired thrust (objectives) of both the black power and feminist movements. That is, the most basic examination of the essence lining of rock music (as a creative thrust) would reveal the relationship of this form to sustaining the present actualness of western culture—as opposed to changing it. For the meta-reality of rock music—as a composite thrust—can be viewed as a projection that functioned in accordance to the basic vibrational thrust of western—or American—culture. Moreover, any attempt to examine the significance of spectacle-diversion cycles would reveal what this phenomenon (rock music) actually means—with regard to helping to sustain the present reality of things—for this progressional continuum derives its significance from the status quo information alignment of the present. Which is to say, the progressional continuity of rock music—in its most natural flow—has nothing to do with making life in the black community any better (in some cases, it is possible to draw the opposite conclusion—that being, the necessity to make the present reality more profitable insures that whatever can be used will be used), for the most basic insight we can gain with regards to the essence alignment of rock music (as a composite thrust) is that rock music is conceived with regards for the source-transfer implications of western culture as an exclusive junction (by white people and about white people—that is, if you are a man). I do not state this viewpoint as a negative factor—but rather as something which seems to be true, and even a light examination of what has happened in rock since the sixties would bear this line of reasoning out; still, it would not be correct to corral the significance of rock, or any projectional thrust for that matter, in one context or light. For the progressional significance of this subject is multi-dynamic, and related to a variety of contexts and realities.

Without doubt, the most significant development to affect the progressional continuity of popular music in the sixties would be the newfound interest of the business and controlling forces of American culture in rock music. It would be impossible to calculate what this interest has meant to the establishment of rock as a composite American music. For if in the beginning rock was perceived as a revolutionary music, in the end, this revolution had to be accepted—but not in the way originally intended. The emergence of rock music—and its subsequent progressions—can be viewed as the thrust responsible for revolutionizing contemporary business techniques and strategy. To understand the realness of this viewpoint is to examine the reality of big business in the early fifties—before the rise of rock—and later in the middle sixties. By 1965, rock music had become one of the most economically profitable avenues in the recording business, and the realness of this success would serve as a transformation factor to big business. By the middle sixties, large recording companies would push rock as an exclusive form—in many cases, both classical and improvised music would be entirely abandoned for rock. Whole companies were reshaped because of the challenge that rock posed—moreover, the recording industry would take polls to find out (1) which segment of the American public buys the most records, and (2) what methods proved successful in advertising their products. In other words, the science that dictates present-day marketing techniques was also solidified at this juncture. Few people seem to have any awareness of the magnitude of reshaping done by large companies in the sixties to connect with the transition that rock posed. More so, few people seem to have any concern that big business has also played an important role in helping to shape the actual reality continuum of rock. But the actual fact is, the progressional thrust of rock music since the late fifties—and especially after the sixties—is directly related to the sophistication of big business, and the solidification of rock as a national spectacle is directly connected with the collective forces of western culture. To understand this phenomenon is to arrive at a very interesting juncture, for if I am correct and if rock music does represent a sanctioned power-alignment creation (on some level), then quite possibly this phenomenon cannot be separated from how we have come to view the progressional implications of rock as a transformation thrust, as well as the assigned values that have been attached to its perception (in vibrational and cosmic terms). Understand, I am not saying that the thrust we refer to as rock has no multi-dynamic potential, nor am I suggesting that rock music has no transformational potential—regardless of level (or focus). I am saying that however we choose to look at the implications of rock as a stimulus for positive movement or growth (in either functional or aesthetical terms), the fact that this thrust has been co-opted by the present forces that dictate American culture cannot simply be ignored. The realness of this utilization does mean something. To ignore this most obvious fact would be ridiculous—or at least to ignore this most obvious fact would not be in the interest of what is most true about this subject.

    Any attempt to deal with the relationship between rock and big business would involve many factors. For example, many of us have come to view rock as a form related to the political developments that characterized the sixties, and on some level this viewpoint is understandable—for it seems on the surface that all of these factors were related. But any real examination of the sixties would reveal that at every juncture—or stage—everything was basically in control. I do not mean to imply that the riots in Watts or Detroit were planned, nor am I saying that people were not in disagreement with what was happening in the country; my point is that the vibrational alignment of American culture was never really threatened at any time. My point is also that **many of the forces that were perceived as revolutionary were not revolutionary at all, but only sequences that functioned in accordance to the spectacle-diversion cycle. The notion that rock music was a political constructivist music can be credited to the ingenuity of the American businessman.** The actualness of rock as a spectacle would function as the most profitable money-making venture for the recording industry in all of its history—and this thrust would both spearhead and dictate how the progressional forces surrounding the American counterculture saw themselves. I do not mean to make light of all the honest work that was done in this period, nor is it my intention to ridicule any group that tried to function in the sixties—not to mention that obviously some real positive activity was able to happen in this time zone as well—but the idea that rock music functioned as a political music is simply not true. The real relationship of rock to the developments that occurred in the sixties would reveal the co-opting of style as a factor to "appear" revolutionary, rather than inspire actual revolution.

Possibly the best way to view the relationship between rock and big business is to examine the progressional development of rock through the sixties until the late seventies. For the most basic thrust progression of rock in this context can be seen quite clearly—that is, rock music as a contemporary vehicle to comment on various social and philosophical developments taking place within the culture, and rock as a social function indicator (i.e., dance, gatherings, etc.). What is interesting, however, is that the progressional thrust development of rock—while commenting on these various aspects of culture—does nothing to help assist real change. In fact, to examine the progressional continuity of rock—from acid to soul, from disco to punk rock—is to see rock as a form connected with the negative thrust to transformation—as opposed to a form that signaled hope and the possibility for positive change (yet quite possibly this type of logic is too narrow). I say this because the present time zone in which we are living can be looked at in a number of ways.

If the interest of the business community in rock music represented how the progressional development of the thrust was to expand (the establishment of rock as an American spectacle), then quite possibly the challenge of the technological community had to do with how this expansion was to be achieved—in actual terms. That is, the sophistication of the technological community would provide the path this expansion was to take with regard to the new technical problems rock would open up. Any attempt to deal with the progressional continuity of this phenomenon would imply some awareness of those technological contributions. For if the emergence of rock would forecast the period of the sixties and seventies in affinity terms, then the magnitude of the thrust would necessitate many new changes in both performance presentation (performing for audiences of twenty thousand or more people) and recording. The impact that the Beatles were to make in the sixties would have been impossible without the breakthroughs that occurred in technology—for it must be understood that technological advances in even one area like amplification would have a strong impact on the "expanding" music. The developments in this one area alone would make the festival concept possible, and the later festivals that developed can be looked at from that same image. In other words, the progressional development of rock music in this context can be traced to several important simultaneous junctions (that being, occurrences that served to encourage more participation in the form): one would be the festival in Monterey, which signaled the actualness of rock as an American spectacle—later, Woodstock as a middle juncture in the progressional continuance of the music—and finally, Altamont as the last festival in this particular progression. All of these gatherings would serve as important alignments for the thrust of rock music, and all of these gatherings would underline the new developments in technology—with regard to the music.

In the fifties, the recording of popular music was a somewhat easy process, requiring not too much time. For a start, very few groups would require more than one or two microphones, and even if they did, there were only two recording tracks to tape the music on. Moreover, all of the music on a given take had to be performed correctly because it was not possible to overdub a track, or erase a mistake; and it goes without saying that the basic fluidity of the process was no way near what it is today. Yet however the recording media in the fifties might now seem, there was a one-to-one relationship between what was performed and what was recorded. To that degree, I view this situation as somewhat positive. This is not to suggest that the recording studios of the fifties are preferable to what we now have in the seventies. My reasons for writing about the reality of recording music in the fifties is to establish some basis for understanding the present situation we are now in. For by the early sixties, at approximately the same period that would bring us the Beatles, there was also a revolution in recording techniques that was of profound importance. The realness of these innovations would have serious positive and negative implications, for the composite essence factor of rock music would at some point become intertwined with what these technical considerations opened up—that is to say, the benefits of technological dynamics would become an essential factor related to the expansion nature of rock music. Where the normal recording situation in the fifties had to do with the musicians practicing their craft, and coming into the studio to record what had been developed from that practice, the development continuance of rock in the sixties would change this most natural progression. Which is to say, the technological advancements of the sixties would alter this progression (even the procedure surrounding recording would be changed). Thus, if the normal studio situation of the fifties had to do with a two-to-four-track studio set-up—by the middle of the sixties, a group of five to six musicians would command as many as 32 (or in some cases 64) tracks to record their music. But this is only the beginning, for the most basic recording procedures surrounding rock since the early sixties would reveal a distinct separation between the recorded product produced for the public and the actual music as separate from the studio. That is, it would be difficult to find any popular song that was actually recorded in one piece, or take—for the development in the late fifties and sixties has transported rock from an "actual" arena to a "synthetic" arena—yet this change is neither positive nor negative, but only a fact. For the contemporary recording procedures surrounding the recording of rock would reveal a given piece of music to actually be a collection of individual solos (sometimes taking as long as three to six months to complete), where the final product has nothing to do with its final shape (and reality)—and in some cases, the final product has nothing to do with what one could hear in actual performance.

It is impossible to speculate on what these innovations will mean for the continuum of the music. But it is clear that something is happening with regards to these new procedures. More so, I have not meant to cast the recent developments concerning "the technology of recording" in negative terms—this is not my point at all. Certainly many of these developments have helped make new possibilities in creative music—e.g., the invention of the 32-track recorder gives the possibility of making clearer records—and it would be unfair to base an evaluation of any initiation on its limited utilization, regardless of context. I have raised this subject only to state that the reality actualness of rock music is connected to many factors—one of which is the developments of the technological community—and all of these factors are important if we are to truly understand something about this thrust. More so, the fact that this relationship was advanced in the sixties greatly contributed to the thrust projection underlying how rock was perceived—as well as the subsequent spread of rock as a "spectacle music."

The economic actualness of rock music is another factor related to how the reality of the form is perceived. For while it is generally acknowledged that rock is the most influential music in this time zone, many of us might not understand what this influence has come to mean in basic economic terms. Certainly everyone has come to view the actualness of the rock superstar as a rich position—or a position synonymous with being a millionaire—but there is more to the economic actualness of rock than only this relationship. **For the economic implications of rock music are directly connected with the position it has in American culture—**

that is, the reality of rock in American society is maintained—and secured—by economic as well as aesthetic considerations. To understand this is to be aware of the many factors that have profited through their relationship with rock. For example, three-fourths of the radio stations in America could not exist without rock music. The revolutionizing of the recording industry is also directly related to this same phenomenon, and the American economy has some dependence as well. The solidification of rock and its related business constituents represents one of the vital money-making sectors of the American business community—and I do not state this as a negative factor. My point is that the meta-reality of rock music is not separate from the position it has secured in western culture, and my point is also that the economic potential of rock has necessitated outside interference (with regard to how a given juncture of the music is perceived) from the business community—as a means to protect their investments. Thus, to view the economic realness of rock music after the time zone of the sixties is to be confronted with a variety of factors.

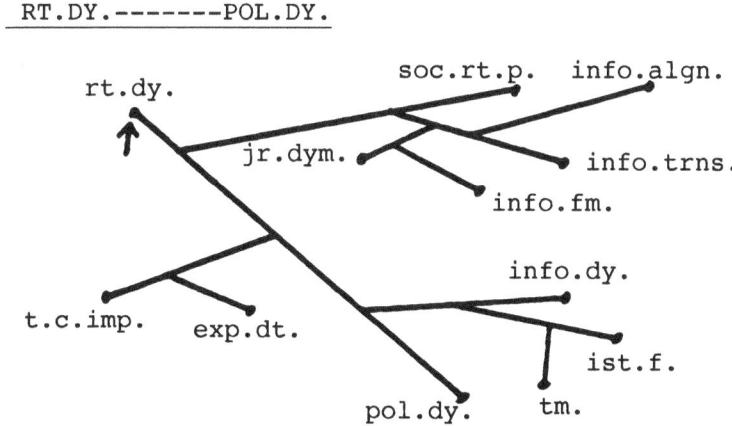

The economic forces that surround rock must also be viewed as another factor that has helped to sustain the present position rock has during this time cycle. By this I am only commenting on the realness of economics as a power factor, as well as an "alignment" consideration. One example of what this power means in physical universe terms would be the use of extended radio manipulation in this period. For it is understood that the success of a given record is directly related to whether or not that record is put in a position where it can be heard. The fact that certain records are allowed to become successful, while others aren't, has to do with many different factors, and certainly one of those factors would be the economic power base related to that record's political connections. The sophistication surrounding advertising in this time zone is directly related to the realness of this phenomenon—and this is true on every level. Thus, any attempt to deal with the economic implications of rock music during this period would reveal the multi-complexual actualness concerning what power really is. For to view the progressional development of rock in the sixties is to witness an all-composite effort on the part of the business community to control the creative taste of western culture. The record companies in this period help shape the music, package the music, advertise the music, control the media's handling of their product, and in many cases put together the actual groups as well. This is, thus, what I mean when I use the term "multi-complexual," for the economic implications surrounding the reality of rock music in this period permeate the total spectrum of involvement.

It would be impossible to detail every progressional thrust of rock music in the time zone of the sixties, for the thrust of that time period represented one of the most dynamic periods for rock music. Unlike the time period of the fifties, which saw the solidification of rock music as an alternative creative popular music, the sixties detailed what this thrust meant in actual terms—in a variety of contexts. More so, the time period of the sixties would shape a whole new generation of young people—which is to say, Americans' memory-lapse button could be utilized. In other words, the transfer-shift junction of the fifties would mean nothing to the next generation of rock musicians or their listening audience (and the actualness of this phenomenon would also affect the late sixties and seventies—for by the end of the sixties, the progression cycle of rock music would see the rise of black popular music as a periodic revalidation agent). By the end of the sixties, the continuum of American rock music would see the spectrum implications of its thrust realized. This would be the period that would see the blending of rock with country music (e.g., Memphis or Nashville)—the blending of rock with extended forms (e.g., *Tommy* or *Jesus Christ Superstar*)—bluegrass rock—English rock (which was actually earlier)—etc. Moreover, this would also be the time period that would actualize the second generation of rock millionaires, for if Elvis Presley had secured his financial position by the end of the fifties, the end of the sixties would see this cycle completed for the members of the Beatles and Stones—in short, the early sixties continuum.

To understand the progression of rock music in the seventies is to view the source-transfer-shift cycle of the early sixties—with regards to the break in the composite solidification of popular music. For the early sixties was the juncture that saw both the rise of rock as a white phenomenon and the suppression of popular black music. All of the subsequent developments that occurred in rock during this juncture were mostly based on the thrust alignment and continuation of rock as a white form. In actual terms, this would be the decade of the Beatles and Stones (Euro-rock continuum) as well as the American school: which is to say that the meta-reality of rock as a western thrust was secured in this period. But there is more to the solidification of white rock than only one aspect, for the seriousness of the sixties would have multi-vibrational consequences. For if I have commented on the physical universe implications of source transfer (as a factor related to the actualization of rock as a white music), there is still the necessity for examining what this transfer meant in vibrational terms. This is so because the vibrational implications of the source-transfer junction of rock would establish the reality continuum of popular music in western culture for the seventies. To understand what this means is to view the actualness of white rock as a thrust functioning in accordance to the composite identity of western culture and western continuance.

When I stated that the cross-transfer shift of rock music established the separateness of white rock—as the only attractive thrust to be utilized by the controlling forces of western culture (in the time zone of the early sixties)—I am also saying that this same juncture established the vibrationaltory thrust we are now dealing with at present. For if the transfer-shift junction of the sixties actualized rock as a separate form from black music—into a form that could function in complete accordance to the western composite affinity thrust—then we must understand that this utilization implies that the affinity thrust of the form is no different from the composite western vibrational and methodological reality platform, and this does seem to be the case. In other words, the "ising" of rock as a white form implied its projectional particulars would now vibrate to the basic affinity thrust of the western vibrational projection—in accordance to the nature underlying its observation and participation criterion. To understand this phenomenon is to understand the progressional continuance of rock in the sixties: that is, rock as a form which addressed its needs to white culture, and rock as a form that could now be harnessed. But what does this really mean in physical universe terms? My point is this: the resultant progressional path of rock in the sixties solidified its own projectional particulars with respect to expansion and/or transformation. This continuum would move to document the vibrational and philosophical reality particulars underlying how western culture perceived of itself. By the same token, if America as a country chose to perceive of herself as being in isolation by the end of the sixties, the same could also be said of the rock community (which is to say, if fantasy became an integral tool to buy time in the late sixties—then its use would be constant throughout the composite thrust of western culture).

The seriousness of black popular music—as a form that deserved more attention—would begin to draw momentum only in the late sixties, and there are many reasons for this. One, the progressional thrust of rock would begin to lose its image momentum in that same period, and two, the transfer-shift junction (feature) of the spectacle-diversion cycle was nearing. Whatever, the time zone of the late sixties would again focus on black popular music, and the intensity of that focus would give new perspectives about American popular music. The basis of this focus would bring into light the developments and changes reshaping black popular music in the sixties, and this would be true for composition as well. For the first ensembles to receive attention from the mass media would not only show the changes reshaping black creativity but also the relationship of those changes to the composite thrust of black creativity—which is to say, however the music was perceived, it could not be separated from the composite black aesthetic. The renewed focus on black creativity that took place in the late sixties would thus serve as a re-examination period for rock music, and it was not uncommon to hear musicians talk of "goin' back to the roots—brother"!

The reality thrust of rock in the early seventies would witness the breakthrough of artists like Stevie Wonder and Al Green to the mass market, and this would also be the period where the latest innovations in dance would be integrated into the composite culture. Ensembles like Earth, Wind & Fire would begin to reach larger audiences—not to mention the sophistication of the new performing circuits that had developed in the black community in this same period—and groups like the Ohio Players would begin to talk of "funk" in terms of its representing a new style (which for many people it did). The emphasis on "funk" in many ways could be looked at in the same context as the "hard bop" thrust of the fifties: that being, a move by the black community to return to the essence of the music, yet the most basic difference this time would be that the lessons of the fifties had been well learned (in other words, if it is about "funk" then everybody will be about "funk"). The late sixties and seventies can be viewed as the period that saw the normalization of rock as a functioning popular music, as well as the period that established how the re-entry of black popular music (to the mass market) could be done without having any problems. For it must be understood that by the sixties-seventies juncture, there was not much difference between the vibrational arenas of black and white music. In other words, however the actual music was perceived, the collective controlling forces of western culture had de-programmed rock as a counter-revolutionary possibility. The only thrust that had "alternative" potential in the late sixties and seventies was the vibrational projection that had emerged from outside America called reggae, and we are still in the cycle where this form is being "focused on." The other notable entry in the early seventies would be the emergence of "disco" music as a form that had synthesized all of the developments in the sixties—especially late sixties—and finally, alternative rock or punk rock as a thrust projection designed in accordance to the spectacle-diversion cycle—later to be called the "new wave" (even though, in fact, its actual reality particulars were no different than what preceded it—it really is a question of who owns the information machinery).

I cannot even pretend my examination of this subject represents a total picture of commercial creativity—for obviously there is much more to say, about every subject area. I have included this section as an attempt to comment on the progressional continuity of present-day music, as a means to examine what popular music really is (on a vibrational and physical universe level), and as a means to deal with the composite thrust of creativity—regardless of focus. The realness of this most dynamic subject is a study in itself.

(Level One) The Phenomenon of Jazz-Rock

The emergence of "jazz-rock" as a movement can be traced back to the end of the sixties—or the beginning of the seventies. Yet I have not meant to imply that no groundwork was laid to develop this thrust earlier, because in actual fact there were many factors leading to the solidification of this forum as an alternative thrust from the post-Coleman movement in the late fifties. Jazz-rock was thus the form that emerged through initiations in both rock music—the actualization of what had been learned in the transition period of this projection in the early and middle sixties—as well as creative improvised music—the harmonic and structural sophistication that had become essential for the creative improvising musician. The resulting form would then employ the best of both worlds, not only in the actual music but total physical universe alignment as well. The use of jazz-rock would allow jazz musicians to continue working in the area of improvised music and enjoy audience support while doing so. The emergence of this projection solved the dilemma of the creative improvising community as well as the reality particulars of the rock musician.

There had long been a community of jazz musicians who yearned for what they would call "a return to the basic essence of creative music." Jazz-rock, for many of these people, represented the path to where this return could be brought about. The return to basic essences to which these musicians referred could best be understood as a call to return to the early functional area of creative black music—rather than proceed and develop the creativity that had emerged in the Coleman, Coltrane, and Taylor continuum. In short—return to a music more metric, with a strong beat—a music that people could again dance to. For it must be understood that many musicians had begun to feel that the developments in the late fifties and early sixties were detrimental for the reality of creative music from the black aesthetic. Many of these musicians had long felt that jazz was becoming a music outside the grasp of the basic public—that is, a form too cerebral and complex to be a positive factor for transformation and a form too abstract and separate to see to the public. More so, their argument was that the loss of public support for creative music was directly related to the developments that emerged in the sixties. In other words, the activity of the post-Coleman threat, to these musicians, was directly related to the emergence of rock as the most commercial and profitable music in this period, and no one could argue with their logic—for, in fact, in many ways they were right. The realness that jazz-rock provided an alternative path that was an important factor to these musicians and the number of instrumentalists who moved into this form—in only a two-to-four-year cycle—only underscores the frustration this segment of the musicians' community must have been dealing with. For it must be understood that at least half of the musicians who functioned in creative music from the affinity insight (1) principle switched to jazz-rock by the end of the sixties.

To understand the extent of switching that took place in this period—involving the rush to jazz-rock—is to become aware of another factor related to this same phenomenon—that being, the deterioration of the composite musicians' community. For the developments that occurred in the music during this period helped to seriously weaken the composite musicians' community. By the middle of the sixties, clearly two camps of musicians had solidified—those who wanted to develop the initiations of post-Ayler thrust dynamics, and those who wanted no part of extended creativity. In short, the newer forms served as a divisive factor between the musicians, and the solidification of this phenomenon can be looked at as the most basic factor that dictated the course of events we are now dealing with in this time zone. Nor was it merely a case of younger musicians against older musicians; for the differences of opinion about the future of the music transcended these types of categories (not to mention, many younger musicians were also opposed to the changes that had come into improvised music—more younger musicians than one might have expected). The move to jazz-rock signaled—for these musicians and the public—that jazz had indeed come home. The emergence of this thrust also represented a breakthrough for work possibilities—because by the end of the sixties, even the word "jazz" had become a stigma for any kind of commercial (or financial) venture. Jazz-rock thus represented a path where this phenomenon could be reshaped and used to the advantage of the musicians.

To rock musicians, the emergence of jazz-rock was as much of a blessing. For while there had been many breakthroughs for rock in the period of the sixties, the resulting social situation had also produced new demands on the form. In other words, as the sophistication of the controlling community evolved in the sixties—and as the realness of the spectacle-diversion cycle on popular music began to take hold—the need for the music to constantly change and draw from other forms was greater than ever. In short, another kind of musician was needed to continue the momentum that had developed in the middle sixties. More so, there was also the realness of the time consideration as a factor related to the changing vibrational needs of the music, the musicians, and the public. For it must be understood that by the beginning of the seventies, rock had entered its twentieth year, which is to say, the needs of the form had changed, as well as the needs of the musicians—who were now moving into their thirties (and forties). Thus, as rock secured its move in the transfer shift from black music, the aesthetics and functional arena of the form would then move towards the transitional definitions of western culture—that is, **rock would now have to advance in accordance to the dictates of spectacle-diversion progressionalism—and as such, be subjected to the nature of its "established" intellectual lines (as viewed through western value systems and tendencies).** The best example of this phenomenon can be seen in the middle sixties. For if we can look at the Beatles as the personification of white musicians who had now developed their own thrust variation in creative black music, then we can also look at what this solidification has posed to the progressional aspect of popular music. That is—the emergence of the *Sgt. Pepper's* album substantiated how the progressional reality surrounding rock was to be perceived, and that breakthrough is important. In other words, after the transfer shift of rhythm and blues was complete in the late fifties, the

Beatles represented the second progressional link factor as to how that transferred information thrust was (is) to proceed. The initiation of the *Sgt. Pepper's* record, as well as some of the other records from that period, substantiated the next alignment reality of popular music from the western thrust. In other words, the most apparent factor the creative community would deal with after *Sgt. Pepper's* would be the concept that rock had now become a sophisticated form of music and as such would have to be dealt with as an "advanced" form, rather than a so-called lightweight or primitive form. Moreover, rock would also vibrate to the progressional factors that surrounded how western culture perceives of advancement—that is, the advancement of the technical considerations, the shifting of the functional arena, the isolation of particulars in a given performance as a means to claim whatever is needed (depending on time zone), etc. My point is that the progression of events in this period would also affect the musicians and type of musicians that could be exploited in rock, and my point is that this situation was conducive for the vibrational-shift change in the composite music as well.

To understand the complexity shift in popular music in the middle sixties is to be aware of several factors that converged on the scene at once. The most significant of those factors would be the rush of musicians from the jazz community to rock music—as well as the expansion of the functional arena of popular music as a more complex factor to justify the new interest of the intellectual critical and defining community, and finally the dictates underlying the spectacle-diversion cycle (and what all of these changes meant to the early rock musicians). More so, all of these factors were accented by the middle sixties, and the result of this phenomenon helped to transform the meta-reality of popular music in the next cycle. To understand the extent of this change, it is necessary to view how developments in this period reshaped the reality of earlier popular music—because nowhere can the difference between this period and the reality of the fifties be better seen than in this comparison. For when I stated that the emergence of jazz-rock was just as much a blessing to rock musicians as to the jazz musicians, it is necessary to understand what this means. The fact is, rock music has long been depicted by the media as a primitive music, having very little to do with serious creativity. What the media was focusing on was the realness that rock did not correspond to the dictates underlying what western culture believed to be "substantial" as a creative form—and to a great extent, rock (or rhythm and blues in this juncture) did not function with regards to the requirements of the intellectual and defining forces of western culture. The realness that this music was separate from the composite western aesthetic was the most basic factor related to why white performers of black popular music in that period had no choice but to attach themselves to black culture on some level (that is—because of rejection). It was in the late fifties that white artists were to form a composite thrust themselves—marking the beginning of the early alternative rebellion movements that were to characterize the sixties, and this move was also directly related to the transfer-shift phenomenon in rock. My point, however, is that the vibrational and aesthetic forces that dictated the meta-reality of rock in the late fifties and sixties were still under the black aesthetic, and thus western culture viewed its particulars as inferior. Because of this, there were many very distorted (imposed) concepts about the ability of the musicians playing rock, and in this context the rock musician was thought to be inferior to the "sanctioned" musician of western art music. **Certainly one of the greatest disservices done to musicians in popular music is the claim that their music requires any less commitment and work than so-called serious music.** The controlling forces that regulate how we have come to view various initiations—whether music or anything else—have often attempted to sustain this warped view of popular music as a factor to secure cultural intimidation for their own interest. The result of this control is that the basic concepts communicated in our culture about popular musicians are distorted and tend to promote a general notion of lack of sophistication as compared to the musician in western art music—who is generally thought of as respectable.

There is also the idea that rock musicians should not be taken seriously because in many instances they cannot read music or can only function in one or two keys. All of these concepts are related to the political and social factors that determine how western culture functions, and as such must be taken seriously. My reason for mentioning this phenomenon is that any true attempt to understand the transition to jazz-rock would also imply that some effort is made to reveal the meta-reality of rock musicians. In other words, the emergence of jazz-rock can be looked at as a positive factor for both jazz and rock musicians, yet for different reasons. Because if jazz-rock would be the form that would lead jazz musicians back into national acceptance, it would also be a vehicle to legitimize rock music—as a serious art form worthy of the critical defining community—and a form that—after its transfer shift completion—functioned in accordance to the dictates of the western defining community as well (thus securing the next arena for spectacle-diversion-transfer progressionalism). To understand what this new extension (jazz-rock) would mean for rock musicians is to be aware of the changes that were becoming apparent on the physical universe level in American culture during the late fifties and early sixties.

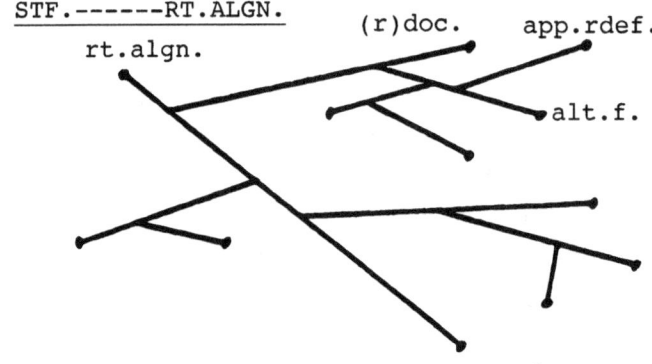

PROJ.DY.------INFO.DY.

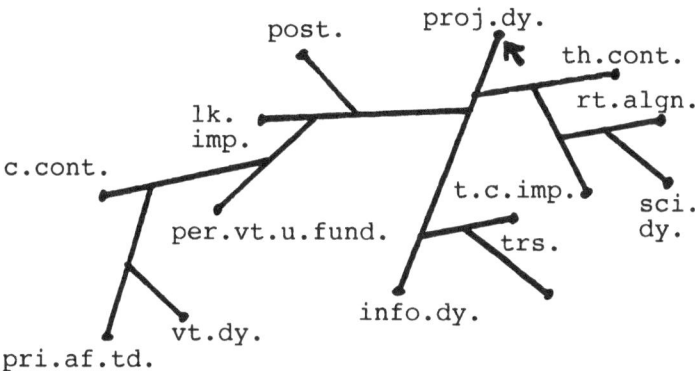

(R)EXPN.------CULT.AF.B.

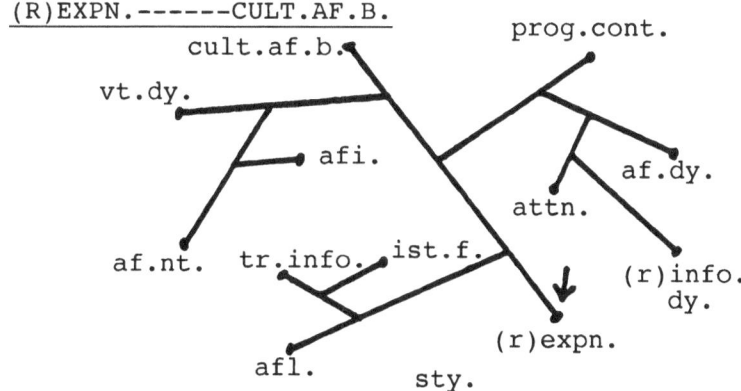

By the end of the sixties, it had become obvious that a new school of musicians had matured in rock music. This maturation could be clearly seen and heard in the changing vibrational reality of the music. The basic factors underlying this change, however, were much more complex than any one focus or movement, but involved several inter-related causes. For as rock music entered the next transfer-shift continuum of the middle sixties, the dictates of the western defining community would make the most basic re-alignment demands felt on the functional arena of the aesthetic, and as such accelerated the surface changes underlying how the music was seen (heard). For when I stated that a whole new school of musicians had emerged in rock music by the early sixties, I am also commenting on the progressional factors that this move necessitated on the music as well. In other words, the progressional development of popular music (rock), as well as the maturation of the next generation of musicians, secured the next composite area dictates for clarifying how the transfer shift in popular music was to proceed. The net result of this phenomenon was that by the end of the sixties, the transfer-shift particulars in popular music had produced a situation where greater emphasis was placed on the individual musician's need, rather than on how a given ensemble should function as a unit. In other words, as popular music entered the transfer shift of the early sixties, the meta-reality that dictated how the music was perceived —from both a spiritual-emotional or technical standpoint—was also changed. More so, by the middle sixties, this change had permeated every level of the music perception (and cultural interpretations). In short, that a whole new generation of musicians had matured on their instruments (as defined in the annals of the western use of that word—"matured" in the sense of successfully learning one's instrument in accordance to the western vibrational and methodological alignment) necessitated a kind of music that would reflect this "sophistication." Jazz-rock, for these musicians, represented a form that could give more room for the individual to utilize the information that had been developing in the transfer-shift time zone of the sixties. This is especially true if one would consider the total social scheme developing in that same period, for jazz-rock was also the form that provided a functional outlet for the individual to utilize the information that was now being taught in the university and classroom situation. In other words, as the defining forces that controlled American culture began to investigate the realness of popular music from the black aesthetic as a serious factor reshaping American culture, and as these same forces began to see the economic implications of what this move implied (as well as the political-social and vibrational consequences of this shift), popular music from the black aesthetic began to be taught in the educational system, as a factor to design how the transfer-shift progressional phenomenon could be applied to the music.

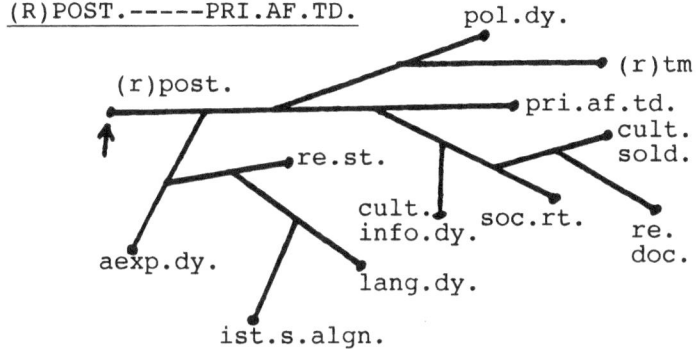

Jazz-rock could best be viewed as the form that addressed itself to the technical implications of the transfer shift of the early sixties. This form (jazz-rock) would enable the musician to utilize existing instrumental knowledge—in a technical or conceptual sense—and would also bring sophistication to the ensemble use of form as well ("sophistication" in the sense that jazz-rock would represent the zone where the latest functional changes could be adopted into the form in accordance with the understanding western culture has of technique or structure—the latest harmonic changes, like the adaptation of Coltrane's use of the pentatonic scale, for instance), and serve as a factor that functions in accordance to present-day western language. Because of the magnitude of transfer-shift progressionalism, jazz-rock would also function as a factor to remove the stigma that western culture has long had for popular music from the black aesthetic (from the time-zone junction of the middle forties to the late fifties—in other words, I am talking about a cyclic process rather than an isolated incident; the particulars of each given transfer cycle are of course different, but the actual phenomenon—especially with regards to black music—has been the same since black people have been in America). To really understand the reality of jazz-rock is to deal with the social and political developments that have been shaping American cultures in the post–Korean War time cycle.

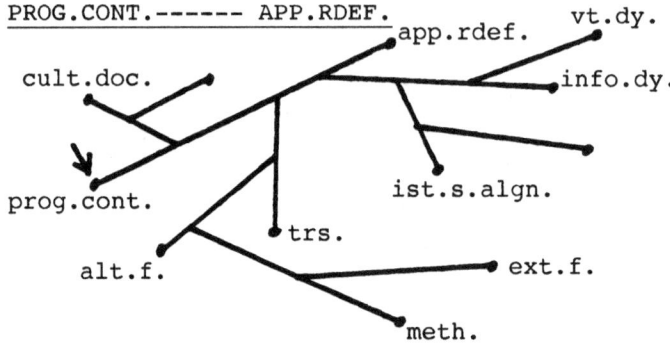

The reality of the jazz-rock musician is much too complex to put in one dimension. For it is clear that many musicians in jazz-rock have grown up with both what they would call "jazz" as well as composite American music. In many cases, the most successful practitioners of jazz-rock have studied creative music of the affinity insight (1) principle, in one form or another, as an accredited educational focus. The effect of this phenomenon could be seen in the changing vibrational and functional reality of the music, even extending to the most basic understanding of instrumentation in popular music. For if the first level of the transfer shift in popular music was manifested by a thrust that over-relied on the use of certain instruments (like the use of the electric guitar, bass, and drums trio and quartet situation that was current in the sixties), by the seventies, one could experience the new sophistication of jazz-rock. That is—a form that could now utilize sophisticated arrangements as well as expanded instrumentation (e.g., groups like the Chicago Transit Authority, later changed to simply Chicago, or Blood, Sweat & Tears). My point is that all of these factors are related to the cross-vibrational shift that has characterized and solidified the meta-reality of the thrust we now refer to as "jazz-rock."

There are many other factors related to the emergence of jazz-rock in the late sixties, and it would be to our advantage to examine every aspect of this subject. For the solidification of jazz-rock as an alternative creative thrust should not be viewed as an isolated phenomenon indigenous only to this time zone—because it isn't. The actualization of jazz-rock goes much deeper than only how a given form is manifested (through style), but instead gives insight into the "actual" reality of the aesthetic from which it derives its "isness." In other words, the existence of jazz-rock gives us some awareness about the meta-reality of creative music—of whatever period—because, more than anything else, no vibrational thrust (form) can exist unless there is some reason for its existence: that is, jazz-rock "actualized" in the late sixties because there was a need for the form—and I am not referring to the situation of creative musicians of the affinity insight (1) principle, or the rock musicians' predicament, I am commenting on the "actual" emergence of the form we now refer to as jazz-rock.

Without doubt, the underlying vibrational basis that determines the actualization of a given thrust can better be viewed by researching the historical progressions of its continuum. In other words, an examination of the historical progressions of a given creative thrust can give insight into what a given reality of the music might mean. The solidification of jazz-rock in the late sixties, when viewed with respect for the historical progressions that surround the meta-reality of creative music, can be understood as an attempt to "is" a form of creativity that could function from both dynamic principles—affinity insight (1) and affinity insight (2)—and as such vibrate to the most basic vibrational and composite factors that governed composite world creative functionalism until the latest dissemination of western (and thus world, because of the position of the west in this period) spiritual and vibrational reality tenets. My point is that the most basic realness of a given thrust seeks to flow in accordance with the dynamics of both affinity-insight principles—that is, a spiritualism that is also functional—depending on how it is used. The move to jazz-rock by so many musicians from the creative music community also indicated a desire to participate in a creative form that had some possibility to function with both dynamic principles—my point is that this move is not without precedent. The historical progressions of creative music—from the black, Asian, and western (or early western) aesthetics—shows that this has always been the "correct" position of creativity—or at least the position most creative cultures (and people) have long tried to function in—or from. I do not advance this concept as a factor to negate the dynamic principles I have already defined in this book—affinity insight (1) and (2)—because, in actual fact, there is no conflict here. My point is that **the optimum position of a given creative thrust is directly related to whether or not it is allowed to manifest the inherent dynamic principles of its meta-reality.** The words I have given to the two vibrational principles that underlie this phenomenon can of course be substituted for other words, but my point is that however these principles are referred to, the optimum position of a given thrust depends on whether or not its projections are able to utilize its underlying dynamic essence (which is what the concept of affinity insight is all about). The most basic factor that influences whether or not the dynamics of a given thrust can be utilized is probably time—or at least the realness that certain time zones seem to promote definite "vibrational particulars" and, by doing so, this phenomenon also seems to inhibit other flows (yet it is clear that however this phenomenon is understood, we are actually commenting on the cosmic arena that determines the realness of "everything"). I mention these considerations only to comment on the cyclic multi-considerations surrounding this subject—of whatever thrust—and on how given periods of the music are perceived; that is, it would not necessarily be to our advantage to merely lock one narrow definition on a given period of creative music, or given strain of creative music, because this does not seem to have anything to do with what is "really" happening on a vibrational and "actual" life level. This viewpoint can become clear by examining the transition cycle of the late forties (the post–Second World War period) and the late sixties (the Vietnam and post-Vietnam cycle) in American culture. **For the solidification of jazz-rock can be viewed as an attempt to re-establish the composite vibrational balance that was lost by many musicians after the initiations of Charlie Parker.** I have written in chapter 1 (*Writings* 1) that the underlying philosophical and vibrational arena of creative music from the black aesthetic was a multi-dynamic composite vibrational thrust that moved with a composite aesthetic reality utilizing both dynamic principles—and I have also commented on the vibrational implications of Charlie Parker's activity, as a thrust that dealt with the progressional realness of transformation (detailing the changing situation of black and white people in America)—but I have not commented on what this phenomenon has meant with regards to the bi-aitional implications of creative music from the black aesthetic. To understand the reality implications of jazz-rock, it would be to our advantage to better understand the position of composite western creativity (from every so-called persuasion) with regard to the dynamic vibrational complications of its aesthetic—as a means to establish a basis for probing into the secrets of this projection.

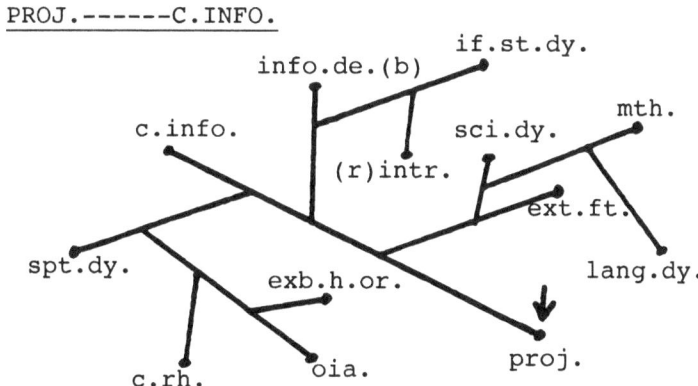

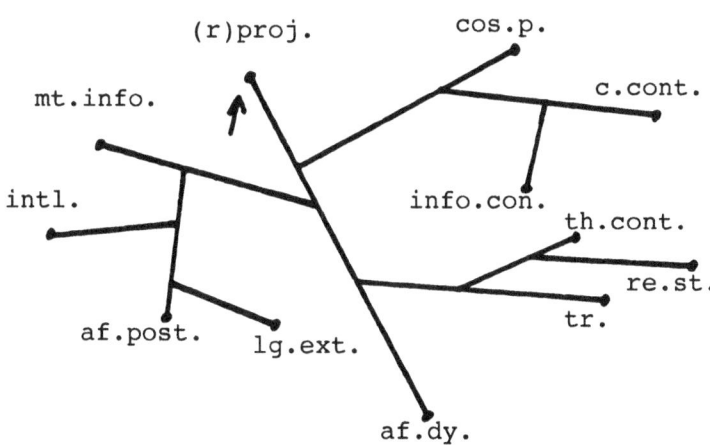

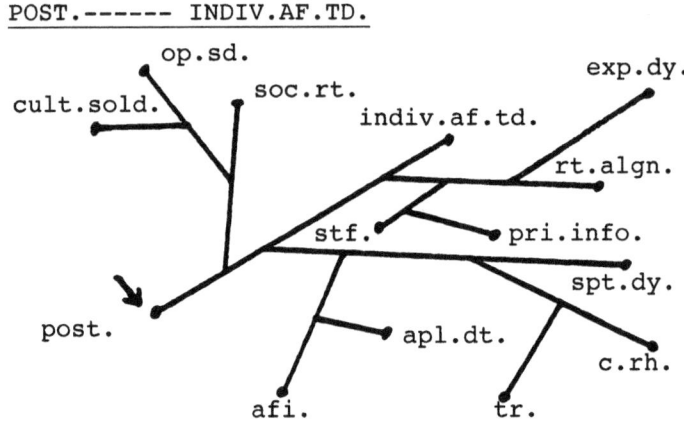

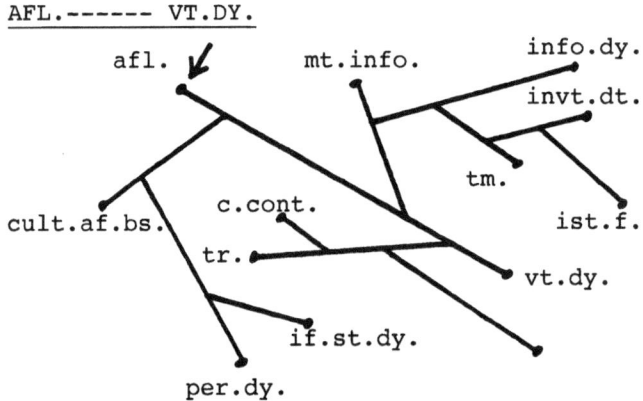

I have written that Charlie Parker's activity established the thrust progression underlying how the affinity insight (1) principle was to be extended (in the middle to late forties time period) in creative music from the black aesthetic, yet it should be noted that there were other musicians functioning in that same period whose activity was just as significant for what it would pose to the composite affinity-insight content of black music. Moreover, many of those musicians were able to continue their extensions while not separating the aesthetic platform of the music—and this difference was no small achievement. In short, musician/composers like Duke Ellington had long understood the significance of bi-aitionalism, and as such his activity was indicative of another understanding of process (and functionalism). So sophisticated was this understanding (of bi-aitionalism) that even after the solidification of the bebop period, he was still able to function through the dynamic spectrum of creative music—as a positive contributor. This has always been the case in creative music from the black aesthetic—especially before the transition cycle of the late forties. Moreover, any real examination of world music would reveal this same creative stance. For while the western defining community would have us look at Duke Ellington's music as "less" than classical music because he has composed compositions like "Sophisticated Lady," many of these same people have not been able to really deal with the reality of their own creativity. Because only a little research would reveal that composers like Bach functioned on every level of his creativity—and as such, wrote popular compositions as well. In fact, before the Schoenbergian transfer cycle, classical music was a popular music—or received like a popular music by the public. **My point is that the idea of "high" and "low" art—as well as the present lack of respect for popular music and the people who participate in popular music—is a relatively new phenomenon. More so, the ability to function in accordance with the bi-aitional implications of creative music should be considered the optimum position for any creative person—that is, the ability to function in the composite dynamic spectrum of the music must be looked at as something positive—not negative.** It is not a question of whether one area of creativity is more important than another area, nor is it a question of whether or not a given dynamic thrust can accurately express the vibrationaltory tone level of a composite culture—it is more a question of understanding that there are as many different people as there are vibrational zones, and this difference should be respected. I have stated throughout the whole of this book that I regard both the affinity insight (1) and affinity insight (2) vibrational principles to be of equal importance (whatever importance means in this context) to transformation and to life. I have also expressed my belief that both of these principles are necessary as well (for the composite implications underlying what creativity is really about). If this is understood, then we must look at the emergence of jazz-rock as a factor related to the cyclic

JR–16

progressions which developed after the Second World War—with regard to social changes on the physical universe level, as well as cosmic change and transformation (that is, new initiations as a factor to transform the forces that have solidified this time zone). **Jazz-rock is thus the form that represents the re-entering of the bi-aitional principle as a factor to participate in the forming of a possible composite alternative creative music (or at least jazz-rock in its pure state—if I can use that term—with respect to the unadulterated intentions it affirms, can be viewed in this context).**

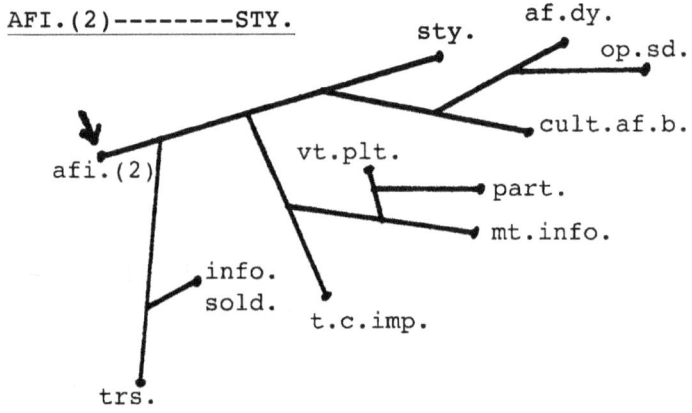

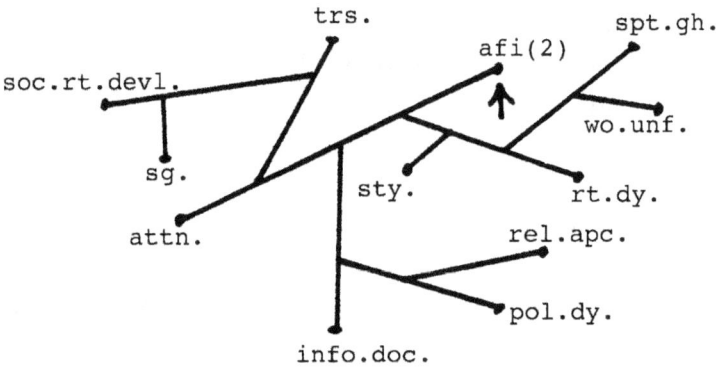

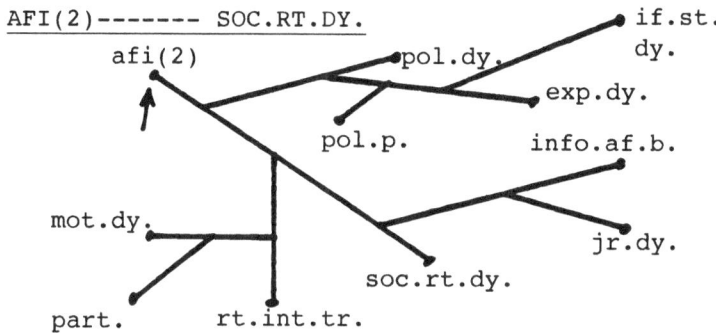

I have not meant to imply that there has been no significant creativity utilizing the affinity insight (2) principle after the emergence of Charlie Parker's activity—because this is not true. My reason for isolating Parker's work had only to do with focusing on the implications of what was raised in his utilization of the extended affinity insight (1) principle, and for what his work necessitated as a creative-thrust (projection) phenomenon for the explorations done in the fifties, sixties, and seventies. But it would be wrong to assume that the utilization of the affinity insight (1) principle in this time period implied a total lack of participation in the composite spectrum of creative improvised music. Because it is possible to trace the emergence of jazz-rock from much of the activity that occurred in the early fifties (or what could be called the first bi-aitional juncture of creative music after the Second World War). The activity I am referring to could be represented by the work of musicians like Horace Silver or Bobby Timmons. These musicians, and many others for that matter, have always functioned with regards to the bi-aitional implications of creative music. It is possible to detail the progressional aspects of jazz-rock to the work that was being done in the early and middle fifties. More so, the meta-reality that contributed to the vibrationaltory particulars that produced jazz-rock is directly connected to the same factors that initiated the activity in the early fifties. Those factors can also shed light on the cyclic shift progressions that have become an integral factor in the progressional continuum of creative music in that period and today. My point is this: **the early work**

that was done by musicians like Silver and Timmons dictated and secured the thrust development of creative music from the affinity insight (2) principle as well as what that securing would mean for a bi-aitional music. Obviously this is so, for if the most basic factor that distinguishes the vibrational and functional position of a given creative thrust has to do with the position of that thrust with regard to its ability to function as a positive factor for its base aesthetic—and what that functionalism means on the physical universe level in terms of its source-initiated definitions—then the work (impact) initiated by that thrust continuum (e.g., the work of Silver, Timmons) has to be evaluated with regard to the dynamic consequences of its influence as well. Musicians like Silver and Timmons dictated and designed how the bi-aitional juncture of extended creative music would function after the initiation of Charlie Parker and the subsequent emergence of bebop—and hard bop. The most basic difference between their activity and the music now happening in this time zone (jazz-rock) is the acceleration and acceptance of present-day rhythmatic generating devices (for dancing) and the use of the latest harmonic advances (or harmonic changes, since these developments are not always necessarily an improvement, let alone advancement), as well as the fact that it was not always possible to dance to some of the music by Silver and Timmons.

It is necessary to again state that I am not saying bi-aitionalism is a phenomenon that started only in the post–Second World War period, because this is not correct—nor is it my point. Yet the most basic alternative factor to emerge in the time zone of the late forties and early fifties would undoubtedly be bebop and its subsequent variations. If anything, the bi-aitional implications of creative music can be looked at as a phenomenon connected to the base affinity of its given aesthetic lining—that is to say, a natural part of its aesthetic (and that has always been the case, especially in the non-western creative thrust). I have attempted, however, to comment on the uniqueness of the bi-aitional projectional phenomenon after the Second World War as a means to detail the progressional particulars that have brought us jazz-rock today (these same factors—but different particulars—can be applied to every period of creative black music in

America with its subsequent progressional effects). In other words, the time-cyclic progressions that shaped the bi-aitional continuum underlying how composers like Timmons and Silver would deal with their activity are directly related to the factors that solidified the bi-aitional developments in the late sixties. The best example of what I am saying can be seen in the vibrational and structural junction of creative music in the early fifties—as compared to the present. The conceptual elements that these musicians worked from drew heavily on the implications of what was realized from the extended language of Charlie Parker's activity as well as a re-adaptation of the language we now commonly refer to as "blues" (but which is more than the word "blues"; not to mention that Parker's language itself drew heavily from the "blues" as well, yet this is not my point)—and in doing so, this relationship dictated the vibrational-affinity alignment that would establish bi-aitional projectional dynamics after the Second World War. My point is that the solidification of bi-aitional particulars in the time zone of the fifties established how the affinity insight (1) principle could continue to be utilized even after the initiations of Charlie Parker's activity, and in doing so this phenomenon provided the foundation of the present composite principle we now have in this time zone. More so, the actual activity from this sector functioned in the same cultural-affinity position of jazz-rock in this time cycle—because creativity from the bi-aitional principle has always had the best chance for being received by the public—and this is true for many different reasons. All of the musicians who have been able to understand the significance of bi-aitional postulation have usually become very successful people. This undoubtedly has to do with the "social reality" position of this phenomenon, for while the meta-reality of the thrust is no different from bebop (musicians like Jimmy Smith are second to none in their understanding of this phenomenon), the functional arena of its science can be dynamically utilized (e.g., dance—or social particulars) and received in the culture as a factor in accordance to cultural life (physical universe)—or pulse of a given community. It should also be stated that awareness of bi-aitional dynamics in creative music does not necessarily mean a complete abandonment of intent—with regards to the challenge of vibrational and/or information dynamics. A musician like

JR–20

Julian "Cannonball" Adderley is a perfect example of a creative force who was able to contribute to the composite spectrum of creative music. His work, for more than twenty years and some, is a perfect example of what can be accomplished by embracing the whole of creative music—from a composite viewpoint.

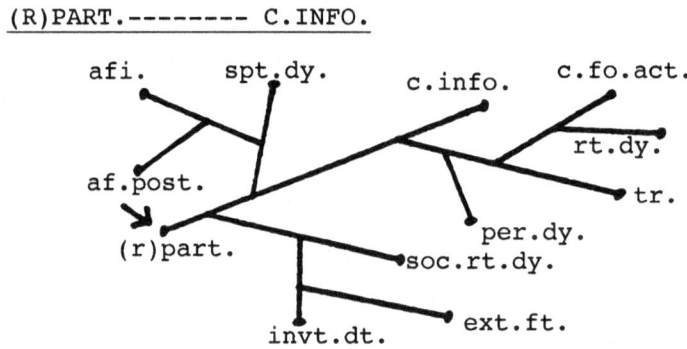

In short, the music that has come to be called jazz-rock in this period has always been manifested in creative music in one form or another. The most basic factor that distinguishes this phenomenon has to do with the particulars underlying how progressionalism unfolds in a given time period. That is, the changing vibrational reality of a culture greatly affects the meta-reality of its creative projections and affinity particulars, and this change can also be viewed as a social and vibrational indicator. In other words, jazz-rock also comments on American culture as a transformational indicator. For it must be understood that the American business community has adopted this thrust—like it has all bi-aitional thrusts—as a factor to control the reality lining underlying how Americans see themselves. Which is to say, the sophistication of the American business community has secured another functional notch with jazz-rock. So profound is this sophistication that jazz-rock can even be distinguished from bi-aitionalism and put in a special category of its own. The most basic physical universe factor that distinguishes jazz-rock from other composite thrusts is the establishment's use of "spectacle" as a factor to dictate the progressional implications of the affinity insight (2) principle. More so, the realness of this manipulation is also connected to the sophistication of source transfer as a factor to dictate and secure the position of western (white) culture and contributions. So intense and real was the controlling machinery pushing jazz-rock that by the middle of the sixties it was practically impossible to make a living playing any other form of music. The progressional factors that led to the abandonment of creative music from the affinity insight (1) principle are directly related to the effectiveness of this machinery. So great was the transition in the sixties that even the word "jazz" had come to symbolize something negative (for both black and white people alike). In short, jazz-rock is important because it personified the latest transition cycle of western culture with regards to source transfer—and in doing so, also solidified the position of the white improvisor, while at the same time commenting on the progressional situation underlying black culture—in other words, jazz-rock can be viewed as a social and vibrational control indicator (in both a positive and negative sense). Obviously this must be so, because if a musician like Lou Donaldson was not able to have his activity received on the level it merited in the fifties, it does not mean his activity didn't exist—and it is important to understand that the activity of the affinity insight (2) principle is basically designed with regards to the emotional and social factors of the culture it is "ised" in (in other words, when Donaldson began to participate in bi-aitional creativity, it was not because of an intellectual whim, nor was it an intellectual music—it was the same thrust we now refer to as jazz-rock today). Jazz-rock is also important because it represents the next solidified juncture of redefinition for the western controlling and defining community—thus providing the basis for continued transition (controlled and uncontrolled) as well as fuel for spectacle. Moreover, the progressional implications of this form, more than any other, reflect the reality junction of the next physical universe cycle that we will soon be dealing with.

My point is this: **jazz-rock is another progressional factor connected to the disintegration of the western composite community as a separate factor from the world group—and in this position, jazz-rock functions as simply another thrust from creative black music.** But because creative black music is allowed to advance only so far into American culture, jazz-rock must be looked at as the form with the most potential for detailing how this disintegration will ultimately affect composite American culture—that is, from a controlled point of view. In other words, the affinity implications of creative black music—manifested in jazz-rock—are a factor that functions to re-align the vibrationaltory lining of western culture. This is so because jazz-rock can now be viewed as a composite thrust rather than a pure and separate black music. This most basic difference has determined its success.

By the end of the sixties, groups like Chicago and Blood, Sweat & Tears had made a noticeable impact on the popular music scene. The seriousness of their impact forecasted the next cycle in popular music, because the most basic factor that determined the activity of both of these ensembles was the fact that all of the musicians had been schooled solidly in creative music from whatever principle—that is, both jazz and rock. Moreover, a musician like Randy Brecker has performed with many different types of creative improvised music, working with some of the best musicians of that period, and in doing so he is not unique—for many of the musicians who participated in the solidification of jazz-rock had also functioned on a dynamic level in extended creative music as well. My reason for mentioning the progressional factors surrounding the development of jazz-rock is only to state that the music coming from these ensembles represented what was possible with a composite understanding of creative music, either with regards to the consideration of improvisation or extended functionalism. All of these considerations—plus the fact that most of these musicians were white—played an important role in establishing the momentum that produced the present period we are in regarding jazz-rock. The basic thrust, then, of this movement would eventually reshape the commercial market by the early seventies, and in doing so also re-establish the business communities' hold on both creativity and functionalism—and while doing so, also allowed a percentage of musicians from the affinity insight (1) principle to move into source transfer. By the middle seventies, it was now possible for many musicians—who couldn't find work in the late fifties and sixties—to perform and have the weight of the controlling forces behind them as well (or at least some of the weight).

This period marked the first time that many of these musicians would be able to support themselves in a decent manner from their creativity. Moreover, some of the musicians from this sector have even seen their music appear on the "top ten records of the month" charts.

As the realness of jazz-rock advanced into the time zone of the middle seventies, there could be no doubt that the transition cycle in popular music had secured the next affinity thrust. Moreover, as the momentum of jazz-rock began to affect the composite reality of popular music, many changes could be seen in the controlling communities' use of the form as well. For it must be understood that by the middle sixties, rock music could be talked of as being on the decline economically (in relationship to what had transpired in the middle sixties), while jazz-rock was still ascending. Many of the musicians in jazz-rock would move into the national arena in this period (in terms of exposure)—and their activity was treated as being on the same commercial level as rock. Today, practically all of the musicians from the creative music community who made the switch to jazz-rock—in the first transfer cycle—are very successful people, at least in an economic sense (that is, if they have attended to their business correctly). The magnitude of the transfer-shift junction in creative music has even confused the basic language consideration of black music. For by the middle seventies, the word "jazz" had been stretched out of proportion to anything recognizable. In short, "jazz" had become respectable in the middle seventies (because nobody knew what the word meant).

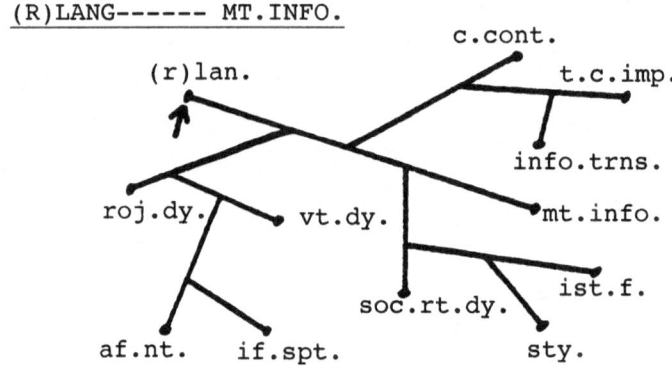

The transfer-shift-continuance phenomenon in popular music can be understood if the reality factor of jazz-rock is taken into account. For the first musicians into jazz-rock (as a movement under that name) were white musicians who had completed their musical training in college around the time period of the early to middle sixties. This is not to say that no black musicians were functioning in a bi-aitional creative thrust as an independent movement, nor have I meant to imply a racial significance to something that might be the consequences of something more multi-complexional. I mention this as a means to separate the progressional development of jazz-rock as a transfer and economic factor. In short, the establishment of jazz-rock in its early period can be viewed as a vehicle for white people to sidetrack the semantical complications of jazz and/or rhythm and blues, and move in accordance to what had become obvious to the business community—that being, the economic potential of the next source-transfer popular music (from black popular music) and how to use it. Obviously this is true. There would have been no need to invent the term "jazz-rock"—let alone the alternative reality it inspired—if the basic desire of the business community had only been to expose people to the music. For it must be understood that while jazz-rock does represent the solidification of the next bi-aitional junction in creative music as a solidified thrust, this form was not necessarily the first emergence of its actual projection. Rather, jazz-rock basically represents the first acceptable bi-aitional form by the controlling forces that dictate life and event progressions in American culture; and to that degree, the source-transfer implications of jazz-rock's position cannot be avoided if we are to truly understand the time zone of the late sixties and seventies.

My point is this: **the time zone of the middle to late sixties was the period where the business community made the decision to finance jazz-rock as a separate creative thrust. It was in this time period that companies like CBS began to search for particular types of groups—as a factor to correspond to the images being formulated for jazz-rock (and also as a factor to justify the economic investments that were to be applied behind this thrust).** The number of ensembles that were hired and recorded in this juncture are too long to categorize in this book, but my point is that the emergence of jazz-rock constituted a decision on the part of the business and controlling community. My point is also that the first wave of musicians chosen to carry the banner for this new thrust were white musicians, and there are several reasons for this. For jazz-rock was basically designed as a vehicle to attract the interest of the white community—that is: **jazz-rock was a vehicle designed to move in accordance to the mis-documentation that is necessary if a given form is to be successful in American culture—a form that also corresponded to western information dynamics and a form that corresponds to how the western controlling community has come to understand (view) the functional and vibrational meta-reality of creative music from the black aesthetic.** The early recruitment of white musicians can thus be understood as a natural progression if the social reality is taken into consideration. Nor have I meant to under-rate the actual abilities of the musicians who participated in the early thrust of jazz-rock, for the actual fact is that all of these musicians could really and did really contribute to the music—and this is a fact. My point is only that the basis which dictated what jazz-rock was and is to be about had to do with its ability to be of commercial value in American (or western) society, and because of that, there were natural limitations placed on how the form could initially be exposed. Only after the form was established as a commercial music did black musicians have a chance to participate in the movement—or at least have their activity distributed and pushed on the same level as white musicians.

It was Miles Davis's recording *Bitches Brew* that established the realness that black musicians had now entered into the jazz-rock movement. The impact of this recording is generally regarded as a factor that outlined transfer-shift progressionalism in creative music during that period. The significance of Miles Davis's entry into popular music cannot be lightly viewed. Because this one factor would have a profound bearing on the composite music scene—affecting many musicians who might not have considered that direction on their own. In fact, many of the musicians who worked with Davis in his *Bitches Brew* period have now become major practitioners of jazz-rock in their own right. I have no way of knowing to what extent Davis consciously molded the dynamic particulars of this composite phenomenon—nor should this necessarily matter. Because the fact is, the bloc that developed from the association with Davis's activity established a definite postulation thrust in the creative continuum of the seventies—a thrust undoubtedly based on the activity Miles initiated. Moreover, that this group was in the position where their activity could also be recorded (and experienced) on the world market is another factor related to how jazz-rock reached its present position. In other words, the influence this thrust was to have in the seventies is directly related to the fact that their activity was made available by the recording companies and commercially pushed to the next level—a move unprecedented in creative music before this juncture.

By the early seventies, the Miles Davis creative thrust could be talked of as the most influential movement of jazz-rock—especially with regards to black musicians—and the black buying audience as well. The work of this one continuum dictated the progressional implications underlying how jazz-rock was to function—and proceed. To understand the impact of this movement is to become aware of the musicians who functioned with Miles Davis at this juncture, for it must be understood that Miles Davis—more so than most musicians—has always associated and worked with some of the best musicians on the planet. We are talking of musicians on the level of Herbie Hancock or Wayne Shorter, for example—that is to say, musicians whose contribution to creative music is undebatable. In fact, so respected were these musicians—because of their proven creative dynamics in bebop (or extended bebop)—that their decision to embrace jazz-rock was another factor to substantiate source-transfer progressionalism in the early seventies. By the middle seventies, all of these musicians had established a creative thrust in jazz-rock of their own, and in doing so, secured the realness of this continuum for the next cycle. For the most part, most of these musicians have changed considerably in the last five to ten years—changed both musically as well as vibrationally. All of these people have become extremely successful, and while doing so have helped reshape the composite arena of popular music at the same time. The collected activity of this group of musicians might be the most important re-aligning factor in popular music during this time cycle—moreover, it is also clear that their activity has affected the composite progression cycle of creative music on every level. And while it is too early to access the impact of their work in its ultimate sense, it is clear that the source-transfer junction of creative music has been affected in a positive way by their decision to embrace jazz-rock.

The most important consideration necessary to understand the Miles Davis transfer-shift phenomenon is the realness that all of these musicians have, in some form or another, undergone vibrational transfer. It is now impossible to evaluate the activity of these musicians on the basis of what they had done in the past—more so, in many cases the awareness of a given artist's earlier work tended to make it somewhat difficult to properly experience his present activity. Because, in a way, these are different people now (or at least they seemed to be different). There are of course some connections between their composite music—even Herbie Hancock continues to perform his composition "Maiden Voyage"—but these similarities are few and in between. For the most part, the source-transfer-shift-cycle phenomenon has been a factor that has completely reshaped the creativity of the "school" that came through Miles Davis. The composite significance of this thrust has been very important for redefining the affinity insight (1) postulation with regards to functionalism in the seventies. Moreover, the potential of jazz-rock as a positive transformation tool rests with how these musicians develop in the next cycle. For the fact that the controlling forces of western culture have allowed the activity from this thrust to dominate this time zone has put these musicians in a very special position. The realness of bi-aitional creativity as a positive transformational tool will depend on how these musicians function in the next cycle. To understand the realness of what this opportunity means is to deal with the seriousness of the controlling factors that surround jazz-rock.

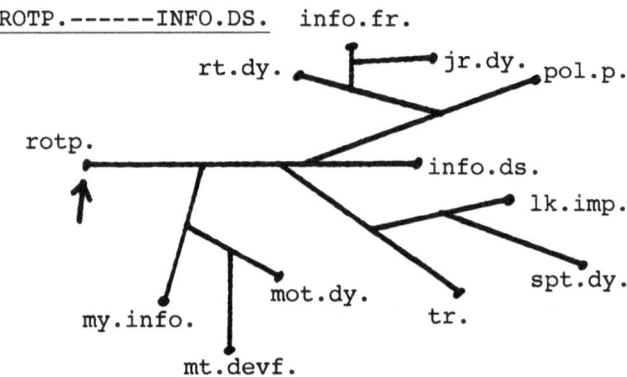

There are several factors connected to the solidification of jazz-rock as the creative force of this time zone (the seventies)—and any real attempt to deal with the reality of popular music would imply that these factors are also discussed on some level. The factors I am referring to are the collective forces that control American culture—manifested through business interests and culture programming. In other words, the political factors that dictate American culture. For it is impossible to look at the emergence of jazz-rock without acknowledging that this movement also represents the triumph of the American business and record industry. This is so because many of the musicians who have embraced jazz-rock have done so for other factors than just the music (e.g., the promise of greater exposure from record company executives, as well as the lure of more money from recording advances). So real has the influence of the business community been on popular music in the seventies that the present cycle we are now living in (the eighties) can be directly reduced to what their tampering has created. **In other words, the reality of popular music taking place in this cycle can also be looked at as being the direct result of the ingenuity of the western controlling forces that shape American culture.** I make this statement not to knock any developments taking place in creativity in the past ten years and some, but because I have no choice. There are of course many different reasons for the over-balance of outside controls in popular music, and I do not mean to imply that the present situation surrounding rock is a recent phenomenon, because it isn't. But the time zone of the sixties and seventies does represent a new level of control by the business community with regards to creativity. To understand how this control was to form in the seventies is to better view the sophistication of the controlling forces shaping American culture, because the reality factor of jazz-rock did not happen by accident, but was instead the result of accurate and precise manipulation by many different forces.

My point is this: **any real understanding of jazz-rock—as a spectacle—would have to take into account the reality aspect of creative music in the transition cycle of the sixties.** In other words, the fact that the business community had successfully designed the transfer shift in the fifties (from rhythm and blues to rock) established a definite economic thrust as well as creative thrust. All through the period of the sixties, the realness of this thrust could be seen, for this period was one of the most dynamic periods in the recording industry. The music that was called rock directly corresponded to the social factors that dictated the affinity alignment and nature of the teenage and hippie generation. Moreover, this generation had proven itself to be one of the best record-buying and concert-supporting generations in the transfer-shift junction of the sixties. All of these factors must have been understood by the business community—for these people are not fools, but instead extremely sophisticated functionalists. I am saying that on the most basic level, any business that hopes to stay in business must deal with preparation—as a factor to continue its existence—and also preparation as a factor to be ready for the next spectacle. The fact that the teenage audience of the sixties was moving into their twenties and thirties in the time zone of the late sixties and seventies necessitated that some preparation be made to greet them, and that is just what happened.

In other words, the most basic factor that determined the business-community progressions in the sixties was the realness that the record-buying public of the late fifties and early sixties was outgrowing the concept and spectacle cycle of rock and roll—as it was designed in the transfer cycle of the late fifties. This is especially true if the total period is examined; for if the early sixties was the junction that saw the critical and defining community embrace rock as a serious music, this was also the same junction that solidified how rock would progress as a sustaining factor for spectacle diversion. My point is that the acceptance of rock by the controlling community in the sixties forecasted the cycle that the music would have to travel—and as such signaled the coming of jazz-rock, both as a new term (for spectacle) and as a factor to correspond with the "sophistication" of the aging public. Thus, the structural sophistication of jazz-rock could validate the critical defining community and also assure the public that they are experiencing an "adult music"—as a form worthy of intellectual conversations. To understand this cycle is also to be aware of the decline of rock as a dynamic spectacle—to only spectacle. It is now fashionable to dislike groups like the Monkees or Bay City Rollers because these ensembles are considered not advanced or mature (yet five years ago, groups like Grand Funk Railroad, who are basically coming from the same tone level, were received as profound artists). By the time zone of the middle seventies, the critical and defining sources of American culture had reshaped the meta-reality particulars concerning how rock was to be written on, and in its place created an intellectualism that functioned to clarify how rock and jazz-rock could proceed.

The exploitation of jazz-rock thus corresponded to the awareness that something was needed to secure the next transition cycle in the seventies. Yet I have not stated this viewpoint to say that no musicians were functioning in this zone before the business community arrived, because many different factors dictate the nature of a time period (I have already stated that the historical progression of bi-aitional creativity is not a new factor). My reason for mentioning the transition cycle in the late sixties is only to state that the most basic factor that determined the subsequent emergence of jazz-rock had to do with the business community—as opposed to a natural development and awareness of the form by the public or greater musicians' community. Moreover, the manipulation of the business and controlling community is too important a factor to simply dismiss if we are sincerely interested in the meta-reality of jazz-rock as an "actuality." **For it is impossible to evaluate jazz-rock without understanding that embedded in the very essence of the music are the ultimatums handed down from record companies informing the artist that either he will perform jazz-rock or risk losing his contract.** So real is the present hold on jazz-rock by the business community that we are forced to understand what this phenomenon means on both aesthetic and functional levels.

It is important to understand that the political reality of jazz-rock is not only manifested in one aspect of the music, but rather in the totality of the phenomenon. I am saying that the outside controlling factors that permeate the reality of jazz-rock do not necessarily stop at any given juncture of the music—or music business—but instead filter through every level of the music. In many instances, record companies now play an integral role in defining the actual music performed by the artist as well. This involvement represents a decrease of responsibility for the creative musician and also signals the gradual takeover of the music by the business community. It is not just a question of a record company helpfully assisting an artist in a recording project—rather, the actual situation that has been developing since the early sixties points to a complete takeover. Today, in many cases, the record company selects the artist, selects the music, selects the arrangements, and directs the operation on every level. As this situation develops, many artists have practically nothing to say about the "product" that finally appears on record under their name for the buying public. At present, there are at least twenty or thirty musicians that I am aware of whose activity today cannot be understood at all unless one accepts that quite possibly that musician has given up the ability to define his own activity. So real is this type of arrangement that the coming transition in popular music must be looked at seriously. **The question is: what is the significance—or reality implications—of a form of creativity that is**

designed by the controlling forces that dictate culture in American society? I do not necessarily mean to imply that everything from this continuum has to be negative either—but if the position of the controlling forces in popular music is on the level I think it is, then we have no choice but to ask these questions (at least we can ask).

There is another aspect of this situation that must be looked at as well. For if I can state that the controlling forces of American culture are now designing popular music—more specifically, jazz-rock—then what does this phenomenon mean with regards to the musicians who have given up their right to be creative? In other words—it would be unfair to simply put down the power structure—or single out record companies—without also commenting on the musicians who have accepted these terms. For together, the power structure and controlled musicians have helped to make this period in progressional American history very close to the period following the emancipation. I am talking about musicians, who at one time performed creative music on a very high level, suddenly by 1974 sounding like TV commercial music. At what point can one say these musicians are also responsible for their activity? I am aware of how different the times are economically—how can I not be—and anyone can understand how there are times in a person's life when compromise is a fact of life . . . (?)—but some of the activity I have been hearing in popular music cannot be justified on any level but economics, and if this is true, then the musicians have no one to blame but themselves. Yet it is important to clarify this viewpoint, for when I stated that I am dismayed at some of the activity I have been hearing of late, I am not trying to look down at another person's creativity—nor am I saying that all jazz-rock is "less" because of my opinion; in other words, there is more to this viewpoint than petty assertions or vehement attacks on jazz-rock. The basic fact I am dealing with is the actual music we are being fed in this period, and the narrowness of the popular music I have been hearing as well (and again, maybe this is only my problem). It is not just the realness that few of the musicians who made the transfer shift to jazz-rock have yet to function on the creative level one would expect, but jazz-rock today has moved more towards a formula music than rock. The fact that the musicians who made the shift had demonstrated they were capable of much more creativity before they made the switch to jazz-rock is what disturbs me. In other words, I find it difficult to believe that the work of the established musician who made the switch to jazz-rock could be so weak when compared to the statements they made before the switch. It is difficult to believe these are the same people who produced such rich music in the fifties and sixties.

    I have tried to include in this series of writings my viewpoint on the actual situation that surrounds creativity and the creative musician, and I have also tried to include the physical universe factor which determines how a given creative thrust can be seen as well. In short, I have tried to take as many factors into account as I can handle, as a means to comment on the reality and meta-reality of creative music—and write something that hopefully means something. Obviously the economic situation surrounding non-rock music has been difficult for quite some time, and I see no change in sight. I most certainly can understand any musician moving to a music which functions in accordance to the affinity insight (2) principle, for this move would have the best chance of being received by the public—and it would also be easier for that musician to make a living. I can also understand any musician who began functioning creatively from the affinity insight (1) principle but later changed and moved to popular forms—for these things do happen—people do change. But the avalanche that occurred in the sixties, and the resultant music that came out of this move, has led me to believe that the time zone of the seventies represents a new low for western culture. I am not saying all of the popular music I have been hearing is not creative, for that is not true either—but I am saying that much of the music I have been hearing has nothing to do with creativity—let alone "necessary postulation." If my viewpoint is correct, then this phenomenon will not be without its "necessary consequences" either.

(Level Three)

1. Has the level of musicianship in rock music been affected by the emergence of jazz-rock?

I believe the emergence of jazz-rock is responsible for many of the dynamic changes that have affected the composite reality of rock music. For the entry of this phenomenon—jazz-rock—has redefined the reality of rock functionalism—on many different levels. The thrust of jazz-rock has helped to alter the harmonic make-up of rock music, and the weight of this movement has also affected the use of dynamic improvisation. Jazz-rock has redefined the application of vocal harmony and musical structure dynamics (i.e., the use of either pyrotechnics in orchestration, or in instrumental execution). The actual reality of musicianship in rock music has been profoundly affected by jazz-rock, and many of the younger players have moved to base their models (for learning) on musicians whose abilities are more dynamically and technically challenging (e.g., Chick Corea or Herbie Hancock). This is so because the technical and functional reality of rock music is now viewed as more relevant to the composite direction popular music has since taken (with regards to style). There are of course exceptions to this movement (e.g., punk rock), but for the most part, the emergence of jazz-rock has helped to open dynamic possibilities for popular music. The only problem, as I am able to understand it, is that the thrust of jazz-rock is not necessarily conducive to the essence continuance of trans-African information and spiritual dynamics—in terms of its separate vibrational identity. Because jazz-rock is susceptible to the current winds of spectacle diversion—as a plastic music (designed from the specific intentions of the business community), rather than a real affirmation of life creativity. It is too early to pass judgment on what this phenomenon will ultimately mean.

2. Which factors do you believe influenced the move towards jazz-rock by the so-called pure jazz community—the aesthetic needs or the economic needs?

I believe that the avalanche of pure bebop musicians to jazz-rock in the seventies had to do with many different factors—especially economics. All of us are affected by the dictates of social reality, and this includes the creative community as well. The non-support of extended creative music most certainly affected the spirit reality of everyone involved—not to mention, many musicians from the extended bebop juncture didn't really like the post-Coleman continuum anyway. The move to jazz-rock is necessarily connected to all of these considerations—and more. For it must be stated that the solidification of jazz-rock was sanctioned by the collective forces of western culture—as a form that could be embraced both commercially and aesthetically—which is to say, as a form that one could participate in and survive in as well. The resulting move that ensued had to do with the attractiveness of what jazz-rock posed, as well as the realness that many of the musicians really had no other place to go. Finally, the challenge of being able to make a living from such a participation was much too irresistible to not take advantage of—for I imagine that musicians like Randy Brecker understood very clearly that they could contribute to the thrust of jazz-rock on a much higher level than what had been happening before—and in this viewpoint they were right. In the final analysis, all that really matters is whether each of us can find an area of participation that agrees with one's nature and purposes—or one's not nature and purposes (depending on the individual).

3. There has long been the understanding that rock musicians are inferior to jazz musicians. Do you agree?

No, I do not agree. It seems to me that comparisons of this nature generally seek to apply alien criteria as a basis to not deal with the real reality of that which they are comparing. This is so because to really deal with the particulars of a given reality is to not have a need for any viewpoint that attempts to downgrade or lessen "real participation." Take the consideration of technique, for example. I have read many magazine articles that have commented on the "technical inferiority of jazz to western art music"—

just as jazz is now viewed as superior to rock. It seems to me that both of these viewpoints violate the real reality position of technique. Because any standard that seeks to evaluate an aspect outside of the context that aspect derives its function from is necessarily meaningless. In other words, to take a consideration (i.e., technique) and put it in a vacuum as a means to claim superiority over another music—or information focus—has no real validity—or meaning. Because there is no such thing as technique in this context. I have met many jazz musicians who are extremely competent musicians (by western criteria) who cannot play rock music—and what does this mean, is the rock musician superior? The most basic factor for any person who participates in creativity, in my opinion, is honesty—and no one type of music has a monopoly on that.

4. What adjustments do you consider valid in any attempt to make an art form communicative?

I don't know if there is any universal criterion that can be used to determine whether or not a given adjustment is valid. I say this because people move in such different ways. It seems to me that as long as any adjustment doesn't take away from how an individual wants to flow, then that adjustment can be pursued. In other words, I believe Cecil Taylor's comment "the artist's first responsibility is to communicate with himself." It is a question of how each individual sees her/himself with regards to his/her understanding of the creative process. It is also a question of each individual's relationship with her/himself, as well as which vibrational zone that individual vibrated towards, that finally determines how an individual will proceed with his/her creativity (and everything else, for that matter). I have met many musicians who later changed their music as an attempt to be more communicative who still had problems communicating. The question for me is not whether or not one should make his activity more communicative, but rather, what is it you wish to communicate. The optimum situation, as I am able to understand it, would be to move in accordance to your own vibrational flow and hopefully communicate that.

5. *How important is it to retain continuity of development with regards to an individual's relationship with creativity?*

Quite frankly, I don't really know. When I think back on those individuals whose activity transformed my life, I am always constantly reminded of the importance of consistency. Yet none of those individuals necessarily had the same type of consistency. It seems to me that what this question is really referring to is really connected with the overall "purpose" of the person creating. Because the continuity of a person's development is not separate from how that person views the creative process as well as his or her life involvement. There are three aspects to this question: (1) continuity with respect to the reality governing how often one practices his or her craft, (2) consistency with respect to a person's level of invention, and (3) consistency with respect to whether or not the route of a given participation is in accordance to the overall objective that person has postulated for him- or herself. On some level, all of us are affected by one aspect or more of this viewpoint, and I imagine that the real challenge of creativity, as a living, is to somehow stay in accordance to that which is "most" about what you are—while trying to grow in the process. As for the nature of a given "continuity of development," it is still difficult to deal with this question in particular terms, because what I might detect as a lack of continuity might not necessarily have anything to do with what is really happening. There is really no way to set a universal criterion for a question of this type. What is continuity of development?—and if we can isolate it, how can there not be a continuity of development (in other words, can the idea of development be separated from the person or persons who are developing—not to mention, how are we to know what a given person wants to develop?). The reality dynamics surrounding one's relationship to continuity is much too complex to comment on—at least in this context.

6. *How does the socio-economic and spiritual climate of a group direct or influence that group's creativity?*

Based on my own experience, I would say that the nature of a given ensemble's composite affinity differs from group to group. I find that a given ensemble (of mine) plays better if everyone in the ensemble has positive feelings about both being there and the music, as well as good feelings about each other. This, of course, is only a subjective viewpoint, and every musician who functions as a leader will undoubtedly have something also to add. I have read that Charlie Mingus, for instance, was not interested in this kind of ensemble climate at all, and any musician who has ever worked for someone will probably have much to say about the particulars underlying how each leader functions with respect to the ensemble's climate. As for the question of socio-economics and its role in the creative ensemble, I believe this consideration has a profound effect on the music as well. For the reality of economics is necessarily intertwined in every aspect of our lives. Thus, if an ensemble is able to work regularly, then that ensemble has a better chance to develop both musically and economically. Many a good group has broken up because of the dynamics of money alone—this is true even though the music itself might have been excellent. As such, it is important that the fairest possible system is developed for paying all members of an ensemble. Because the sooner this problem is solved, the better it is for all concerned. Finally, the question of spirituality is another context that is difficult to gauge. On the surface, one would assume that if all of the members of a given ensemble were spiritual people, concerned about spiritual things, then the music of that ensemble would be a spiritual music. Yet this is not necessarily true. What this probably means is that "projected spirituality" really has to do with magic, and magic is not something that can be necessarily learned—at least in some areas anyway. Instead, this area of spirituality might be reserved for those "who are appointed." I can only speculate about "these matters." Nevertheless, I have seen many musicians who do not see themselves as spiritual people play some of the most spiritual music I have ever experienced, and, on the other side, I have heard music from certain musicians who talk only about spirituality and spiritual music that did not touch me spiritually at all (which again means nothing). This is a complex question for me.

7. Is there a parallel development between popular music and so-called jazz in the reality of its historical continuity, and has each continuum helped to clarify the reality of the other?

Yes. There has always been a direct connection between popular and art creativity, as well as the dynamic principles underlining what these continuums really are. This is so because both musics—and principles—are affirming the same reality. Moreover, the separation of so-called art and popular music is a recent development and does not correspond to the dictates of world culture. I believe that the coming fifty years will see a re-solidification of life music, and to some extent that has already started. Nevertheless, there is a dynamic inter-relation between so-called art and popular music, and the nature of that relationship does comment on the natural compatibility of composite creativity. In a sense, the emergence of jazz-rock can be viewed as an attempt to solidify composite creativity. For the thrust continuum of black creativity was a unified music until the solidification of bebop. A composer such as Duke Ellington has long been noted for his insistence on functioning in the composite spectrum of the music—and in this he was not alone. Even Bach and Beethoven wrote popular music for their culture—music to dance to, music to sing to, etc. I believe that the present insistence western culture has on separating art and popular music reflects an inability to deal with the reality of ideas and spirituality and its real relationship to living (and social reality)—and feeling (i.e., sexuality and emotionalism). Somehow, the west sees the mind as godly while condemning the body as sinful.

8. Is the song form a useful medium in contemporary music?

I would say that any form—as long as that form serves the needs of the people using it—is useful. It seems to me that we have, in this culture (western culture), come to the juncture when some attempt must be made to re-examine the reality of "participation." I believe the creative person should be able to use everything that exists—as he or she sees (or hears) it. Not to mention the fact that there have been so many wonderful contributions to creative music via the song form. The song form will always have a part to play in creative music—at least this is what I feel.

Many of the avant-garde musicians from the sixties moved to abandon this most basic area of creative music—with the understanding being that the song form could not necessarily transmit the dynamics of their viewpoint. Fortunately, this viewpoint has begun to either change or open up, and the eighties promise to see the total inclusion of the song form as a necessary medium. It seems to me that the reality of extended functionalism doesn't so much call for the dismissal of a given approach, as much as the emphasis on particular approaches. In the final analysis, the reality of one's material is really related to the needs of the particular person, rather than the so-called problems of a given medium. Because, finally, every form has its own dynamics, and its own positive and negative attributes. The song form is as meaningful and dynamic as any other region of creative functionalism.

9. *What is jazz-rock?*

Since improvised music has always functioned with respect to the dynamics of both the affinity insight (1) and affinity insight (2) principles, as it is expressed in both extended functionalism and popular music, I must assume that jazz-rock is basically an attitude. This is a term that comments on the marketability of a given projection, and this is also a term that vibrationally gives insight into the present dictates of western culture dynamics. For the many musicians from so-called pure jazz who adopted this term, jazz-rock represented a path back to a music that could again be accepted by the general public—and this of course is exactly what happened. For the American businessperson, jazz-rock is probably viewed as another spectacle in the long chain of events that has solidified western information dynamics, that has also functioned as a profitable venture. I view this phenomenon as a move to establish a bi-aitional music and composite aesthetic, as well as a music that can be made to affirm the present reality of things. I mean this both positively and negatively. I believe the real intentions behind the emergence of this phenomenon (jazz-rock) are not necessarily the same as what has resulted from its use. In other words, after all is said and done, the musicians in this medium are really attempting to be involved in a positive creativity that can be embraced by the greater public. The imposed manipulation and applied definitions from the controlling and defining community of western culture is an extra added feature of this phenomenon.

10. You have written about the multi-synthesis between western art music and black creativity in a positive (or somewhat positive) light, and yet you hesitate about the same synthesis in popular music. Why?

If I have somehow communicated that the basic thrust of multi-synthesis now occurring in popular music is negative, it is undoubtedly because of my unhappiness about the position of non-white people in this multi-synthesis. For the dynamic reality of popular music in this time period really accents the racism that non-white people are dealing with. This is true for how the music is projected—the disrespect of all things not viewed as white, and the valiant use of accented manipulation, etc.—and probably my resentment of this phenomenon has muted my positive feelings about the projectional continuity of popular music. Nevertheless, in the long run, I view the composite reality of popular music as positive. I believe that sooner or later the multi-implications of composite music will help to change life on this planet for the better.

11. How do you view the acoustic implications of rock music—and the so-called disco phenomenon?

I believe the dynamics of contemporary rock music have profoundly altered the relationship that many young people could have for composite creativity—especially acoustically. Since the sixties, live performances of rock have moved to totally violate any human standard for sound dynamics and volume. The music is performed at such a loud volume that to endure a complete performance is to damage some aspect of one's hearing—and this is very serious. For the past twenty years, many people in this culture have slowly become numb to the sheer volume of commercial music, because the use of loud sounds today now permeates the culture, in practically every social context. Certainly I do not claim to know what this phenomenon will pose for the next cycle of western living, but I do feel that the effects of this phenomenon cannot possibly be positive. In the past five years, the emerging disco scene has also embraced this use of loud music. As such, the reality of "having a good time dancing" involves exposure to such high levels of sound volume that the effects of that time "will last forever." It is important to understand that the physics of a given sound have the potential to do dynamic good as well as bad. I believe the present volume level of commercial music is very dangerous. Even if it were stopped at this moment, serious damage has already been done. We can only imagine what the future holds.

12. How do you view the emergence of disco music in the seventies?

It seems to me that the emergence of disco music (and the disco itself) has solidified another output for social-reality participation, and this must be viewed positively. The realness of life in this time period necessitates that people have an opportunity to "get away from it all"—and in some cases to "simply have some fun." The emergence of the disco must really be viewed in sociological terms, because the reality of this phenomenon transcends the particulars of creativity—or music. From what I have been able to understand, the disco is something of an emotional platform for balancing the pressures of contemporary living, where the music is not about anything, but at least "it's loud." The realness of the disco—and all other "cos"—seems to represent a reaction to the dictates of western manipulation (yet even in this context, the nature of present-day social reaction is strange, for the people who cause the reaction are the same people responsible for creating the disco). I do believe that the volume of sound in this context is frightening—but then again, these are frightening times.

13. Has the source-transfer realness of present-day rock music really solidified its own vibrational continuance from black creativity?

This is a somewhat difficult question in that the present nature of dynamic commercial manipulation keeps changing terms every other week—and in doing so, keeps the progressional continuance of popular music always in a state of flux. Yes, I believe the source-transfer solidification of rock music in the white community has solidified its own vibrational continuum—in fact, I believe this continuum was solidified in the middle to late fifties. But the present nature of western manipulation tends to diminish the realness of the phenomenon through present-day marketing techniques (that change focus every four months). In a way, the advantages of the white musician are also the disadvantages—because the option-spread dynamics of the white popular musician are invariably co-opted into the spectacle-diversion information complex as a means to "become successful" (that being, "make money and be a star"). For this reason, the composite continuum of white rock must always look to black creativity as a means to be "validly revolutionary" or "non-establishment"—but all of this is short-lived. Black creativity in popular music is exploited as a means to "get over"—because in the final analysis, the dictates of western culture have created a situation where no one minds being "establishment," as long as they also have the coins. The success of white rock is also its dilemma.

14. To what extent has Madison Avenue helped to solidify rock music, and what does this manipulation really mean in terms of the vibrational actualness of the music?

The move to rock by white people in the fifties was not designed by Madison Avenue, but was instead an expression of natural attraction. The realness of this attraction had to do with what the meta-implications of the music implied to the progressional continuity of composite America—and especially to the composite young people of America. The institutionalization of rock was solidified because of the foresight of the American business community—and the realness of this decision has been dynamically profitable. By the same token, the adaptation of rock by big business has necessarily affected the vibrational reality of the music. For the thrust of this marriage has profoundly altered the vibrational and affinity nature of rock music—and in doing so, "has helped to make rock music as American as apple pie." In vibrational terms, the meta-reality of popular music must be viewed as an affirmation of the American aesthetic reality—this is so or it wouldn't be accorded the treatment it now receives—yet I have not meant to sound negative. My point is only that the present reality of rock is directly in accordance to the reality dictates of western composite information. Rock as such can be viewed as the music of "today"—and this is positive if today is what "it is about." I view the manipulation of the western business community in rock music as not being in accordance to the dynamic implications of the music (from its own terms).

15. *What ramifications has the move to jazz-rock made to the composite reality of so-called mainstream jazz in terms of continuance and also in terms of option dynamics for future creative postulation?*

At this point in time (the early eighties), I think it is much too early to speculate on just what the emergence of jazz-rock in the early seventies will mean for the next continuum of the music. Hopefully the emergence of this form will prove to be a positive factor for the continuance of the music. Obviously this must be true. Already, the realness of this phenomenon has broadened the scope of popular creativity—which is to say, there are positive benefits of this movement that cannot be overlooked. Many of the so-called articles on the music seem to suggest that the realness of jazz-rock will have a positive effect on the overall state of all black creativity—that is, jazz-rock will help attract people to bebop. Yet it seems to me that the opposite is also true, for whenever I hear the radio in this period, what they now call jazz is what I thought was rock. In fact, the distance between what was jazz and what is now jazz is so wide that I have grave doubts that mainstream jazz, as I understood the term (in the fifties and sixties), will ever be the same. Possibly, I am simply over-reacting. But in the final analysis, the music has to go the route of the people—or the businesspeople (what!!!!? hum m m m m m m?).

16. *Have the economic dynamics of popular music affected the motivation implications of young musicians?*

I believe the present "state" of things has indeed affected everyone—regardless of age—and this is especially true of younger musicians. There can be no denying the importance of economics, and the emergence of the "businessperson musician" in itself must be viewed as positive. At the same time, the present reality of option dynamics has moved to encourage younger musicians to pursue only those areas that might be beneficial economically rather than aesthetically—and this influence is profound enough for what it poses to older musicians, let alone younger ones. Because in the case of older musicians, the move to commercial music is not the result of not knowing about other forms of music, nor does this move take away from what that individual has learned throughout the whole of his or her involvement with composite creativity. Instead, the move towards commerciality by older musicians represents a decision based on what that person (or those persons) wants to do. The problem for younger musicians in this time period is that even before one has a chance to really learn about composite creativity, the objective of economics has already influenced the nature of one's scope. As such, the younger musician in this time zone is in a very dangerous position—this is true even though he or she might stand a good chance of making lots of money—because "the reality of intentions" in this time zone can easily be distorted.

17. Why are so many musicians who were once associated with so-called jazz now attempting to separate themselves from the word, and in its place put rock or popular music? Is the word "jazz" a stigma?

The move by musicians in this time zone to separate themselves from the word "jazz" is both complex and diverse. For on the most basic level, jazz has never been socially viewed as an acceptable form of creative music, and nothing has changed in this time zone. Many younger musicians have separated from jazz because, to them, "jazz" is a word that functions as a negative factor to their ability to be successful—and in that context, they are right. It is now better to be viewed as either a popular commercial musician or a rock musician if one wants to attain public acceptance—and financial rewards as well. But the exodus from the word "jazz" is not only limited to younger musicians, and this phenomenon is much more widespread than any one sector of the musicians' community. This is so because while most people have long rejected the music called jazz, nobody knows what the word really means or really refers to. The whole of this book has tried to focus on what I now call creative music—rather than jazz—because of this very same problem. Yet on the other hand, there are many musicians who feel this term does accurately comment on their music. Because of this confusion—or widespread disagreement—many musicians have moved to change their nomenclature as a means to forge their own separate destinies.

18. What effect has the rapid rise and exploitation of new artists in popular music had on the social-reality particulars surrounding the learning of one's trade?

The present state of western culture has profoundly altered the reality of learning—in music and every other area. One of the most basic areas that has been affected is the "reality of apprenticeship"—involving both the time spent on one's craft and the time spent learning under more experienced musicians (towards solidifying a viewpoint). Many young musicians are now so affected by the accelerated pace of western living that they are moved to "make a name" for themselves long before they have had the time or life to have a viewpoint—about music or anything else. The realness of this phenomenon is related to the "Coke-generation image"— that being, the over-emphasis on youth as the focal point for living. In the final analysis, the accelerated move to become famous has profoundly affected the vibrational state of western creativity—and especially western commercial creativity. Yet this acceleration does satisfy the "image dynamics" of western culture. I believe that the thrust of this phenomenon carries consequences for what it signals about the future of "perceived" western creativity and information dynamics. This is so because "when the children are at the controls" it tells something about the path degree of its culture.

19. What attributes have distinguished the second generation of fusion musicians from the first generation?

The first generation of fusion musicians (of commercial music) were individuals who had functioned in mostly mainstream jazz but later in the late sixties or seventies made the switch to jazz-rock. The thrust of their activity secured the reality of the jazz-rock continuum and also provided the functionalism for later generations. Many of those individuals have now gone on to become very successful throughout the whole of popular music. The second generation of fusion musicians have come to view themselves as jazz-rock musicians in their first emergence, and later simply commercial or rock musicians. The second generation of fusion players seem to be consciously attempting to get as far away from jazz as possible. In fact, many of these people have only surface awareness of jazz-rock—which they view as jazz. In many ways, I believe the reality dictates of the second generation of jazz-rock musicians are no different from those of the normal rock or commercial musician. In other words, the solidification of the second generation of jazz-rock musicians is really the solidification of the rock or commercial musician—there is no such thing as the second generation of jazz-rock music. What we have instead is a category that can be used in this time period to "get over" (or become successful). The significance of second-generation jazz-rock has only to do with how long the term can be used before discardment. The reality of this continuum has to do with producing a commercial music that can be received positively throughout the composite society—a music that can be bended so as to be able to tap "whatever the focus of the moment is directed on"—as a means to continue. This is the goal of all popular musicians, and this goal is also positively directed towards doing whatever has to be done in the present dictates of western living. As such, there is no need to separate the particulars of the second-generation jazz-rock musician from the composite community of all popular music.

TRANSFORMATION

(Level One) The Reality of the Creative Woman

It is somewhat difficult to comment accurately on the reality of the creative woman with regards to music—either today or from a historical context—because so little information has been developed on this most important subject. Yet the seriousness of this area of information is such that no real attempt to view composite creativity can afford to ignore this subject—that is, the reality dynamics of the creative woman are necessarily related to any transformational view of creativity—and this is true on every level. Moreover, if the basic thrust of this series of books has attempted to focus on the particulars of postulation dynamics—as it has involved the separateness of the white improvisor, European improvisor, or black notated composer—then there is still a need to detail the reality particulars of creative women as a means to better view the special situation women now find themselves in as we move to the next transformation cycle. We are now in a period where many changes are taking place on the physical universe level, and hopefully this phenomenon is more than only surface restructuring but, rather, the beginning of actual change. More so, the creativity we are experiencing in this period is directly related to the changing vibrational factors which personified the last two thousand years and some on this planet—having to do with the solidification of western culture as the dominant factor in this time zone, and also having to do with what this dominance would mean on the physical universe level for both western and non-western people. Any attempt, then, to deal with the progressional implications of earth culture would detail how western controlling factors have functioned with regards to both non-white people and women—and not necessarily in this order. My point is that there are definite signs in this period that give insight into the nature of the coming transformation, and among those signs are the reality dynamics of women as a creative force to be reckoned with in the next cycle (as well as the reality dynamics of feminism as a creative force to be reckoned with from previous cycles to the present).

The seriousness of creative statements by women in this cycle has already begun to affect the basic physical universe situation we now find ourselves in during this period—especially in the west—and the next time cycle will see this phenomenon expand to every level of our society. There are, of course, many obstacles still to be overcome, but already the momentum of the last ten years has established a definite thrust. The creative woman is now redefining her collective universe, and the work emerging in this time zone will help shape the next cycle in creative music. What is important in this period is whether or not men and women are prepared for what these statements will mean, for the developments shaping the middle to late seventies seem to forecast a new functional and vibrational attitude with regard to creativity. So profound is this phenomenon that the composite creative progressionalism of the next cycle will most surely be affected. In other words, there can be no doubt that women will participate in shaping what the next creative thrust will be—and mean, as well. It would be to our advantage if some attempt is made in this period to deal with the reality of creative women—both as a factor to better understand the next transition of creativity, as well as why change is inevitable.

What is the reality of women in creative music (?)—or at least, what observations can be made with regard to the participation of women in creative music? Based on my experiences, the present planet situation is designed to make it practically impossible for a woman to pursue creativity for a life's commitment—or at least in the same context as men. It is almost impossible for a woman to secure a strong enough position in society to make a living from her work—this is true even though, in spite of the odds, there are many women who have succeeded in making their activity known and "ised." Still, the situation women are faced with in this and previous time zones cannot be looked at as fair in comparison to the composite culture—by any means. To understand the collective factors that have produced this reality posture is to gain insight into what is really happening with the male creative community, as well as the sophistication of the controlling forces surrounding the music. This is so because the defining and controlling community that determines and regulates perception dynamics (and interpretations and/or focuses) has always dealt with women unfairly. To understand this phenomenon is to be made aware of the dichotomy between how creative people—especially musicians—perceive themselves and how they actually function. In other words, one might think it strange that musicians—especially the super-mystical and self-appointed leaders who emerged in the sixties—could at the same time function as chauvinist and oppressor—but in fact this does seem to be the case. Nor does it seem to matter that musicians tend to think of themselves as closer to knowingness than most people—because, in the final analysis, women have always been treated "differently" by their male contemporaries. So real is this situation that certain basic conclusions cannot be avoided, and so real is the suppression of women a fact that any attempt to understand transformation would imply a total reshaping of society. Because one thing is clear: **the most basic understanding that western society has with regard to creativity is that women are not capable of making creative statements on the same level as men.** It is this understanding that permeated the fabric of western culture in this time zone (yet I have not meant to imply that this distortion is solely western, because this does not seem to be the case either), and it is also this understanding that best gives insight into the vibrational factors dictating how "culture" is maintained in this time zone. For when I wrote that obviously some women have fought and secured prominent positions with regard to having their work received by the greater public, it is necessary to understand what this means. In other words, it is not society's fault that these people have succeeded in their given fields. Everything is set up to either keep this from happening or limit it as much as possible. But the reality aspect of the creative woman is much more profound than any one context—there is much more to be looked at.

The best way to really understand the present situation of women in creative music is to look at the actual physical universe "scene" surrounding the music. It is on this most basic level that the distortions of the composite culture thrust can be viewed as an actualness rather than as theory. For if I have written that the western defining and controlling thrust believes in the innate inferiority of women as creative beings (forces), then we must understand the ramifications of this sentiment as it applies to every strata of our society—especially with regard to the physical universe act of functioning (or living). We are also forced to deal with these injustices in this time zone if our commitment to transformation is serious. It is not a question of understanding some mystical equation or the implication of some strange mathematical theorem—but rather, the physical universe situation surrounding creative women in this period can be reduced quite quickly to the distortions of the male controlling and defining community. To understand this is to arrive at what seems to be the only logical starting point for rebuilding. The result of the present reality—in human terms—is manifested on every level and impossible to write on as a single entity. There are, however, several factors related to the reality aspect of creative women that can be commented on with regard to the progressional effect of sexism—as a factor related to the impediment of women participants—and as a central link related to the institution of "art" in this time zone. Even on this most basic level—entry or initial exposure to creative music—women are put at a disadvantage. For the first misconception women have to deal with, in any encounter to participate in the "scene," is the understanding that her real motives are social rather than aesthetic. By the same token, if a woman has developed her creativity to the point where her work has to be taken seriously—on whatever level—it is not uncommon to hear musicians say that "yes, she can play—in fact, she plays like a man."

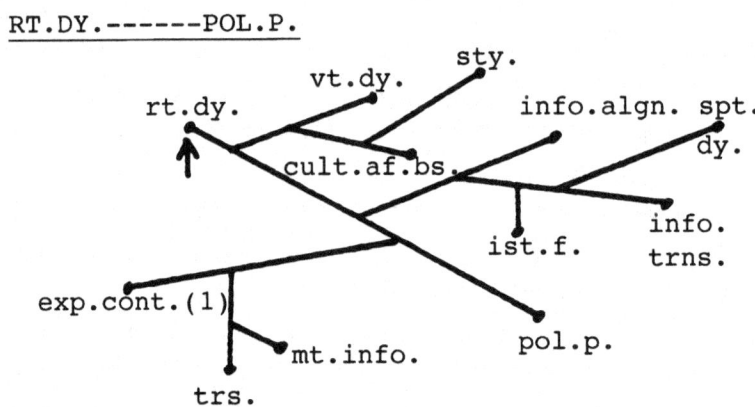

It is in the social and political forces surrounding the music where the creative woman's situation can best be understood. This is so because the social and political progressions—as related to recording and performing, or reviews—are directly connected with how far one is allowed to penetrate into the scene, either from a historical progressional aspect (contributing to the culture and having that contribution documented as such) or economically (and the influence connected to power). All of these considerations must be operative if one is to be successful—in the sense of how success is defined on the physical universe level (in this time and culture). Moreover, one cannot underestimate the significance of the social factors surrounding creative music either, because few musicians are able to complete their activity without the help of other musicians. But what does this mean with regard to women?

To understand the social implications surrounding the progressional development of a given individual in creative music is to be made aware of how sexism is used to ostracize women as participants. In short, everything is geared to make it as difficult as possible for women to succeed in creative music. The progressional development I am referring to has to do with actual musicians' communities and how new musicians are integrated into the composite scene. Moreover, I am not referring to isolated progressions in selected areas around the country, but instead an attitude that permeates the entire scene—regardless of area—in creative music. Rather than proceed with generalities and run the risk of obscuring this phenomenon, one has only to view the reality particulars of New York City to understand what this subject means in actual terms. In New York, like most large cities, musicians invariably find out about new musicians from a given appearance in clubs (i.e., sitting in), and invariably the word spreads within days that a new player has arrived on the scene. So sophisticated is the musicians' network that few things pertaining to the music escape scrutiny. If the reality platform of the "session" context proved to be the major outlet for new talent from the thirties until the late fifties—providing a direct link for the musicians' communicating network—this same function could also be seen forming in the alternative performing outlets (e.g., lofts) in the late sixties and seventies. Through these channels, a young musician can advance his activity and have the possibility of increasing work potential. Understandably, the competition in these situations can be quite intense and serious—for one's very career is intertwined with the successes or failures associated with these outlets. Moreover, the social significance of the musicians' scene is not limited only to performing or sessions. In fact, the environment of the "session" or alternative performing scene serves many other purposes. This is so because of the social demands surrounding how to make a living from creative music. My point is that sessions provide a chance for new musicians to gain exposure as well as establish necessary social contacts as a basis to continue or expand one's working or creative situation. To understand this phenomenon is to understand that when a new group is formed, it is not only a matter of music, but rather involves a combination of factors— among which might be friendship. This is what I mean when I write of the social implications surrounding creative music—the realness that many developments, including personal relationships, are the result of social factors as well as musical considerations. In other words, the progressional dynamics surrounding a given musicians' community are much more significant than is generally understood. Any attempt to understand the reality aspect of the creative woman must involve this consideration as an important factor related to the collective forces sustaining the present situation in music. This is so because, while none of the social actions I have written about are negative in themselves, there is another factor connected to present-day social reality that cannot be avoided. That factor quite simply is racism and/or sexism.

It is extremely difficult for women to penetrate the established barriers around creative music communities—this is true in every form of creative music—because for many musicians, the entry of women is seen as a threat to the social and vibrational order of things. To understand this mentality, it is necessary to examine the forces that dictate how given thrusts of the music were interpreted for the greater public—in short, it is necessary to examine what is really happening in the vibrational hierarchy of creative music today. It is not uncommon to see a woman serving in the role of provider while the musician she lives with struggles in the fight for recognition of his music, but it is rare to see women having the opportunity to participate in creative music—rarer still to see men working while the woman struggles to get her music accepted—and it goes on. Because of this, both improvised and notated music cannot be talked of as manifesting a complete—or actual—reality thrust. For as long as women are not allowed to participate in the making of the music—and having a chance to assist in forming the direction of the activity—it is ridiculous to assume that creative music is representing and manifesting the vibrations of the total reality spectrum (in this period or any period). The actual fact is: **creative music has long functioned directly in accordance to the needs and whims of masculine vibrational tendencies (from the beginning of this historical cycle—from early Egypt until now). In this regard, there is no difference between the situation surrounding western art music today and what has transpired in creative music from the black aesthetic (though there are basic differences in how this situation was established).** It is clear that when we talk of western art music in this period, we are speaking of a form designed with the active participation of men in the functioning role (decisions)—and by the same token, creative music from the black aesthetic does not fare much better. For black music has long functioned according to the needs of black male musicians (and western culture misinterpretations)—yet the factors related to the meta-reality which produced this phenomenon are different from western art music. The reasons for this difference are: 1) the social factors surrounding black people's struggle since being brought to these shores; 2) the physical unattractiveness involving what musicians had to endure (as an involvement thought to be on the low end of society's spectrum); 3) the influence of the church as a re-unification factor; 4) the implications of the affinity insight (1) principle after World War Two, and what this phenomenon would imply for creative black music; 5) the fact that the power forces designing the whole of the emerging American music scene was masculine, and, as such, provided the cross-transfer continuance of this same mentality (and way of being) in the black community; 6) the realness that black men and black culture in America in actual fact can also be looked at as a patriarchal thrust as compared to a universal thrust;

and, finally, 7) the limitations that surrounded the actuality of "family" (those being, the realness of children and the functional systems—or lack of systems—initiated to keep a family or center afloat). Thus, any attempt to understand the progressional implications surrounding the creative woman would imply some insight into what these considerations mean in theoretical as well as practical terms. This is so because I am not writing of a recent development shaping, say, the last ten or twenty years, but rather a phenomenon that can be traced to the beginning of record-keeping (or at least this seems to be the case). In short, the collective forces working to the disadvantage of creative women have been enormous—and the implications of this subject represent one of the greatest challenges we will be faced with in the coming period.

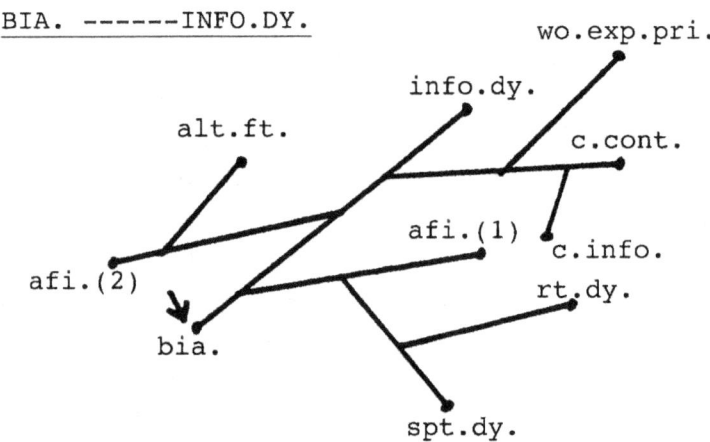

Given the historical progressions surrounding creative music—and the overwhelming barriers erected to exclude women—I find many of the present concepts concerning the participation of women in creative music to be very interesting. For example, one of the most common ideas floating in and out the creative music scene is the notion that few women support creative music of the affinity insight (1) principle—but, rather, are only attracted to popular music. This type of thinking can also be found in discussions concerning audience attendance at concerts; yet few musicians care to examine what is really happening in the social-ritual progressions surrounding the music (i.e., the scene). For in actual fact, not only are very few women allowed to participate in making the music, but few women are allowed to experience the music as listeners without being hassled on some level (however, this might not accurately explain the lack of support of women in, say, creative improvised music either, for the popular music scene in most instances reflects the same attitude as the creative music scene—yet there are differences that can be discussed). **Quite possibly, the factors related to the low turnout of women in the post-Webern or post-Ayler junction of the music is the realness that: (1) no efforts have been made to include women; (2) the meta-reality of the music might not be perceived of as relevant to where women want to go; or (3) women are in the same position as everyone else in western culture and as such cannot support the music because of the sophistication of media, and the lack of awareness that this condition promotes.** Whatever, I do not see this situation changing unless efforts are made to educate people about what sexism poses for one as a person, and what this consideration means with regard to composite creativity.

I believe that the lack of women in creative music of the affinity insight (1) principle is directly related to the flaws in the essence factor of western information dynamics (and its interpretations). That is to say: I believe it would be wrong to attribute the lack of participation of women in creative music as only a reflection of the social-political forces surrounding the music without also commenting on the realness of what this exclusion implies with regard to the aesthetic basis of western information and its focuses (i.e., creative music). Until sexism is eradicated, I see no immediate chance to gain insight into our potential—as earth people. More so, the realness of both sexism and racism stand as major blockages to real transformation. It is not just a question of women having the right to be creative—obviously this is what is needed—but it is also necessary for men to understand that without the participation of women in creative music, an important factor is missing from the music. In other words, the fact that half of the population is denied the opportunity to be creative is also reflected in the actual music—and however one chooses to understand this phenomenon, the resulting creativity we are left with has to be looked at as being less that what it should (and could) be. It is not just a question of writing about the actual effects of prejudice, with regard to how a given work (or moment) of music is or can be seen; rather, it is necessary to understand what has been happening on a planet and vibrational level to better deal with what can happen as we move into the next cycle. Nor can I comment accurately on what this change will mean in music terms, for while I have opinions about what the inclusion of women will mean in the future, in actual fact, I have no credentials to make blanket generalizations on this most important subject (in short, we are approaching the boundaries of what I can write on in this context). Moreover, in the final analysis, whether the inclusion of women will mean a change in the next cycle of the music or not is irrelevant. For the most basic point I have been trying to make is that there can be no excuse for sexism—regardless of context or focus. None of us can really talk—or write—with authority about how post-transformation composite creativity will sound—not to mention how a given segment in the music community will function. This is obviously true, and we would indeed be naive to merely presume that the effect of a composite creative thrust would be mono-dimensional. The fact is, women—like men, like the rest of the planet (e.g., flowers, rocks, trees)—cannot simply be lumped together as manifesting only one thrust. The seriousness of the forming world group hints at a multi-dimensional, all-encompassing creative music. We can be sure that the challenge of the next period will reflect the diversity that this experience (living) necessitates. In short, the contributions of women cannot now or later be confused with monochromatic perceptions (i.e., their contribution will be this—or this).

AF.DY.------POST.

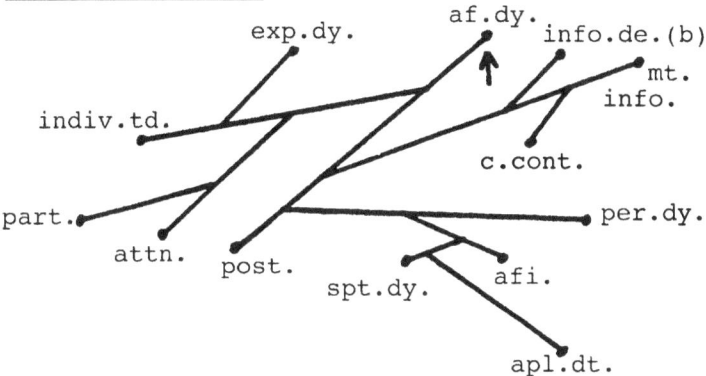

A.PR.------PROG.CONT.

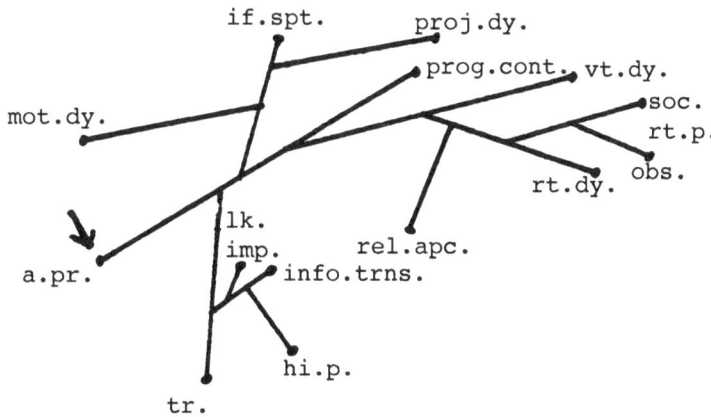

SPT.DY.------ PART.

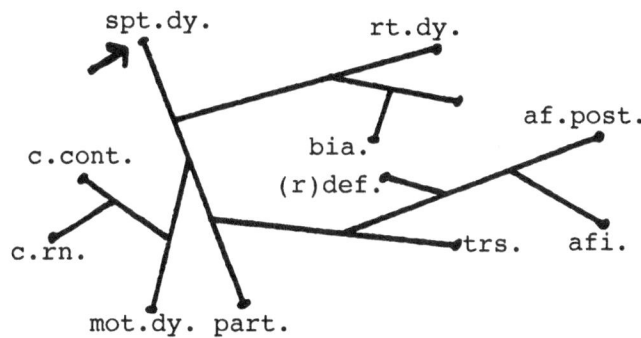

TRF(CW)–12

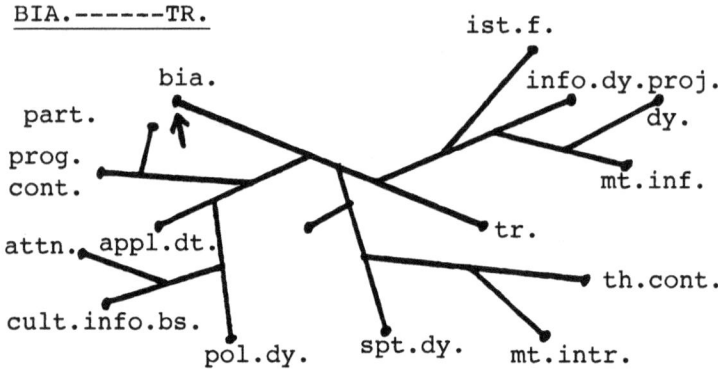

However one chooses to understand the situation surrounding creative women—no matter whether from a social, historical, or political context—it is important to make distinctions between how a given period of creativity is perceived in transitional documented terms (i.e., words as a weapon for redocumentation, and words as a means to make someone feel "less" than they are) and what actually took place. In other words, while it is certainly possible—and necessary—to write of the discrimination directed against women, it would be a great mistake to assume that no contributions have been brought to creative music by women composers or musicians. This has never been the case, and only a light research of the historical records would correct this mis-viewpoint. In every period of creative music—in creativity, period—there have been many important contributions by creative women. We have finally entered the time zone where hopefully some of this information will be made available to the general public. Much of the prejudice against women that has been disseminated throughout the greater culture is the result of a lack of awareness about the true historical progressions of creativity—whatever strain. For this reason, we cannot underestimate the seriousness of establishing correct information in our school system. There is a clear relationship between what information one is exposed to and how a given individual chooses to function in his or her life. This relationship is true for every sector of humanity: in other words, there is a real need for non-racist and non-sexist information.

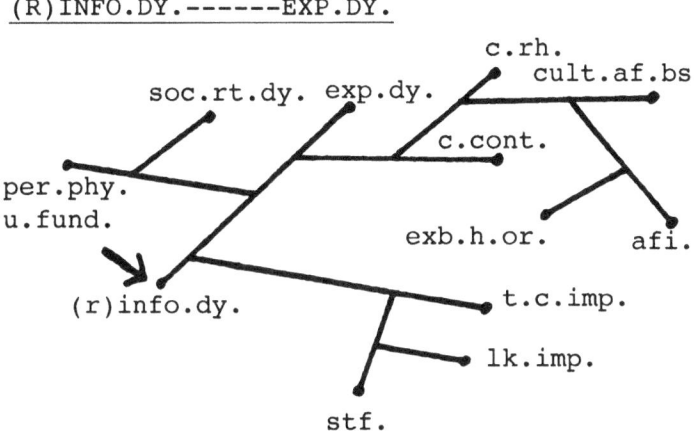

It is important to research the progressions of creative music from the black aesthetic as a means to better understand the realness of transformation with regard to the creative woman. For I have already stated my belief that the seeds underlying black creativity represent the most important unification factor in this time zone. I believe this because the essence factor which dictated the progressional implications of black creative music was a bi-aitional composite thrust. I am saying that the composite vibrational lining of black music is of a different nature than that of western art music. Because the actual fact is, women have been instrumental in the very forming of the music. This is not to excuse the actualness of sexism—obviously this consideration permeates every level of life perception and participation (in this time period)—but only to point out that, historically, the contribution of creative women is a fact. It is not just a question of stating that there have been many creative women in improvised music, because obviously this is true. My reason for commenting on the distinction between the position of women in creative improvised music and in the world of notated music, has to do with the realness of the progressional continuity of improvised music. For more than merely participating in improvised music, there has been a substantial amount of creative women who have contributed to the actual lining of the music as well. More so, those contributions have never been restricted to only one period of a given thrust (form), but rather the activity of creative women has affected the total vibrational and actual make-up of trans-African creativity.

To understand the concept of composite continuance (what the concept of "culture" implies), it is necessary to examine the composite thrust of creative music from the black aesthetic. We must investigate the vibrational reality underlying creative black music as it was "ised" in its early period, as well as what this reality has meant to the progressional—and projectional—continuum of the music. This is necessary because the vibrational affinity relationship of creative improvised music today has moved into a somewhat esoteric position—where few people are affected by the scope of its dynamic principles (in proportion to the total society)—and as such the reality of extended black improvised music is not necessarily indicative of the total thrust projection of black creativity. To understand the vibrational and social effect of creative black music is to be aware of the composite alignment of the music—in all of its different periods—and how that alignment functioned from and with black culture—and was received by the people. In Chapter 1 (Book 1), I wrote on how the emergence of the affinity insight (1) principle (in the thrust personified by the music of Charlie Parker) moved toward alienating a large part of the listening public, and in doing so became less effective as a regenerative factor—but this was not the case with the earlier projections (forms) of black music, and there are many reasons why. This is not to say that the activity of Charlie Parker—or the period of music referred to as bebop—didn't actualize from a real thrust (or cosmic objective), because obviously it did; but we must also remember that every form of black music—including the forms before bebop—has been subjected to the spectacle-diversion syndrome—and all survived and continued to influence the broad spectrum of African and American culture. The distinguishing factor that accents bebop—and creativity from the affinity insight (1) principle (as solidified from the continuum we now call bebop)—has to do with the implications underlying what bebop posed with regard to the source-transfer function after World War Two—and what this relationship would mean to the source-transfer junction of world music. The suppression of bebop, and the later blocking off of creative black music by the collective controlling forces dictating American culture, had to do with what bebop posed in relationship to both words (i.e., ideas for transformation, and the position black creativity would have in reconstruction, whether on a physical or vibrational universe level), and how this relationship could be used—positively and negatively—to promote a world music. The suppression of black music of the affinity insight (1) continuum was possible only because of much preparation by the controlling forces—the most important of this preparation affecting the affinity thrust of black society—and the most important of this preparation also affecting the bi-aitional implications of black creativity (of the affinity insight (2) principle as well). But the success of this suppression also signals something else—because as I have already stated, this was not the first time the controlling forces surrounding black music sought to undermine African invention (in fact, the suppression of black creativity is an integral cyclic function connected to the spectacle-diversion syndrome in American culture). **The suppression of bebop was possible only because the thrust projection of the form represented the most serious break yet with the composite black community—as equal participants in the defining and making of the music.** In other words, the life potential of a given creative thrust is directly related to what access people have to that thrust—or another way of saying this would be, the potential of a given thrust is directly connected to the bi-aitional implications underlying how it is utilized. For however difficult the early period in America has been to black people, the early forms of black creativity show very clearly the active participation of both men and women in the creative process—both in the actual music and also in the forming and extended aspects underlying how a given thrust was to develop. Because of composite participation, the vibrational-affinity pull of the creativity indeed reflected the meta-reality of composite black people in that period. More so, the actual creativity "ised" through that context is the basis (source initiation) and foundation we are still drawing from. That is—black creativity in its most basic state must be viewed as a bi-aitional creative thrust. Yet there is more to this subject than only one strata—for the emergence of black creativity in America signaled several very real junctures, and every creative projection that has emerged from this context must be looked at in accordance to what zones it has unleashed to the greater public. My point is this: the concept of new music in a vacuum does not mean very much.

If the concept of "new" is to have any meaning, it cannot be grounded solely in intellectual terms, but rather in "actual" terms. Creative music from the black aesthetic—as it has been "ised" in the Americas—is significant because the vibrational and physical universe factors surrounding its solidification were "new"—that is, representative of what was actually in the air at that time (as well as in accordance to the social reality of its time), and as such affirming the actualness of its reality. In short, the activity that solidified this thrust can be called new—which is to say, the bi-aitional thrust that "ised" creative black music has multi-complexual implications (and these implications also reflect on the significance of the creative woman's contribution). For it is important to understand that not only did the earlier period of black creative music establish a real new music, but the seeds underlying the base aesthetic of black creativity contained everything creative black music now utilizes today. In some ways, the original construction of the music can be looked at as much more advanced than what we now have—much more was created in the early period of the music than is generally recognized. For however the progressional implications of creative black music are now perceived, the fact remains that bi-aitionalism was and is the most distinguishing factor related to the solidification of black music as a transformation force, as well as spiritual force. The importance of all-inclusive participation in creativity is no light matter—the very cornerstone of alternative reconstruction is based on this consideration.

(R)PART------ TR.

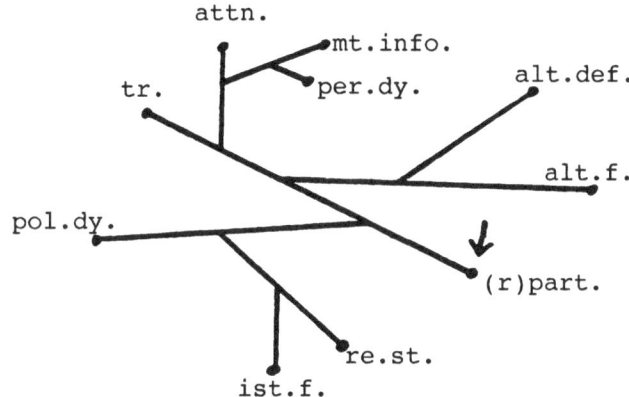

BIA.---- EXT.FT.

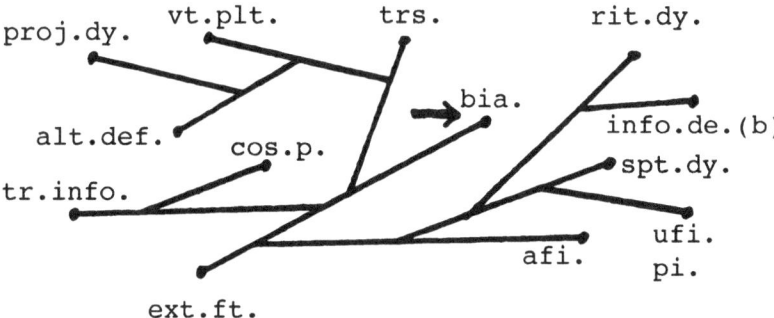

To gain insight into the implications of creative women in improvised music is to in fact be confronted with the dynamic consequence of bi-aitionalism as well as the essence factor of creativity. The most basic difference that has distinguished creative black music from that of western art music has been not just the use of improvisation, but instead the science that has developed from its composite aesthetic. In other words, it is clear that we can talk of how composers in the early period of western art music utilized particular aspects of improvisation—and it is clear that, abstractly, we could talk of improvisation as probably the first kind of music (i.e., before notation, people probably just made music from whatever)—but it is with creative music from the black aesthetic (not from America, but from what was raised in the source-initiation continuum of black culture) where one can see the seriousness of the science that surrounds this phenomenon. The dynamic functionalism (and participation)—involving improvisation and notation—that developed through black culture comments on what I believe are the most essential ingredients for establishing post-transformation culture. Moreover, when I wrote that the nature of this phenomenon was conceived and developed in accordance with bi-aitionalism, it is necessary to elaborate on what this really means. My point is this: if the aesthetic lining of black music functions with regard to scientific particulars that are not separate from composite fundamentals, then the creative arena actualized from its particulars (style or form) must reflect this same balance. We can thus view bi-aitionalism as a humanizing agent, or we can view bi-aitionalism as a mystical factor—it is even possible to view the significance of bi-aitionalism as a social and political factor—all of these viewpoints are valid.

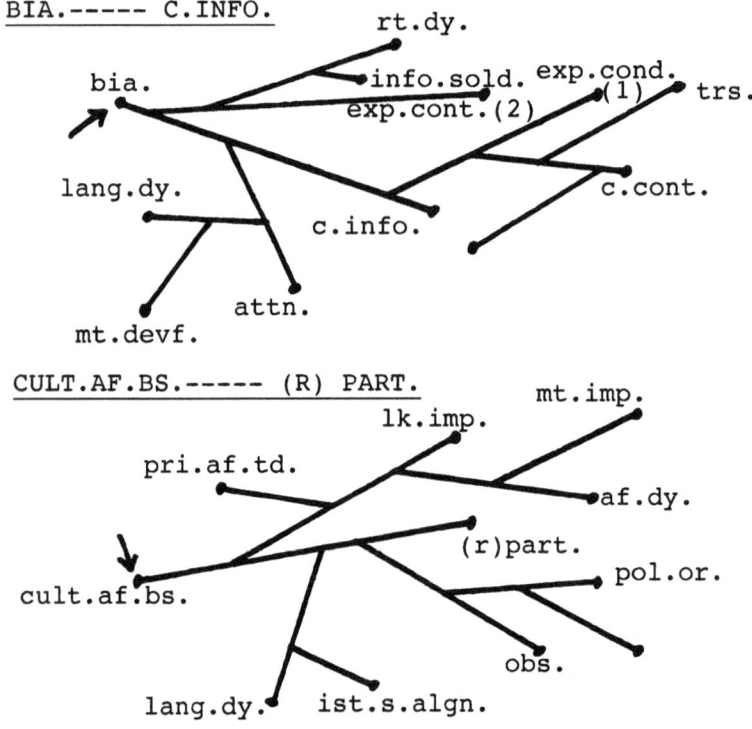

AF.POST.------MT.INFO.

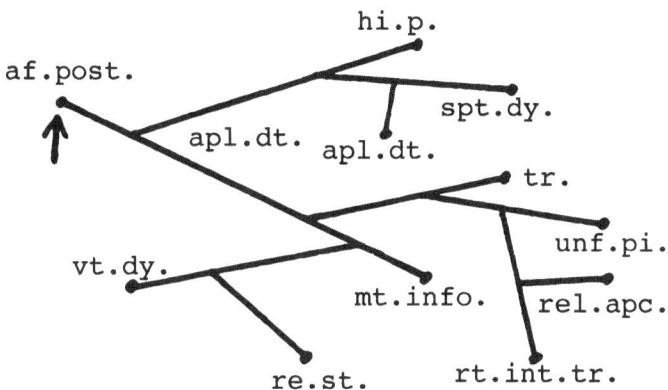

While it is possible to view many individual women who have helped shape creative black music with regard to multi-complexual progressionalism, it is important to avoid introducing any aspect as a word. The fact is, to view the activity of a musician like Bessie Smith is to understand that not only was her activity significant for what she did—but her work is also significant for how it reshaped the progression cycle of composite alternative functionalism on many different levels (e.g., the relationship of vocal implications to a given period to instrumental language—or inflection as a compositional consideration). In short, when one talks of improvisation—as "ised" through black music—it is important to view this subject on more than one level, because the thrust of this subject is not mono-dimensional, but rather multi-dynamic and profound. We must also be made to understand that the utilization of improvisation in the composite thrust of black music is directly related to the mystical potential of black music as a transformation force designed through the composite forces of black culture (people).

AFTD.----- ACC.DY.

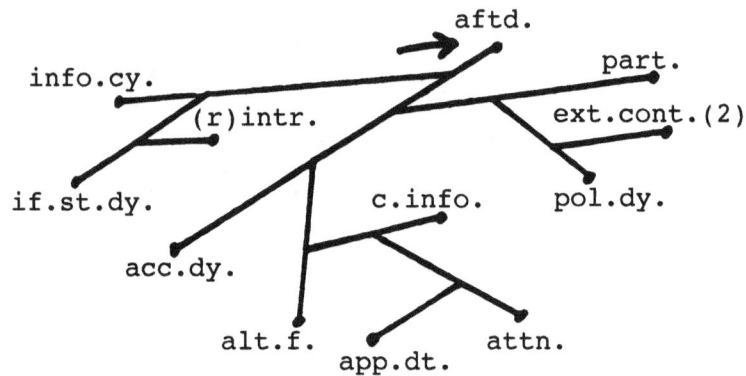

SF.RZ.------EXP.INFO.B.

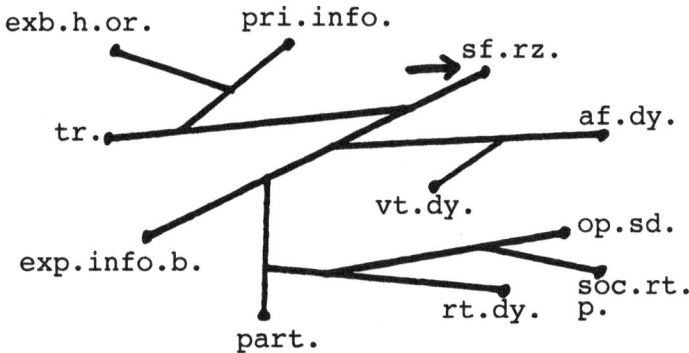

It is possible to better understand the bi-aitional implications of black creativity—in its formative period—by examining the physical universe situation surrounding how black creativity was to develop in America. For it is in the early transfer junction (i.e., Africa to America) of black creativity that one can view how this continuum extended to the present. My point is, **the progressional factors surrounding how black creativity was to develop, as well as the progressional factors that dictated how given creative thrusts were integrated into the new American experience, were actualized in the transfer-junction period of the music.** Any attempt to gain insight into the essence factor of black creativity must imply some attempt to examine the composite make-up underlying "what"

black creativity really is and "how" black creativity really is. Because the most basic factor distinguishing how any given creative projection can be understood has to do with the position of that projection to spiritual considerations. The best way to examine black creativity in this context would be to view the progressional development of black people with regard to the necessary changes that took place in their life participation and vibrational nature—since coming to America.

The influence of the church on black music is generally acknowledged by most people, yet very few writers have chosen to deal with the implications underlying what this relationship really means, and there are many reasons for this. For if a form in western terms derives its position in society by and through the complex underlying western information dynamics exclusively, it is possible that few writers are equipped to deal with creativity actualized from a different criterion. My point is that when I wrote that the most basic factor that dictated how black culture was to expand was the church, I am really stating that the creativity actualized from this context must be looked at for what it really is—that is, religious music. To understand this viewpoint is to deal with the meta-reality of black music. For while I have accented the progressional implications of bi-aitionalism in its most separate state—i.e., the affinity insight (1) principle as opposed to the affinity insight (2) principle—as a basis to comment on the dynamic spectrum of black creativity, the composite arena dictating how any form of black creativity functions is not separate from what is implied in the concept of bi-aitionalism—or unification (or the teachings of the church—the real teachings of the church). It is this factor that permeates black culture as well as black creativity, and this factor has also shaped how given creative strains could be actualized as a positive and life-giving consideration, rather than as only entertainment. The position of the church in the black community—especially in the transition cycle involving the forming of America—is not something to be taken lightly. The church was the single most powerful institution in the black community in that period, and for the most part, this is the position it still has today. But there is much more to look at here—we have only scratched the surface.

TRF(CW)—22

SPT.GH. ----- HI.P.

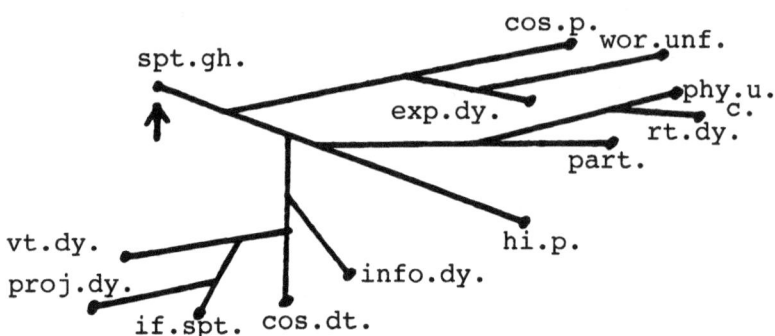

When I wrote that the church was the most powerful institution in the black community, I was also commenting on another important consideration concerning the music. For not only did the church provide a social function, but all of the activity designed within its walls vibrated to the social responsibility of its position. My point is that in the very beginning of American black creativity—as a composite thrust—there was a social responsibility, and more so—black creativity is based on a functioning methodology, that being with regard to the community. To understand the realness of this methodology is to have some indication of the factors influencing the essence factor of black creativity. It is at this junction where one can begin to deal with the actualness of bi-aitionalism as a real factor shaping the music. The aesthetic ramifications of black creativity were designed and practiced by both men and women musicians, and the architecture and science that provided the framework for the source transfer and world embracing of black music—as a transformation vehicle—resulted from the work done by men and women restructuralists. **To understand the significance of the creative woman—with regard to how a given projection might be advanced—it is only necessary to examine the aesthetic lining of creative music from the black aesthetic.** One thing is clear: if the functional lining of creative music reveals the most sophisticated use of "actual" participation (improvisation)—dynamic participation (improvisation and its use in different structural contexts), collective participation and spiritual participation (improvisation with

regard to the cosmic forces which determine whatever there is to be determined)—then, quite possibly, we already have some idea about the profound impact of women in creative music. History would only accent this point. For the problem is not really what would be the effects of a given creative strain if women were allowed to participate; the problem is what would be the effect of a given male ego if this knowledge were made available. For the most basic factor that can be drawn from the essence implications of creative music from the black aesthetic is the actualness of creativity as a human factor—or creativity as a means to serve humanity. The composite continuum of creative music from the black aesthetic was conceived with regard to what it posed as a life source in accordance to the implications of bi-aitionalism—spiritualism—functionalism—dynamicism—humanitarianism—momentum (or actualism—the realness that one is on the planet at the moment he or she is aware of that moment—this is especially real in improvisation—that is, actually being conscious of the realness of the moment in and through improvisation)—and this is only the beginning of what creative music is.

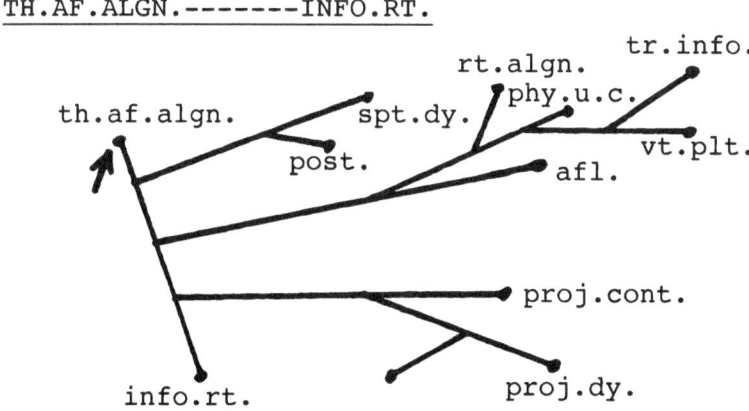

TRF(CW)-24

TH.AF.ALGN.------INFO.RT.

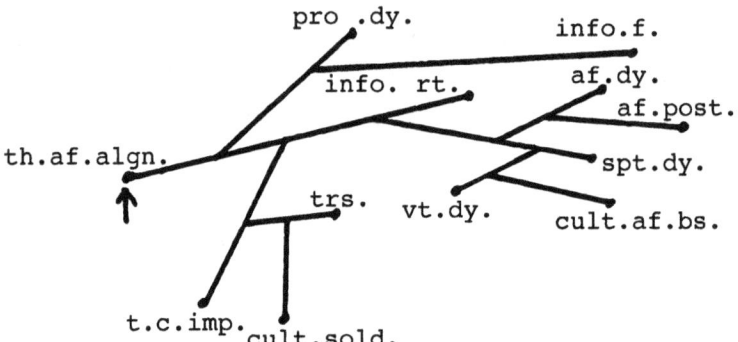

UNF.PI.------TH.CONT.DY

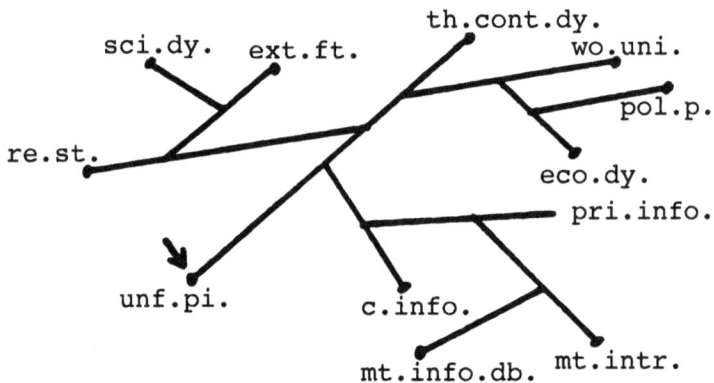

RE.ST.------WO.UNI.

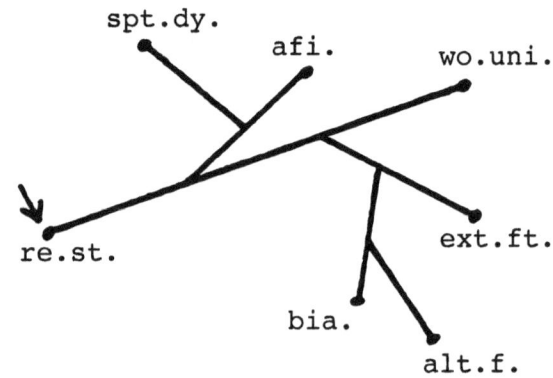

When I wrote that the essence factor of creative music from the black aesthetic is conceived with regard to a world humanism, it is important to elaborate on what this means in relationship to the creative woman. My point is this: not only have women been instrumental in shaping creative music from the affinity insight (2) principle—as it relates to developing continuums (projections) for particular physical universe situations, whether the work songs, or dance, etc.—but this influence is also equally felt on creativity from the affinity insight (1) principle. Creative music as a factor to function with regard to the spiritual dictates of black culture is directly related to the actualness of bi-aitionalism. By the same token, this fact can also be applied to the dynamics of form and the wealth of creativity that have emerged through trans-African projectional dynamics (regardless of time period). I am saying that every form that has emerged in black creativity has a masculine and feminine interpretation (that is used by both men and women), as well as a dynamic feminine and masculine source projection. To understand this viewpoint is to better view the secret implications of black creativity, as well as the dynamic vibrational tenets—underlying what a given form is, or can be. Take, for example, the use of what is commonly called "falsetto" in black vocal music. Many people have come to think of falsetto as only a stylistic inflection, rather than an approach that carries both mystical and vibrational overtones. Nevertheless, the actualness of "falsetto" singing is a perfect example of a given methodological thrust that is utilized by the composite culture regardless of unreal (or unnatural) barriers concerning the separation of what is feminine or masculine exclusively—nor is this one example unique.

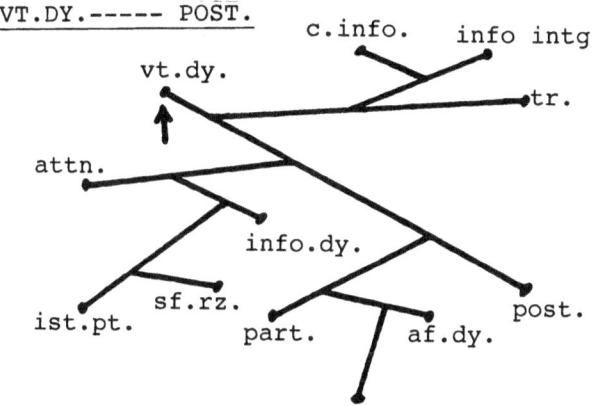

The composite essence factor of creative music from the black aesthetic also comments on—and indeed helps to maintain—the reality dictates underlying how given aspects are to be viewed by society. In other words, creative black music was conceived as a factor to function with regard to maintaining society and unification. The bi-aitional implications of creative music from the black aesthetic comment on what a given continuum can ultimately mean with regard to its physical universe manifestation. This can be seen in the early period of the music, where all of the emphasis—because of the physical universe situation (with respect to slavery)—was on holding the family unit together. During that period, the music, church, etc., functioned as a solidarity and spiritual factor for strength to endure adversity, and a consolidating and healing factor that helped maintain the family and community structure. The bi-aitional implications of this maintenance can be seen as a source-initiation phenomenon that underlined how the responsibility of the creative arts were to be viewed—and this is still true today. For when I write that black music is a spiritual music, I am not simply commenting on some vague notion that has little or nothing to do with actual life (whose effect has nothing to do with anything); I am instead commenting on something real. The fact is, the essence center of black creativity—from its early period until now—reveals what this solidarity and spiritual factor would mean on every level. The responsibility and maintenance I am referring to—with regard to the relationship of black art to black culture—has to do with how a given form transmits the moral and ethical implications that it celebrates—either through "doing" or "experiencing." **For one of the most important truths that the bi-aitional juncture of the music seems to stress is that the particulars of a given forum (thrust) must have both spiritual and ethical connotations that can be passed on to the community—to the people.** In other words, in its most real state, the bi-aitional actualness of a given form comments on given (or all-inclusive) ethical considerations as well—and the implications of this gives insight into the spiritual and ethical reality of trans-African creativity (in its source-initiated context).

BIA.------V.SY.

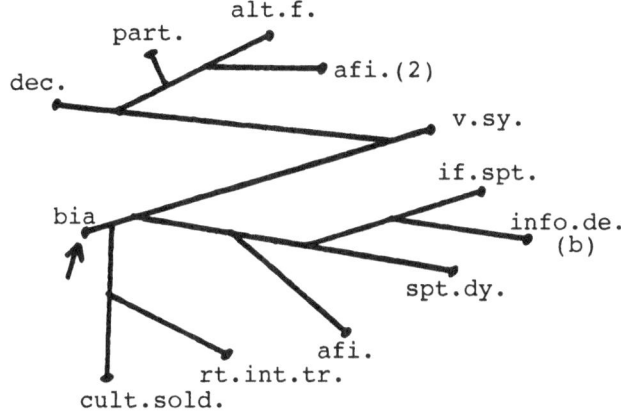

VT.ATT.-----IST.S.ALGN.

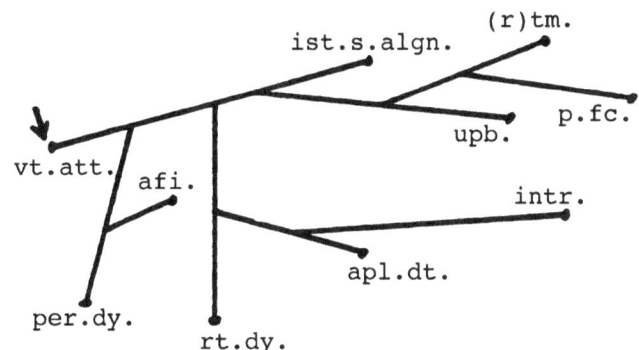

TRF(CW)-28

WO.EXP.PRI.------VT.PLT.

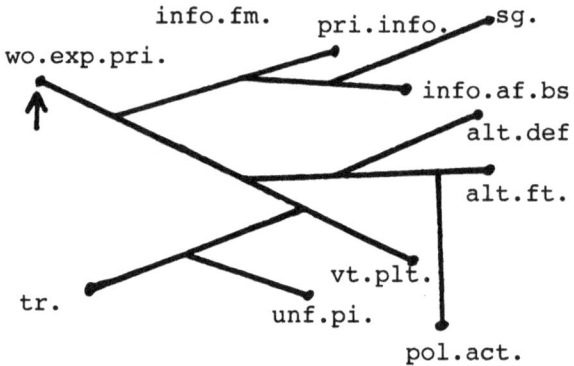

WO.MTH.------ C.INFO.

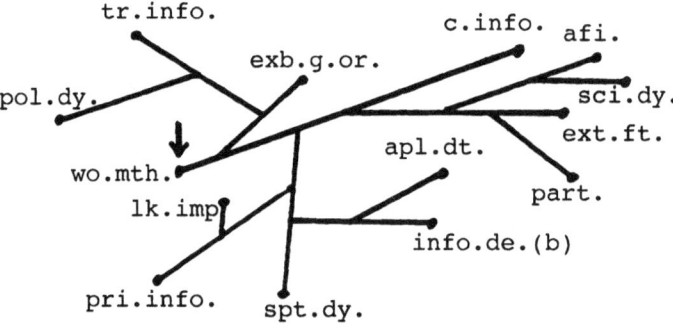

Quite possibly the best way to understand the significance of bi-aitionalism—as a unification, spiritual and ethical insight factor—might be to examine the post–World War Two juncture in American history as a basis to review the progressional aspect of black music. It was in this juncture that the music we refer to as bebop solidified, and it was also in this junction when the multi-complications surrounding American life produced the social-reality tendencies that served to further separate women from composite participation. More so, that bebop was to provide the next link for transformation makes this examination all the more necessary. Because if my observations are accurate, and if this was the juncture that solidified the affinity insight (1) and affinity insight (2) principles as separate thrusts—as a phenomenon that commented on the then-forming composite world group re-information order, in both cultural terms and intellectual/dynamic terms—then quite possibly there is something else to be learned about the seriousness of bi-aitionalism. For if bebop provided the framework for the spectacle-diversion cycle in American culture, as well as the dynamics to override existentialism, we can ask ourselves: what did this phenomenon mean with regard to what has happened to black culture since that time? This can be asked because I believe the resulting progressions that surrounded the dissemination of black creativity from the late forties until now shed light on the seriousness of what happens when women are not allowed to participate in the music. Yet it is necessary to lay a broader basis before expanding on this statement. For the implications of bi-aitionalism are much more far-reaching than only one context.

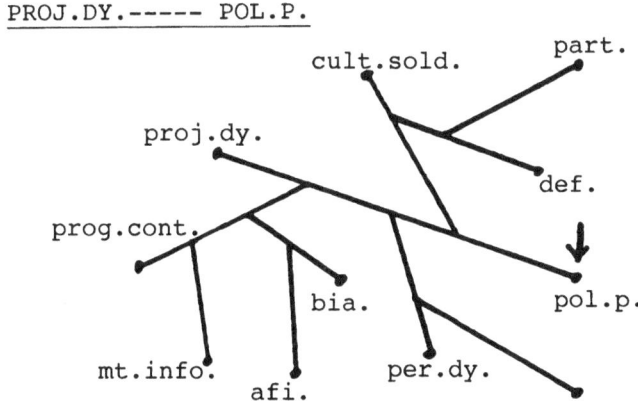

Possibly the best way to deal with the significance of bi-aitionalism would be to examine the social and vibrational factors that stabilized black culture in the post-Reconstruction juncture of American culture. This is so because the vibrational and social patterns that emerged in the black community—even encompassing the subsequent migrations to the north—were operative until the effects of the coming world wars. Before we can understand the significance of bebop, it is necessary to understand what forces were functioning to solidify the black community in that period. It is my belief that the greatest single factor that solidified the thrust of black American continuance was and is the church—as a body for functionalism as well as aesthetic awareness. In other words, the church up until the end of World War Two functioned as the strongest defining factor for unifying the black community on every level. The effects of this position can be viewed on every level of black culture as well—including creative music. If we can look at the body of music that has come from the black church in an unbiased way, there can be no doubt as to its originality and purpose. More so, the creativity—and thrust projection—that was "ised" from this context has also functioned as the strongest and "realest" creativity related to the life progression of black people as a composite group. I am referring to the spirituals and hymns, which many of us have now come to take for granted, as examples of some of the most important creativity "ised" in American culture. This is a music (continuum) that fulfills the dynamic implications underlying what a thrust projection could be, in the sense that its vibrational and reality dictates were directly related to black people's ability to endure early American history. Moreover, every vibrational thrust of black music can be viewed by its relationship to the composite vibrational platform developed in and through the church structure surrounding black culture. To understand this is to gain some insight into the profound impact of the church in black society, and this information can also help to establish some basis for dealing with the meta-reality of bebop. For the music we refer to as bebop was the solidification of several vibrational and social developments that were not necessarily contained within the set social arena of the post-Reconstruction period. Moreover, the solidification of bebop would shed light on the changing vibrational and social order of the black community, as well as dictate how that change would be manifested through the dynamics of style (affinity dynamics). In short, the entry of this thrust projection would be viewed as a threat to the existing order of life in the black community—and, in many ways, this view was justified. To understand this phenomenon is to see what the music we refer to as bebop really is.

My point is this: the elements that were to dictate the vibrational lining of bebop also shed light on the world complications of the form. If, in the first book (underlying philosophical basis), I wrote of bebop as a signal that the second transformational implications of the music had solidified, my point was meant that bebop was the form which provided the creative thrust for shaping how the next transformational cycle in western culture would materialize. Another way of saying this would be that the solidification of bebop would accelerate a move towards the next restructuralist cycle in creative music by providing insight into what that change would mean in both actual and vibrational terms. Thus, the reality implications of bebop would transcend any form of regionalism—on whatever level—because the aesthetic-lining form would penetrate—and indeed reshape—world music. But there is more to my point than this. For if the meta-reality of bebop would transcend the social order of black people in the forties, the question is, how would this form be viewed with regard to its multi-complexual complications by the church, and what would the net effects of this dynamicism be with regard to the black community?

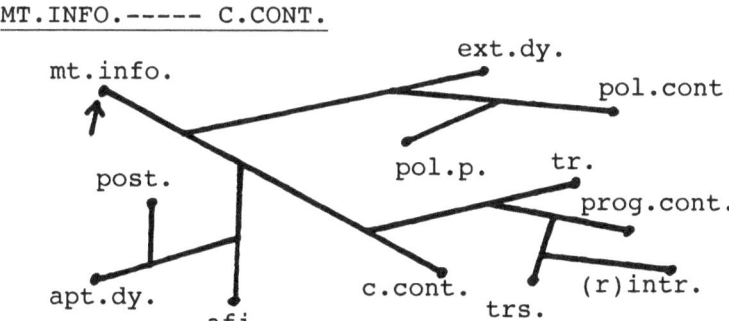

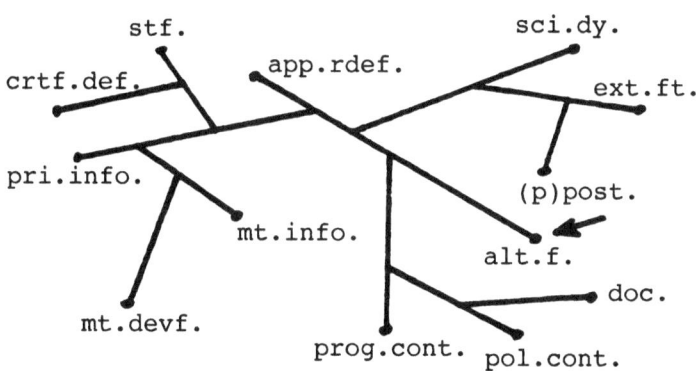

When I stated that bebop was "ised" from outside the traditional order of the church, I am only referring to the collective factors related to the social and political developments in the black community after Reconstruction. In short, if we can look at the emergence of the church as personifying how the unified black cultural and community thrust would advance after slavery, it is possible to see the progressional forming of bebop as a movement that extended both in and outside of the church. The seriousness of its outside significance, however, would have a direct bearing on bi-aitionalism. For the most distinguishing factors surrounding the "actual arena" of church-related activity was the realness of bi-aitionalism as an integral defining agent—on every level. By the time the thrust known as bebop solidified, the social-political, as well as the vibrational and projectional, significance of the form had also become real: **that being—the actualness that a thrust had developed with multi-composite overtones which did not necessarily correspond to the vibrational particulars surrounding church music—more so, the social realness which surrounded the form would make it extremely difficult for women to participate in the music.** If we can talk of black church music as a form that allowed for full participation—or a thrust that corresponded to the dictates of the composite black community—we could look at the solidification of bebop as a form against the social grain of its day—as well as a form perceived in sexist terms (even though the exclusion of women had more to do with the social reality of that time zone than with the music).

The social implications underlying how bebop was perceived in the black community served as a stimulus for increasing the distance between the music and church. I have not meant, however, to narrow the relationship of the music and the black community to any one-dimensional criterion; obviously there are many other factors connected to this phenomenon (e.g., the emerging influence of the defining and controlling factors surrounding black music—in other words, jazz writers—and the sophistication of "gradualism" and how this tool has been applied to the music). But we cannot underestimate the seriousness of this separation—for many of the developments surrounding creative music in this time zone are in fact related to this juncture. My point is this: **there is a relationship between** the emergence of the black middle class in the transfer-shift juncture of black American culture during the forties, and the solidification of bebop as a so-called art music—and this relationship directly sheds light on the meta-reality of bebop (both in its social and vibrational context) as well as the social actualness of extended functionalism. To understand this viewpoint is to understand that the suppression of bebop was systematically desired by both black and white people. For if we can say that the aesthetic implications of bebop represented a threat to the white controlling order of that period, we can also add that the repercussions underlying how this threat was perceived would affect the black middle class as well. The social limitations surrounding how bebop was seen in the black community would thus be another factor contributing to the overall feeling that bebop had somehow gone outside of what is acceptable—as a black music, and as such could not be embraced as a socially positive or aesthetically uplifting projection.

For many people, the actualness that bebop did not really encourage composite participation was only further proof of its decadence. To this group, bebop was seen as a thrust that did not conform to the teachings of the church and, as such, represented a threat to the established order (or desired order). On a practical physical universe level, few women, in the time zone between 1945 and 1955, would naturally find themselves gravitating towards playing bebop. For the most basic alignment encouraged in the church was for participation in the source-transfer shift of classical (western art) music and black music (i.e., spirituals). Because of the social and vibrational actualness of the situation, few women had the chance to participate in bebop as compared to men (yet there were, of course, exceptions)—moreover, few women were inclined to support the music as listeners. In fact, bebop developed within and apart from the social order of black culture at the same time; and however this phenomenon is now viewed, the bi-aitional implications surrounding this phenomenon cannot be underestimated if we are to better view the present period of creative music.

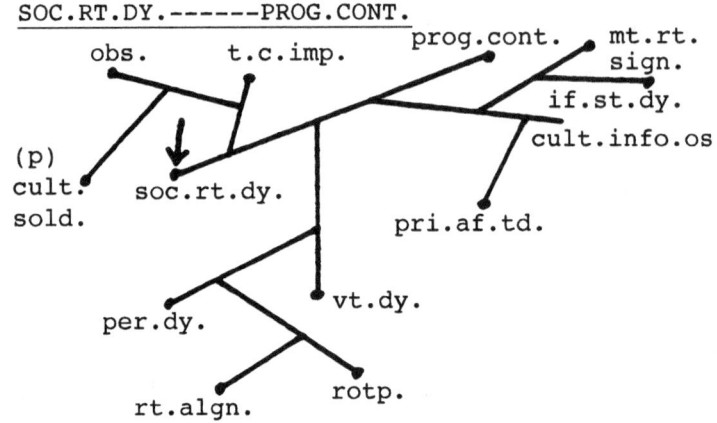

The transfer junction that witnessed the composite thrust breakdown in creative black music is important to examine for many reasons. For if I am correct, and the realness of bebop did, because of its world implications, dictate how bi-aitionalism would be channeled (into two basic thrust projections), then it is at this same juncture where we can begin to see the cosmic significance of what this break would mean—in physical and vibrational universe terms. In other words, I have already commented on the positive implications of bebop—as an alternative world creative thrust that carried profound implications for the world expansion principle—but the magnitude of the transfer-shift period in the middle forties would also have serious consequences—engulfing both positive and negative overtones. It is my opinion that the most important factor to establish a basis for the ensuing alternative progressions of the fifties and sixties—as far as creativity is concerned—was the solidification of the projection we now call bebop. The dynamic implications of this form would reveal what transfer-shift progressionalism would mean on both an aesthetic and physical universe level. The realness that the social reality surrounding bebop was also sexist would be an important consideration affecting the potential of creative music in the fifties and sixties time cycle. Many of the negative social factors surrounding the reality of popular music in this period are directly related to this same phenomenon. So real is the relationship of the emergence of bebop as a form signaling world implications (yet without social responsibility with regard to women) to the resulting vibrational and physical universe situations we now find ourselves in at present, that it is possible to gain insight into the social and cosmic implications of bi-aitionalism. In other words, if the present physical universe situation can be looked at with regard to the suppression of bi-aitionalism, then it should also be possible to draw conclusions—on some level—as to what this subject must mean if implemented.

To understand the realness of bi-ationalism is to deal with social and ethical considerations related to how given cultural—or communal—thrusts are perceived in functional terms. This is so because the solidification of bi-ationalism must be examined in aesthetic and practical (physical universe) terms if we are to really view the subject. In the early part of this section, I wrote of the progressional implications surrounding the spread of black creative music throughout America and what this expansion means in aesthetic and vibrational terms. The fact is—no matter how the social and political reality of American culture functioned with regard to black culture—it is possible to view the progressional thrust of black music in the post-Reconstruction period as an example of the highest alignment of cultural solidification. To gain insight into what this cultural phenomenon really means is to deal with the dynamic implications of bi-aitionalism as a positive aesthetic and profound functional influence on culture—this is what I am interested in. For if I have commented on the role of the church in helping to solidify how the progressional expansion of black culture was to expand, it is necessary to understand what this expansion means with regard to the aesthetic implications of re-alignment. One fact is clear: the composite actualness of creative music from the black aesthetic does comment on—and indeed is intertwined with—the realness of ethics (as a factor dictating how a given people or persons should vibrationally and functionally interact on the spectrum of social and actual levels) and what this means on a functional and spiritual level (ethics as a consideration reflecting on the spirituality underlying what a given thrust really is). To understand this viewpoint is to have some awareness of the seriousness of bi-aitionalism, and how important it is for the whole of humanity that everyone is allowed to contribute to the maintenance and dynamics of cultural business. All of the subsequent developments that took place after bebop can be understood with regard to the social ramifications related to the momentum surrounding world reformation—because of the "so-called progressive jazz source thrust." I have not meant to imply that bebop was the only post–World War Two factor to define composite creative progressionalism—but I have meant to state that the progressional thrust of creative black music, especially after Reconstruction and the industrial period following World Wars One and Two, cannot be underestimated on any level—or context.

The breakdown in the composite development of creative music is directly related to the present situation we now find ourselves in—especially with regard to popular music. For the resulting factor that has come to solidify both popular and creative music—as opposed to church music—is the realness of male domination and what this imbalance has meant with regard to the natural social dynamics of society. The suppression and ostracizing of women is directly related to the present vibrational reality underlying how postulation is utilized in this period. One needs only to look at the lyrics of the average rock composition to understand what I am saying. I do not mean to imply that the suppression of women—in creativity or any other aspect of society—is a recent development or only related to the time zone of the forties, because that would be a ridiculous assertion. But I do believe that the second transfer junction of creative music provided a distinct path that is related to the present situation we now find ourselves in. In other words, the exclusion of creative women has affected the vibrational dictates underlying how given thrusts of the music are perceived, and unless this suppression is corrected, there can be no real hope for either composite transformation—on a global or national level—or cosmic transformation—as a mystical and ethical restoration consideration. The significance of the creative woman is connected with the realness of world transformation.

(Level Two)

In this book I have attempted to deal with the reality particulars and implications of creativity, as well as how we are the effects of misinformation about this subject—even to the extent of how to perceive creativity. For the most part, I have focused on the implications of this subject as a basis to solidify a more universal perspective about ourselves—yet however we choose to look at these questions, in no way can creativity be divorced from the actual physical universe realness of existence on this planet. In other words, it is important to understand the physical universe considerations that help shape what a given culture thrust means (regardless of time zone). For the physical universe reality is the platform that dictates how given creative thrusts will function with regards to culture (and this realm of being). My reason for writing this book is to outline some of these questions while at the same time hopefully lay a basis to deal with a practical physical universe stance concerning how change can be brought about. Of all the considerations I have tried to deal with in this book, none is more important than the concept and realness of transformation: transformation as what seems to be a natural progression—if I can use the word "progression"—in the physical universe sense (the appearance of things as they seem to be, and the appearance of change as it seems to be manifested on the physical universal plane). Any attempt to deal with the realness of creativity must reveal some aspect of what this subject really means with regards to real essence. For to understand the real arena of creativity is to deal with transformation as well as the implications of what this subject raises in the total context of living.

 The concept of transformation has several meanings depending on its use, but ultimately this is the word I use to speak of vibrational-cosmic and physical universe change cycles that take place on the chemical and vibrational universe level. In other words, transformation is a phenomenon which corresponds to my belief that cosmic cycles have long played an important part in physical universe progressionalism on this planet. Quite possibly the last real transformation that determined the nature of this time period was the destruction of African civilization—and/or the decline of Indian civilization—and the subsequent emergence of western civilization as the defining agent of this time cycle. In other words, the concept of transformation—in this sense—would have to do with the initiation of a given vibrational-essence thrust in a dominant position, as well as what that initiation implies on the physical universe level (i.e., expansion). The natural thrust of any transformation moves to permeate the vibrational lining of a given time zone (that being, how a given culture or people sees itself), and as such the solidification of western civilization can be looked at as a definitive time-block continuum that can be used as a basis for establishing the nature of the next change cycle (i.e., transformation).

Yet I have not meant to qualify transformation as a phenomenon that only comments on physical universe realignment shifts in a given time zone, for the dynamics of this concept embrace more than only one function. This is so because while "transformation" is the word I use to comment on physical universe shifts, this same concept also addresses itself to the underlying factors which precede what that given shift will be. In other words, the concept of transformation would also have to do with the vibrationaltory cosmic factors that dictate how the physical universe is perceived and is. The best example of what I mean by transformational vibrational and cosmic factors in this context can be seen in the interrelationship of different religious doctrines on the planet. For however different a given doctrine might seem from the others, in the final analysis, all of the many different religious strains on the planet are very similar—in many respects. I believe the surface differences of a given religious thrust can be traced to the vibrationaltory cosmic factors that are related to transformation. In short, the concept of transformation has to do with the nature underlying how given cycles are realized, as well as what that realization poses for the vibrational and methodological attitudes of its culture. Thus, whether one considers him/herself a Buddhist or a Christian in actual fact makes little difference, for in the final analysis, both religions seek the same basic affinity relationship with the cosmic arena—both teach of god, and both seek to help people function as one entity and with love. The developments that have moved to solidify the various social and cultural (religious) doctrines are also connected to the concept of transformation.

Any attempt to gain insight into the meta-reality potential of creative music would necessitate that some effort is made to examine transformation. For as we move into the next century, it is clear that the physical universe is undergoing many different levels of change (transition). At present, all of the various culture groups on the planet have moved into source shift as the first step towards re-alignment. I believe we have already begun moving into the next transformational cycle, even though it might not be apparent on the surface. For the first condition that must be met before transformation is possible has already occurred: that being, the disintegration of composite cultural tendencies (as a center factor to align or celebrate vibrational dynamics) as the first signal that the realness of transition has been met—and the nature of a given transition will inevitably reveal some insight into the total consequences of that disintegration. In other words, all of the signals that have been occurring for the last two hundred years can be read as favorable for "actual" transformation. If this is true, then it would be in our interest to better understand what this phenomenon means on a practical planet level as well as cosmic vibrational level. Whatever we can understand about this phenomenon today can better prepare us for what must be done tomorrow—for while I believe we have much time to prepare for what this shift will mean, I also do not believe we have much time to prepare for what this shift will mean.

TRF(II)–4

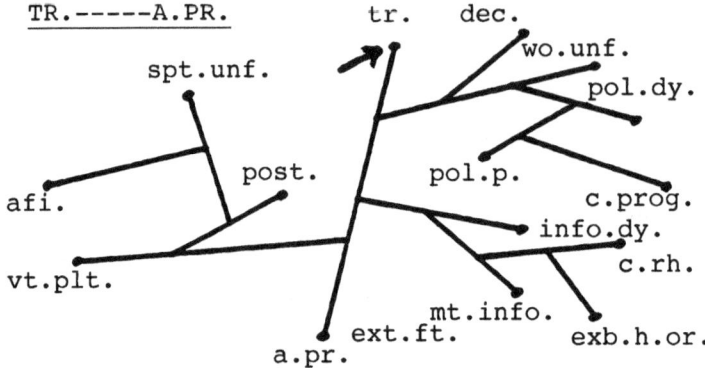

Quite possibly Buckminster Fuller was one of the first people to recognize what this next transformation would mean on a practical physical universe level. Fuller has long been aware of the realness of technology—as an important factor reshaping our daily planet existence—and I am in complete agreement with his views concerning how this consideration has shaped our present planet position. For when I write of transformation in this section of the book, I am commenting on the realness that technology has produced a situation conducive to the solidification of a composite world aesthetic. All of the natural interchange that has been an integral part of the planet between different culture groups, etc., has been speeded up because of the sophistication of present-day technology. It is now possible to fly from Paris to Washington, D.C., in approximately three and a half hours—and this is only the beginning. Television and the recording industry have completely eliminated independent creative strains in every country on the planet. So great is the impact of media in this time zone that few people are aware of its profound effect on progressional continuance and composite humanity. The end result of these developments has moved to weaken the factors which solidified the last transformation cycle that brought us African, western, and Asian culture thrusts, and in its place are the seeds of a new composite world group. The realness of transformation is of such significance that we have no choice but to investigate what this phenomenon might imply for the next time cycle—for the advances in technology are clear enough, but how the controlling culture intends to use these tools is not.

For if the next transformation cycle can be understood by viewing the developments in technology over the past thirty years and some, there is also the realness that only a select group of people are in control of what these advances will mean on a physical universe level. In other words, while practically every country on the planet utilizes television, the functional utilization of this medium is controlled by only a select group of people who are not necessarily representative of the composite world group. In this position, the sophistication of technology can be viewed as both a positive and negative factor—depending on its use. Certainly the western political position has benefited from the utilization of technology in this present time cycle, for nine-tenths of these developments have come through and from the western functional and vibrational position (and there are many reasons for this if the planet situation is taken into account—and yet, at the same time, I do not mean to take anything away from the achievement of the western functional and technological community either, for the advances that have occurred through this thrust represent what is most positive and negative about western civilization). Nevertheless, the realness of the present physical universe situation cannot be simply dismissed as unimportant—because it is important. The nature of the next transformation might well rest on how profoundly we understand those forces now dictating planet progressions in this time zone.

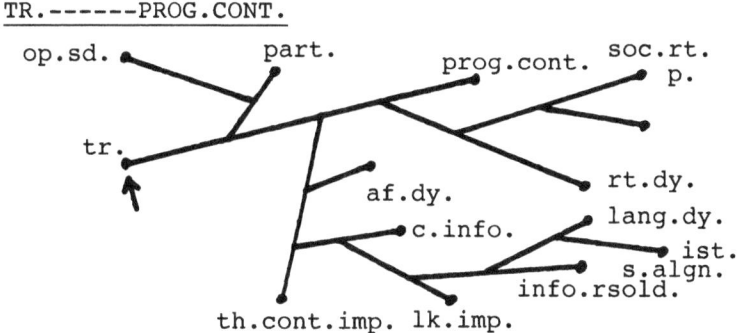

TRF(II)—6

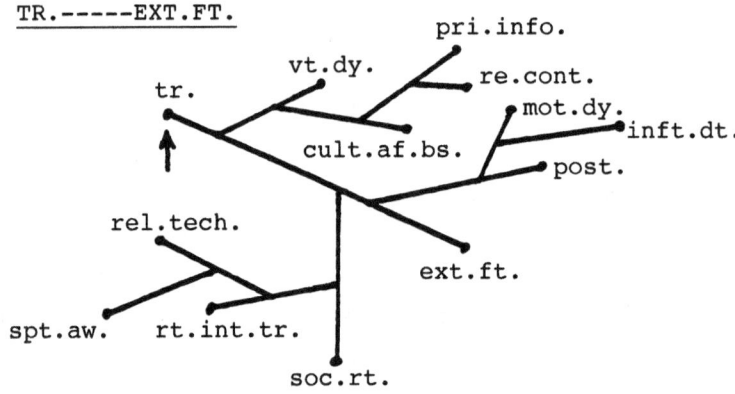

The concept of transformation must be looked at from as many contexts as possible, because this phenomenon is not a mono-dimensional sequence, but rather a multi-dynamic movement that will affect the total planet. Not only will we have to deal with the seriousness of transformation as a solidifying factor, but also as a disintegrating factor. For if we can talk of the sophistication underlying how technology is reshaping the planet in this time zone, we must also understand that the western methodological and vibrational pull is accented because of these same factors. In other words, any attempt to understand transformation would necessitate that this phenomenon is dealt with on some level, for I am not simply writing about concepts that have no relevance to life on the physical universe. To understand the dynamic implications of this subject is to only apply practical application; that being—how to function in the noblest sense of the word for positive change. In short, the concept of transformation must also involve application. To state otherwise would imply that the considerations governing the nature of transformation function as a factor isolated from composite life—or that transformation by its very nature only implies one type of change, and this viewpoint is false (or at least I don't believe this viewpoint). For if "transformation" is the word I have given to the multi-factors that dictate vibrational and physical universe realignment on a planet level, it is important to state that I also believe that actual events on the physical universe level determine whether or not the positive or negative attributes of that re-alignment will be dominant.

In other words, I believe we have something to say about our destiny—although whatever we do, it couldn't have been any other way. The realness of transformation can best be understood as a cosmic factor, while the resulting physical universe situation can be looked at as how we have chosen to utilize that cosmic factor (which does not seem to be cosmic). If this is indeed the case, then the realness of transformation does signal choice on our part. That is, **if the cosmic factors that dictate change have provided a situation that can be shaped in a number of ways, and if we are in the position to decide just what the shape will be, then that position must imply some degree of responsibility on our part.** Whether or not we meet the challenge that transformation necessitates is a question which can be discussed and debated, but the actual fact is that transformation does not depend on whether we choose to accept the challenge or not. In other words, the "reality of change" which dictates what cosmic and vibrational forces we will have to deal with on this planet is much greater than one factor. Our ability to survive on this planet depends on how well we adapt ourselves to what these changes will be—for not only do we not control these forces, but, ultimately, "transformation is not about us." The best we can do with the cosmic forces reshaping this planet is to align and adapt ourselves to these changes as a means to better understand the positive implications of this experience.

The seriousness of transformation in the next cycle will constitute basis for a complete re-evaluation of creativity as well as total physical universe reality. In that light, the subject of transformation will comment on the physical universe particulars underlying the present situation we find ourselves in today. The fact that white people are in a controlling position, with two-thirds of the people on the planet living within the effects of that position, will also be subjected to change. More so, the magnitude of the potential change can be looked at as the strongest signal that the western position on the planet is moving to a decline. In short, the solidification of the factors that stabilized the western vibrational and affinity composite reality will be weakened as we move into the next cycle. This does not necessarily mean that western civilization will be over in the next cycle—for events on the physical universe level do not seem to have anything to do with "start" or "stop"—but I do believe that transformation, by its very definition, functions as a factor to reshape a given vibrational or physical universe situation. The realness of this phenomenon will comment on the changing nature of political and social dynamics—and what this means in actual terms.

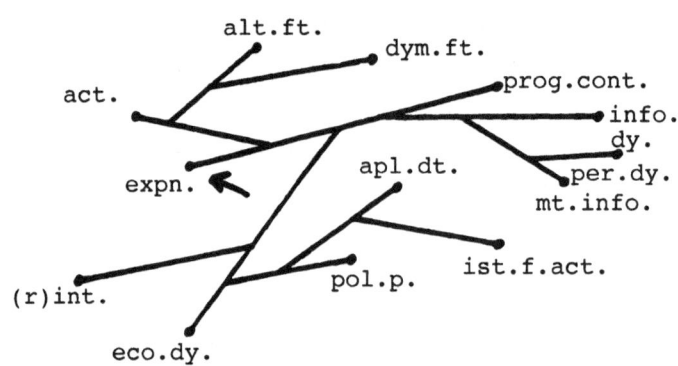

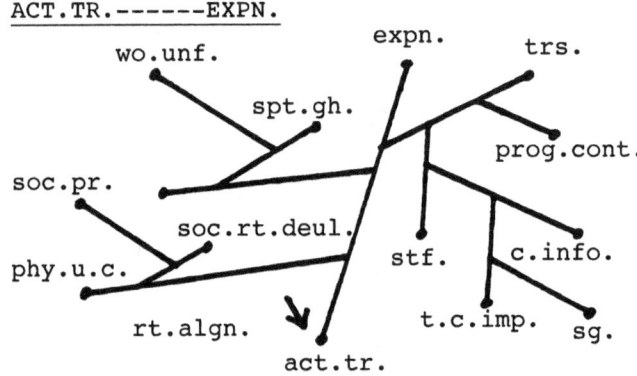

The phenomenon of transformation is not limited to any one factor (context), because any real discussion of this subject must take into account the physical universe reality factor of change—whether it is manifested in tragedy (in the sense of events whose natural progression serves as a basis where human beings will have to go through whatever changes are necessary in order to endure and learn from it), or whether it is manifested through the cosmic realm. For the concept of transformation that I am trying to comment on will touch upon every aspect that we are aware of—and many we are not aware of. **I am commenting on a force that, in its normal state, will move to change a given vibrational and physical universe cycle without regard for what we think we understand.** This transformation might manifest itself through what we have come to call plagues, war, etc.—and whether we choose to attribute these changes to the problems inherent in the western over-balance on the planet—or the implications of justice in terms of whether one cares to place this consideration on the whole of what is happening on this planet during this time zone—or the inherent progressional factors which are simply "like it is" because "it is like it is"—all of us will be forced to deal with the "actualness" of change (whether or not we have our theories together). For however one chooses to deal with the consideration of transformation, in the final analysis, this consideration seems to be in accordance with the logical-illogical progression of events happening on the physical universe plane—having very little to do with what we think should be happening, but rather connected to the all-cosmic realness of what is actually happening.

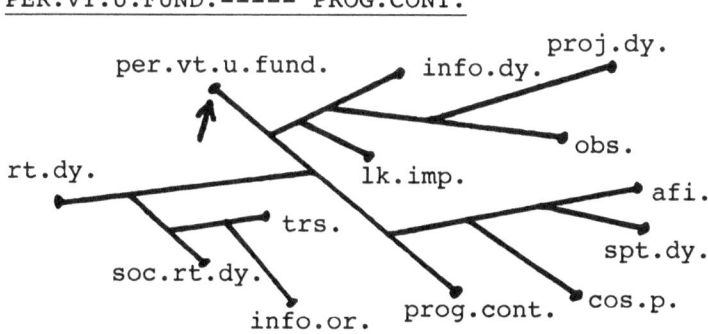

TRF(II)–10

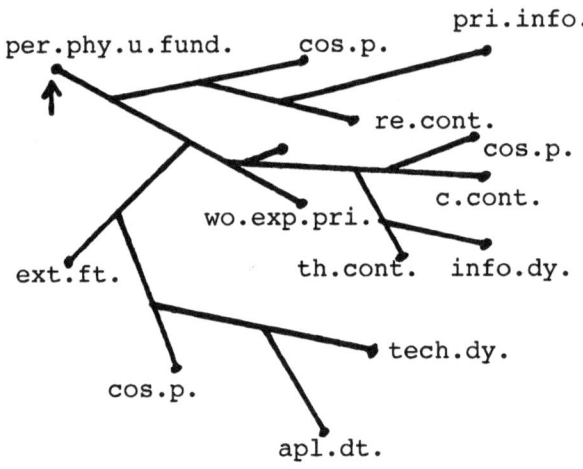

Everything in this period seems to point to a transformation of some kind. Not just the alignment of one or two situations on the planet (e.g., the position of western culture as compared to the world group), but instead a multitude of factors. Yet transformation will not take place in a week or a year either, for this is a cyclic shift phenomenon that utilizes many dynamic considerations—including time. Already, the philosophical and vibrational basis underlying how events are understood in the west is changing, and I have always believed that the movement towards a composite aesthetic is directly connected to the dictates of transformation.

Nor am I only referring to developments in western culture at the expense of the world group, for the changes that are slowly happening in this period are reshaping every culture and vibrational group. If I have chosen to accent the situation of western culture in this series of books, it is only because of my familiarity with its problems (because of my own position in western culture)—and because of the uniqueness of western culture's present political position.

The most basic factor related to the realness of transition is the breakdown of the composite spiritual affinity structure of a given culture. When this occurs, transition is inevitable—more so, the nature of a succession of transitions can also shed light on the progressional position of a given period in time—thus commenting on transformation. This is exactly what is now happening in this time period. For the breakdown in the composite spiritual arena of western civilization has arrived at the juncture of "reacting to nothing." The realness of "being without center" gives the clearest picture of the present time zone we are now in as a collective group, and the consequences of this position are what we are dealing with today. To understand this viewpoint is to understand the significance of the composite spiritual arena that dictates what culture is supposed to mean. For the realness of the cosmic arena serves as an underlying sustaining factor that addresses itself to interpreting how events are perceived—the relationship between the progression of events and what that progression means to the essence factor that motivates how people function (as a group) together—and also how the emotional implications of a given action are perceived. The disintegration of the center factor in western culture is directly connected to the distortions of aesthetic and cosmic laws—for the basis underlying the concept of culture has to do with "agreement." More so, the extent of the disintegration of present-day western culture must be looked at in relationship to the position western culture now has with regard to the world group—that is, the transition western culture is presently undergoing is affecting the composite planet. So great is disagreement in the western composite-affinity stance—and so real are cosmic change cycles occurring in their own right (even the weather cycles are changing, and the summers seem to be getting shorter while the winter expands—and maybe even this phenomenon is not separate from the experiments which have developed from the misuse of extended functionalism)—that, together, the planet does seem to be moving into a change that signals more than simply transition, but rather actual transformation. Either this is so or the dynamics surrounding transition have changed—or expanded. Whatever, the present cycle we are living in seems to be a time zone to prepare (shape) the next cycle of progressional continuance.

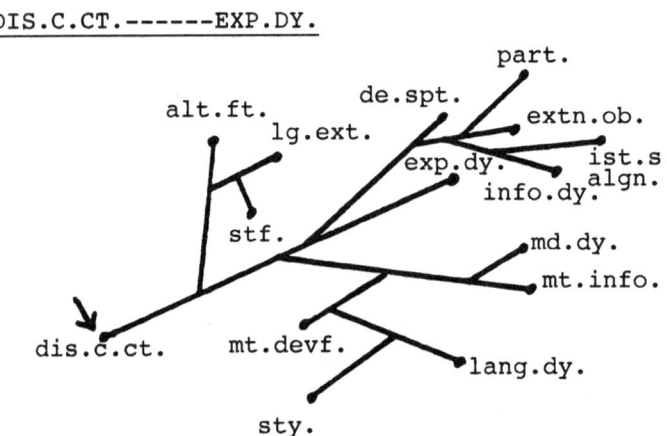

The break in present-day western composite spirituality is responsible for the subsequent variations of the philosophic and religious thrusts which gathered momentum after the fall of Greek civilization, and these developments are directly related to the overall ineffectiveness of real spiritualism in this time zone. As such, the last fifteen years have seen an acceleration towards eastern religions as a substitute for the spiritual vacuum of western culture. So profound has the move towards alternative religious movements been, that the underlying motivation factor of this phenomenon could be spectacle-diversion progressionalism; nevertheless, it would not be necessarily in our interest to ignore the real fact that this phenomenon does mean something. For the present-day accent on spiritualism does seem to comment on what results when the center factor of a given culture moves into decline—but there is still more here. Probably the most important thing we can learn from the mass embracing of eastern religion is that, whatever the actual motivating factor, this move does signal the realness of source-transfer progressionalism—and this move also accents the dynamics of source transfer as a factor that is instrumental in establishing alternative composite culture. I do not mean to question the intentions of any one given individual in terms of that person's position with regard to source-transfer progressionalism, because whether a person is dealing with the dynamics of religious or spiritual knowledge or simply following cultural patterns in a particular time zone, in the final analysis, is not relevant. What is relevant is the fact that so many people have come to accept that the only way to perceive their spiritual needs and beliefs involves seeking other spiritual outlets—especially non-western (sanctioned) religion movements.

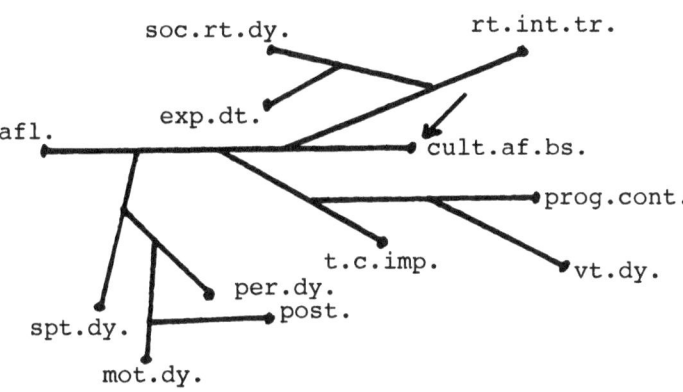

In the past ten years, there have been many new spiritual groups—or spiritual consciousness groups—in America. Many of these groups are connected to eastern spiritual thrusts, but there are some new western movements as well. Whatever their differences, the time zone of the sixties proved to be quite valuable for new recruits, for this period personified the schism that had developed in composite American culture because of the war, or social reality, etc. It would be impossible to estimate the strength of any of the organizations that developed in this period, for undoubtedly this factor would vary from group to group—but if the Scientology organization is any example of the sophistication of alternative spiritual movements, then these organizations are indeed powerful. However any of these movements are seen (e.g., Hare Krishna, the church of the Reverend Sun Myung Moon, etc.), it is clear that their presence comments on the time zone we are now in during this period. It is also clear that ultimately their work is connected to the realness of the disintegration of the western composite affinity stance, and, in that regard, these movements are related to transformation. For the "actualness" of their activity seeks to re-align the basic affinity thrust of western culture; and whether or not one chooses to view their work as constructivist in a positive sense or not, in the final analysis, the end result of this activity is conducive for real change.

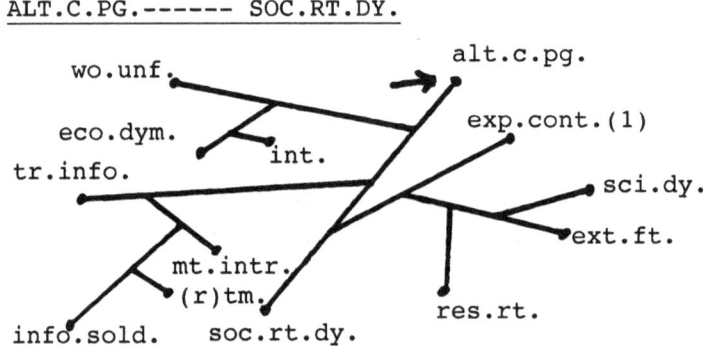

The western cultural continuum functions as a factor to impede actual creativity, and in its place offers spectacle diversion. In this position, the actual life force is finally stripped of the ability to "ise" creativity, and deprived of the most valuable tool for "being." The end result of this condition is what we are dealing with today, and the present reality will not be changed by either a white hope or the next Charlie Parker. For it is not a question of whether an alternative creative form can supply a creative language to change the tone level of western culture, because the significance of language does do just that—it is more a question of designing a situation that is conducive for all the people of a given culture to be able to participate in composite life dynamics. The realness of whether we can meet the challenge of transformation is directly tied to total participation. What this means can better be understood by looking at the situation women have been confronted with for the past thousand years. In other words, the realness that women have been denied the opportunity to participate in the spectrum of creativity must be looked at and understood for what it really is. It has never been a question of whether or not women are qualified to be creative—for in actuality, who among us can truly say they are "qualified" to be creative—but rather, the situation of women in creative music can be looked at as the logical result of male suppression—and what's more, this factor is still very prevalent today. Because of this phenomenon, it is very difficult to look through the historical progressions of western art music and find work from creative women composers—even though there were more composers than one might expect. In other words, any attempt to understand the realness of transformation would imply that the situation of women is dealt with.

It is common knowledge that, whatever the creative form or aesthetic, men have always made a great distinction between how they see their activity and how they view activity from women. This is particularly true in western culture, for the underlying basis that determines how the aesthetic itself is viewed excluded women. More so, by the time western art music solidified as an art form, only the composer was a necessary "person"—that is, only the composer functioned from a truly creative stance, and in this functional area both men and women functioned in minor roles (i.e., interpreters). The factors that sustain this predicament are directly in accordance with the controlling forces that dictated western culture on all levels, and, as such, the suppression of non-European people and women was consistent after the solidification of the aesthetic and functional arena of extended western art music. But there was one big difference—that being, the methodological and vibrational arena of western art music was conceived directly in accordance with the male sensibility and vibrational needs, rather than for the composite needs of both men and women. For the science that determined how western art music was to flow was designed through an exclusive power-elite community that did not include the masses—men or women—but rather, a select group of forces (all of whom were men) that defined the reality and meta-reality of western art music and its related information complex.

TRF(II)–16

I have not meant to imply that the vibrational lining of western art music has no relationship to women at all, because obviously it must have some relationship. For when we talk of initiations from the western creative thrust, we are referring to activity that personifies the "essence factor" of the European and trans-European life-vibrational pull—and if this is true, then there can be no separating women from men. But I do mean to imply that however the inclusion of women in the general reality is perceived, it was not an inclusion that involved equal participation in the establishment of the functional arena concerning how the culture would work—either on the physical plane (i.e., society) or the aesthetic plane (i.e., creativity—in particular, music). The nature of this distinction is significant if we are to truly understand the position of women with regards to western civilization. More so, what this phenomenon means for transformation is also clear, for the next change cycle will most certainly begin to deal with what has happened to women—and, to some extent, this research has already begun.

It would also be wrong to assume that no women have contributed to western art music. For the historical records show these contributions to be a fact. The last ten to fifteen years have seen much research into the historical progressions surrounding black initiations and the contributions of women, and many people will be surprised at what this research has revealed even though, by academic standards, the research for information in these areas has only just begun). The fact is, women have contributed to every period of western creativity—whether we are talking of literature, painting, or music. Every month, there is another book released revealing new people for us to learn about—in short, even with the suppressive position women have functioned under, there have been many valuable contributions, and in practically every case, men (and women) would have us believe each new discovery initiation (from creative women whose works are finally attracting attention) should be evaluated in the same way that men evaluate their own work. In short, the controlling factors of western culture have now turned their attention on works from creative women, and unless this sector (the critics) is watched, their evaluations will design the course for the next cycle of source transfer. That is, **source transfer**

as an attempt to have women evaluate their work in the same way that white men see their activity—and if this shift is accomplished, creative women will continually have their activity looked at as being "less" than the great "masters" of western art music. In many ways, this process has already started, for I am constantly learning about creative women whose work was discovered only lately—suddenly having a performance by a major orchestra (usually on the token women's concert of the year—this also corresponds to the token black night for symphony orchestras)—and the next day, I will invariably read a review that assigns the composer to the position of following a great white man composer—and in doing so, undercuts the value of the composer's contribution. In short, even in this period (and most of us like to think of the present as advanced in some way), the collective forces of western culture function as a negative factor with regards to the "actualness" of creativity from every sector of the planet—especially if the creator is not a white man.

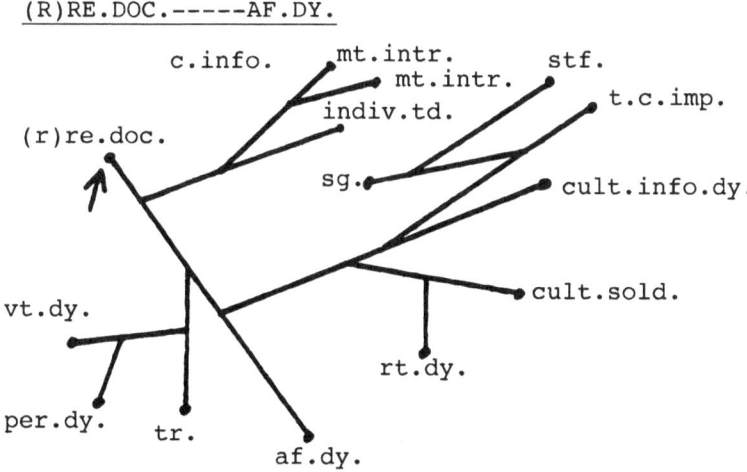

TRF(II)–18

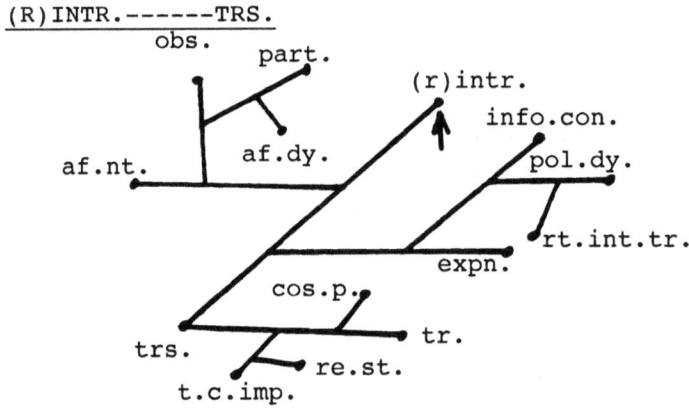

If the Egyptian Empire cycle is the most basic point of reference for documenting the present vibrational cycle we are now in, then there are several factors we cannot avoid looking at. For however one chooses to look at the planet progressions from early Egypt until the present, one factor has remained consistent—that is, the transformation cycle that began in Egypt and continued until the present has utilized the basic underlying controlling factor of patriotical extension—or movement in accordance to the patriotical vibrational defining factor. If this factor has indeed determined the nature of planet activity in the past thousand and some years, then quite possibly the germ factor of transformation must address itself to what this phenomenon has implied on a planet level. For regardless of culture thrust, the most distinctive factor that has been consistent since the advent of the Egyptian Empire has been the patriotical society—so real has this one factor been that it is possible to label the last transformational cycle as the patriotical-extension cycle. In other words, the reality dynamics of women on the planet have to be looked at in relationship to the patriotical implications underlying this transformational cycle, and the realness of the coming transformation (in its most positive state) would imply a re-alignment of this phenomenon. The most important factor that this change must necessitate is the power and realness of definition—for the functional arena that maintains the present reality of western culture is directly connected to words. My point is that the first level of securing a reality must involve the rejection of alien definitions—as a means for designing a more meaningful alternative-reality position, to participate in the challenge of re-ordering the next composite reality.

The present cycle we are now living in is thus the time zone where practical re-ordering of physical universe transfer-shift phenomena can be actualized. This is a period where functional movements must challenge the political and vibrational order of western culture. It is possible to look at the gains that have been made in this cycle already, for clearly the reality implications of the creative woman have begun to change. Transformation in this context, then, would shed light on the lack of performing outlets for creative women, and transformation would also provide insight into the nature of the next forming composite aesthetic—and what this implies for trans-feminism. Transformation in this context is also directly related to the needs of the world group—that is, while the basis of this book has focused on the needs of the world community, the position women are now in on this planet cannot be separated from what this means as well. In other words, it is possible to substitute the word "women" in place of "black" in almost every section of this book—because the basic problems are the same in many instances—yet I have not meant to imply that all problems (regardless of focus) are the same, because this is not true. Without doubt, the research taking place in this time zone will be of positive assistance to transformation as we move deeper into this cycle. For the restoration of honest historical information about life on this planet will be an important factor that will help determine how to proceed in the future—with regards to the challenge of positive world change.

To really view the dynamic implications of extended functionalism and transformational politics, it is necessary to first understand the reality of participation—as this consideration relates to alternative unification and/or positive functionalism. This is so because the significance of a given participation is not limited to only one context or specific focus. As such, the success of the next cycle of alternative functionalism will not only have to do with whether or not certain accomplishments are solidified, but will also concern the reality dynamics underlying how those accomplishments were approached (and practiced). For the purpose of this series of books,

I have attempted to view the dynamics of participation in terms of its transformational undertones, and in doing so, I have formulated what I now call the concept of "the responsibility of the position" as a basis to begin viewing the nature of alternative functionalism in the last twenty years especially—and as a means to attempt understanding what extended participation could mean in the future, if approached correctly. Certainly I do not present this concept—or any of the concepts in this book—as necessarily true or completed, because it is not the purpose of this book to establish universal laws (in any real terms). Instead, I see this viewpoint as consistent with the approach I have taken throughout this book. That being, ideas I have been thinking about—and nothing more. Nevertheless, the concept of "the responsibility of the position" is relevant in the sense that it does attempt to examine the "reality of participation" in alternative terms—and this is needed. I believe many of the mistakes that took place in dynamic functionalism during the sixties can be viewed with respect to what a given action posed to the concept of "the responsibility of the position"—but first it is necessary to define terms.

"The responsibility of the position" is my term to comment on the dynamic implication degrees of participation with respect to what a given participation means when executed (1) to the individual, (2) to the greater collective or movement that generates the dictates of that individual, and finally (3) to the greater country or planet space. My point is this: **the reality of a given participation has multi-dimensional implications that must be taken into account whenever a given functionalism (or procedure) is adopted.** It is one thing for an individual to take a given course of action as a means to function with respect to what he or she interprets as correct in one's own universe, but it is quite another thing to commit a greater group of people on a given course of action—and this difference reflects on more than what is obvious. I believe the present state of western culture can be viewed as directly related to the reality of its decision-making policies, and I also believe that the specifics of many other important decisions have been utilized only for what those decisions posed to "the responsibility of the first degree" (which is really the third degree, but this I will explain later on).

My point is this: **the dynamics of transformational participation will necessitate a higher context for motivation than only individual interest—and this is especially true for transformational activity. What we need now, more than ever, are leaders whose visions and motivations are focused on what is best (and most positive) and of the greatest good for all humanity and planet earth.** In other words, what we now need are individuals who will work for composite unification and dynamic change—that benefits everybody on the planet, as opposed to only certain sectors of the planet. When I wrote that the first degree of "the responsibility of the position" was really the third degree (in all-cosmic motivation), I meant only that the individual's needs and reality, while of course important, pale when viewed in the composite context of all humanity—and as such, the dynamics of the individual's reality platform, while representing the first degree of awareness and participation, must be viewed as the third degree of "high motivation." Yet in assigning "degrees" to this phenomenon I have not meant to disrespect any aspect of positive motivation and/or involvement.

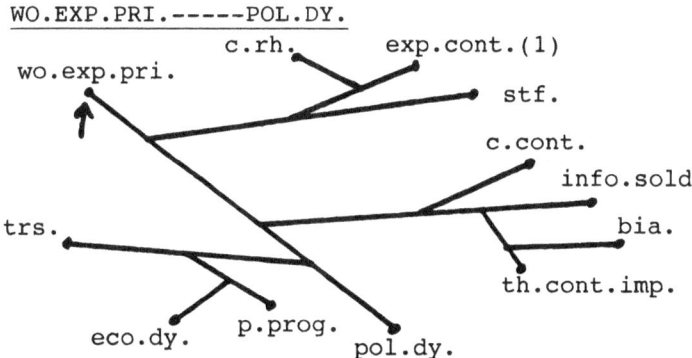

The present reality of participation in western culture can be viewed as profoundly detrimental to transformational expansion or spiritual resolidification and/or world unification—and this is true regardless of level of functionalism or specifics. If we are to ever hope for positive change, then some attempt must be made by the composite people on this planet to come to terms with the third degree of "the responsibility of the position"—because this degree of participation is the highest degree for the "greater good of all humanity." To really view the realness of this concept, it is necessary to apply its criterion of examination to the basic thrust of this book—that being, information dynamics and the reality of creative music. For instance, nine-tenths of the "reality of interpretations" surrounding the dynamics of creative music that we are dealing with today are interpretations conceived with respect to what that writer deemed to be accurate about first-degree postulation—as opposed to viewing creative music in a composite context. Moreover, by basing a viewpoint from this level of awareness, jazz journalists continually make the mistake of imposing alien information dynamics on black creativity—because the essence of world creativity is not about existential postulation (and the reality continuum of black creativity—and its affinity dynamics—is not separate from the dictates of composite black creativity and world creativity). The end result of this mis-awareness is that more distortions are put on black creativity—and this phenomenon also impedes the possibility of positive world change. But this is only one example of this concept—there is much more to look at.

The importance of higher motivation for functionalism can especially be understood by viewing the composite dynamics of present-day information transference. For the development of contemporary media is much too significant to be allowed to continually distort relevant cultural information. I believe the present-day music journalist should be concerned about helping to solidify a more positive understanding of composite earth creativity—as opposed to the present state of name-calling and ego postulation. This is especially important when one understands that only a small sector of the greater community has access to any medium of information transference. In other words, **there is a responsibility that must be recognized for those special individuals whose natural—or unnatural—desire is to affect the greater "state of things" in dynamic terms. There is also a responsibility attached to forming a so-called revolutionary movement—having to do with altering people's lives; there is a responsibility for those individuals whose natural vibrational alignment has helped to make them successful in politics or social causes; there is a responsibility attached to those whose desires are to**

lead—and it is time this is recognized. For instance, America is generally considered to be the richest nation on the planet in this time zone. If that is true—and it seems to be—then America has a responsibility to help elevate life on the composite planet. It is important that western culture begins to think in these terms, for the future of this planet is not separate from whether or not real consciousness can be developed. I believe the concept of "the responsibility of the position" can help to clarify the present reality of competitiveness in western culture, for the realness of a given participation is not limited to whether or not it is the so-called best, but instead concerns whether all involved contributes the best of what each person is—because in cosmic terms, there is no such thing as the best (in this sense, anyway). Thus, in real terms, the reality of a given degree is related to how it ultimately serves its users: that is, the reality of the first degree (the individual) is positive as long as it serves to further individual excellence and growth; the reality of the second degree in this context has to do with how a given participation helps to further the intentions of its particular movement; and the reality of the third degree has to do with what a given participation poses for its composite context (which in this case is the whole of this planet). But in every degree, the ultimate effect of its focus should not "discredit" or disenfranchise the composite dictates of "the responsibility of the position"—because I feel that the total is more important than anything. This is not to say that any given participation should not be approached because the individual or movement has no importance—obviously all of these contexts are important. Instead, the reality of a given participation must be approached with respect for its separate and composite dictates—either this is done or one runs the risk of a particular governing the "dictates" of aspect-essence information distortion—and this phenomenon has nothing to do with real understanding (let alone real insight).

The seriousness of what is implied in transformation forces us to look at the general planet situation we are experiencing at present—as a means to better understand what must be done. We are forced to examine the political reality of the present time zone as well, for it is already clear that this consideration must be completely redesigned.

More so, when I talk of transformation, it must be understood that I am talking of change on a composite planet level rather than isolated areas of earth—for the realness of the problems humanity faces transcends race or nationality. There can be no uplifting of only some of the people of the planet if we are serious about the challenge of transformation. Real change can only come about from a collective effort from all humanity. For to deal with the present political reality is to be confronted with one definite fact that cannot be ignored: "as long as white people are controlling three-fourths of this planet, there can never be real equality"—in other words, the realness of transformation would have to address itself to this most basic problem. The concept of transformation must deal with the present situation in Africa and be a vibrational and functional factor to assist positive change. Any attempt to view the progressions that have been shaping events in this continent for the last thousand years would reveal the importance of Africa as the most basic factor related to the transformation cycle we are now in. In other words, the destruction of Africa was directly related to the subsequent emergence of western civilization as the dominant controlling factor for this time zone. It is my opinion that the fate of Africa is directly connected to the fate of black people everywhere on the planet—and the events which are shaping the next cycle in Africa will be important to all of us for what it will reveal about the next cycle.

The political consequences of change seem to forecast another systematic balance until actual transformation is completed. That is, to view the present power relationship on the planet is to be aware of the western exclusive controlling position. These basic alignment powers are America, Europe, and the Soviet Union. All of the other areas on the planet can be viewed in terms of what relationship each has with one of these controlling powers. As we progress into the next change cycle, this balance of power will undoubtedly be changed, for already China has emerged as a power to be reckoned with, and the next fifty years will see the collective forces of South America and Africa—not to mention, events in the Middle East have shown that western culture is not all-powerful, but rather a vibrational culture thrust that can be brought to its knees unless its has sufficient amounts of oil to run its mines—in short, the Middle East has also now become an important power. Transformation in this context will address itself to the nature of power flows—whether in regards to cross-vibrational movements or within a given country's own reality—and hopefully this phenomenon will shed light on how politics can be made to function in a more human and noble role. For the next cycle, people must learn how to share space on the physical universe level without trying to destroy each other. The realness of what this means implies another understanding of functionalism.

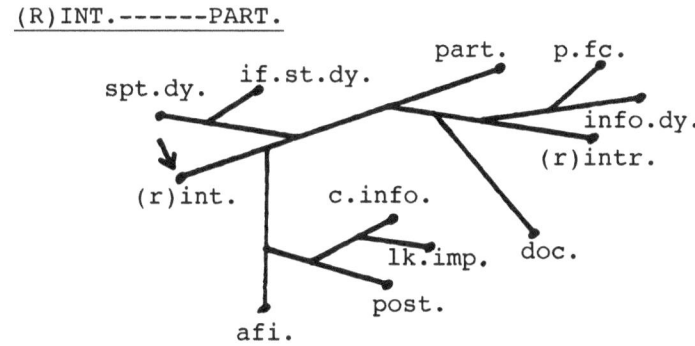

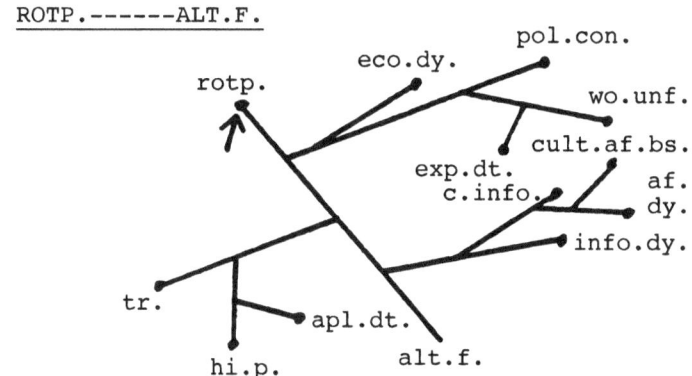

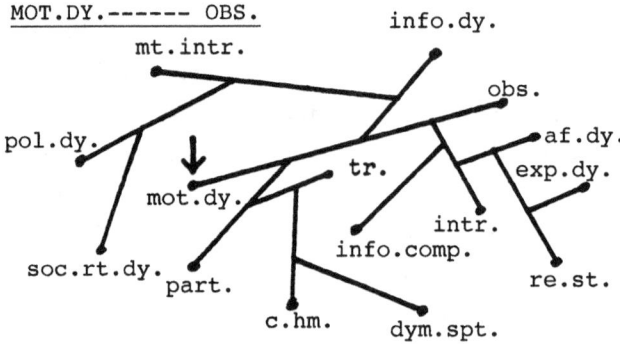

I cannot endorse the extension of western political ideologies as a basis for forming the alternative composite world group—in fact, my understanding of transformation suggests completely abandoning the present-day view of "isolated" functionalism, and adopting instead a "consolidated" functionalism that could move in accordance to the dynamics of both essence and theory. If this is understood, then it follows that the basis of scientific socialism would also have to be rejected as a desirable goal and utilized instead as only a necessary path to pursue until the "essence" factor of "consolidated" functionalism can be realized. For the implications of scientific socialism, Marxism, etc., do not necessarily lay the seeds for a revolutionary transformation, but instead these philosophies are conceived with respect to the present physical universe "particulars"—in a practical sense—whereas a "consolidated" functionalism moving in accordance with the vibrational lining of transformation (in the positive sense of the word) would carry the seeds for real change. That being—**"a renewed and vital spiritual and practical physical universe stance which could serve as a positive tool for rebuilding our lives and for discovering humanity and God."** In my opinion, there is no challenge greater than this—for the very basis of present-day western living contains unhealthy tendencies—reflecting on separations that have come about because of an inability to understand "essence." Transformation will thus be the cycle where information dynamics are re-examined and dealt with, and hopefully this re-examination will form the basis for the next cycle.

The realness of transformation also seems to imply a reordering of the physical nature of the planet. In other words, the next transfer-cycle phenomenon seems to hint at the nature of individual changes that will transpire—on the vibrational and physical universe level. For the magnitude of change necessary to bring about real growth will undoubtedly challenge our very understanding of existence in the next cycle, because the dynamic implications of this phenomenon includes tragedy as well. The next ten to fifty years seems to hint at the nature of what tragedies we will be forced to deal with as change accelerates: whether these forces are manifested in the ecological situation of the planet, war, or the plague. The realness that tragedy is also shaping the next cycle can be understood by looking at the factors now controlling the planet in this time zone. For it is obvious that the controlling forces now dictating earth order are not about to relinquish their hold on the planet unless forced to. More so, it is also obvious—with the present situation being as it is—that everything in this time zone is being designed for confrontation—on the most basic level. Yet I have not meant to paint a picture of despair either, for there are many other forces that balance the composite theatre of factors on this planet. My reason for mentioning this phenomenon is only to deal with the dynamics of change—and face up to the realness that inherent in multi-progressionalism is the real factor of tragedy. Yet I do not mean to accent the realness of tragedy in the future, for the present situation we are now dealing with is tragic enough—which is to say, tragedy is not exclusively connected to transformation, but rather a phenomenon that can be viewed in its separateness.

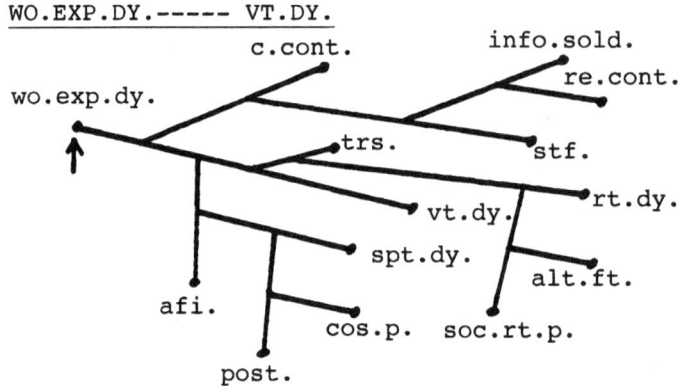

Moreover, the consideration of tragedy should not be viewed as an isolated act that has no relationship to real life—rather, this phenomenon must be viewed as the consequences related to how we have chosen to treat given situations. My position is that the next cycle will see the disintegration of the composite western controlling position, and however tragic one chooses to interpret this (disintegration) change, in actual fact, the realness of a given physical universe reality has very little to do with our interpretations. I do believe, however, that whatever the given physical universe situation is (regardless of time zone), that " 'it' is not about tragedy"; or the actualness of what is happening on the planet is not about one aspect of how it might be viewed. But there is another factor connected to this phenomenon that must also be discussed, for the actualness of how we see ourselves on the planet can serve as a distortion—in many instances—for truly understanding what is really happening on a planet level. The factor I am referring to has to do with the underlying forces that dictate how given events occur as well as our relationship to those events. My point is this: the realness of coming events on the physical universe level will not be so much the result of particulars happening in this period—the sexual revolution, the relationship between black and white people, rich and poor people, etc.—as much as the realness of cosmic cycles. **In other words, the concept and existence of music and/or political reality, etc. are not factors that cause transformation so much as factors that are caused**

by transformation. This difference is significant. For my opinion of transformation is not that once a given cycle is solidified, suddenly everyone will love one another and all will be wonderful, etc.—but instead, the concept of transformation has to do with the vibrational and cosmic factors which dictate the nature underlying how change is to occur—as that change is connected to the all-cosmic considerations of "what is." In other words, the "reality of planet progressionalism" seems to imply that given progressions function in accordance to vibrational and cosmic factors—as those factors relate to what that given time zone is about. As such, it is possible to look at the cycle that took place during the Egyptian period, the great Chinese period, the migration cycle, the Ice Age, the western cycle, etc., etc., and understand what I mean when I refer to the nature underlying a given transformational cycle. My point is that the solidification of a given transformational cycle is not an end in itself but rather the completion of a given vibrational zone and nothing more. In other words, when I write of the seriousness of the next transformational cycle, I do not mean to imply that any particular cycle is the final cycle, for this is not the case (or at least this is not what I think). The next transformation cycle will merely address itself to the present physical universe alignment coordinates and transform what that alignment means in dynamic terms. After this transformation cycle is completed, I imagine we will have new options as a basis for learning and hopefully growing—I also imagine that we will have new negative forces to deal with as well (not new—but fresh). Whatever, my most basic point is that I have not used the word "transformation" as a final fate, but rather as a junction that will give us new options to deal with—transformation as a cleansing factor that serves to re-energize "the new frontier."

TRF(II)-30

EXP.DY.------ALT.C.PROG.

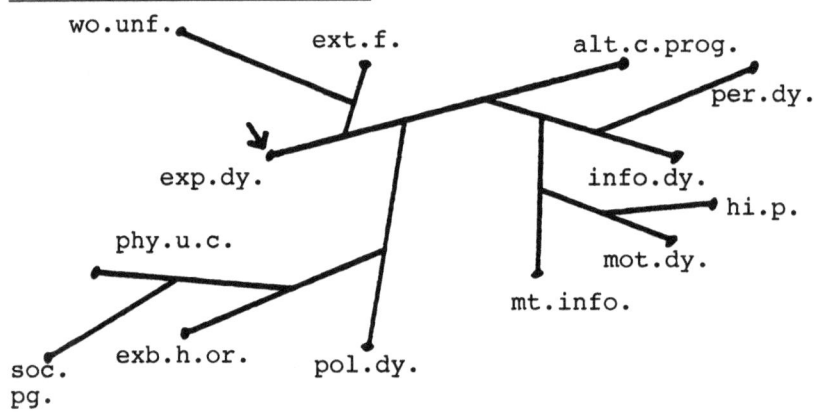

DE.SPTL.------ CR.INFO.DY.

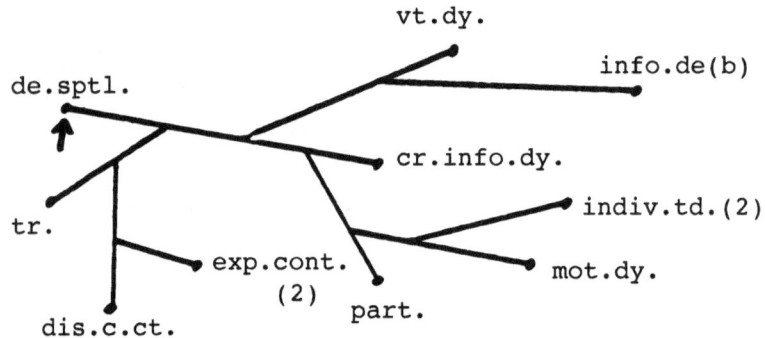

PROJ.DY.------MT.INFO.

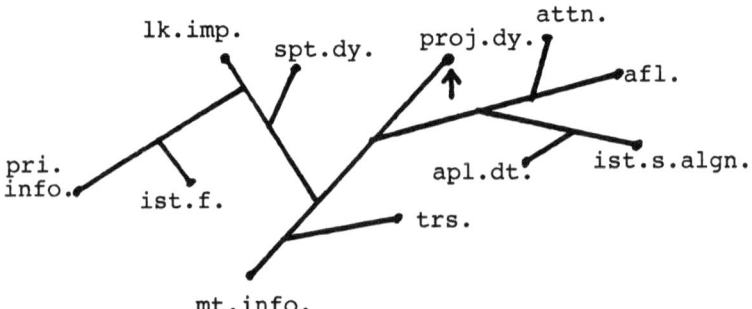

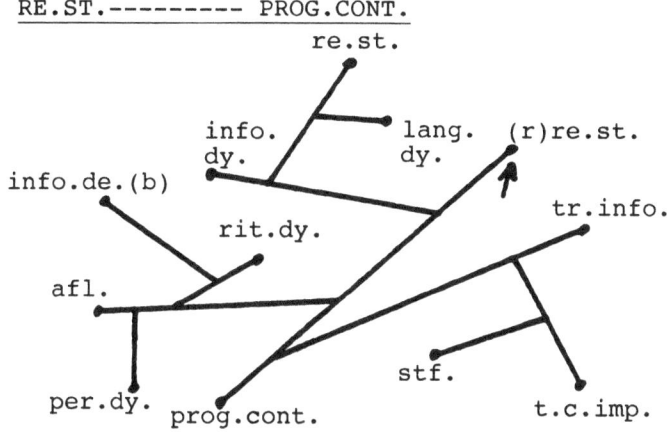

If, on the first level, transformation has to do with the unification of human beings on the planet, then undoubtedly the next level of transformation would have to do with establishing the underlying basis and tenet structure for determining how to function as a group. In other words, it is not enough to merely eradicate prejudice to proclaim ourselves ready to function on the next level, for prejudice is only one symptom of what is happening on a planet level. More so, I am not in agreement with the idea that by focusing on a given area we can solve the dynamic implications underlying how a particular situation affects us on a planet level. In other words, the solving of an aspect doesn't necessarily have anything to do with the dynamic consequences that determined the nature of an aspect. My point is that the solving of an aspect can be useful for a given time zone only if its solving will prepare a situation that provides an "overview" of its reality context. It is for this same reason that the methodological arena of creativity in this time cycle has moved into distortion, for if the basis of agreement can only be found in how a given aspect is viewed (i.e., harmony-rhythm), then this condition is held together only by words—and as such, is at the mercy of a given whim, or of a twist in how a given word is utilized (which depends on where a particular intention is coming from, as far as what I will call positive and negative intentions—not to mention, there is also the realness that people simply do not see things the same way, so there is a natural conflict in language as well). Yet I do not mean to under-value the realness of agreement—on whatever level. For not only is this a necessary condition that we must strive for, but this condition is the first level that must be secured if there is to be any real gain in positive functional activity. But it is important to understand the two most basic conditions of transformation: those being, transformation as a factor to aid positive activity, and transformation as a factor to aid the securing of an alternative composite affinity stance.

The first level of transformation must address itself to the seriousness of positive functional activity as a means for establishing what we—as a collective people—want in the next cycle. Transformation in this context would shed light on our "agreements" as well as how those agreements could solidify into a positive functional tool. Undoubtedly, the most important reconsideration that must be correctly aligned would be the nature underlying how given functional aspects are viewed. In other words, the first level of transformation in this context would serve as a factor to clarify perception dynamics; and this juncture will hopefully perceive with respect to the essence factor of a given initiation. The composite identity of a given aspect can better be understood when its criterion is seated in empirical and spiritual terms—with a proper integration between the two. When this integration is secured, we will have a better basis for establishing culture.

To understand the reality dynamics of perceived transformation—of the second degree—one has only to look at the present planet situation. All of the alternative functional movements that developed in the sixties have been rendered helpless in the seventies because of their inability to foresee the consequences of their activity, as well as the perception implications of their activity (as transmitted through "words"). To understand the present situation of alternative functional activism in America during the late seventies is to see that intellectualism is basically non-functional. More so, the present time zone can be looked at as being the direct result of the inability of these groups to function in accordance with the most basic essence factor that motivated the transition in the sixties—that being, what was and is happening to people on this planet, and the actualness that cosmic considerations in the sixties had produced a situation conducive for real change. In short, the separations that occurred in the political movements in the sixties served as a factor to weaken composite transition, and eventually this same factor led to the emergence of the particulars we are now dealing with. The present situation of the planet is also directly connected to the limitation of western information dynamics—regardless of focus. More so, the political dictates of western expansionalism are maintained because of the block western language poses for transformational thinking. In the final analysis, all of these factors can be reduced to the consequences of aspect-essence transfer progressionalism—that is, the challenge of transformation preparations must necessitate a re-examining of how we have come to view both language and "perception dynamics."

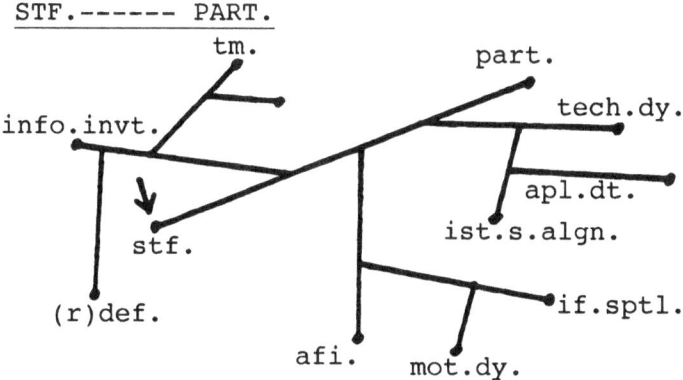

When I stated that the first level of transformation has to do with the establishment of a composite affinity stance, I am not saying that any given community or racial group should not respect their tradition, nor am I suggesting that any group see themselves as "less" than they are. I am only commenting on the realness that the magnitude of the next cycle seems to suggest a move towards unification on a level that is unprecedented in this time zone. More so, when I stated that the basis of that unification would have to do with "agreement," I was referring to the most basic affinity-alignment particulars everyone has in common. For the truth seems to be that if the next transformation cycle is to be realized in its most optimum state, then everyone must work to shape this (present) cycle—for we have already moved into the next transfer cycle (on the way to real transformation). More so, it is important to establish unification in this time zone if we truly want a better life in the next period, for the optimum condition of any cycle would comment on whether or not all of the people in its parameter are able to participate in their lives on the highest level (whatever "highest level" means). To secure that position in the next vibrational and transformational cycle tomorrow implies that preparation is made on our part today. I write this because I do not agree with the idea of "transformation in a vacuum" either. For however people see their differences, there are also similarities that cannot be avoided—that being, the realness that all of us are on this planet, and most people have hope for a better future (where conditions on the physical universe level can be upgraded, and that life on this planet can mean something more than "a walk in space").

If the first level of transformation comments on the seriousness of unification as a necessary factor for survival, it is important to realize that this level cannot be substantiated by itself. In other words, the realness of unification is a factor that predates the possibility of transformation—and should not be confused with "actual" transformation. There are many examples of what I mean by this. For surely the concept of scientific socialism can be viewed as an idea that attempts to deal with the present planet situation as a basis for moving towards transformation. My point is that the "realness" of any approach—as a tool for transformation—must reveal whether or not it takes into account the actual fact of people's lives, and functions in accordance with the cosmic and vibrational principles of justice (not just the word). In other words, scientific socialism must be evaluated by how close it comes to recognizing that fact, as well as by whether considerations are merely tools to attain a given position or instead used as knowledge that is part of a doctrine for real transformation to build on. I state this as opposed to the concept of waiting idly for transformation without actively participating—or becoming involved. For the most basic factor that can distinguish scientific socialism from the sequences that determine the aspect-essence cycle is whether or not this concept functions as a progressive force rather than a destructive agent (with regards to the people on this planet). My point is that **the** seeds underlying positive transitional doctrine can serve as a factor for advancing into the next cycle—more so, if this condition is met, then scientific socialism can be viewed as a positive functional thrust. But this condition also implies that the underlying aesthetic and affinity arena of world culture is also affected, for it is clear that functionalism and intellectualism in themselves are not necessarily pointed towards positive solutions—but are instead considerations that are designed within the limitations of words, and can be reshaped at a given whim. I am saying that the basis underlying how any functional and/or aesthetic phenomenon is made real must shed light on the vibrational and cosmic consequences of its variables (extensions)—that is, whether or not a movement can be looked at as a positive force (for the welfare of the people on this planet) or negative (for the welfare of some of the people on this planet). Because it is not enough to proclaim only a conceptual unification—and it is not enough to proclaim "equal-equal." These concepts must have some larger context from which to derive "real" meaning; and if that is true, then whatever we learn from this subject can give insight into the second level of transformation.

The second level of transformation would have to do with the solidification of an alternative composite spiritual and cosmic stance. The establishment of this objective can reveal another alignment for world religion as a factor for building real unification rather than diversion. It is important to understand that the breakdown happening in this present period is directly connected to what factors moved to weaken the composite vibrational identity of western culture. The factors I speak of in this context have to do with the solidification of non-white people as a force that must be dealt with, and the acceleration of dynamic feminism (among other factors). In other words, the forces that underlined the developments that brought black people and women to the present juncture are also connected to the same factors that have weakened the affinity lining of western culture. The end results of these developments have made the established religious institutions seem outmoded, for the affinity needs of people in this time zone are different (on the surface) from what people were dealing with two hundred years ago. Yet I do not mean to negate the teachings of any particular religion—this is not my point at all. It is not a question of whether a given religious strain is "real" or not, but rather understanding that the planet itself actually determines whether or not something is made "real." The spiritual alignment of a given culture is directly related to the vibrational and dynamic factors which outline how a given time zone is understood. Thus, if the concept of transformation has anything to do with "actualness" of change, then this concept must also imply that the composite results of that change be addressed with regards for what they mean on a dynamic (i.e., cosmic-spiritual-practical) level. The solidification of an alternative spiritual affinity alignment is directly related to the concept of transformation.

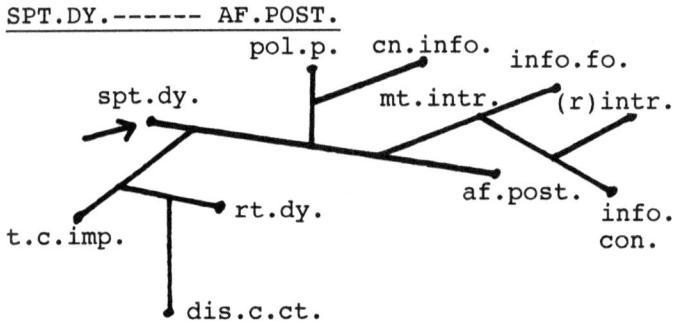

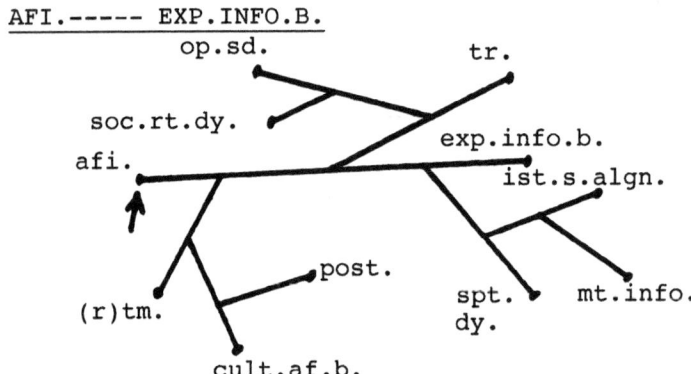

There are many other factors related to the need for an alternative spiritual alignment, and it would be wrong to accent only certain aspects of this most complex subject. For it is clear that the spiritual alignment of a given time zone is the most basic factor to substantiate how a given culture sees itself. The realness of an alternative composite spiritual thrust in this context is a factor that must be viewed on more than one level if we are to truly understand what this consideration means. Because there are other variables which must be mentioned in this context as well—including the sophistication of western technology, the profound influence of media, and finally the realness of change (or the realness of how cycles appear to change). For to understand the actuality of a given vibrational and physical universe change is to view what are essentially cosmic matters—that is, we can only speculate as to what all this really means (or doesn't mean)—and should not necessarily conclude that it is "about meaning." In other words, however we choose to attempt viewing different progressions on a physical universe level, we must not make the mistake of confusing planet activity with "activity"—but rather, use our observations to better understand what we can do to be in accord with the affinity alignments we profess to care about.

In many ways, it is already possible to view how the next transformation cycle is forming. For the vibrational nature of this time period appears to be changing on some level. By the same token, I have not meant to emphasize any one factor or focus as the principal direction either—because I have no way of knowing this information. But based on the most generalized observations, something does seem to be changing—or more accurately, "something" is moving towards real change—and this can be seen on practically every level in this time period. Whether or not events in this period are the seeds underlining the next vibrational change cycle, in the final analysis, every participation gives insight into the composite state of its culture's reality—or potential reality. Because even though this time zone is wracked by violence and racism, and even though the political structure is still functioning in its traditional context, there is also the realness that people are struggling to understand one another—and there is also sufficient evidence outlining dynamic positive activity throughout the culture and planet. The seriousness of unification cannot be taken lightly, for if there is any one factor that accents the realness that "perceived transformation" is even a possibility, that factor would be unification. My point is that even though we are given proof—in the newspaper, on television—that racism is alive and well, the actual life situation seems to reveal that many other factors are also happening. The reality of this multi-factor will eventually affect people in their relationships with one another—and hopefully we are moving to a period of greater understanding and tolerance. Transformation in this context would involve not only a re-examination of our relationship to other people, but also our relationship to the all-cosmic implications of this phenomenon (life). In other words, if the spiritual aspect of our existence necessitates a deeper commitment towards other people—and the planet—then the nature of what this commitment means must also shed light on the vibrational dictates that will personify the next spiritual alignment. My point is that the present vibrationaltory factors we are now dealing with give insight into how the next composite spiritual arena is to be actualized as well—and, as such, what we learn from this phenomenon can better prepare us to deal with transformation. The realness that spiritual and vibrationaltory factors are moving to a composite affinity alignment can give us some idea about the next cycle. **In this context, we can say that transformation involves not only a re-examination of our relationship with the spiritual aspects of our existence, but also the formulation of "new gods"—in the sense that a composite alignment would necessitate a new way of dealing with spiritualism and the basis determining how spiritualism is communicated and perceived as well. The resurrection of new gods will probably be inevitable if transformation is to function as a composite healing and unifying factor. I am also talking about a spiritual alignment that would embrace all things and all people, with the distinguishing factor being that people would know this spiritual thrust was "about—or with—them."**

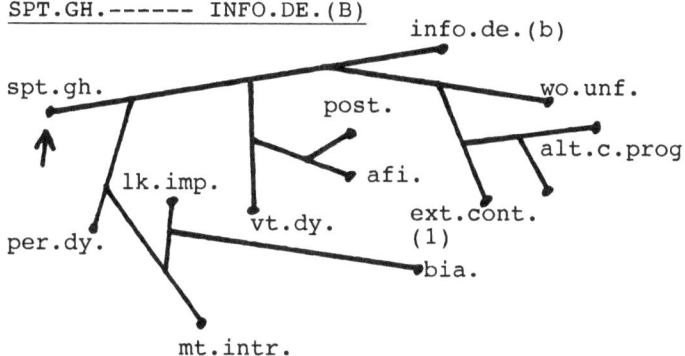

It is important to maintain a balanced outlook with regards to the reality of spiritualism—especially after events in the last two hundred years. It would be tragic if we confused the present reality of religion with the essence factor surrounding what spiritualism could be in its most positive state. More so, the use of spiritualism as a diversion factor in the sixties did not help much either; for by the end of this period, spiritualism and pseudo-mysticism had become a tired excuse for style. It was in this period when the Jesus freaks and cult movements were at their peak—not to mention, this was also the same time zone that saw the emergence of the "what is your sign?" movement. While I have tried to deal with the problems surrounding how this subject is currently perceived, it is important to separate the essence factor of this subject from the distorting elements that have gathered as a response to progressional "particulars" (on the social-physical universe level). In other words, it might not be to our advantage to simply dismiss the "cosmic implications of being" if we truly want to understand more—or if we truly want to function in accordance with the highest considerations we think we understand. Because of this, we are forced to attempt understanding—on whatever level is real for each individual—of spiritualism and what this subject implies for our actual life progression, as well as spiritualism and its relationship to the all-cosmic mystic life consideration—in the sense that our lives on this planet are not one-dimensional. Nor am I advocating some sort of mystic existentialism. I am looking for a viewpoint that substantiates our spiritual and vibrational health as well as aids in the establishment of a functional doctrine for "continuance" on the physical universe level. My most basic understanding of spiritualism is simply that this consideration is possibly the most profound unification factor on the planet. This consideration affects how people flow—whatever the level—having to do with knowingness as well as the effects of that knowingness on a practical level. Spiritualism is the strongest factor to accent similarities as well, and this vibrational factor is the most powerful cosmic tool for accenting "agreements" rather than differences.

In this time zone, the concept of spiritualism is usually connected to a religion, although this is not always the case (especially in the last transition period). I believe the optimum situation for dynamic spiritualism would be a world religion—or at least a religion that respected all of the different source-initiated thrusts that we now have, as a factor to move towards composite transformation. The dynamics of this change have already solidified for the last two hundred years, and have seen a breakdown in every isolated religious thrust (and focus).

The spiritual extensions that emerged in the last cycle have been a positive stimulating agent for re-examining the total phenomenon of spirituality, and I see this re-examination as important. The most basic factors that point to the need for a world's religion are the same factors that are changing the physical and vibrational flows in this time zone. In other words, the changes that have come about because of the sophistication in technology have helped to create a situation conducive for extended dynamic change—and even the religious community is not immune to what this change necessitates on a practical and vibrational level.

On the most basic level, it is important to understand the relationship of creativity to the physical space consideration that shapes how given creative strains are to be actualized. For it is clear that the present situation of creative music could best be summed up by the word "isolation." In other words, the most basic general statement that one could make on creative music in this time zone would be that creative music functions as a factor isolated from the public. The phenomenon of transformation can help us look at the factors that personified this situation, and the realness of the next cycle is directly connected to whether or not this situation is corrected. We can no longer afford to not challenge the present forces that are dictating events in this time zone. Thus the "isolation of creativity" in this time zone must be examined on every level as a means to better understand how this situation developed. For to look at the esoteric blockage that developed around creative music in the last one hundred years is to view several factors connected to the present reality platform of western culture. Moreover, all of these developments shed light on how the controlling forces have functioned—either on the vibrational plane (i.e., criticism) or the practical physical universe level (i.e., economics). Any real attempt to understand the present situation of creativity on this planet must also give insight into the forces we will eventually have to deal with in the coming cycle.

On the physical universe level, it is important to understand what has resulted from the isolation of creativity in physical universe terms. In short, decentralization is a challenge that is directly coupled to transformation. The isolation of creative music is sustained by the functional arena involving how western culture works, rather than a phenomenon which naturally happened. For the most part, the public's relationship with creative music is conditioned by the physical universe factors that determine whether or not a given area is exposed to the music. The isolation of the music is related to the distance between the music and the public as well as how we have been taught to deal with class structure in American society. The fact that the basic cultural flow of American society is directed to one sector of the country (i.e., New York City) and the fact that the majority of people are the effect of the power forces controlling how the country collectively sees itself, must be considered a factor that has helped distort the realness of composite western information dynamics. The realness of decentralization is directly connected to transformation, and because of this, creativity is used to accent our differences rather than what we are as a group. This situation will not change unless we begin to understand how the forces that maintain "present reality" are utilized. For to understand the reality of separation is to view the solidification of criticism, regionalism, and, finally, class and racism. The seriousness of decentralization cannot be dismissed on any level, for there are two basic effects that this phenomenon perpetrates: (1) that the accent on creativity from New York and other large centers serves as a factor to redirect a person's sensibilities outside his/her work, and (2) in doing so, deprives a region of its creative people. The end result of this situation is what we are dealing with today—that being, only certain parts of given regions house the creativity, while the rest of the country is "less." I do not mean to imply there are no creative people outside of New York City, London, or Paris—for obviously this is not true—but I do mean to state that the present physical universe set-up—as designed through the western position (tendencies) in this time zone—is not conducive for healthy creative communities throughout the planet, but rather for specialized centers in select regions.

The centralization of creativity is directly related to economic developments in the last one hundred years. In short, the only sector of the community that benefits from the present reality context of creativity is the business community. A decentralization in this context would necessitate another understanding of the individual (or group) and, in doing so, serve as a unification factor for the establishment of alternative outlets—and this is what is needed. More so, the move towards decentralization would have a devastating effect on the economic reality that surrounds the music—for if the people of a given community would support the creativity in their region as well as the creativity that passes through their community, this would represent the first attempt to re-order the economic controlling forces surrounding the music. In short, the concept of decentralization is directly coupled to the realness of redistribution on a composite level. What is really needed in the next cycle is a more balanced physical universe alignment with regards to creative outlets—not only for the music but for the entire creative spectrum.

Without doubt, the realness of transformation implies another understanding of functionalism on the physical universe level. The concept of politics will have to be totally realigned as well, for this consideration is directly connected to the present predicament we find ourselves in. Our total understanding of politics must be completely re-aligned to function as a positive and meaningful factor for the next cycle. This is not to say there should be no concept of order, nor am I suggesting that people should function without regards for the composite society—in other words, I am not advocating an idealistic anarchism. My point instead is that the basis which determines our understanding of this consideration (politics) must be re-evaluated. For the concept of government will not necessarily mean the same thing in a transformational context as what we have at present, and we will have to address ourselves to what this difference means in the future. In short, the reality of political functionalism will be subjected to radical change in the coming transformation. The consideration of politics cannot afford to be separated from the cosmic and spiritual laws that determine the vibrational lining of its reality. This subject must be an outgrowth of the composite spiritual arena of its thrust continuum (i.e., functional agreements that move in accordance to what a given community professes to be about). There is also a practical level which must be confronted if we are to truly understand post-transformational functional politics, for it is not merely a question of words, but rather the realness that each person should have the right to participate in their lives in accordance to what is most "real" to that person. To deal with the reality of politics is to comment on the realness of functional ideology and what this consideration poses for actual change. Questions like "what will replace money?" or "what is to prevent a person from taking something from another person?" or "who is to decide what course is the best course for a given group?," etc., etc., are practical questions that must of course be dealt with if we are talking of alternative functional systems for culture (politics). But I have accented the need for post-transformational perception because the essence basis of this subject is related to—and comments on—the vibrational platform underlying what these considerations are (as well as what these considerations could potentially mean in another vibrational reality). Because the basics that determine how a given consideration is perceived are directly related to the vibrational reality underlying how that culture sees itself (on a cosmic and vibrational level)—"what that culture group is really about." It then is necessary to examine what these considerations (politics) imply in their purest state.

  To believe that all of a sudden the next transformation will simply change our lives and make everything wonderful is of course a nice thought. But the realness of change cycles is a factor not separate from what physical and vibrational progressionalism really is—which is to say, the considerations governing our understanding of transformation must be grounded in realistic terms. In other words, people are not going to just simply come together and love one another. There is a need for functional politics to deal with dynamic new solutions—regardless of focus or levels—and we must move to creatively find ways to resolidify dynamic functionalism. We must re-examine what political dynamics really means if we are to ever change them in the future. My point is that the most basic factor underlying how a given political consideration can be utilized is the cosmic and spiritual implications of that culture's spiritual tenets.

If there is one factor that gives insight into the "actualness" of a given culture—as to where that culture group is really at with regards to tone level—that factor would have to do with the position of a culture's cosmic vibrational secrets (which line its spiritual and information complex) regarding how those secrets are implemented on a practical and just level (i.e., in the functional and actual life of people). In other words, the next consideration of politics cannot be simply arrived at through intellectual scrutiny, but rather "revealed" as a factor connected to the composite spiritual and vibrational arena of its given cultural group. It is not a question of "which comes first, the chicken or the egg"—but rather, understanding that the best homes are built on foundations. I disagree with the notion that utilities could function as an alternative center factor—or at least I disagree with this notion as a substitute for culture (agreement). I believe many dynamic solutions must be utilized in pre-transformational progressionalism, and I realize the practicality of functional equal as a pre-rallying point for establishing quick participation; but the seriousness of transformation implies a re-alignment that involves how essence is understood—and what essence really means. The basic premise I have been working with in this book is that the underlying philosophical basis of a given phenomenon actually determines how people will approach understanding its particulars—whether that phenomenon is utilities or whether that phenomenon is connected to how particular focuses are culturally achieved. Because on one level, while functional aspects, as manifested through utilities, could serve as a rallying factor for certain sectors of existence (i.e., factors that must be dealt with in our normal physical universe life track—talking, eating, reading, dealing with other people—whatever the situation or level), it is the total—or actual—understanding of what that aspect "really" means that reflects on the vibrational and methodological and cosmic implications of its culture group. For without the uplifting of consciousness, we are doomed to have to deal solely with "proportion" (which is one thing on a theoretical level, but quite another in actual life). In short, there can be no replacement for what "essence" really means. Which is to say—the most basic factor that we as a collective people need to understand is the significance of "essence"—and/or "purpose" in a dynamic sense. How we deal with that information will shed light on the spiritual and cosmic particulars of the next forming transformation.

(Level Three)

1. By "world culture group" what do you mean?

I have used the term "world culture group" in three most basic contexts: (1) as a phrase to comment on the composite beingness of all of the cultures on this planet; (2) as a term to solidify a broader understanding of what multi-cultural dynamics really means; and finally (3) as a phrase to comment on the hopeful forming of a new coalition that functions for what is best for composite humanity. The solidification of this coalition represents only the beginning of what world culture could really mean in its most optimistic sense, for the attainment of this "state of awareness" is directly related to the hope of composite spirituality and new politics. In the final analysis, all of us must be concerned about the composite state of this planet, because Earth is what we are really dealing with (in this time zone, anyway). "World culture group" in this context, then, is the first degree of awareness towards real universalism and dynamic change.

2. Is it possible to achieve "world culture" without the destruction of western civilization?

Before the possibility of world culture and planet unification can begin, there must first be a change in the composite order of both world economics and politics. If this is true, then the implications of this change would profoundly alter the present state of things—having to do with the redistribution of land, wealth, food, and information dynamics (knowledge and availability of knowledge). With the present climate of the world being as it is, I doubt very seriously if the rich countries will make the sacrifices that real transformation entails, and yet unless the gains from rich countries are compositely distributed, there can never be the possibility of world culture—or for that matter, a decent living for all people on the planet. This is not to say that I am advocating that western culture simply give away all of its wealth and put itself at the mercy of the planet—because the world's situation is much too complex for a move of this kind (not to mention, the business community supporting western culture wouldn't give away its wealth anyway). But certainly some kind of plan could be drawn up that moved to gradually balance the reality of international functionalism by installing a real concern about unification. In the end, only composite humanity will be able to change the reality of living on this planet—and this must be understood. Unless some attempt is made to share the resources of this planet, we are all doomed to the worse kind of failure. The real question that must be asked is: is it possible to have peace and world unification without the help of every country and nation on this planet? I am sure the answer is no.

3. Does the concept of sound pollution have any meaning in this time zone?

Yes. Probably few people would take the concept of sound pollution seriously—since, on the surface, the term sounds like it came from Madison Avenue—but the actual fact is that in many of our cities, the level of sound has become a hazard to healthy living. I believe some efforts must be made to correct the unimpeded levels of sound that permeate our environment. It is important to understand that the physical dynamics of sound is not simply a harmless tool, but instead a serious factor that must be dealt with. To understand the laws surrounding what creativity is, is to understand how to hopefully channel some aspect of those laws to positively assist living. The fact is, however, even the dynamics of a given sound can be very dangerous—especially when improperly used. We live in a culture that regularly subjects each person to a variety of sounds, and we are profoundly affected by the vibrational implications of what this means—whether we know it or not. It seems to me that the many levels of Muzak we now experience are harmful on a number of levels, and I also question the volume of police cars and fire trucks—although I realize there must be some kind of signal to help these people do their jobs. I also wonder about the sound implications of the subway—especially in New York City. It takes a couple of hours before my head stops ringing every time I use the subway. There is also the problem of sound volume at rock concerts and in the disco music scene. Many people are seriously damaging their ears—and what about this new fashion that involves playing one's transistor radio as loud as possible?

4. Would the significance of creative music from the black aesthetic have to do with its ability to be a positive factor in influencing the composite vibrational attraction of western culture?

Yes. I would say that one of the most significant factors about black creativity in this time zone is what it has posed for the acceleration of world unification and composition information dynamics. I believe the ultimate significance of a given projection will not lie in what particular individuals will produce—or have produced—but instead will involve what effect—if any—that projection has had in helping to advance the well-being of composite humanity. At present, the information focus of this time zone moves to over-accent the dynamics of individual offerings, but the specifics of a given offering will not constitute the basis of world culture information interpretation. It is my hope that the progressional continuity of creative music will be viewed as a positive factor for bringing about world change—but we will only know this when real transformation is achieved. Certainly the dynamic position of black creativity will be viewed for how it has compositely affected the total world group. It remains to be seen if that effect is somehow solidified into a real world attitude—positive world attitude—because many other factors come into play if we are to investigate world information transference. But the significance of affinity dynamics, as transferred through the vibrational lining of black creativity, can be viewed as an important factor that has affected the composite reality continuum of this time period, and I believe this phenomenon is directly related to how trans-African creativity will ultimately be evaluated.

5. In the past, creative music has been dominated by men (or at least, the cultural documentation that has been made available to the greater public says creativity has been dominated by men—which is different). Does this domination reflect an inherent emotional aspect of the music, and if so, what does this mean with regard to women?

The present vibrational arena of creative music does indeed reflect an unbalanced emotional and affinity state that is overly masculine—but I do not view this phenomenon as indicative of the inherent vibrational reality of the music as much as symptomatic of the composite social-political reality that permeates this period in time. Because of the present social-reality alignment, it is understandable that many women might tend to think of creative music as adverse to their vibrational needs (I have already stated my belief that men and women do have different vibrational flows), and as such be disinclined to want to participate in the music. But I don't believe that creativity (or any particular creative projection) has anything to do with any one group—whether that group is white, black, American, European, men or women—or another; in fact, this whole way of thinking runs contrary to what creativity is really about. I believe the present vibrational state of creative music is as it is because women have been denied the possibility to participate, but this denial is separate from the meta-implications of creativity. In other words, the creativity is before the denial, because creativity has to do with being born and living. The suppression of creative women must be viewed as one of the most serious areas of manipulation. Because to tamper with the affinity-dynamic affirmation of "doing"—which is what creativity is—is to strike at the essence of a person.

6. How will creative music define harmony and rhythm after the transformation?

It is difficult to get specific with this question because there is of course no way to really know. It seems to me that after transformation, the first order of business is to redefine terms—that is, information dynamics and information-degree implications. From that intention, the functional science of creativity must be recalibrated into a more meaningful position with composite information, and it is at this point where the dynamics of harmony and rhythm can be dealt with. It seems to me that a proper calibration of rhythm and harmony would show the real reality position of a given use of material to its multi-information function. With that completed, a transformational culture could establish its healing music, its ritual music, secular music, etc. My point being that the consideration of harmony and rhythm are not just playthings for the composer, nor are these considerations only related to the reality particulars of a given piece of music. Rather, the real reality position of harmony and rhythm are inter-connected with the composite alignment of cultural multi-information and multi-information dynamics. However these considerations (harmony and rhythm) are aligned after the transformation, it is my hope that new creative methodology will not be allowed to over-accent the contributions of the individual—so that each new offering (participation) will be viewed as a positive reflection of the greater culture (for everyone).

7. Has the increased dependence on mechanization had an effect on creativity in the west?

Yes. In fact, the dynamics of mechanization have altered the composite state of creativity on many different levels. This dependence has even profoundly affected how the music is recorded—and this is especially so in commercial music. For the use of over-dubbing and multi-tracking has helped produce a kind of synthetic music that is very different from what the same musicians could produce live. The emergence of the synthesizer and the electric piano, while being positive on one hand, has helped to retard basic piano technique in many of the young musicians to where, in the end, few pianists today are able to get their own sound from the instrument—and this is a dangerous trend. The dynamics of contemporary sound systems have also changed the composite music, and while this development has provided positive stimulation in some fields (e.g., new bass techniques), it has made problems in many others (e.g., ensemble dynamics and timbral subtlety). Finally, the gradual dependence on mechanization has moved to undermine the affinity-dimension implications of the music, for the use of a given technological breakthrough has its own inherent dynamics—which are different from what it seeks to replace or extend. I write this not as a means to put down technology or extended mechanization, but to only point out that the nature of a given mechanization has multi-dimensional rewards and consequences.

8. Has society's search for instant solutions affected creativity?

The search for instant solutions in this time period has affected everything—regardless of level and/or focus. This is true whether we are commenting on creativity or the dynamics of planet ecology. If we are to ever change life on this planet, then the seriousness of this phenomenon must be addressed in every context. In many cases, the acceleration of "doing" is related to the composite realness of present-day information availability—through the media—and contemporary living. On one hand, the emergence of extended technology has helped to transform our lives in positive terms, while on the other hand, the accelerated nature of contemporary living—which is an outgrowth of extended technology (among other things)—has made living impossible. Moreover, the search for instant solutions is related to the composite tone level of western culture—and its perceived survival.

For the realness of this phenomenon is not separate from the economic dynamics of western living. In creativity, the search for instant solutions (for economic gain) has helped to accelerate the commercial music industry. The thrust of this industry has moved to exploit the dynamics of black creativity on every possible level, and while this exploitation is currently viewed as positive—by those who want to cite the impact of black creativity on composite western culture—in the end, I believe the present manipulation of popular creativity will have a negative impact on progressional continuance. Finally, the search for instant solutions has created a society that vibrates only to "surface particulars," as opposed to information of substance. For this reason, I view this tendency as not positive.

9. Is cultural separation detrimental to the potential of creative music?

I believe that multi-culturalism is inevitable and directly related to transformation—yet it is important to explain this viewpoint in detail, because I am not simply endorsing one route of continuance at the expense of actual life. Certainly the dynamic continuum of a given cultural group is important and also related to positive change, nor have I meant to discredit any particular social or national group—because to do so would violate the cosmic basis of everything. As such, I am grateful to experience the creativity of any vibrational strain, because every strain affirms some aspect of our collective lives. By cultural separation, however, I am commenting on the total thrust continuance of a creative projection, and how the ultimate function of a given projection cannot be separated from the particulars of its route. My position is this: the real reality of earth life seems to clearly imply that there can be no separation between anything—but rather, the reality position underlying a given phenomenon has to do with "where" that phenomenon is at in its own timetable, and as well where that phenomenon is at in the overall cosmic timetable of everything, and, finally, what that phenomenon expresses as "cosmic purpose." It then is not a question of disrespecting any information position or separate cultural continuity, but of recognizing the inevitable nature of progressional (and/or affinity) convergence and dynamic unification. Not to mention, even in this context nothing is static, for the solidification of transformational unification only means it will be from this point (transformational) that future new separations will occur. For this reason, I view cultural separation—especially imposed separation, as opposed to the natural dynamics that dictate progressional continuity—as not necessarily conducive to positive progressionalism. In other words, I believe that given continuances—including human beings, and how life is on this planet—should not be regulated vibrationally only with respect to a so-called concept of separate culture, but instead this phenomenon should be viewed in accordance to the natural tendencies of its own dynamics. Because, to me, the truth of a given phenomenon has to do with how that phenomenon actually flows, or how that phenomenon actually vibrates, and what zones that phenomenon actually attracts. I find those criteria more related to what is really happening on this planet, as opposed to the concept of an all-separate culture. More important—and this is the real reason the concept of isolated culturalism cannot be accepted—the natural continuance of a given phenomenon—how it moves in its natural flow—in many cases transcends the dictates of isolated cultural zones. Which is to say, the imposed precepts of isolated culturalism are only as real as when they are happening—that being, when a given phenomenon happens to be in that position—and nothing more.

10. Why have so few women been considered important contributors or initiators of contemporary creative music?

I am not really sure this is a true statement—if my experiences are valid—because I have experienced many dynamic individuals (whose activity must be considered important) in the last fifteen years and some, and of those individuals, many were women. This is not to say that a given woman's or man's activity must necessarily vibrate to what this question poses, because I totally disagree with the legitimacy of this question myself. To really deal with this question, one must first look at the composite reality of western culture to establish a broader base from which to view progressional continuance. First of all, I have never agreed with the notion that "the historical continuum of western culture is only an affirmation of the white male vibrational identity" and, as such, women cannot be blamed for any of the negative features of western culture—or its positive contributions as well. However the suppression of women is viewed, my point is that to comment on a given culture—and its development—is to comment on the composite vibrational sensibility of what that culture really is. In that context, it is impossible to separate the inter-dynamic and multi-dynamic realness of men and women. But it is at this point where the complexity comes in, because the history of this period in time seems to document a profound inability on the part of men to deal with women. The dynamics of this inability have, of course, had to do with much more than words—in other words, I am commenting on injustice and subrogation, not to mention brutality, etc. Even worse, the vibrational nature of this relationship has moved to underline the reality of present-day definitions—which is to say, if we are to understand this question, then we must first understand what position this question has to the very thing that has created the problems people are dealing with in this period. This is so because "who is important?"—and what does "important" have to do with honestly participating in one's creativity and life? It seems to me that the reality of this question has to do with both its agreement by men and women and with the affinity-dynamic implications underlying what "who is asking the question" means. Why have so few women been considered important contributors or initiators in contemporary music—or in traditional music for that matter? The answer is simple: Men somehow cannot deal with creative women, and men have also helped to erect an information alignment that will forever keep their work from being accepted. Because nine-tenths of our understanding about this subject—creativity—has nothing to do with creativity, but instead ego and competitiveness. Whose work is important? Who is the best? Who is in first place? Me, that's who! History is full of this kind of nonsense, and no one in the final analysis really benefits from mis-information.

11. What kind of vibrational and actual effects will women have on transformational creativity?

It is really impossible to forecast what changes will occur in creativity when women are completely participating in shaping the music—for how can I really know? But it does seem that somehow the emergence of the creative woman will profoundly alter the music on many different levels. I find myself thinking that the composite participation of women will change the overall dynamic sensibility of the music—and yet by stating this, I have not meant to limit the dynamic implications of this question. One thing is clear: the emergence of the creative woman in real terms will mean that, for the first time in this cycle, western creativity will be about "its people," and this change alone will be as dynamic as anything could possibly be. Ultimately, as to what this change will mean, I wait like everyone else. Somehow I find myself hoping that the total inclusion of women will be the first real solidification of transformational progressionalism—having to do with the clarification of "striving for excellence," "the concept of the artist," and the beginning of "culture time"—that being, a move to solidify a creativity of and about life and culture, or life and world identity—and consciousness. Yet it might be somewhat unfair to ask all of this from the creative woman—I mean, if this doesn't happen, what will someone say then. I would like to hope that future civilizations will be able to tolerate the real dynamics of both functioning and un-functioning men and women. This is a person's right as well.

12. Is electronics the future of creative music?

No. I believe that creative music—as we understand this term—has only to do with there being people to be creative. In other words, the future of creative music is directly related to whether or not this planet is able to sustain life, and whether or not people are able to find some way to live together (of course, even if people are not living together, there will still be creative music). The emergence of electronics is only another tool for the creative person. This is not to say electronic music is not important— because it is, but the progressional continuance of earth creativity does not depend on only one information continuum. The present-day accented emphasis on electronic music and technology has moved to unbalance the composite state of things. I believe the abandonment of acoustic instruments for only electronic instruments would be a profound mistake. Electronics—as exciting as it is—is only one route for dynamic creativity, among many other routes. To believe that electronic music is the future of creativity is to be totally misinformed, because people are the future of creative music—and, ultimately, the cosmos is the real juncture that designates if there is to even be a future for anything to "happen" in.

13. Are there any institutions developing that approach, teaching creative music in alignment with the aesthetic of the music?

At this point in my life, I cannot say—because I don't know. On some level, I imagine there is something positive happening at every institution for music, but there is no one place—or school—that I would completely endorse as representing transformational education. From what I have heard, there are several centers of learning in the New York area—programs like the one solidified by the collective black artist group in New York, or the curriculum offered by schools like Wesleyan University. I do believe that, slowly, the reality of education is improving, but the change seems to be very slow—and too isolated to speak of as a movement per se. One of the problems with the university context is that it is too isolated from the real reality of the greater society. I find myself thinking that the university must come down from the mountaintop and create dynamic new programs to positively help build real culture and awareness. It is for this reason that I am optimistic about most of the independent efforts to establish alternative schools and/or programs. Because there is another level of involvement by these groups. The challenge of the next cycle is to really move towards elevating this country—in terms of real information—and creating a new world order. This should be the goal of transformational education—in fact, this should have been the goal of un-transformational education.

14. Do you view the United Nations as an important forum for bringing about change?

I believe the hope of positive change is dependent on whether or not collectives like the United Nations are more respected by all Earth countries. This is so because the U.N. is one of the few forums representing the whole of this planet. The problem with the United Nations in this period is that it has so little power to either enact a given change or directive, or to enforce that directive. It is interesting that neither the United States nor the Soviet Union really dominates the reality of this great body as we might have presumed on the surface—and there are reasons for this. The fact is, the progressional policies of both the United States and the Soviet Union are conceived only with respect to their own self-interest—and not that of the composite world group—and the realness of this difference has long made itself felt in the direction the U.N. has since taken. I view the United Nations as the most important forum we have in this time period to bring about world change, but the challenge of this role will not be easy. For the reality of effective decisions from this body is not separate from the basic dilemma that surrounds present-day economics. The wealth of this planet is at present divided mainly into six divisions, and this must be changed. The divisions at present are: (1) the United States; (2) the Soviet Union; (3) Western Europe; (4) western satellite powers (e.g., Canada, Australia); (5) Japan; and (6) China. This is not to say the

Middle East does not also enjoy some aspect of wealth—especially in this time period—because obviously it does; the same can be said of particular regions in Africa and South America. But the six divisions I have cited are real centers of wealth and cultural affluence; and these same divisions are also profoundly inter-related throughout the whole of earth, multi-business manipulation. The effectiveness of the United Nations is not separate from what this phenomenon poses—and it is my hope that the future will see this body become greater and more powerful than any of its individual parts.

15. Why is the composite pooling of world information important for transformation?

The composite pooling of world information is important for transformation because no one region of information is about "it"—or "all of it." If we are to ever deal with the realness of this experience (living), then we must come to terms with the available information that already exists. The solidification of a world information position would help clarify the dynamic implication of information focuses—having to do with the restoration of a more benevolent approach to functionalism as well as spiritualism—and this is important. But even more important, the solidification of a world information attitude would have a direct bearing on solving many of the misunderstandings we have about each other. The thrust of composite information could help alleviate the need for war—because no one goes to war with him- or herself. And the realness of composite information would help solidify a real basis for moving towards greater areas of information focus. In other words, composite information, like world culture, can move to help people better approach dealing with living. I believe the diversity of earth information can move to open everyone to the wonder of "actual living." For the cross-realness of world information is related to the composite dynamics of information transference.

16. To what degree can a given progressionalism be viewed as extending transition into transformation? Is there a clear point that can be cited?

I believe the reality of transition and transformation are vibrational cycles that are determined by higher forces—having probably nothing to do with this use of words, but instead fulfilling some aspect of cosmic all-purpose. To what extent a given cycle should be viewed as transition—as opposed to transformation—would first depend on the particulars of its vibrational dictates, as well as how long those dictates have underlined the reality of a (its) given time period. In other words, the reality of a transition would have to do with viewing "what happened" after it "happened" rather than before—because there is no way to know what is going to happen until it happens. I view all of the progressions, from the solidification of Greece to Rome—to the eventual spread into Europe—to America, as part of one transformational cycle, with each change representing some aspect of transition. At this point in my life, I tend to view a given continuum that has lasted for at least two thousand years as real enough to call a vibrational period—hence, a transformation block of time. It does seem that a given progressionalism can be observed with respect to what has happened in history as a basis to comment on "what seems to be happening" with that progression—although we can never really know until it happens. My belief that we are slowly moving towards real transformation is based from my observations about the past. This is so because the state that lends itself to transformation has happened many times before.

17. What are some of the specifics that the decade of the eighties will have to address if positive transformation is to be attained?

It seems to me that the redistribution of both wealth and basic necessities must be viewed as especially critical as we move into the eighties. Many of us have come to view the saying that "people are starving in other parts of the world" as a joke, or only something to say to get the children to eat. But in fact, there are many countries that are barely surviving—countries whose present state is not separate from the economic decisions that western super-powers have made. Sooner or later, the intensity of living is going to see a dynamic reaction to the present state of western culture—not only American but in all of western culture. I believe each decade will see the realness of world unification become more important—for the survival of the planet. I view the eighties as extremely important for what it will play in shaping the nature of the next transformation. Either the thrust of this period will complete what was intended in the sixties, or the restoration of dynamic western continuance will move into its most critical cycle yet. As such, I believe the specifics of the eighties' functionalism must involve dynamic changes in social reality: concerning the plight of poor people, the solidification of a positive platform towards resurrecting culture, the move to a more logical use of energy, and the emergence of a real spiritual position. I believe the eighties will be very important for what it will reveal about the future continuance of western culture.

18. *Can there be such a thing as existential ethics—or vibrational ethics?*

I believe the first real impression of a "way to be" or "code of behavior" is manifested in one's own vibrational make-up. In other words, the realness of vibrational ethics is really the first level of awareness—or meaning—about social and vibrational participation. From this context it is possible to begin viewing the composite reality of participation—for the concept of "destroying each other" is also universally recognized as "not in the highest realm of doing"—and this is true in every culture. The concept of the "ten commandments" can be found in practically every religious movement—which is to say, it seems as if we are all born with a similar code of conduct and honor—and I believe this means something. For the hopeful realness of transformation is related to "what is most similar about all of us" rather than what is most different. The realness of vibrational ethics is really all we have at present in western so-called culture, because the present "state of affairs" that we are living in has nothing to do with anything but words (and anyone knows that one can "say anything"—which is exactly what has happened). Thus, the reality of vibrational ethics and sensitivity is all we have to guide the particulars of our own life path—the hope being that affinity attraction can help deliver us to where we belong—or would like to belong. Yes, I do believe there is such a thing as vibrational ethics (which is really related to the precepts of vibrational dictates)—before a given phenomenon can be "approached."

19. Are there any steps that can be taken to make a given sector or group spiritual? In other words, what are the precepts for re-establishing culturalization in this time period?.

It seems to me that the re-establishment of real culture cannot simply be decided—especially by one or two people—but instead involves several dynamic factors (some of which have nothing to do with human beings). The first of those factors would undoubtedly be (1) that the greater cosmics must first determine if a given time-space environment is to be anything—let alone a culture; (2) the information continuum of that time-space environment must be compositely calibrated into its proper functional and spiritual degrees (another way of writing this is to say that the environment must have its information "put in tune" with the greater laws of the universe—which is an expression of cosmic law); and finally, (3) living in that resultant context must be made "real" (which is to say, life expression and participation in "the act of living" is not only an affirmation of some theoretical implication but instead a natural expression of its affinity state). As such, before any attempt to solidify a culture can take place in this time period there must first be a unification of all of the principles of "its space environment." What this means is that the effectiveness of any transformation pedagogy is directly related to whether its affinity scope includes the composite nature of its citizenry. Either there is some real degree of unification or the concept of real culture—"high culture"—can never solidify as a real "way of living."

20. What relationship can history have to dynamic future continuance?

To really examine the nature of progressional continuance is to begin seeing how similar given cycles of time are—and this is only the beginning. I believe that, in some instances, many earlier cultures had a higher way of living than what we now have today, and the study of world history can help one better understand what has been both lost and gained. To examine documentation from cultures like Egypt, Greece, or India in their high cycles is to see a way of living that is much higher on many levels than what we now have in this time cycle. The study of history can help us better understand how we have gotten to this point in time, as well as how we can get out of this point in time. I believe there are many aspects of world culture that we must relearn, if the level of life on this planet is to ever change. Among those areas are (1) the realness of religion and dynamic spirituality; (2) the use of the ritual (as participation with respect to "the greater forces" and not only the individual); and (3) the restoration of ethics. This is not to say that every period in history was necessarily on the highest level—because this is not the case, but I do believe the study of world history contains much information of positive value.

21. In your opinion, what has been the single most important factor to affect popular music in the seventies?

This is a difficult question because the reality continuance of popular music in the decade of the seventies was both complex and varied. However, there is one factor that can be isolated from the general continuum of popular music dynamics, and that is the extended implications of the projection we call reggae. I believe that the solidification of this music represents an important entry in popular music—and points to serious matters. This is a projection that has transformation potential in that: 1) the projection was solidified from spiritual intention, 2) reggae confronts head-on the state of present-day political dynamics, 3) the form shows a responsibility in its lyrics (promoting unification and world consciousness, 4) it seeks to reinstate the importance of history and world progressionalism, and 5) it functions to restore the attention focus of African and trans-African people to our real essence and savior—Mother Africa. The thrust of this projection is not separate from new tendencies developing in popular music (e.g., rap music). I believe reggae is a very important music.

GLOSSARY

Accelerated Dynamics: (1) a time period that experiences an increased rate of dynamic particulars; (2) the phenomenon of increased motion and information awareness or exchange; (3) information or dynamic particulars which are occurring at a faster rate than the concept of "progressional continuance" (which is my phrase for the "normal" pulse flow of information and/or affinity dynamics); (4) the phenomenon of moving faster towards affinity insight—or self-realization—than what is otherwise viewed as normal.

Accelerated Functionalism: (1) a "particular" that advances the nature or effectiveness of a given discipline; (2) the phenomenon of a given discipline expanding at what is perceived to be faster or greater than normal.

Activism: (1) the act of participating in a given discipline; (2) the act of participating in a given moment or collective with the intent to making a "particular" result solidify.

Actual Terms: (1) my phrase for "concrete terms"; (2) in the physical universe sense of a given phenomenon act; (3) a term used to bring in a physical universe or "solid" example of a given concept or statement; (4) a term for either clarifying or simplifying the concept being dealt with.

Actual Transformation: (1) the state of "total change" in both the physical and vibrational universe; (2) the arrival of transformation whether or not it was intended; (3) the phenomenon of transformation solidified because the precepts of the phenomenon (or focus) under review adhered to the dictates of what transformation is; (4) the phenomenon of total physical and vibrational universe change.

Affinity Alignment: (1) the way of one's vibrational nature or sensibility; (2) how a given nature is manifested in both doing or perceiving—in terms of its vibrational and actual slant.

Affinity Compression: (1) a move to lessen an individual's vibrational make-up; (2) the reality of isolating affinity dynamics for the purpose of limiting a given individual's vibrational or spiritual realness; (3) the phenomenon of stagnating a culture or individual's ability to gain self-realization or affinity-insight awareness about their lives—or life purpose; (4) the phenomenon of suppressing affinity dynamics.

Affinity Convergence: (1) the phenomenon of different vibrational sensibilities coming together; (2) the solidification of different so-called affinity tendencies; (3) vibrational unification or point of.

Affinity Dictates: (1) the reality of information as it applies to the particulars of a given sensibility; (2) the realness of information or observation tenets as it involves the laws which govern fundamentals and affinity postulation, and what this means for a given vibrational observation or participation; (3) that being, the laws which support a given reality of information and/or information affinity basis; (4) in other words, whatever one does there are fundamental laws that are related to whether or not a given focus can be successfully utilized—this is also true for the nature, or vibrational realness, of those fundamentals.

Affinity Dynamics: (1) vibrational diversity or the spectrum of possibilities related to a given vibrational position; (2) the related vibrational spectrum of a given phenomenon—that being, areas that are related to the vibrational particulars of a given phenomenon; (3) the scope of a person's life options, as related to vibrational attraction and what this phenomenon means with respect to that person's vibrational make-up.

Affinity Insight: (1) the uncovering of necessary information through self-realization; (2) the phenomenon of spiritual awareness as uncovered by an individual tapping his or her "life experiences" and vibrational make-up; (3) the secrets of a given information continuum as made real by affinity dynamic awareness.

Affinity Insight (1): (1) the realization of spiritual and necessary information about the whole of a given route of participation or culture, or cultural group, by or through self-realization; (2) self-realization as a basis to understand the reality of a given phenomenon as that phenomenon pertains to the greater culture or space; (3) the uncovering of spiritual information as to the "composite state of things."

Affinity Insight (2): (1) the use of self-realization as a basis to connect to one's own "life realness"; (2) the phenomenon of individual awareness as developed by the individual to better understand how to live; (3) taking one's spirit and beingness into one's self as a basis to connect with "the IT" as a means to better understand one's life or life purpose—or desired purpose.

Affinity Nature: (1) the reality of a person's feeling and vibrational make-up; (2) the reality of a phenomenon's inherent tendencies; (3) the reality of a given individual's basic feeling and vibrational tendencies.

Affinity Negation: (1) the move to not acknowledge the "way" of a person's vibrational nature; (2) the realness of isolating the reality interpretation of a given phenomenon in a way that doesn't correspond to the composite platform of affinity dynamics; (3) the isolated vibrational focus of a given area of information as a basis to undermine that same information's composite value.

Affinity Postulation: (1) the phenomenon of "reaching" for "understanding" without the information tenets that are accepted as true, but instead "reaching" with respect to what one feels and senses; (2) postulation with respect to affinity dynamics and affinity insight; (3) learning with respect to one's basic nature (or way of doing "things") and/or feeling.

Affinity Tendencies: (1) the nature of principle information that a given individual normally vibrates (or draws) from; (2) a concept which observes that given individuals over a period of time in "normal situations" are attracted to particular aspects of principle information rather than composite information interpretation; (3) the nature of a continuous "attraction" to a particular vibrational focus.

Affinity Transfer: (1) the phenomenon of changing vibrational continuum interpretations; (2) the refocus and interpretation of principle information with respect to its affinity nature—usually taking an extended time period to become solidified; (3) the natural exchange of principle information with respect to its focus particulars and vibrational dynamics.

Agreement: (1) vibrationally conducive to; (2) in accordance with; (3) a phenomenon whose vibrational properties and "way of being"—with respect to interpretation of the reality of procedure—are within the accepted nature and reality position of those individuals or "things" that are dealing with it.

All-Purpose: (1) a term to emphasize that the actual realness of a given phenomenon has to do with cosmic or spiritual matters; (2) a term to stress that even though I have observed a given information line or observation route to the best of my ability, I am also aware that its real "reason to be" goes much further than its surface; (3) a term used to comment on the destiny implications, or greater spiritual purpose, of a given phenomenon.

Alternative Activism: (1) participation that is outside of what is perceived to be in accordance to the "accepted" reality of things; (2) participation that is not viewed as politically conducive to sustaining the "vibrational" or physical universe reality of things; (3) participation that utilized different information tenets or vibrational tenets from what is perceived to be the "accepted" reality of procedure.

Alternative Composite Progressionalism: (1) my term for the time continuum changes which are taking place, involving total information tenets (that being spiritual and empirical)—as those tenets relate to given cultures or movements or vibrational phenomena—that are separate from the cultural manipulated version of "sanctioned progressionalism"—or its interpretation; (2) a term to comment on the dynamics of progressionalism, as a given focus is accented to the degree that it becomes necessary to include the fact that other movements (or focuses) were also happening as well (and the thrusts of some of those focuses were and are in opposition to the dictates of the accented focus mentioned).

Alternative Definitions: (1) definitions that are equally as real but not accepted or realized; (2) definitions that are related to other regions of affinity dynamics; (3) definitions that are related to other areas of its principle information reality and in some cases give a completely opposite interpretation from its other alternative type.

Alternative Functionalism: (1) disciplines that are perceived as not being in alignment to what is accepted as "correct" or "culturally sustaining"; (2) disciplines that are the outgrowth of alternative information and/or affinity positions; (3) disciplines whose "participation intentions" are not perceived or practiced as a means to affirm what is generally believed to be true for only one region of information, but instead participation that is directed towards uncovering other aspects of principle information and information dynamics.

Application Dictates: (1) a term used in the integration schematics to denote the reality of application for its given concept mixture; (2) a term in the integration schematics to clarify that the reality of a given set of ingredients must be calibrated into actual use (as opposed to simply using in any manner or order).

Applied Redefinitions: (1) the move to reinterpret what a given area of information means; (2) the point underlying when a given information interpretation is changed—and for what reason; (3) the move to focus on another aspect of a given definition's vibrational dynamics; (4) the conscious move to change what a given area or focus of information means—or could mean.

Aspect Essence: (1) the phenomenon of focusing on one part of a given area of principle information as a means to proclaim a universal interpretation; (2) a phenomenon that accents the particulars of a given focus on principle information to the degree where it moves to distort what that principle information really means—or could mean; (3) a phenomenon related to information manipulation in the west involving how given areas—and interpretations—of information are kept in perpetual motion as a means to sustain what is considered to be "interesting" at the expense of what is "most spiritual."

Attachment: (1) to be aligned with or the act of aligning with; (2) to be in agreement with and in being so, to come together with; (3) to not be in agreement with but to come together anyway.

Attitude: (1) vibrational persuasion or way of being; (2) having to do with the vibrational state underlying how a given person or composite culture approaches "phenomenon."

Attraction: (1) to be drawn towards a given focus; (2) to naturally be moving towards a given phenomenon because of either interest or not interest or vibrational interest; (3) the coming together of different phenomena because those phenomena were supposed to come together because of cosmic matters.

Basic Science: (1) in this context involves the use of this term in present-day western culture—that being, extended empirical investigation without respect for (or awareness of) spiritual dynamics; (2) extended functionalism that moves to investigate "the reality of things" as that "thing" works but not as that "thing" is.

Bi-aitional: (1) my term for viewing the reality of principle information with respect to the realness of two basic vibrational continuums, that being the masculine and feminine vibrational principle.

Circular Information Dynamics: (1) the phenomenon of changing the focus of a given principle information interpretation to the detriment to its real reality; (2) the phenomenon of continually refocusing on principle information as a basis to accelerate information dynamics.

Collected Forces of Western Culture: (1) by this term I am referring to all of the agencies that have been constructed to perpetuate the reality of western culture—whatever that perpetuation involves. In other words, the western media, and its educators, the so-called right and left wing (and new left), the western scientific community, western politics, western information interpretation and regulation, etc.

Composite Activism: (1) participation that functions with respect to humanity and composite information; (2) participation with respect to physical universe objectives and spiritual dynamics; (3) the realness of different so-called sectors of humanity working towards the same objective; (4) participation with respect to composite information dynamics—thereby having positive relevance to the composite community.

Composite Affinity Alignment: (1) a vibrational relationship to principle information that attempts to respect and reflect the greater dynamics of composite humanity; (2) a vibrational relationship to information that brings together empirical information dictates with spiritual intent or insight; (3) a vibrational relationship to information that seeks to better understand and include composite humanity within the tenets of its particular focus; (4) the bringing together of composite humanity by establishing an all-encompassing information basis for information and information transference.

Composite Continuance: (1) repeated involvement with respect to both composite information and composite humanity; (2) the reality of time progressionalism as it involves composite humanity; (3) the nature of time changes as it involves composite information.

Composite Culture Attitude: (1) the reality of a culture's vibrational sensibility as it concerns all of the different vibrational persuasions in that culture; (2) the state of a given culture's composite vibrational nature and way of being.

Composite Focused Activism: (1) participation directed at a "particular" that also seeks to reflect the composite concerns of humanity; (2) participation by different kinds of people—both vibrationally and socially—on a particular area of interest; (3) composite participation on a given focus as a means to interpret that focus for the greater good of composite society. Composite participation and/or interest in a given area of information or physical universe particulars.

Composite Humanity: (1) all humanity—men, women, and children, regardless of planet sector; (2) with respect to all humanity.

Composite Information: (1) information that gives insight into the physical universe principle reality of a given phenomenon and also its accompanied vibrational or spiritual universe particulars; (2)

information that respects and reveals the multi-dynamic realness of a given phenomenon.

Composite Research: (1) research with respect to the past and present; (2) research with respect to composite information and interpretation; (3) investigation with respect to composite perception dynamics.

Controlled Information: (1) interpretations that have been sanctioned for the greater public to assimilate and believe; (2) interpretations which have consciously been manipulated as a means to suppress affinity dynamics and/or alternative definitions.

Cosmic Assignment: (1) a term to acknowledge that the "particulars" of a given phenomenon really have to do with "the greater forces" or quite simply "GOD," rather than something that can be only "talked about" or "written on"; (2) a term to acknowledge that some phenomena and/or focuses are indicative of the intent of forces that are greater than humanity or "what humanity can do."

Cosmic Dictates: (1) a term to acknowledge that the fundamentals or particulars underlying a given focus transcend the "intentions" of humanity and instead involve "the greater forces" or "GOD"; (2) a term to acknowledge that the reality of a given set of dictates is related to increased "understanding—or not understanding" of the cosmic realness of everything.

Cosmic Particulars: (1) that being, the reality of a given focus has nothing to do with our information dynamics but instead has to do with spiritual matters; (2) the point of a given interpretation or focus that transcends words and moves into the "real."

Criticism: (1) the phenomenon of commenting as to the reality particulars and/or dynamics of another person's participation; (2) the move to isolate a person's participation as a basis to apply value judgments—even if those judgments are outside the actual reality of that person's affinity participation; (3) an existential observation tool that moves to isolate a given phenomenon's "way of being—or participation" as a means to determine the success of that "beingness or participation"; (4) a unique tool of western information dynamics that involves the imposition of observation criteria (without spiritual dictates) as a means to isolate whether or not a given postulation is in accordance to its dictates.

Cross-Transfer Definitions: (1) interpretations which are solidified and applied when a given continuum of information moves into its change (or affinity refocus) cycle; (2) interpretations that are made "real" as a given continuum of information changes its vibrational or physical universe perceived focus; (3) definitions that had no or little meaning (or different meaning) in a given information continuum that are suddenly elevated into prominence because of the change of that information's use (on the physical universe level or political level).

Cross-Transfer Progressionalism: (1) the reality of continuums coming together and moving apart (and while doing so, taking or exchanging information dynamics in the process); (2) the reality of alternative continuums and the point of interchange between their reality or vibrational ingredients.

Cultural Transfer Shift(s): (1) those cycles in time which underline the phenomenon of different cultures changing or exchanging information and/or information dynamics; (2) the phenomenon of a given culture coming to an end while at the same moment another culture is emerging based on the same information or information dynamics—and what this inter-relationship means.

Culture Affinity Basis: (1) the reality of a culture vibrational and postulation make-up and what this phenomenon means for the establishment of that culture's "way of doing things"; (2) the vibrational particulars which underlie a given culture's reality and vibrational way of living.

Culture Information Basis: (1) the reality of a given culture's idea nature and its accompanied dynamics; (2) the affinity dynamic nature of a culture's intellectual "way of being."

Culture Information Dynamics: (1) the natural and unnatural possibilities that are related to a given culture's idea alignment in terms of "participation spectrum" and "vibrational postulation spectrum"; (2) the variety of focuses or "things" that are related to a culture's information reality—or position; (3) the spectrum of "focuses" or "things" that are related to—and the result of—a culture's relationship with its information.

Culture Information Focus: (1) the agreed-upon interpretation of a particular area of information by those individuals responsible for establishing cultural information; (2) the reality of how a given focus of information reflects the dynamic solidification of its culture's idea nature.

Culture Order: (1) the establishment of whatever devices are necessary to insure that a given culture can function in whatever way that culture desires to function; (2) the move to functionally insure that a culture can "work" the way its founders intended; (3) the reality of those devices which have been designed to solidify "how a culture works" with respect to that culture's political reality and/or dynamics.

Culture Solidification: (1) the establishment of the physical universe situation for a way that affirms the collective intent and desire of those individuals in that space, for the purpose of living in accordance to what is perceived to be "most real."

Decentralization: (1) the move to open up the reality dynamics of a given phenomenon as a means to have the greater spectrum of its forces able to equally have both input and relevance; (2) the move to spread the resources of a given phenomenon to all areas of its principle space, and in doing so, opening up the greater dynamics of the composite space.

Definition: (1) meaning of; (2) the reality of.

Despiritualization: (1) the phenomenon of having something viewed in less spiritual or vibrational terms; (2) the move to solidify the reality of a given spiritual phenomenon in terms that adhere to what is now called rational or logical—that being, the reality of "how something is" as opposed to "how something really is"; (3) the move to take away or not acknowledge—or not even be aware of—the magic or spiritual realness of a given focus.

Disintegration of a Culture's Center: (1) the phenomenon of a culture's vibrational and informational tenets moving to complete destruction; (2) the realness of a culture's idea and affinity support structure being overthrown.

Documentation: (1) the recording of information and particulars as a means to have that information available for future study or use.

Dynamic Functionalism: (1) a discipline that is pursued with respect to its number dynamics as well as spiritual dynamics; (2) a discipline that can bring about a spectrum of information awareness because of its ability to tap the system's particulars of a given phenomenon as well as vibrational dynamics related to that same phenomenon; (3) disciplines that are pursued because they are related to advancing the state of composite humanity; (4) disciplines that are pursued because their tenets are from—and moving towards—composite humanity (that is, disciplines that are about positive transformation).

Dynamic Separation: (1) the isolation of information to the degree that its particulars are viewed without respect for the whole of its principle platform and the creation of a dynamic functionalism from those separate focuses; (2) the intense focus of particulars as a means to view its fundamental law as a means to solidify that procedure for "spectrum participation and investigation"—all of this being done separately or not separately from its spiritualism.

Dynamic Spiritualism: (1) a spiritualism that is all-purpose—involving every aspect of one's life and living; (2) a spiritualism that moves to solidify living in accordance to the secrets and intentions of the greater forces; (3) a spiritualism or mystery system that serves to help humanity to come together for positive acts; (4) a spiritualism that moves to "ritualize" the reality of participation.

Economic Dynamics: (1) the reality and multi-particulars that involve how "contractual dynamics" are solidified and in what form.

Establishing High Order: (1) solidifying composite all spiritual and dynamic functional context, in accordance to transformational precepts; (2) solidifying the spiritual and information dynamics of a given state (and its related pedagogy all system); (3) solidifying the "most" spiritual and vibrational platform with the co-ordinates of the "moment" (or integration mix).

Existential Definition: (1) a definition that views the realness of a given phenomenon with respect to what happened on the physical universe level; (2) an observational phenomenon that views the nature of an occurrence from outside of that occurrence based on how that occurrence is perceived to have happened.

Existential Observation: (1) observation with respect to "how" something seems to be—as separate from the spiritual context of that something; (2) observation with respect to what appears to be happening (in terms of the physicality of that something—and how it "is"—in terms of its "movement" or "low system"), but not in terms of the composite all spiritual nature of that "something."

Existentialism: (1) the phenomenon and state of being that arises when spiritualism is subjected to logical analysis without respect for its proper affinity adjustments, which results in despiritualism and emphasis instead on the "particulars" of a physical universe occurrence—with the understanding being that "something that happens is really what has happened" as opposed to "something that happens is an expression of . . . greater forces."

Expansion Condition: (1) a concept that has to do with how change is solidified in cultural terms; (2) having to do with the reality of intentions surrounding how change is perceived and moved towards.

Expansion Condition (1): the reality and concept of expansion as it relates to composite focus (that being humanity and all spiritualism).

Expansion Condition (2): the reality and dynamics of expansion as it relates to the individual desiring that expansion.

Expansion Dictates: (1) the reality of procedure as it involves expansion; (2) the infra-structure particulars—in their correct order—underlying expansion dynamics (in a given context).

Expansion Dynamics: (1) a term that has to do with the conceptual or vibrational factors that are related to a particular point or kind of expansion. In other words, a given approach or area of expansionism carries its own vibrational or actual implications.

Expansion Information Basis: (1) the phenomenon of increasing the idea spectrum of a given information line as a means to better understand the multi-complexual realness of principle information; (2) the attempt of increasing the affinity dynamic postulates related to what a given information line really means or could mean; (3) the solidification of an idea platform that has relevance to all of the people in its culture, and in doing so, having the dynamics related to what this phenomenon poses to information dictates.

Expansionism: (1) the phenomenon of growing in a given period of time, or the inherent additives that result from a "solidification" in a given time; (2) the move to encompass more territories and/or information without regard for whether or not the inhabitants of those said territories are in agreement with that encompassing; (3) the conscious move to increase the territories or "stuff" of a given culture as a means to "grow"—or support a "growth" that has already occurred.

Extended Dynamics: (1) the uncovering of more information or vibrational possibilities as that phenomenon relates to the reality of investigation; (2) the solidification of more insight about the reality of participation and/or living as that insight relates to a given discipline's meta-secrets or methodological possibilities.

Extended Functionalism: (1) a discipline that provides more insight as to the spiritual and actual particulars underlying what is normally perceived to be "real"; (2) a discipline whose infra-structure and/or particulars are related to, and gives insight into, the dynamics of positive transformation; (3) a discipline whose utilization can provide greater affinity insight as well as composite positive assistance for bringing about positive insight and change; (4) the act of advancing a given discipline to where its meta-reality can begin to provide some of these attributes.

Extension: (1) to move deeper into or towards; (2) coming into, closer to.

Form: (1) how something is; (2) the structure concerning how something seems to be or how something happens; (3) the context, and its related laws, that house a given phenomenon; (4) the spiritual platform that houses a given phenomenon; (5) the physical universe materialization of a vibrational ritual—that being, the context of a participation as well as what that participation means.

Fundamental Dynamics: (1) the focus particulars related to what a given discipline is, or could be in its optimum state; (2) the spiritual and "actual" possibilities that are related to a given "law," or discipline's reality.

Fundamental Particulars: (1) a principle focus or aspect of a given discipline's dictates; (2) the reality of a given discipline's separate parts.

Gradualism: (1) the phenomenon of re-defining information and/or particulars to have that information be viewed in accordance to the intent of its re-definers; (2) the phenomenon of changing information or contributions by groups or nations as a means to have that information or achievement perceived (or re-documented) as coming from the culture of those who changed the information; (3) the act of claiming ownership of concepts and/or achievements done by others as a means either to claim superiority or to claim historical "right of" or "linkage to."

High Purpose: (1) participation with respect to what is most positive for humanity; (2) participation with respect to what is perceived to be "most positive" for humanity; (3) spiritual participation that is done for what is most real for the greater forces; (4) cosmic phenomena that are about cosmic phenomena.

Improvisation: (1) a discipline that involves the science of creative postulation as it unfolds in "actual" time; (2) a discipline that utilizes the dynamics of moment postulation in both the context of individual postulation and its related affinity dynamics, as well as cultural vibrational transference; (3) the science and multi-discipline of existing—having to do with the appearance of "moments" and making life choices (either with respect to "particulars" or spiritual growth) and the gradual awareness of how best to proceed with that information in "rapid-moment-decision contexts."

Individual Dynamic Reality: (1) that being those "particulars" of the greatest positive attributes in a given individual's physical universe reality; (2) a concept that accents the realness of the individual and what that individual's vibrational spectrum could be in its most positive sense, as related to the particulars of his or her physical universe reality.

Individual Dynamics: that being, the "natural" or "particular" vibrational properties that each individual has—and is born with (or can acquire, depending on the situation)—having to do with the areas that individual is attracted to, the areas that individual can excel at, the information that individual can relate to (and later contribute to as well). Having to do with "what is most" or "can be most" about a given individual in his or her most positive state.

Individual Tendencies: (1) having to do with what region of principle information a given individual is continually drawn to, and functions from (in his or her natural feeling and "postulation" nature); (2) a concept which observes that given individuals vibrate to different areas of the same information because every information continuum is related to its particular "nature spectrum"—and this phenomenon also corresponds to the different types (or so-called types) of people.

Information Affinity Basis: (1) that being, the vibrational particulars which determine what a given idea structure is to really mean. My viewpoint is that the dynamics of vibrational postulates come before the actual idea or concept interpretation; (2) the affinity or vibrational nature that determines what aspect is to be affirmed of a given principle information line.

Information Alignment: the reality of a given idea or concept as it connects to principle information, and also the reality of a given interpretation as it affirms its vibrational basis.

Information Compression: (1) same as affinity compression but also involves the physical universe removal (or put-down) of given areas of information which are not in the interest of those who choose to do the compression; (2) the blockage of information.

Information Convergence: (1) the coming together of different continuums of information—either involving principle information dynamics or particulars; (2) the phenomenon of information expansion and/or affinity linkage.

Information Degrees: my term for information tenets. I have chosen this term because it moves to involve the reality of spiritualism more than the word "tenet." By "degree" I am saying that each aspect of a given information line moves to both substantiate the reality of its principle focus as well as its spiritual designation. I view the term "tenet" as more related to intellectual dynamics—having to do with the dynamics which support a given focus's particulars but not its affinity basis.

Information Dissemination: (1) the phenomenon concerning how given ideas and concepts are spread on the physical universe level; (2) the phenomenon that underlines how given practices are transmitted to the greater culture or through a sustained time cycle; (3) the spread of information.

Information Documentation: (1) the recording of knowledge—whatever the context or focus—as a means to have it taught or later re-examined; (2) having to do with the reality of recorded concepts and ideas and how it is passed on through different time cycles.

Information Focus: (1) the particular emphasis on a given aspect of principle information; (2) the point of a given intention as manifested in actual terms; (3) the reality underlying how a given principle information line is perceived in actual terms (that being, the reality concerning what factors and affinities underlie how a given information line is repeatedly perceived and practiced).

Information Focus Distortion: (1) that being, the particular point in a given information tenet structure that is consciously or not consciously distorted as a means to have an understanding that corresponds to what one wants to believe, rather than what that information seems to be saying; (2) the point in a given information complex that is misused or not understood, or not viewed correctly.

Information Forum: (1) the reality of what information is available in a given context; (2) the solidification of what information is to be made available in a given context—and in what terms; (3) a platform for information—or given information—that can or cannot be experienced by the greater public.

Information Integration: (1) solidifying given areas of information—regardless of thrust alignment or affinity nature; (2) bringing given continuums of information together.

Information Interpretation: the reality of attempting to deduce what a given idea or concept means—with respect to both that concept's principle information greater context, as well as its particular degrees.

Information Order: (1) the reality structure that underlies a given area of information; (2) the focus ingredient that establishes a given area of information; (3) "how" a given type of information is, and "how" it should be in its most correct alignment.

Information Projection: (1) this term refers to the actualness of a given viewpoint and what that viewpoint poses for its greater information multi-complex. In other words, a projection in this context is indicative of "one particular" manifestation of a given principle information complex; (2) that being, an actual example or particular of a principle information multi-complex.

Information Reality: (1) viewing the actualness of a given information concept with respect to its physical universe realness; (2) an informational example in concrete physical universe terms; (3) that being, "how a given information is" in the physical universe context of its existence.

Information Solidification: (1) bringing all aspects of a given focus (or set) of information particulars together; (2) completing the infrastructure of a given information continuum as a means to make it (the information) real—or correct; (3) the same as information integration (but in a more progressional sense).

Information Transference: the changing of information—either from person to person (whether vibrational or actual) or culture to culture.

Infra-Spirituality: (1) that being, the reality of spirituality as it involves the particulars of a given discipline; (2) how a given part of a particular discipline also has spiritual connotations; (3) finding the "god" of a given discipline or point of activism.

Infra-Structure Dynamics: (1) that being, the possibilities related to the particulars of a given system in terms of what the procedure of that discipline implies for other focus spectrums; (2) having to do with the ritual implications of a given participation—that being, every aspect of a given structure carries a physical universe and vibrational multi-implication.

Intellectualism: (1) having to do with the reality of ideas and the dynamics of inter-relationship seeded by the vibrational concern (or attraction) to what is perceived to be "interesting" or logically true, as opposed to what is spiritually true; (2) the reality of ideas without regard for its spiritual context; (3) the dynamics of concepts and isolated information focus with the intent to understand as separate from spiritual insight.

Intention: having to do with the reality of a given motive.

Interpretation: (1) having to do with extracting the meaning of a given phenomenon or information line; (2) the reality of providing the context and tools to receive insight into the state of a given phenomenon; (3) having to do with viewing what a given principle information line means or could mean for the beings in a given affinity focus—or spectrum; (4) having to do with providing insight into how a given spiritual and vibrational actualness can be solidified—and understood—on the physical universe level, and practiced.

Investigation Dictates: (1) the reality of correct observation as it relates to a particular focus; (2) the reality of perception dynamics as this concept involves establishing correct criteria for examination; (3) investigation with respect to the tenets of what is being investigated; (4) the reality of proper investigation as it involves procedure.

Isolated Activism: (1) participation with respect to the particulars of a given focus; (2) participation with respect to one or "whatever is defined" area of interest or focus, for the purpose of achieving a desired result; (3) participation that is practiced without respect for the composite physical or vibrational universe situation but instead is directed to deal with the immediacy of a particular (or particular set of) focus or focuses.

Isolated Focus: (1) that being, to view the "particulars" of a given phenomenon rather than the composite picture; (2) to focus on only certain aspects of a given phenomenon as a means to deal or not deal with that aspect.

Isolated Focus Activism: (1) that being, participation with respect to the interest of particular sectors or people, rather than the composite sector; (2) participation that is undertaken from the reality of a particular focus rather than a composite focus.

Isolated Focus Dictates: (1) the pedagogical structure underlying a given focus; (2) the reality of fundamental information that supports a given focus; (3) taking into account—in the perception of a given focus—its underlying information tenets; (4) the reality underlying how a given focus must be observed with respect to its fundamental support systems.

Isolated Particulars: (1) having to do with separating a given idea or focus from its principle information multi-focus as a basis to only deal with a given independent idea; (2) that being, a particular focus that is separated and viewed with respect to whatever the intentions of the viewer are.

Isolated Systematic Alignment: (1) that being, the independent logic systems which are solidified as a basis to view the particulars of a given focus—as opposed to an all-encompassing logic system; (2) the reality of linkage as it involves different isolated idea focuses (as made or viewed separately from its vibrational foundation).

Journalism Dynamics: the possibilities inherent in the reality of present-day journalism—involving its interpretation dynamics, its focus (or not focus) dynamics, its semantical dynamics, and its ability to profoundly affect the greater culture (both positively and negatively—especially negatively).

Language: (1) the reality of symbols as a basis to codify particulars; (2) the reality of symbols as a basis to transmit intention; (3) the reality of procedure as a basis to convey information.

Language Dynamics: (1) that being, the inherent possibilities that are related to the particulars of a given functionalism (or set of symbols) in terms of what can be successfully communicated through its particular use; (2) having to do with what the use of a given language poses for dynamic postulation as well as spiritual insight; (3) having to do with how a given communication discipline can also affect and determine the option-spread possibilities of the person or culture utilizing the discipline.

Linkage Implications: (1) the possibilities related to the coupling or inter-relationship of two phenomena and/or focuses; (2) the reality of possibilities as it relates to the coupling and/or inter-relationship of two different phenomena and/or focuses.

Logical Dissolution: (1) that being, the rational result of; (2) that being, the rational consequences of—as a result of using a particular technique and/or discipline or act; (3) in accordance to the context that has been defined—or dissolution in accordance to the context that has been defined.

Manipulation: (1) having to do with controlling the meaning of—or use of—how a given phenomenon is viewed or utilized; (2) having to do with the intention to utilize a given phenomenon in a way to achieve a desired result that is not necessarily related to what that same phenomenon would achieve if utilized differently; (3) the conscious use of materials and things as a means to solidify and/or establish a given result or results.

Media Dynamics: (1) the reality and vibrational dynamics related to how the media works; (2) how the media is, and how it can be; (3) the inherent possibilities related to the reality of accelerated information transference and its established institutions.

Meta-Implications: (1) vibrational related possibilities or consequences; (2) cosmic or vibrational relationships (and possibilities).

Meta-Reality: (1) the vibrational or cosmic "living" or "being" context of a given phenomenon; (2) a term that injects cosmic or spiritual being matters as a consideration not separate from what is being discussed; (3) having to do with the spiritual or vibrational weight of a given idea or focus.

Meta-Reality Significance: (1) the vibrational or spiritual meaning of a given postulation or focus; (2) having to do with what a given function or focus will ultimately mean in vibrational or spiritual terms.

Methodology: (1) the reality particulars of a given function or discipline; (2) the science of a given discipline and how to execute a given function; (3) how something is done and the discipline to make it happen again; (4) the spiritual and vibrational procedures necessary to gain insight into the "all motion" realness of the physical and vibrational universe; (5) the reality of doing in its most highest context with the establishment of ritual as the most correct or effective procedure to make a particular "thing" happen.

Mono-Dimensional: (1) the reality of one context or one observation plane; (2) a concept that has to do with viewing a given phenomenon in only one affinity and/or actual context; (3) the reality of a given phenomenon as it is viewed in only one or two (or a limited amount of) contexts—and in doing so moves to limit that phenomenon's affinity and/or actual life options and/or "being" options.

Motivation Dynamics: (1) the reality of intention as it applies to a participation; (2) the spectrum of intentions related to a given participation.

Multi-Dimensional: (1) many dimensions on many different levels; (2) dynamically complex and related to many different factors and/or contexts; (3) means more than only one interpretation and extends into many other areas, and things.

Multi-Information: (1) information that is not only about one particular focus but instead is relevant and meaningful on many different levels; (2) information—ideas and concepts—that have relevance on many different levels and/or focuses.

Multi-Informational Degree Basis: (1) a western information phenomenon that utilizes dynamic information in a way that enables a given word or statement to be utilized and interpreted in as many ways as is necessary for the real purpose to be actualized; (2) a phenomenon that helps to keep the reality of western information dynamics in constant motion.

Multi-Transfer Shift Activity: a concept that observes the different dynamic contexts which dictate the reality of a given discipline's effectiveness.

Multiple Diversification: (1) a term that comments as to the many different possibilities related to a given phenomenon; (2) a term that comments on a given phenomenon's dynamic possibilities as well as the realness that those possibilities are not limited to any one particular level.

Multiple Interpretation: (1) to decipher meaning on several different levels; (2) a term that comments on how a given focus is interpreted and on how many different levels.

Observation: (1) to view something; (2) the reality of viewing a phenomenon as a means to understand it (or some aspect of it).

Option Spread: (1) the opportunities available for a given person on the physical universe level; (2) the life pursuance possibilities of a given individual in terms of his ability to achieve either information, economic gain, cultural recognition, and/or cultural participation.

Participation: (1) the reality of "doing something"; (2) to be a part of and actively functioning; (3) the act of doing something.

Particular Focus: (1) a particular subject; (2) an isolated subject that is being viewed for whatever reason.

Particular Progressionalism: (1) an isolated continuum; (2) having to do with the reality of a given continuum of either information or people (culture) or vibrational "way of doing things."

Perceived Physical Universe Fundamental: that being the perception of a given discipline or focus as indicative of a fundamental or primary law that underlies how the all-motion dynamics of earth—and/or the heavens—are made "real" (or work).

Perception Dynamics: (1) the reality of observation with respect to the variables—and spectrum of possibilities—underlying a given way of looking at "things"; (2) the vibrational and "actual" factors that underlie a given observation context (or platform).

Physical Universe Context: (1) having to do with viewing a given phenomenon with respect to what that phenomenon reveals as it is made real in actual concrete terms; (2) in concrete terms or in "actual" context.

Physical Universe Fundamental: (1) a law that seems to be dynamically and cosmically related to how the actualness of this experience (living and the appearance of things as they seem to be and the realness of vibrations as it seems to be) is made real; (2) a law or discipline that expresses some aspect of how the physical universe is able to be as it is.

Physical Universe Particular: (1) that being, a focus or particular that can be viewed in concrete terms as a basis to participate in that context; (2) a given focus that is concrete with respect to the dimension we refer to as the physical universe.

Political Consciousness: (1) awareness of what is taking place in the reality of politics; (2) the awareness of what politics means—or could mean as an expression of dynamic spiritualism; (3) the awareness of politics and how given realities are solidified and/or maintained.

Political Dynamics: (1) the inherent possibilities that are related to the political context of a given physical universe space; (2) the related possibilities of a given political system as it concerns cultural option dynamics—spiritual dynamics, social dynamics, and particular focus dynamics.

Political Order: (1) the securing of a given political philosophy and reality posture and its actualization on the physical universe level; (2) establishing a given reality context in accordance to a given political system (or philosophy).

Political Policies: (1) involves the reality of what laws are established in a given political state; (2) involves the particulars of a given political system as it relates to what is viewed as correct, positive and beneficial, as opposed to what is labeled negative, not correct and "against the state."

Political Significance: (1) has to do with what a given action poses to the reality of the political arena it takes place in; (2) has to do with what a given postulation poses to the reality of its given political space; (3) has to do with the reality of "meaning" as it relates to political tenets and/or dynamics.

Political State: that being the reality of politics as it shapes the particulars of its culture's actual living.

Postulation: (1) the act of bringing something forth as in expressing an idea or a feeling; (2) the reality of what one aspires to and works towards—that being the creation of an objective and/or focus that did not exist before; (3) the phenomenon of vibrationally expressing the actualness of a given phenomenon from one's own affinity particulars (or culture affinity particulars); (4) the expression of a cosmic and/or vibrational dictate that is manifested and/or made real through dynamic existence—as in "doing" or "movement."

Primary Affinity Tendencies: (1) a concept that views the reality of vibrational postulation with respect to (a) what is called traditionalism, (b) stylism, and (c) restructuralism.

Primary Intention: (1) the basic motivation of; (2) what a given phenomenon really makes happen when utilized and the purpose behind who decides whether it is to be utilized (or explored) or not.

Progressional Continuance: (1) a term that views physical universe reality changes and/or events with respect to sequential time blocks and/or parameters (and/or time cycles); (2) looking at given time periods with respect to blocks of tendencies (and/or variables) as a basis to view the world expansion principle.

Progressional Extended Functionalism: (1) the phenomenon of viewing a given discipline and/or science and how it moves into greater areas of its dynamics; (2) the reality continuance of advanced discipline in its own right (that is, how a given advanced discipline has continued its existence as separate from the composite arena of a given continuum and/or discipline).

Progressional Significance: (1) the meaning and/or value of a given phenomenon as that phenomenon advances different time periods; (2) the reality of change and the reality of a given phenomenon's significance as it advances through change cycles and/or time periods.

Progressional Transfer Cycles: a concept that refers to those periods in time which are conducive to or "about" the interchange of composite information and/or information dynamics.

Projection: (1) a term that is used to comment on information off-shoots as it involves ideas and concept lines from a principle information continuum; (2) a style or isolated information focus continuum; (3) in music, "projection" is my word for style or music type.

Projectional Continuance: (1) the continuation of a given style of idea type focus throughout a given time period or periods; (2) the use or realness of a given projection in the larger context of time or time changes.

Projectional Dynamics: (1) the diversity or possibilities related and/or based from the reality of a given projection; (2) the possibilities connected to a given projection; (3) a term to comment on the spiritual dictates related to the particulars of a given discipline, and what those dictates translate into as actual and/or vibrational terms.

Race: (1) the compilation of a people in a given physical universe space for an extended period in time to the degree that their physical traits and affinity spectrum traits move to affirm a particular identity; (2) the vibrational attraction phenomenon that underlies a given group of people with respect to their affinity dynamic dictates and destiny; (3) an applied precept concerning the reality of isolated particulars as this concept involves the family of humanity and existence; (4) the dynamic realization and/or actualization of affinity dynamics—as made real in human beings and/or all living things (and non-so-called living things) that expresses some or all aspects of the cosmic realness of "it" and/or "is" and/or "this."

Reality Alignment: (1) the physical universe application or view of; (2) the physical universe context and use of; (3) viewing a given phenomenon with respect to what that phenomenon would mean on the physical universe level—if utilized, or as a context to view from.

Reality Dynamics: (1) the possibilities or diverse particulars of a given physical universe situation; (2) the related possibilities of a given physical universe context.

Reality Implications: (1) the related information and/or phenomenon possibilities to a given physical universe situation; (2) what a given physical universe situation poses for extended circumstances.

Reality Initiative Traits: (1) what is most common to the reality of postulation as it concerns a particular physical universe space; (2) the "way of doing things" in a given physical universe space and/or culture.

Reality Options: (1) that being, the opportunities or avenues of participation in a given physical universe space and/or culture; (2) having to do with what living opportunities are available for a person or persons in a given physical universe context.

Recontinuance: (1) the continuance of a given phenomenon that seemingly was not there before; (2) the re-appearance of a given "way of doing things" or "viewpoint"—"law system"—that seemingly was not there before; (3) a cosmic phenomenon that underlies how given areas of information (or "things") are brought into and out of being in accordance to factors that have nothing to do with what we know about.

Redefinitions: (1) giving a definition and new definition; (2) changing the meaning of a given definition and/or focus.

Redocumentation: (1) changing what is documented; (2) either rewriting or correcting what has been documented.

Related Procedure: (1) a term used in the integration schematics to denote that a given combination of terms should be utilized at that point in its solidification; (2) a term to denote the usage of a given set of variables in the information schematic.

Relevant Application: (1) the reality of what is "most real" to a given application; (2) application with respect to the cosmic dictates of positive utilization; (3) application with respect to what is most effective.

Relevant Technology: (1) technology that is solidified in accordance to spiritual and dynamic dictates; (2) the use of technology with respect to what is "most" (for humanity) about that technology; (3) technology that is related to what one professes to be about—or would like to be about (both dynamically and spiritually).

Restructuralism: (1) the reality of realigning how a given system or structure works; (2) changing the surface particulars of a given structure but keeping the fundamentals that gave that structure its laws; (3) changing the particulars of a system as well as its dictates.

Responsibility Ratio: having to do with what extent and/or degree a given person or culture is to be held accountable for the reality and/or particulars of a given focus and/or discipline and/or reality; (2) the spectrum of an individual's responsibility in a given context.

Retrograde Affinity Tendencies: that being, those vibrational urges which, if allowed, would pursue their particulars in focuses that are considered in the past.

Ritual Dynamics: (1) the possibilities and diverse particulars related to the use of a given ritual; (2) the dynamic possibilities that underlie what a given ritual is or does or makes happen.

Scientific Dynamics: (1) the possibilities and/or particular discoveries that are related to a given use or reality of science; (2) the particulars related to a given type of area or science.

Self-Realization: (1) having to do with the individual becoming aware of who he or she really is—as made real through both physical universe particulars and spiritual insight; (2) spiritual discovery.

Social Programs: (1) organizations established to help uplift given aspects of social reality; (2) organizations for bringing about positive changes—and participation—in social reality.

Social Reality: (1) the particulars related to events on the physical universe level; (2) the "way of life" on the physical universe level as it involves living and functioning in a given space.

Social Reality Development: (1) the reality of bringing about positive reforms in social reality; (2) positive participation—or effect—for a given social reality context (or sector).

Social Reality Dynamics: (1) the possibilities and particulars related to a given social reality context and/or physical universe context; (2) the particulars related to what and how a given social reality space is—as far as achievement possibilities and/or postulation possibilities.

Social Reality Interpretation: (1) "meanings" that have solidified in a given social reality context (that have been accepted) for the greater culture; (2) the meanings that are to be accepted in a given social reality context.

Social Reality Particular(s): (1) the actualness of a given focus or focuses that is related to—or draws its ability to be from—its social reality context; (2) that being, the reality of a given focus as that focus is made real from its social reality basis.

Source Initiation: (1) the point and/or reality from which a given initiation solidifies; (2) the reality concerning when a given particular solidifies.

Source Projection: (1) a style or language that has solidified from its historical continuum; (2) an information line that has come into being from its greater information basis; (3) a term that views a given style or focus with respect to its greater continuum position (as related to either principle information or historical point of solidification).

Source Shift: (1) the phenomenon of a given continuum (that being "reality or way of doing things") suddenly realigning its path or "surface nature"; (2) the phenomenon of a projection changing its path and taking the attributes of another continuum; (3) having to do with the phenomenon of two or more continuums entering into a "time or cosmic" cycle whereby either one or all of the continuums will attach it or their self to the "particulars" of the other, and proceed from that point.

Source Transfer: (1) the phenomenon of a given continuum—or documented continuum which is more accurate—adopting tenets and/or particulars from another continuum; (2) the point of a continuum change of information and/or particulars; (3) the phenomenon of a continuum adopting or simply taking the attributes (and way of being) of other continuums.

Spectacle Diversion: (1) a concept involving the rotation of a culture's information dynamics and/or forces as a means to have "people involved" but not involved in "something"; (2) rotating "information dynamics" as a phenomenon to give the impression of either "high culture" or "real involvement."

Spiritual Awareness: (1) the act of having some insight as to the reality of spiritualness and/or spiritual dynamics; (2) understanding something about spiritualism, and what is real "for the person" understanding.

Spiritual Dynamics: (1) the reality of possibilities and/or "things" that are related to or brought about from spiritualism; (2) having to do with what can happen through spirituality.

Spiritual Growth: "becoming" as made real through learning about and "being in" a spiritual state or trying to be in a spiritual state—or "becoming" because of one's relationship to spiritualism.

Spiritual Unification: (1) the bringing together of concrete and abstract information and affinity dynamics as a means to "be" in accordance to "greater forces"—or as a means to solidify the proper platform for real "insight"; (2) the bringing together of all religions as a means to establish a composite "all religion."

Style: (1) the appearance of a projection or "way to be"; (2) the reality of a particular interpretation line as that line is actualized into physicality; (3) the manifestation of a particular information dynamic focus into concrete terms; (4) the reality of "ways to be" as it involves actualizing the particulars of a proven information and/or vibrational continuum.

Technological (or Technology) Dynamics: (1) the reality of possibilities—or variables—related to a given functionalism (or related to composite technology); (2) the vibrational and "actual" dynamics related to a given technology (or to composite technology—with respect to its composite position in "all information").

Terminology: (1) the reality of a definition; (2) the reality of how a given language is made real and for what reason; (3) the reality of a given definition as it is made real from its vibrational and/or spiritual base.

Theoretical Science: (1) the reality of ideas as a focus to dynamic methodology for extended functionalism and/or scientific discipline.

Thrust Affinity Alignment: (1) that being, the reality of a given continuum (vibrational and physical universe) way of being; (2) the dynamics of a particular continuum and how it is constructed.

Thrust Continuance: (1) the time advancement or advancing reality of a composite continuum or vibrational and empirical continuum; (2) the reality of a continuum as it advances through time.

Thrust Continuance Dynamics: (1) the dynamic possibilities related to a given continuum as it moves through time—in terms of that continuum's information order and/or vibrational alignment.

Time Continuance Implications: (1) having to do with what results to a given phenomenon in the course of a particular time cycle and/or progression; (2) the possibilities related to a given phenomenon in a given period of time.

Time Lag: (1) the phenomenon of a given particular and/or focus as viewed past the interpretation dynamics of its allotted or designated time period; (2) the reality of a given phenomenon when viewed after the time cycle that made it real; (3) the effects of a given phenomenon and/or focus when viewed and/or perceived past its actual time parameter.

Time Presence: (1) the phenomenon of participation with respect to and awareness of the reality of "actualness" and what that means with regards to events in time and moment awareness; (2) "doing" with respect to (and awareness of) the vibrational realness of the moments in that "doing"—as that "doing" relates to what we call time and what we call motion; (3) the spiritualness of "doing" and also the related vibrational dynamics of "all motion" (or "actual motion").

Trans-Definition: (1) an interpretation that carries over different time periods and/or so-called culture groups; (2) an interpretation that actualizes cosmic significances and as such cannot be simply ignored or stopped because of physical universe particulars or information dynamics.

Transformation: (1) a concept that involves total physical and vibrational universe change; (2) the close of a given or particular physical and vibrational universe cycle and the beginning of the next.

Trans-Information: (1) information that spans physical universe territories, having to do with the laws of this "state" and the experiencing of this "state"; (2) information that is universal and "all real"—regardless of time or culture; (3) information that is not about a given culture and/or focus but instead is cosmically directed because it is "real."

Transition: (1) the change of a given and/or particular state in terms of its surface information and/or focus dynamics—but not its total "beingness"; (2) the change of some aspects of a given physical universe and/or vibrational universe state.

Underlying Philosophical Basis: (1) the reality of a given phenomenon's idea and focus bases—having to do with viewing the factors which support what a given information interpretation means, or is supposed to mean.

Unification: (1) the affinity solidification of humanity as a means to live in accordance to the dictates of dynamic spiritualism; (2) the actual and/or vibrational bringing together of a given phenomenon; (3) a state of composite intentions.

Utilization: (1) the use of a given terminology mix in the information schematics; (2) in other words, the point in the schematics where the given terms should be utilized.

Value System: (1) the ethical and spiritual weight of a particular focus or participation; (2) the reality of a given focus with respect to whether its implementation advances the particulars of spiritual well-being and positive composite well-being, or not; (3) the reality of a given "state of being" and/or phenomenon as evaluated with respect to its assignment and/or desired assignment.

Vibrational Affinity and/or Attitude: (1) the reality of a vibrational state with respect for how a given attitude colors what can or can't be achieved or completed; (2) the reality of given feelings and what those feelings mean in actual terms—as far as whether or not a given objective can be achieved or understood.

Vibrational Attitude: (1) that being, the real attitude before the "words," or before the particular focus that the attitude is directed on; (2) the "way" of a particular vibrational way of being.

Vibrational Dynamics: (1) the possibilities and diverse focuses related to a given vibrational "way of being" (or way of "not" being).

Vibrational Implications: (1) the related possibilities and "things" connected to a given vibrational state and/or position that aren't necessarily connected to the basic focus or reality "stuff" of what that vibration really is—when viewed in its separate state and/or basic reality tone—but can be activated if that vibrational state is utilized or not utilized correctly.

Vibrational Platform: (1) having to do with utilizing the reality of a particular vibrational position as a basis from which to mount either a participation or a focus; (2) the reality of basing an assumption and/or action from a particular vibrational focus—or focuses.

Vibrational Postulation: (1) the same as affinity postulation but not as "deep"; (2) the same as affinity postulation but semantically having less to do with an individual's vibrational and affinity nature and more to do with the act of postulation as this phenomenon happens with respect to other factors (e.g., like the greater culture).

Vibrational Science: (1) that being, the reality of mystical or high spiritual or vibrational (e.g., music or what is called art) discipline with respect to its law position or moving to understand its law position—as made real through multi-information dynamics and high spiritualism; (2) observation and participation in vibrational discipline as that discipline unfolds some aspect of the dynamic functionalism and/or order of the universe (or what we call the universe); (3) vibrationally doing as a means to cosmically grow and love.

Vibrational Tendencies: (1) the reality of possibilities—or attractions—as related to vibrational dynamics; having to do with postulation or "vibrational reception"; (2) the reality of vibrational tendencies as related to the individual (i.e., see individual vibrational tendencies) or environment—or focus dictates.

Vibrational Universe Particulars: (1) the reality of a given focus that is seeded in vibrational terms; (2) the reality of a given focus as it unfolds some aspect of its vibrational universe dynamics.

World Change: (1) the re-alignment of earth in terms of how people live and how people perceive of living—and the reality of postulation and participation.

World Expansion Principle: (1) the reality of change as it affirms the dynamic particulars underlying composite physical universe change.

World Methodology: (1) the reality of a given procedure when viewed in its greater context; (2) a term to underline that a given focus or particular cannot be viewed as the result of one or two countries but, instead, is the property of or related to composite humanity.

World Unification: (1) bringing people and "things" together—harmony with what the "experience of living could mean" in its most positive state.

www.ingramcontent.com/pod-product-compliance
Lightning Source LLC
Chambersburg PA
CBHW071849290426
44110CB00013B/1084